Preface

1. Aims of the book

This book is designed to provide a thorough understanding of Management Accounting and is particularly relevant for:

a) Students preparing themselves for the Professional Examinations of the following bodies: Institute of Chartered Accountants, Chartered Association of Certified Accountants, Chartered Institute of Management Accountants, Chartered Institute of Public Finance and Accountancy, the Institute of Chartered Secretaries and Administrators, and the Institute of Company Accountants.

b) Undergraduates reading Accounting, Business Studies and allied subjects where Management Accounting is part of the curriculum and students on BTEC Higher Level courses.

c) Managers and others in industry, commerce, local authorities and public corporation who wish to obtain a working knowledge of management accounting to aid them in their own work and to facilitate communication with accountants.

2. Scope and coverage of the book

The book provides comprehensive coverage of the Management Accounting Syllabuses of the major Professional Bodies listed above. In so doing it will be found that there is coverage of the typical Management Accounting syllabus included in Degree and Diploma courses.

Management Accounting is a broadly based, eclectic subject drawing upon relevant concepts and principles from Economics, Statistics, Operational Research, Management, Behavioural Science, Information Systems as well as from Cost and Financial Accounting. At appropriate points in the book the principles and theories from other disciplines relevant to Management Accounting are explained together with the problems associated with implementing the theoretical ideas in practical Management Accounting situations.

Students approach the study of Management Accounting with differing backgrounds. For example, some Professional Bodies have separate Cost Accounting examinations whilst others include Cost Accounting in the Management Accounting examinations. Because of this some students will find that a small amount of the more basic material in the book is repeated from earlier studies. Examples include: cost ascertainment principles, elementary standard costing and variance analysis. In each case it will be found that the material is dealt with in a more critical fashion and the subject is extended to deal with the more exacting requirements of the Management Accounting syllabuses.

3. Teaching approach

The book has been written in a standardised format with numbered paragraphs, end of chapter summaries, with review questions and examination questions at the end of each chapter. This approach has been tested and found effective by thousands of students and the book can be used for independent study or in conjunction with tuition at a college. Management Accounting is a large and ever expanding subject and students are recommended to read widely. To assist this process each chapter has suggestions for additional reading. It will be seen that these include publications on selected topics by the Professional Bodies,and students, particularly those preparing for professional examinations, are strongly recommended to read some or all of these publications.

4. How to use the book effectively

For ease of study the book is divided into self contained chapters with numbered paragraphs. Each chapter is followed by self review questions, cross referenced to appropriate paragraphs. You should attempt to answer the self review questions unaided then check your answer with the text.

At appropriate points in the text (after Chapters 3, 7, 12, 18 and 23) there are Assessment and Revision Sections. These contain carefully selected examination questions drawn from the most recent professional examinations. The questions have been chosen not merely to repeat the material in the chapters, but to extend knowledge and understanding. Fully-worked answers are provided in an Appendix to the book, but again you are recommended to attempt the questions yourself before looking at the answers.

Each Assessment and Revision Section also contains a further selection of examination questions, without answers. These can be used by lecturers for classwork and assignments when the book is being used as a course text, or as extra practice when the book is used for independent study.

5. Sequence of study

The book should be studied in the sequence of the chapters. The sequence has been arranged so that there is a progressive accumulation of knowledge and any given chapter either includes all the principles necessary or draws upon a previous chapter(s).

6. Case studies and further examination questions

The book also contains a series of Management Accounting Case Studies contributed by G.S. Clinton, of the University of Aberystwyth.

The Case Studies can be studied with profit by all readers but will be of most value when used in conjunction with a lecturer. They will be found to be a useful means of reinforcing subject knowledge and demonstrate the integrated nature of Management Accounting problems in realistic settings.

A separate answer guide is available free to lecturers who adopt the book as a course text. The guide contains full answers to all the questions and suggested solutions to the Case Studies.

Notes on the 4th Edition

The response to earlier editions has been extremely gratifying and I would like to express my appreciation of the constructive feedback from lecturers and students world-wide.

Particular features of the 4th edition are:

a) There have been numerous detailed revisions and extensions of coverage including: more material on marginal and cumulative average learning curves; annuity depreciation and performance measurement; benchmarking.

b) Questions have been included from the latest professional examinations.

c) Learning objectives have been set for each chapter.

d) A separate Lecturers' Supplement is available free to lecturers who adopt the book as a course text. Application should be made to the publishers on departmental headed notepaper. The supplement contains:

❐ Guidance notes on the Case Studies

❐ Solutions to examination questions

❐ OHP masters of key diagrams from the book.

T Lucey
1996

Contents

Tables

Appendices

1 What is management accounting?

1. Objectives

After studying this chapter you will:

❒ have been introduced to the scope and principles of management accounting (MA);

❒ know how MA relates to cost accounting and financial accounting;

❒ understand key themes of MA, such as future orientation, goal congruence, economic reality, decision making;

❒ have been introduced to the rest of the book.

2. Management accounting defined

In the sense that management will be interested in any information produced by an accounting system, all accounting could be said to be management accounting whether it was for example, published accounts mainly for external consumption or routine product costs for internal use. However, for practical purposes, such a description is too broad and imprecise. Although there are many definitions of management accounting the following CIMA definition would gain general acceptance.

Management accounting

An integral part of management concerned with identifying, presenting and interpreting information used for:

❒ formulating strategy;

❒ planning and controlling activities;

❒ decision taking;

❒ optimising the use of resources;

❒ disclosure to shareholders and others external to the entity;

❒ disclosure to employees;

❒ safeguarding assets.

The above involves participation in management to ensure that there is effective:

❒ formulation of plans to meet objectives (strategic planning);

❒ formulation of short-term operation plans (budgeting/ profit; planning);

❒ acquisition and use of finance (financial management) and recording of transactions (financial accounting and cost accounting);

❒ communication of financial and operating information;

❒ corrective action to bring plans and results into line (financial control);

❒ reviewing and reporting on systems and operations (internal audit, management audit). See Figure 1.1.

Terminology

1

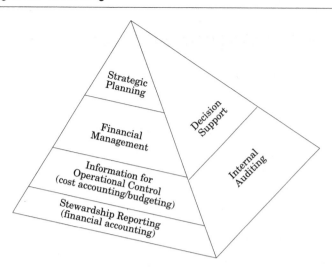

Figure 1.1 Elements of management accounting

Management accounting therefore is primarily concerned with data gathering (from internal and external sources) analysing, processing, interpreting and communicating the resulting information for use within the organisation so that management can more effectively plan, make decisions and control operations.

To carry out this task efficiently the management accountant will use data from the financial and cost accounting systems, he will conduct special investigations to gather required data, he will use accounting techniques and appropriate techniques from statistics and operations research, he will take account of the human element in all activities, he will be aware of the underlying economic logic, he will do all these things and many others so that at all times he will produce information which is **relevant for the intended purpose**.

3. Relationship of management accounting, cost accounting and financial accounting

Financial accounting evolved from the stewardship function and is concerned in the main with such matters as: financial record keeping, the preparation of final accounts, dealing with debtors and creditors, the raising of finance, and dealing with all aspects of taxation. Financial accounting has a different emphasis to management accounting and, whilst outside the scope of this book, it is important that the concepts underlying financial accounting are thoroughly understood.

However, there is no realistic dividing line between cost accounting and management accounting particularly with regard to the provision of information for planning and control. Cost accounting is at a more basic level than management accounting and in many organisations is primarily concerned with the ascertainment of product costs. Because the cost accounting system is an important source of data for management accounting purposes, students must be totally familiar with basic cost accounting principles and methods and their conventions and limitations. A chapter covering the outlines of cost ascertainment and basic cost accounting principles is included in this book for revision purposes but students are recommended to study a comprehensive book on cost accounting (for example: *Costing*, T Lucey, *Letts Educational (formerly DP Publications)*) before tackling this book.

4. Major themes of management accounting

There are a number of important themes which pervade all aspects of management accounting and which are covered in detail at various points in the book. These themes are briefly introduced below under the following headings – Future Orientation, Economic Reality, Goal Congruence, Information Systems, Statistical and Operational Research Techniques, Uncertainty. These themes are developed and exemplified throughout the book.

5. Future orientation

Much of the work of the management accountant is concerned with the future, for example, the provision of information for policy formulation, for planning, and for decision making. In detail these activities may involve – forecasting future costs and revenues – estimating future rates of taxation, interest and inflation – considering the reactions of markets and competitors to the introduction of new products or prices – analysing the likely changes in cost structures and productivity consequent upon the introduction of new methods and equipment – assessing the effect of government policies on the operations of the organisation, and many other similar considerations.

Because of this future orientation, information from conventionally prepared historical records (for example, last period's product costs) is only of value if it provides a guide to future outcomes. This factor is a considerable influence (or should be!) on the methods used for coding, recording and aggregating data used in the financial and cost accounting systems of the organisation.

6. Economic reality

Accounting data and information are used to represent the underlying economic activities of the organisation which include: buying materials, selling products, manufacturing, and financing the organisation. Accordingly, it is essential that the records of past performance and the information derived from the records which is used to guide future planning and decision making, represents the underlying economic realities in a clear and unambiguous manner unfettered by accounting conventions.

As a simple illustration of this principle assume that a firm has some raw material called Zeon in stock which cost £500 per ton to purchase. A new contract is being considered which could use Zeon. What is the appropriate cost to include for Zeon in the following circumstances?

a) Where Zeon is in regular use for many existing products and use for the new contract would require an immediate replenishment order at a cost of £600 per ton, and

b) Where Zeon has no alternative productive use but could be sold for scrap at £200 per ton?

Assuming (a) applied the appropriate price to use would be the replacement cost of £600 per ton and if (b) were applicable then the scrap value of £200 per ton would be the appropriate figure to use. It will be noted that the recorded historical cost is not relevant in either case.

7. Goal congruence

This rather ugly piece of jargon simply means that the management accounting system should encourage all employees, including management, to act in a fashion which contributes to the overall objectives of the organisation, ie the employees' objectives and the organisation's objectives would, in ideal circumstances, coincide. More broadly the theme which is stressed repeatedly throughout this book is that the behavioural aspects of management accounting are of supreme importance. The systems and the approach adopted by the management accountant should motivate staff by means of genuine participation, good communications, rapid feedback and in many other ways, all of which are dealt with in detail later in the book.

8. Information systems

An organisation comprises a number of information systems or networks, frequently computer based. Sometimes there are separate information systems dealing with sales, production, personnel, financial and other matters, sometimes there is integration of these sub-systems. Rarely, if ever, is the information system a totally integrated one dealing with all aspects of management's requirements for planning, control and decision making. In many organisations the management accounting information system is the most developed of all the information systems and it is therefore critical that management accounting systems are designed in accordance with the principles of systems theory otherwise they will be less efficient. An example of this could be where a poorly designed budget system causes a manager to act in a manner which, although advantageous to his department, is detrimental to the overall objectives of the organisation. This is an example of *sub-optimality*.

9. Statistical and operational research techniques

Certain aspects of management accounting, particularly in the areas of planning and decision making, lend themselves to the use of appropriate statistical and operational research techniques. The use of such techniques does not alter the underlying objectives of management accounting but helps to improve or refine a particular solution. Frequently these techniques are implemented by means of computer packages and the accountant's role is to provide relevant input data and to interpret and present the results produced. There are numerous areas where such techniques have been found to assist management accounting. Examples include: statistical forecasting for cost and sales extrapolations, linear programming for resource allocation problems such as production planning, economic order quantity models to help solve inventory control problems and so on.

It is important the management accountant has sufficient familiarity with such techniques to recognise where their use will be beneficial and cost effective. The use of relevant techniques should be seen as a normal part of the work of the modern management accountant and accordingly this book deals with some key techniques at appropriate points throughout the book. Because of their particular importance in planning, control and decision making certain techniques (for example, linear programming and statistical forecasting) are dealt with in this book but for full coverage of statistical and operational research techniques students are advised to refer to an appropriate text (for example: *Quantitative Techniques*, T Lucey, *Letts Educational (formerly DP Publications)*).

10. Uncertainty

Conditions of certainty are said to exist when a single point estimate can be made which will be exactly achieved. Conversely, uncertainty exists where there are various possible outcomes or results or values. It will be apparent that uncertainty, to a greater or lesser degree, is present in most aspects of management accounting, particularly in the areas of planning and decision making. The influence of uncertainty usually increases the longer the planning or decision period but it is frequently present in short run circumstances as well.

There may be uncertainties about the measurement of data, the economic climate, wage rates, performance levels, material costs, the actions of competitors, the rate of inflation or indeed any of the myriads of factors involved in a typical decision.

Accordingly, the management accountant must recognise the all pervasive influence of uncertainty and incorporate its effects into his analysis of a problem. This may involve statistical tests or in depth investigations on uncertain source data, the use of probabilistic analysis when processing the data, and/or presenting and interpreting the results for the decision maker in ways that show the effects of uncertainty. In many circumstances it can be positively misleading to show a single figure of profit or contribution when many of the factors involved are likely to be subject to uncertainty.

11. Central role of decision making

Underlying all the activities of management and therefore all the activities of the management accounting, is decision making.

Planning, control systems, performance appraisal, resource allocation and all the other facets of the managerial task, directly or indirectly involve decision making. This is a key point to bear in mind when studying the whole of the book and not just the sections involved with particular decision making techniques.

12. Inflation and management accounting

Inflation is but one element, albeit an important one, of the general problem of uncertainty. As pointed out earlier in the chapter the management accountant must consider the effects of uncertainty in every facet of his work and this applies equally to inflation.

Although the Accounting Profession has had difficulties in developing a comprehensive system of accounting for inflation in published accounts, this is no excuse for the management accountant to ignore the effects of inflation when preparing information for planning, control and decision making for use within the firm.

The general effect of inflation, assuming normal accounting procedures and no special adjustments, is that there is an overstatement of profits and an understatement of asset values. These features lead to several undesirable effects which include: higher tax payments (the fiscal drift effect beloved by governments), liquidity problems and an erosion of real income. As a primary task of the management accountant is to show economic realities it is important that the changing value of money is reflected in the information provided to management. Whilst the effects of inflation impinge on every aspects of accounting there are areas where its effects may be particularly significant, eg investment appraisal, pricing decisions, performance appraisal and budgeting, and accordingly there are sections on dealing with inflation in these areas at appropriate points throughout the book.

13. Changing role of the management accountant

There have been dramatic changes in the nature of industry over the past ten years and it is likely that the 1990s will bring even more change. The environment and industrial conditions have become more volatile, there is increasing usage of micro-electronics in the factory and office, there is increase and ever-changing competitive threats especially from overseas. In addition, the role of the management accountant as the sole or primary supplier of information to management is being challenged by other information specialists, including systems analysts, operational researchers, managerial economists and business studies graduates. To meet these challenges the management accountant must be adaptable with a sufficient knowledge of a range of relevant disciplines so as to be able to provide the right information at the right time. He must be prepared to keep up-to-date and master new concepts, principles and techniques. At all times he must be critical of existing systems and information to ensure their continuing relevance in the future. The position of management accountants in the future will not be a comfortable one but it will be challenging and worthwhile.

A particular challenge that the management accountant must face is the growth in the use of Advanced Manufacturing Technology (AMT) in what are termed World Class Manufacturers (WCM).

AMT means that production is assisted and controlled by computers, automation is used extensively and radical production administration methods are used. This means that Management Accounting must adapt and rethink traditional methods to ensure its usefulness in the new manufacturing environment.

The drive for efficiency and accountability is not confined to the private sector. Developments such as the Market and Budget Holders in the National Health Services, Local Management in Schools, Government Agencies and so on focus attention on costs, efficiency, budgets and performance in the Public Sector, all of which require Management Accounting expertise.

14. Management accounting and computers

Nowadays much of the routine aspects of management accounting is dealt with by computers. This includes; cost analysis and forecasting, all forms of ledger keeping, product cost calculations, routine reports production, variance analysis and so on. In addition there is a tendency for computers to be used for more and more of the sophisticated aspects of management accounting such as the provision of information for planning and decision making. Accordingly it is vital that the management accountant becomes fully conversant with computers and understands their advantages and disadvantages in dealing with management accounting. As more and more of the routine work is dealt with by computers, interpretation of results and professional judgement will play an increasing role.

The final chapter of this book deals with the application of computers in management accounting and information systems generally and, in addition to studying this chapter and other material on computers, students are urged to gain as much practical experience as possible with computers.

15. Scope of the book

The book has been written to provide a comprehensive, integrated coverage of management accounting. The book structure is shown in Figure 1.2 from which it will be seen that, after initial study of certain fundamentals, the book is arranged in four main sections that cover the key areas of work with which the management accountant is involved – planning, control, decision making, and performance appraisal. Each section covers the necessary theoretical background before discussing the ways that the particular topic is dealt with in practice. In this way the student is better able to understand the limitations of some of the techniques and procedures that are conventionally used whilst at the same time appreciating the practical difficulties involved in implementing a theoretically optimum solution.

16. Summary

a) Management accounting is concerned with the provision and interpretation of information which assists management in planning, controlling, decision making and appraising performance.

b) The key feature of information is that it must be relevant for the intended purpose.

c) The information supplied by the management accountant is future oriented and must reflect economic realities unfettered by accounting conventions.

d) The management accountant must be aware of the behavioural consequences of his actions and information. Goal congruence must be encouraged.

e) Management accounting systems should be designed in accordance with system principles and are improved by the judicious use of appropriate statistical and operational research techniques.

f) Uncertainty exists in all business situations and the information supplied by the management accountant must reflect the uncertainties and variabilities of the situation.

g) Regardless of whether or not inflation adjustments are made in the organisation's published accounts, the requirement to show economic reality dictates that the management accountant should take account of the changing value of money.

h) The structure and scope of the book is shown in Figure 1.2.

17. Points to note

a) The concept of 'consistency'. so necessary for many aspects of accountancy, is inappropriate for management accounting purposes. The only consistent rule is that the information must be relevant for the intended purpose. This may mean, for example, that for different purposes an asset might be valued in several ways. It might be historical cost, net book value, replacement cost, resale value, scrap value, whichever is the most relevant for the intended purpose.

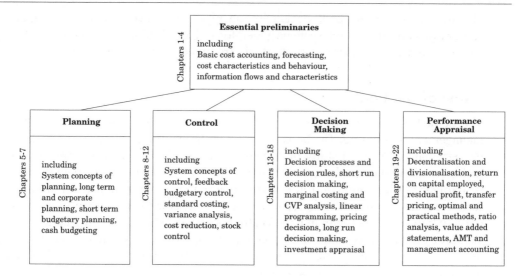

Figure 1.2 Structure and scope of book.

b) The management accountant has no exclusive rights to be the sole supplier of information to management. Other specialists, for example, systems analysts, operational researchers, economists and so on are increasingly providing information for planning and decision making purposes. If the management accountant is to maintain his pre-eminent position in this area it is essential that he takes a broadly based multi-disciplinary view of business operations and is able to appreciate the contributions made by disciplines such as operations research, economics, computer science, and the behavioural sciences.

Additional reading

Topics in Management Accounting; *Arnold, Carsberg & Scapens* – Philip Allan
Accounting for Management Control; *Emmanuel & Otley* – Chapman & Hall
An Insight into Management Accounting; *Sizer* – Pitman

Self review questions

1. Define management accounting. (2)
2. What is the key characteristic of all information supplied by the management accountant? (3)
3. Why must the information produced by the management accountant concerned with the future? (5)
4. Why must the information produced by the management accountant reflect economic reality? (6)
5. What is goal congruence? (7)
6. In what areas of management accounting can statistical and operational research techniques be employed? (9)
7. Why is the treatment of uncertainty important? (10)
8. Why must the effects of inflation be considered? (12)
9. What are some of the developments which are extending the scope of management accounting? (13)

2 Cost accounting and cost ascertainment – a revision

1. Objectives

After studying this chapter you will:

❑ have revised your knowledge of cost accounting

❑ be able to define basic cost accounting terminology;

❑ know how overheads are established and used in product costing;

❑ understand the difference between absorption and marginal costing;

❑ be able to deal with secondary apportionment of service department costs;

❑ know the principles of job, batch and contract costing;

❑ have a sound knowledge of process costing;

❑ understand the principles of activity-based costing.

2. Historical emphasis

The whole process of cost ascertainment is directed towards the establishment of what it actually cost to produce an article, run a department or complete a job. The costs involved are *past costs*, ie those that have already been incurred. Thus the cost ascertainment process (like financial accounting) is concerned with collecting, classifying, recording, analysing and reporting upon the financial consequences of past actions. For many purposes it is vital to know the results of past activities (for example; for control, inventory valuations and profit determination) but this historic emphasis is in sharp contrast to the future orientation of much management accounting work; for example, the provision of information for planning and decision making.

It is *future costs and revenues* which are relevant for these purposes so that past costs are only of importance if they provide a guide to the future. It is because of this, and the fact that cost ascertainment involves numerous conventions and assumptions, that any information derived from the cost accounting system is critically examined and, if necessary, adjusted before it is used for management accounting purposes. This is an important point which should be borne in mind whilst studying this chapter.

3. Some basic definitions

Before the procedures of cost ascertainment are discussed, certain preliminary definitions need to be dealt with.

Cost unit This is a unit of output or service to which costs can be related. The unit chosen is what is most relevant for the activities of the organisation.

Examples

Units of production   Tables, TV sets, tons of cement, litres of paint, a job, a contract, a barrel of beer.

Units of service   Consulting hours, guest-nights, kilowatt hours, passenger-mile.

Within a given organisation there may be several different cost units in order to cost various products or activities.

As costs are incurred they are classified in various way by means of the accounts coding system. An important, primary classification is that into *direct costs* and *indirect costs*.

Direct costs. These costs comprising direct materials, direct labour, and direct expenses, are those which can be directly identified with a job, a product or a service.

Examples

Direct materials	Raw materials used in the product; parts and assemblies incorporated into the finished product; bricks, timber, cement used on a contract.
Direct labour	Wages paid to production workers for work directly related to production, salaries directly attributable to a saleable service (for example, a draughtsman's salary in a contract design office).
Direct expense	Expenses incurred specifically for a particular job, project or saleable service (for example, royalties paid per unit for a copyright design, tool hire for a particular job).

The total of direct costs is known as *prime cost* thus

Direct materials + direct labour + direct expenses = prime cost

Indirect costs. All material, labour and expense expenditure which cannot be identified with the product are termed indirect costs. The total of indirect costs is known as *overhead* which is normally separated into categories such as Production Overheads, Administration Overheads, Selling Overheads and so on.

It will be clear that the sum of direct and indirect costs will equal total cost, thus:

Prime cost + overheads = total cost

4. Establishing overheads

The process of establishing overheads is more involved than for direct costs. The conventional process includes defining a number of cost centres and then allocating or apportioning costs to the cost centres. These terms are defined below:

Cost centre: a production or service location, function, activity or item of equipment whose costs may be attributed to cost units. Terminology.

Thus, via the cost centre coding system, costs are gathered together according to their incidence. The gathering together of the indirect costs results in the establishment of the overheads relating to each cost centre which is an essential preliminary to spreading the overheads over cost units.

Cost allocation. This is the term used where the whole of a cost, without splitting or separation, can be attributed to a cost unit or cost centre.

All direct costs being identifiable with a cost unit can be allocated without difficulty. Allocation is less frequent with indirect costs but for some items it is possible. For example, fuel oil for a heating boiler which supplies heat to the whole factory could be allocated to the Boiler cost centre.

Apportionment. This process, which is common for indirect costs, involves the splitting or sharing of a common cost over the receiving cost centres on some basis which is deemed to reflect the benefits received. The following table gives examples of typical bases of apportionment.

Basis	Costs which may be apportioned on this basis
Floor Area	Rates, Rent, Heating, Cleaning, Lighting, Building Depreciation
Volume or Space Occupied	Heating, Lighting, Building Depreciation
Number of Employees in each Cost Centre	Canteen, Welfare, Personnel, General Administration, Industrial Relations, Safety
Book (or Replacement) Value of Plant, Equipment, Premises, etc.	Insurance, Depreciation
Stores Requisitions	Store-Keeping
Weight of Materials	Store-Keeping, Materials Handling

Note

The process of apportionment, although commonly used for cost ascertainment purposes, is a convention only and as such its accuracy cannot be tested. Furthermore, the use of data which involves apportionments for planning, control or decision making purposes is likely to give misleading results. Accordingly the management accountant must carefully analyse the methods by which cost data are prepared and make appropriate adjustments before using such data for management accounting purposes.

5. Overhead absorption

Overheads form part of total cost but cannot be directly identified with a given cost unit in the way that direct costs can be. Accordingly, overheads are spread over the cost units by the process known as *overhead absorption* or *overhead recovery*.

This is conventionally done by calculating an overhead absorption rate (OAR) based on the estimated overheads for a cost centre and the expected number of direct labour hours or machines hours for the cost centre. Labour and machine hours are the most common bases chosen for production cost centres. It is conventionally assumed that time based methods such as these more accurately reflect the incidence of overheads in labour or machine intensive departments, respectively, but note that this view is challenged by newer developments such as Activity-based Costing dealt with later.

Basic Cost Ascertainment. Having defined the various terms the build up of total cost can be shown.

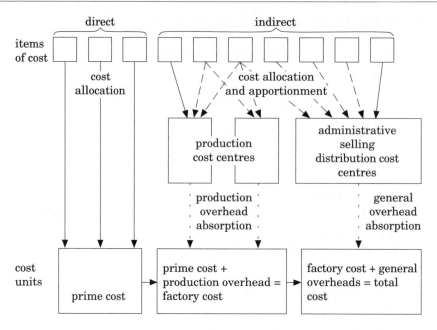

Figure 2.1 The conventional build-up of total cost.

6. Absorption costing

The procedure outlined so far by which all overheads are absorbed into production is known as *absorption costing* or sometimes total absorption costing. Because total overheads contain items which are fixed in nature (those which do not change when the level of activity changes, eg rates) and items known as *variable costs* (those which vary more or less directly with activity changes, eg raw material usage), absorption costing has implications for stock valuation and performance measurement which are subject to criticism from some accountants. An alternative method of costing, known as *marginal costing,* excludes fixed costs from the absorption process and charges them in total against the period's results. The implications of these two alternative approaches are explored in the following paragraphs and later in the book.

7. Marginal costing

Marginal costing distinguishes between fixed costs and variable costs. The marginal cost of a product is its variable cost, ie it includes direct labour, direct materials, direct expenses and the variable part of overheads. Marginal costing can be defined as

> *'the accounting system in which variable costs are changed to cost units and fixed costs of the period are written-off in full against the aggregate contribution. Its special value is in decision making'.*   *Terminology.*

The term 'contribution' mentioned in the formal definition is the term given to the difference between Sales and Marginal Cost.

Thus:

Marginal cost

> **= Variable cost**

> **= Direct labour + Direct material + Direct expense + Variable overheads**

Contribution

> **= Sales – Marginal cost**

The term marginal cost sometimes refers to the marginal cost per unit and sometimes to the total marginal costs of a department or batch or operation. The meaning is usually clear from the context.

Note: Alternative names for marginal costing are the 'contribution approach' and 'direct costing'.

There are two main uses for marginal costing principles:

a) As a basis for providing information to management for planning and decision making. It is particularly appropriate for short run decisions involving changes in volume or activity and the resulting cost changes. This is an important area of study for students and it is dealt with in detail later in the book.

b) It can also be used in the routine cost accounting system for the calculation of costs and the valuation of stocks. Used in this fashion, it is an alternative to total absorption costing. This facet of marginal costing is dealt with below.

8. Marginal costing and absorption costing

Absorption costing, sometimes known as total absorption costing, is the basis of all financial accounting statements and was the basis used for the first part of this chapter. Using absorption costing, all costs are absorbed into production and thus operating statements do not distinguish between fixed and variable costs.

Consequently the valuation of stocks and work-in-progress contains both fixed and variable elements. On the other hand, using marginal costing, fixed costs are not absorbed into the cost of production. they are treated as period costs and written off each period in the Costing Profit and Loss account. The effect of this is that finished goods and work-in-progress are valued at marginal cost only, ie the variable elements of cost, usually prime cost plus variable overhead. At the end of a period the marginal cost of sales is deducted from sales revenue to show the contribution, from which fixed costs are deducted to show net profit.

The two approaches are illustrated below using the following data:

Example 1

In a period, 20,000 units of Z were produced and sold. Costs and revenues were:

	£
Sales	100,000
Production costs: Variable	35,000
Fixed	15,000
Administrative + Selling overheads: Fixed	25,000

Operating statements

Absorption costing approach	£	*Marginal costing approach*	£	£
Sales	100,000	Sales		100,000
less Production cost of sales	50,000	less Marginal cost		35,000
= Gross Profit	50,000	= Contribution		65,000
less Admin + Selling Overheads	25,000	less Fixed costs		
		Production	15,000	
		Admin S + D	25,000	40,000
= Net profit	£25,000	= Net profit		£25,000

The above illustration, although simple, illustrates the general characteristics of both approaches.

The key figure arising in the Marginal statement is the contribution of £65,000. The total amount of contribution arising from Product Z (and other products, if any) forms a pool from which fixed costs are met. Any surplus arising after fixed costs are met becomes the Net Profit.

9. Changes in the level of activity

When changes occur in the level of activity, the absorption costing approach may cause some confusion. In example 1 the activity level was 20,000 units and using the absorption approach, the profit per unit and cost per unit can be calculated as follows:

		£
Selling Price per unit		5
less Total cost per unit =	£75,000	
	20,000	3.75
Profit per unit		£1.25

If these figures were used as guides to results at any activity level other than 20,000, they would be incorrect and may mislead. For example, if the level of activity of Example 1 changed to 25,000 units, it might be assumed that the total profits would be 25,000 × £1.25 = £31,150. However, the results are likely to be as follows:

Operating Statement (Absorption approach)

		£
Sales (25,000 × £5)		125,000
less Production Cost (£35,000 × 125% + 15,000)		58,750
= Gross Profit		66,250
less Admin + Selling overheads		25,000
= Net Profit		£41,250

The difference is, of course caused by the incorrect treatment of the fixed cost. In such circumstances the use of the marginal approach presents a clearer picture. Based on the data in Example 1 the marginal cost per unit and the contribution per unit are calculated as follows:

$$\text{Marginal cost per unit} = \frac{£35,000}{20,000}$$

$$= \textbf{£1.75}$$

$$\text{Contribution per unit} = \text{Sales Price} - \text{Marginal cost per unit}$$
$$= £5 - £1.75$$
$$= \textbf{£3.25}$$

If, once again, the activity is increased to 25,000 units, the expected profit would be:

$$= (25,000 \text{ units} \times \text{Contribution per unit}) - \text{Fixed costs}$$
$$= (25,000 \times £3.25) - £40,000$$
$$= £41,250$$

and the operating statement on marginal costing lines would be

		£
Sales		125,000
less Marginal cost (25,000 × 1.75)		43,750
= Contribution		£81,250
less Fixed costs		40,000
Net profit		£41,250

Note: Students will note that the marginal cost and contribution per unit are assumed to be constant and that the fixed costs remain unchanged.

10. Stocks and marginal costing

Although the method of presentation was different, both marginal and absorption costing produced the same net profit for the data in Example 1. This was because there was no stock at the beginning or end of the period. Because the two methods differ in their valuation of stock, they produce different profit figures when stocks arise. This is illustrated below.

Example 2

Assume the same data as Example 1 except that only 18,000 of the 20,000 units produced were sold, 2,000 units being carried forward as stock to the next period.

Operating statements based upon marginal costing and absorption costing principles are shown below.

Operating statements

Absorption costing			*Marginal costing*		
		£			£
Sales (18,000 × £5)		90,000	Sales		90,000
	£			£	
less Production			*less* Marginal cost	35,000	
Cost of sales	50,000		– Closing stock		
– Closing stock			(2,000 × £.175)	3,500	31,500
(2,000 × £2.50)	5,000	45,000			
= Gross profit		£45,000	= Contribution		£58,500
less Admin + Selling			*less* Fixed costs		
overheads		25,000	Production	15,000	
			Admin S + D	25,000	40,000
= Net Profit		£20,000			£18,500

a) The closing stock valuations using the two approaches are:

Absorption Costing = Average Production Cost (including fixed costs)

$$= \frac{£50,000}{20,000} = £2.50$$

Marginal Costing = Marginal production cost, ie variable costs only

$$= \frac{£35,000}{20,000} = £1.75$$

b) By including fixed costs in stock valuation, absorption costing transfers some of this period's fixed costs into next period when they will be charged against the revenue derived from the stock carried forward (assuming it is sold). Marginal costing always writes off all fixed costs in the period they are incurred.

c) In a period with increasing stocks (as the one illustrated) absorption costing will show higher profits than marginal costing. Conversely in a period of decreasing stocks marginal costing will show the higher profits. The difference is of course, entirely due to the different treatment of fixed costs in the stock valuation.

11. Marginal costing or absorption costing?

The arguments below relate to the use of these techniques in the routine cost accounting system of the organisation and not to their use for decision making or control.

Arguments for the use of marginal costing in routine costing:

a) Simple to operate.

b) No apportionments, which are frequently on an arbitrary basis, of fixed costs to products or departments. Many fixed costs are indivisible by their nature, eg Managing Director's Salary.

c) Where sales are constant, but production fluctuates (possibly an unlikely circumstance) marginal costing shows a constant net profit whereas absorption costing shows variable amounts of profit.

d) Under or over absorption of overheads is almost entirely avoided. The usual reason for under/over absorption is the inclusion of fixed costs into overhead absorption rates and the level of activity being different to that planned.

e) Fixed costs are incurred on a time basis, eg salaries, rent, rates etc., and do not relate to activity. Therefore it is logical to write them off in the period they are incurred and this is done using marginal costing.

f) Accounts prepared using marginal costing more nearly approach the actual cash flow position.

Arguments for the use of total absorption in routine costing:

a) Fixed costs are a substantial and increasing proportion of costs in modern industry. Production cannot be achieved without incurring fixed costs which thus form an inescapable part of the cost of production, so should be included in stock valuations. Marginal costing may give the impression that fixed costs are somehow divorced from production.

b) Where production is constant but sales fluctuate, net profit fluctuations are less with absorption costing than with marginal costing.

c) Where stock building is a necessary part of operations, eg timber seasoning, spirit maturing, firework manufacture, the inclusion of fixed costs in stock valuation is necessary and desirable. Otherwise a series of fictitious losses will be shown in earlier periods to be offset eventually by excessive profits when the goods are sold.

d) The calculation of marginal cost and the concentration upon contribution may lead to the firm setting prices which are below total cost although producing some contribution. Absorption cost makes this less likely because of the automatic inclusion of fixed charges.

e) SSAP 9 (Stocks and Works in Progress) recommends the use of absorption costing for financial accounts because costs and revenues must be matched in the period when the revenue arises, not when the costs are incurred. Also it recommends that stock valuations must include production overheads incurred in the normal course of business even if such overheads are time related, ie fixed. The production overheads must be based upon normal activity levels.

12. Conclusions regarding marginal and absorption costing

No generalised, all embracing answer can be given as to which technique should be used. Having regard to all the factors, the accountant should make a judgement as to which technique is more appropriate for the requirements of a particular organisation. Although any technique can be used for internal purposes, SSAP 9 is quite clear that absorption costing must be the basis of the financial accounts.

It would appear that the use of a full marginal costing system in the routine cost ascertainment procedures of an organisation is relatively rare. This does not mean that marginal costing principles are unimportant. An understanding of the behaviour of costs and the implications of contribution is vital for accountants and managers. The use of marginal costing principles in planning and decision making, dealt with later in the book is universal and is of considerable importance.

13. Multi-period example of marginal and absorption costing

To bring together the various points covered in the chapter, a fully worked example is shown below.

Example 3

Stock, production and sales data for Industrial Detergents Ltd are given below.

		Period 1	Period 2	Period 3	Period 4
Production	(litres)	60,000	70,000	55,000	65,000
Sales	(litres)	60,000	55,000	65,000	70,000
Opening Stock	(litres)	–	–	15,000	5,000
Closing Stock	(litres)	–	15,000	5,000	–

The company has a single product, for which the financial data, based on an activity level of 60,000 litres/period, are as follows:

	Cost per litre £
Direct Material	2.50
Direct Labour	3.00
Production Overheads	
= 200% of direct labour	6.00
= Total cost/litre	£11.50
Selling price per litre	£18.00

Administrative overheads are fixed at £100,000 per period and half of the production overheads are fixed.

From the above information prepare operating statements on marginal and absorption costing principles.

Solution

The first step is to establish the amount of fixed production overheads per period. The cost data shown above are based on 60,000 litres.

$$
\begin{aligned}
\text{Labour for 60,000 litres} &= 60,000 \times £3 &= £180,000 \\
\text{Total production overheads} &= 200\% \times £180,000 &= £360,000 \\
\therefore \text{Fixed production overheads} &= \frac{£360,000}{2} &= £180,000
\end{aligned}
$$

The variable overhead recovery rate is accordingly 100% of direct wages so that marginal cost per litre can be established as follows:

	£
Material	2.50
Labour	3.00
Variable overhead	
100% of wages	3.00
	£8.50

Operating Statement using Marginal Costing

	Period 1		Period 2		Period 3		Period 4	
	£		£		£		£	
Sales	1,080,000		990,000		1,170,000		1,260,000	
Marginal cost of								
production	510,000			595,000		467,500		552,500
+ opening stock	–			–		127,500		42,500
– closing stock	–			127,500		42,500		–
= Marginal cost of								
sales	510,000		467,500		552,500		595,000	
Contribution	570,000		522,500		617,500		665,000	
Fixed costs								
(Admin + Production)	280,000		280,000		280,000		280,000	
Net profit	£290,000		£242,500		£337,500		£385,000	

Note: Stocks are valued at marginal cost.

Operating Statement using Absorption costing in Accordance with SSAP 9

	Period 1		Period 2		Period 3		Period 4	
	£		£		£		£	
Sales	1,080,000		990,000		1,170,000		1,260,000	
Total cost of								
production	690,000			805,000		632,500		747,500
+ opening stock	–			–		172,500		57,500
– closing stock	–			172,500		57,500		–
= Total cost of sales	690,000		632,500		747,500		805,000	
Gross profit	390,000		357,500		422,500		455,000	
Administration costs	100,000		100,000		100,000		100,000	
Net profit	£290,000		£257,500		£322,500		£355,000	
Planned activity level	60,000		60,000		60,000		60,000	
Actual activity level	60,000		70,000		55,000		65,000	
Difference	–		+ 10,000		– 5,000		+ 5,000	
Overhead over or								
Under) absorption	–		+ £30,000		(£15,000)		+ £15,000	

Notes:

a) Stocks are valued at full production cost including fixed production overheads, ie in this example £11.50 per litre. This represents the cost at normal activity levels in accordance with SSAP 9 recommendations.

b) The amount of over or under absorbed overhead represents the over or under recovery of fixed overheads caused when activity is above or below the planned activity level. In this example the fixed overheads are recovered at £3 per litre. ∴ in period 2 production was 70,000 litres as compared with 60,000 planned so the over absorption was 10,000 litres at £3 per litre = £30,000.

c) The over/under absorption could be taken direct to P & L a/c or, more usually, taken to a suspense account from which the net balance at the end of the year would be written off to P & L.

d) The amount over absorbed would be deducted from total cost; the amount under absorbed would be added to total cost.

e) Because in this example, production and sales were equal over the periods concerned the profits using the two techniques can be reconciled thus:

Profits using Marginal Costing

	£
Period 1	290,000
2	242,500
3	337,500
4	385,000
	£1,255,000

Profits using Absorption Costing

	£
Period 1	290,000
2	257,500
3	322,500
4	355,000
+ Net over absorption	30,000
	£1,255,000

14. Elements of cost – material, labour and overheads

There are a number of costing problems associated with the three elements of cost and these are dealt with below.

Materials. For many organisations the expenditure on materials is a large proportion of total cost and it is essential that all aspects of material control are dealt with efficiently. This involves purchasing, receipt, storage and accounting functions.

There are two main areas with which accountants are concerned. Firstly, the management of the investment in materials and stocks through inventory control procedures which are dealt with in this book under the general section dealing with Control.

Secondly, the costing problems involved in pricing issues of materials to production. The pricing system should be consistent and realistic and should not involve undue administrative complications.

The major pricing systems are FIFO (First in First Out), LIFO (Last in First Out), Average price and Standard price.

FIFO — Issues are priced at the price of the oldest batch in stock until all units have been issued when the next oldest batch is used. It is an actual cost system which has the effect of charging the oldest prices to production and valuing stocks at the more recent. The system is recommended by SSAP 9 and is acceptable to the Inland Revenue.

LIFO — Issues are priced at the price of the most recent batch until a new batch is received. It is an actual cost system which causes product costs to be based fairly closely on current prices and stocks to be valued at the oldest prices. It is not recommended by SSAP 9 and is not acceptable to the Inland Revenue. Like FIFO it is administratively cumbersome because it requires the recording system to keep track of batches.

Average Price — This is a perpetual weighted average system where the issue price is calculated after each receipt taking into account both quantities and money value. This system has an effect on product costs and stock valuation somewhere between LIFO and FIFO. The system makes cost comparisons between jobs somewhat easier and is simpler to administer. It is recommended by SSAP 9 and acceptable to the Inland Revenue.

Standard Price — This is a predetermined price based on consideration of all factors which are expected to affect the price. If a realistic price can be set then purchasing efficiency can be monitored to some extent.

Pricing methods – a summary. Apart from the rare occasions when the specific price paid for materials can be charged into product costs, the price charges will be based on a pricing convention such as described above. It is because of this that product costs from the costing system which are to be used for planning and decision making purposes need to be used with discretion by the management accountant. For planning and decision making purposes the appropriate material cost may be the future replacement cost, the net realisable value or the value of the material in some alternative use (opportunity cost). Rarely will the historical cost be appropriate.

15. Labour cost

Payment systems for production workers are frequently complex and difficult to administer. Although there are innumerable variations they are essentially of two types; those where straight time rates are paid and wages are not related to production levels, and those where payment is related directly or indirectly to production levels.

Obviously, where the payment system is related in some way to activity, for example, by straight or differential piecework or by individual and/or group bonus systems, labour costs will have some variable characteristics but rarely, if ever, will labour costs behave in a truly variable, linear fashion. The existence of guaranteed minima, in-lieu bonuses, high day rate systems, the tendency for more production workers to become salaried employees, all have implications for the management accountant when considering labour costs in planning and decision making.

16. Service cost centres

As previous described, overheads are aggregated by the process of classification, allocation and apportionment and are then spread over the cost units produced, by the process known as overhead absorption.

A typical complication which occurs in most costing systems relates to service cost centres. These are departments which, although providing essential services to production departments and each other, do not take part in actual production, eg maintenance and stores. Naturally, service cost centres incur costs which may be allocated to them (eg storeman's wages to stores) or apportioned to them (eg an appropriate share of the rates, heating costs to the maintenance shop) by the normal cost accounting process.

The service department costs have to be shared over the production departments by the process of *secondary apportionment,* the base for which is chosen so as to reflect the use made of each service. This process is necessary so that all the service department costs are eventually included in the costs of the production cost units. Typical bases for the secondary apportionment, ie the apportionment of service costs to production cost centres, are shown below:

Service Department	Possible Bases for the Secondary Apportionment of Service Department Costs to Production Cost Centres
Stores	No. of Requisitions Weight of Materials Issues No. of Items Issued
Maintenance	Maintenance Labour Hours Maintenance Wages Plant Values
Power Generation	Metered Usage Notional Capacity
Personnel	No. of Employees per Department Gross Wages per Department

The necessity for secondary apportionment disappears when Activity Based Costing (ABC) is used. With ABC most of the costs of support services can be traced direct to the product. This is explained in more detail when ABC is covered.

17. Service department costs with reciprocal servicing

Prior to the secondary apportionment of costs to production departments it is necessary to establish the costs of each service department. Particular problems arise when service departments provide reciprocal servicing for each other as well as for Production. For example assume that Maintenance (M) do work for Power Generation (PG) who supply power to maintenance. The total cost of M cannot be found until the charge for PG's services is known whilst PG's costs cannot be found until the charge for

M's work is known. There are three conventional methods of breaking this circular problem; continuous allotment, the elimination method and the algebraic method using simultaneous equations which is illustrated below in Example 3.

Example 3

A factory has two service departments maintenance (M) and Power Generation (PG) and three production departments (P1, P2 and P3). There is reciprocal servicing as well as servicing the production departments. It has been agreed that the most appropriate bases of apportionment for service departments costs are: Capital equipment values for maintenance and motor horse power for power generation. The appropriate data are summarised below.

Department	M	PG	P1	P2	P3
Overheads	£4,800	£14,600	£14,000	£22,000	£33,000
Capital values		£100,000	£550,000	£760,000	£640,000
Proportion	–	5%	25%	38%	32%
Horse power	9000	–	24000	16200	10800
Proportion	15%	–	40%	27%	18%

It is required to establish the total overheads of the production departments.

Solution using simultaneous equations

Let m = Total overheads for maintenance when the power generation charges have been allotted.

Let pg = Total overheads for power generation when the maintenance charges have been allotted.

$$\therefore m = 4800 + 0.15pg$$
$$pg = 14600 + 0.05m$$

which rearranged give

$$m - 0.15pg = 4800 \qquad \text{Equation I}$$
$$pg - 0.05m = 1460 \qquad \text{Equation II}$$

These equations are solved in the normal manner (in this case Equation II is multiplied by 20 and added to Equation I) thus

$$m - 0.15\,pg = 4800 \qquad \text{Equation I}$$
$$\underline{20pg - m = 292,000} \qquad 20 \times \text{Equation II}$$
$$19.85pg = 296,800$$
$$\therefore pg = £14952$$

and by substitution, m is found to be £7,043.

These values of notional overheads are used to make the final secondary apportionments thus (rounded to the nearest £).

	Departments				
	M	PG	P1	P2	P3
Original Allotment	£4,800	£14,600	£14,000	£22,000	£33,000
Notional overheads for M apportioned over serviced departments	–7,043	352	1,761	2,676	2,254
Notional overheads for PQ apportioned over serviced departments	2,243	–14,952	5,981	4,037	2,691
	–	–	£21,742	£28,713	£37,945

The final apportioned overheads equal the original total allotments, ie £88,400.

Notes:

a) The processes of primary and secondary apportionments and establishing the costs of service departments are conventions only and as such their accuracy cannot be tested. The use of such data for decision making should therefore be subject to close scrutiny to ensure its appropriateness for the intended purpose.

b) Reciprocal service cost problems can also be solved using matrix algebra, which is described in detail in 'Quantitative Techniques' Ibid.

18. Costing methods

These are methods of costing which are designed to suit the way products are manufactured or processed or the way that services are provided. Examples of costing methods are: job costing, batch costing, contract costing and process costing which are explained below. It must be clearly understood that, whatever costing method is used, basic costing principles relating to classification, allocation, apportionment and absorption will be used

19. Job costing

The main purposes of job costing are to establish the profit or loss on each completed job and to provide a valuation of uncompleted jobs, ie the Work-in-Progress (WIP). This done by creating a Job Cost Card for each job on which would be entered the following details:

❐ Direct Labour costs – including time based and piecework earnings.

❐ Direct Material costs – based on stores issues, special purchases, bills of materials.

❐ Direct expenses – expenses incurred specifically for the particular job, eg tool hire, royalties.

Based on these details and labour and machine time bookings the production departmental overheads would be calculated using the times recorded and the predetermined overhead absorption rates for labour or machine time as appropriate. A job is normally valued at factory cost until it is dispatched when an appropriate amount of selling and administration overheads would be added usually as a percentage of the works cost. The total of the partly complete job cost cards represent the firms work-in-progress and on completion the costs are removed from W-I-P and charged to the Cost of Sales account (DR Cost of Sales CR WIP).

20. Batch costing

This is a form of costing which is used where a quantity of identical articles are produced together as a batch. The general procedures are very similar to costing jobs. The batch would be treated as a job during manufacture and the various costs (material, labour and overheads) collected in the usual manner. On completion of the batch the total batch cost would be divided by the number of good articles produced so as to provide the average cost per article. Batch costing procedures are common in a variety of industries including clothing, footwear, engineering components.

21. Contract costing

This has many similarities to job costing and is usually adopted for work which is: site based, of a relatively long duration and undertaken to the customer's special requirements. Because of the self contained nature of most site operations more costs than normal can be identified as direct and thus charged to the contract, eg telephones on site, design and planning salaries, site vehicle costs.

A particular feature associated with contracts is the provision for progress payments to be made by the client which are necessary because of the length and value of some contracts. The basis for these interim payments is an architect's certificate of work satisfactorily completed. The amount paid is usually the certified value less a percentage retention which is released by the client when the contract is fully completed. Because contracts often extend over more than one financial year it is necessary to estimate the profit on uncompleted contracts so as to avoid undue fluctuation in company results. The profit to be taken is conservatively estimated to allow for any unforeseen difficulties and costs. Anticipated losses should be allowed for, in full, as early as possible.

The recommended approach for estimating attributable profit for the year and the resulting Balance Sheet entries is given in SSAP 9 Stocks and Long-Term Contracts.

22. Process costing

This form of costing is appropriate where the product follows a series of sequential, frequently automatic processes, eg paper making, refining, paint manufacture, food processing. The essence of process costing is the averaging of the total costs of each process over the total throughput of that process (including partly completed units) and charging the cost of the output of one process as the raw material input to the next process. Any partly complete units at the end of the period are, for cost calculation purposes, expressed as 'equivalent units'. This merely means the equivalent number of fully complete units which the partly complete units represents. For example, assume that at the end of a period the output of a process was as follows:

1300 fully complete units and 400 partly complete with the following progress:

Material	80% complete
Labour	60% complete
Overheads	50% complete

The number of equivalent units is:

	Fully complete units	+	Equivalent units in WIP	=	Total effective production
Material	1300	+	400 × 80%	=	1620
Labour	1300	+	400 × 60%	=	1540
Overheads	1300	+	400 × 50%	=	1500

The cost of each element of the total effective production is calculated from the material, labour and overhead costs of the period, aggregated, and a total cost per unit calculated.

23. Process losses

With many forms of processing the quantity, weight or volume of the *output* will be less than the quantity weight or volume of the material *input*. Where differences arise, there are three possibilities:

❐ losses as expected, ie *Normal Process Losses;*

❐ losses greater than expected, ie *Abnormal Process Losses;*

❐ losses less than expected ie *Abnormal Process Gains.*

When there are Normal losses these are borne by the good production. It is an important costing principle that abnormal conditions are excluded from routine reporting. Accordingly, the cost effects of abnormal losses or gains will be excluded from the Process account. This is done by costing the abnormal losses or gains on the same basis as good production ie they will carry a proportion of the normal losses.

24. Opening work in progress

It follows that where there are partly completed units at the end of one period (the closing WIP) there will be opening work in progress at the beginning of the next period. This opening work in progress will be partially complete and will have value brought forward from the previous period, sometimes sub-divided into the various elements of material, labour and overheads, each with a given degree of completion and value. Naturally in most practical situations there is both opening and closing work in progress and in such cases the problem arises of how to value the closing work in progress and the completed units transferred out.

There are two approaches to this problem; the FIFO method and the Average cost method.

FIFO method of valuation

Using this method it is assumed that units are dealt with on a first in – first out basis so that it is assumed that the first work done in a period is the completion of the opening WIP. The effect of this is that the closing WIP is valued at current period costs and part of the previous period's costs brought forward in the opening WIP valuation is attached to the cost of completed units.

Average cost method of valuation

Using this method an average unit cost is calculated using the total of the opening WIP valuation *plus* the current period costs. The effect of this is that both closing WIP and completed units are valued using the same average unit cost. This means that the previous period's costs (contained in the opening WIP valuation) influence the closing WIP valuation which is carried forward to the next period. It is for this reason that it is sometimes argued that the average cost method makes the comparison of performance between periods more difficult than when the FIFO method is used.

An alternative view is that the Average cost method is a useful device when costs fluctuate from period to period. Neither of the valuation methods can be said to be 'incorrect' or 'correct', they are simply two different conventions which produce different answers. When costs are stable from one period to another and/or where the work-in-progress is a small proportion of throughput then the two systems produce similar results.

Examples follow which contrast the results obtained using both methods of valuation.

Example 4

Process 2 received units from Process 1   and after carrying out work on the units transfers them to Process 3. For one accounting period the relevant data were as follows:

> Opening WIP   200 units (25% complete) valued at £2,500
>
> 800 units received from Process 1 valued at £4,300
>
> 840 units were transferred to Process 3
>
> Closing WIP   160 units (50% complete)

The costs for the period were £16,580 and no units were scrapped.

It is required to prepare the Process accounts for Process 2 using:

i)   the FIFO method of valuation,

ii) the average cost method of valuation.

Solution to Example 4 using FIFO method

Calculation of effective units of production

	Units
Completed units transferred out	840
+ Work contained in closing WIP (160 × 50%)	80
	920
− Work contained in opening WIP (200 × 25%)	50
∴ Effective units for period	870

$$\therefore \text{Period cost per unit} = \frac{\text{Total cost for period ie Process costs + transfers in}}{\text{Effective units for period}}$$

$$= \frac{16,580 + 4,300}{870}$$

$$= \textbf{£24.}$$

This figure is used to give the closing WIP valuation, ie

$160 \times 50\% \times £24 = £1,920.$

The valuation of the number of complete units transferred to Process 3 is found from the balance on the process account as follows:

Process 2 Account

	Units	£		Units	£
Opening WIP b/f	200	2,500			
Receipts from Process 1	800	4,300	Transfers to Process 3	840	21,460
Process costs		16,580	Closing WIP c/f	160	1,920
	1,000	23,380		1,000	23,380

Note on Example 4 (FIFO method):

The transfer value of £21,460 is the balance on the account and is £1,300 greater than the period cost per unit already calculated ie £21,460 – (840 × £24) = £1,300.

This is the amount by which the opening WIP valuation (based on the *previous* period's costs) is greater than the current period costs ie

$£2,500 – (200 \times 25\% \times £24) = £1,300.$

Thus, it would be seen that only the current period cost levels, ie the £24 per unit, are carried forward to the next period in the closing WIP valuation.

Solution to Example 4 using average cost method

Using this system the effective units are the transfers to the next process (840 units) plus the work contained in the closing WIP (80 units ie 50% of 160 units) that is a total of 920 *units.*

The costs involved are the total of the opening WIP valuation + the valuation of units transferred in + the process 2 costs ie

$£2,500 + 4,300 + 16,580 = £23,380.$

$$\therefore \text{average cost per unit} = \frac{23,380}{920} = £25.413.$$

This is used to value both the closing stock and transfers out thus:

Closing stock valuation = 160 × 50% × £25.413 = £2,033.

Transfers to Process 3 = 840 × £25.413 = £21,347.

The process account is as follows:

	Units	£		Units	£
Opening WIP b/f	200	2,500			
Receipts from Process 1	800	4,300	Transfers to Process 3	840	21,347
Process costs		16,580	Closing WIP c/f	160	2,033
	1,000	23,380		1,000	23,380

Notes on Example 4 (average cost method):

1. It will be seen that the effect of the average cost method is, in this example, to increase the value of closing stock and reduce the value of transfers to Process 3. This is because the previous period cost levels (as contained in the opening WIP valuation) were *higher* than the current cost levels. If the previous period cost levels were *lower* than current levels the average cost method would cause the closing WIP valuations to be lower than when using the FIFO system.

2. The above example has deliberately been kept simple to show clearly the principles involved. Examples follow which show the added complications of abnormal and normal scrap and where the elements (material, labour and overheads) of the opening and closing WIP are involved. It must be stressed however, that these added complications merely increase the amount of arithmetic involved, they do not alter the basic principles explained above so it is important that these are thoroughly understood before proceeding further.

Example 5

This example illustrates the treatment of opening and closing WIP where the WIP is broken down into its various elements.

The following data relate to Process Y for accounting period 2.

At the beginning of period 2, there were 800 units partly completed which had the following values:

	Value £	Percentage complete
Input material (from Process X)	8,200	100
Material introduced	5,600	55
Labour	3,200	60
Overheads	2,400	45

During the period 4,300 units were transferred from Process X at a value of £46,500 and other costs were:

	£
Material introduced	24,000
Labour	19,500
Overhead	18,200

At the end of the period, the closing WIP was 600 units which were at the following stage of completion:

Input material	100% complete
Material introduced	50% complete
Labour	45% complete
Overheads	40% complete

The balance of 4,500 units was transferred to Finished Goods.

Calculate the value of units transferred to Finished Goods and the value of WIP and prepare the Process account using

i) the FIFO method and

ii) the average cost method.

Solution to Example 5 using FIFO method

As previously, the first step is to calculate the effective units of production for the period. This follows identical principles to Example 4 except that in this example it is necessary to consider the four elements of the units (Input material, material introduced, labour and overheads) instead of simply the units as a whole. When the effective production is ascertained the cost per unit, for each element, can be calculated.

Calculation of effective units and cost per unit

Cost Element	Completed Units	+	Equiv. Units in Closing WIP	–	Equiv. Units in Opening WIP	=	Total Effective Production	Costs £	Cost per Unit £
Input Material	4500	+	600	–	800	=	4300	46500	10.814
Material Intro.	4500	+	300	–	440	=	4360	24000	5.505
Labour	4500	+	270	–	480	=	4290	19500	4.545
Overheads	4500	+	240	–	360	=	4380	18200	4.155

∴ *Closing stock valuation = 600 units*

				£		£
Input material	=	100% complete	=	600×10.814	=	6,488
Material introduced	=	50% complete	=	300×5.505	=	1,651
Labour	=	45% complete	=	270×4.545	=	1,227
Overheads	=	40% complete	=	240×4.155	=	997
						£10,363

This value is used in the Process Account in the normal way with the value of the Transfers to Finished Goods being the balance on the account.

Process account – Process Y (FIFO)

	Units	£		Units	£
Opening WIP b/f	800	19,400			
Transfers in from ProcessX	4,300	46,500	Transfers to Finished Goods	4,500	117,237
Material introduced		24,000			
Labour		19,500	Closing WIP c/f	600	10,363
Overheads		18,200			
	5,100	127,600		5,100	127,600

Solution to example 5 using average cost method

Calculation of effective units and cost per unit

Cost Elements	Equivalent units in Closing WIP	+	Fully Complete Units	=	Total Effective Production (a)	Opening WIP Values	+	Period Costs	=	Total Cost (b)	Cost per Unit (b). (a)
Input Material	600 × 100% = 600	+	4500	=	5100	£8200	+	£46500	=	£54700	£10.725
Material Intro	600 × 50% = 300	+	4500	=	4800	5600	+	24000	=	29600	6.167
Labour	600 × 45% = 270	+	4500	=	4770	3200	+	19500	=	22700	4.759
Overheads	600 × 40% = 240	+	4500	=	4740	2400	+	18200	=	20600	4.346
						£19400	+	£108200	=	£127600	£25.997

∴ Value of completed production = 4,500 × £25.997 = £116,987.

The value of the closing WIP can be found either by deducting the value of completed production from total costs or, more tediously, by calculating the various element values, as follows:

Value of closing WIP

= Total cost – value of completed production

= £127,600 – 116,987 = £10,613

or this can be calculated by using the various element values

ie

600	×	£10.725	=	6,435.00
300	×	£6.167	=	1,850.10
270	×	£4.759	=	1,284.93
240	×	£4.346	=	1,043.04
				£10,613.07

(slight rounding error)

The process account can now be completed

Process account – Process Y (average cost)

	Units	£		Units	£
Opening WIP b/f	800	19,400	Transfers to Finished Goods	4,500	116,987
Transfers in from Process X	4,300	46,500			
Material introduced		24,000			
Labour		19,500	Closing WIP c/f	600	10,613
Overheads		18,200			
	5,100	127,600		5,100	127,600

Example 6

This is a more complicated example which brings together the various facets of process costing covered in the chapter. It includes opening and closing WIP and normal and abnormal losses where the scrapped units are not fully complete.

The following data relate to Process 2 for one accounting period. Process 2 receives units from Process 1 and, after processing, transfers them to Process 3.

Opening WIP 600 units

	Value	Percentage complete
	£	%
Input material	720	100
Material introduced	500	60
Labour	340	50
Overheads	270	40

Transfers from Process 1: 4,100 units valued at £5,200.

Transfers to Process 3: 3,500 units

	£
Materials introduced	2,956
Labour	2,200
Overheads	1,900

Closing stock 800 units at the following stage of completion

Input material	100% complete
Material introduced	60% complete
Labour	50% complete
Overheads	40% complete

400 units were scrapped at the following stage of completion

Input material	100% complete
Material introduced	100% complete
Labour	40% complete
Overheads	30% complete

The normal loss is 10% of production and the scrapped units realised 40p each.

It is required to prepare the Process Account for Process 2 using

i)   the FIFO method,

ii) the average cost method.

Solution to example 6 using FIFO method

The first stage is to calculate the amount of normal loss to see whether there is any abnormal loss or gain involved.

The production for the period is calculated as follows:

Opening WIP	600	units
+ transfers in	4,100	
	4,700	
– closing WIP	800	
∴ Production	3,900	units

∴ Normal loss is 10% of 3,900 = 390, and as the actual number scrapped were 400, there were 10 units of abnormal loss.

The calculation of effective units for cost calculation purposes follows the same principles as in Examples 4 and 5 except that the number of units abnormal loss must be included in the total effective production because, as explained, abnormal losses are costed on the same basis as good production.

Calculation of effective units and cost per unit

Cost Element	Completed Units	+	Equiv. Units in Closing WIP	+	Equiv Units in Abnormal loss	–	Equiv. Units in Opening WIP	=	Total Effective Production	Costs £	Cost per Unit £
Input Material	3500	+	800	+	10	–	600	=	3710	5200	1.402
Material Intro.	3500	+	480	+	10	–	360	=	3630	*2800	0.771
Labour	3500	+	400	+	4	–	300	=	3604	2200	0.610
Overheads	3500	+	320	+	3	–	240	=	3583	1900	0.530

(*This is the cost of the material introduced, £2,956, less the resale value of the normal loss, £156 ie 390 @ 40p each. The resale value of the 10 units of abnormal loss is credited to the abnormal loss account **not** the process account.)

The costs per unit calculated are then used to evaluate the value of the closing WIP and the abnormal loss.

Closing WIP valuation

		£
Input material	800 equivalent units @ £1.402	1121.60
Material introduced	480 equivalent units @ 0.771	370.08
Labour	400 equivalent units @ 0.610	244.00
Overheads	320 equivalent units @ 0.530	169.60
		£1,905.28
		say £1,905.

Abnormal loss valuation

		£
Input material	10 equivalent units @ £1.402	14.02
Material introduced	10 equivalent units @ 0.771	7.71
Labour	4 equivalent units @ 0.610	2.44
Overheads	3 equivalent units @ 0.530	1.59
		25.76
		say £26.

The process account can now be prepared.

Process 2 Account(FIFO)

	Units	£		Units	£
Opening WIP	600	1830			
Transfers from Process 1	4100	5200	Normal loss	390	156
Material		2956	Abnormal loss	10	26
Labour		2200	Transfers to Process 3	3500	11999
Overheads		1900	Closing WIP	800	1905
	4700	£14086		4700	£14086

Solution to example 7 using average cost

Calculation of effective units and cost per unit

Cost Element	Equiv. Units in Closing WIP	+	Equiv. Units in Abnormal loss	+	Complete units	=	Effective Production	Opening WIP value £	+	Period cost £	=	Total Costs £	Cost per Unit £
Input Material	800	+	10	+	3500	=	4310	720	+	5200	=	5920	1.373
Material Intro.	480	+	10	+	3500	=	3990	500	+	2800	=	3300	0.827
Labour	400	+	4	+	3500	=	3904	340	+	2200	=	2540	0.651
Overheads	320	+	3	+	3500	=	3823	270	+	1900	=	2170	0.568

The various costs per unit are used to evaluate the closing WIP, abnormal loss and the completed production:

Closing WIP equivalent units		Cost per unit		Value
800	×	1.373	=	1,098.40
480	×	0.827	=	396.96
400	×	0.651	=	260.40
320	×	0.568	=	181.76
				1,937.52

say £1,938.

Abnormal loss

10	×	1.373	=	13.73
10	×	0.827	=	8.27
4	×	0.651	=	2.60
3	×	0.568	=	1.70
				26.30

say £26.

Completed production

3,500	×	1.373	=	4,805.50
3,500	×	0.827	=	2,894.50
3,500	×	0.651	=	2,278.50
3,500	×	0.568	=	1,988.00
				£11966.50

say £11,966.

These values are used in the Process account.

Process 2 Account (Average Cost)

	Units	£		Units	£
Opening WIP	600	1830			
			Normal loss	390	156
Transfers from Process 1	4100	5200	Abnormal loss	10	26
Material		2956	Transfers to Process 3	3500	11966
Labour		2200			
Overheads		1900	Closing WIP	800	1938
	4700	£14086		4700	£14086

Note: If instead of the abnormal loss, there had been an abnormal gain the treatment would be as follows for both Average cost and the FIFO methods. The total effective production would be found as in Example 5 *less* the number of abnormal gain units. These units would be evaluated at the cost per unit calculated and the Process account *debited* with the abnormal gain units and their value. It follows that abnormal gain units will always be fully complete whereas abnormal loss units may be partially or fully complete.

25. Joint product and by-product costing

Joint and by-products frequently arise from the production process. Although the dividing line between the two is difficult to determine, a *joint product* is usually the term used when two or more products arise simultaneously in the course of processing, each of which has a significant sales value in relation to one another. Where one of the products arises incidentally in the course of manufacture and has relatively little sales value it is termed a *by-product,* eg sawdust and bark in timber processing.

The most common method of dealing with by-products is to credit the net realisable value of the by-product against the total cost of production. Because of the greater value of joint products more elaborate costing systems are used. The various products become separately identifiable, at a point known as the 'split-off point'. Up to that point all costs are joint costs and, after it, any cost incurred for a particular product is readily identifiable with that product.

26. Apportioning joint costs

For income determination and stock valuation purposes it is conventional to apportion the common costs (ie those prior to split-off point) between the joint products. The two methods most frequently used are: the physical unit basis (where costs were apportioned in proportion to the weight or volume of the products), and the sales value basis (where costs are apportioned according to the sales value of the products). These two methods are illustrated in Example 7.

Example 7

A process produces three joint products, M, N and O. The appropriate data were as follows:

M – 400 Kgs sold at £12.50 Kg	Sales value =	£5,000
N – 300 Kgs sold at £20 Kg	Sales value =	£6,000
O – 200 Kgs sold at £25 Kg	Sales value =	£5,000
		£16,000

Total joint costs were £11,000

Cost apportionment

Physical unit basis

				Apportionment		Costs Apportioned £
M	400 Kgs	$\frac{400}{900}$	×	£11,000	=	4,889
N	300 Kgs	$\frac{300}{900}$	×	£11,000	=	3,667
O	200 Kgs	$\frac{200}{900}$	×	£11,000	=	2,444
	900 Kgs					£11,000

Sales value basis £

M	£5,000	$\frac{5,000}{16,000}$	×	£11,000	=	3,437
N	£6,000	$\frac{6,000}{16,000}$	×	£11,000	=	4,126
O	£5,000	$\frac{5,000}{16,000}$	×	£11,000	=	3,437
	£16,000					£11,000

Notes:

a) It will be seen that the two methods can product substantially different results giving, in this example, gross profit percentages of 2%, 39% and 51% on the physical unit basis and a constant 31% on the sales value basis. The sales value basis always produces a constant margin.

b) On occasions, products are not saleable at the split-off point and need further processing before a sales value can be established. In such circumstances the post split-off costs are deducted from the final sales value so as to establish a notional sales value at the split-off point which is used for the cost apportionment.

c) It will be apparent that any method of apportioning joint costs is only a convention and accordingly is of no value for decision making.

27. Problems with traditional product costing

Conventional costing systems, which are still widely used, were developed in the early part of this century to deal with product costing in the typical factory which then existed. This had the following characteristics:

❑ Direct costs (material and labour) were a high proportion of total costs;

❑ Relatively small number of support functions (eg planning, purchasing, financial, quality control etc) which meant low overheads;

❑ Low level of mechanisation with the consequence that simple labour based production was the norm;

❑ Large runs of relatively standardised products;

❑ Slow rate of change both of products and methods.

Based on these characteristics, product costs were calculated by adding on to direct costs a proportion of overheads deemed to be related to the units produced. Overheads were charged to products on a *production volume* related basis, usually direct labour hours (or direct wages) or machine hours. Implicit in this system is the assumption that all overheads are related primarily to production volume.

However, manufacturing methods, organisation and cost patterns have changed dramatically. Nowadays manufacture is automated and computerised, there is greater diversity, and overheads are a much higher proportion of total costs. Direct labour is nowadays often only 5-15% of total costs in a modern factory. More specifically, there has been a growth in the costs of service support functions which assist the efficient production of a range of high quality products. Examples of these functions include: scheduling, production control, data processing, industrial engineering and so on. The important feature of these types of overheads is that they are largely unaffected by production volume. Instead they vary in the longer term according to the *range* and *complexity* of products manufactured rather than the simple volume of output.

Conventional product costing – which absorbs support overhead costs simply on production volume (measured by labour or machine hours or units) – tends to *overcost high volume products*, which cause relatively little diversity, and *undercost low volume products*, which cause greater diversity and so call upon the support services more.

In an attempt to make overhead attribution more realistic, there have been various product costing developments in recent years. One of the most influential has been *Activity-Based Costing*.

28. Activity-based costing (ABC)

The ideas behind ABC have been around for many years but ABC has been brought into recent prominence by the work of the Harvard Business School, especially Professors Kaplan and Cooper.

At its simplest level ABC can be thought of as a method of charging overheads to cost units on the basis of benefits received from the particular indirect activity eg ordering, planning, setting and so on. ABC seeks not only to attribute overheads to product costs on a more realistic basis than simply production volume, but also attempts to show the relationship between overhead costs and the activities that cause them.

There are some similarities between ABC and traditional systems but a key difference is the way that the costs of support activities are collected and then charged or traced to cost units.

In outline an ABC system is developed and used as follows.

Step 1   Identify the main activities in the organisation.

Examples include: materials handling, purchasing, reception, despatch, machining, assembly and so on.

Step 2   Identify the factors which determine the costs of an activity. These are known as *cost drivers*.

Examples include: number of purchase orders, number of orders delivered, number of set-ups and so on.

Step 3   Collect the costs of each activity. These are known as *cost pools* and are directly equivalent to conventional cost centres.

Step 4   Charge support overheads to products on the basis of their usage of the activity, expressed in terms of the chosen cost driver(s). For example, if the total costs of Purchasing were £200,000 and there were 1,000 Purchase orders (the chosen cost driver), products would be charged £200 per purchase order. Thus a batch generating 3 purchase orders would be charged 3 × £200 = £600 for Purchasing overheads.

Figure 2.2 shows the outline of ABC contrasted with conventional product costing.

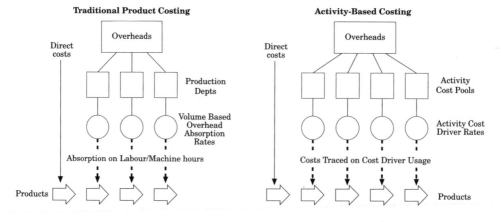

Figure 2.2. Traditional product costing and activity-based costing compared

It will be seen from the diagram that there are considerable similarities between the two systems. In both systems, direct costs go straight to the product and overheads are traced to the product using a two stage allocation process. However, it is in the second stage of the overhead allocation process that significant differences arise. In a traditional system overheads would be charged to products using at the most two absorption bases (labour hours and/or machine hours). On the other hand, ABC systems use many drivers as absorption bases (eg number of set-ups, number of orders, number of despatches and so on). Because of this, ABC cost driver rates should produce more realistic product costs, especially where support overheads are high.

Having examined the main principles of ABC, more detailed points can be considered.

29. Cost classifications

Using traditional systems, variable costs are those that change with production volume. Examples include: direct material, power costs and so on. Fixed costs are those which do not change with production volume. This includes the majority of costs including most overheads.

Using ABC, Kaplan and Cooper advocate classifying overhead costs in a different way. They propose: ***short-term variable costs, long-term variable costs*** and *fixed costs.*

❑ *Short-term variable costs*

These are costs that do vary with production volume and would be those also classified as variable under traditional methods. A typical example would be power costs. These vary in direct relationship to production volume, expressed as machine hours.

It is suggested that short-term variable overhead costs are traced to products using production volume-related cost drivers as appropriate. Examples include: direct labour hours, machine hours, direct material cost or weight. Unlike traditional systems where only one or two absorption bases are used, ABC recognises that there could be several cost drivers whenever labour hours, machine hours and material costs are used in different proportions by products. In most organisations, there will only be a small proportion of overheads that can be classed as short-term variable costs.

❑ *Long-term variable costs*

These are overhead costs which do not vary with production volume but do vary with other measures of activity, but not immediately. For example, costs for support activities such as stock handling, production scheduling, set-ups etc are fixed in the shorter term but vary in the longer term according to the range and complexity of the products manufactured. ABC requires these costs be traced to products by *transaction based cost drivers.*

Most support overheads can be classified as long-term variable costs and thus traced to products using appropriate cost drivers. In traditional systems most of these costs would be classified as fixed.

❏ *Fixed costs*

Using ABC these are classified as costs which do not vary, for a given time period with any activity indicator. An example would be the salary of the Managing Director. Research by Kaplan and Cooper suggests that these costs are a relatively small proportion of the total costs.

30. Transaction-based cost drivers

A key idea behind ABC is to focus attention on what factors cause or drive costs, known as cost drivers.

Cost drivers can be defined as:

Activities or transactions which are significant determinants of cost.

There are difficulties in choosing realistic cost drivers and Cooper warns:

'There are no simple rules that pertain to the selection of cost drivers. The best approach is to identify the resources that constitute a significant proportion of the product costs and determine their cost behaviour. If several are long-term variable costs, a transaction-based cost system should be considered.

Examples of transaction-based cost drivers are given below.

Support Department Costs (ie Cost Pools)	*Possible Cost Driver*
Production scheduling	No of production runs
Set-up costs	No of production runs
Material handling	No of production runs
Finished goods stock handling & despatch costs	No of orders delivered
Purchasing costs	No of purchase orders
Raw materials stock handling	No of orders received

The development of ABC and the designation of cost pools and appropriate cost-drivers forces the organisation to ask the following important questions:

❏ What does this department achieve?

Does, for example, the department add value or does it simply add cost? Why is it needed? Can we do without it?

❏ What causes the activity for which the department is responsible?

This question can force a re-appraisal of the underlying causes of costs. As Johnson has said 'people cannot manage costs, they can only manage the activities which cause costs'.

Focusing on the drivers which cause overheads and tracing overheads to products on the usage of cost drivers enables a higher proportion of overheads to be product related. Using traditional systems most support overheads cannot be related to products except in the most general arbitrary way. It is this feature of ABC which, it is claimed, produces greater realism.

31. Examples of ABC and traditional costing

Example 8

Assume that a firm makes four products A, B, C and D. Data for the past period are as follows:

Product	Output units	No of production runs in period	Direct labour hrs per unit	Machine hours per unit	Material cost per unit	Material components per unit
A	25	3	2	2	£30	8
B	25	4	4	4	£75	5
C	250	7	2	2	£30	8
D	250	10	4	4	£75	6
		24				

Direct labour costs £7 per hour:

Overhead costs	£
Short-run variable costs	8,250
Long-run variable costs:	
Scheduling costs	7,680
Set-up costs	3,600
Material handling costs	7,650
	27,180

Find the unit production cost

a) Using conventional product costing using a labour hour or machine hour overhead absorption rate.

b) Using ABC with the following cost drivers:

Short-term variable costs:	Machine hours
Scheduling costs:	No of production runs
Set-up costs:	No of production runs
Materials handling costs:	No of components

c) Compare the results from the two methods.

Solution

a) Conventional costing

Total machine hours in period

Product		Hours
A	25 × 2 =	50
B	25 × 4 =	100
C	250 × 2 =	500
D	250 × 4 =	1,000
		1,650

$$\therefore \text{ OAR based on machine hours} = \frac{£27,180}{1,650} = £16.47 \text{ per machine hour}$$

Cost summary

	A	B	C	D	Total
	£	£	£	£	£
Direct materials	750	1,875	7,500	18,750	
Direct labour	350	700	3,500	7,000	
Prime costs	1,100	2,575	11,000	25,750	40,425
Overheads @ £16.47 per hour	824	1,647	8,235	16,470	27,177
Total cost	1,924	4,222	19,235	42,220	67,602
Units produced	25	25	250	250	
Cost per unit (rounded)	£77	£169	£77	£169	

b) Using ABC

Calculation of cost driver rates

Cost driver rates

Short-term variable costs $\dfrac{£8,250}{1,650}$ machine hours = £5 per machine hour

Scheduling costs $\dfrac{7,680}{24}$ production runs = £320 per production run

Set-up costs $\dfrac{3,600}{24}$ production runs = £150 per production run

Materials handling costs $\dfrac{£7,650}{3,825}$ components* = £2 per component

* Number of components in period = $25 \times 8 + 25 \times 5 + 250 \times 8 + 250 \times 6 = 3,825$

Cost summary

	A	B	C	D	Total
	£	£	£	£	£
Prime cost	1,100	2,575	11,000	25,750	40,425
Short run variable costs @ £5 per machine hour	250	500	2,500	5,000	8,250
Scheduling @ £320 per run	960	1,280	2,240	3,200	7,680
Set-up @ £150 per run	450	600	1,050	1,500	3,600
Materials handling @ £2 per component	400	250	4,000	3,000	7,650
Total cost	3,160	5,205	20,790	38,450	*67,605
Units produced	25	25	250	250	
Cost per unit	£126.4	£208.2	£83.16	£153.8	

* Slight difference in total cost due to rounding.

c) Comparing the results we obtain

Products	A	B	C	D
	£	£	£	£
Unit cost: conventional	77	169	77	169
Unit cost: ABC	126.4	208.2	83.16	153.8
Percentage change using ABC	+64%	+23%	+8%	–9%

It will be seen that ABC charges more overheads to lower volume production and tends to charge relatively less to higher volume production, especially Product D in this case.

The above example has deliberately been kept simple in order to show the principles of the ABC method.

32. Merits of ABC

The following are the main claims made regarding ABC:

a) More realistic product costs are provided especially in Advanced Manufacturing Technology (AMT) factories where support overheads are a significant proportion of total costs.

b) More overheads can be traced to the product. In modern factories there are a growing number of non-factory floor activities. ABC is concerned with all activities so takes product costing beyond the traditional factory floor basis.

c) ABC recognises that it is *activities* which cause cost, not products and it is products which consume activities.

d) ABC focuses attention on the real nature of cost behaviour and helps in reducing costs and identifying activities which do not add value to the product.

e) ABC recognises the complexity and diversity of modern production by the use of multiple cost drivers, many of which are transaction based rather than based solely on production volume.

f) ABC provides a reliable indication of long-run variable product cost which is relevant to strategic decision making.

g) ABC is flexible enough to trace costs to processes, customers, areas of managerial responsibility, as well as product costs.

h) ABC provides useful financial measures (eg cost driver rates) and non-financial measures (eg transaction volumes).

33. Criticisms of ABC

a) A full ABC system with numerous cost pools with multiple cost drivers is undeniably more complex than traditional systems and will thus be more expensive to administer.

b) ABC was originally developed by CAMI, the US based consortium of very large manufacturing firms, consulting groups and universities. Much of their work is defence related and pricing is on a cost-plus basis hence the need to show accurate product costs. The applicability of ABC to companies who have to use market-based pricing and do not have the same high technology structure has been questioned.

c) Many practical problems are unresolved. Examples include: common costs, cost driver selection, non-linearity of cost driver rates etc.

34. ABC and service organisations

Although the discussion above has used manufacturing as a background this was for convenience only.

The principles of ABC, ie identification of activities and cost drivers, the classification of costs, the distinction between activities that add value and those that do not are equally applicable to the service sector. By linking costs to services by transaction-based cost drivers, ABC should assist in providing more accurate costs of individual services.

To date there is little published material on ABC in the service sector although it has been applied in banking and an airline.

35. Activity-based budgeting

The general principles of activity analysis can also be applied to budgeting systems. This is dealt with later in the book after the general principles of budgeting have been covered.

36. Summary

a) Cost accounting systems are largely concerned with the analysis of past costs and operations. Management accounting is largely (but not exclusively) concerned with future costs and revenues.

b) Cost units should be chosen that are the most relevant for the activities of the particular organisation.

c) The total of direct cost + direct labour + direct expense is Prime Cost. The total of indirect costs is Overhead.

d) Overheads are conventionally established by defining cost centres and then allocating and apportioning costs to the cost centres using bases of apportionment which are deemed to reflect the benefits received. The process of apportionment is a convention only.

e) Overheads are spread over cost units by using overhead absorption rates usually based on labour or machine hours.

f) Where all costs, both fixed and variable, are included in production costs, the system is known as absorption or total absorption costing. Where fixed costs are excluded from production costs and charged against the period's results, the system is known as marginal costing.

g) Contribution is the difference between sales and marginal cost (ie all the variable costs).

h) Where there are no opening and closing stocks marginal and absorption costing produce the same net profit. Because the two systems differ in their valuation of stock, differences in net profit arise when stocks exist.

i) The major pricing systems for charging materials to production are FIFO, LIFO, Average price and Standard price. Although widely used in cost ascertainment the use of such systems for management accounting purposes has doubtful validity.

j) Labour remuneration systems vary widely but are either wholly time based or related, directly or indirectly, to production levels. Labour costs rarely behave in a truly variable, linear fashion.

k) A particular problem which arises with the ascertainment of overheads is dealing with service department costs where there is reciprocal servicing.

l) The major costing methods are: job costing, batch costing, contract costing and process costing.

m) Job, batch and contract costing have broad similarities. Because of the large scale and long term nature of many contracts, conventional arrangements are made to include a proportion of the total contract profit into each years accounts.

n) Process costing involves the averaging of total costs over the total throughput of the process, including any partly completed units.

o) Process losses may be Normal losses, Abnormal losses or there may be Abnormal gains.

p) There are two valuation methods used in Process accounts. The FIFO method and Average Cost method.

q) Where a process produces joint-products or by-products it is conventional to apportion the common costs on either the physical unit basis or the sales value basis.

r) Activity Based Costing (ABC) treats direct costs the same as traditional product costing.

s) Using ABC, support overheads are traced to product costs based on the usage of cost drivers.

t) ABC classifies costs into: short-term variable, long-term variable and fixed.

u) ABC is equally applicable to Service organisations and activity-based analysis can be used in budgeting.

37. Points to note

a) In most organisations the cost accounting system has been developed to aid routine purposes. It does not follow that the system will produce appropriate information for management accounting purposes.

b) The cost accounting system of the organisation must itself be cost effective. Is the cost accounting system of your organisation just another part of overheads or does it make a positive contribution to organisational efficiency? Is it being adapted to cope with changes in technology?

Additional reading

Cost accounting: a managerial emphasis; *Horngren* – Prentice-Hall

Costing; *Lucey* – Letts Educational (formerly DP Publications)

Management accounting; evolution not revolution; *Bromwich & Bhimani* – CIMA

Activity-based costing; *Inness & Milchell* – CIMA

Self review questions

1. Why should the management accountant critically examine the bases and assumptions used to produce information from the cost accounting system? (2)
2. Define cost unit, direct cost, indirect cost and prime cost. (3)
3. What is the process by which overheads are established? (4)
4. What is overhead absorption and typically how is this done? (5)
5. Distinguish between absorption and marginal costing. (6)
6. What is contribution? (7)
7. What is the difference between stock valuations using absorption and marginal costing? (8)
8. If stocks are increasing will absorption or marginal costing show the higher profits? Why? (10)
9. What does SSAP 9 recommend as the basis of Stock Valuation? (11)
10. Describe the FIFO, LIFO, Average price, and Standard price systems of pricing stock issues. (14)
11. What are some typical bases on which service department costs are apportioned to production cost centres?
12. What are three methods of dealing with service department costs where reciprocal servicing takes place? (17)
13. Describe Job, Batch and Contract Costing. (19-21)
14. When is Process Costing used and what are equivalent units? (22)
15. Distinguish between Normal and Abnormal Process Losses and Abnormal Gains. (23)
16. What are the FIFO and Average Cost methods of valuing WIP? (24)
17. What are the problems of traditional product costing? (27)
18. What is the key principle of Activity-Based Costing (ABC)? (28)
19. How are costs classified using ABC? (29)
20. What is a cost driver and what is it used for? (30)
21. What are the merits claimed for ABC? (32)

3 Cost behaviour

1. Objectives

After studying this chapter you will:

☐ understand why the study of cost behaviour is necessary;
☐ know the key cost classifications of fixed, variable and semi-variable;
☐ be able to distinguish between linear and curvi-linear cost patterns;
☐ understand the main approaches to cost forecasting;
☐ know the main techniques of regression analysis: high-low, scattergraphs and least squares;
☐ have been introduced to multiple linear regression analysis;
☐ understand both marginal and cumulative average learning curves.

2. What will our costs be next year?

This deceptively simple sounding question – and many others of a like nature – is typical of the problems that the management accountant has to face. Such questions can occur in virtually every aspect of his work and knowledge of the patterns of cost behaviour and ways that future costs (and, of course, other factors such as sales) can be predicted is a fundamental requirement for the management accountant, particularly when he is supplying information for planning and decision making.

3. Cost classification

The classification of costs into fixed and variable, according to their behaviour and characteristics, is an essential preliminary to being able to make any form of cost prediction.

The behaviour of a cost in relation to changes in the level of activity forms the basis of the usual accounting classifications thus:

❏ a *Fixed Cost* is one which, within certain output limits, tends to be unaffected by variations in the level of activity.

❏ a *Variable Cost* is one which tends to vary in direct proportion to variations in the level of activity.

Such a classification should not be a once off exercise to sort costs into rigid absolute categories for all time and for all conditions. The accountant must look at the actual and forecast behaviour of the cost, and the purpose for which the cost is intended so that there is a flexible approach to the classification of costs.

The normal process of cost classification into fixed and variable is only valid within specific, limiting assumptions, ie

a) When the time period being considered is relatively short, typically a year. Over longer periods, methods, technology and other factors alter, causing changes in the classification of costs and in their behaviour.

b) When the activity variation being considered is relatively small; for example, normal capacity ± 10%. Outside a limited activity range costs are unlikely to behave in accordance with their original classification.

c) Over the time period being considered the state of technology, management policies and the methods employed are deemed to remain unchanged.

4. Problems associated with conventional cost classifications

There are numerous pitfalls contained in the conventional classifications of fixed and variable cost and the management accountant must constantly keep these in mind to avoid taking too superficial a view of cost classification and prediction.

Typical of the problems involved are the following:

a) The usual assumption regarding the behaviour of variable costs is that they behave in a linear fashion, ie a variable cost is deemed to alter in direct proportion to changes in volume. This may be correct, but a cost may also vary in a non-linear, or curvi-linear, fashion or may change in a series of steps. Whatever the cost function, linear, curvi-linear or stepped, it should be established by analysis of the cost in question and not by some overall, simplistic assumption.

b) Fixed costs can and do change, for example, local rates virtually always increase each year as do many other fixed costs. The main point is that although costs which are classified as fixed often alter, they do so usually because of factors other than changes in volume. The adherence to quite arbitrary conventions may cause a cost to be classified as fixed, semi-fixed, or variable in different organisations or even in different parts of the same organisation. An example of such a cost is depreciation which, by convention, may be deemed to range from wholly time related through to being directly related to the amount produced.

So that the individual characteristics of costs are not overlooked and in consequence dealt with incorrectly it is useful to subdivide fixed costs into four categories:

  i) The time period classification. Those types of cost which are not likely to change significantly in the short term, usually a year. In the long term all costs may change or become avoidable.

  ii) The volume classification. Costs which are fixed for small, but not large changes in output or capacity.

  iii) The joint classification. Where a cost is incurred jointly with another cost and is only capable of being altered jointly. For example, if an organisation leases a showroom which has a warehouse attached then the fixed cost element applies to both parts of the asset acquired whether or not they are both wanted.

  iv) The policy classification. These are costs which are fixed by management policy and bear no causal relationship to volume or time. They are usually items which are dealt with by appropriation budgets, eg expenditure on advertising, research and development. These types of costs are sometimes known as programmed fixed costs and typically are reviewed annually.

It will be apparent that a cost may be classed as fixed for some purposes and not others and the management accountant must continually appraise the classification of a cost to ensure its appropriateness for the intended purpose.

c) Rarely can a cost be classified as purely variable or purely fixed even though such classifications are, for simplicity, frequently made. More often a cost displays both fixed and variable characteristics and is termed a semi-fixed, or semi-variable, or a mixed cost. With all such costs it is necessary to separate the fixed and variable elements so as to be able to make predictions about the behaviour of the cost in relation to the changes being considered. Various methods are possible which can be sub divided into two categories; by judgement, and by statistical methods.

  i) By judgement. The characteristics of the cost are established by studying the cost coding system and discussing with the managers and departments involved those costs which cannot be readily identified as fixed or variable. Typically the manager would be asked what the cost in question would be if there was little or no activity and in this way a crude estimate of the fixed element would be obtained.

  ii) By statistical methods. These methods are of varying sophistication but all rely on some form of analysis of past data of the behaviour of the cost being studied.

These methods include: the high-low points method, the scatter chart, regression analysis and are described in detail later in the chapter.

d) Irregularity of behaviour. Unfortunately, costs do not behave in regular patterns and care must be taken not to classify say, a variable cost as having a regular, linear function for all activity levels when further analysis might show that it is linear between 90% – 115% of normal activity and thereafter has a curvi-linear function.

e) Multiple causes of variation. Different variable costs (or the variable portions of semi-fixed costs) react to different activity measures. For example, direct wages may vary with the number of orders received, distribution costs may vary with the deliveries made and so on. It is an oversimplification, frequently made in examinations, that all variable costs vary in relation to the same measure of activity and this may give misleading results. Activity analysis states that many costs, especially support overhead costs, do not vary with production volume but are related to the scope and complexity of production.

In summary, it must be realised that the conventional accounting classification of fixed and variable costs being defined in relation to one factor, that of production volume, is simplistic and is, at best, only a crude approximation of reality.

5. Typical cost patterns

Having considered some of the problems inherent in cost classification some typical cost patterns are shown below in diagrammatic form.

Variable cost patterns – Linear

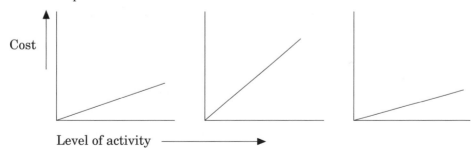

Figure 3.1 Examples of linear variable cost

This pattern is the simplest possible and represents costs which vary in direct proportion to the level of activity. Examples include: direct materials, royalties per unit, power usage (without a standing charge).

A perfectly linear variable cost over all activity levels, as shown in Figure 3.1 is extremely unlikely. More realistically, a cost may be linear (or a linear approximation assumed) only over the normal range of activity levels and extrapolations outside this range are likely to have less validity. See Figure 3.2.

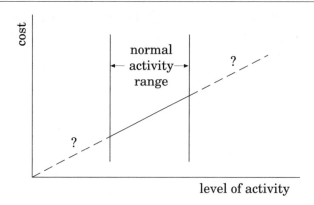

Figure 3.2 Normal Activity Range

Notes:

a) The slope of the line, usually represented by b, is the variable cost per unit of activity.

b) The activity level in units is usually represented by *x*. Accordingly a variable cost with a linear relationship is expressed thus:

$$y = bx$$

where *y* is the expected cost.

6. Variable cost patterns – curvi-linear

Where costs do not vary in direct proportion to activity changes the function is non-linear or curvi-linear thus:

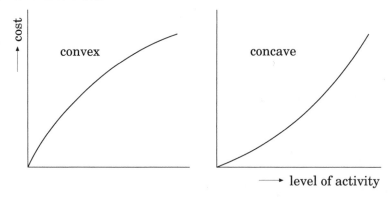

Figure 3.3 Curvi-Linear Variable Costs

Convex – where each extra unit of output causes a less than proportionate increase in cost, ie economies of scale operate.

Concave – where each extra unit of output causes a more than proportionate increase in cost, ie diminishing returns operate.

Many variable costs may display curvi-linear characteristics. for example, in some processes the amount of waste material remains more or less constant so that when output increases the unit cost for material reduces (economies of scale).

Conversely, when it is necessary to pay increasing differential piece rates so as to increase output, diminishing returns operate and some form of concave curvi-linear function will result.

If a given curve has particular characteristics it may be categorised as a known statistical function by the technique of curve fitting. There are numerous statistical functions which could represent cost behaviour, for example, logarithmic, simple exponential, gompertz and the parabola which is one of the more common types and is illustrated below.

7. Curvi-linear variable costs – the parabola

Where the slope of the cost function changes uniformly with variations in the level of activity (as shown in Fig. 3.3) the curve is known as a Parabola and is expressed algebraically thus:

$$\text{Variable Cost} = bx + cx^2 + dx^3 + \dots + px^n$$

where: $b, c, d, \dots, p$ are constants

and: x is the level of activity.

Example

Analysis of cost and activity data shows that the variable costs of Part No. 329 can be represented by the function:

$$\text{Variable cost of Part No. 329} = £bx + cx^2 + dx^3$$

where: b = material cost per unit   = £3
          c = labour cost per unit   = £0.8
          d = variable overheads per unit   = £0.06

Calculate

i) Variable cost when production is 10 units

ii) Variable cost when production is 15 units

Solution

i) Production 10 units

Variable cost $= £(3 \times 10) + (0.8 \times 10^2) + (0.06 \times 10^3)$

$= £170$

ii) Production 15 units

Variable cost $= £(3 \times 15) + (0.8 \times 15^2) + (0.06 \times 15^3)$

$= £427.5$

It will be seen that there is a more than proportionate increase in cost compared with the increase in production thus demonstrating that the function is concave, ie there are diminishing returns. The values of the constants determine whether the function is concave or convex.

8. Linear approximations

Frequently a linear approximation is made even when it is known that the underlying cost function is curvi-linear (or indeed any other function). This is shown in Fig. 3.4.

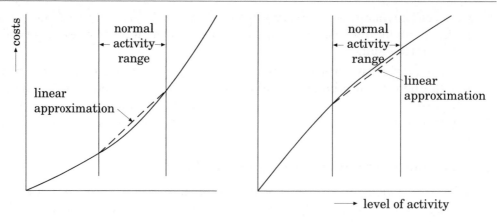

Figure 3.4 *Linear approximations of curvi-linear functions*

Such approximations greatly simplify calculations and there is empirical evidence from cost studies that they are reasonably accurate providing that there is only a limited range of activity variation covering a short time period.

Care should be taken, in practice and in examinations, not to make the assumption of linearity where this could produce misleading results.

9. Other cost patterns

Some typical cost patterns are shown below:

Fixed cost patterns

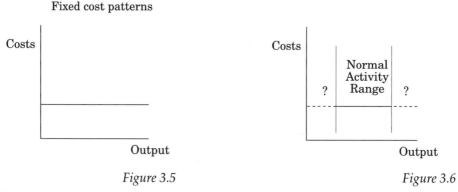

Figure 3.5   *Figure 3.6*

Notes:

i) Fig. 3.5 depicts the conventional assumption for a fixed cost constant at all levels of activity. However, a cost is unlikely to be fixed at all levels and Fig. 3.6 shows a more realistic situation.

ii) Examples of fixed costs include: rates, time based depreciation, most salaries, rent.

iii) A fixed cost can be described algebraically as $y = a$, where y is the cost and a is a constant.

Semi-variable cost patterns

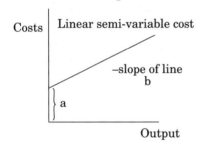

Figure 3.7   Figure 3.8

Notes:

i)   The variable element of a semi-variable cost may be *linear,* as shown in Fig. 3.7, or *curvi-linear* as shown in Fig. 3.8.

ii) Examples of semi-variable cost include: power and telephone charges, computer bureau costs with a standing charge and extra costs for the level of service, some direct wage schemes with a piecework and guaranteed minimum payment system.

iii) These costs can be represented algebraically as follows.

Linear semi-variable cost

$$y = a + bx$$

Curvi-linear semi-variable cost (where the variable portion can be approximated by a parabola)

$$y = a + bx + cx^2 + \dots px^n$$

'Stepped' costs

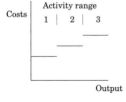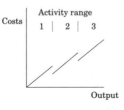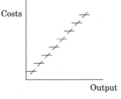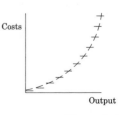

Figure 3.9   Figure 3.10   Figure 3.11   Figure 3.12

Notes:

a)   These are costs which have continuous characteristics – of a fixed or variable nature – for a given range of activity then, when the activity changes, the cost varies sharply producing a discontinuous function.

b)   If the range of activity being considered lies within one step, say activity range 2 on Figs. 3.9 and 3.10, then for analysis purposes the cost can be considered as fixed or variable as appropriate within the given activity range.

c)   Two typical examples of step costs are, supervisory salaries (up to a certain activity level, one is sufficient but there comes a point when an additional supervisor becomes necessary see Fig 3.9) and bought in material costs when there are discounts see Fig. 3.10.

d) There is not a simple algebraic expression for step costs but where the steps are relatively small it is usual to make a linear approximation (Figs. 3.11 and 3.12). When that is done the cost analysis can be carried out algebraically.

The above diagrams illustrate some commonly encountered cost functions but, of course, many others exist. A given cost may be purely variable up to a certain activity level when it reaches a ceiling and can then be considered as fixed. There may be declining (or increasing) rates paid say, as commission, within fixed minima and maxima; there may be costs which have linear characteristics for one activity range, curvi-linear for another and which are fixed at a third. In all cases the *individual characteristics* of the specific cost must be analysed in order to be able to make realistic predictions. Overall, simplistic assumptions about cost characteristics are very unlikely to produce accurate forecasts and in many cases the quality of planning and decision making is directly related to the accuracy of the forecasts involved.

10. Cost forecasting

So far in this chapter the various problems associated with cost classification have been dealt with and typical cost behaviour patterns have been described.

This background is vital to the management accountant when he is attempting to forecast future cost behaviour for use in planning and decision making.

There are three broad approaches to the problem of cost forecasting:

i) that based on extrapolation of historical costs and data, frequently using statistical analysis of varying degrees of sophistication,

ii) the accounts classification method, and

iii) the industrial engineering approach.

These are dealt with below.

11. Industrial engineering approach

Where there are no previous cost records, for example, the launching of a completely new product or where conditions have changed substantially, any form of statistical analysis is likely to be of little or no value. It is in such circumstances that the engineering approach can be used. This method uses a detailed, elemental approach to establish the required level of inputs (materials, labour, facilities, capital equipment) for a particular level of output. These physical inputs are then converted into money costs. The engineering approach is lengthy and can be expensive but when used for the right purposes it can be quite accurate.

It is most appropriate for estimating production costs and where there are clear, physical relationships between inputs and outputs. In addition to separating the fixed and variable elements of cost the method will also establish efficiency targets for different levels of activity which can be used for subsequent monitoring and control purposes.

The engineering approach is not so useful when there is a less direct relationship between costs, activity levels and outputs; for example, maintenance – administration and other overhead items.

The engineering approach uses work study and production engineering techniques and seeks to establish what a cost should be. It will be apparent that this is the same approach which is used to establish the basis of standard costs.

12. The accounts classification method

This method involves examination of the accounting records and classifying each item on the basis of its assumed behaviour, eg rent and rates as fixed, material cost as variable.

Considerable difficulties arise with the large number of costs which are semi-variable. For each of these costs an estimate must be made of the fixed and variable components. This may be relatively easy for some costs (electricity charges can be analysed into fixed and variable charges by studying published tariffs) but much more difficult for others, for example, maintenance.

The accounts classification method is quick and inexpensive but suffers from several limitations:

a) The initial classification has a considerable subjective element.

b) The method of dealing with semi-variable costs is often arbitrary.

c) By their nature, step costs are likely to be forced into either a fixed or variable category with a subsequent loss of accuracy.

d) For this method it is normal to use the latest details from the cost accounts which naturally relate to past events. These may not be representative of future conditions which are of prime importance as far as cost forecasting is concerned.

13. Forecasting using historical data

Frequently data will be available on the past costs incurred, performance levels, output, sales and similar matters which are used as a basis for forecasting future values. Numerous techniques have been developed to help with this process ranging from simple arithmetic and visual methods to advanced, computer based statistical systems. The more important ones from the point of view of the management accountant are dealt with later in this chapter. Regardless of the sophistication of the technique uses there is the presumption that the past will provide some guidance to the future, as indeed it often does. However, before using any method based on historical data for extrapolation into the future the data must be critically examined to ensure their appropriateness for the intended purpose.

Typical of the steps to be taken are the following.

a) Check the time period over which the data were collected.

The time scale chosen should be long enough for periodic costs to be included but short enough to avoid the averaging of variations in the level of activity. Averages tend to hide the underlying relationships between cost and level of activity.

b) Check that non-volume factors are comparable.

Most cost forecasting exercises are carried out to explore the effect on cost of changes in the level of activity. However many other factors influence cost: for example, changes in technology, production and administrative methods, changes in efficiency, changes in material, labour and other input costs, strikes, weather conditions and numerous other factors. These non volume factors tend to obscure the cost fluctuations due to volume alone and the data must be examined closely to ensure that the non volume factors were broadly similar in the past to the forecasted future conditions. Frequently adjustments have to be made to the data before it can be used for forecasting purposes. Unexamined and unadjusted historical data will only be suitable for forecasting purposes in the most exceptional circumstances.

c) Examine the accounting methods and policies used for the data.

The ways in which the data are collected and the accounting policies used can introduce bias in the data which may require adjustment.

Examples include: the ways in which apportionments have been made, the treatment of by-products, depreciation policies, cost data being out of phase with the activity to which they relate (eg wages and bonuses paid in arrears).

d) Choice of the independent variable.

To make cost predictions some form of cost function is required. This will contain a dependent variable, usually called y, (ie the cost) and one or more independent variables usually called x.

The dependent variable is expressed as a function of the independent variable thus

$$y = f(x)$$

for example, the cost of petrol consumed (the dependent variable) could be expressed as a function of the miles travelled (the independent variable) thus:

cost of petrol = f(miles travelled)

Frequently for accounting purposes only one independent variable is used but more than one independent variable may be employed, in which case more sophisticated statistical techniques will be necessary. At the stage of reviewing the basic data it is necessary to establish whether one independent variable will result in acceptable accuracy and, if so, which of the possible independent variables should be chosen? Should it be units of production, labour hours, sales volume, machine hours, weight processed, orders handled? For examination purposes the independent variable is usually clearly stated but in practice it is frequently very difficult to select a single independent variable which provides acceptable accuracy.

14. Linear regression lines

If it is decided that a linear relationship is a reasonable representation of the cost function there are numerous methods of establishing the fixed and variable characteristics so as to be able to forecast the anticipated future cost. The methods described in detail in this book are the 'high-low' technique, the visual method using scattergraphs, and the least squares method of simple linear regression analysis. In addition there is some discussion on multiple regression analysis. The methods are described below.

15. 'High–low' technique

The recorded cost and activity data are plotted on a graph and the two points representing the highest cost and the lowest cost respectively are joined by a straight line.

The slope of the line represents the variable cost per unit and the intercept with the vertical axis represents the fixed cost. This is illustrated in Figure 3.13.

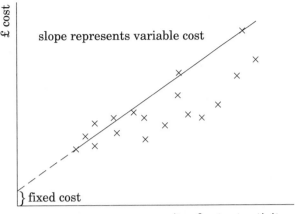

units of output activity

Figure 3.13 High-Low Graph

The high–low method is simple, crude and because it relies on two extreme points, it may not be very representative of the data. For example the line in Figure 3.13, probably overstates the variable cost and understates the fixed cost of the data represented. Graphical methods need not be used for the high-low system. Simple arithmetic readily gives the required answers.

For example, assume the following data have been collected on production levels and associated costs

	Production level (units)	Costs £
Lowest level	2,000	8,000
Highest level	4,000	12,000

$$\therefore \text{Variable costs per unit} = \frac{\text{Difference in costs}}{\text{Difference in activity}} = \frac{£4,000}{2,000}$$

$$= £2 \text{ per unit}$$

The fixed element can be calculated by deducting the total variable cost from the cost at either level, as follows:

$$\text{Fixed Cost} = \text{Total Cost} - \text{Variable Costs}$$
$$= £8,000 - (2,000 \times £2) = £4,000$$

The high–low method ignores all other observations save for the two extreme values and is likely to be unrepresentative of all the data. Its use is not recommended because of its inherent limitations.

16. The scattergraph method

Cost and activity data are plotted in a similar manner to that above and a line drawn at an angle which is judged to be the best representation of the slope of the plottings.

This is illustrated in Fig. 3.14.

The dotted line is drawn to show the intersection with the vertical axis and thus gives an estimate of the fixed content of the cost being considered, in this case £400. The slope of the line, ie the variable element, is found as follows:

$$\text{cost @ zero activity} \quad = \quad £400$$
$$\text{cost @ 100 units activity} \quad = \quad £1,250$$
$$\frac{1,250 - 400}{100 - 0} \quad = \quad £8.5$$

∴ the estimate cost function = £400 + 8.5x where x = units of output, ie the independent variable.

The graphical method is simple to use and provides a visual indication of approximate cost behaviour. Because each individual is likely to draw a different line with a different slope the method is subjective and approximate. A more objective and accurate approach is to calculate the line of best fit mathematically using the least squares method.

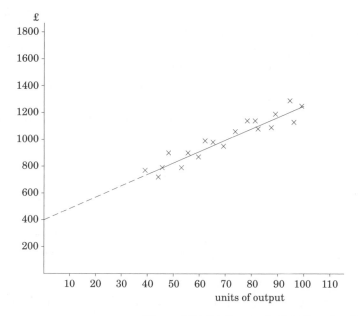

Figure 3.14 Scattergraph showing visual line of best fit

17. Least squares method of regression analysis

When it has been established that a causal relationship exists in the data and that a linear function is appropriate the statistical technique known as least squares is frequently used to establish values for the coefficients a and b (representing fixed and variable cost respectively) in the linear cost function

$$y = a + bx$$

where y is total cost – the dependent variable

and x is the agreed measure of activity – the independent variable

There are many computer packages available to calculate the coefficients but for simple regression analysis (ie as illustrated above with one independent variable) the coefficients are easily calculated using one of the following approaches, either:

Solve the following two equations

$$\Sigma y = an + b\Sigma x \ldots\ldots\text{.I}$$
$$\Sigma xy = a\Sigma x + b\Sigma x^2 \ldots\ldots\text{II}$$

These are known as the *normal equations*

Alternatively, transpose the normal equations and calculate the coefficients directly.

$$a = \frac{\Sigma y \Sigma x^2 - \Sigma x \Sigma xy}{n\Sigma x^2 - (\Sigma x)^2}$$

$$b = \frac{n\Sigma xy - \Sigma y \Sigma x}{n\Sigma x^2 - (\Sigma x)^2}$$

Both approaches are illustrated in the following example.

Example 1

The following data have been collected on costs and output:

Output ('000s)	1	2	3	4	5	6	7
Costs (£'000s)	14	17	15	23	18	22	31

Calculate the coefficients in the linear cost function

$$y = a + bx$$

using

i) the Normal Equations and ii) the coefficient formulae.

Solution

Output (x)	Costs (y)	xy	x^2
1	14	14	1
2	17	34	4
3	15	45	9
4	23	92	16
5	18	90	25
6	22	132	36
7	31	217	49
$\Sigma x = 28$	$\Sigma y = 140$	$\Sigma xy = 624$	$\Sigma x^2 = 140$

where $n = 7$ (ie number of pairs of readings)

i) Using the normal equations

$$140 = 7a + 28b \quad \ldots\ldots \text{ I}$$
$$624 = 28a + 140b \quad \ldots\ldots \text{ II}$$

and eliminating one coefficient thus

$$624 = 28a + 140b \quad \ldots\ldots \text{ II}$$
$$\underline{560 = 28a + 112b \quad \ldots\ldots 1 \times 4}$$
$$64 = \phantom{28a + {}} 28b$$

∴ $b = 2.286$ and, substituting this value in one of the equations, the value of a is found to be 10.86

∴ Regression line is: $y = 10.86 + 2.286x$

ii) Using the coefficient formulae

$$a = \frac{(140 \times 140) - (28 \times 624)}{7(140) - 28^2} = 10.86$$

$$b = \frac{7(624) - (28 \times 140)}{7(140) - 28^2} = 2.286$$

When the coefficients have been calculated the cost function can be used for forecasting simply by inserting the appropriate level of activity, ie a value for x, and calculating the resulting total cost.

For example, where are the predicted costs at output levels of:

a)   4,500 units (ie 4.5 in '000s), and

b)   8,000 units (ie 8 in '000s)?

a) $y = 10.86 + 2.286 (4.5)$ $= £21,147$

Note: A prediction *within* the range of the original observations (1 to 7 in Example 1) is known as an *interpolation*.

b) $y = 10.86 + 2.286 (8)$ $= £29,148$

Note: A prediction outside the range of original observations is known as an *extrapolation*.

18. Using least squares in practice

A line of best fit can be calculated for any set of data however widely scattered by mechanically using the least squares method. However the values of fixed and variable costs obtained may be of little practical use unless:

a)   There is a clear causal relationship between the data.

b)   There is good evidence of correlation.

c)   The line of best fit calculated is a good predictor of the trend in data.

These three factors are dealt with below.

19. Causal relationship

There must be a cause and effect relationship between the variables. This can only be established by a knowledge of the practicalities of the situation being studied. Correlation calculations merely tell us if two variables move together, not if the movement of one causes the movement of the other. There is, unfortunately, no simple test which enables causal relationships to be determined.

20. Correlation

Having established that a causal relationship exists between the data, it is worthwhile to test for evidence of good correlation prior to carrying out a least squares calculation.

This can be done by carrying out a significance test of the correlation between the two variables using a t-test.

This is illustrated using the data from Example 1 above.

x	y	x^2	y^2	xy
1	14	1	196	14
2	17	4	289	34
3	15	9	225	45
4	23	16	529	92
5	18	25	324	90
6	22	36	484	132
7	31	49	961	217
$\sum = 28$	140	140	30,008	624

∴ the calculated t value is

$$t = r \frac{\sqrt{n-2}}{\sqrt{1-r^2}}$$

where:

$$r = \frac{n\Sigma xy - \Sigma x \Sigma y}{\sqrt{n\Sigma x^2 - (\Sigma x)^2}\sqrt{n\Sigma y^2 - (\Sigma y)^2}}$$

$$= \frac{7 \times 624 - 28 \times 140}{\sqrt{7 \times 140 - 28^2}\sqrt{7 \times 3008 - 140^2}}$$

$$= 0.839$$

∴

$$t = 0.839 \frac{\sqrt{7-2}}{\sqrt{1-0.839^2}} = 3.45$$

The values of t from statistical tables for 5 degrees of freedom are:

at the 95% level = 2.57

at the 99% level = 4.03

∴ we may conclude that as the calculated t value is greater than the value at the 95% level there is evidence of real correlation at the 95% level of significance but not at the 99% level.

21. Predictive quality of the calculated regression line

Having calculated the regression line we now wish to know if the calculated regression coefficients have good predictive qualities. This is done by calculating the *coefficient of determination* (r^2).

This coefficient calculates what proportion of the variation in the actual values of y (costs in the example above) may be predicted by changes in the value of x (activity in this example)

$$\therefore r^2 = \frac{\textbf{Explained Variation}}{\textbf{Total Variation}}$$

and as r has been calculated above

$$r^2 = 0.839^2$$

$$= \textbf{0.704 or 70.4\%}$$

This can be interpreted in the example above that 70.4% of the variations in costs may be predicted by changes in the output level. Alternatively, factors other than output changes influence costs to the extent of $(100 - 70.4)\%$, ie 29.6%.

Note: Alternative methods exist for assessing the predictive quality of the regression line. One common method is to calculate confidence intervals for the value of the regression coefficient, b. These intervals show for a given probability, say 95%, the range which contains the true variable cost.

How to calculate confidence intervals and other more advanced aspects of regression analysis are described in detail in *Quantitative Techniques*, T. Lucey, Letts Educational (formerly DP Publications).

22. Multiple linear regression analysis

There are occasions when the accuracy of cost prediction can be improved by basing the forecast on two or more independent variables rather than the single variable used so far. For example, assume that it has been discovered that total costs depend on a linear function of labour hours, weight handled, and machine hours, then the cost function would be:

$$y = a + bx_1 + cx_2 + dx_3 + \mu$$

Where a, b, c and d are coefficients similar to those discussed previously.

μ is a disturbance term that includes the net effect of other factors,

$$\text{and} \quad x_1 = \text{labour hours}$$
$$x_2 = \text{weight handled}$$
$$x_3 = \text{machine hours}$$
$$\text{and} \quad y = \text{total cost}$$

The manual calculation of multiple regression coefficients is laborious but most computer systems have statistical packages which can calculate the values of the individual coefficients, their standard errors, the overall value of y, confidence intervals for the regression line and so on.

As an example of the application of multiple regression consider a firm which has found that its total overheads are dependent on labour hours, machine hours and units produced. Analysis has produced the following multiple regression formula:

$$y = £25,000 + 7.3x_1 + 4.8x_2 + 3.1x_3$$

where: y = total overheads

x_1 = labour hours

x_2 = machine hours

x_3 = units produced

What are the predicted overheads in a period when there were 16,500 labour hours, 7,300 machine hours and 13,400 units were produced?

Solution

$$y = £25,000 + 7.3(16,500) + 4.8(7,300) + 3.1(13,400)$$
$$= £222,030$$

In a similar manner to the methods shown for simple regression, the coefficient of multiple determination and the standard errors of the individual coefficients can be calculated. Those wishing to study this in greater detail are advised to see *Quantitative Techniques*, Ibid.

23. The learning curve

Cost predictions especially those relating to direct labour costs should allow for the effects of learning process. During the early stages or producing a new part or carrying out a new process, experience and skill is gained, productivity increases and there is a reduction of time taken per unit.

There are two forms of learning curve model, the *cumulative average* model and the *marginal* model. Both models use the same general formula, but with some changes in the definitions of the formula elements. The learning curve is a non-linear function for which the general formula is:

$$y = ax^b$$

where a = number of labour hours for the first unit

x = cumulative number of units

b = the learning coefficient.

It is the definition of y which determines the model to be used as follows:

When the *cumulative average model* is used:

y = cumulative average time per unit for x units

When the *marginal model* is used:

y = marginal time for the xth unit

The two approaches are described in detail below.

24. Cumulative average learning curves

Studies have shown that there is a tendency for the time per unit to reduce at some constant rate as production mounts. For example, a 90% learning curve means that as cumulative production quantities double the cumulative average time per unit falls by 10%. An 80% learning curve would mean that a doubling of production causes a 20% fall in the cumulative average time per unit, and so on.

This is illustrated in Table 1 which is based on a product with an 80% learning curve where the first unit of production takes 50 hours.

Note that the cumulative average time of 25.6 hours when cumulative production is 8 units is *not* the time taken for the 8th unit; it is the average over all production to date,

i.e. $\dfrac{204.8}{8} = 25.6$.

Cumulative production	Cumulative time taken	Cumulative average time per unit	
(Units)	(Hours)	(Hours)	
1	50	50	
2	80	40	$(50 \times 80\%)$
4	128	32	$(50 \times 80\% \times 80\%)$
8	204.8	25.6	$(50 \times 80\% \times 80\% \times 80\%)$

Table 1 Illustration of 80% cumulative average learning curve.

If it is required to find the time the 8th unit takes, it is necessary to find the cumulative time for 7 units of cumulative production and deduct it from the cumulative time for 8 units. This is illustrated below after the learning curve formula is explained.

25. Cumulative average learning curves by formula

When the cumulative average model is used the formula is as follows:

$$y = ax^b$$

where: y = cumulative average labour hours per unit

a = number of labour hours for the first unit

x = cumulative number of units

b = the learning coefficient

The learning coefficient is calculated as follows:

$$b = \frac{\log(1 - \text{Proportionate decrease})}{\log 2}$$

thus for a 20% decrease (i.e. an 80% learning curve)

$$b = \frac{\log(1 - 0.2)}{\log 2} = \frac{-0.09691}{0.30103} = -0.322$$

The formula is used to solve questions based on the product in Table 1.

a) What is the cumulative average time per unit when cumulative production is 8 units and 16 units?

b) How long did unit 8 take to manufacture?

Solutions

a) When cumulative production is 8 units:

$$y = 50 \times 8^{-0.322}$$

∴ cumulative average time= 25.6 hours (confirming the value in Table 1)

When cumulative production is 16 units:

$$y = 50 \times 16^{-0.322}$$

∴ cumulative average time per unit= **20.48 hours**

(this can be verified by multiplying 25.6 hours by 80%)

b) *Time taken to manufacture the 8th unit.*

As explained above, this is found by deducting the cumulative time for 7 units from the cumulative time for 8 units.

The cumulative time for 8 units is already known from Table 1, i.e. 204.8 hours, but it is necessary to calculate the cumulative time for 7 units, as follows:

Cumulative average time for 7 units= $50 \times 7^{-0.322}$ = 26.72 hours

Thus cumulative time for 7 units = 26.72×7 = 187.04 hours

∴ Time for 8th unit = 204.8 − 187.04 hours = **17.76 hours**

26. Marginal leaning curve model

This model is based on the assumption that the time for the marginal, or last, unit reduces by a given percentage when cumulative production doubles.

This is illustrated in Table 2, based on the same product used for Table 1, i.e. an 80% learning curve where the first unit takes 50 hours.

Cumulative production (Units)	Cumulative time taken (Hours)	Time taken for marginal unit (Hours)	
1	50	50	
2	90	40	$(50 \times 80\%)$
4	?	32	$(50 \times 80\% \times 80\%)$
8	?	25.6	$(50 \times 80\% \times 80\% \times 80\%)$

Table 2 illustration of the 80% marginal learning curve

Although the figures in the right-hand column are the same as in Table 1 their meaning is quite different. In Table 2 the 50, 40, 32 and 25.6 hours are the times the 1st, 2nd, 4th and 8th unit take to manufacture, not an overall average. It will also be seen that it is not directly possible to find the cumulative production time at the 4 and 8 units production levels. This is because we do not yet know the marginal times for the 3rd, 5th, 6th and 7th units. These can be found using the formula, and this process is demonstrated below.

27. Marginal learning curves by formula

As already explained, the general learning curve formula is applicable, but y is defined differently as follows:

$$y = ax^b$$

where y = time for the marginal unit, and all other elements are as previously defined, and the learning coefficient is calculated in the same manner.

Once again the formula is used to solve questions based on the product in Tables 1 and 2.

a) How long did unit 8 take to manufacture?

b) What was the cumulative production time when cumulative production is 8 units?

Solutions

a) Time to manufacture 8th unit

$$y = 50 \times 8^{-0.322}$$

$$= 25.6 \text{ hours (confirming the value in Table 2)}$$

b) Cumulative production time when cumulative production is 8 units.

The cumulative production time cannot be found directly. It is necessary to find the times to manufacture each of the units 1 to 8 separately and total them. The times for units 1, 2, 4 and 8 are already known from Table 2, but it is necessary to calculate the times for units 3, 5, 6 and 7 and then add all the times together.

Time for unit 3 $= 50 \times 3^{-0.322}$ $= 35.1$ hours

Time for unit 5 $= 50 \times 5^{-0.322}$ $= 29.78$ hours

Time for unit 6 $= 50 \times 6^{-0.322}$ $= 28.08$ hours

Time for unit 7 $= 50 \times 7^{-0.322}$ $= 26.72$ hours

Thus the cumulative time for a cumulative production of 8 units is

$50 + 40 + 35.1 + 32 + 29.78 + 28.08 + 26.72 + 25.6 = \textbf{267.28 hours}$

It will be apparent that this process is tedious, so if large quantities were being produced, computer assistance would be required to carry out these calculations if they were thought necessary.

28. Cumulative average and marginal models compared

Although the same general formula is applicable there are substantial differences in results, depending on the definition for y in the formula $y = ax^b$. In general, when the marginal model is used the reduction in time taken for production is *less* than the cumulative average model for any given learning curve. This can be proved by examining the total time for 8 units in the examples above:

With an 80% learning curve:

Total time for 8 units using cumulative average model = **204.8 hours**

Total time for 8 units using marginal model = **267.28**

Thus 80% learning curves (or any other values) are not equivalent in the two models.

Great care must therefore be taken to use the correct model. Remember, this is entirely dependent on the meaning given to y in the general formula.

29. Practical example of learning curve

A Production Planning Department is considering the production Schedules for Period 9. In particular they wish to calculate the time to be allocated for the manufacture of a batch of 100 of a computer-controlled machine tool called ROBO X1. The first ROBO X1 took 80 hours to make and it is known from past experience that there is a learning effect. From past records the following information is available:

Cumulative production (Units)	Cumulative time taken (Hours)	Time per unit (Hours)
600	18,153.6	30.256
1,200	32,676	27.23

They calculate that the cumulative production at the beginning of Period 9 will be 3,000 units.

Required:

a) What type of learning curve model do the records suggest?

b) What value of learning curve do the records show?

c) Calculate the learning coefficient.

d) Calculate the time allowance necessary for the batch of 100 in Period 9.

Solution

a) **Type of learning curve model.**

From the data supplied it is clear that the time per unit is a cumulative average because the cumulative time is production multiplied by time per unit, e.g:

$$600 \times 30.256 = \mathbf{18{,}153.6}$$

∴ a cumulative average model is being used.

b) Value of the learning curve:

$$\frac{27.23}{30.256} = 0.9$$

∴ there is a 90% learning curve.

c) **Learning coefficient for a 90% learning curve**

$$b = \frac{\log (1 - \text{Proportionate decrease})}{\log 2}$$

$$= \frac{\log (1 - 0.1)}{\log 2}$$

$$= \frac{-0.04576}{0.30103}$$

$$= -0.152$$

d) Time allowance for a batch of 100 in Period 9 when cumulative production at start is 3,000 units.

The time allowance will be the difference between the cumulative time for 3,000 units and the cumulative time for 3,100 units, thus:

At 3,000 units

Cumulative average per unit = $80 \times 3{,}000^{-0.152} = 23.69$ hours

∴ cumulative time = $3{,}000 \times 23.69 = \mathbf{71{,}070}$ **hours**

At 3,100 units

Cumulative average per unit = $80 \times 3{,}100^{-0.152} = 23.57$ hours

∴ cumulative time = $3{,}100 \times 23.57 = \mathbf{73{,}067}$ **hours**

Thus the time allowance for the batch of 100 = 73,067 - 71,070 = **1,997 hours**

Note that in the above example and in the earlier explanation of learning curves it has been assumed that regular reduction in labour times occur in strict accordance with the theoretical models. In practice, of course, it is very unlikely that this will happen. Although learning does take place and reductions in labour times per unit do occur, the consistency and regularity of the theoretical models are not likely to be encountered.

30. Applications of learning curve theory

The original studies of learning curves were in connection with aircraft construction in World War 2. Aircraft manufacture is labour intensive and complex and these features are characteristic of industries where learning curves might reasonably be applied; for example, shipbuilding, electronics, construction and so on. The more capital intensive an industry, the more automated, the greater the use of robots and so on, the less likely there is to be any form of regular learning curve. Where they are applicable, learning curves typically vary between 70% and 90%. Although 80% learning curves are commonly encountered, as previously illustrated, students are advised that any value may be encountered in an examination so it is essential to be able to calculate the learning coefficient from first principles.

Where learning takes place with a regular pattern it is important to take account of the reduction in labour hours and costs per unit. This is important in such areas as; production planning and work scheduling, standard costing, overhead absorption (where this is based on labour hours), pricing policy (where this is based on costs).

The learning curve effect is usually applied to the skilled labour element of manufacturing. With AMT this is reduced so that the conventional learning curve effect is of diminishing significance although it is beloved by examiners!

The *experience curve*, in contrast, describes the process of acquiring skills and ability through working in a particular environment and dealing with new production technologies and applies to management as well as other employees. The experience curve or cost experience curve describes the general learning effect on the organisation and expresses the way that the average cost per unit of production changes over time due to technological and organisational changes, not just 'learning' by skilled workers. The experience curve has little relevance for short-term standard setting and product costing. It is more relevant to strategic planning and may be of value in Target Costing, described later in the book.

31. Cost behaviour and time scale

The methods and techniques illustrated in this chapter are most appropriate for short run planning and decision making purposes. This means that the relationship between costs and activity and the classifications of the costs themselves are only likely to hold good over a relatively short time span. What is a 'relatively short time span' depends on the particular circumstances, it may be three months, six months, a year; it is unlikely to be as long as five years. Over longer time periods, unpredictable factors are bound to occur, technology will improve, materials may become scarce, so that predictions of cost behaviour, based on examination of historical data, are likely to be increasingly unreliable. For longer term forecasting, qualitative factors and judgement play an increasing role. For example, in the Delphi Method of forecasting a panel of experts independently answers a sequence of questionnaires in which the answers to one questionnaire are used to produce the next questionnaire. Thus information is shared and subsequent judgement become more refined. In this way qualitative judgements are used in a systematic fashion to produce long-term forecasts.

32. Summary

a) The ability to predict costs (and other factors such as sales) is a vital part of supplying information for planning and decision making.

b) An essential preliminary to cost prediction is the consideration of what costs (or parts of cost) are fixed and which are variable.

c) There are difficulties with the usual cost classifications. Variable costs are not always linear, fixed costs can and do change, and many costs are semi-fixed or semi-variable.

d) Costs frequently do not behave in regular fashions and a cost may be linear, curvi-linear or stepped at different activity levels.

e) Cost extrapolations outside normal activity ranges are likely to be less accurate.

f) A convex function is one in which there are economies of scale. A concave function is one where diminishing returns operate.

g) A common curvi-linear function is a parabola which has the form

$$f = bx + cx^2 + dx^3 \ldots\ldots px^n$$

h) For simplicity, linear approximations of curvi-linear functions are frequently made.

i) There are three approaches to cost forecasting; extrapolation based on historical data using statistical techniques, accounts classification, and the industrial engineering approach.

j) Before using any statistical technique the data to be worked on should be checked for their appropriateness.

k) Common methods used for linear regression analysis are the 'high-low' technique, scattergraphs, and the lest square method of simple, linear regression analysis.

l) The least squares methods produces values for the coefficients a and b in the linear function,

$$y = a + bx$$

m) The coefficients are found by solving the Normal Equations or directly by using transpositions of the Normal Equations.

n) Although the coefficients can always be calculated, they are of little value for predictive purposes unless there is a causal relationship in the data, there is evidence of correlation, and the line of best fit is a good predictor of the trend.

o) The correlation between the two variables can be established by using a t-test and the predictive quality of the trend line can be assessed by calculating the coefficient of determination, r^2.

p) Multiple regression analysis is where the function has two or more independent variables. The use of multiple regression may be necessary where total cost is a function of two or more activity indicators, eg labour hours, tonnage produced, and machine hours.

q) A learning curve is the term given to the function representing the reduction in time taken per unit due to direct labour gaining experience and skill.

r) Learning curve are represented by the function $y = ax^b$. In marginal models $y =$ the time for the last unit to be made. In cumulative average models $y =$ average time per unit over the cumulative production to date.

s) When longer term forecasting is required extrapolations from historical data become less relevant, and judgement and qualitative factors become increasingly important.

33. Points to note

a) Forecasting is a large and complex subject and the intending management accountant is advised to master the introduction contained in this chapter and pursue the subject in one of the specialist books on the subject.

b) A factor which should always be considered when making cost and revenue forecasts is the rate of inflation. In general, the management accountant is concerned with values in real terms so care must be taken to allow for the projected rate of inflation particularly when considering such items as labour and material costs, selling prices, and bought in services.

Additional reading

Applied regression analysis; *Draper and Smith* – Wiley

Forecasting methods in business and management; *Firth* – Arnold

Statistical cost analysis; *Johnston* – McGraw Hill

Quantitative Techniques; *Lucey* – Letts Educational (formerly DP Publications)

Forecasting costs and prices; *Morrell* – CIMA

Forecasting for Business; *Wood and Fildes* – Longman

Self review questions

1. For cost prediction purposes what are the essential cost classifications? (3)
2. Why must the management accountant continually review conventional cost classifications and the conventional assumptions regarding cost behaviour? (4)
3. Why is it unlikely that all variable costs vary in relation to the same measure of activity? (4)
4. What is a concave function? – a convex function? (6)
5. What is the formula for a parabolic cost function with four independent variables? (7)
6. Why are linear approximations used? (8)
7. What is a stepped cost? (9)
8. What is the accounts classification method of cost forecasting? (12)
9. What questions should be asked regarding the data to be used for forecasting? (13)
10. Describe the 'high-low' technique (15)
11. How is a scattergraph drawn and used? (16)
12. Give the Normal Equations used in the least squares method. (17)
13. What is a causal relationship? (19)

14. How is a significance test of the correlation between the two variables used for regression analysis?
15. What is the coefficient of determination and what is its meaning? (21)
16. Why is multiple regression analysis used? (22)
17. Distinguish between a marginal and cumulative average learning curve. (23)
18. How is the coefficient b calculated in the learning curve formula $y = ax^b$? (25)
19. Why are statistical and other techniques based on historical data of less validity for long-term forecasting? (24)

Assessment and revision section 1

Examination questions with answers

A1. (i) Cost may be classified in a number of ways including classification by behaviour, by function, by expense type, by controllability and by relevance.

(ii) Management accounting should assist in EACH of the planning, control and decision making processes in an organisation.

Discuss the ways in which relationships between statements (i) and (ii) are relevant in the design of an effective management accounting system.

ACCA, Information for Control and Decision Making.

A2. Discuss the following statement giving examples to illustrate the meaning and relevance of each of points (i) and (ii).

A management accounting system may not realise its full potential because information is:

(i) insufficiently relevant   (ii) subject to bias (i.e., not neutral in nature)

ACCA, Information for Control and Decision Making.

A3. PQR Limited produces two joint products - P and Q - together with a by-product R, from a single main process (process 1). Product P is sold at the point of separation for £5 per kg whereas product Q is sold for £7 per kg after further processing into product Q2. By-product R is sold without further processing for £1.75 per kg.

Process 1 is closely monitored by a team of chemists who planned the output per 1,000 kg of input materials to be as follows:

Product P	500 kg
Product Q	350 kg
Product R	100 kg
Toxic waste	50 kg

The toxic waste is disposed of at a cost of £1.50 per kg, and arises at the end of processing.

Process 2, which is used for further processing of product Q into product Q2, has the following cost structure:

Fixed costs	£6,000 per week
Variable costs	£1.50 per kg processed

The following actual data relate to the first week of accounting period 10:

Process 1

Opening work in process		Nil
Materials input	10,000 kg	£15,000
Direct labour		£10,000
Variable overhead		£4,000
Fixed overhead		£6,000

Outputs:

Product P	4,800 kg
Product Q	3,600 kg
Product R	1,000 kg
Toxic waste	600 kg
Closing work in process	Nil

Process 2

Opening work in process	Nil
Input of product Q	3,600 kg
Output of product Q2	3,300 kg
Closing work in process	300 kg, 50% converted

Conversion costs were incurred in accordance with the planned cost structure.

Required:

a) Prepare the main process account for the first week of period 10 using the final sales value method to attribute pre-separation costs to joint products.

b) Prepare the toxic waste accounts and process 2 account for the first week of period 10.

c) Comment on the method used by PQR Limited to attribute pre-separation costs to its joint products.

d) Advise the management of PQR Limited whether or not, on purely financial grounds, it should continue to process product Q into product Q2

   (i) if product Q could be sold at the point of separation for £4.30 per kg *and*

   (ii) if 60% of the weekly fixed costs of process 2 were avoided by not processing product Q further.

CIMA, Operational Cost Accounting.

A4. The following budgeted information relates to Brunti plc for the forthcoming period:

	Products		
	XYI	YZT	ABW
	(000)	(000)	(000)
Sales and production (units)	50	40	30
	£	£	£
Selling price (per unit)	45	95	73
Prime cost (per unit)	32	84	65
	Hours	Hours	Hours
Machine department (machine hours per unit)	2	5	4
Assembly department (direct labour hours per unit)	7	3	2

Overheads allocated and apportioned to production departments (including service cost centre costs) were to be recovered in product costs as follows:

Machine department at £1.20 per machine hour

Assembly department at £.825 per direct labour hour

You ascertain that the above overheads could be re-analysed into cost pools as follows:

Cost pool	£000	Cost Driver	Quantity for period
Machining services	357	Machined hours	420,000
Assembly services	318	Direct labour hours	530,000
Set up costs	26	Set ups	520
Order processing	156	Customer orders	32,000
Purchasing	84	Suppliers orders	11,200
	941		

You have also been provided with the following estimates for the period:

	Products		
	XYI	YZT	ABW
	(000)	(000)	(000)
Number of set-ups	120	200	200
Customer orders	8,000	8,000	16,000
Suppliers orders	3,000	4,000	4,200

Required:

a) Prepare and present profit statements using:

(i) conventional absorption costing, and

(ii) activity-based costing.

b) Comment on why activity-based costing is considered to present a fairer valuation of the product cost per unit.

ACCA, Managerial Finance.

A5. The following budget and actual data relates to Cassiop plc for the past three periods:

Budget	Period 1	Period 2	Period 3
Sales (units)	10,000	14,000	12,200
Production (units)	8,000	14,200	12,400
Fixed overheads	£10,400	£19,170	£17,360
Actual			
Sales (units)	9,600	12,400	10,200
Production (units)	8,400	13,600	9,200
Fixed overheads	£11,200	£18,320	£16,740

The value of the opening and closing stock of the units produced is arrived at by using FIFO. The budgeted and actual opening stock for period 1 was 2,600 units and its valuation included £3,315 of fixed overheads. The company absorbs its fixed overheads via a predetermined fixed overhead rate per unit which is the same for each period. It is assumed that variable costs per unit and selling prices per unit remained the same for each of the periods.

Required:

a) Calculate the under- or over-recovery of fixed overhead for each period and indicate how it will affect the profit or loss.

b) Absorption costing will produce a higher profit than marginal costing. Explain why you agree or disagree with this statement, making reference to the data provided above as appropriate.

c) Explain briefly why absorption costing is usually considered to be unsuitable as an aid for decision-making. Justify your answer.

ACCA, Managerial Finance.

A6. Trimake Limited makes three main products, using broadly the same production methods and equipment for each. A conventional product costing system is used at present, although an Activity Based Costing (ABC) system is being considered. Details of the three products for a typical period are:

	Hours per unit		Materials per unit	Volumes
	Labour hours	Machine hours	£	Units
Product X	$\frac{1}{2}$	$1\frac{1}{2}$	20	750
Product Y	$1\frac{1}{2}$	1	12	1,250
Product Z	1	3	25	7,000

Direct labour costs £6 per hour and production overheads are absorbed on a machine hour basis. The rate for the period is £28 per machine hour.

a) You are required to calculate the cost per unit for each product using conventional methods.

Further analysis shows that the total of production overheads can be divided as follows:

	%
Costs relating to set-ups	35
Costs relating to machinery	20
Costs relating to materials handling	15
Cost relating to inspection	30
Total production overhead	100%

The following activity volumes are associated with the product line for the period as a whole.

Total activities for the period

	Number of set-ups	Number of movements of materials	Number of inspections
Product X	75	12	150
Product Y	115	21	180
Product Z	480	87	670
	670	120	1,000

You are required:

b) to calculate the cost per unit for each product using ABC principles;

c) to comment on the reasons for any differences in the costs in your answers to a) and b).

CIMA, Management Accounting Techniques.

A7. The learning curve is a simple mathematical model but its application to management accounting problems requires careful thought.

Required:

Having regard to the above statement,

a) explain the 'cumulative average time' model commonly used to represent learning curve effects.

b) sketch TWO diagrams to illustrate, in regard to a new product, the relative impacts of 70%, 80% and 90% learning curves on

- ❐ cumulative average hours per unit,
- ❐ cumulative hours taken.

c) compare and contrast the learning curve with the experience curve; explain the circumstances when each may be most relevant.

CIMA, Management Accounting Applications (part question).

Examination questions without answers

B1. Large service organisations, such as banks and hospitals, used to be noted for their lack of standard costing systems, and their relatively unsophisticated budgeting and control systems compared with large manufacturing organisations. But this is changing and many large service organisations are new revising their use of management accounting techniques.

Required:

a) Explain which features of large-scale service organisations encourage the application of Activity Based approaches to the analysis of cost information.

b) Explain which features of service organisations may create problems for the application of Activity Based Costing.

c) Explain the uses for activity-based cost information in service industries.

CIMA, Management Accounting Control Systems (part question).

B2. Sapu plc make and sell a number of products. Products A and B are products for which market prices are available at which Sapu plc can obtain a share of the market as detailed below. Estimated data for the forthcoming period is as follows:

(i) Product data

	Product A	Product B	Other products
Production/sales (units)	5,000	10,000	40,000
	£000	£000	£000
Total direct material cost	80	300	2,020
Total direct labour cost	40	100	660

(ii) Variable overhead cost is £1,500,000 of which 40% is related to the acquisition, storage and use of direct materials and 60% is related to the control and use of direct labour.

(iii) It is current practice in Sapu plc to absorb variable overhead cost into product units using overall company wide percentages on direct material cost and direct labour cost as the absorption bases.

(iv) Market prices for Products A and B are £75 and £95 per unit respectively.

(v) Sapu plc require a minimum estimated contribution: sales ratio of 40% before proceeding with the production/sale of any product.

Required:

a) Prepare estimated unit product costs for Product A and Product B where variable overhead is charged to product units as follows:

   (i) Using the existing absorption basis as detailed above.

   (ii) Using an activity-based costing approach where cost drivers have been estimated for material and labour related overhead costs as follows:

	Product A	Product B	Other products
Direct material related overheads - cost driver is material bulk. The bulk proportions per unit are:	4	1	1.5
Direct labour related overheads - cost driver is number of labour operations (not directly time related). Labour operations per product unit	6	1	2

b) Prepare an analysis of the decision strategy which Sapu plc may implement with regard to the production and sale of Products A and B. Use unit costs as calculated in a)(i) and a)(ii) together with other information given in the question in your analysis. Your answer should include relevant calculations and discussion and be prepared in a form suitable for presentation to management.

ACCA, Information for Control and Decision Making (part question).

B3. The manufacture of one of the products of A Ltd requires three separate processes. In the last of the three processes, costs, production and stock for the month just ended were:

1) Transfers from Process 2: 180,000 units at a cost of £394,200

2) Process 3 costs: materials £110,520, conversion costs £76,506

3) Work in progress at the beginning of the month: 20,000 units at a cost of £55,160 (based on FIFO pricing method). Units were 70% complete for materials, and 40% complete for conversion costs.

4) Work in progress at the end of the month: 18,000 units which were 90% complete for materials, and 70% complete for conversion costs.

5) Product inspected when it is complete. Normally no losses are expected but during the month 60 units were rejected and sold for £1.50 per unit.

Required:

a) Prepare the Process 3 account for the month just ended.

b) Explain how, and why, your calculations would be affected if the 60 units lost were treated as normal losses.

c) Explain how your calculations would be affected by the use of weighted average pricing instead of FIFO.

ACCA Cost and Management Accounting 1.

B4. a) Describe the characteristics of service costing.

b) A transport business with a fleet of four similar vehicles is working at 80% of practical capacity for three-quarters of the time. For the remainder of the time operations are at 60% of practical capacity. Measured in operating hours, practical capacity of the business is 8,000 per annum; this is equivalent to 160,000 kilometres. Operating costs of the business are as follows:

Vehicle depreciation, £4,000 per vehicle, per annum.

Basic maintenance, £110 per vehicle, per monthly service.

Spares/replacement parts, £100 per '000 kilometres.

Vehicle licence, £140 per vehicle, per annum.

Vehicle insurance, £450 per vehicle, per annum.

Tyre replacements after 40,000 kilometres, six at £90 each.

Fuel, £0.40 per litre.

Average kilometres per litre, 4.0.

Drivers, £8,000 per annum each (four drivers are employed at all times, on a time rate basis)

General administration costs, £19,700 per annum (these are absorbed into the cost of jobs at 25% of total cost before general administration).

Required:

i) Define the term 'cost unit' and discuss appropriate cost unit(s) for the transport business.

ii) Demonstrate on a graph the total cost per kilometre from 60% to 100% of practical capacity (plot costs at intervals of 8,000 kilometres).

iii) If jobs are costed based upon unit costs per kilometre (to 3 decimal places of a £) at 80% of practical capacity, calculate the extent of the fixed overhead under-absorption in a year.

iv) Calculate the variable and total costs that would be charged to a job if it requires one vehicle driving 64 kilometres.

ACCA, Cost and Management Accounting I.

B5. FRN Ltd is a small company which produces a single product - a light aircraft called the RUSTLER. The RUSTLER is similar in capability and performance to aircraft produced by a number of other manufacturers, although the RUSTLER does have certain features which make it particularly useful for certain special purposes. In a given three-month period, all customers buying RUSTLERS are charged s single uniform price.

The construction of the RUSTLER by FRN Ltd is mainly an assembly operation using bought-in components. Most of FRN Ltd's factory staff are engaged on terms which include a fixed basic wage, an hourly rate and overtime bonuses. It is not possible to increase factory size or equipment levels within a three-month period.

You have been engaged as a consultant to advise FRN Ltd's management on output and product pricing during the coming three-month period. During this period the maximum output is 30 RUSTLERs. Your initial research indicates that the revenues and variable costs associated with output of 1 RUSTLER and 30 RUSTLERs during the period are:

Output of RUSTLERs	1	30
	£	£
Revenues	100,000	2,134,000
Variable costs	30,000	2,497,000

You may assume that the relationships of revenues and variable costs to output are curvilinear ones that may be described by formulae based on the equation

$$y = ax^n$$

Required:

a) Draw a diagram in order to illustrate the behaviour of revenue and variable costs over the whole range of possible levels of output.

b) Determine two mathematical formulae to describe the relationship between
  – output and revenues,
  – output and variable costs.

c) Determine the level of output and the price per RUSTLER that will maximise profit during the period.

d) Give likely reasons why revenues and variable costs behave in relation to output in the way they do.

CIMA, Management Accounting Applications

4 Information and management accounting

1. Objectives

After studying this chapter you will:

❑ be able to distinguish between data and information;

❑ know the attributes of information;

❑ be able to define communication terms such as noise, redundancy, perception;

❑ understand the relationship between the costs and value of information;

❑ know the desirable properties of accounting information;

❑ understand how uncertainty affects information.

2. Data and information

The terms 'data' and 'information' are commonly used interchangeably but from a technical viewpoint they can be distinguished from each other. Data can be defined as groups of non random symbols which represent quantities, events, actions and things. Data are made up of characters which may be alphabetic or numeric or special symbols.

Information is data which have been processed into a form which is meaningful to the recipient and which is of real or perceived value for the intended purpose which, as far as the management accountant is concerned, is likely to be for planning, control or decision making. Thus data are the raw materials from which information is produced. It also follows that what is information for one purpose or level in the organisation may be used as data for further processing into information for a different purpose and level.

Note:

This latter point is a key element in management accounting. Information produced must be relevant for the intended purpose otherwise it is useless. This means that, for example, a cost prepared for use in today's selling price quotation may need to be reanalysed and reprocessed to be able to use it for a make or buy decision. This approach is summed up in the well known management accounting phrase, 'different costs for different purposes'. The relevancy requirement may make much of the information produced by the costing system (eg product costs) inappropriate for management accounting purposes without further analysis. This requirement emphasises the need for the management accounting system to be flexible so that the information produced by the system is use specific.

3. Information attributes

From a system's viewpoint information possesses a number of attributes

a) It reduces uncertainty. Rapid feedback of information helps to reduce uncertainty. This is the main rationale for the introduction of any information system.

b) It may be true or false. If the recipient of false information believes it to be true the effect is the same as if it were true.

c) It may be incremental. It may update or add new increments to information already available.

d) It may be a correction of past false information.

e) It may confirm existing information. Note that such information may be of value because it increases the recipient's perception of the correctness of the information.

f) It has surprise value. This is the attribute which above all determines the information content of a message or report. The greater the probability of an event occurring the smaller will be the amount of information in a message saying that the event has occurred. The greater the surprise, the more informative the message.

The message, 'It will be dark tonight' has no surprise value and hence contains no information.

4. Communications systems

Data arise from both internal and external sources and frequently are derived from the day to day operations of the organisation – buying and using materials, selling to customers, making products, receiving and paying cash and so forth. Invoices and other documents are coded, analysed and the data recorded. Subsequently the data are processed perhaps using particular decision or planning techniques, comparisons are made, inferences are drawn and information for a particular purpose is produced. This information is used to prepare a report or statement or a display on a terminal which is then communicated to the manager for his use.

The above very brief outline describes a typical communication system of which the management accounting system is but one example. The various parts of a typical communication system are shown in Figure 4.1 related to a management accounting example and several important terms are described.

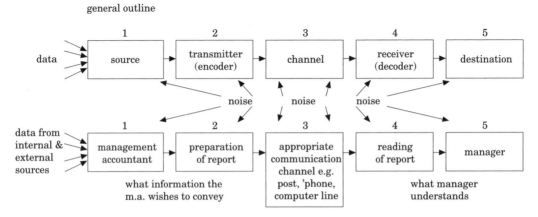

Figure 4.1 Communication Systems

5. Noise

This is the term used in communication theory for any influences or factors which cause the message at the receiver being different to the message transmitted. In a general business sense, noise makes the perceived content of a message different from that intended to be conveyed. Noise may arise from numerous factors including: wrong coding, poor presentation, bad form design, illegible writing, misinterpretation, actual physical noise, unexplained jargon. It is clearly important that noise is kept to a minimum and the management accountant should examine each of the gathering, processing, transmitting and receiving stages so that maximum effectiveness is achieved.

6. Redundancy

This means that more symbols, figures or words are used to represent the message than is strictly necessary.

However, the additional material helps the presence of errors to be detected and, in some instances, can provide for the correction of those errors. The effects of noise can be reduced by the use of some redundancy. Redundancy may consist of repetition of words or figures, multiple copies, confirmatory letters following telephone calls, hard copy printouts following a visual display etc. Normal messages in English exhibit varying degrees of redundancy and it is this fact which makes poor handwriting decipherable and enables the comprehension of messages. Too much redundancy is to be avoided as the amount of repetition and/or extraneous material may obscure the essential information contained in a message.

7. Perception

For our purpose this can be defined as the understanding a person obtains from a message or report.

This is an obvious area of importance to the management accountant must of whose output is in the form of reports and statements. A communication can have at least three meanings:

a) What the sender intended to send

b) What is actually contained in the message, and

c) What meaning the receiver understands from the message.

The process of perception in any individual varies from time to time and people attach meanings to messages in accordance with their attitudes, past experiences, and their knowledge of the source of the message. Because only the receivers perception of a message is relevant – he presumably will be taking some action based on the message – it is vital for the sender to reduce possible ambiguities and noise so as to bring the understanding of the receiver as close as possible to that of the sender. The receiver's perception will be enhances if the following points are observed.

a) Avoidance of unfamiliar technical or accounting jargon. Where its use is unavoidable clear explanations should be provided.

b) Collaboration with the receiver on the content, format and presentation of reports and statements.

c) Regular feedback of comments and criticisms from the managers to the management accountant on the effectiveness of the information system.

d) Gain the confidence of the managers involved by showing that the management accounting system is supportive and not threatening and can be relied upon to produce relevant, accurate and timely information.

e) The avoidance of excessive detail. Detail should not be confused with accuracy. Every superfluous character means more processing, more delay, extra assimilation and possibly poorer decisions. The basic rule, as with the volume of information, is as little as possible consistent with effective managerial action.

8. Value of information

Information has no value in itself; its value derives from the changes in decision behaviour caused by the information being available. It follows from this that more detailed information, more accurate information, earlier information is not necessarily better information. Only if it improves the resulting decisions is it better information. The production of information only incurs costs which are frequently considerable. Benefits only arise from actions. A typical relationship between costs and values is shown in Figure 4.2.

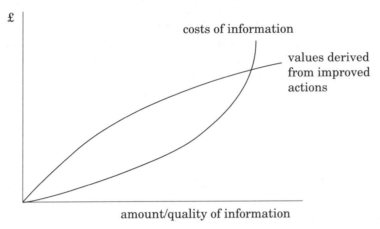

Figure 4.2 Information – Cost and Value

It follows from economic principles that additional information should be produced only if the additional expected value is greater than the additional expected costs.

Remember – information can only produce costs and only actions can produce benefits.

9. Desirable properties of management accounting information

Investigations into information systems, including accounting ones, have shown that much of the information produced is ignored by the managers concerned. It follows that information which is ignored cannot influence the decision making process and therefore can have no value. To ensure that management accounting information is used effectively the following actors must be considered.

a) **Economic reality.** The information should correctly reflect the underlying economic realities. This is the prime requirement and may mean adjusting conventionally prepared accounting information to show more effectively the real economic consequences.

b) **Relevance.** The information must be relevant for the person and purpose intended. As an example, information prepared for performance and control purposes should cover only those items for which the manager is responsible.

c) **Timing.** The information must be produced in time for it to be used effectively.

d) **Accuracy.** The information should be sufficiently accurate for the intended purpose. A reputation for accuracy will enhance the value of the information to the recipient and will make it more likely to be used.

   Note: There is no such thing as absolute accuracy. What is required is information, prepared according to correct principles, that can be relied upon for the intended purpose. This may mean that a realistic, speedily prepared estimate may be more useful than a more precise answer produced some time later.

e) **Understandability.** The information must be capable of being understood by the recipient. Typical of the ways to increase comprehension are the following:

i) avoidance of unexplained terminology

ii) use of charts, diagrams and tabulated information where appropriate

iii) use of exception reporting and comparative figures

iv) good report and statement layouts

v) a reasonable, but not excessive, amount of redundancy

vi) eliciting the recipient's views and suggestions regarding the understandability of the information.

f) **Detail.** Frequently the amount of detail in a statement or report will depend on the recipients level in the organisation. There is a tendency for information to be aggregated (summarised, totalled, precised) more and more according to the recipient's level in the hierarchy. There are usually sound reasons for this but it should be remembered that aggregation reduces the information content of a message or report. The amount of detail should be that which is sufficient for the intended purpose.

10. Uncertainty and management accounting information

Uncertainty to a greater or lesser degree is present in all planning and decision making situations. It may be the possibility of machine failure, it may be the difficulties of forecasting inflation or exchange rates, it may be the effects of competitors, changing tastes, government actions – the list is endless.

Accordingly, it is vital that the preparer of information for planning and decision making purposes presents the information in a manner which helps the manager to understand the effects of uncertainty on the problem being considered and in particular, now uncertainty is likely to affect the range of possible outcomes.

Information which is presented showing a single valued outcome with no indication of possible uncertainties can be positively misleading for the manager concerned. Some of the ways in which the effects of uncertainties can be presented in reports, statements and analyses are given below.

a) Presenting results and outcomes as ranges of values rather than single point estimates. This may be as a simple range (highest – lowest) or it may be by presenting the outcome(s) as a distribution of values represented by the mean or most likely value and a measure of the dispersion of the distribution – usually the standard deviation.

b) Using three point estimates (high, low and most likely) for analysis and presentation purposes.

c) Associating probabilities with the values and outcomes. The probabilities are likely to be subjective probabilities, ie the quantification of judgement rather than objective or statistical probabilities but in spite of this, such probabilities can provide valuable insights to the underlying uncertainties.

d) The use of sensitivity analysis. This is a process by which the factors involved in the situation (eg sales volume, cost per unit, inflation rate, selling price per unit and so on) are varied one at a time and the effect on the outcome noted. In this way sensitive factors – those that influence outcomes most – are identified so that they may receive further attention and analysis before a final decision is taken.

e) The use of confidence limits. This is particularly appropriate when forecasts are being supplied. Instead of merely a single line representing say, a forecasted cost, confidence limits each side of the line can be calculated so that the uncertainty inherent in the forecast is clearly shown. Narrow confidence limits would demonstrate a higher degree of certainty than confidence limits which are widely spaced.

Note:

The treatment of uncertainty, subjective probability, sensitivity analysis, and confidence limits is dealt with in more detail in *Quantitative Techniques*, T. Lucey, Letts Educational (formerly DP Publications).

11. Summary

a) Information is data processed into a form relevant for the intended purpose.

b) Information reduces uncertainty and has surprise value.

c) The major elements of a communications system are: source – transmitter – channel – receiver – destination.

d) Noise is the term used for factors which cause the message received to be different from that transmitted.

e) Redundancy means that more figures or words are used than is absolutely necessary. Some redundancy is useful but too much is to be avoided.

f) The perception of messages and information by the receiver is all important for the management accountant and good form design, avoidance of jargon, avoidance of excessive detail, all help to improve perception.

g) The value of information can only come from better decisions or planning brought about by the information.

h) For maximum effectiveness, information produced by the management accounting system should: reflect economic reality, be relevant, timely, accurate, and understandable to the recipient.

i) Uncertainty is always present and the effects of uncertainty should be reflected in information produced by the management accountant. This might be by the use of ranges of outcomes, three point estimates, the use of probabilities, sensitivity analysis, the use of confidence limits and so on.

12. Points to note

a) It must be remembers that *all* information is incomplete and to some extent inaccurate. It follows from this that many so called 'optimal' solutions are only optimal in relation to the (imperfect) information on which they are based.

b) Much management information is now produced by computer. This has many advantages, eg greater depth of analysis, use of statistical and operational techniques, speed and so on. However, great care must still be taken to ensure that the information produced is *relevant for the intended purpose.* Speediness and volume of information are no substitutes for relevance.

Additional reading

Report writing in business; *Bentley* – CIMA

Cybernetics and management; *Beer* – English Universities Press

Accounting Information Systems; *Bodnar* – Allyn & Bacon

Management Information systems; *Lucey* – Letts Educational (formerly DP Publications)

Self review questions

1. Distinguish between data and information. (2)
2. Give six attributes of information. (3)
3. What are the elements in a communication system? (4)
4. What is noise? (5)
5. What is redundancy and why is a certain amount necessary in a message? (6)
6. How can the receiver's perception be increased? (7)
7. How is the value of information derived? (8)
8. Give five desirable properties of management accounting information. (9)
9. How can the effects of uncertainty be incorporated in reports and statements? (10)

Planning

The Management Accountant is one of the major providers of information for planning purposes and to do this effectively it is essential that he understand the nature of planning, how plans are established, the distinction between long-term and short-term planning, the place of budgeting in the planning process, how to derive individual budgets and the overall Master Budget, and how planning relates to control.

The following four chapters cover these and related matters and commence with an introduction to some important system concepts which are highly relevant to the planning and subsequent control process.

Statistical and Operational research techniques can provide invaluable assistance in planning. Examples include the statistical aids to forecasting cost behaviour already dealt with in Chapter 3 and such operational research techniques as Linear Programming dealt with later in the book.

5 Planning – system concepts

1. Objectives

After studying this chapter you will:

- ❑ understand the relevance of systems theory to planning;
- ❑ know the distinction between deterministic, probabilistic and adaptive systems;
- ❑ be able to describe open and closed systems
- ❑ understand sub-optimality;
- ❑ know that planning and control are related.

2. What is a system?

Systems exist in every facet of life. There are mechanical systems, biological systems, information systems, social systems, organisational systems and innumerable others. Two simple and typical definitions are:

'A system is a set of interrelated components directed to some purpose'.

'A system is a set of parts co-ordinated to accomplish a set of goals'.

Various other definitions existing but they all contain the essential elements of parts and relationships and, in the case of organisational systems, they seek to accomplish agreed objectives.

3. Systems approach

The systems approach avoids taking a piecemeal approach to problems and directs the activities of the components or sub systems of the total system towards meeting overall objectives. The systems approach recognises that changes cannot be made to some parts of the system without considering the effect on the system as a whole and that the overall system characteristics are greater than the sum of the separate parts. This latter is known as the synergy or the 2 + 2 = 5 effect.

In relation to a particular organisation the systems approach would require consideration of the following factors:

a) the system must be defined. This requires establishing the *boundaries* (real or arbitrary) which encompass the system being studied.

b) The *real objectives* of the system must be specified.

c) The environment in which the system operates, the interactions with the environment, and the constraints which it imposes.

d) The indicators which will be used to measure the performance of the system as a whole.

e) The current and anticipated resources available to operate the system.

f) The parts of the system (ie the sub systems) their relationships, activities and objectives must be studied to ensure conformity with overall system objectives.

g) The way that the system is managed, ie the planning and controlling of the system through information networks.

Note: It will be seen how the systems approach aligns closely to good management practice. It is objective oriented, an overall view is taken and the effects of the environment are considered.

4. Types of systems

For our purposes the three most relevant types of systems are deterministic, stochastic and adaptive.

Deterministic or mechanistic systems. These are the simplest systems which are perfectly predictable, ie given the inputs the outputs can be predicted accurately. Machines and computer programs are examples of deterministic systems.

Stochastic or probabilistic systems. In these systems some states can be predicted from a previous state but only in terms of probable behaviour. Predictions will always have a certain degree of error because of the existence of random variations in the values of the system components caused by internal and external influences. For example, in an inventory control system the *average* stock or *average* demand can be predicted but the exact value of these factors at a future time cannot be predicted. Various control systems (eg Inventory Control, Production Control, Quality Control) are installed to detect and control the variations in order that they do not become of such magnitude as to endanger the fulfilment of the system objectives.

Adaptive or self organising or cybernetic systems. These are highly complex systems which adapt to the environment by altering their structure and/or parts and/or behaviour. This adaption is of the system itself and not merely the alteration of some parameter (eg a stock level) within the system. This class of system includes all living systems – animals, plants, social groups and organisations. It is a primary task of management to ensure that organisations continually adapt to changes in the environment to ensure survival and development. It is the essence of long-term planning that recognition is given to the fact that organisations are adaptive systems and that environmental influences are all important.

5. System relationships with the environment

The environment of a system is all other systems outside its own boundaries. Thus the environment of an organisation are the systems (ie the markets, suppliers, competitors, distribution and so on) in the sector of the economy in which it operates. The environment of a production system in an organisation is the other interacting systems within the organisation.

Systems may be *closed* or *open.*

Closed systems: These are systems which are self contained and do not exchange material, information or energy with the environment. In the strict sense no business or organisation system can be a closed system but for many planning and control purposes, systems are designed to be relatively closed with only minimal interactions with their environment. This greatly aids the prediction and monitoring of system performance.

Open systems: These are systems which interact and exchange information, energy and materials with their environment. To ensure survival (the primary organisational objective) adaption to changes in the environment is vital and only open systems have this capability.

These various types of systems are shown in Figure 5.1.

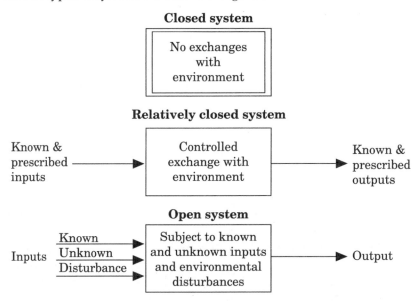

Figure 5.1 Relationship with Environment

Thus it will be seen that an organisation is an open, adaptive system containing within it a number of sub-systems which may be adaptive, probabilistic or deterministic.

6. Sub-optimisation

This is where the objectives of sub-systems are pursued to the detriment of the overall system goals. Each sub-system may be working at peak efficiency but this does not necessarily mean that the system as a whole is acting optimally. Sub-optimisation is probably more common than is realised and may be caused by departmental pressures and rivalries, poor communications, lack of co-ordination, poor information systems, or lack of centralised direction and control. The avoidance of sub-optimisation is an important objective of the planning and control process. The key way of avoiding sub-optimisation is to ensure that the overall objectives of the organisation dominate the objectives of each of the sub systems. This factor must be borne in mind when planning, controlling and monitoring performance.

7. Planning and control

Planning precedes control and planning without consideration of the type, frequency and method of control will largely be a waste of time. It follows from this, that part of the planning process involves the design of an appropriate control system. Control is an important element of the work of the management accountant and is dealt with in detail in a major section later in the book after this section on planning. Students should study the following section on planning having regard to the necessity to develop concurrently appropriate control mechanisms in order to monitor the implementation of the agreed plans.

8. Summary

a) Various definitions exist of a system but all contain the essential elements of parts and relationships.

b) The systems approach directs attention to overall objectives and thus attempts to avoid sub-optimality.

c) Three of the most relevant types of system are, deterministic or mechanistic, stochastic or probabilistic, and adaptive or cybernetic.

d) Open system interact with the environment, closed systems are self contained.

e) Sub-optimisation means that the objectives of sub-systems (eg departments) are pursued to the detriment of overall objectives.

f) Part of the planning process includes consideration of an appropriate control system.

9. Points to note

a) There are few, if any, organisations where sub-optimal activities do not take place. As a primary provider of planning and control information the management accountant must seek to highlight such activities so that corrective action can be taken.

b) Do not dismiss the basic system principles as obvious, common-sense platitudes. How many recent company failures are due to lack of recognition of the fact that the organisation (ie the system) must adapt to changes in the environment in order to survive?

Additional reading

Management accounting: a conceptual approach; *Amey & Egginton* – Longman

Planning and control systems – a framework for analysis;
Anthony – Harvard University Press

Systems behaviour; *Beishon*– Harper & Row

Corporate Resource Allocation; *Tompkins* – Blackwell

Self review questions

1. Define a system. (2)
2. What factors constitute the systems approach? (3)
3. Define a deterministic, a stochastic, and a cybernetic system. (4)
4. What is the difference between an open and closed system? (5)
5. What is sub-optimisation and why should it be avoided? (6)
6. When should a control system be considered? (7)

6 Long-term planning

1. Objectives

After studying this chapter you will:

❏ be able to define planning;

❏ know the differences between strategic, tactical and operational planning;

❏ understand how a corporate plan is developed;

❏ know how objectives are developed;

❏ be able to describe SWOT analysis;

❏ know the types and sources of planning information;

❏ understand how corporate planning relates to budgeting;

❏ be able to describe planning models.

2. Planning defined

Planning is an inescapable part of all rational human activity. Because of its importance to organisations their planning processes have become refined and structured in order to improve their efficiency.

Planning can be defined as:

> 'The establishment of objectives , and the formulation, evaluation and selection of the policies, strategies, tactics and action required to achieve these objectives. Planning comprises long-term/strategic planning, and short-term operational planning. The latter usually refers to a period of one year'.   Terminology.

Thus it will be seen that the overall process of planning covers both the long and short term. Short-term tactical planning or budgeting works within a framework set by the long-term plans and is dealt with in the next chapter.

The relationships between the various levels of planning and indicative time scales are shown in Figure 6.1.

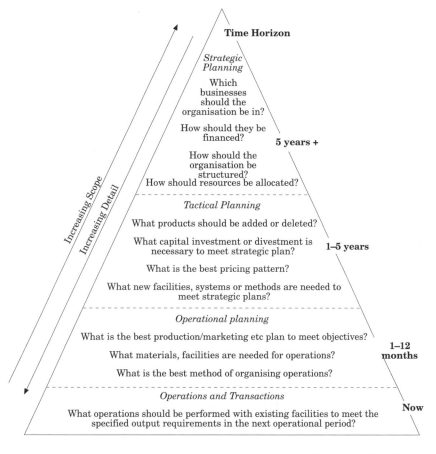

Figure 6.1 Levels of planning

3. Long-term strategic planning

This is variously termed 'long range planning', 'strategic planning' or, when applied to organisations, 'corporate planning'. long-term planning covers periods longer than one year and typically embraces 3, 5, 10 years or even longer periods. It can be defined as follows:

> *'The formulation, evaluation and selection of strategies for the purpose of preparing a long-term plan of action to attain objectives. Also known as corporate planning and long range planning'.* Terminology.

Note:

Because the readers of this manual are likely to be more concerned with long-term planning in organisations, the term Corporate Planning (CP) will be used subsequently.

4. How is the corporate plan developed?

The process of CP consists of various stages which focus attention on four key areas: the environment, the objectives, the factors which influence the achievement of the objectives, and the choice of strategies and tactics to achieve the objectives.

Figure 6.2 shows an overview of CP.

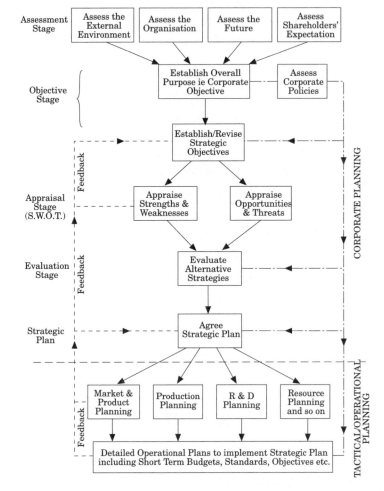

Figure 6.2 Overview of corporate planning

5. The assessment stage

This is also known as a *position audit* and seeks to provide detailed answers to the following questions.

What is the existing state of the organisation and the environment in which it operates?

What is the environment in which the organisation will have to operate in the future?

The four aspects of the assessment stage are:

❐ *The external environment*

This includes an assessment of:

○ Economic, political, social and technological factors affecting the organisation.

○ Detailed analysis of competitive activity for established products and product developments.

○ An assessment of current marketing and distribution policies, the degree of market penetration and acceptability and possible market development and product diversification.

○ Analysis of resources available to the organisation including finance, raw materials, skilled labour.

❐ *The organisation*

○ This is a detailed study of the organisation's strengths and weaknesses, its results, limitations and constraints. Typical of the factors to be studied are:

○ Analysis of production facilities, age and sophistication of plant, bottlenecks.

○ Analysis of personnel, their qualities, skills, age profiles, industrial relation policies and record.

○ Analysis of trading results, profits, turnover, contributions for product groups, sales areas and divisions.

○ Analysis of research and development activities including projects in progress.

○ Analysis of financial procedure, investment policies, working capital management.

❐ *The future*

Clearly the most difficult to assess yet the most crucial over the medium to long term covered by the CP period. There is a very wide range of factors to be considered, including:

○ Economic forecasts of GNP, Disposable income, Markets, Inflation, Taxation.

○ Political problems relating to raw materials, energy, embargoes, tariffs.

○ Social trends in taste, purchasing power, leisure.

○ Technological forecasting regarding likely developments affecting the organisation.

○ Competitors likely actions, mergers and acquisitions.

❐ *The expectations*

A major influence on corporate objectives are the expectations of the groups involved, known as the stakeholders.

○ Employees – their expectation of job security and satisfaction, income, pensions, leisure.

○ Customers – their expectations of quality, delivery, price, product availability.

○ Shareholders – their expectations of dividends, capital growth.

○ General Public – their expectations regarding environmental and pollution matters, the contribution of the organisation to the economy.

6. The objectives stage

This is the key stage in the CP process and seeks to answer the question, Where does the organisation want to go?

The essence of CP (as in the system approach outlined earlier) is to define objectives first then consider how they can be achieved. This approach avoids major errors of sub-optimisation by ensuring that the long-term corporate objectives are defined before the short term tactical objectives covering various facets of operations. The short-term objectives and targets contribute towards the achievement of the long-term corporate objectives thus encouraging co-ordination and goal congruence on the part of management.

There are very real problems in establishing corporate objectives because of the multi-faceted nature of modern business.

Drucker suggests that there are eight areas in which objectives of performance and results have to be set, ie

❑ Market standing

❑ Innovation

❑ Productivity

❑ Physical and financial resources

❑ Profitability

❑ Manager performance and development

❑ Worker performance and attitude

❑ Public responsibility

The setting of objectives is a detailed, iterative task involving much discussion but eventually objectives must be set, within each area, in clear quantifiable terms.

For example within the 'Market Standing' area specific statements would need to be made about such matters as:

❑ Target sales of each product

❑ Target sales of product ranges

❑ Target market share of each product

❑ Target market share of product ranges

❑ Target home/export sales of each product/product range

❑ Target proportions of sales by distribution channel/industrial sector

❑ Target proportion of sales from new/existing products

❑ Target new market development,

... and so on

Similar detailed objectives will be set for each of the other areas. The area most familiar to accountants, relating to profitability and finance, would include: target return on capital employed, earnings per share, operating profit, dividends, asset growth and so on.

It will be apparent that objectives covering the whole range of organisational activities are extremely diverse and because of this it is unlikely that a single performance measure, such as Return on Capital Employed, could adequately represent the whole spectrum of corporate objectives. It has been convincingly argued by Simon and others that satisficing rather than classical profit maximising behaviour is more usual. This means that the aim is to obtain a satisfactory level of achievement across a set of objectives rather than attempting to optimise a single measure.

Top management will also establish corporate policies which provide guidelines on the manner in which the organisation expects its objectives to be achieved. Policy statements reflect the organisation's culture and belief system and can be powerful influences on the ways activities are carried out and decisions taken. Consider, for example, the difference in policies between two local authorities; one a Conservative controlled rural area and the other a Labour controlled inner-city authority.

7. The appraisal stage

This is colloquially known as SWOT analysis (ie Strengths, Weaknesses, Opportunities, Threats). By a process of discussion, analysis and comparison of internal factors, the planning team should attempt to rank what are considered to be the main strengths and weaknesses of the organisation. These could be found in any area of the organisation. They could, for example, relate to; the price, range, reliability (or otherwise) of the products; the training, age structure, morale of the workforce; size, age, capability of equipment and so on. Although all the details are not known it seems clear that a detailed analysis of this type was undertaken by John Egan (now Sir John) when he first took over Jaguar Cars. This identified product reliability and quality as the major weakness which was remedied in a highly professional manner, resulting in the turn-round of the whole company.

Next the planning team should consider the environment within which the organisation operates to try to identify the trends and factors which will have material effect on the organisation in the medium to long term. This process will involve considerable discussion with outside experts and analysts, perhaps special investigations, examination of national and international statistics and so on. Depending on the size and scope of the organisation the appraisal could include local, national or international factors. Threats and opportunities maybe identified in various aspects of the environment, for example:

a) Political factors such as privatisation, changes of government at home and abroad, legislation, wars and so on.

b) Market factors such as new and current competitors, market share, changes in distribution (eg city centre to out of town shopping) and so on.

c) Economic and social factors such as unemployment, inflation, social mobility and so on.

d) Technology factors such as automation and robotics, new materials, process and so on.

It has to be recognised that all these appraisals mean trying to peer into a misty and uncertain future. When change is in a continuous pattern it is possible to project existing trends and thus make reasonable assumptions as to the actions and reactions required. The problem is that much change is discontinuous and unexpected. With truth it has been said that the only thing we know for certain about the future is that the unexpected will happen. This unpredictability means that judgement and intuition always play a part in long-term forecastings. Statistical forecasting, of whatever level of sophistication, is based on the implicit assumption that existing trends, patterns and cycles will continue in the future. Of course, they may but on the other hand they may not.

8. Evaluating alternatives

By this stage the planning team will be aware of:

a) the scale of the strategic task ahead;

b) the major forecasted trends and factors which are expected to influence the organisation either as threats or opportunities;

c) the aspects of the organisation which are strong and those which are weak.

The team are now able to consider alternative corporate strategies which will form the basis of the agreed corporate plan. The strategies should be sufficiently clear so that they can be evaluated as to whether they have been achieved or not, but not so specific that they constrain the organisation. Specific targets can only be set at tactical and operational levels for shorter periods of, say, up to one year.

The information system of the organisation can be of considerable assistance to the planning team when considering alternative strategies. The team will continually require answers to a series of questions beginning, 'What would happen if...?' Possible answers to these, and similar questions, are provided by the process termed *modelling* which is dealt with in the later part of this chapter.

9. The corporate plan

By this time there will be a consensus on the strategies for the organisation so that the remaining stages add increasing amounts of practical detail. The task is to prepare action plans for the various departments and functions of the organisation. These plans will contain targets and will be in sufficient detail so that tactical level management know the task they have to perform. The plan should show not only the new tasks, but how existing operations will dovetail into the new targets over, say, the next five years. The strategic plan will be used by tactical management to prepare operational plans, budgets, set short term targets and so on.

10. Monitoring and control

There is little point in any planning exercise if progress is not monitored after the plans have been implemented. This is to see whether activities need to be adjusted to bring them into line with the original strategies or to see whether, because of unforeseen circumstances, it is time to review the strategies themselves.

Monitoring and control at all levels works by the feedback of information which is a major function of the information system of the organisation and is dealt with in detail later in the book.

11. Formal and informal planning

In the 1960's and 70's the vogue was for highly formal planning systems and for formal information systems to support them. Informal planning and information systems were thought of as imprecise and somehow amateurish. Experience and major unforeseen disturbances such as the oil price explosion of the mid 1970's, the stock market crash of 1987, the collapse of the property market in 1990 and others showed that highly structured systems are slow to respond to change, perpetuate static organisational assumptions and offer little or no protection from unpredictability. Indeed a survey by Grinyer and Norburn found no correlation between formal planning procedures and financial performance; instead informality and diversity of information, especially from external sources, seemed to be the critical factor.

Informal systems are more flexible and adaptable. They deal with information which is more current and significant and, because of the social contact involved, they can convey nuances which formal systems cannot handle. They do, however, suffer from bias, noise and do not always provide a complete picture. What is required is a blend of formal and informal so that the completeness, accuracy and detail of the formal systems complement the flexibility the adaptability of the informal. To achieve the right mixture is difficult for both managers and information specialists but to be aware that there is no single, all-embracing, simple solution, is an important first step.

Various reviews of formal planning procedures suggest that they encourage inflexibility whereas the real requirements, especially at the strategic level, are responsiveness and adaptability. The greatest care must be taken to ensure that the environment is continually scanned and monitored so that the organisation can adapt in progressive, controlled fashion. This is always more efficient than enforced traumatic changes made after a period of stagnation.

12. Type and sources of planning information

By now it should be apparent that planning requires a great deal of information. The types of information and their sources will naturally vary from organisation to organisation but there is one general principle. For long-term planning, environmental information is of critical importance. At lower levels, and in the short-term, internal information is important but for planning the long-term direction of the organisation and ensuring survival and success, external information is all important.

The following paragraphs give examples of the *types* of information that might be required for strategic planning and typical *sources* of such information.

Types of *external* information

❏ *Markets and competition*

Is the market segment increasing or decreasing? Where should our products/services be positioned? What are our competitors doing? etc.

❐ *Demographic trends*

How is the population structure changing? Can we deal with an ageing population? Is the age profile of our customers changing? etc.

❐ *Economic conditions*

What are the forecasts for growth, inflation, GDP etc? What will be effect of the European Community Single market? etc.

❐ *Industrial structure*

Is there a process of rationalisation/concentration taking place? What will be the consequences of privatisation? How many new firms are entering the industry? etc.

❐ *Social factors*

What will be the effect of the changing family patterns, the role of women in society? What changes are expected in attitudes towards consumption and savings? etc.

❐ *Political factors*

What will be the effect of political decisions? Is there likely to be political instability (especially important in overseas markets)? etc.

❐ *Technological change*

Can the organisation adapt to/take advantage of new technology? How will it affect the organisation? etc.

Types of *internal* information

❐ *Marketing and sales information* on performance, revenues, market shares, distribution channels etc.

❐ *Production and operational information* on assets, capacities, lead times, quality standards etc.

❐ *Financial information* on profits, costs, margins, cash flows, investments etc.

❐ *Personnel information* on labour skills and availability, training, labour relations etc.

❐ *Research and development information* on new products and developments, patents, knowledge base etc.

Typical *sources* of information

❐ *External*

○ Formal: Published reports, government statistics, scientific and technical abstracts, company reports, commercial data banks, Trade Associations, special investigations.

○ Informal: Discussions, social contact of all types, media coverage, conferences, business and holiday trips at home and abroad, correspondence.

❐ *Internal*

    ○ Formal: All outputs of the organisation's MIS including control and monitoring reports, forecasting and enquiry systems, modelling and simulation, investigative reports, budgets, job descriptions, organisation charts, correspondence, video displays.

    ○ Informal: Discussions, meetings, social contact, telephone conversations, personal record keeping, correspondence.

Note:

The above are not exhaustive lists but are indicative of typical sources.

In spite of the wealth of external information available and its obvious importance in planning there is evidence that organisations fail to explore the sources in a thorough comprehensive manner.

> A survey conducted by UWIST, Cardiff of 27 South Wales engineering firms with turnovers ranging from £1m – 50m employing 9000 people in total, found that 50% based market forecasts solely on the opinions of the existing sales force. Only 4 out of 27 took advantage of information services available externally.

13. The need for flexibility

Corporate plans are developed using forecasts, judgements and assumptions about an increasingly uncertain future. This uncertainty must be recognised and frequently forecasts and assumptions are shown as ranges of values rather than as single point estimates. The inherent uncertainty also requires that the plan itself may need modification and adjustment in the light of unexpected, major occurrences. The process of CP must be dynamic and flexible and not static and inflexible.

The process of reviewing the plan would be done regularly and typically plans might require updating:

a) When an unexpected event occurs which has a significant effect on the organisation, eg the sudden loss of a large market or source of supply of raw materials caused by a coup or war, the merger of major competitors, a major technological breakthrough.

b) In the light of the organisation's actual progress. This would form part of the annual review of the plan when the year's results were known.

c) At longer term intervals (say 3/5 years), the underlying objectives may require redefining with appropriate revisions to corporate strategies.

14. Advantages of CP

a) The processes and discussions involved in setting corporate objectives clarify policies and strategies and provide the essential framework for realistic operational planning and budgeting.

b) The processes of CP and the associated operational planning help to co-ordinate the differing aspects of the organisation and helps to avoid sub-optimality.

   c) Having CP as a background avoids undue concentration on short-term factors and facilitates those policies which by their nature are long-term in nature, eg capital investment, organisational restructuring, acquisitions and divestments, career planning.

   d) The CP process exposes weaknesses in the organisation's information systems and forces improvements to be made.

   e) The all important psychological effect on motivation of having clear targets may be substantial. Furthermore, goal congruence by middle and senior management may be improved.

15. Disadvantages of CP

   a) The processes may become somewhat bureaucratic and absorb a considerable amount of management time.

   b) Unrealistic objectives may be a disincentive.

   c) A corporate plan which is rigidly applied may make the organisation inflexible and less capable of responding to major changes.

In spite of the possible disadvantages and the genuine problems of developing and monitoring corporate plans it appears that an increasing number of organisations think that the process is worthwhile.

16. CP and the systems approach

The systems approach outlined previously emphasises objective setting, the necessity of taking an overall view, the avoidance of sub-optimisation and the installation of appropriate controls to monitor performance against the plan. It will be apparent that CP aligns itself very closely indeed to the systems approach and is the prime organisational example of systems principles being applied in practice.

17. CP and budgeting

A budget is a short-term plan (usually extending over a year) developed within the framework of the medium to long-term CP. The budgetary process, encompassing budgetary planning and budgetary control, is the way that the CP is implemented, period by period. The budgetary process is dealt with in detail in the next chapter.

18. Computer-based planning models

The preparation of a full CP complete with comprehensive statements of all the financial consequences is a daunting task to carry out manually. It becomes even more difficult and time consuming to prepare if it is also required to show the effects of changes in the assumptions upon which the plan has been based. For example, an apparently minor change in the assumed inflation rate from 10% to 12% projected over the life of the CP is likely to involve many thousands of calculations, changes in operating, statements, balance sheets, cash flow projections and many other such alterations.

It is because of this that many organisations use computer-based models to assist in the overall CP process. The models are sometimes called corporate models or financial models or planning models. Very simply these models are computer programs which depict the operations and relationships of the organisation. Usually the model consists of a large number of interrelated equations representing various facets of the organisations activities. Input of primary assumptions (eg sales level, sales price, wages cost etc., etc.,) into the model enables the resulting operating statements, projections, balance sheets, to be quickly and easily produced by the machine.

The real power and advantage of such computer-based models is not merely to produce a single result but is to enable management to ask and obtain answers to questions of the following types:

'What would happen if ......?'

'What would be the result of ......?'

For example, what would be the result of the sales volume growing by 5% p.a., costs increasing by 6% p.a. and selling prices increasing by 4%?

The computer would speedily calculate the results of such a question and it is this facility to test out various possibilities that makes this development so important for the management accountant.

It should be recognised that whilst computer-based models help to illustrate and quantify the uncertainties attached to long-term planning they do not eliminate them. Managerial judgement and expertise are still key factors.

Figure 6.3 provides a broad classification of different management models.

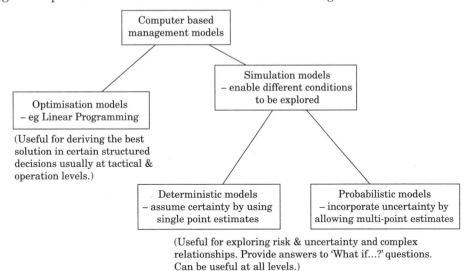

Figure 6.3 Classification of management models

19. Model development

To develop a model which is realistic and has adequate predictive qualities is a collaborative effort between management and information specialists such as systems analysts, accountants and so on.

The key points are:

❏ The model should have a purpose and be objective oriented.

❏ Model building is an iterative, creative process with the aim of identifying those variables and relation-ships which must be included in the model so that it is capable of predicting overall system performance. It is not essential or indeed possible, to include all variables in a model. The variables in a model of greatest importance are those which govern, to a greater or lesser extent, the achievement of the specified objectives. There are the critical variables.

❏ The best model is the simplest one with the fewest variables that has adequate predictive qualities. To obtain this ideal there must be a thorough understanding of the system. The management who operate the system have this understanding and must be involved in the model building, otherwise over elaborate and overly mathematical models may result if this exercise is left to systems professionals.

Figure 6.4 shows an outline of the way models are developed and used.

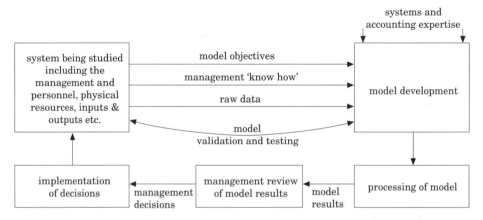

Figure 6.4 Model development and use

20. Summary

a) Planning is an essential part of business activity and can be defined as the process of setting objectives and deciding upon the ways that these will be achieved.

b) Long-term strategic planning or corporate planning covers periods longer than one year and typically involves the 5 to 10 year term.

c) Strategic or corporate planning consists of several stages; the assessment stage, the objective stage, the appraisal stage (SWOT analysis) and the evaluation stage.

d) The assessment stage answers the question 'Where is the organisation now?, by examining the external environment, the organisation itself, the future, and the expectations of the major groups involved.

e) The objective stages answers the question 'Where does the organisation wish to go? After much analysis and discussion objectives would be set in each area of corporate activity and responsibility.

f) The appraisal stage considers, in detail, the strengths, weaknesses, opportunities and threats facing the organisation.

g) The evaluation stage considers the alternative strategies open to the organisation.

h) When the Corporate Plan is agreed, detailed short-term or operational planning takes place usually covering one year periods.

i) The uncertainty of the future must be recognised and the Corporate Plan must be flexible and capable of revision if required.

j) Corporate planning has a number of advantages including: the clarification of policies and strategies, the avoidance of sub-optimality, taking a long-term view, the exposure of weaknesses, and motivational effects.

k) The disadvantages include: time consuming, makes for inflexibility, possible bureaucratic procedures.

l) Corporate planning is the prime organisation example of the systems approach in action.

m) Computer-based planning models enables various options and assumptions to be tested easily and speedily.

21. Points to note

a) To be effective Corporate Planning must have the total support and involvement of top management. It is not a process to be left to technical specialists. Their assistance and advice can be extremely useful but management involvement is essential.

b) Budgetary and short-term planning are unlikely to be very effective unless such operational planning takes place within a properly thought out, long-term plan for the organisation.

c) Excessive detail should be avoided in the CP. Argenti recommends that the CP should provide 'a coarse grained, strategic structure for the long-term future'.

Additional reading

Corporate Strategy; *Ansoff* – Sidgwick & Jackson

Practical Corporate Planning; *Argenti* – Allen & Unwin

Financial Modelling in Corporate Management; *Bryant* – Wiley

Understanding Organisations; *Hardy* – Penguin

Exploring Corporate Strategy; *Johnson & Scholes* – Prentice Hall

Strategic Management; *Thompson* – Chapman & Hall

Self review questions

1. Define planning. (2)
2. What are the stages in Corporate Planning? (4)
3. What does the position audit seek to do? (5)
4. What are the various stages in the position audit? (5)
5. What are the areas in which Drucker suggests objectives should be set? (6)
6. What is SWOT analysis? (7)
7. What types of information are required for strategic planning? (12)
8. What are the advantages and disadvantages of corporate planning? (14 & 15)
9. What are computer-based planning models and how can they assist the corporate planning process? (15)

7 Budgeting

1. Objectives

After studying this chapter you will:

☐ understand budgeting and budgetary planning;

☐ know the major benefits of budgeting;

☐ be able to define the principal budget factor;

☐ know the stages in developing budgets;

☐ understand the inter-relationships between budgets;

☐ be able to derive a cash budget;

☐ know the principles of flexible budgeting;

☐ understand how uncertainty can be incorporated into budgeting;

☐ know the principles of zero-based budgeting;

☐ understand programme planning and budgeting systems.

2. Budgetary planning

Short-term tactical planning or budgetary planning is the process of preparing detailed, short-term (usually 1 year) plans for the functions, activities and departments of the organisation thus converting the long-term Corporate Plan into action. In general plans are developed using physical values, for example, the number of units to be produced, the number of hours to be worked, the amount of materials to be consumed and so on. When monetary values are attached the plan becomes a budget. Budgets are prepared for departments, for functions such as production, inspection, marketing, or for financial and resource items such as capital expenditure, cash, materials, etc.

The annual process of budgeting should be seen as stages in the progressive fulfilment of the long-term plan for the organisation. The budgetary process steers the organisation towards the long-term objectives defined in the Corporate Plan.

3. The benefits of budgeting

Benefits do not automatically arise from the budgetary process, they have to be worked for. Narrowly conceived budgetary systems or those which are insensitively applied may produce dysfunctional effects, ie behaviour and actions from management and staff which oppose or do not contribute to the fulfilment of organisational objectives. Well organised and thought out schemes can however bring positive and significant benefits. These are dealt with below under the following headings: co-ordination, clarification of authority and responsibility, communication, control, motivation and goal congruence, and performance evaluation.

4. Co-ordination

The budgeting process requires that feasible, detailed budgets are developed covering each activity, department or function in the organisation. This can only be done when the effects of one department's budget are related to the budget of another department. In this way the budgeting process provides for the co-ordination of the activities, departments and functions of the organisation so that each aspects of the operation contributes to the overall plan. This is expressed in the form of a Master Budget which summarises all the supporting budgets (fully described in para. 19).

A well co-ordinated budgeting system helps to ensure that, for example, inventory and purchasing plans are geared to production requirements, that production schedules are related to sales budgets, that arrangements are made for overdraft facilities (if necessary) to coincide with the cash flow budget and similar relationships. Co-ordination is necessary to avoid sub-optimality.

5. Clarification of authority and responsibility

Budgeting (with standard costing) is known as *responsibility accounting*. This means that plans and the resulting information on the performance of the plans is expressed in terms of human responsibilities because it is people that control operations not reports.

The process of budgeting, particularly for the control aspects, makes it necessary for the organisation to be organised into responsibility or budget centres with clear statements of the responsibilities of each manager who has a budget. The adoption of a budget authorises the plans contained within it. This process enables management by exception to be practised. This is where a subordinate is given a clearly defined role with the requisite authority and resources to carry out that part of the overall plan assigned to him and, if activities do not proceed according to plan, the variations are reported to a higher authority. Thus the full budgeting process forces the organisation to clarify roles and responsibilities of its managers and is an excellent example of management by exception in practice.

6. Communication

The full budgetary process involves liaison and discussion between all levels of management. It is an important, formal avenue of communication between top and lower levels of management regarding the organisation's long-term objectives and the practical problems of implementing those objectives. When the Master Budget and supporting budgets are agreed and finalised they provide the formal means of communicating the agreed plans embodied in the budgets to all the staff involved. As well as vertical communication between levels, the budgetary process requires lateral communication between functions and departments to ensure that activities are co-ordinated.

7. Control

This aspect of budgeting is the one most likely to be encountered by the ordinary staff member. The process of comparing actual results with planned or budgeted results and reporting upon variations, which is the principle of budgetary control, sets a control discipline which helps to accomplish the plans within agreed expenditure limits. In most practical circumstances the same budgets appear to serve as both plans and controls. However, students should be aware that this need not be the case and separate budgets for planning and for control could be developed.

As Charnes and Cooper have remarked

'a good plan ..... does not necessarily yield a good control'.

The reason for this is that two distinctly different functions are involved. Planning is concerned with internal resource allocation to achieve certain objectives whereas control is concerned with the task of co-ordinating and using the allocated resources (labour, machinery, space, finance) to achieve predetermined levels of efficiency. There are, of course, very real practical problems in developing separate budgets but the fact remains that a single budget used for both planning and control, which appears to be the norm, is attempting to achieve two different objectives which may conflict.

8. Motivation and goal congruence

A well organised budgeting system which encourages the genuine participation and involvement of operating management in the preparation of budgets and the establishment of agreed performance levels, has been found to have a motivating effect. The success of a budgeting system should be judged by the extent to which it encourages goal congruence by the budget holders. This is a recognition of the fact that it is the behavioural aspects of budgeting, rather than the technical ones, which are of primary importance. If the budgetary system is not acceptable to the people who are involved with it, it is likely to be manipulated or opposed to such an extent that it will become unworkable. There are many factors to be considered in relating to the behavioural aspects of budgeting and these are developed in greater detail in the chapter on budgetary control.

9. Performance evaluation

A manager's performance is often judged partly by his ability to meet budgets. When considering a manager for promotion or for a salary increase or for some other form of recognition, a manager's budget record and his ability to meet the targets incorporated in budgets is often an important factor. Budgets used as a target can also assist a manager in monitoring his own performance. The knowledge that a budget will be used for performance evaluation causes changes in the manager's attitude to the whole budgeting process. These, and other behavioural factors concerned with budgeting are dealt with in the chapter on Budgetary Control.

10. Conditions for successful budgeting

There are benefits to be gain from budgeting systems but, as previously pointed out, these do not automatically arise. It has been found that a budgeting system is more likely to be successful when the following conditions are found:

a) The involvement and support of top management.

b) Clear cut definition of long-term, corporate objectives within which the budgeting system will operate.

c) A realistic organisation structure with clearly defined responsibilities.

d) Genuine and full involvement of the line managers in all aspects of the budgeting process. This is likely to include a staff development and education programme in the meaning and use of budgets.

e) An appropriate accounting and information system which will include: the records of expenditure and performance related to responsibility, a prompt and accurate reporting system showing actual against budget, the ability to provide more detailed information or advice on request; in short the accounting system should be seen as supportive and not threatening.

f) Regular revisions of budgets and targets (where necessary).

g) Budgets should be administered in a flexible manner. Changes in conditions may call for changes in plans and the resulting budgets. Rigid adherence to budgets which are clearly inappropriate for current conditions will cause the whole budgeting system to lose credibility and effectiveness. Indeed, if budgets are not subject to revision they are effectively decisions and not plans.

11. Principal budget factor

The principal budget factor (or limiting factor or key factor) is a factor which, at any given time, is an overriding planning limitation on the activities of the organisation. The principal budget factor may be production capacity, shortage of labour, materials, finance or, commonly, the level of demand for the goods or services. Because such a constraint will have a pervasive effect on all operational plans and budgets the limiting factor for the planning period must be identified so that the various budgets can be developed having regard to the expected limitation.

The factor can and does change – when one constraint is removed some other limitation will occur otherwise there would be no limit to the organisation's activities.

The assumption of a single principal budget factor is often too simplistic. In a complex organisation, for example, a divisionalised multi-product company, two or more factors may operate simultaneously. In such cases care must be taken to optimise the contribution to the organisation as a whole and not merely try to maximise contribution related to any one limiting factor which would cause sub-optimality. Where several constraints arise simultaneously the use of mathematical programming techniques, such as linear programming which is described later, can be invaluable in determining the optimum use of resources.

12. Preparing the budget

Figure 7.1 shows an outline of the overall budgetary process. This is time consuming but vital task. The diagram shows the process as a sequential series of steps but in practice the process is less straightforward. Steps are repeated, revisions are made and there is considerable discussion and argument. Generally a budget committee meet at regular intervals and would be serviced by a budget officer, usually the accountant. The committee's task to co-ordinate and review the budget programme, establish procedures and timetables, product and update a budget manual (described below) explaining the objectives, role and procedures involved in the budgetary system, in short to oversee the administration of the whole process. It is *not* the committee's task to prepare individual budgets for particular departments or functions.

It is a cardinal feature of budgeting that managers are personally involved with the development of their own budgets and accept responsibility for them. This is a key element in motivating managers and encouraging goal congruence.

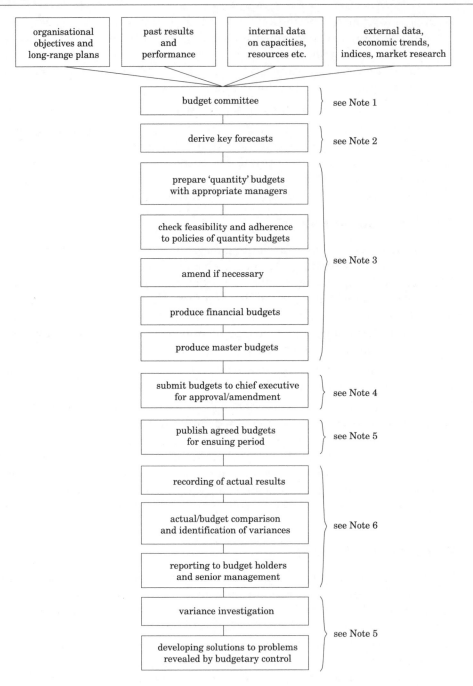

Figure 7.1 Outline of the budgetary process

It is unrealistic to expect a manager to accept responsibility for an externally prepared budget which is imposed on him.

Notes on Figure 7.1

1. The budget committee is given responsibility for the task of developing and co-ordinating budgets. The membership varies between organisations but usually comprises people from various functions of the company. The committee would be serviced by the budget officer, usually the accountant. His responsibility is to administer the budget when agreed and to provide technical assistance and data during the budget preparation. The budget planning process takes place prior to the budget period and where budgets are prepared on a rolling basis, budget planning is a regular, continuous activity.

2. An essential preliminary to making plans and budgets is to prepare forecasts. A forecast is a prediction of future events which are expected to happen, whereas a budget is a planned series of actions to achieve a given result. Invariably the primary forecast, from which most of the subsequent planning derives, is the sales forecast. Forecasting is a large and complex field frequently involving advanced statistical and mathematical techniques.

3. These steps comprise the bulk of the planning process. Co-ordination and communication between functions is essential to ensure interlocking, feasible budgets which accord to company policies and objectives. Many of these steps need to be repeated during the budget development as inconsistencies become apparent. The testing of one budget against another for feasibility and practicability is a key element in co-ordinating the budget process.

4. The Budget, comprising the individual departmental and functional budgets and the master budget, is submitted to the Chief Executive or the Board of Directors for examination and approval after any revisions thought necessary. When approved, the budget becomes an executive order and shows for each budget centre an approved level of expenditure. (A budget centre is a section of the organisation so designated for budgetary purposes. It may be a cost centre, a group of cost centres or a department. It will be the responsibility of a designated person, the budget holder).

5. The agreed budgets are published and distributed to all the budget holders and budget centres. In this way budgets serve as a means of communicating plans and objectives downwards. In addition, that part of the budgetary process concerned with monitoring results, known as budgetary control provides upward feedback on the progress made towards meeting plans.

6. These are the main stages in budgetary control. They take place after the actual events, usually on a monthly basis. Speedy production of budgetary control statements and immediate investigation of revealed variances provide the best basis for bringing operations into line with the plan, or where there have been substantial changes in circumstances, making agreed alterations to the plan.

7. The investigations into the variances and their causes provide the link between budgetary control and budgetary planning. The experience of operations, levels of performance and difficulties are fed to the budget committee so that the planning process is continually refined.

13. The budget manual

As one of the objectives of budgeting is to improve communications it is important that a manual is produced so that everyone in the organisation can refer to the manual for guidance and information about the budgetary process. The budget manual does not contain the actual budgets for the ensuing period – it is more of an instruction/information manual about the way budgeting operates in the particular organisation and the reasons for having budgeting. Contents obviously vary from organisation to organisation but the following are examples of the information such a manual should contain.

Manual contents

❐ Foreword	– preferably by Chief Executive/Managing Director
❐ Objectives/explanation of the budgetary process	– explanation of budgetary planning and control
	– objectives of each stage of the budgetary process
	– relationship to long-term planning
❐ Organisation Structures and responsibilities	– structure of the organisation showing titles, responsibilities and relationships
	– titles and names of current budget holders
❐ Main budgets and relationship	– outline of all main budgets and their accounting relationships
	– explanation of key budgets (eg Master Budget, Cash Budget, Sales Budget)
❐ Budget development	– Budget committee, membership and terms of reference
	– sequence of budget preparation
	– timetable for budget preparation and publication
❐ Accounting procedures	– name and terms of reference of the budget officer (usually the accountant)
	– coding lists
	– sample forms
	– timetable for accounting procedures, production of reports, closing dates.

14. Budget relationships

The various budgets found in an organisation and their relationships will be specific to that organisation and are unlikely to be found elsewhere in exactly the same form. In spite of this there are broad similarities in the budgets prepared in various types of organisations. As an example, Figure 7.2 shows the major budgets found in a typical manufacturing concern with their main relationships.

Notes:

a) Only the main functional budgets are shown. Usually these are subdivided into departmental budgets for day to day control purposes.

b) The diagram shows only the major formal accounting relationships. It does not purport to show the links and communication flows necessary during budget preparation which are obviously many and varied.

15. Categories of budgets

Budgets may be categorised in numerous ways but for a typical manufacturing organisation they could be grouped as follows:

a) Budgets in the *sales* area, ie the Sales Budget and those budgets which are functionally related to the Sales Budget, eg selling and distribution cost budgets and, to some extent, the advertising and promotion budgets.

b) Budgets in the *production* area, ie the Production Budget and the related production input budgets (labour, materials, production services).

c) Budgets for *services*. These are the budgets relating to the general services of the organisation, eg administration, personnel, welfare.

d) Budgets determined by *policy*. These are budgets which are less directly related to day to day activities and are usually determined by top management. Monies and resources would be allocated for these budgets, usually on a longer term basis than normal operating budgets, in order that long-term objectives can be met. The main examples of these types of budget are the Capital Expenditure Budget, the Research and Development Budget, and, to some extent, the Advertising Budget. The activities covered by these budgets are, of course, related to current operations but their major emphasis is more far reaching and is to ensure that the organisation is able to meet future challenges by developing new products and techniques, increasing productivity by investment, and preparing for new markets. Although these budgets are reviewed periodically they usually cover periods longer than one year, which is the typical duration for normal operating budgets.

e) The *summary budgets*. These are budgets which derive from the various budgets outlined above and provide valuable summaries of the effects of the organisation's plans. The two budgets in this category are the Master Budget and the Cash Flow Budget.

These various categories are expanded below:

16. Sales and related budgets

For many organisations the principal budget factor is sales volume so that the sales budget is the primary budget from which the majority of the other budgets are derived.

Before the sales budget can be developed it is necessary to make a sales forecast. A forecast is a prediction or estimate of the events which are likely to occur in the future. The forecast becomes a budget only if management accepts it as the objective. Frequently, consideration of the forecasted sales leads management to make adjustment to their plans so that the agreed sales budget differs from the original sales forecast.

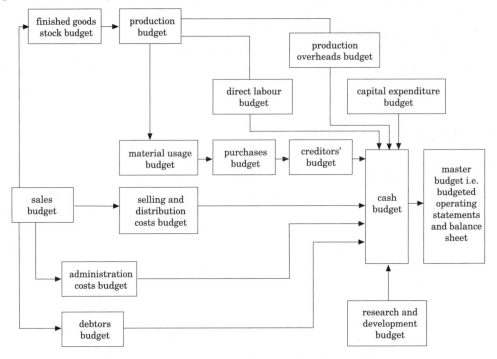

Figure 7.2 Major budgets and their relationships

Sales forecasting is a complex and difficult task and involves consideration of numerous factors, including:

a) Past sales patterns – absolutes and trends.

b) General economic indicators, eg GDP, personal income, consumer spending patterns, unemployment, inflation.

c) Results of market research studies and test marketing.

d) Advertising and promotion policies and anticipated expenditures.

e) Pricing and discount policies to be adopted.

f) Distribution and quality of sales outlets and personnel.

g) Interaction with competitors on quality, pricing, advertising, product range, availability.

h) Impact on new technology, where appropriate.

i) Consumer tastes and legislation.

j) Environmental, ecological, and safety factors, where appropriate.

Having regard to the sales forecast and the productive capacity of the organisation the sales budget will be prepared which will be subdivided in several ways – by personal responsibility, by sales area, by product or product group. When the sales budget has been drawn up and agreed it becomes the organisation's plan which the sales managers will try to turn into actual sales.

When the sales budget has been finalised the related budgets such as the selling cost budget, the distribution cost budget and similar supporting budgets can be developed relatively easily. A budget which is also related, to a greater or lesser extent, to the level of sales is the advertising and promotion budget. This budget is, however, likely to be set by a policy decision of senior management.

17. Production and related budgets

If the principal budget factor was lack of production capacity then this budget would be the first to be prepared. More normally, when sales volume is the constraint, the production budget would be prepared after the sales budget and would be co-ordinated with that budget and the finished goods stock budget.

The production budget will show the quantities and costs involved for each product and product group and will be scheduled to dovetail with the sales and inventory budgets. This co-ordinating process is likely to show shortfalls or excesses in capacity at various times over the budget period. Where temporary shortfalls are anticipated then consideration would be given to extra overtime or shift working, subcontracting, buying in more parts or machine hire or some other short-term way of increasing output. Where there is a more significant shortfall this means that production capacity is the limiting factor and consideration will have to be given to providing more substantial increase in capacity (which will have implications for the Capital Expenditure Budget).

When production capacity exceeds the anticipated sales level for significant periods then consideration will have to be given to product diversification, additional promotional effort, reducing selling prices (if demand is considered to be price elastic) or, if all else fails, selling off the excess production capacity.

When the production budget is finalised the production input budgets (labour, materials, production services) are developed based on the budgeted activity levels, existing stock positions and projected labour, material and service costs. Where standardised goods and services are produced then the production input budgets can be developed relatively easily but in jobbing type industries the process is much less precise. In such circumstances some percentage of the sales budget is used for the various inputs. This percentage is based on previous experience but will, of course, only be valid if the pattern and mix of production in the future is broadly the same as in the past.

18. Budgets for services

Within this area there may be a number of individual budgets depending on the size and complexity of the support functions of the organisation although for small organisations a single administration budget may be found acceptable. The major problem in determining the size of these budgets is their indirect relationship with the level of activity, whether expressed as sales volume or units produced. Because of this they are frequently determined by adjusting last year's budget by a percentage. This process, sometimes known as incremental budgeting, obviously lacks any rigour and may conceal inefficiencies. Consequently it requires careful study by the Budget Committee before it can be deemed to be acceptable.

It is in the area of support overheads which tend to be related to the scope and complexity of production rather than volume that Activity-Based Budgeting may be of value. This is dealt with in Chapter 9.

19. Budgets determined by policy

These budgets, which include Capital Expenditure, Research and Development, Advertising, have some relationship to current operations but also contain substantial elements which are of a long-term nature determined by top management policy. As an example, the Capital Expenditure Budget may contain authorisations for expenditure in connection with replacements and/or enhancements of facilities for current product lines and also provision for equipment and facilities to cope with new products or new methods to be introduced in the future. It is because of this that these budgets may well move in different directions to the normal operating budgets. For example, a declining Sales Budget may cause management to increase the Advertising and/or Research and Development, and/or Capital Expenditure budgets.

The policy budgets are the key ways in which current facilities, products and operations are progressively adjusted in order to meet the long-term objectives specified in the Corporate Plan.

20. The summary budgets

The two main summary budgets are the master budget and the cash budget.

a) The master budget is usually presented in the form of budgeted operating statements, a budgeted trading and profit and loss account and a budgeted balance sheet. The master budget represents a consolidation of all the supporting budgets and represents the financial effects of the total plan for the business as a whole. Each of the parts of the master budget is prepared in the conventional manner except that budgeted costs, revenues, investments and so on, are used instead of historical figures.

The master budget, supported by the subsidiary budgets, is presented to top management for approval. If approval is given the master budget becomes the financial summary of the agreed plan for the budget period being considered, usually for the year ahead. Often however the master budget is not given immediate approval in which case amendments will have to be made in the underlying budgets (eg the sales budget, the production budget, etc) in order to bring about the desired effects on the master budget. Such amendments should, of course, only be made if they are realistically capable of attainment.

b) Cash budget. Liquidity and cash flow management are key factors in the successful operation of any organisation and it is with good reason that the cash budget should receive close attention from both accountants and managers.

The cash budget shows the effect of budgeted activities – selling, buying, paying wages, investing in capital equipment and so on – on the cash flow of the organisation. Cash budgeting is a continuous activity with budgets being rolled forward as time progresses. The budgets are usually subdivided into reasonably short periods – months or weeks.

Cash budgets are prepared in order to ensure that there will be just sufficient cash in hand to cope adequately with budgeted activities. The cash budget may show that there is likely to be a deficiency of cash in some future period – in which case overdraft or loans will have to be arranged or activities curtailed – or alternatively the budget may show that there is likely to be a cash surplus, in which case appropriate investment or use for the surplus can be planned rather than merely leaving the cash idle in a current account.

The typical cash budget has the general form shown in Figure 7.3.

Cash Budget

	Period 1	Period 2	Period 3	etc.
Opening Cash Balance b/f	XXX	YYY	ZZZ	AAA
+ Receipts from Debtors				
+ Sales of Capital Items				
+ Any Loans Received				
+ Proceeds for Share Issues				
+ Any other Cash Receipts				
= Total Cash Available				
– Payments to Creditors				
– Cash Purchases				
– Wages and Salaries				
– Loan Repayments				
– Capital Expenditure				
– Dividends				
– Taxation				
– Any Other Cash Disbursements				
= Closing Cash Balance c/f	YYY	ZZZ	AAA	

Figure 7.3

Cash budgets are good examples of *rolling budgets,* ie where the process of continuous budgeting takes place whereby regularly each period (week, month, quarter as appropriate) a new future period is added to the budget whilst the earliest period is deleted. In this way the rolling budget is continually revised so as to reflect the most up to date position. The process of continuous budgeting could, of course, be carried out for any type of budget, not just cash budgets.

21. Cash budget example

The opening cash balance on 1 January was expected to be £30,000. The sales budgeted were as follows:

	£
November	80,000
December	90,000
January	75,000
February	75,000
March	80,000

Analysis of records shows that debtors settle according to the following pattern:

60%	within the month of sale.
25%	the month following.
15%	the month following.

Extracts from the Purchases budget were as follows:

	£
December	60,000
January	55,000
February	45,000
March	55,000

All purchases are on credit and past experience shows that 90% are settled in the month of purchase and the balance settled the month after.

Wages are £15,000 per month and overheads of £20,000 per month (including £5,000 depreciation) are settled monthly.

Taxation of £8,000 has to be settled in February and the company will receive settlement of an insurance claim of £25,000 in March.

Prepare a cash budget for January, February and March.

Solution

Workings   *Receipts from sales*

January cash

	£
November (15% × 80,000)	12,000
December (25% × 90,000)	22,500
January (60% × 75,000)	45,000
	79,500

February cash

	£
December (15% × 90,000)	13,500
January (25% × 75,000)	18,750
February (60% × 75,000)	45,000
	77,250

March cash

	£
January (15% × 75,000)	11,250
February (25% × 75,000)	18,750
March (60% × 80,000)	48,000
	78,000

Payments for purchases:

January cash

	£
December (10% × 60,000)	6,000
January (90% × 55,000)	49,500
	55,500

February cash

	£
January (10% × 55,000)	5,500
February (90% × 45,000)	40,500
	46,000

March cash

	£
February (10% × 45,000)	4,500
March (90% × 55,000)	49,500
	54,000

Cash Budget

	January £	*February* £	*March* £
Opening balance	30,000	24,000	17,250
Receipts from sales	79,500	77,250	78,000
Insurance claim			25,000
= Total Cash Available	109,500	101,250	120,250
Payments			
Purchases	55,500	46,000	54,000
Wages	15,000	15,000	15,000
Overheads (less dep'n)	15,000	15,000	15,000
Taxation		8,000	
Total Payments	85,500	84,000	84,000
Closing balance c/f	24,000	17,250	36,250

22. Reconciliation of cash balance and profits

Organisations prepare both cash budgets and operating budgets which show the budgeted profits for each period. These two forms of statements are prepared on totally different bases; the cash budget on the practical, objective basis of measuring positive and negative cash flows whereas budgeted profits are based on the normal conventions of accounting. These include, for example, the accruals concept, the charging of cost which do not create a cash flow – eg depreciation, the distinctions between capital and revenue expenditure and so on.

It is sometimes required to reconcile the budgeted cash and profit figures and the simplest approach to this is to use the Bank Reconciliation Statement approach and commence with one of the figures, say the budgeted cash balance, and then add or subtract the various elements in the budgets so as to agree with the figure of budgeted profit.

In practice there are innumerable items which cause differences between the two figures but the following examples include the major categories:

Sales/Purchases used in profit calculation whereas actual receipts from debtors and payments to creditors used in cash budgets.

Various items in cash budgets which do not appear in profit calculations, eg capital expenditure, taxation and dividends, increases and decreases in loans, sales or fixed assets etc.

Notional cost items such as depreciation and imputed charges appear in profit statements but not in cash budgets.

Changes in credit policies and stock levels affect cash budgets but not profit statements.

Accruals and prepayments are normal features of profit statements but do not appear in cash budgets.

23. Budgets and flexible budget

A budget or, as it is sometimes known, a fixed budget, can be defined thus

> *'A plan expressed in money. It is prepared and approved prior to the budget period and may show income expenditure and the capital to be employed. It may be drawn up showing incremental effects on former budgeted or actual figures or be compiled by zero-based budgeting'.*   *Terminology.*

A flexible budget is one which is designed to adjust the budgeted cost levels to suit the level of activity actually attained. This is achieved by analysing each item of cost contained in the budget into fixed and variable elements. In this way an estimate can be made of the expected costs for the actual activity level experienced. This process is often known as 'flexing' the budget. The procedure for developing a flexible budget is, in principle, quite simple but the results are only accurate if the costs behave in the predicted fashions. Too often simplistic assumptions are made about cost behaviour which are unrealistic.

Examples include – the frequent arbitrary assumption of cost linearity – the assumption of continuity when the cost may actually behave in a stepped or discontinuous manner – the often arbitrary classifications used to determine the fixed and variable elements of costs – the fact that often all variable costs are flexed in relation to the same activity indicator (eg sales or output) when in reality different variable costs vary in sympathy with different activity indicators. This latter point is the rationale behind Activity-Based Accounting. Activity-Based Costing has already been dealt with and Activity-Based Budgeting is dealt with in Chapter 9, Budgetary Control.

A flexible budget is useful for the control aspect of budgeting but as it is an important part of the planning process to consider what control procedures will be necessary, it is usual to carry out the required cost analyses and breakdowns at the planning stage so that the budget may be flexed in due course if this is necessary.

The following simplified example illustrates the general principle.

A machinery department produces a variety of components and its output is measured in standard hours produced (SHP). The anticipated production level is 2000 SHP. This level has been agreed as the basis for the other budgets throughout the organisation and for the Master budget.

The Machinery Department's costs, their classification and behaviour in relation to output levels, have been studied and, after discussion, have been agreed with the departmental manager, who is the budget holder, and his superior, the Works Manager.

Budget

Period 09	*Budget Holder:* A.N. Other
Department: MACHINING	Budget Relationships
Activity Level. 2000 Standard Hours	*Upwards:* Factory cost
	Downwards: Nil

Nature of Expense	Budgeted cost for anticipated activity level of 2000 standard hours	Cost Classification	Cost Function (x = activity level)
	£		
Materials	10,000	Variable (linear)	$5x$
Wages	8,200	Semi-variable (linear)	$2,600 \times 2.8x$
Salaries	3,200	Fixed	
Maintenance	4,600	Semi-variable (curvi-linear)	$1,000 + 0.0009x^2$
Consumable Materials	2,500	Variable (curvi-linear)	$0.000625x^2$
•	•	•	•
•	•	•	•
•	•	•	•

Notes:

a) Only a few items of cost are shown. In practice there is likely to be far more detail.

b) It has been assumed that the variable and semi-variable items vary in relation to the same activity indicator, ie Standard Hours Produced. Although this is a common assumption, particularly in examinations, it is not always an accurate reflection of reality.

Such a budget with its cost breakdowns can be flexed for any required activity level. For example, the budgeted cost allowances for 1,800 and 2,200 SHP are shown below compared with the original 2,000 SHP.

Cost	Cost Function	Activity Level		
		1800 SHP	2000 SHP	2200 SHP
		£		
Materials	$5x$	9,000	10,000	11,000
Wages	$2,600 + 2.8x$	7,640	8,200	8,760
Salaries	$3,200 + 0x$	3,200	3,200	3,200
Maintenance	$1,000 + 0.0009x^2$	3,916	4,600	5,356
Consumables	$0.000625x^2$	2,025	2,500	3,025

The point must be stressed again that any such cost projection is only as good as the original cost classifications and functions. It has been said with considerable truth that the budgeting process is more a test of forecasting skill than anything else.

24. Level of attainment

It is relatively easy to determine the level of activity of an organisation or a department but much more difficult to determine the level of attainment to be incorporated into the budget for the planned level of activity. Conventionally the most appropriate level is often described as a tough but realistically attainable standard of achievement. It has to be recognised that the level of attainment incorporated into the budget is likely to influence the motivation of the managers responsible for the achievement of the target. Ideally, the level of attainment should be such that perfect goal congruence is achieved both between individual and organisational goals and between departmental and organisational objectives but this is unlikely to happen.

If impossibly high levels of attainment are incorporated into budgets then it is likely that there will be strong disincentives to management involvement with the budgetary process and a corresponding low level of motivation and goal congruence. If levels are set which are too low than a condition will exist which is called *budgetary slack*. This means that managers can easily keep within the budgeted cost levels for the level of activity even though there may be many inefficiencies. Budgetary slack exists more widely than is realised and is often characterised by the spending sprees which occur towards the end of the budget period so that departments 'spend up to their budget'.

25. Budget variability and uncertainty

Due to the uncertainty attached to the level of attainment (and many of the other factors in budget preparation) attempts have been made to recognise these inherent variabilities by the use of subjective probabilities and elementary probability and statistical theory in budget preparation. Several approaches are possible, for example, instead of the traditional single point estimates, three estimates could be made of the level expected for each factor, pessimistic, most likely and optimistic, each with a subjective probability attached. Alternatively, control bands could be calculated for budget values based on the statistical concept of confidence limits which are calculated from the mean or most likely value of the budget and a measure of the budget's dispersion, the estimated standard deviation.

A simple illustration follows:

Example

A department's budget consists of three items: sales, variable costs and fixed costs. Discussions with management, supported by analysis of records, has produced the following data:

| Expected Sales for period: | Most Likely | £20,000 | Probability 0.7 |
| | Optimistic | £25,000 | Probability 0.3 |

Variable costs (for £20,000 sales level)

	Optimistic	£12,000	P = 0.2
	Most likely	£14,000	P = 0.6
	Pessimistic	£15,000	P = 0.2

Variable costs (for £25,000 sales level)

	Optimistic	£14,000	P = 0.3
	Most likely	£16,800	P = 0.5
	Pessimistic	£18,500	P = 0.2
	Fixed Costs	£4,000	

What is the expected value of budgeted profit?

What is the range of possible outcomes?

Solution

		£
Sales		20,000
less Expected value of variable costs		
$(12,000 \times 0.2 + 14,000 \times 0.6 + 15,000 \times 0.2)$	=	13,800
= Contribution		6,200
Sales		25,000
less Expected value of variable costs		
$(14,000 \times 0.3 + 16,800 \times 0.5 + 18,500 \times 0.2)$		16,300
= contribution		8,700
∴ Expected contribution		
$= (6,200 \times 0.7) + (8,700 \times 0.3)$	=	6,950
less Fixed Costs		4,000
∴ Expected value of budgeted profit	=	£2,950

The range of outcome is from:

lowest   £20,000 sales combined with the pessimistic variable cost of £15,000

highest   £25,000 sales combined with the optimistic variable cost of £14,000, ie

from   £20,000 – £15,000   = £5,000 contribution   = £1,000 profit

to   £25,000 – £14,000   = £11,000 contribution   = £7,000 profit

Note: The procedure for establishing a control band of values is illustrated in connection with budgetary control in a later chapter.

26. Alternative approaches to budgeting

Whilst there are undoubted advantages in properly planned conventional budgeting systems, too often budgeting tends to reinforce the status quo and budgets are often merely extrapolations of the past (including its inefficiencies). Cost levels are frequently determined by what was spent last year plus a percentage for inflation. This process is known as an incremental budgeting and is commonly encountered in both public and private sector organisations.

In stable conditions where there are few changes in the environment in which the organisation operates and objectives remain unchanged then *incremental budgeting* is a reasonable procedure. However, care will always be needed to ensure that existing expenditure levels – to which will be added an increment – do not conceal gross inefficiencies. Using incremental budgeting, change is inhibited and rarely are the relationships between costs, benefits and objectives subjected to any searching scrutiny. In an attempt to overcome these very real problems, alternative approaches to budgeting have been developed, particularly in North American, two of which Zero-base Budgeting and the Programme Planning and Budgeting System, are described below.

27. Zero-based budgeting (ZBB) or priority based budgeting

ZBB is a cost-benefit approach whereby it is assumed that the cost allowance for an item is zero, and will remain so until the manager responsible justifies the existence of the cost item and the benefits the expenditure brings. In this way a questioning attitude is developed whereby each cost item and its level has to be justified in relation to the way it helps to meet objectives and how the expenditure benefits the organisation. This is a forward looking approach as opposed to the all too common method of extrapolating past activities and costs, which is a feature of the incremental budgeting approach.

ZBB is formally defined by the CIMA thus;

> '*A method of budgeting whereby all activities are re-evaluated each time a budget is set. Discrete levels of each activity are valued and a combination chosen to match the funds available.*'   *Terminology.*

The use of ZBB was pioneered by P Phyrr in the United States in the early 1970s and has gained wide acceptance probably because it is a simple idea obviously based on common-sense. ZBB is concerned with the evaluation of the costs and benefits of alternatives and, implicit in the technique, is the concept of opportunity cost.

28. Where can ZBB be applied?

ZBB can be applied in both profit seeking and non-profit seeking organisations. The technique gained wide publicity when the then President Carter directed that all US government departments adopt ZBB.

In a manufacturing firm, ZBB is best applied to service and support expenditure including; administration, marketing, personnel, information and computer services, research and development, finance and accounting, production planning and so on. These activities are less easily quantifiable by conventional methods and are more discretionary in nature. Manufacturing costs such as direct materials and labour and production overheads can be more easily controlled by well established methods which compare production outputs with resource inputs rather than using ZBB. Budgeting and controlling manufacturing expenditure uses techniques such as work study and standard costing which are described later in the manual.

ZBB can successfully be applied to service industries and to a wide range of non-profit seeking organisations. For example local and central government departments, educational establishments, hospitals and so on. ZBB could be applied in any organisation where alternative levels of provision for each activity are possible and the costs and benefits can be separately identified. ZBB is concerned with alternatives and means that established activities have to be compared with alternative uses of the same resources. ZBB takes away the implied right of existing activities to continue to receive resources, unless it can be shown that this is the best use of those resources.

29. Implementing ZBB

There are several formal stages involved in implementing a ZBB system but of greater importance is the development of an appropriate questioning attitude by all concerned. There must be a 'value for money' approach which challenges existing practices and expenditures and searching questions must be asked at each stage; typical of which are the following:

a) Does the activity need to be carried out at all? What would be the effects, if any, if it ceased?

b) How does the activity – existing or proposed – contribute to the organisation's objectives?

c) What is the correct level of provision? Has too much or too little been provided in the past?

d) What is the best way to provide the function? Have all alternative possibilities been considered?

e) How much should the activity cost? Is this expenditure worth the benefits achieved?

f) Is the activity essential or one of the frills?

and so on.

30. Stages in implementing ZBB

The overall process of implementing a ZBB system can be sub-divided into three stages thus:

a) **Definition of decision packages**

A decision package is a comprehensive description of a facet of the organisation's activities or functions which can be individually evaluated. The decision package is specified by the managers concerned and must show details of the anticipated costs and results expected expressed in terms of tasks accomplished and benefits achieved.

Two types of decision package are possible:

❐ *Mutually-exclusive decision packages.*

These are *alternative* forms of activity, tasks and expenditure to carry out the same job. The best option among the mutually exclusive packages is selected by comparing costs and benefits, and the other packages are then discarded. Naturally, mutually-exclusive packages would only be prepared when there are quite clearly different approaches for dealing with the same function. As an example, an organisation with a distribution problem might consider two alternative decision packages: Package 1 might be an in-house fleet of lorries, whereas Package 2 could involve contracts with independent hauliers.

❐ *Incremental decision packages*

These packages reflect different levels of effort in dealing with a particular activity. There will be what is known as the *base package,* which represents the minimum feasible level of activity, and other packages which describe higher activity levels at given costs and resulting benefits. As an example, a base package for a Personnel Department might provide for staff engagement and termination procedures and payroll administration. Incremental packages might include; education and training, welfare and social activities, pension administration, trade union liaison and negotiations etc. Each package would have its costs and benefits clearly tabulated.

b) **Packages are evaluated and ranked**

When the decision packages have been prepared, management will then rank all the packages on the basis of their benefits to the organisation. This is a process of allocating scarce resources between different activities, some of which already exist and other that are new.

Minimum requirements which are essential to get the job done and activities necessary to meet legal or safety obligations will naturally receive high priority. It will be found that the ranking process focuses management's attention on discretionary or optional activities.

Because of the large number of packages prepared throughout the organisation the ranking process can become onerous and time consuming for senior management. One way of reducing this problem is for lower level managers to rank the packages for their own budget centre and for these rankings to be consolidated, with others, at the next level up the hierarchy. Alternatively, there could be a cut-off limit for expenditure so that packages for a lower amount, say less than £2,000, could be ranked within the department and need not be referred higher.

c) **Resources are allocated**

When the overall budgeted expenditure level is decided upon the packages would be accepted in the ranked priority sequence up to the agreed expenditure level.

Where the ranking of lower cost packages has been delegated to departments the proportion of the expenditure budget remaining after the more expensive packages have been ranked would be allocated to individual departments. The departments would then rank their own small packages up to their allocated expenditure level.

31. Advantages of ZBB

a) Properly carried out, it should result in a more efficient allocation of resources to activities and departments.

b) ZBB focuses attention on value for money and makes explicit the relationship between the input of resources and the output of benefits.

c) It develops a questioning attitude and makes it easier to identify inefficient, obsolete or less cost-effective operations.

d) The ZBB process leads to greater staff and management knowledge of the operations and activities of the organisations and can increase motivation.

e) It is a systematic way of challenging the status quo and obliges the organisation to examine alternative activities and existing cost behaviour patterns and expenditure levels.

32. Disadvantages of ZBB

a) It is a time consuming process which can generate volumes of paper work especially for the decision packages.

b) There is considerable management skill required in both drawing up decision packages and for the ranking process. These skills may not exist in the organisation.

c) It may encourage the wrong impression that all decisions have to be made in the budget. Circumstances change and new opportunities and threats can arise at any time and organisations must be flexible enough to deal rapidly with these circumstances when they occur.

d) ZBB is not always acceptable to staff or management or trade unions who may prefer the cosy status quo and who see the detailed examination of alternatives, costs and benefits as a threat not a challenge.

e) There are considerable problems in ranking packages and there are inevitably many subjective judgements. Political pressures within organisations also contribute to the problem of ranking different types of activity, especially where there are qualitative rather than quantitative benefits.

f) It may emphasise short-term benefits to the detriment of longer term ones which in the end may be more important.

Undoubtedly the major drawback to ZBB is the amount of time the system takes. One way of obtaining the benefits of ZBB is to apply it selectively on a rolling basis throughout the organisation. This year Marketing, next year, Personnel, the year after Research and Development and so on. In this way, over a period, all activities will receive a thorough scrutiny, the benefits of which should last for years.

ZBB is particularly appropriate for non-profit making organisations where quality of service is all important. These types of organisations do not necessarily apply all the detail of ZBB but try to follow its basic philosophy by undertaking reviews of base estimates rather than using the simple incremental approach. As an example, a survey by Skousen in 1990 found that 54% of UK local authorities claimed to challenge base estimates each year.

33. Programme planning and budgeting systems (PPBS)

Non-profit seeking organisations such as local and central government, hospitals, charities and so on, often prepare detailed conventional budgets showing the different categories of expenditure, classification by classification. A particular problem of such organisations is that the measurement of outputs is difficult and sometimes impossible. As a consequence the budgeting process frequently just compares current expenditure to budgeted expenditure with little or no attempt to compare expenditure against performance achieved. By contrast, in profit seeking organisations the comparison of expenditure on resource inputs to outputs in terms of revenue and profits is much more straightforward.

In addition to the problems of relating inputs to benefits achieved, non-profit seeking organisations also have difficulties with long-term strategic planning and realistic resource allocation. The short-term financial process of annual expenditure budgets is, on occasions, also being used for long-term policy planning with obvious disadvantages.

In an attempt to overcome these problems the PPBS system was evolved.

PPBS is a sophisticated concept developed in North America and is usually considered in relation to State and Federal government activities although there is no reason why the system principles could not be more widely applied.

PPBS is based on systems theory and is output and objective oriented with a substantial emphasis on resource allocation based on economic analysis. The system is based, not on traditional organisational structures and divisions, but on 'programmes' – grouping of activities with common objectives. PPBS is similar to the corporate planning process for profit-seeking organisations, described in Chapter 6, but it is not identical. As with corporate planning, conventional short-term budgeting – year by year – takes place within the PPBS long-term framework.

PPBS requires that the organisation prepares a long-term plan relating to the objectives of the organisation subdivided into programmes. These programmes are expressed in terms of objectives to be achieved over the medium to long-term, say 3 to 5 years. The key point is that the programmes are objective related and spread across several conventional departments. The total estimated costs are for the programme as a whole and are not initially expressed in relation to departments. When the various programmes for the organisation have been agreed they form the long-term plan for the organisation. PPBS covers activities spanning several years and conventional annual expenditure budgeting would take place within this framework. Each year the departments contributing to a given programme would prepare, and be monitored by, normal expenditure budgets for their share of the programme's activities for the year in question.

PPBS requires a sophisticated information system able to monitor progress towards meeting systems objectives. The PPBS reporting system should be able to report upon results in terms of the programmes of activities unlike conventional reporting which is geared to existing organisational sub-divisions and usually deals only with expenditures.

34. A PPBS example

Assume that a Local Authority operates PPBS and has a programme concerned with the welfare of children. The programme might extend over 5 years and objectives would be agreed covering all aspects of children's welfare, including:

a) Births, health, diseases, dental care and so on

b) Nursery school attendance, primary and secondary school attendance, achievements and so on

c) Home conditions parental care, one parent family problems, etc

d) Discipline and behavioural aspects

e) Sports and leisure activities and provision

f) Safety and counselling services

and so on.

It will be immediately apparent that numerous departments would contribute to the 'Children's Programme' and this can be represented diagrammatically as shown in Figure 7.4.

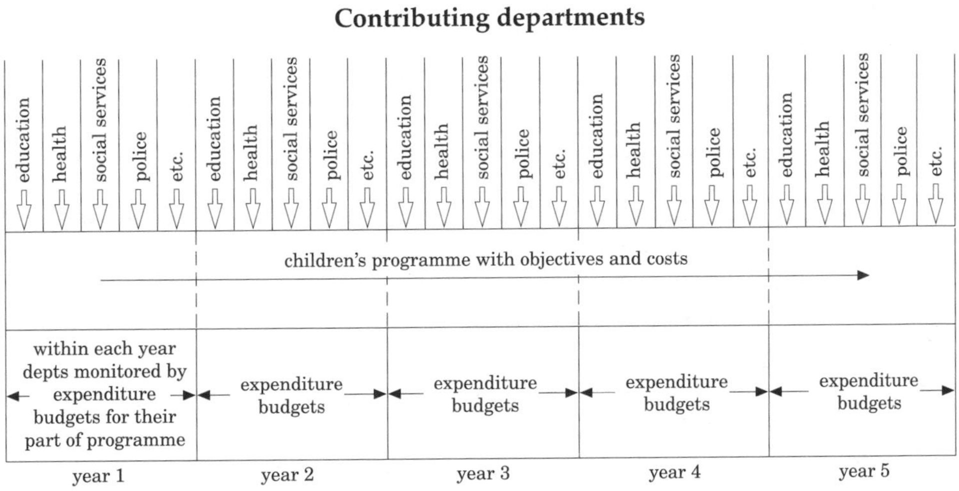

Contributing departments

Figure 7.4

35. Summary

a) Budgetary or short-term planning is the process by which the long-term corporate plan is converted into action.

b) Properly organised budgetary systems can bring substantial benefits including: co-ordination, clarification of responsibilities, communication, control, motivation, and goal congruence.

c) Properly developed budgets co-ordinate departments and activities and thus help to avoid sub-optimality.

d) The budgetary process is an important formal means of horizontal and vertical communication.

e) The budgetary process includes the all important control aspect. Although the same budgets frequently appear to serve for both planning and control, separate planning and control budgets could be prepared.

f) The success of a budgetary system should be judged by the extent it encourages goal congruence.

g) The budgeting system is likely to be successful if it has top management support, clear definitions, full involvements, appropriate accounting systems, and is administered in a flexible manner.

h) The principal budget factor is the factor which imposes the overall limitation on the activities of the organisation. In complex organisations the assumption of a single limiting factor may be too simplistic.

i) The whole budgetary process is detailed with many steps and is shown in Figure 7.1.

j) The Budget Manual is an important aid to communications and is an instructional/information manual not a list of agreed financial budgets.

k) All budgets are related and interconnect so as to form part of the Master Budget.

l) Key summary budgets are the Cash Budget and the Master Budget which are effectively summaries of all other budgets.

m) The control of cash and liquidity is a continuous process and cash budgets are updated frequently, usually on a rolling basis.

n) A fixed budget is designed to remain unchanged irrespective of activity changes whereas a flexible budget (by analysis of the fixed and variable nature of costs) adjusts to the level of activity attained.

o) It is difficult to determine the level of attainment to be included in budgets. If set too high there will be low motivation, if set too low there will be budgetary slack.

p) Many of the factors in budget preparation are subject to variation and this should be recognised. Possible ways include the use of probability and elementary statistical concepts.

q) Zero base budgeting is a method of budgeting whereby all activities are re-evaluated (costs c.f. benefits) each budget period.

r) ZBB requires activities to be specified in terms of decision packages which may be mutually exclusive or incremental.

s) ZBB should result in more efficient allocation of resources to activities and engenders a value for money attitude.

t) ZBB creates voluminous quantities of paperwork and takes considerable managerial time to implement.

u) PPBS is a radical approach to budgeting based on 'programmes', which are groupings of activities with common objectives. It is mainly used in public authorities and government departments.

36. Points to note

a) Mechanically applied budgeting systems reinforce existing structures, responsibilities and methods and may inhibit change.

b) Budgeting systems are no substitute for good management. Too often budgeting systems concentrate almost entirely on internal factors whilst neglecting the all important interactions and necessary adaptions to the environment.

Additional reading

Budget Planning and Control Systems; *Amey* – Pitman

Management Control Systems, Anthony; *Dearden & Bedford* – Irwin

Readings in Accounting for Management Control; *Emmanuel, Otley & Merchant* – Chapman & Hall

Management Control in Non-Profit Organisations; *Anthony & Herzlinger* – Irwin

Design of Cost Management Systems; *Cooper & Kaplan* – Prentice Hall

Accounting and Human Behaviour; *Hopwood* – Prentice Hall

Self review questions

1. What is the difference between a plan and a budget? (2)
2. In what ways does budgeting help co-ordination? (4)
3. How does the budgetary process assist communication? (6)
4. What are the conditions for successful budgeting? (9)
5. What is the principal budget factor and why must it be identified? (11)
6. What are the steps in the budgetary process? (12)
7. Give the contents of a typical budget manual. (13)
8. Show the relationships of the main budgets with the Master Budget. (14)
9. What is the Master Budget? (20)
10. Why is the Cash Budget important and what is a typical format? (20)
11. Distinguish between fixed and flexible budgets. (23)
12. How is a flexible budget adjusted? (23)
13. What is budgetary slack? (24)
14. How can the variability of budget factors be dealt with? (25)
15. What is zero base budgeting and what is its objective? (26)
16. What is a decision package? (30)
17. Why is ranking necessary and how is it done? (30)
18. What are the advantages of ZBB? (31)
19. What are the disadvantages of ZBB? (32)
20. Define PPBS. (33)

Assessment and revision section 2

Examination questions with answers

A1. It has been said that we live in an age of discontinuity and that the only thing we know for certain about the future is that it will not be the same as the past.

In spite of this, many statistical and accounting techniques are based on extrapolations of past performance into the future in order to provide information for planning and decision making.

You are required

a) to discuss the problems of extrapolating past performance into the future;

b) to explain how you can forecast in circumstances where the future is likely to be different from the past.

CIMA, Management Accounting Techniques.

A2. Lack of co-ordination between strategic planning and operational planning may result in *unrealistic plans, inconsistent goals. poor communication and inadequate performance measurement.*

a) State key features or characteristics which should be incorporated in each of strategic planning and operational planning.

b) Name and comment on examples of the cost implications of each of the factors shown in italics in the above statement which may occur from lack of relevant and appropriate operational planning. Your answer should be in the context of a strategic planning goal of sustaining competitive advantage at minimum cost through speedy delivery of quality products to customers.

ACCA, Information for Control and Decision Making.

A3. a) An extensive literature on the behavioural aspects of budgeting discusses the propensity of managers to create budgetary slack.

You are required to explain *three* ways in which managers may attempt to create budgetary slack, and how senior managers can identify these attempts to distort the budgetary system.

b) Managerial behaviour can be quite different from that discussed in a).

You are required to explain circumstances in which managers may be motivated to set themselves very high, possibly unachievable budgets.

c) Sections a) and b) above are examples of differing managerial behaviour in disparate situations. There are theories which attempt to explain the consequences for the design of management accounting systems of disparate situations, one of which is contingency theory.

You are required to explain:

❐ the contingency theory of management accounting

❐ the effects of environmental uncertainty on the choice of managerial control systems and on information systems for managerial control.

CIMA, Management Accounting - Control and Audit.

A4. The budgeted balance sheet data of Kwan Tong Umbago Ltd is as follows:

1 March 19X5

Fixed assets	Cost	Depreciation to date	Net
	£	£	£
Land and buildings	500,000	–	500,000
Machinery and equipment	124,000	84,500	39,500
Motor vehicles	42,000	16,400	25,600
	666,000	100,900	565,100

Working capital:

Current assets

Stock of raw materials (100 units)		4,320	
Stock of finished goods (110 units)*		10,450	
Debtors (January £7,680 February £10,400)		18,080	
Cash and bank		6,790	
		39,640	

Less current liabilities

Creditors (raw materials)		3,900	35,740
			600,840

Represented by:

Ordinary share capital (fully paid) £1 shares	500,000
Share premium	60,000
Profit and loss account	40,840
	600,840

*The stock of finished goods was valued at marginal cost.

The estimates for the next four month period are as follows:

	March	April	May	June
Sales (units)	80	84	96	94
Production (units)	70	75	90	90
Purchases of raw materials (units)	80	80	85	85
Wages and variable overheads at £65 per unit	£4,550	£4,875	£5,580	£5,580
Fixed overheads	£1,200	£1,200	£1,200	£1,200

The company intends to sell each unit for £219 and has estimated that it will have to pay £45 per unit for raw materials. One unit of raw material is needed for each unit of finished product.

All sales and purchases of raw materials are on credit. Debtors are allowed two month's credit and suppliers of raw materials are paid after one month's credit. The wages, variable overheads and fixed overheads are paid in the month in which they are incurred.

Cash from a loan secured on the land and buildings of £120,000 at an interest rate of 7.5% is due to be received on 1 May. Machinery costing £112,000 will be received in May and paid for in June.

The loan interest is payable half yearly from September onwards. An interim dividend to 31 March 19X5 of £12,500 will be paid in June.

Depreciation for the four months, including that on the new machinery is:

- Machinery and equipment £15,733
- Motor vehicles £3,500

The company uses the FIFO method of stock valuation. Ignore taxation.

Required:

a) Calculate and present the raw materials budget and finished goods budget in terms of units, for each month from March to June inclusive, and

b) the corresponding sales budgets, the production cost budgets and the budgeted closing debtors, creditors and stocks in terms of value.

c) Prepare and present a cash budget for each of the four months.

d) Prepare a master budget i.e. a budgeted trading and profit and loss account for the four months to 30 June 19X5, and budgeted balance sheet as at 30 June 19X5.

e) Advise the company about possible ways in which it can improve its cash management.

ACCA, Managerial Finance.

A5. The Finance Director of A & B plc is about to renegotiate the companyís overdraft facility. The company currently has annual sales of

Product A: 50,000 units at £4.50 per unit.
Product B: 60,000 units at £6.50 per unit.
Product C: 75,000 units at £3.50 per unit.

Other information is as follows:

	Product A	Product B	Product C
Cost of sales	50%	60%	30%
Stock conversion period (months)	1.5	2	1
Average debtors credit (months)	2.0	3	1.5
Average suppliers credit (months)	2.5	2.5	1.5
Forecast increase in sales volume	25%	20%	30%

The forecast increase in sales volume is expected to result from aggressive marketing and not as a result of a price reduction. The costs associated with marketing and other administrative activities are included in the average suppliers (creditors) conversion rates.

The Finance Director forecasts three possible scenarios. These are described below. All variations are from the current position.

1. The conversion rates of stock, debtors and creditors will remain unchanged.

2. The conversion rates for debtors for all three products will deteriorate by 25% because longer credit periods will have to be offered to customers to gain the new business. The conversion rates for stock and creditors will remain unchanged.

3. Much of the extra business will be gained by entering a new market of cash-paying customers. As a result, the debtors conversion period for all three products will improve by 25%. The conversion rate for stock will remain unchanged, but the rate for creditors is likely to fall slightly to 2.4 months for Products A and B and to 1.2 months for Product C.

   a) *You are required:*

      (i) to calculate the net current operating assets (stock, debtors and creditors) and the likely future requirements based on the three scenarios presented above;

      (ii) to comment on other information which the Finance Director might require before he renegotiates the company's overdraft requirements.

   b) A detailed forecast based on new marketing data reveals that the overdraft can be substantially reduced in around 6 months' time. In fact, surplus funds will be available for periods of between 1 and 6 months.

You are required to describe *three* possible uses for these surplus funds.

CIMA, Management Accounting - Financial Management.

A6. You are the Management Accountant of a medium-sized company. You have been asked to provide budgetary information and advice to the Board of Directors for a meeting where they will decide the pricing of an important product for the next period. The following information is available from the records:

	Previous period £000	Current period £000
Sales:		
(100,000 units at £13 each)	1,300	(106,000 units at £13 each) 1,378.0
Costs	1,000	1,077.4
Profit	300	300.6

You find that between the previous and current periods there was 4% general cost inflation and it is forecast that costs will rise a further 6% in the next period. As a matter of policy, the firm did not increase the selling price in the current period although competitors raised their prices by 4% to allow for the increased costs. A survey by economic consultants was commissioned and has found that the demand for the product is elastic with an estimated price elasticity of demand of 1.5. This means that volume would fall by $1\frac{1}{2}$ times the rate of real price increase.

Various options are to be considered by the Board and *you are required:*

a) to show the budgeted position if the firm maintains the £13 selling price for the next period (when it is expected that competitors will increase their prices by 6%);

b) to show the budgeted position if the firm also raises its price by 6%;

c) to write a short report to the Board, with appropriate figures, recommending whether the firm should maintain the £13 selling price or raise it by 6%;

d) to state what assumptions you have used in your answers.

CIMA, Management Accounting Techniques.

Examination questions without answers

B1. Dr Bentley in Defining Management's Information Needs (CIMA MIS Series) says that the information systems designer should not

i) just ask the manager what he wants.

ii) tell the manager what he needs.

iii) give the manager what is available.

You are required

a) to explain why the system designer is recommended to avoid the three steps mentioned above;

b) to describe how management's information needs could be defined;

c) to describe the characteristics that information should possess for it to have value.

CIMA, Management Accounting Techniques.

B2. A company is preparing budgets for the year ahead for two of its raw materials that are used in various products which it manufactures. Current year material usage standards are as follows:

Kilos per thousand units of product

	Product 1	*Product 2*	*Product 3*	*Product 4*	*Product 5*
Material A	25	70	15	–	55
Material B	30	5	–	20	–

It has been decided to change standards on Material B for the following year to reflect the favourable usage variances that are occurring for that material on all products. Usage variances on Material B are 10% of standard costs.

Budgeted sales quantities for the following year are:

	Product 1	*Product 2*	*Product 3*	*Product 4*	*Product 5*
('000 units)	600	350	1,850	1,200	900

Production quantities are to be budgeted in line with sales, apart from Product 5 where an increase in stock of 30% is required by the end of the budget year. Stocks of the five products at the beginning of the budget year are expected to be:

	Product 1	*Product 2*	*Product 3*	*Product 4*	*Product 5*
('000 units)	140	80	260	180	100

Stocks of Materials A and B at the end of the budget year are to be 10% of the year's budgeted usage. Stocks at the end of the current year are expected to be:

	Kilos
Material A	10,030
Material B	4,260

Required:

a) Describe the benefits that can be derived from a budgeting system.

b) Prepare material usage and purchases budgets (kilos only) for each of Materials A and B for the year ahead.

c) Prepare summary journal entries for the Material A stock account for the current period.

ACCA, Cost and Management Accounting I.

B3. DEF Ltd manufactures a product called the D. A single batch of Ds is produced each month. D production is labour-intensive and is known to involve an 80% learning curve effect. The D is perishable; therefore, stocks cannot be held for a significant period.

In recent months output and sales have been at the rate of 1,200 Ds per month. The selling price has been £8 per unit and the variable cost of production (mostly labour related) has been £6.50 per unit. Market research has indicated that the elasticity of demand for the D is 1.25.

It has been suggested that it would be advantageous to change the unit selling price of the D from its present level. As DEF Ltd's management accountant, you have been asked to advise on this suggestion.

You may assume that when elasticity of demand is 1.25 then demand, d, and unit selling price, p, may be related by the following equation:

$$d = \left(\frac{2,325}{p}\right)^{1.25}$$

You may assume that when an 80% learning curve effect applies, then batch size, B, and variable cost per unit, h, may be related by the following equation (a being a constant):

$$h = \frac{a}{B^{0.322}}$$

You are required

a) to calculate the contribution that will be earned if the unit selling price is set at each of the following figures - £10.00, £8.00, £6.00, and £5.00; identify which of these alternative selling prices gives the largest contribution;

b) to draw a diagram (which need not be perfectly to scale) illustrating the relationship between output, unit variable cost and unit selling price;

c) to write a memorandum in reply to a statement made by DEF Ltd's finance director, as follows:

'This exercise is just a mathematician's delight and has nothing to do with real accounting, or the real world for that matter.'

CIMA, Management Accounting – Decision Making.

B4. **You are required** to:

a) compare the operation of fixed budgets (or cash limits) within public sector organisations or local government authorities with the budgeting procedures normally used in commercial organisations, listing three advantages and three disadvantages from the public sector or local government point of view;

b) explain the use of a budget manual and give an indication of the likely contents. Your explanation must be related to one of the following:

i) a private sector organisation;

ii) a public sector organisation;

iii) a local government authority.

CIMA, Cost Accounting.

B5. A company manufactures a range of products by passing materials through a number of processes. A number of service departments provide support to the production processes.

a) Define responsibility accounting and comment on the application of responsibility accounting in the context of the above situation.

b) Explain how responsibility may be shared in respect of the cost of the maintenance department and suggest ways in which the management accounting system may assist in recognising such shared responsibility.

c) Explain ways in which the provision of more information need not lead to more effective management of a cost centre.

ACCA, Cost and Management Accounting.

Control

The next five chapters cover the important topic of control and control systems. The implementation of plans without well designed control systems is largely a waste of time so that the management accountant must be considering the problems of implementation and control at the planning stage.

The essence of control is the comparison of performance against plan or target. The monitoring of progress and the comparisons with target reveal variations from the original plan which can either be used to guide activities back towards the original plan or, if the monitoring of actual results and conditions shows that unforeseen conditions have arisen, can be used to revise the original plans. This latter process is of great strategic importance and is part of general plan reviews which are vital in volatile, uncertain conditions.

8 Control – concepts and system principles

1. Objectives

After studying this chapter you will:

❑ understand the principles of control;

❑ know the elements in the control cycle;

❑ be able to describe the various forms of feedback;

❑ know the importance of timing in control systems;

❑ understand the Law of Requisite Variety;

❑ be able to describe Pareto analysis;

❑ know what is meant by feedforward.

2. Control defined

Control is concerned with the efficient use of resources to achieve a previously determined objective, or set of objectives, contained within a plan. It will be recalled that a plan is the method by which it has been decided that the objectives will be most effectively achieved. In an organisational sense, control is exercised by the feedback of information on performance compared with plan. Thus it will be seen that planning and control are inextricably linked and indeed in practice the distinction between the two functions is often blurred.

3. Types of control systems

The main accounting control systems are budgetary control and standard costing, dealt with in the following chapters. These are important quantitative control systems but they are by no means the only ones found in a typical organisation. Other quantitative control systems include: Quality Control, Production Control and Inventory Control.

In addition to the quantitative systems outlined above there are also control systems concerned with qualitative factors. Two important examples are systems for monitoring product quality and schemes of staff appraisal.

An organisation is a network of interacting control systems which, in the ideal world, should complement one another and should help to steer the activities of the organisation towards meeting the corporate objectives. Perhaps inevitably this is not always the case and sometimes the systems may be in direct conflict. An example of this is where a narrowly conceived and rigidly applied budgetary control system which concentrated on short term cost reductions might cause a lack of staff recruitment and development with an inevitable long term reduction in overall staff efficiency.

4. Basic elements of control

Control is the activity which measures deviations from planned performance and provides information upon which corrective action can be taken (if required) either to alter future performance so as to conform to the original plan, or to modify the original plans.

The elements of the control cycle are:

a) A standard specifying the expected performance. This can be in the form of a budget, a procedure, a stock level, an output rate or some other target.

b) A measurement of actual performance. This should be made in an accurate, speedy, unbiased manner and using relevant units or measures. For example, time taken, £'s spent, units produced, efficiency ratings and so on.

c) Comparison of (a) and (b). Frequently the comparison is accompanied by an analysis which attempts to isolate the reasons for any variations. A well known example of this is the accounting process of variance analysis, described in Chapter 10.

d) Feedback of deviations or variations to a control unit. In an organisational context the 'control unit' would be a manager. This type of feedback is 'single-loop' feedback which is described more fully in the next paragraph.

e) Actions by the control unit to alter performance in accordance with the plan.

f) Feedback to a higher level control unit regarding large variations between performance and plan and upon the results of the lower level control unit's actions.

This is 'double-loop' feedback which is also described more fully in the next paragraph.

5. Feedback loops

Control is exercised in organisational systems by feedback loops which gather information on past performance from the output side of a system, department or process, which is used to govern future performance by adjusting the input side of the system.

Systems theory gives special names to certain parts of the control and feedback cycle – illustrated in Figure 8.1 and explained below.

Sensor

These are the measuring and recording devices of the system. In mechanical systems this is some form of automatic metering but in organisational systems the usual sensor is some form of paperwork. Care must be taken to ensure that the sensor is appropriate for the system, is sufficiently accurate and timely and does not introduce bias.

Comparator

This is the means by which the comparison of actual results and the plan is achieved. Typically in information systems this is done by a clerk or by a computer program.

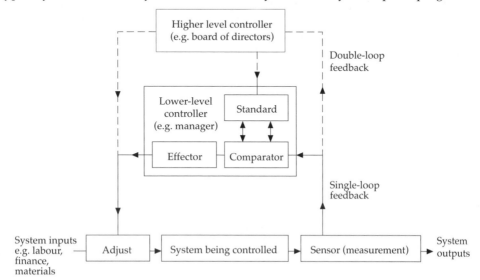

Figure 8.1 Control and Feedback Cycle

Effector

In an information system the usual effector is a manager or supervisor acting on the report containing the results of the comparisons and issuing the instructions for adjustments to be made.

Single loop feedback

Single-loop feedback, usually expressed simply as 'feedback', is the conventional feedback of relatively small variations between actual and plan in order that corrective action can be taken to bring performance in line with the plan. The implications of this is that existing performance standards and plans remain unchanged. This type of feedback is that associated with the normal budgetary control or standard costing statement.

Double loop feedback

This is a higher order of feedback designed to ensure that plans, budgets, organisational structures and the control systems themselves are revised to meet changes in conditions. Ross Ashby maintains that double-loop feedback is essential if a system is to adapt to a changing environment and, as already pointed out, adaptability is the primary characteristic of organisations that survive. The business environment abounds with uncertainties – competitor's actions, inflation, industrial disputes, changes in tastes and technology, new legislation – and the monitoring of trends and performance so that appropriate adjustments can be made to plans is likely to be more productive than the rigid adherence to historical plans and budgets which were prepared in earlier and different circumstances.

6. Negative feedback

This is feedback which seeks to dampen and reduce fluctuations around a norm or standard. Control systems incorporating negative feedback are inherently more stable and are more likely to conform to previously agreed levels or standards. A typical example is that of a Stock Control system with a planned level of stock holding. In such systems the monitoring of stock levels and usage rates and the ordering of replenishments at appropriate times seeks to maintain stocks at the planned level. This is depicted in Figure 8.2.

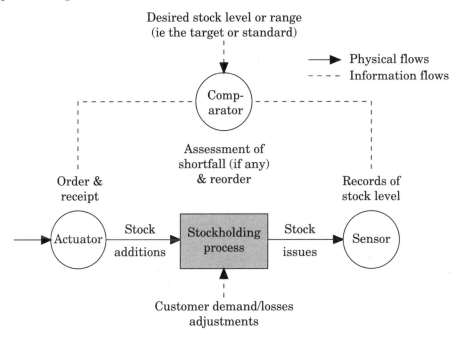

Figure 8.2 Feedback in stock control

Negative feedback produces corrective action in the *opposite direction to the deviation*. See Figure 8.3 on the following page.

A homeostat is a control device for holding a process or system within desired limits so that it becomes self regulating. A control system using negative feedback is homeostatic in nature but it may be far from a perfect homeostat.

7. Positive feedback

Positive feedback causes the system to amplify an adjustment or action. Positive feedback acts in the *same direction as the measured deviation*. Negative feedback is more commonly found in control systems but positive feedback does sometimes occur in information systems. An example is where advertising expenditure is linked to sales –

as sales increase beyond the original expectation, positive feedback causes the advertising appropriation to be increased.

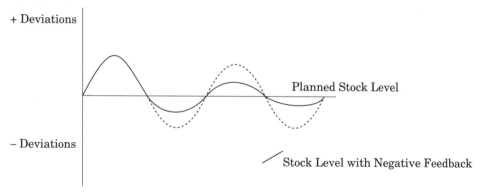

Figure 8.3 Effect of negative feedback

Unplanned positive feedback, perhaps caused by excessive delays in producing information, can cause system instability and loss of control.

8. Closed loop and open loop systems

A closed loop system is one where output measurement is fed back so that appropriate adjustments are made to the input side of the system. Some mechanical systems, eg thermostats in heating installations, are totally closed loop systems.

Organisational and business systems containing feedback control loops which have been designed as an integral part of the system are essentially closed loop systems although influences other than output monitoring can effect decisions.

Open loop systems are where no feedback loop exists and control is external to the system and not an internal part of it. This means that control is not an automatic process within the system but has to be dealt with by external intervention. Because of the obvious dangers of such imperfectly controlled systems, open loop systems are not consciously designed into business organisations but some of the effects of an open loop system may accidentally occur. Where the feedback control loop breaks down (eg reports not prepared, not read, or prepared too late for action etc.) the effects of an open loop system would be achieved.

9. Timing of control action

Control action is likely to be most effective when the time lag between the output and corrective action – via the information loop – is as short as possible. Not only will the control action be able to commence earlier but it will be more appropriate. Too great a time lag may cause the resulting control action to be the opposite of what it should be.

Figure 8.4 shows the effect of time lag in control actions which transforms what should be negative feedback (ie damping oscillations) to positive feedback (ie amplifying oscillations).

Two factors which influence the speed of control are the organisational structure and the reporting period.

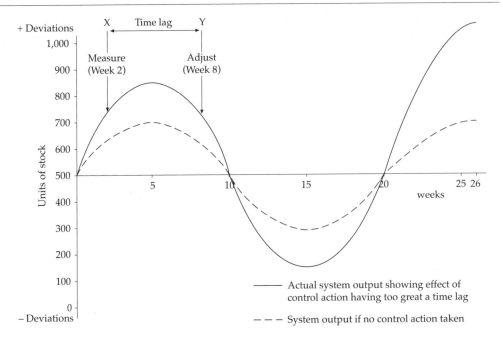

Figure 8.4 Effect of Time Lag in Control Actions

Point X: Measurement – Above standard and rising

Point Y: Adjustment – As consequence of measurement at
           point X, adjust in downwards direction

(Note that the system at point Y is already moving downward.
Adjustment, because of time lag, exaggerates oscillation.)

If an item of information has to pass through several levels of organisation's hierarchy before effective action can be taken then there will inevitably be delays.

Peter Drucker has said that decisions should always be made at the lowest possible level, consistent with the nature of the decision and as close to the scene of action as possible. Effective control and organisational protocol may thus be in conflict.

There is a tendency for some types of control information for example budgetary control and standard costing reports, to be produced in accordance with conventional accounting periods – monthly or four weekly – for all levels in the organisation. Because of the procedures involved, such reports are frequently not available until halfway through the next period and consequently much of the information is out-of-date and is misleading as a guide to action. There is no complete answer to this problem but there should be recognition that the most effective control period is not necessarily the same as an accounting period. At lower levels in the organisation, rapid feedback of a relatively small range of matters is likely to be more effective whilst at higher levels there is less immediacy.

10. Control systems and reward structures

The targets and levels of performance which are developed at the planning stage are used subsequently during the control process to monitor performance and to provide guidance as to the corrections required, if any. Performance targets should be set so that goal congruence is encouraged, ie the employee is given the maximum incentive to work towards the firm's goals. Control is effective when it induces behaviour which is in accord with achievement of the firm's objectives as specified in the planning budget. Where the organisation's reward-penalty system is consistent with the control systems there is evidence from Stedry, Arrow and others, that goal striving behaviour is encouraged.

The reward-penalty system of an organisation is the whole range of benefits and advantages which can be offered to, or withheld from, an employee. Typically these could include: promotions, wage and salary increments, bonuses, share options, profit sharing, company cars and other 'perks, holidays and so on.

If the control system is seen to be unconnected to the reward-penalty system of the organisation it will be perceived to be of little importance by the managers concerned and consequently it will tend to be ignored and so, by inference, will the organisation's objectives.

The incentive element discussed above is but one of the behavioural aspects of control systems, albeit an important one. Other behavioural considerations related directly to budgetary control are dealt with in the next chapter.

11. Law of requisite variety

Complex systems such as commercial and industrial firms, public authorities and other types of organisations contain a large number of elements and pursue a range of objectives. The law of requisite variety, discussed by Beer, Ashby and others, states that for full control the control system should contain variety at least equal to the system it is wished to control. The effect of this is that relatively simple control systems such as, for example, budgetary control, cannot be expected to control the multi-faceted activities of a complex organisation. At best such control systems may only control a relatively narrow aspect of the organisation's activities.

The developments in Activity-Based Accounting and the growth in the use of a range of performance indicators, financial and non-financial, relating to quality, reliability, lead times and so on can be seen as a conscious effort to broaden control systems. Some of these have already been dealt with, others are covered in later chapters.

A major source of the disturbances and variations in organisations is the influence of external variables upon the achievement of the firm's objectives. Many of these external factors are non-controllable so would not be included in a conventional control system which concentrates on controllable internal factors. However where external factors interact with internal variables it is necessary to include them in the overall control system in order that the interactions can be monitored. Examples of external factors which, although uncontrollable by the organisation, are likely to make changes necessary within the organisation, are a sudden increase in advertising expenditure by a competitor or the introduction of a discount campaign by a competitor.

12. Concentration of control effort

The full control cycle – continual monitoring of results, comparisons with plans, analysis of variations and reporting – is an expensive and time consuming process.

Accordingly it is important that the effort is concentrated where it can be most effective such as areas of high expenditure, vital operations and process, departments whose objectives are vital elements in the fulfilment of overall objectives and other similar areas.

A good example of this is the use of Pareto analysis (sometimes called ABC analysis or the 80/20 rule) in stock control. It is commonly found that 20% of the items account for 80% of the total inventory value and accordingly the major control effort would be concentrated on these items and correspondingly less time spent on detailed analysis and control of items which have insignificant values. The application of this simple concept is, of course, much wider than just inventory control and its use makes it more likely that control activities will be cost effective.

13. Feedforward

Close examination of any socio-technical system such as a private or public sector organisation will show that there are two types of control loop; *feedback loops* which monitor past results to detect and correct disturbances to the plan and *feedforward loops* which react to immediate or forthcoming dangers by making adjustments to the system in advance in order to cope with the problem in good time. In any organisation it is unlikely that pure feedforward or pure feedback control would operate in isolation. Feedback control on its own may be too slow and feedforward control too risky, so that some balance between the two is desirable. *Feedback monitors, feedforward warns.*

Figure 8.5 shows an outline of the two types of control.

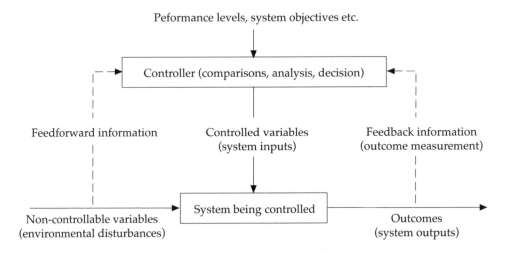

Figure 8.5 Feed forward and feedback loops

Feedforward uses flair and insight and relies heavily on information about the environment to anticipate critical changes in the non-controllable variables before they have an effect on the system. Feedforward is open-loop and does not feed back through the process as does closed-loop feedback control. The ability to sense impending problems and to take prior corrective action, which is the essence of feedforward control, are also the hallmarks of successful managers and businessmen.

14. Examples of feedforward

Practical examples of feedforward include the following: news of political instability in a country which was a major supplier of an important raw metal would cause astute buyers to buy before prices went up and their own stocks were depleted (in contrast a pure feedback system would not react until stocks had actually fallen), a company hearing of a possible industrial dispute would make alternative production arrangements, such as sub-contracting or engaging non-union labour, in advance of the withdrawal of labour and so on.

Figure 8.6 provides an example of feedforward and feedback in a marketing system.

Figure 8.6 Feedforward feedback in a marketing system

15. Summary

a) Control is concerned with the efficient use of resources to achieve a plan.

b) Major quantitative control systems are budgetary control, standard costing, inventory control, production control.

c) The elements of control are: a standard, measurement of actual, comparison, feedback, adjustment.

d) Control in organisations is carried out using information feedback loops.

e) Single loop feedback is the feedback of relatively small variations of actual compared to plan.

f) Negative feedback produces correction action in the opposite direction to that of the deviation.

g) Closed loop systems are those in which the control mechanism or system is an integral part of the system whereas in an open loop system control is external to the system.

h) Control actions must be correctly phased otherwise the action may become the opposite of that intended.

i) Where the reward-penalty system is consistent with the organisation's control system, goal striving behaviour is encouraged.

j) The law of requisite variety states that the control system should contain variety at least equal to the system it is wished to control.

k) Feedforward loops react to immediate or future disturbances in order to take corrective action.

16. Points to note

a) In practice it is very difficult to distinguish between control variations which arise from uncertainties in the environment and poor forecasting, and those due to sub-standard performance on the part of the manager concerned.

b) In Chapter 1 it was stressed that the overriding requirement for the management accountant was to produce information which is relevant for the intended purpose. This principle applies also to control information and it is vitally necessary that the information produced by the control system is based on genuine economic realities and not upon arbitrary conventions and assumptions.

c) When a variation between performance and plan occurs (eg a standard costing variance) always ask 'Is this due to managerial inefficiency or some other form of sub-standard performance or does the variation arise because the plan is inappropriate for current conditions?

Additional reading

Management Accounting, a conceptual approach; *Amey & Egginton* – Longman

Management Control Systems; Anthon;, *Dearden & Bedford* – Irwin

Performance Measurement in the Manufacturing sector – CIMA

Performance Measurement in Service Businesses – CIMA

Management, Control and Information; *Dew & Gee* – Macmillan

Measuring Corporate Performance; *Lothian* – CIMA

Management Information Systems; *Lucey* – Letts Educational (formerly DP Publications)

Self review questions

1. What is the relationship of planning and control? (2)
2. What are the elements of the control cycle? (4)
3. Draw a feedback loop. (5)
4. What is the distinction between single and double level feedback? (5)
5. Describe negative feedback. (6)
6. Distinguish between closed loop and open loop systems. (8)

7.   What is the reward-penalty system of the organisation? (10)
8.   Define the law of requisite variety. (11)
9.   What is the 80/20 rule? Why is it important? (11)
10. What is feedforward? (13)

9 Budgetary control

1. Objectives

After studying this chapter you will:

❒ understand the principles of budgetary control;

❒ know that flexible budgets are necessary for control to be effective;

❒ be aware of the hierarchy of control reporting;

❒ be able to design a budgetary control report;

❒ know what is meant by a significant variance;

❒ be able to calculate control limits;

❒ understand the vital importance of the behavioural aspects of budgeting;

❒ be able to describe activity-based budgeting

❒ understand the application of budgeting in not-for-profit organisations.

2. Responsibility accounting and budgetary control

Budgetary control, with budgetary planning described in Chapter 7, is part of the overall system of responsibility accounting within an organisation.

Responsibility accounting is a system of accounting in which costs and revenues are analysed in accordance with areas of personal responsibilities so that the performance of the budget holders can be monitored in financial terms.

Once the plans for the department have been agreed and embodied in a budget (ie budgetary planning), the budgetary control process begins. The process follows the classical control cycle whereby each period, usually monthly, the actual costs incurred are compared with the planned costs and the differences or variances are highlighted. Budgetary control is an example of management by exception where attention is directed to the few items which are not proceeding according to plan. The usual method of feedback is via budgetary control reports to the manager concerned (ie the effector) with copies to his superior.

The aim of budgetary control is to provide a formal basis for monitoring the progress of the organisation as a whole and of its component parts, towards the achievement of the objectives specified in the planning budgets. The budgetary control system provides some of the feedback necessary to be able to make corrections to current operations and activities in order to meet the original objectives and plans (ie single-loop feedback) and also some of the feedback upon which alterations to the plans are made, if necessary (ie double-loop feedback).

Budgetary control should not be viewed merely as a penny pinching, cost saving exercise but as a positive and integral part of the organisation's planning and control activities which should give due regard to organisational objectives, the needs and aspirations of the personnel involved, and to longer term as well as short term considerations.

3. Flexible budgets for control

To be able to make valid comparisons between actual costs incurred and a realistic budget allowance it is necessary for there to be flexible budgets. It will be recalled from Chapter 7 that these are budgets with each item of cost analysed into fixed and variable elements so that when the actual activity level is known the budget can be 'flexed' to produce a target cost allowance against which actual costs can be legitimately compared. From a control viewpoint a fixed budget is likely to be inappropriate unless by pure chance the actual level of activity turns out to be the same as the planned level. Thus the only feasible type of budget for control purposes is a flexible budget and all subsequent references in this chapter to 'budgets' mean 'flexible budgets'.

4. Controllable and non-controllable items

The basis of responsibility accounting is the partitioning of the whole organisation into responsibility or control centres. In the feedback comparisons the manager of a responsibility centre, the budget holder, should not be held responsible for an item over which he has no control.

Thus the items over which a manager has significant, though not necessarily complete, influence within a given time span are deemed controllable items and other items as non controllable. The terms, controllable and non controllable, only have meaning related to a particular responsibility centre. What is non-controllable for a lower level budget centre will be controllable at some higher level. It is important that budgetary control reports are consistent with the assigned responsibility at each level of the organisation and that a budget holder is only held responsible for items which he can genuinely influence.

Non controllable items may sometimes be included in the feedback reports purely for information and communication. This is particularly appropriate for higher level responsibility centres.

Every elements which appeared in the planning budgets will be controllable by someone in the organisation and should thus appear in their budget. This applies equally to such matters as working capital, cash flow, research and development, capital expenditure as well as to the more normal items such as wages, salaries and expenditure on materials.

5. The hierarchy of control

The system of responsibility accounting and budgetary control feedback is designed round the organisation structure of the firm. The feedback reports of the system should be designed to reflect the different levels of the organisation and the duties and scope of responsibility of the managers concerned. Each level of reporting should be interrelated with levels which are above and below the one concerned. In this way each manager is kept informed of his own performance and of the progress of budget holders junior to him for whom he is responsible. He also knows that managers senior to him will receive reports, suitably summarised and edited, on his own performance. This linked, hierarchical reporting system would, of course, be supported by regular meetings between budget holders and their superiors to review progress and performance and to discuss actions to be taken and the results of actions already taken.

The procedures outlined above are the very core of the control process from which it is to be hoped that appropriate corrective actions will result.

As an example, Figure 9.1 shows several typical levels of reporting from Production Supervisors through to the Managing Director. As each item of cost is reported at the ascending levels its treatment becomes less and less detailed with the scope of the budgetary control report becoming broader and broader in line with the increase in responsibilities.

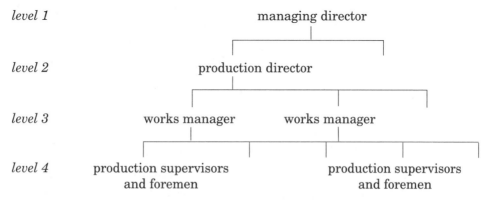

Figure 9.1 The hierarchy of reporting

Figure 9.2 (on the following page) shows for one item of cost, direct labour, the typical aggregation process that takes place as the level ascends together with the increase in scope of the budget reports for the particular budget holder. The reports range from those containing all the cost performance data of the whole organisation prepared for the Managing Director to the directly controllable production costs and expenses of a small section in one factory for a factory foreman.

6. Effective control reports

The budgetary control report is a major vehicle in the feedback process and to ensure maximum effectiveness it is important that its design, content, timing and general impact are given careful consideration. The general characteristics of information have been dealt with in Chapter 4 from which it will be remembered that it is actions which produce benefits whilst information only produces costs. It follows that a budgetary control report which is ignored or misunderstood will not lead to effective actions and so will be useless.

		Budget v Actual
Level 1	Managing Director	Total labour costs (plus costs and performance for whole organisation)
Level 2	Production Director	Total labour cost analysed works by works (plus costs and performance for the production function)
Level 3	Works Manager	Labour costs for works analysed by section, product group and labour type supported by summary of standard cost variances (plus costs and performance for the works)
Level 4	Production Supervisor	Labour costs analysed by section, by product group, by labour type and by operation. Supported by detailed standard costing variance analysis (plus costs and performance for section).

Figure 9.2 Report interrelationships for labour costs and scope of reports

The key items which should be shown are:

a) The budgeted level of costs and revenues for the period and year to date.

b) The actual level of costs and revenues for the period and year to date.

c) The variances between (a) and (b) together with the trends in variances.

d) An indication of what variances are significant together with, where possible, analysis and comment which can be used to bring the variances under control.

The recipients of budgetary control reports should be encouraged to make constructive criticisms of all aspects of the reporting procedure so that it is improved and made more effective.

A typical budgetary control report is shown in Figure 9.3 (following page)ß. It should be noted that the budgeted amounts would be the flexed budget allowances appropriate to the actual level of activity achieved.

7. The significance of variances

As pointed out in the previous chapter it is good practice to concentrate control efforts where they will be most useful. Rather than dissipating scarce and expensive managerial and accounting time into detailed investigations of all variances it is more cost-effective to focus attention on those variances which are considered *significant*. This means that there should be some way of deciding what is a 'significant variance'.

From a practical viewpoint a variance can be considered significant when it is of such a magnitude, relative to the budget or standard, that it will influence management's actions and decisions.

```
┌─────────────────────────────────────────────────────────────────────────────┐
│                    BUDGETARY CONTROL REPORT NO  ....                         │
│                                                                              │
│   BUDGET CENTRE    ----------------   DATE PREPARED ---------------------     │
│   BUDGET HOLDER    ----------------   BUDGETED ACTIVITY LEVEL ----------      │
│                         UP    -----                                          │
│   REPORT RELATIONSHIP   DOWN  -----   ACTUAL ACTIVITY LEVEL -----------       │
│                      ACCOUNTING PERIOD ------------------                     │
├────────────────┬──────────────────┬──────────────────┬─────────┬──────────┬─────────┤
│ BUDGETED ITEM  │  CURRENT PERIOD  │   YEAR TO DATE   │ TREND OF│SIGNIFICANT?│COMMENTS│
│                │                  │                  │ VARIANCE│          │        │
│ CODE│DESCRIPTION│BUDGET│ACTUAL│VARIANCE│BUDGET│ACTUAL│VARIANCE│        │          │        │
└────────────────┴──────────────────┴──────────────────┴─────────┴──────────┴─────────┘
```

Figure 9.3 Typical budgetary control report

Variances may arise for a number of reasons of which the following three are the most important.

a) Failure to meet a correctly set and agreed budget or standard.

b) An incorrectly set or out of date budget or standard.

c) Random deviations.

Variances arising from reasons (a) and (b), if of sufficient relative magnitude, are variances which require further investigation and possible management action. This action may be to bring operations into line with the agreed plans or it may be to make adjustments to the plan itself. Random deviations, ie variations which have arisen by chance are, by definition, uncontrollable.

The problem remains of how to determine whether a variation from a budget or standard is attributable to chance and therefore not significant or whether it is due to a controllable cause and is of sufficient magnitude to be classed as significant.

8. Budgets and standards as ranges

Typically a budget allowance or a standard cost is shown as a single figure but more realistically it should be considered as a band or range of values with the budgeted allowance or standard as the centre value.

This is illustrated in Figure 9.4 (following page).

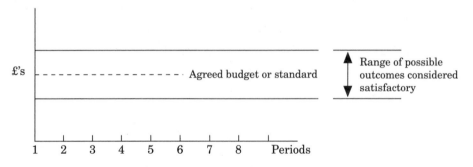

Figure 9.4

If the actual result falls within the band it is considered satisfactory and the variance would be deemed to be not significant. If the actual result was outside the range it would be considered to be significant and a fuller investigation would probably be mounted. When used in this way the range of values shown in Figure 4 is known as a *Control Band* and the upper and lower limits known as *Control Limits*.

9. Setting control limits

The control limits may be set by estimation or statistical analysis.

a) Estimation. This approach is the most commonly used and bases the control limits on judgement and experience. Typically a figure of ± 5% is used and variances within this range would be deemed not significant. Although obviously lacking any statistical rigour this approach is a pragmatic one and implicitly uses the same concepts as more sophisticated methods.

b) Statistical analysis. Up until now the term 'significant' has been used in a general sense. More precisely a variance which is statistically significant is one which is of such a magnitude that it is unlikely to have arisen by chance.

Statistical probability tests based on the properties of normal distributions can be used to determine whether differences from budget or standard arise from chance (ie not significant) or from controllable causes (ie significant).

To be able to set control limits which can be used to determine statistical significance is dependent on a number of statistical assumptions and upon being able to calculate or estimate the standard deviation.

The major assumptions are:

i) The actual values which are compared with the budgeted allowance or standard are drawn from a single, homogeneous population.

ii) The budgeted allowance or standard is the arithmetic mean of the population. This means that the budget or standard is set at an attainable level.

iii) Any variations from budget are deemed to arise from chance.

These various assumptions are necessary in order to utilise the known properties of the normal distribution.

Therefore assuming that the population (used in the statistical sense) of actual values is normally distributed about the mean (or budget), control limits can be set at any required level, for example:

5 % control limits are set at mean ± 1.96 standard deviations

2 % control limits are set at mean ± 2.33 standard deviations

1 % control limits are set at mean ± 2.57 standard deviations

0.2% control limits are set at mean ± 3.09 standard deviations

For example, the budgeted allowance for a given cost is £2,500 and from analysis of past records of cost behaviour the standard deviation is estimated to be £90.

❏ what are the 2% control limits?

❏ what is the meaning of such limits?

❏ show the limits graphically.

Now: 2% control limits   = mean ± 2.33 s.d.

= £2,500 ± 2.33 (90)

= £2,500 ± 210 (to nearest whole number)

Thus: Upper control limit   = £2,500 + 210 = £2,710

Lower control limit   = £2,500 – 210 = £2,290

Meaning of control limits. If chance alone causes variations from standard, then 98% of deviations should fall within the range of the mean (or budget) ± 2.33 standard deviations. If a deviation falls outside these limits, ie above £2,710 or below £2,290 then the variance is said to be *significant at the 2% level.*

Graph of control limits

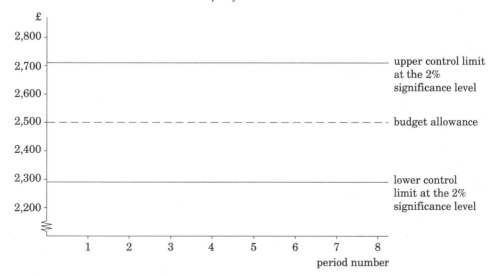

Although setting control limits by statistical methods appears to be more rigorous it must be realised that some of the necessary statistical assumptions regarding the distribution of actual values may not be valid in practice and also that the calculation or estimation of the standard deviation may be difficult.

10. To investigate or not to investigate

Judgement will always be required whether to investigate the causes of a variance. Investigations cost money and may cause operational disruptions whilst the benefits gained may be slight. Mechanical rules could be set up to decide upon an investigation, for example, 'investigate all variances which fall outside the control limits described previously'. Such rules formalise the decision process but are not necessarily cost-effective in deciding whether a system is out of control. If it was required to derive a quantitative decision rule whether to investigate or not this could be done using elementary decision theory, provided the necessary information was available. To illustrate this, assume the following factors:

p = probability of budget being found to be under control when a variance is investigated.

$1 - p$ = probability of budget being found to be out of control when a variance is investigated.

I = Investigation costs

B = Benefits gained from an investigation.

These factors can be set out as follows:

	Budget under control (p)	Budget out of control ($1 - p$)	Expected value of decision
Decision			
Investigate	$-I$	$B - I$	$-pI + (1 - p)(B - I)$
Do not investigate	0	0	0

Example

Detailed records have been kept of a department's budget variances, the average costs of previous investigations and the benefits gained when an out of control state is corrected; thus:

p = probability of budget been found to be under control = 0.8; I = £240; B = £2,000.

Assuming that past conditions will apply in the future is it worth investigating a significant variance?

Solution

EV of decision to investigate $= -(0.8 \times 240) + (1 - 0.8)(2,000 - 240)$

$$= + £160$$

∴ worthwhile to investigate.

It will be realised that the above procedure is only superficially objective. It presupposes knowledge of probabilities, costs and revenues that is unlikely to be encountered in practice. As previously stated, judgement will always be required.

Note:

The whole of the above section on the significance of variances, the setting of control limits and the decision to investigate variances is applicable to both budgets and standard costs, which are dealt with in the following chapter.

11. Quantities not prices

The statistical concepts covered in the preceding paragraphs deal with the random variations which arise from the human element. This could be variations in the time taken to produce a part or the different amounts of material used by an operative. Because of human factors there will always be some variances even if there is no specific cause. This makes variances which arise from human induced quantity fluctuations more suitable for statistical analysis. These variances include: labour and overhead efficiency, material usage and overhead volume.

Price and expenditure variances are different in character to quantity variances and are less suitable for the type of statistical analysis described.

12. Behavioural aspects of budgeting

An understanding only of the technical aspects of the budgetary process is not sufficient for the management accountant. The human, social and organisational factors which are involved at all stages in budgeting are of critical importance and cannot be ignored. There has been considerable research into the behavioural aspects of budgeting but as with many other facets of human behaviour the findings are complex, imperfectly understood and sometimes contradictory so broad generalisations are difficult to make. On one point there does seem to be agreement and that is that budgeting is not considered by participants as a neutral, objective, purely technical process which is a view adopted by many accountants.

The human, subjective elements cannot be overemphasised – budgeting is not a mechanistic, technical procedure. Its success is totally dependent upon the goodwill and co-operation of the participants. Without this budgeting will become merely a paper exercise with no real impact on the operations of the organisation except perhaps negatively.

Many of the behavioural problems with budgeting arise from managements' attempts to make the budget perform different functions; some of which are to an extent incompatible. These functions include:

a)   acting as a target.

b)   acting as a plan.

c)   being a control measure.

d)   a means of motivating managers.

e)   acting as a device for measuring performance.

f)   promoting a goal congruence.

g)   acting as a medium of communication and co-ordination.

h)   acting as a framework for the delegation of authority

and so on.

It will be apparent from the above list that it is almost inevitable that difficulties will arise in setting and using budgets which attempt to cope with so many disparate tasks.

The following paragraphs explore some of the more relevant behavioural research findings about budgets and the budgeting process.

13. **Budgets as targets**

Numerous researchers (for example Argyris, Hofstede, French, Kay and Meyer) have found that clearly defined quantitative targets can improve motivation and thus produce better performance than if no target existed. This raises the problem of the level of performance to be incorporated as the target. Should the budget targets reflect senior management's expectations or employee aspirations (ie the level of performance the employee hopes to attain)?

Hofstede's research indicated that:

a) very easy targets will be achieved but do not motivate managers to achieve their full potential;

b) very difficult targets will not be accepted and cause managers to give up trying, so that their performance will be lower than if realistic targets had been set;

c) the best performance levels are likely to be achieved by setting the toughest target that will be accepted by the manager as his own personal goal, ie equivalent to the manager's aspiration level.

Research has shown that budgets do not necessarily lead to improved performance and that the budget level which leads to the best performance is unlikely to be set on the majority of occasions. If budgets are set at the level which will achieve maximum performance then adverse variances are likely. These must be treated sympathetically; if they are used as a pressure device budget holders will try to obtain looser budgets in the future either by under performing or by political bargaining. These easier budgets will produce fewer adverse variances but overall performance will be lower.

Aspiration levels are not constant and are affected by the budget holders previous performance compared with the budget level. Becker and Green found that:

a) where performance is well below the budget then the budget should be revised downward sufficiently for it to be perceived as attainable. If this is not done the budget holder will become discouraged and his aspiration level, and future performance, will fall;

b) where performance is just below the budget level (resulting in an adverse variance) sympathetic and non-punitive feedback of results will normally lead to an increase in aspiration level and performance;

c) where performance meets or slightly exceeds the level in the budget it is likely that the aspiration level will increase and the budget holder's potential performance will be greater. In these circumstances a budget revision could be made.

14. **Motivation**

Motivation is the need to achieve a selected target or objective and the resulting drive and determination that influences actions directed towards the selected target. It is clearly desirable that managers and supervisors are motivated by the budgeting system and there is some evidence that clearly defined targets and objectives can influence motivation in a positive manner.

Research shows that although budgeting systems sometimes gave positive motivational effects all too often they produce undesirable negative reactions.

The adverse effects can occur at both the planning and the implementation stages thus:

At the *planning stage* managers may

a) build in slack unnecessarily;

b) complain of lack of time for budgeting;

c) argue that a formal budget is too restrictive and that they should be allowed more flexibility in making operational decisions;

d) not co-ordinate their budgets with those of other budget centres;

e) base future plans purely on past results with no examination of alternative options and new ideas;

f) set out to show the budget is unworkable especially if they have not been connected with the budget's preparation and it has been decided for them by senior management.

At the *implementation stage* managers may

a) not co-operate and co-ordinate with other budget holders;

b) put in just enough effort to achieve budget targets without trying to beat those targets;

c) tolerate poor and inaccurate recording and classification of costs;

d) ensure that they spend up to their budget, even if not necessary, to ensure it is not tightened in the future;

e) concentrate on short-term factors to the detriment of more important longer term consequences;

f) seek to blame the budgeting system for any problems which occur.

It is obviously of importance that accountants and senior management try to develop and implement budgeting systems in a manner that is acceptable to the budget holders and produces positive effects.

However, Argyris in his researches often found that budgets were considered as pressure devices and were viewed as part of a management policing system. Naturally enough in such circumstances the budgeting system had a demotivating effect – the opposite to that intended. To foster motivation, acceptance by the managers concerned of their budgets and of the levels of performance contained in the budgets is absolutely vital.

The effect on motivation of incentives should not be underestimated. As pointed out in the previous chapter, research studies carried out by Stedry and others show that there are positive gains in motivation when the reward – penalty systems of the organisation is consistent with its control system.

There is an intuitive feeling that participation by budget holders in the budget and target setting process is likely to affect motivation and this aspect of budgeting has been extensively researched.

15. Participation in budgeting

Participation in budget and target setting means that, before budgets are finalised, there are frank discussions with budget holders who are thus in a position to influence the levels of their budgets and targets. Thus defined, it would seem to be self evidently a good thing but the research does not produce a clear cut picture.

Some studies show that participation leads to more positive attitudes and higher performance whilst others find the opposite. For example studies by Kenis and Collins showed a positive correlation of attitude and performance with participation whilst other studies by such researchers as, Bryan and Locke, Stedry and others showed a negative relationship between participation and performance.

An additional problem is that different organisations use the word participation to describe quite different activities. These can range from true participation, which is where the budget holder can exert real influence, to what is described by Argyris as 'pseudo-participation'. This is where budgets are discussed with lower level management but with the primary aim of obtaining formal acceptance of budgets and performance levels previously determined by top management.

16. Making participation work better

The research has identified various factors which help the organisation to decide whether or not participation is worthwhile and, if so, how it can be made most effective. The factors include; the cultural setting of the organisation, the work situation, the management style of the organisation, the relationship between supervisors and the supervised, the extent of decentralisation, the type of structure and business, and so on.

As examples; Stedry found that a more authoritarian and less participative management style led to higher performance, Hopwood found that in constrained and programmed environments, participation was much less effective than those where flexibility and motivation were important.

Where individuals feel that they have more control over their own destinies and the organisation has genuine decentralised decision making participation appears to have positive effects. Conversely some people do not welcome independence and respond more positively to a more authoritative and less participative approach. It does seem that participation in the right circumstances can improve the budget holder's attitude to the budget system and make it more likely that he will accept the targets contained in the budget. However, it is apparent from the research that participation must be used with care and applied selectively having regard to social and behavioural factors. On occasions, imposed budgets and an authoritarian style will lead to higher performance.

17. Goal congruence

This is there the goals of individuals and groups coincide with the goals and objectives of the organisation so that individuals and groups acting in their own self interest are also acting in accordance with the higher organisational goals. This ideal is difficult to achieve in its entirety but recognition must be given to the fact that organisational objectives cannot be set and implemented through the budgeting system without consideration of the interaction of local group and departmental objectives.

Hopwood's researches suggest that there are numerous problems in achieving goal congruence. Objectives are rarely clearly defined and there may be numerous objectives in the one organisation, some of which may conflict. Further, different managers may perceive their objectives differently and imperfect information, departmental rivalries, different and conflicting reward structures and other practical realities make perfect goal congruence extremely unlikely.

Ideally, budgets should help to achieve the overall objectives of the organisation, at least in the short term. However, Hopwood suggests that although the accounting system of budgeting is often dominant as a means of setting short-term goals, it has severely limited capacity to do so because it emphasises profit to the exclusion of other goals even though estimates of costs and revenues are subject to political manipulation by budget centre managers.

18. Budgets and performance evaluation

Budgets are one of the accounting measures which are used to assess a manager's performance. The reward system of the organisation (ie pay, promotion, etc) is often linked to the achievement of certain levels of performance, frequently measured in accounting terms. It is conventionally assumed that by establishing formal performance measurement and rewarding individuals for their performance they will be encouraged to maximise their contribution towards the organisation's objectives. In this way it is assumed that goal congruence will be achieved. On the other hand, if performance measures and the way they are used, motivate managers in ways that do not contribute to organisational objectives this is a dysfunctional consequence and leads to a lack of goal congruence.

Unfortunately, the research evidence suggests that all too often accounting performance measures lead to a lack of goal congruence. Managers seek to improve their performance on the basis of the indicator used even though this is not in the best interests of the organisation as a whole. For example Likert found that concentration on short term cost reductions produced damaging longer term effects on labour turnover and absenteeism which were dysfunctional. This problem occurs not only with budgets but with other types of accounting measurement. For example, assessing management performance by the Return on Capital Employed (discussed in detail later in the book) has been found by Dearden to cause managers to delay making new investments which are in the interests of the organisation as a whole but which would cause their own R.O.C.E. to fall. This is a clear example of sub-optimality discussed earlier.

We should not be surprised that concentration on a single measure or target causes problems. The Law of Requisite Variety, explained in the previous chapter, states that for full control the control system must have as much variety as the system being controlled so that concentration on a single measure (a budget level, return on capital employed or whatever) cannot hope to control adequately a complex system. Numerous organisations have attempted to deal with the problem of assessing managerial performance using multiple criteria and one of the pioneers was the General Electric Company of America.

General Electric identified eight key result areas which are summarised below:

❑ Productivity

❑ Personnel development

❑ Profitability

❑ Market position

❑ Product leadership

❑ Employee attitudes

❑ Public responsibility

❑ Balance between short- and long-term goals.

Within each key area various performance targets were established and a manager would be expected to achieve a satisfactory performance level across all eight facets. A high score on profitability would not compensate for poor performance elsewhere.

19. How budgets are used

Behavioural problems also arise from the way that senior management use the budgeting system. Budgets and indeed all accounting information should be interpreted and used with care and tact.

Hopwood found three distinct styles of using budget and cost data:

a) Budget-constraint style:

This is where the accounting information was primarily to ensure adherence to short-term cost levels. Adverse cost variances would be used to censure a budget holder regardless of performance elsewhere.

b) Profit-conscious style:

Here the emphasis was on the long run effectiveness of the budget holder's contribution to the organisation's goals. In this case the minimisation of long run costs was seen as most desirable.

c) Non-accounting style:

Accounting data played only a minor role in assessing performance.

Hopwood found that the first two styles were more effective in concentrating attention on costs than the non-accounting style. There was evidence that the profit-conscious style promoted a more positive attitude whereas the short-term emphasis on cost levels caused tensions, budget manipulation and a less active involvement with the financial well being of organisation.

From this and other research it is clear that accountants must use budget and accounting data in a supportive not threatening manner without an over emphasis on short-term budget compliance. Accounting information should assist managers to manage their departments more efficiently. It should not be seen as negative and something which is used to find faults. If the budgeting and accounting systems are seen as providing genuine assistance to a manager there will be fewer behavioural problems, motivation will increase, and dysfunctional effects minimised.

20. Benefits and problems of budgeting

Budgetary planning and control systems, in varying degrees of complexity and coverage, can be found in most organisations of any size in both the public and private sectors. There are genuine benefits to be gained from the use of such systems but these benefits do not automatically accrue. They have to be worked for and there must be continual appraisal of all aspects of the budgetary system and of its administration. An awareness of the problems which may be encountered and of the factors which prevent the most effective use of budgetary systems is also valuable in order that, where possible, these may be overcome.

21. Benefits of budgeting

a) It is the major formal way in which the organisational objectives are translated into specific plans, tasks and objectives related to individual managers and supervisors. It should provide clear guidelines for current operations.

b) It is an important medium of communication for organisational plans and objectives and of the progress towards meeting those objectives.

c) The development of budgets (done properly) helps to achieve co-ordination between the various departments and functions of the organisation.

d) The involvement of all levels of management with setting budgets, the acceptance of defined targets, the two way flow of information and other facets of a properly organised budgeting system all help to promote a coalition of interest and to increase motivation.

e) Management's time can be saved and attention directed to areas of most concern by the 'exception principle' which is at the heart of budgetary control.

f) Performance of all levels is systematically reported and monitored thus aiding the control of current activities.

g) The investigation of operations and procedures, which is part of budgetary planning and the subsequent monitoring of expenditure, may lead to reduced costs and greater efficiency.

h) The regular systematic monitoring of results compared to plan (ie the budget) provides information upon which either, to adjust current operations to bring them into line with the previous plan or, to make adjustments to the plan itself where this becomes necessary.

i) The integration of budgets makes possible better cash and working capital management and makes stock and buying policies more realistic.

22. Problems associated with budgeting

Various problems and difficulties which may occur in connection with budgeting are given below but it does not necessarily follow that they will occur in any given organisation.

a) There may be too much reliance on the technique as a substitute for good management.

b) The budgetary system, perhaps because of undue pressure or poor human relations, may cause antagonism and decrease motivation.

c) Variances are just as frequently due to changing circumstances, poor forecasting or general uncertainties as due to managerial performance.

d) Budgets are developed round existing organisational structures and departments which may be inappropriate for current conditions and may not reflect the underlying economic realities.

e) The very existence of well documented plans and budgets may cause inertia and lack of flexibility in adapting to change.

f) There is a major problem in setting the levels of attainment to be included in budgets and standards. Although much research has been done in this area by Stedry, Becker and Green and others, knowledge is still incomplete. There are many factors to be considered including: the aspiration level of individuals, group pressures, the extent of participation, past performances and so on. This is an unresolved problem which is present in every budgetary and standard costing system.

g) The inherent lags and delays in the system. For example the actual results for June are typically available mid to late July and would be compared with June's budget which itself would be based on estimates and forecasts which were made up to 12 months previously. The resulting variances may then be used to guide management's actions for August. Because of these delays and lags there is the real possibility that the budgets and resulting variances are of little value as a guide to current operations.

Conventional budgeting, as described so far, concentrates on expenditures by budget centres under conventional cost headings eg salaries, telephone, travelling expenses and so on. These are known as *Line Item Budgets* as there is a line for each expenditure item.

Traditional budgeting systems have been criticised as it is claimed that they do not support the drive for continuous improvement, nor do they relate expenditures to the activities which cause them. It is claimed that budgeting based on activity analysis overcomes some of these problems.

23. Activity-based budgeting (ABB)

ABB, sometimes termed Activity Cost Management, is a planning and control system which seeks to support the objective of continuous improvement. It is a development of conventional budgeting systems and is based on activity analysis techniques. It will be recalled that these were described when Activity-Based Costing (ABC) was covered previously. In outline this required the identification of the *activities* of the organisation, establishing the factors which cause costs the cost drivers, and then collecting the costs of the activities in *cost pools*.

ABB recognises that:

a) It is activities which drive costs and the aim is to control the causes (drivers) of costs directly rather than the costs themselves. In the long-run, costs will be managed and better understood.

b) Not all activities add value so it is essential to differentiate and examine activities for their value-adding potential.

c) The majority of activities in a department are driven by demands and decisions beyond the immediate control of the budget holder. Conventional budgets, expressed in financial terms against established cost headings, ignore this causal relationship.

d) More immediate and relevant performance measures are required than are found in conventional budgeting systems. These consist exclusively of traditional financial measures which are insufficient to fulfil the objective of continuous improvement. Additional measures are required which should focus on factors which drive activities, the quality of the activities undertaken, the responsiveness to change and so on.

In an article in Management Accounting in January 1991 Brimson and Fraser claim that ABB provided stronger links between an organisation's strategic objectives and the objectives of the individual activities within a business for which departmental managers are responsible. Additionally, they point out that an important strength of ABB is its ability to tackle cross-organisational issues by a participative approach and activity analysis techniques, all of which promote continuous improvement.

The outline of ABB given by Brimson and Fraser is shown in Figure 9.5.

24. Features of ABB

The key features of ABB can be summarised thus:

a) A clear link between strategic objectives and planning and the tactical planning of the ABB process;

b) The use of activity analysis to relate costs to activities;

c) The identification of cost improvement opportunities;

d) A focused, participative approach by all levels to guide and sustain continuous improvement.

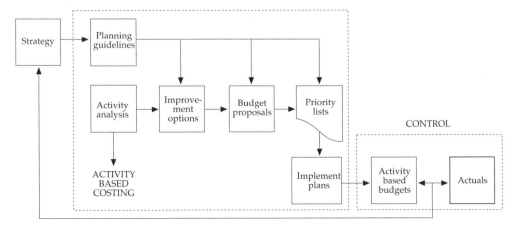

Figure 9.5

In developing activity-based budgets there will inevitably be subjective judgements and approximations. Any activity costs calculated will not be precise but this is not the real point. The objective is to develop an analysis which produces relevant information and pointers for management. It will, for example, highlight the approximate cost of activities, encourage new thinking (can the activity be carried out more effectively?, does the activity represent value for money?), assist management in resource allocation and so on.

25. Illustration of ABB

A Purchasing Department has two main activities; investigating and liaising with suppliers and issuing purchase orders. Two major cost drivers have been identified: the number of suppliers and the number of purchase orders placed. The resources and costs of the department have largely been spread over the two main cost drivers. The balance of costs have been termed 'Department sustaining costs'. These include some general clerical costs and part of the manager's costs. Based on the activity expected for the next period, cost driver volumes of 270 suppliers and 1,850 purchase orders have been forecast. Using these volumes and cost analysis, cost driver units and resource item costs have been budgeted for the department after discussion with the Departmental manager. The budget is as shown on the following page.

Notes:

a) The apportionment of costs to activities will, of course, be partly subjective. The object however is that the resource has to be justified in supporting one or more of the activities or the sustaining function. There is no place to hide the costs.

b) ABB highlights the cost of activities and thus encourages new thinking.

c) ABB enables a more focused view of cost control because the activity level is taken into account. Trends can be monitored and comparison with other organisations can be made. This is known as *benchmarking*.

d) The cost driver rates of £150 and £30 are used in calculating the product costs in the Activity-Based Costing system.

e) The identification of activities and their costs helps to focus attention on those activities which add value and those that do not.

Budget for Purchasing Department

Cost	Cost Drivers	No of suppliers	No of purchase orders	Dept sustaining cost	Total
		£	£	£	£
Management salaries		12,000	2,000	18,000	32,000
Clerical salaries		3,000	21,500	6,500	31,000
Space costs		1,000	14,500	2,000	17,500
Consumables, travelling etc		17,500	3,000	4,500	25,000
Information technology		3,000	8,500	1,000	12,500
Other costs		4,000	6,000	7,500	17,500
Total		40,500	55,500	39,500	135,500
Activity volumes		270	1,850	–	–
Cost/unit of cost driver		£150	£30	£39,500	

26. Possible problems with activity-based analysis

An activity-based approach may not be always suitable for month-to-month monitoring because of short-term fluctuations. If, for example, the number of purchase orders goes up by 20% in a month and resources stay the same the cost per order will decrease. However, if the increase in activity lasts long enough there is likely to be the need for more staff, overtime and so on. The inevitable variability in the cost per activity directs attention to whether resources are being used effectively and what levels may be required in the future.

There is also the need to guard against the notion that a selected cost driver provides a comprehensive basis for controlling costs. The cost levels of most activities are determinable in a more complex manner than can be explained by a single work load measure. Over-concentration on one performance measure can produce dysfuntional effects. In the Purchasing Department illustration above, the staff can decrease the cost per purchase order simply by splitting large orders into several smaller ones yet this could well have adverse longer-term effects.

27. Budgeting in non-profit organisations

Non-profit organisations (NPOs) include central and local government, schools and colleges, charities, hospitals and a range of other organisations.

Although many of the principles of budgeting apply equally to NPOs and to profit-seeking organisations a key difference is that the latter organisations' budgets focus on the relationships between inputs (expenditure) and outputs (sales revenue). In NPOs outputs are much more difficult to measure so traditionally budgeting has been concerned with inputs only. In effect, the budgetary system is concerned with making sure that for each expenditure heading actual spending does not exceed the budget authorised cash limit. This has been criticised by Farry for concentrating on what the money is spent on rather than what is obtained for the money.

Another problem for NPOs is that many of their activities and the level of costs, are determined elsewhere and thus are much less controllable. Take, for example, the budget for a Local Managed School. A major item, often accounting for 70% of costs, is teachers' salaries. The level of salaries is determined nationally and legislation and norms largely govern the number of teachers. As a consequence, a high proportion of costs are not controllable to any significant degree at the school level.

28. Types of budgets in NPOs

As NPOs vary considerably in size, structure and objectives it is inevitable that the budgets prepared also vary.

However a major influence on budgeting for NPOs comes from the typical budgets prepared in Local Authorities and Government Departments. These typically include:

a) the Capital Budget covering capital expenditure during the year;

b) the Revenue Budget, covering the 'running costs' of the authority;

c) the Manpower or Personnel Budget;

d) the Cash Budget usually combining short-term cash control and longer-term financing sources (including grants, taxes, sales etc).

The budgets become the key tool of financial management. Control is exercised during budget preparation and during the operating period.

29. Budgeting systems used in NPOs

Many approaches are used in NPOs, including zero-based budgeting and PPBS (covered earlier) and incremental budgeting. In spite of the theoretical advantages claimed for zero-based budgeting and for PPBS, incremental budgeting is traditionally used. In general the new budget tends to be based on the current estimates plus an amount extra for inflation and any known mandatory extensions of service and perhaps with a reduction for planned cost-cutting economics.

The incremental approach is defended by the following arguments.

a) Most activities are fundamental or determined by legislation so will continue year after year.

b) A thorough analysis, each year of all policies, activities and costs (eg in zero-based budgeting) is impossible and probably unnecessary anyway.

c) The marginal changes in the budget tend to be the only 'controllable' parts.

d) Inter-departmental conflicts are avoided by narrowing down the areas open to the incremental changes.

30. Criticisms of traditional budgeting in NPOs

As is to be expected there are several criticisms of traditional budgeting systems in NPOs. These include:

a) A one-year planning cycle is too short for many activities;

b) Incremental budgeting focuses attention on expenditure headings (eg salaries, heating etc) rather than the purposes for which the spending will be incurred;

c) the budgets lack flexibility and do not encourage efficiency or economy. Too often an increase in spending on inputs is automatically assumed to imply an increase in the provision of the service's outputs. Experience and common sense suggest that this is far from true.

Throughout the 1980s and early 1990s the UK Government has attempted to make all public sector organisations more efficient and cost-effective. This has been done in numerous ways. Examples include: competitive tendering for services such as refuse collection, maintenance and so on, the creation of Trust Hospitals and a market for health care in the National Health Service, the Local Management of Schools.

The general process has been termed getting Value-For-Money (VFM). VFM and VFM audits are covered later in the book.

31. Summary

a) Budgetary control is part of the organisation's system of responsibility accounting.

b) Flexible budgets are essential to produce realistic budget allowances against which to compare actual results.

c) A budget holder can only be held responsible for controllable items, ie those items over which he has significant influence.

d) Budgets and the subsequent reporting procedures are developed in accordance with the organisation structure of the firm.

e) The design, content and timing of budgetary control reports must be given careful consideration to ensure maximum effectiveness.

f) To concentrate attention it is necessary to determine what are significant variances.

g) Budgets or standards should more properly be considered as a range of values round the agreed budget or standard.

h) Control limited can be set by estimation or statistical analysis based on certain assumptions and the properties of the normal distribution.

i) Variances which are within the control limits are not significant and those outside would be deemed significant.

j) Typical control limits are:

    5% control limits   mean ± 1.96 s.d.
    1% control limits   mean ± 2.57 s.d.

k) The behavioural aspects of budgeting are of critical importance even though imperfectly understood.

l) Goal congruence should be encouraged and is where individual and organisational goals coincide.

m) Where budgets are seen merely as pressure devices and as part of a management policing system, motivation likely to decrease. Real participation promotes a coalition of interests which increases goal congruence and motivation.

n) Dysfunctional behaviour is any behaviour which reduces organisational efficiency and should be minimised where possible.

o) The major benefits of budgeting systems, assuming they are properly planned and administered are: communication, co-ordination, motivation, the promotion of goal congruence, better control and possible cost reductions.

p) The main problems which may be encountered with budgetary systems include: antagonism and demotivation, difficulties in determining real variances, may cause inflexibility, setting the appropriate level of attainment, lags and delays in the system.

q) Activity-Based Budgeting (or Activity Cost Management) recognises that it is activities that need to be controlled as these cause the costs.

r) ABB provides a clear link between strategic objectives and tactical planning and seeks to foster continuous improvement.

s) Budgeting in Non-Profit Organisations (NPOs) has many similarities to profit-seeking organisations, but there is a greater concentration on inputs (expenditures) partly because outputs are often difficult to measure.

32. Points to note

a) The type of responsibility centres discussed in this chapter are budget centres, which may be a single cost centre or a group of cost centres. With increasing amounts of responsibility accorded to managers, responsibility centres may be termed profit centres or investment centres. These latter types of responsibility centres are dealt with in the section on Performance Appraisal.

b) Care must be taken that, with so much attention directed to the exceptions or variances, the levels of the standards and budgets themselves are not neglected.

c) Even if a variance is deemed to be significant it does not follow that there will be a full investigation. The decision to investigate or not is a cost/benefit exercise whereby the investigation costs are compared with the likely benefits.

d) The variance control chart shown in the chapter is similar to those used in Quality Control Procedures. In such applications measurements of, say, the diameter of a component are plotted on the chart so that the trend of deviations can be seen easily and this enables corrections to be made, if necessary, even before a deviation goes beyond the control limits.

e) Most readers of this book will be accountants or intending accountants so that it is worth pointing out that one of the common attitudes of accountants is a potential source of friction particularly when related to control systems. Accountants regard it as a success when they are able to show evidence of waste or inefficiency and a considerable part of their training is directed to this end. To the line managers and staff involved in the control system these events are effectively failures or mistakes and it is a natural reaction, to a greater or lesser extent, to resent failures being pointed out.

Additional reading

Management Control in Non-Profit Organisations; *Anthony & Young* – Irwin

Management Accounting And Behavioural Science; *Caplan – Addison* Wesley

Management, Control and Information; Dew & Gee – Macmillan

Accounting for Management Control; *Emmanuel, Otley & Merchant* – Chapman & Hall

The Game Of Budget Control; *Hofstede* – Tavistock

Accounting and Human Behaviour; *Hopwood* – Prentice Hall

Management Accounting in the Public Sector; *Pendlebury* – Butterworth-Heinemann

Budget Control and Cost Behaviour; *Stedry* – Prentice Hall

Self review questions

1. What is responsibility accounting? (2)
2. What is the major aim of budgetary control? (2)
3. What type of budgets should be used in budgetary control? (3)
4. Distinguish between controllable and non-controllable items. (4)
5. What relationship is there between the organisation structure and budgetary control? (5)
6. What are the key items which should appear on a budgetary control report? (6)
7. How do variances arise? (7)
8. What is a significant variance? (7)
9. How can control limits be set? (8)
10. What are the major assumptions necessary in order to set control limits by statistical methods? (9)
11. What are the different functions a budget attempts to achieve? (12)

12. What level of target should be incorporated into a budget? (13)
13. What is a person's aspiration level? (13)
14. What is motivation and how is it affected by the budget process? (14)
15. What is participation and is it always effective? (15)
16. What is pseudo-participation? (15)
17. In what circumstances is participation most effective? (16)
18. What is goal congruence and why is it difficult to achieve? (17)
19. What are the behavioural problems associated with accounting measures for performance evaluation? (18)
20. How can Requisite Variety be included in performance measurement? (18)
21. What are the behavioural consequences of the way that budgets are used? (19)
22. Give six benefits of a properly organised budgeting system. (21)
23. What problems may be encountered in implementing and operating a budgeting system? (22)
24. What is Activity-Based Budgeting (ABB)? (23)
25. What are the features of ABB? (24)
26. What are the major differences between budgeting in non-profit organisations and those that are profit seeking? (27)
27. What types of budget are found? (28)
28. What are the criticisms made of traditional budgeting in NPOs ? (30)

10 Standard costing I

1. Objectives

After studying this chapter you will:

❒ understand the technique of standard costing and its objectives;

❒ know the various types of standards;

❒ understand how standards are developed;

❒ realise the importance of the behavioural aspects of standard costing;

❒ understand the principles of variance analysis;

❒ know the relationship between variances;

❒ be able to calculate material, labour and overhead variances;

❒ know the reasons why variances arise and how they are dealt with in the accounts;

❒ be able to calculate the activity, capacity and efficiency ratios.

2. Standard costing explained

Standard costing is an important control technique which follows the feedback control cycle discussed previously. Standard costing establishes predetermined estimates of the cost of products or services, collects actual costs and output data and compares the actual results with the predetermined estimates. The predetermined costs are known as *standard costs* and the difference between standard and actual is known as a *variance*. The process by which the total variance or difference between standard and actual cost is subdivided is known as *variance analysis*.

In practice, standard costing is a detailed process requiring considerable accounting and technical development work before it can be used effectively. It can be used in a variety of costing situations, batch and mass production, process manufacture, transport, certain aspects of repetitive clerical work and even in jobbing manufacture where there is some standardisation of components or parts. In principle there is no reason why standard costing should not be applied in service industries providing that a realistic cost unit can be established. Undoubtedly, however, the greatest benefit is gained when the manufacturing or production process involves a substantial degree of repetition. The major applications in practice are in mass production and repetitive assembly work.

3. Objectives of standard costing

a) To provide a formal basis for assessing performance and efficiency.

b) To control costs by establishing standards and analysing variances.

c) To enable the principle of 'management by exception' to be practised at the detailed, operational level.

d) To assist in setting budgets.

e) The standard costs are readily available substitutes for actual average unit costs and can be used for stock and work-in-progress valuations, profit planning and decision making, and as a basis of pricing where 'cost-plus' systems are used.

f) To assist in assigning responsibility for non-standard performance in order to correct deficiencies or to capitalise on benefits.

g) To motivate staff and management.

h) To provide a basis for estimating.

i) To provide guidance on possible ways of improving performance.

4. Standard cost defined

This can be formally defined as:

> '*A standard expressed in money. It is built up from an assessment of the value of cost elements. Its main uses are providing bases for performance measurement, control by exception reporting, valuing stock and establishing selling prices*'.   Terminology.

A standard cost should be based on sound technical and engineering studies, specified production methods, work study and work measurement, clearly defined material specifications, and price and wage rate projections. The above represents the position under ideal circumstances and standards produced following such a thorough process are likely to be accepted as truly representative and realistic. However, standards produced less rigorously can also be of some value particularly in service areas and in industries where a detailed engineering basis is inappropriate.

It will be noted that a standard cost is not an average of past costs. These are likely to contain the results of past mistakes and inefficiencies. Furthermore, changes in methods, technology and prices make comparisons with the past of doubtful value for control purposes and for assessing current efficiency.

5. Types of standard

There are various types of standards which could be established and the type or types to be used in a particular organisation is dependent upon the requirements and objectives of the standard costing system. The type of standard used naturally affects the nature and scale of the variances and the meaning which can be attributed to them.

Four main types of standard are described: basic, ideal, attainable, and current.

Basic Standards: These are long term standards which could remain unchanged over the years. They could be used to show trends over time for such items as material prices, labour rates and efficiency and the long term effects of changing methods. Also they could be used as a basis for setting current standards. Basic standards would not normally form part of the reporting system as any variances produced would have little or no meaning being an unknown mixture of controllable and uncontrollable factors.

Ideal Standards: These are based on optimal operating conditions, no breakdowns, no wastage, no stoppages or idle time. Ideal standards would be adjusted periodically to reflect improvements in materials, methods and technology. Clearly such standards would be unattainable in practice and accordingly ideal standards are unlikely to be used for routine reporting purposes. If they were used there would continually be adverse variances which are likely to affect morale and motivation. Ideal standards may however be considered as long term targets and used for long term development purposes but are of little value for day-to-day control activities.

Attainable Standard: This is by far the most commonly encountered standard. Such a standard is based on efficient (but not perfect) operating conditions. Allowances would be made for normal material losses, fatigue and machine and tool breakdowns. Attainable standards should be based on high performance levels which can, with effort, be achieved. Such standards aim to provide tough but realistic targets and as such should motivate staff; they can be used for product costing, for cost control, for stock valuation, for estimating and as a basis for budgeting. Attainable Standards would be revised periodically (usually annually) to reflect the conditions, prices, methods etc. which are expected to prevail during the ensuing control period.

These standards are the ones normally used for routine control purposes and from which variances are calculated. If the standard remains a realistic target over the whole of the control period then the cumulative sum of the variances should be small and any variances calculated will represent controllable matters which, if significant, would merit attention. Unless otherwise stated subsequent references in this book to standards mean attainable standards.

Current Standard: This is a standard which is set for use over a short period to reflect current conditions. Where conditions are stable then a current standard will be the same as an attainable standard but where, for example, a temporary problem exists with material quality or there is an unexpected price rise, then a current standard could be set covering, say, two or three months to deal with the particular circumstances. It follows that any variances arising when a current standard is used will be controllable variances.

A particular example of the use of current standards is in inflationary circumstances where current standards could be set, perhaps on a month by month basis, using the performance levels agreed for the attainable standard for the year with the price levels adjusted by suitable indices for month by month control.

Note: As mentioned in the previous chapter there are very real problems in determining the level of attainment in budgets or standards. It follows therefore, to a greater or lesser extent, all standards contain a subjective element.

6. Standards and budgets

Both standards and budgets are concerned with setting performance and cost levels for control purposes. They therefore are similar in principle although they differ in scope. Standards are a unit concept, ie they apply to particular products, to individual operations or processes. Budgets are concerned with totals; they lay down cost limits for functions and departments and for the firm as a whole. As an illustration the standard material cost of the various products in a firm could be as follows:

		Standard material cost/unit	Planned production	Total material cost
		£		£
Product	X321	3.50	5,000 units	17,500
Product	Y592	7.25	1,500 units	10,875
Product	Y728	1.50	2,500 units	3,750
etc	etc	etc	etc	etc
etc	etc	etc	etc	etc

Overall total = Materials budget = £275,000

In this way the detailed unit standards are used as the basis for developing realistic budgets. This is particularly so for direct material and direct labour costs which are more amenable to close control through standard costing whereas overheads would normally be controlled by functional and departmental budgets. Further differences are that budgets would be revised on a periodic basis, frequently as an annual exercise, whereas standards are revised only when they are inappropriate for current operating conditions. Such revisions may take place more or less frequently than budget revisions. The accounting treatment of standards and budgets also differs. Budgets are memorandum figures and do not form part of the double entry accounting system whereas standards and the resulting variances are included.

7. Setting standards

Standards which can be used for control purposes rest on a foundation of properly organised, standardised methods and procedures and a comprehensive information system. It is little point trying to develop a standard cost for a product if the production method is not decided upon. A standard cost implies that a target or standard exists for every single element which contributes to the product; the types, usage and prices of materials and parts, the grades, rates of pay and times for the labour involved, the production methods and layouts, the tools and jigs and so on. Considerable effort is involved in establishing standard costs and keeping them up to date.

Traditionally, the standard cost for each part or product is recorded on a standard cost card and an example is given later in this chapter. With the increased usage of computers for costing purposes frequently nowadays there is no physical standard cost card. When a computer is used, the standard costs are recorded on a magnetic disk or tape file and can be accessed and processed as required. Whether a computer or manual system is used, there are no differences in the principles of standard costing, although there are many differences in the method of day to day operation. The following paragraphs explain some of the detailed procedures involved in setting standards.

8. Setting standards – materials

The materials content of a product: raw materials, sub-assemblies, piece parts, finishing materials etc is derived from technical and engineering specifications, frequently in the form of a Bill of Materials. The standard quantities required include an allowance for normal and inevitable losses in production, that is, machining loss, evaporation, and expected levels of breakages and rejections. The process of analysis is valuable in itself because savings and alternative materials and ways of using materials are frequently discovered.

The responsibility for providing material prices is that of the buying department. The prices used are not the past costs, but the forecast expected costs for the relevant budget period. The expected costs should take into account trends in material prices, anticipated changes in purchasing policies, quantity and cash discounts, carriage and packing charges and any other factor which will influence material costs.

9. Setting standards – labour

Without detailed operation and process specifications it would be impossible to establish standard labour time. The agreed methods of manufacture are the basis of setting the standard labour times. The techniques of work measurement are involved, frequently combined with work study projections based on elemental analysis when a part is not yet in production. The labour standards must specify the exact grades of labour to be used as well as the times involved. Planned labour times are expressed in standard hours (or standard minutes). The concept of a standard hour or minute is important and can be defined as:

> 'The quantity of work achievable at standard performance in an hour or minute'.
>
> *Terminology.*

Frequently output is expressed as so many 'standard hours' or 'standard minutes' rather than a quantity of parts. When the times and grades of labour have been established a forecast of the relevant wage rates for the control period can be made, usually by the Personnel Department.

Note: In setting the time element of a labour standard full account must be taken of any learning effects so that the standard set will be a realistic one under operational conditions. The 'learning curve' and its effect on labour times was described in Chapter 3.

10. Setting standards – overheads

It will be recalled from Chapter 2 how overhead absorption rates are established. These predetermined overhead absorption rates become the standards for overheads for each cost centre using the budgeted standard labour hours as the activity base. For realistic control, overheads must be analysed into their fixed and variable overheads thus:

$$\text{Standard Variable O.A.R} = \frac{\text{Budgeted variable overheads for cost centre}}{\text{Budgeted standard labour hours for cost centre}}$$

and

$$\text{Standard Fixed O.A.R.} = \frac{\text{Budgeted fixed overheads for cost centre}}{\text{Budgeted standard labour hours for cost centre}}$$

The level of activity adopted, expressed in standard labour hours, is the budgeted expected annual activity level which is the basis of the Master budget. For reporting and control purposes this would be classed as 100% capacity.

11. Setting standards – sales price and margin

Fundamental to any form of standard costing, budgeting and profit planning is the anticipated selling price for the product. The setting of the selling price is frequently a top level decision and is based on a variety of factors including: the anticipated market demand, competing products, manufacturing costs, inflation estimates and so on. Finally, after discussion and investigation, a selling price is established at which it is planned to sell the product during the period concerned. This becomes the standard selling price. The standard sales margin is the difference between the standard cost and the standard selling price. Where a standard marginal costing system is used, the standard contribution is calculated following normal marginal costing principles.

Notes:

a) Normally when 'standard cost' is mentioned it means *total standard cost*, ie total absorption cost principles are used incorporating fixed and variable costs. Standard marginal costing is also employed, but students should assume that total absorption cost principles are involved whenever the term standard cost is used without qualification. This nomenclature is adopted in this book. When marginal costing principles are used the term *standard marginal cost* is used.

b) The problems of setting selling prices and the ways that the Management Accountant can assist in the pricing decision are dealt with in detail later in the book.

c) It follows that a standard costing system works within a framework of a budgeting system. A budgetary control system without a standard costing system is quite usual but a standard costing system without the discipline and structure provided by a budgetary system could not be recommended.

12. Responsibility for setting standards

The line managers who have to work with and accept the standards must be involved in establishing them. There are strong behavioural and motivational factors involved in this process as mentioned in the previous chapter. Work study staff, engineers, accountants and other specialists provide technical assistance and information but the line managers must be involved in the critical part of standard setting, that of agreeing the level of attainment to be included in the standard.

13. The standard cost card

The process of setting standards results in the establishment of the standard cost for the product. The makeup of the standard cost is recorded on a standard cost card. In practice there may be numerous detail cards together with a summary card for a given product, or the standard cost details may be on a computer file. The principles, however, remain the same. A simple standard cost card is shown on the following page.

14. Revision of standards

To show trends and to be able to compare performance and costs between different periods, standards would be rarely changed. On the other hand, for day to day control and motivation purposes, standards which reflect the most up to date position are required and consequently revisions would need to be made continually. The above positions reflect the extremes of the situation. There is no doubt that standards which are right up to date provide a better target and are more meaningful to the foremen and managers involved, but the extent and frequency of standard revision is a matter of judgement.

Minor changes in rates, prices and usage are frequently ignored for a time, but their cumulative effect soon becomes significant and changes need to be made. Prior to computer maintained standard cost files, standard cost revisions were a time consuming chore as it was necessary to ensure that all the effects of a change were recorded. For example, a price change of a common raw material would necessitate alterations to

a) the standard cost cards of all products, parts and assemblies using the material;

b) any price lists, stock sheets and catalogues involving the material and products derived from the material;

Because of such factors, commonly all standard costs are revised together at regular, periodic intervals such as every six or twelve months, rather than on an individual, random basis.

15. Behavioural aspects of standards

The points made in the previous chapter regarding the importance of the human aspects of budgeting apply equally to standard costing. Both techniques employ similar principles and both rely absolutely upon the people who have to work to the budgets and standards. Because of the detailed nature of standard costing and its involvement with foremen and production workers, communication becomes of even greater importance. Production workers frequently regard any form of performance evaluation with deep suspicion and if a cost-conscious, positive attitude is to be developed, close attention must be paid to the behavioural aspects of the system. Full participation, realistic standards, prompt and accurate reporting, no undue pressure or censure – all contribute to an acceptable system. Remember if the system is not accepted by the people involved it will be unworkable.

Standard Cost Card					
Part no *X291*	Description *stub joint*		Batch quantity *100*		
Tool Ref. *T5983*	Work study ref. *WS255*		Drawing no. *D59215*		
	Revision date *3/12/95*		Revised by *G.R.P.*		
Cost type and quantity	Standard price or rate	Dept 7	Dept 19	Dept 15	Total
		£	£	£	£
Direct materials					
2.5Kg P101	£14.8kg	37.00	37.50		37.50
1000 units A539	£3.75 100		37.50		37.50
					74.50
Direct Labour					
Machine Operation					
Grade 15					
4.8 hrs	£2.5 hr	12.00			12.00
9.2 hrs	£2.5 hr		23.00		23.00
Assembly					
Grade 8					
16.4 hrs	£1.75 hr			28.70	28.70
					63.70
Production Overhead					
Machine Hour Rate	£11 hr	52.80	101.12		153.92
Labour Hour Rate	£6 hr			98.40	98.40
		101.80	161.62	127.10	252.32

Standard cost summary	
	£
Direct materials	74.50
Direct labour	63.70
Production overheads	252.32
Standard cost per 100	390.52

Figure 10.1 Standard cost card

16. Control through variance analysis

An important objective of standard costing is to be able to monitor current operational performance against standards by the use of variance analysis. This procedure follows the control cycle explained earlier and is identical in principle to that used in budgetary control except that the analysis of variances is much more detailed.

It will be recalled that a variance is a difference between standard cost and actual cost. The term variance is rarely used on its own.

Invariably it is qualified in some way, for example: labour efficiency variance, direct material yield variance and so on. The process by which the total difference between standard and actual costs is analysed is known as *variance analysis*. Variances arise from differences between standard and actual quantities, efficiencies and proportions and/or differences between standard and actual rates or prices. These are the *causes* of variances; the *reasons* for the differences have to be established by investigation.

Notes:

a) Variances may be *adverse* ie where actual cost is greater than standard or they may be *favourable* where actual cost is less than standard. Alternative terms are *minus* or *plus* variances, respectively.

b) The accounting use of the term variance should not be confused with the statistical variance which is a measure of the dispersion of a statistical population. In statistical terminology, an accounting variance would be known as a deviation.

17. The purpose of variance analysis

The only purpose of variance analysis is to provide practical pointers to the causes of off-standard performance so that management can improve operations, increase efficiency, utilise resources more effectively and reduce costs. It follows that overly elaborate variance analysis which is not understood, variances that are not acted upon and variances which are calculated too long after the event do not fulfil the central purpose of standard costing. The types of variances which are identified must be those which fulfil the needs of the organisation.

The only criterion for the calculation of a variance is its usefulness – if it is not useful for management purposes, it should not be produced. Most text books (and this one is no exception!) give lists of commonly encountered variances but it cannot be emphasised too strongly that these should not be automatically produced unless they provide specific, relevant and useful information. It is highly likely, in a given organisation, that specialised variances will be found to be most relevant and that some or all of the conventionally encountered variances will be of little value.

18. Responsibility identification through variance analysis

In ideal circumstances, variances are analysed in sufficient detail so that responsibility can be assigned to a particular individual for a specific variance. This is a worthwhile objective which, if achieved, considerably assists cost control. Because of the importance of this principle, standard costing and budgetary control are known as *responsibility accounting*. A particular example of this principle is the conventional assumptions behind the subdivision of the direct materials cost variance, that is, the total difference in material costs between actual and standard. The total variance comprises a price component, which is deemed to be the responsibility of the buyer, and a usage component, which is deemed to be the responsibility of the foreman or line manager.

However, it must be realised that in practice divisions of responsibility are rarely perfectly clear cut. There are many interdependencies and shared responsibilities in a typical organisation which make simplistic assumptions about the location of responsibilities highly suspect. For example, where Department A receives parts and materials from another section within the organisation, the labour efficiency of Department A is to some extent dependent on the regular and timely flows of correct specification parts and materials from elsewhere. This means that labour efficiency, and the resulting variances, which are conventionally deemed to be the sole responsibility of Department A are to some extent uncontrollable by the management of Department A. This is only a simple example of an interdependency and other more subtle examples can be found in most organisations.

19. The relationship of variances

The overall objective of variance analysis is to subdivide the total difference between budgeted profit and actual profit for the period into the detailed differences (relating to material, labour, overheads and sales) which go to make up the total difference. The particular variances which are computed in any given organisation are those which are relevant to its operations and which will aid control. Figure 10.2 (opposite page) shows a hierarchy of commonly encountered variances but, as pointed out above, relevance and specific appropriateness to management are the only criteria which justify the calculation of any variance, not the fact that it is frequently mentioned in textbooks and examinations.

Notes on Figure 10.2:

a) Each variance and sub-variance is described in detail in the paragraphs which follow.

b) For simplicity the full title of each variance is not shown in each box. The full titles are easily derived from the chart. For example, under the Direct Materials Total Variance is found the Direct Materials Price Variance, the Direct Materials Usage Variance and so on.

c) The chart is arithmetically consistent, ie the total of the linked variances equals the senior variance shown. For example.

$$\frac{\text{Variance overhead}}{\text{expenditure variance}} + \frac{\text{Overhead efficiency}}{\text{variance}} = \frac{\text{Variable overhead}}{\text{variance}}$$

d) The price and quantity aspects of each variance are shown clearly on the chart and can be summarised as shown in the table below.

Cost element	Price variances	Quantity variances
Direct wages	Rate	Efficiency
Direct materials	Price	Usage
Variable overheads	Expenditure	Efficiency
Fixed overheads	Expenditure	Volume

e) The 'operating profit' variance is the difference between budgeted and actual operating profit for a period. This variance can be calculated directly and it is the sum of all variances, ie cost variances and sales variances. The operating profit variance is not entered in a ledger account because budgeted profit does not appear therein. **All other variances do appear in ledger accounts.**

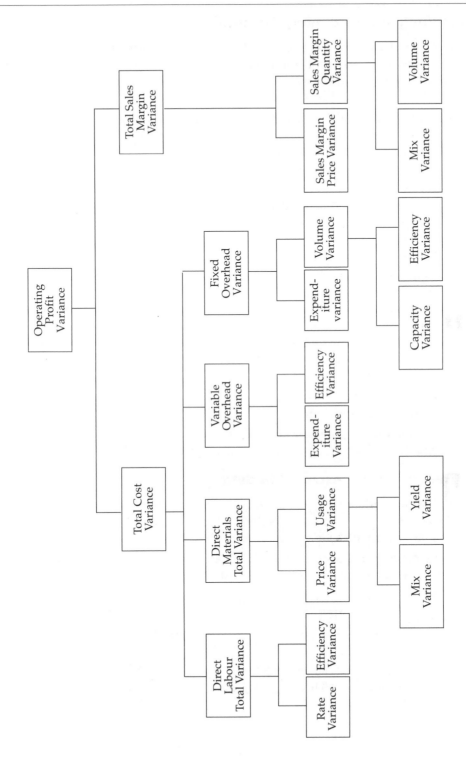

Figure 10.2 Chart of commonly encountered variances

20. Making variance analysis useful

It is not sufficient merely to be able to describe and calculate variances. To make variance analysis into a useful aid to management it is necessary to probe and investigate the variances and the data used to calculate them. Typical of the questions which should be asked are the following:

a) Is there any relationship between the variances? For example, there may be pleasure in observing a favourable materials price variance caused by purchase of a job lot of material, but if this favourable variance is more than offset by adverse usage and labour variances caused by the poor quality material, then there is little cause for rejoicing.

b) Can further information than merely the variance be provided for management? Remember, variance analysis is but a means to an end. Management's task is to find the reasons for the variances and to take action to bring operations into line with the plan.

c) Is the variance significant and worth reporting? This is an important matter for the management accountant because it is vital to direct attention to areas where there is a substantial variation between actual and standard. The meaning of significant variances and the methods by which they can be identified have been dealt with previously in connection with budgetary control. The methods and principles described are equally applicable to standard costing variances as well as those which arise in budgetary control.

d) Are the variances being reported quickly enough to the right people, with sufficient or too much detail, with explanatory notes and background data?

e) Do the variances and trends indicate that the standards need amendment? This is the double loop or higher order feedback previously described.

21. The variances described in detail

Each of the variances shown in Figure 10.2 is described in the following paragraphs. Each variance is defined and explained, a formula and typical causes of the variance are given together with a worked example.

The worked examples for the basic material and labour variances are based on the following extract from the Standard Cost Card for Part No. 50Y and actual results for period 2.

Extract from a Standard Cost Card for a Part No. 50Y

Standard Cost/Unit

£

Raw materials 60 kgs @ £3.5 Kg	210
Direct labour 15 hrs @ £2.75/hour	41.25
	251.25

Actual Results for Period 2

Production	140 parts
Direct Material Purchases	8,000 Kgs at a cost of £30,000
Opening stock direct material	1,800 Kgs
Closing stock direct material	1,450 Kgs
Direct wages	5,805 for 2,150 hours

22. The basic materials variances

This paragraph deals with the Direct Materials Total Variance and the primary sub divisions, the Direct Materials Price Variance and the Direct Materials Usage Variance.

A particular problem arises with material variances because materials could be charged to production either at actual prices or standard prices. This affects when the prices variance is calculated, ie either at the time of purchase or at the time of usage. Although both these approaches are possible, the procedure where materials are charged to production at standard price has many advantages and will be adopted in this book.

This method means that variances are calculated as soon as they arise, (ie a price variance when the material is purchased) and that they are more easily related to an individual's responsibility (ie a price variance would be the buyer's responsibility). Accordingly for materials variances (and ALL other variances), price variances are calculated first and thereafter the material is at standard price. The individual material variances can now be considered.

Direct material total variance – definition

> 'The difference between the standard direct material cost of the actual production volume and the actual cost of direct material.'

Direct material price variance – definition

> 'The difference between the standard price and actual purchase price for the actual quantity of material.'

Direct material usage variance – definition

> The difference between the standard quantity specified for the actual production and the actual quantity used, at standard purchase price'.

Actual purchase quantity × Actual price
(ie Total purchase cost)
minus
Actual purchase quantity × STANDARD PRICE
} PRICE VARIANCE

Actual quantity used for actual production × STANDARD PRICE
minus
STANDARD QUANTITY FOR ACTUAL PRODUCTION × STANDARD PRICE
} USAGE VARIANCE

} TOTAL DIRECT MATERIAL COST VARIANCE

Example 1 (based on data from para 21)

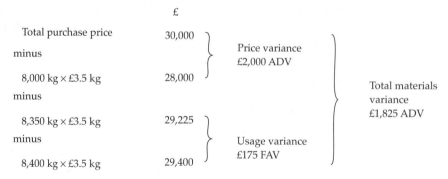

£

Total purchase price   30,000

minus   Price variance £2,000 ADV

8,000 kg × £3.5 kg   28,000

minus   Total materials variance £1,825 ADV

8,350 kg × £3.5 kg   29,225

minus   Usage variance £175 FAV

8,400 kg × £3.5 kg   29,400

Notes:

a) Although rules can be given regarding the sequence of the formulae so that a minus variance is always adverse and a plus is favourable, it is easier and less error prone to determine the direction of the variance by common sense, ie if the price/usage is less than standard the variance is favourable, if more, then the variance is adverse.

b) The price variance is based on the actual quantity purchased and is extracted first. Thereafter the *actual price is never used for variance calculations.*

c) In the above example, the actual usage (8,350 Kgs) was calculated as follows:

Opening Stock + Purchases – Closing Stock = Usage

ie 1,800 + 8,000 – 1,450 = 8,350 Kgs

d) It follows from the above calculations that a price variance could arise even if there was no usage, provided that there were purchases during the period.

e) Students should note how the formulae develop from actual values (in lower case) progressively to STANDARD VALUES (in capitals). This layout is used throughout the book.

Typical causes of material variances

❐ Price variances

    a) Paying higher or lower prices than planned.

    b) Losing or gaining quantity discounts by buying in smaller or larger quantities than planned.

    c) Buying lower or higher quality than planned.

    d) Buying substitute material due to unavailability of planned material. (Both (c) and (d) may affect usage variances).

❐ Usage variances

    a) Greater or lower yield from material than planned.

    b) Gains or losses due to use of substitute or higher/lower quality than planned.

    c) Greater or lower rate of scrap than anticipated.

Notes:

a) As can be seen from the variance chart, Figure 10.2, the usage variance can be further divided into mix and yield variances. This is only done when useful information can be thus provided. An example is given in the next chapter.

b) The rule given above that price variances are extracted first, is the normal procedure but it should be realised that is a convention only. The effect of this convention is that the cross hatched area of Figure 10.3 is arbitrarily assigned to the price variance because that variance is isolated first. Where actual prices do not differ significantly from standard there is no real problem.

However, where there is a significant difference between actual and standard prices then the usage/quantity variance will not be valued in economically realistic terms. This problem exists throughout variance analysis and means that the sequence of variance analysis (conventionally price or rate first) determines to which variance the 'increment x increment' amount is assigned. This means that many variances have an inbuilt imprecision which should be remembered when interpreting variances.

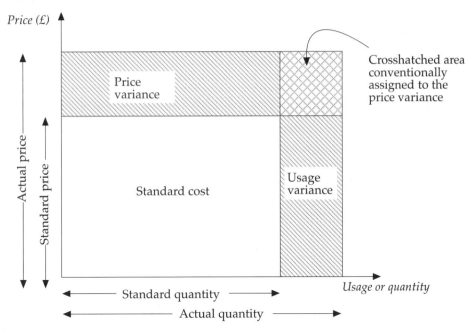

Figure 10.3 Diagrammatic representation of Price and Usage Variances

23. Labour variances

This paragraph deals with the Direct Labour Total Variance, The Direct Labour Rate Variance (the 'price' variance), and the Direct Labour Efficiency Variance (the 'usage' variance). These are defined below:

Direct Labour Total Variance – definition

> 'The difference between the standard direct labour cost and the actual direct labour cost, incurred for the production achieved'.

Direct Labour Rate Variance – definition

> 'The difference between the standard and actual direct labour rate per hour for the total hours worked'.

Direct Labour Efficiency Variance – definition

> 'The difference between the standard hours for the actual production achieved and the hours actually worked, valued at the standard labour rate'.

The formulae are given below and follow a similar pattern to the material variances.

Formulae

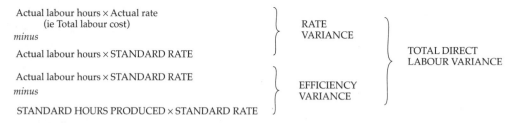

Actual labour hours × Actual rate
(ie Total labour cost)
minus
Actual labour hours × STANDARD RATE
} RATE VARIANCE

Actual labour hours × STANDARD RATE
minus
STANDARD HOURS PRODUCED × STANDARD RATE
} EFFICIENCY VARIANCE

} TOTAL DIRECT LABOUR VARIANCE

Notes:

a) It will be seen that the second line of the rate variance and the first line of the efficiency variance are identical.

b) Where appropriate records exist and it is considered that useful information will result, an idle time variance can be calculated by multiplying the hours of idle time by the standard rate. The variance so calculated, together with the efficiency variance, forms the labour usage variance. Where no idle time variance is calculated, as in the formulae shown above, the efficiency variance is equivalent to the labour usage variance. As with labour efficiency, the effect of idle time on variable and fixed overheads can also be calculated.

Example 2 (based on data from para 21.)

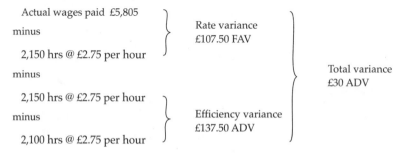

Actual wages paid £5,805
minus
2,150 hrs @ £2.75 per hour
} Rate variance £107.50 FAV

2,150 hrs @ £2.75 per hour
minus
2,100 hrs @ £2.75 per hour
} Efficiency variance £137.50 ADV

} Total variance £30 ADV

The total variance should be verified by calculating the difference between actual wages paid, £5805 and the standard labour costs of the actual production, £5775, ie £30 ADV.

Typical causes of labour variances:

❑ Rate

    a) Higher rates being paid than planned due to wage award.

    b) Higher or lower grade of worker being used than planned.

    c) Payment of unplanned overtime or bonus.

❑ Efficiency

    a) Use of incorrect grade of labour.

    b) Poor workshop organisation or supervision.

    c) Incorrect materials and/or machine problems.

Note: It will be apparent that the assumption behind the labour efficiency variance is that labour is a variable cost and that output is directly related to labour hours. In modern circumstances where output may be machine dominated and the amount of labour may be more or less constant, the calculation of such a variance is unlikely to produce any useful information for control purposes.

24. Basic variance analysis

So far only the basic material and labour variances have been dealt with. The illustrations have been deliberately kept simple in order to emphasise the major principles of variance analysis. There is considerable similarity between the methods of calculating all types of variance and students are advised to master the first part of this chapter before proceeding to the overhead and other variances which follow. An important general principle which should be apparent at this stage is that actual prices or rates are never used in variance analysis, except to calculate the price or rate variance which is always done first.

25. Introduction to overhead variance analysis

Before dealing with the individual variances it is necessary to recall some of the earlier material in the book. Overheads are absorbed into costs by means of predetermined overhead absorption rates (OAR) which are calculated by dividing the budgeted overheads for the period by the activity level anticipated. The activity level can be expressed in various ways (units, weight, sales etc.), but by far the most useful concept is that of the Standard Hour. It will be recalled that the 'Standard Hour' is a unit measure of production and is the most commonly used measure of activity level. thus:

$$\text{Total overhead absorbed} = \text{OAR} \times \text{SHP}$$

where SHP is the number of Standard Hours of Production.

Where the Standard costing system uses total absorption costing principles (ie where both fixed and variable overheads are absorbed into production costs) the total overheads absorbed can be subdivided into Fixed Overhead Absorption Rates (FOAR) and Variable Overhead Absorption Rates (VOAR) thus:

$$\text{Fixed overheads absorbed} = \text{FOAR} \times \text{SHP}$$
$$\text{Variable overheads absorbed} = \text{VOAR} \times \text{SHP}$$
$$\text{Total overheads absorbed} = (\text{FOAR} + \text{VOAR}) \times \text{SHP}$$

When standard marginal costing is used, only variable overheads are absorbed into production costs and thus only variances relating to variable overheads arise; fixed overheads being dealt with by the budgetary control system. Thus it will be seen that overhead variance analysis is considerably simplified when standard marginal costing is employed.

There are several possible approaches to overhead variance analysis and one commonly encountered approach, that shown in Figure 10.2, is described with worked examples and diagrammatic representations. Students should be aware that much of conventional overhead variance analysis is subject to criticism as being of little value for control purposes. The various criticisms that can be made are dealt with after the conventional principles have been explained and exemplified. The various examples are based on the following data.

Budget for *Department No. 13*

for period No. 5

Fixed overheads	£15,360
Variable overheads	£20,480
Labour hours	5,120
Standard hours of Production	5,120

Actual for period

Fixed overheads	£15,850
Variable overheads	£21,220
Labour hours	5,100
Standard hours produced	5,050

From the budget the overhead absorption rates have been calculated using standard hours as the absorption base.

$$\text{F.O.A.R.} = \frac{\text{Budgeted fixed overheads}}{\text{Budgeted activity (Std. Hrs)}} = \frac{£15,360}{5,120} = £3 \text{ per hour}$$

$$\text{V.O.A.R} = \frac{\text{Budgeted variable overheads}}{\text{Budgeted activity (Std. Hrs)}} = \frac{20,480}{5,120} = £4 \text{ per hour}$$

and the total absorption rate is $£3 + 4 = £7$ per hour

Notes:

a) It will be seen that *budgeted labour hours* and the *budgeted standard hours* production are the same. This is the normal planning basis. If actual labour hours and the standard hours actually produced also were the same, then efficiency would be exactly as planned and no efficiency variances would arise. It will be seen from the data that this is not the case on this occasion.

b) It will be apparent that because absorption rates for fixed overheads have been calculated the examples will be based on total absorption costing principles.

26. Variable overhead variances

This paragraph describes the variable overhead variance, the variable overhead expenditure variance and the variable overhead efficiency variance.

Variable overhead variance – definition

The difference between the actual variable overheads incurred and the variable overheads absorbed.

(This variance is simply the over or under absorption of overheads.)

Variable overhead expenditure variance – definition

The difference between the actual variable overheads incurred and the allowed variable overheads based on the actual hours worked.

Variable overhead efficiency variance – definition

The difference between the allowed variable overheads and the absorbed variable overhead.

Formulae

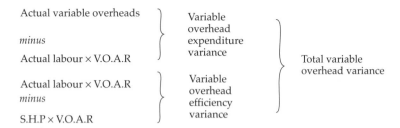

Note: It will be realised that, based on the VOAR, the budget is flexed to suit the actual hours worked.

Example 3 *(based on data from para 25.)*

As usual, the total variance can be verified by taking the difference between what the variable overheads actually cost and the amount absorbed by the actual production.

$$£21,220 - 20,200 = £1,020$$

Variable overhead variances can be depicted as shown in Figure 10.4.

27. Fixed overhead variances

This paragraph describes one approach to fixed overhead variance analysis and covers the Fixed overhead Variance, the Fixed Overhead Expenditure Variance, the Fixed Overhead Volume Variance and its sub variances, the Capacity Variance and the Efficiency or Productivity Variance.

Fixed overhead total variance – definition

The total difference between the fixed overhead absorbed by the actual production and the actual fixed overhead for the period.

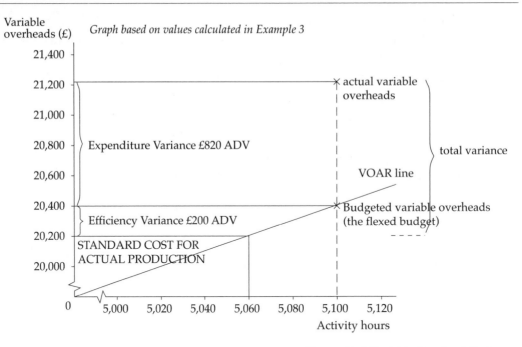

Figure 10.4 Variable Overhead Variances

Note:

As with the variable overhead variance the fixed overhead total variance simply represents under or over absorption of overheads.

Fixed overhead expenditure variance – definition

> The difference between actual fixed overheads and allowed or budgeted fixed overheads for the period.

Fixed overhead volume variance – definition

> The difference between the fixed overhead absorbed by the actual production and budgeted fixed overheads for the period.

The volume variance arises from the actual volume of production differing from the planned volume. If required, the volume variance can be subdivided into an efficiency variance and a capacity variance.

Fixed overhead efficiency variance – definition

> This is the difference between the standard hours of production achieved and the actual labour hours, valued at the F.O.A.R.

Fixed overhead capacity variance

> This is the difference between the budgeted hours and actual hours, valued at the F.O.A.R.

The formulae for these variances are as follows:

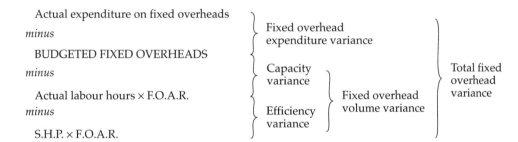

Example 4 (based on data from para 25.)

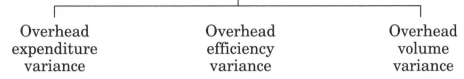

Actual expenditure   £15,850

minus

BUDGETED EXPENDITURE   £15,360

minus

Actual hours × F.O.A.R.   £15,300
(5100 × £3)

minus

S.H.P. × F.O.A.R.   £15,150
(5050 × £3)

Expenditure variance
£490 ADV

Capacity variance
£60 ADV

Efficiency variance
£150 ADV

Volume variance
£210 ADV

Total variance
£700 ADV

Once again the total variance can be verified by comparing actual expenditure and the amount of fixed overheads absorbed by the actual production,

ie £15,850 − 15,150 = £700 ADV

The fixed overhead variances can be depicted as shown in Figure 10.5 (following page).

28. Alternative overhead variances

The overhead variances illustrated so far have been based on the separation of the total overheads into fixed and variable components. An alternative, and simpler, approach is to calculate variances based on the total overheads, that is fixed and variable combined.

In such circumstances the following variances could be calculated

Overhead total variance

| Overhead expenditure variance | Overhead efficiency variance | Overhead volume variance |

Overhead total variance – definition

'The difference between the standard overhead cost specified for the production achieved, and the actual cost incurred'.

Overhead expenditure variance –definition

'The difference between budgeted and actual overhead expenditure'.

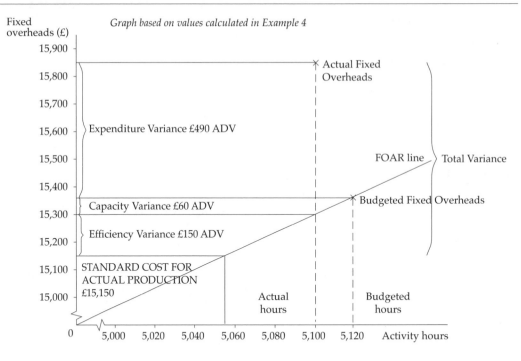

Figure 10.5 Fixed Overhead Variances

Overhead efficiency variance – definition

'The difference between the standard over head rate for the production achieved and the standard overhead rate for the actual hours taken'.

Overhead volume variance – definition

'The difference between the standard overhead cost of the actual hours taken and the flexed budget allowance for the actual hours taken'.

Formulae

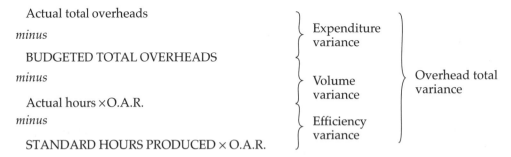

where O.A.R. is the total overhead absorption rate.

Example 5 (based on the data in Para 25.)

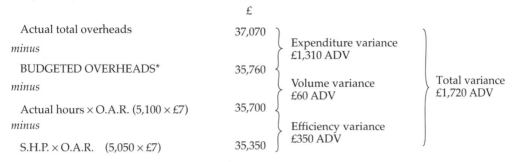

	£		
Actual total overheads	37,070	Expenditure variance £1,310 ADV	
minus			
BUDGETED OVERHEADS*	35,760		Total variance £1,720 ADV
minus		Volume variance £60 ADV	
Actual hours × O.A.R. (5,100 × £7)	35,700		
minus		Efficiency variance £350 ADV	
S.H.P. × O.A.R. (5,050 × £7)	35,350		

This can be verified by calculating the difference between actual total overheads and the total overheads absorbed by the actual production. £37,070 – 35,350 = £1,720 ADV

*The budgeted overheads are calculated by the normal process of flexing a budget, ie

Budgeted total overheads   =   Budgeted Fixed overheads + Actual hours × V.O.A.R

$\qquad\qquad\qquad\qquad$ =   £15,360 + 5,100 × £4 = £35,760

It will be seen that the volume variance is equivalent to the under-recovery of the fixed overheads caused by working 5100 instead of the budgeted 5120 hours, ie

(Actual hours – budgeted hours) × F.O.A.R. = (5,100 – 5,120) × £3 = £60 ADV

The above variances can be depicted as shown in Figure 10.6.

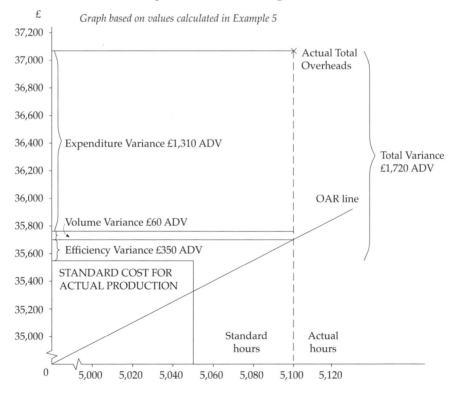

Figure 10.6 Total Overhead Variances

Note: It will be realised that this second approach to overhead variance analysis is merely an aggregation of the approach outlined previously in para 27.

29. Reasons for overhead variances

Overhead variances largely arise because of the conventions of the overhead absorption process. Overhead absorption rates are calculated from estimates of expenditure and activity levels and variances arise from differences in both these factors. In addition, because overheads are frequently absorbed into production by means of labour hours, overhead variances need to be calculated to reconcile the total difference between standard and actual cost. Apart from the expenditure variances, overhead variances are of limited value for control purposes.

30. A critique of overhead variances

It will be recalled from earlier in the chapter that the variances which should be calculated are those which help management to control operations. Such variances indicate the direction of the movement away from standard (adverse or favourable) and provide a realistic valuation of the amount of the difference. An example is an adverse materials usage variance of say, £500. This tells the manager that an extra £500 of materials, valued at standard price, have been used in production. The meaning of this information is clear and the manager has a realistic valuation of the improvement he might make by bringing operations in line with standard, assuming that the standard price is a reasonable figure.

How do overhead variances measure up to these criteria? In general, the answer is, not very well. The following are some of the specific criticisms that can be made of overhead variance analysis especially the fixed overhead content.

a) A major factor in calculating overhead variances is the overhead recovery rates. These rates arise from the conventions of cost ascertainment whereby costs are absorbed into cost units by means of labour hour or machine hour rates. The use of such rates for the quite different purpose of cost control has obvious limitations.

b) Both the numerator and denominator of a department overhead absorption rate contain subjective and possibly quite arbitrary values. The fixed costs in the numerator may include apportionments of general company fixed costs to the various departments and the choice of the output level for the denominator is arbitrary. These and other factors determine the amount of the overhead absorption rate which in turn determines the values assigned to the overhead variances.

c) The volume variance purports to show the effect of not working to planned capacity but its use in this respect is extremely limited. Together with the expenditure variance however it does show to what extent the overhead absorption system has adequately absorbed overheads for cost ascertainment purposes. It will be realised that this is simply a book balancing exercise, largely dependent on the accuracy of the original estimates used in calculating absorption rates, and does not assist managerial decision making or operational control. A more useful variance in this area would be one which valued losses or gains in output in terms of realisable contribution rather than variances based on absorption rates which have arbitrary elements and which were designed for a quite different purpose.

d) The variances relating to variable overheads do not have the major flaws inherent in those relating to fixed overheads but some problems still remain. The valuations are still related to overhead absorption rates which have the same caveats as mentioned above. A more serious problem, which considerably limits their usefulness for operational control purposes, is the implicit assumption that all the numerous items which go to make up variable overheads vary directly in proportion to the same activity indicator, conventionally labour hours. It may be a realistic assumption that, say, direct materials vary in proportion to output but it is far too simplistic a view that all the items making up variable overheads (eg indirect materials, power, lighting, supervision, maintenance and so on) vary in proportion to one activity indicator.

e) The expenditure variance (the difference between actual expenditure and the flexed budget) is probably the most useful of the overhead variances and is the one which would generally be considered to be controllable by the responsibility centre's management. However, it too has limitations. The overhead expenditure variance is analogous to the total variance for direct costs in that it consists of both a price and a usage component. The expenditure variance can arise from either price increases, eg increase in electricity charges, salary increases or by changes in quantity, eg more telephone calls, more staff, or some combination of price and quantity differences. Accordingly, without further analysis, perhaps by detailed item-by-item budgetary comparisons, the overall expenditure variance is of limited value for control purposes.

31. How are variances dealt with in the accounts?

It is general practice at the end of a control period to write off all variances to the Costing Profit and Loss account and to carry all items in the Cost Accounts at standard cost. Provided that the variances are relatively small this is a reasonable practice and is one which should be adopted. However, certain difficulties may arise from this practice particularly when the variances are significant; for example:

a) Typically, material price variances are isolated at the time of purchase and materials are thereafter maintained at standard price. This process breaks the normal matching rule used in calculating the profits of an accounting period, ie the accruals concept.

b) Where the variances are significant, the valuations (at standard cost) of materials, work-in-progress, and finished goods stocks may not be considered acceptable for balance sheet purposes. In such circumstances it may be necessary to apportion variances over the various categories to achieve more acceptable valuations.

c) Where significant favourable price, usage and efficiency variances arise and stock exist, this could mean that an unrealised profit may be taken. Because of this, favourable variances are sometimes retained in the accounts until the relevant production is actually sold.

32. Control ratios

As an alternative to overhead efficiency and volume variances ratios can be calculated using the same basic data of budgeted and actual labour hours and standard hours produced.

The three ratios are:

$$\text{Activity ratio} = \frac{\text{Standard hours produced}}{\text{Budgeted labour hours}} \times 100$$

$$\text{Capacity ratio} = \frac{\text{Actual labour hours worked}}{\text{Budgeted labour hours}} \times 100$$

$$\text{Efficiency ratio} = \frac{\text{Standard hours produced}}{\text{Actual labour hours worked}} \times 100$$

Based on the data from para 25. the three ratios can be calculated.

Data Budgeted labour hours   5,120

      Actual labour hours   5,100

      Standard hours produced   5,050

$$\text{Activity Ratio} = \frac{5,050}{5,120} \times 100 = 98.6\%$$

$$\text{Capacity Ratio} = \frac{5,100}{5,120} \times 100 = 99.6\%$$

$$\text{Efficiency Ratio} = \frac{5,050}{5,100} \times 100 = 99\%$$

These ratios are statements in relative terms of the absolute measures provided by variances.

The Activity ratio is equivalent to the Fixed Overhead Volume variance.

The Capacity ratio is equivalent to the Fixed Overhead Capacity variance.

The Efficiency ratio is equivalent to the Fixed and Variable Overhead and Labour Efficiency variances.

33. Summary

a) Standard costing involves comparing actual costs with predetermined costs and analysing the differences, known as variances.

b) There are four main types of standard: Basic standards, ideal standards, attainable standards and current standards.

c) Basic standards are long term standards which remain unchanged for long periods; ideal standards represent perfect working conditions and performances; attainable standards are currently attainable standards based on high but not impossible performance levels. Attainable standards are the most common.

d) Standards relate to individual items, processes and products; budgets relate to totals.

e) Setting standards is a detailed, lengthy process usually based on engineering and technical studies of times, materials and methods. Standards are set for each of the elements which make up the standard cost: labour, materials and overheads.

f) Accountants, work study engineers and other specialists provide technical advice and information, but do not set the standards. This is the responsibility of the line managers and their superiors.

g) The culmination of the standard setting process is the preparation of a standard cost for the product showing the target cost for the following periods.

h) Difficulties arise with the too frequent revision of standards. Consequently it is common practice to revise them on a periodic basis, half yearly or yearly.

i) The behavioural aspects of standard costing, like budgeting, are all important. The system must be acceptable to the people who will have to operate it.

j) Variance analysis is the process of analysing the total difference between planned and actual performance into its constituent parts.

k) Variance analysis must be useful to management otherwise it is pointless.

l) Variances should be calculated in accordance with responsibilities but this is often difficult.

m) Although there are different names, each type of variance; materials, wages and overheads has a price element and a quantity element.

n) The relationship between variances must be considered. Variances should not be considered in isolation. Invariably there are interdependencies which conventional variance analysis does not reveal.

o) The basic materials variances measure the differences between actual and standard price and actual and standard usage.

p) Price variances are always extracted first. Thereafter all variance calculations use standard price.

q) The basic labour variances measure the difference between actual and standard wage rates and actual and standard labour efficiency.

r) An important factor in overhead absorption and overhead variance analysis is the activity level. Frequently this is measured in standard hours. A standard hour is a unit measure of production, not of time.

s) Using total absorption principles both fixed and variable overheads are absorbed into production, so variances relating to both fixed and variable overheads will arise. Using standard marginal costing only variable overheads are absorbed into production overheads so that fixed overhead variances cannot arise.

t) Variable overhead variances reflect differences in variable overhead expenditure and labour efficiency. Fixed overhead variances also reflect differences in expenditure and labour efficiency and in addition differences between the planned capacity (activity level) and actual capacity. Apart from the expenditure variances the usefulness of overhead variances is questionable except for balancing purposes.

u) The Total Cost Variance, shown in Figure 10.1, is merely the total of all the variances, ie the Direct Materials cost variance, the Direct Wages cost variance and the Variable and Fixed Overhead variances.

34. Points to note

a) Variances are related to responsibilities. It follows, therefore, that a manager should only be held responsible for a variance when he has control over the resource or cost element being considered.

b) It must be stressed that variance analysis merely directs attention to the cause of off-standard performances. It does not solve the problem, nor does it establish the reasons behind the variance. These are management tasks.

c) The variances described are ones commonly found, but many others exist. It would be impossible to describe or remember all the possible variances, but of far greater importance is to understand the principles underlying variance analysis; once this is done any given variance can be calculated easily.

d) The relationships between variances must always be considered. Rarely is a single variance of great significance. Is a favourable variance offset by a larger adverse one?

e) Although budgetary control and standard costing are techniques which use the same underlying principle, an important difference is that standard costs and variances form part of the double entry system whereas budgetary control is in memorandum form.

f) The overhead volume variances can be criticised because information which is intended for product costing purposes (ie absorption of fixed overheads into cost units) is used as a basis for control information. Fixed overheads are based more on time than activity so that it becomes very difficult to trace responsibility for an adverse volume variance. Because of this, the fixed overhead expenditure variance is probably the most relevant fixed overhead variance for control purposes.

g) Standard costing can only exist realistically within the framework of a budgeting system. On the other hand budgetary control systems are frequently found without a standard costing system. Standard costing should only be employed when it suits the product, type of manufacture and the organisation and when its use is cost-effective.

h) The significance of variances and variance control bands have been dealt with in the chapter on Budgetary Control. The principles and techniques described apply equally to standard costing variances.

i) Although it is conventional to value usage and efficiency variances at standard prices or rates students should be aware that they could alternatively be valued at actual price. It is argued that such a procedure gives a valuation that is economically realistic, more up to date and is thus a better guide for management action.

Additional reading

Management Accounting; *Amey & Egginton* – Longman

Cost Accounting – a Managerial Emphasis; *Horngren & Foster* – Prentice Hall

Advanced Management Accounting; *Kaplan & Atkinson* – Prentice Hall

Management Accounting – Review of Recent Developments; *Scapens* – Macmillan

Self review questions

1. What is standard costing? (2)
2. What are the objectives of standard costing? (3)
3. Define standard cost. (4)
4. What are the four main types of standard? (5)
5. What is the relationship between budgets and standards? (6)
6. What factors need to be considered when setting standards? (7-9)
7. What is a 'standard hour'? (9)
8. Whose responsibility is it ultimately for setting the attainment level in a standard? (12)
9. Describe a standard cost card. (13)
10. Why are the behavioural aspects of standard costing so important? (15)
11. What is the purpose of variance analysis and what variances should be calculated? (17)
12. Why is the location of responsibility for variances desirable but difficult to achieve? (18)
13. What is the operating profit variance and how could this be analysed? (19)
14. How can the significance of a variance be established? (20)
15. Define the common materials variances and give their formulae. (22)
16. Define the common labour variances and give their formulae. (23)
17. What is the basis of overhead variance analysis? (25)
18. What are typical variable overhead variances and what are their formulae? (26)
19. Describe a four way variance analysis of fixed overheads. (27)
20. What is a possible alternative approach to overhead variance analysis? (28)
21. Why do overhead variances arise? (29)
22. What specific criticisms can be made of overhead variances as a means of management control? (30)
23. What happens to variances at the period end? (31)
24. Describe the control ratios. (32)

11 Standard costing II

1. Objectives

After studying this chapter you will:

❏ be able to calculate mix and yield variances;

❏ know the differences between the individual price and weighted average price methods;

❏ understand the deficiencies of mix and yield variances;

❏ be able to calculate sales margin variances;

❏ know the principles of standard marginal costing;

❏ understand the principles of planning and operational variances;

❏ be able to describe the advantages and disadvantages of standard costing;

❏ know the principles of value analysis, work study and O & M.

2. More detailed material variances

The basic material variances were described in the previous chapter. In certain circumstances it is conventional for sub-variances to be calculated, known as the Direct Materials Mix Variance and the Direct Materials Yield Variance. Typical circumstances in which such calculations are considered appropriate are those where the production process involves mixing different material inputs to make the required output. Examples include: the manufacture of fertilisers, steel, plastics, food products and so on. A feature of such processes is the existence of process losses through impurities, evaporation, breakages, machinery failures and other such factors which affect the yield from the process.

There are several methods of calculating mix and yield variances; some treat the mix variance as part of the price variance, others that there should be a combined mix/price variance, whilst another approach is that the mix and yield variances are sub-variances of the usage variance. This latter approach is illustrated in Figure 2 in the previous chapter and is the system included in the CIMA Terminology of Management Accounting.

There are two alternative ways of sub-dividing the usage variance. One uses the individual standard prices of the ingredients whilst the other uses a weighted average price for all ingredients. For the variance calculations these prices are applied to slightly different ingredient quantities. Both methods produce the same mix and yield variances in total; all that differs is the amount attributed to each constituent ingredient.

For identification the methods will be termed the 'individual price' and the 'weighted average price' methods and both are defined and illustrated below using the same data for comparative purposes. The individual price method (which is that in the CIMA terminology) is illustrated first.

Definitions (Individual price method)

Direct Materials Mix Variance

'A subset of the direct usage variance, applicable when materials are applied in a standard proportion. Shows the effect on cost on variations from the standard proportion'. *Terminology.*

Direct Materials Yield Variance

'A subset of the direct materials usage variance applicable when materials are combined in standard proportion'. *Terminology.*

3. Mix and yield formulae (individual price method)

Direct Materials Mixture Variance	=	STANDARD COST of the actual quantity of the actual mixture	minus	STANDARD COST of the actual quantity of the STANDARD MIXTURE
Direct Materials Yield Variance	=	STANDARD COST of the actual quantity of the STANDARD MIXTURE	minus	STANDARD COST of the STANDARD QUANTITY of the STANDARD MIXTURE

Notes:

a) Because the price variance is always dealt with first, the mix and yield variances use only standard prices.

b) Note how the expressions move from actual to STANDARD values and that the second part of the mix variance is the same as the first in the yield variance.

c) The yield variance measures abnormal process losses or gains.

Example 1

A fertiliser is made by mixing and processing three ingredients, P, N and Q. The standard cost data are:

	Ingredient	Standard Proportions	Standard Cost
	P	50%	£20 per tonne
	N	40%	£25 per tonne
	Q	10%	£42 per tonne

A standard process loss of 5% is anticipated.

In a period the output was 93.1 tonnes and the inputs were as follows:

Ingredient		Actual usage	Actual price	Actual cost
	P	49 tonnes	£16 per tonne	784
	N	43 tonnes	£27 per tonne	1,161
	Q	8 tonnes	£48 per tonne	384
				£2,329

Calculate all relevant material variances using the individual price method.

Solution

The total variance is calculated thus:

Standard cost for 1 tonne

Ingredient				
	P	0.5 tonne @ £20	=	£10
	N	0.4 tonne @ £25	=	£10
	Q	0.1 tonne @ £42	=	£4.2
				£24.2

1 tonne of input at standard produces 0.95 tonnes of output so the standard cost per tonne of output is

$$£24.2 \times \frac{100}{95} = £25.473684$$

∴ Standard cost of actual output = $93.1 \times £25.473684$ = £2,371.6

Actual cost of output = £2,329

Total Variance = £42.6(FAV)

The three relevant variances are: Price, Mix and Yield which are to be calculated in that order. The usage variance is merely the total of the mix and yield variances.

The summary of the variance calculations is given below followed by explanatory notes.

a) Actual usage
   Actual mix   £2,329
   Actual price

b) Actual usage
   Actual mix   £2,391
   STANDARD price

c) Actual usage
   STANDARD mix   £2,420
   STANDARD price

d) STANDARD usage
   STANDARD mix   £2,371.6
   STANDARD price

DIRECT MATERIALS PRICE VARIANCE £62 FAV

MIXTURE VARIANCE £29 FAV

YIELD VARIANCE £48.4 ADV

USAGE VARIANCE £19.4 ADV

DIRECT MATERIALS COST VARIANCE £42.6 FAV

It will be seen how the factors involved, usage-mix-price, start all at actual and move stage by stage to become all at STANDARD. This is the key to remembering the method of calculation.

Notes:

a) Actual usage, actual mix, actual price is the cost given in the question, ie £2,329.

b) The actual usage in the actual proportions is evaluated at the standard price, ie

$$£(49 \times 20) + (43 \times 25) + (8 \times 42) = \textbf{£2,391}$$

c) The standard mix is found by putting the actual total quantity (100 tonnes) into the standard proportions (50%, 40% and 10%), ie 50P, 40N and 10Q.

   These are evaluated at the standard prices and compared with the values from (b).

Ingredient	Actual usage Tonnes	Total usage in STANDARD PROPORTIONS Tonnes	Difference Tonnes	STANDARD PRICE £	Variance £
P	49	50	+1	20	20 FAV
N	43	40	−3	25	75 ADV
Q	8	10	+2	42	84 FAV
	100	100		TOTAL MIX VARIANCE	29 FAV

d) The standard usage is found by working back from the actual output (93.1 tonnes) to determine what the standard total quantity of inputs should be, assuming a normal process loss of 5%.

$$\text{ie standard output quantity} = 95\% \text{ of standard input quantity}$$

$$\therefore \text{Standard input quantity} = \frac{100}{95} \times \text{actual output quantity}$$

$$= \frac{100}{95} \times 93.1$$

$$= \textbf{98 tonnes}$$

This value is pro rated in the standard proportions, calculated at the standard price and compared with the values from (c) thus:

Ingredient	Tonnes	Total usage in STANDARD PROPORTIONS	Standard USAGE for output in STD PROPORTIONS tonnes	Difference tonnes	STANDARD PRICE £	Variance £
P	50	(98 × 50%)	49	−1	20	20.0 ADV
N	40	(98 × 40%)	39.2	−0.8	25	20.0 ADV
Q	10	(98 × 10%)	9.8	−0.2	42	8.4 ADV
	100		98	TOTAL YIELD VARIANCE		48.4 ADV

The alternative 'weighted average price' method is now defined and illustrated.

4. Alternative method for mix and yield variances

Definitions (weighted average price method)

Direct Materials Mix Variance

The difference between the standard quantity of inputs for the output achieved and the actual quantity used priced at the difference between individual standard prices and weighted average standard price.

Direct Materials Yield Variance

The difference between the standard quantity of inputs for the output achieved and the actual quantity used priced at the weighted average standard price.

Example 1 is reworked below based on these alternative definitions.

The Total Variance is £42.6 ADV and the Price Variance is calculated in exactly the same manner and is, as previously, £62 Favourable.

To calculate the weighted average mix and yield variances the input quantity differences and the weighted average standard ingredient price have to be calculated.

Ingredient	STANDARD USAGE for output in STD proportions Tonnes	Actual usage Tonnes	Input differences Tonnes
P	49	49	–
N	39.2	43	−3.8
Q	9.8	8	+1.8
	98	100	−2.0

Weighted Average Standard ingredient price.

From the original data the standard cost of 1 tonne is:

			£
Ingredient	P 0.5 × £20	=	10
	N 0.4 × £25	=	10
	Q 0.1 × £42	=	4.2
			24.2

∴ Weighted average ingredient cost is £24.2 per tonne

These values are used in the variance calculations

MIX VARIANCE:

INGREDIENT	INPUT DIFFERENCES × Tonnes	STANDARD PRICE less WEIGHTED AVERAGE PRICE	=	VARIANCE
		£		£
P	–	–		
N	– 3.8	(£25 – 24.2) = 0.80		3.04 ADV
Q	+ 1.8	(£42 – 24.2) = 17.80		
				32.04 FAV
		TOTAL MIX VARIANCE		29.00 FAV

YIELD VARIANCE:

INGREDIENT	INPUT DIFFERENCES × Tonnes	WEIGHTED AVERAGE STANDARD PRICE	=	VARIANCE
		£		£
P	–			
N	– 3.8	24.2		91.96 ADV
Q	+ 1.8	24.2		43.56 FAV
		TOTAL MIX VARIANCE		48.40 ADV

Thus it will be seen that the alternative approaches produce the same total mix and yield variances but differ in the amount attributed to each ingredient. Which is the correct method?

No one method of calculating variances or any given variance is more correct than any other. The 'correct' variances are those which assist management to make the right decisions. Accordingly, management would use whichever of the above methods is deemed to provide the most relevant information if, in fact, mix and yield variances are thought to provide any useful information. However, students should be aware that there are serious doubts about the usefulness and meaning of conventionally prepared mix and yield variances. These doubts are explored below.

5. Problems with conventional mix and yield variances

The standard mix is, by definition, the cheapest possible combination of materials, which fulfils the technical requirements of the output, having regard to the relative prices and characteristics of the materials and the process yield expected when the standard was set. Typical conventional variances, as the example calculated above, show the effect of changes from the original standard (based on implicit assumptions discussed below) but give no indication of whether the results were optimal given the relative prices, qualities and availability of materials at the time of production. Where substitutability of materials is possible and/or where the characteristics of materials are variable and/or where there are relative price changes then the optimal mix may be continually changing and a static, historical standard, as implied in conventional variance calculations, is unlikely to be appropriate.

The choice of the optimum mix of materials in any given circumstances is a subtle one involving the balancing of current material prices, availability and characteristics, the extent of technical substitutability and the requirements of the finished production. Because of this many process industries use computer based linear programming techniques (described in a later chapter) on a continual basis to select the optimal mix for the current production.

The likelihood that the original standard will be out of date is but one problem with conventional mix and yield variance analysis. Other problems are as follows:

a) The conventional analysis presupposes a constant correlation between physical inputs and output regardless of the mix of inputs, ie if the mix of inputs changes the same relationship is assumed between the new mix and output as between the original standard mix and output. Such an assumption is illogical and contravenes the concept of an optimum mix.

b) The conventional analysis ignores the technical acceptability of the output by assuming that the output is acceptable regardless of the input mix of materials.

c) Conventionally a linear substitutability between material inputs assumed. If this reasoning were pursued to the extreme it would result in a mix consisting of one material only, the cheapest! This mix would produce a large, favourable mix variance which seems a strange measure of what would be a production impossibility.

d) Based on the premise that the standard represents the optimum position, conventional analysis should never produce a favourable mix variance because the lower standard cost of the actual mix means that it should have been the original standard in the first place, assuming the technical acceptability of the output. Examination questions based on conventional analysis which produce favourable mix variances are therefore internally inconsistent. The figures in Example 1 earlier in the chapter were chosen to give a favourable mix variance to illustrate this point.

e) Even when the current circumstances are exactly as envisaged (ie same prices, technical qualities etc) if one of the sub-variances (mix or yield) is adverse then the other will be favourable and vice versa. Accordingly even in such stable conditions there would seem to be little value in calculating the sub-variances. The usage variance will be adverse at all conditions other than standard.

f) The conventional analysis abstracts any differences between actual and standard prices first, and then uses standard price for the mix and yield variances. However, when prices vary from standard it is these very changes in relative prices which may make changes in mix and yield worthwhile. The exclusion of them from mix and yield calculations makes it more difficult to judge the correctness, or otherwise, of managerial decisions.

It will be seen from the above that conventional mix and yield variance analysis has serious deficiencies and is unlikely to produce information that assists management. Useful variance analysis is possible in this area but it cannot be achieved by the mechanical application of a few simple formulae. It will always be based on a thorough understanding of the principles and objectives of variance analysis and of the technical and commercial factors affecting the process being considered. Typical of the factors to be considered are:

i) The relative prices, availabilities and technical characteristics of the input materials at the time of the mix.

ii) The extent of the technical substitutability of materials.

iii) The planned yield from any given actual mix of materials, not merely the yield from the standard mix.

iv) The interdependencies between the material variances and the other process inputs. For example, a given material mix, based on relative prices and other factors may show an overall favourable materials variance but which may be more than outweighed by extra labour costs.

6. Sales margin variances

A number of the more commonly encountered cost variances have now been dealt with and it will be recalled that the objective of cost variance analysis was to help management to control costs. However, costs are only one factor contributing to the achievement of planned profits. Another important factor is the margin on sales; either the profit margin when absorption costing is used or the contribution margin when marginal costing is used.

Accordingly sales margin variances can be calculated and because cost variance analysis extracts all the differences between planned and actual costs, the products are always treated at standard manufacturing cost for the purpose of sales margin variance analysis.

Part of Figure 10.2 from the preceding chapter is reproduced below showing the sales margin variances.

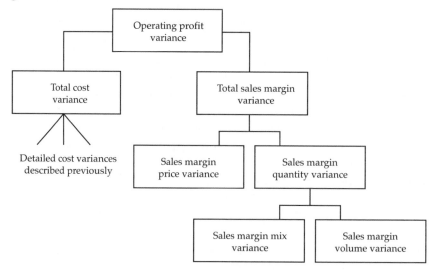

Extract from Figure 10.2. Preceding chapter

Notes:

a) The standard sales margin is the difference between the standard selling price of a produce and its standard cost and is the same as the standard profit for the product.

b) The 'standard cost' referred to above is the 'total standard cost', ie it includes both fixed and variable costs. When fixed costs are excluded it becomes the standard marginal cost and the difference between standard selling price and standard marginal cost is known as the standard sales contribution.

7. Sales margin variances – definitions

Total sales margin variance

> The difference between the budgeted margin from sales and the actual margin when the cost of sales is valued at the standard cost of production.

Sales margin price variance

> That portion of the total sales margin variance which is the difference between the standard margin per unit and the actual margin per unit for the number of units sold in the period.

Note: This is a normal price variance and could equally well be described as the 'sales turnover price variance'.

Sales margin quantity variance

> The portion of the total sales margin variance which is the difference between the budgeted number of units sold and the actual number sold valued at the standard margin per unit.

Note:

This is a normal usage variance, analogous to the direct materials usage variance previously described.

When more than one product is sold, the Sales Margin Quantity Variance can be subdivided into a Mix Variance and a Volume Variance. The mix variance shows the effect on profits of variations from the planned sales mixture, and the volume variance shows the effect of the unit volume varying from standard. These sub-variances are defined below.

Sales margin mixture variance

> That portion of the sales margin quantity variance which is the difference between the actual total number of units at the actual mix and the actual total number of units at standard mix valued at the standard margin per unit.

Sales margin volume variance

> That portion of the sales margin quantity variance which is the difference between the actual total quantity of units sold and the budgeted total number of units at the standard mix valued at the standard margin per unit.

The formulae for these variances are given below.

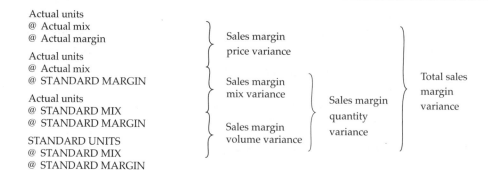

Note:

There is considerable similarity in approach between these variances and the direct materials variances shown previously.

Example 2

A company makes and sells three products Q, R, and S. During a period, budget and actual results were as follows:

	Budget					Actual				
Product	Total Sales	Unit			Total Margin	Total Sales	Unit			Total Margin
		Volume	Price	Margin			Volume	Price	Margin	
	£	units	£	£	£	£	units	£	£	£
Q	18,000	600	30	10	6,000	14,560	520	28	8	4,160
R	13,500	300	45	15	4,500	14,210	290	49	19	5,510
S	6,500	100	65	25	2,500	5,670	90	63	23	2,070
	38,000	1,000			13,000	34,440	900			11,740

Solution

Notes:

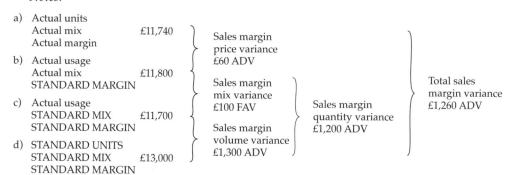

The similarity of these calculations and those for material variances can be seen by comparing the above solution with that for Example 1 in para 3.

Notes:

a) This is the actual total margin as shown in the original data, ie £11,740.

b) This is the actual units in the actual proportions but at budgeted margins, ie

$$£(520 \times 10) + (290 \times 15) + (90 \times 25) = £11,800$$

c) This is the actual number of units sold (900) but at the standard proportions (60%, 30%, 10%), valued at standard

$$£(540 \times 10) + (270 \times 15) + (90 \times 25) = £11,700$$

d) This is the total budgeted margin as given in the question, ie £13,000.

As usual, the total variance can be verified by comparing the budgeted position with the actual position, ie

$$£11,740 - £13,000 = £1,260 \text{ ADV}$$

Note: In similar fashion to the material mix and yield variances, the sales margin mix variance and the volume variance can alternatively be calculated using the weighted average standard margin rather than the individual standard margins as used above.

8. Limitations of sales margin variance analysis

The purpose of all variance analysis is to aid management control. To do this variances must be relevant and within a manager's control. Because there are so many external factors involved, the control of sales volume, sales margins and sales mix is extremely difficult and it is somewhat doubtful whether full variance analysis in this area is useful. In certain circumstances however, some of the variances may provide useful information; for example, where the sales price is under the control of the selling organisation and prices are stable, then the sales margin price variance could be useful, alternatively, when a manager is responsible for two or more products which are substitutes for one another (different qualities of paint) then the mix variance would show the effect of changes in demand and therefore might be useful.

Note: In the above example the standard proportions were based on the number of units. On occasions where there are substantial differences in the selling prices of the various products within a firm (eg bicycle tyres and tractor tyres) standardising on the number of units could produce distortions. In such cases the proportions for the standard mix would be based on sales turnover, not units. This procedure would only alter the balance between the mix and volume variances. The overall quantity variance would remain unchanged.

9. Sales variances c.f. sales margin variances

Historically variance analysis in the sales are commenced with variances based on sales turnover, ie if actual sales were above budget there was a favourable sales variance even if profits fell, perhaps because the sales of low profit items had increased. Although information on variations in sales turnover is important, nowadays it is likely to be supplied by detailed sales analyses, not through variance analysis. Management need to have information about profit performance related to budget and for this reason sales margin variances are generally of much greater importance and so have been described in the preceding paragraphs.

10. **Standard marginal costing**

Most standard costing systems are based on total absorption cost principles and the standards and variances described in the last two chapters are typical of such systems. Standard costing can also incorporate marginal cost principles and is then termed *standard marginal costing*. It will be recalled that marginal costing involves the separation of costs, and those which remain unaffected by activity changes, known as fixed costs. Fixed costs are not absorbed into individual units of production and are deducted in total from the contribution (sales – marginal cost) earned from units sold. Standard marginal costing incorporates these principles and has the following characteristics.

a) Standards are developed in the normal manner and entered as usual on the standard cost card, except that fixed costs do not appear. The standard cost card includes

❒ Direct materials

❒ Direct labour

❒ Direct expenses

❒ Variable overheads (ie no fixed costs)

b) A standard contribution is set for each product and added to the standard margin cost. This sets the standard selling price. The standard contribution becomes the standard sales margin.

c) A budgeted profit statement is prepared for the next period with budgeted levels of sales and fixed overheads. Typically this would appear as follows:

Budgeted Profit Statement for Period

		£
	Budgeted sales	XXX
	(Budgeted no. of units × standard selling price)	
less	Budgeted cost of sales	XXX
	(Budgeted no. of units × standard marginal cost per unit)	
=	Budgeted Contribution	XXX
less	Budgeted fixed cost	XXX
	Budgeted profit	XXX

d) Variance analysis is simplified because of the disappearance of the fixed overhead volume variance and its sub-variances, the capacity and efficiency variances. All other variances are identical or very similar. The different categories are listed below.

Types of variance	Characteristics of standard marginal cost variances
DIRECT MATERIALS DIRECT LABOUR VARIABLE OVERHEADS	} Identical to ABSORPTION STANDARD COST VARIANCES
FIXED OVERHEADS	Only variance is the FIXED OVERHEAD EXPENDITURE VARIANCE. All other fixed overhead variances disappear.
SALES VARIANCES	With the exception that the STANDARD SALES MARGIN is now the STANDARD CONTRIBUTION. The variances are calculated in an identical manner. The new titles are: ❏ Sales contribution variance 　(was sales margin variance) ❏ Sales contribution variance 　(was sales margin variance ❏ Sales contribution price variance 　(was sales margin price variance) ❏ Sales contribution quantity variance 　(was sales margin quantity variance) ❏ Sales contribution mixture variance 　(was sales margin mixture variance) ❏ Sales contribution volume variance 　(was sales margin volume variance)

11. Standard marginal costing example

Example 3

The following data relate to the budget and actual results of a firm which produces and sells a single product and which employs standard marginal costing.

Budget			Actual		
Production	12,000	units	Production	11,200	
Sales	12,000	units	Sales	11,200	
		£			£
Sales		192,000	Sales		190,400
less Standard Marginal Cost			less Actual Marginal Cost		
	£			£	
– materials	48,000		– materials	50,400	
– labour	60,000		– labour	50,400	
– variable overheads	36,000	144,000	– variable overheads	39,200	140,000
= Contribution		48,000	= Contribution		50,400
less Fixed Costs		25,000	less Fixed Costs		28,400
= Profit		23,000	= Profit		22,000

Extracts from the Standard Cost Card for the products are:

	£
Material 4 Kgs @ £1 Kg	4
Labour 2 hours @ £2.50	5
Variable overheads 2 hours @ £1.50	3
= Standard marginal cost	12
Standard contribution	4
Standard selling price	16

During the period 44,800 Kgs of material were used and 21,000 labour hours were worked.

Calculate all relevant variances and show a reconciliation between budgeted and actual profit.

Solution

The total variance is the Operating Profit variance which is the difference between budgeted and actual profit, ie

$$£23,000 – 22,000 = £1,000 \text{ ADV}$$

The total of all other variances will equal this amount.

The cost variances are extracted first.

Material variances

	£		
Actual price Actual quantity	£50,400	Price variance £5,600 ADV	Materials variance £5,600 ADV
Actual quantity STANDARD PRICE (44,800 @ £1)	£44,800	Usage variance NIL	
STANDARD QUANTITY STANDARD PRICE (44,800 @ £1)	£44,800		

Labour variances

Actual hours Actual rate	£50,400	Rate variance £2,100 FAV	Labour variance £5,600 FAV
Actual hours STANDARD RATE (21,000 @ £2.50)	£52,500	Efficiency variance £3,500 FAV	
STANDARD HOURS STANDARD RATE (22,400 @ £2.50)	£56,000		

Variable overhead variances

Actual variable overheads	£39,200	Expenditure variance £7,700 ADV	Variable overhead variance £5,600 ADV
Actual hours × VOAR (21,000 × £1.50)	£31,500	Efficiency variance £2,100 FAV	
SHP × VOAR (22,400 × £1.50)	£33,600		

Fixed overhead expenditure variance

= £28,400 − 25,000 = £3400 ADV

Summary of Cost Variances

	£	
Materials	5,600	ADV
Labour	5,600	FAV
Variable overheads	5,600	ADV
Fixed overheads	3,400	ADV
Total	£9,000	ADV

Sales variances (when standard contribution is £4 per unit and standard selling price is £16).

Actual contribution when Sales valued at std cost (£190,400 − (11,200 × 12)	£56,000	Price variance £11,200 FAV	Total contribution variance £8,000 ADV
Actual hours @ STANDARD CONTRIBUTION	£44,800	Quantity variance £3,200 ADV	
BUDGETED UNITS STANDARD CONTRIBUTION (12,000 × £4)	£48,000		

Variance Summary

	£	
Total cost variance	9,000	ADV
Total sales variance	8,000	FAV
= Operating Profit variance	£1,000	ADV

12. Planning and operational variances

The approach to variance analysis so far explained is the traditional one whereby actual performance is compared with a predetermined standard and a variance calculated. If the standard, which will have been prepared some time previously, is still a realistic target in current conditions then the calculated variances will be of some value. However, if there have been uncontrollable changes in internal or external operating conditions then the standard may not now be a realistic one and the calculated variances will be of little or no value and may even be misleading.

This is a real problem particularly in volatile conditions and an attempt to overcome this is to separate out the total variances into *planning variances* and *operating variances*.

Planning variances seek to explain the extent to which the original standard needs to be adjusted in order to reflect changes in operating conditions between the current situation and that envisaged when the standard was originally calculated. In effect it means that the original standard is brought up to date so that it is a realistic target in current conditions.

Operating variances indicate the extent to which attainable targets (ie the adjusted standards) have been achieved. Operating variances would be calculated after the planning variances have been established and are thus a realistic way of assessing performance.

The separation of that part of the total variation which is due to planning deficiencies makes possible a clearer definition of what is an attainable, current target. In traditional variance analysis there is the implicit assumption that the whole of the variance is due to operating deficiencies and that the planning associated with setting the original standard was perfectly accurate, which is hardly realistic.

One of the leading exponents of the theory of planning variances, Professor Demski, has argued that because of the traditional emphasis on the comparison between actual and planned results, without regard to changes in planned results, the traditional accounting method does not act as an opportunity cost system. He argues that variances ought to be calculated by taking as the comparison level, not the original budget or standard, but a budget or standard which can be seen with hindsight, to be the optimum that should have been achievable. The original budget and standards are known as *ex-ante* standards, the ones that are set which are deemed to be currently attainable are known as *ex-post* standards.

13. Opportunity cost approach using ex-ante and ex-post standards

The opportunity cost approach seeks to calculate variances that provide a realistic measurement of the gains or losses arising from controllable operating results, ie the operating variances. The ex-post standards, ie the planning variances, are largely uncontrollable by operating management so are best separated in order to show more clearly the efficiency or inefficiency of operations.

The relationships are shown in Figure 11.1.

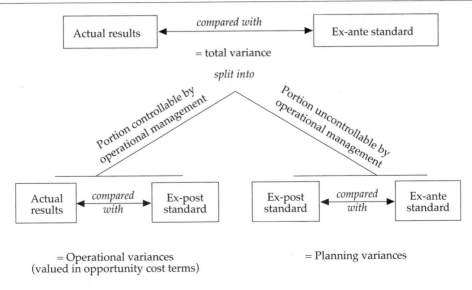

Figure 11.1 Planning and Operational Variances

The following examples illustrates the calculation of planning and operational variances.

14. Examples of planning and operating variances

Example 4

A raw material, Zeta, is used in the production of Alpha and an extract from the standard cost card for Alpha showing the rates of usage and expected price is as follows:

Alpha Standard Cost Card (extract)

material per unit 10 Kgs of Zeta @ £6 Kg = £60 = standard material cost.

During the current period 270 units of Alpha were produced and the usage was 2,850 Kgs with an actual material cost of £16,530. Due to world wide price movements Zeta was freely available at £5.5 Kg during the period.

Calculate

i) the traditional variances

ii) the planning and operating variances.

Solution

i) *Traditional variances*

		£	
Material Price Variance	=	570	FAV
£16,530 – (2,850 × £6)			
Material Usage Variance			
(2,850 – 2,700) × £6	=	900	ADV
∴ Total material cost variance	=	**£330**	**ADV**

ii) *Planning Variance (uncontrollable)*

		£	
$(2,700 \times £6) - (2,700 \times £5.5)$	=	1,350	FAV

Operating Variances (controllable)
Operating Price variance

		£	
$£16,530 - (2,850 \times £5.5)$	=	855	ADV

Operating Usage variance

$(2,850 - 2,700) \times £5.5$	=	825	ADV
Total Operating Material Variance	=	**£1,680**	**ADV**

Planning variance + Operating variances = Traditional variance
= £1,350 FAV + 1680 ADV = **£330 ADV.**

Notes:

a) The planning variance shows the total difference due to uncontrollable factors, ie the world wide price change, and is the difference between the old standard price and the new standard price for the standard quantity of material that should be used. If the planning variance is correct all that is left are controllable factors which are analysed by the operating variances.

b) The operating variances follow the normal procedures for material variances except that the new standard price of £5.5 is used. It will be noted that the operating price variance shows that there have been purchasing inefficiencies which contrasts with the traditional price variance which showed apparent purchasing efficiency.

Example 5

In a four week period Acme Ltd budgeted to make and sell 800 units of its single product with a budget as follows:

Budget for 4 week period

	£
Production and Sales (8,000 units at £15 each)	120,000
less Variable costs (8,000 at £5 each)	40,000
= Contribution	80,000
less Fixed Costs	45,000
= Profit	35,000

Due to storm damage there was an external power line failure and 3 days production out of the possible 20 days were lost. The actual results were:

	£
Production and Sales (7,150 units at £15 each)	107,250
less Variable costs (7,150 at £5 each)	35,750
= Contribution	71,500
less Fixed Costs	45,000
= Profit	26,500

Calculate

i) the traditional variances

ii) the planning and operational variances

Solution

i) Traditional Variances

Inspection shows that there has been no change in selling prices, variable costs and margin so the only variance is the sales volume variance, ie

(Original Budget – Actual Sales) × Standard Margin = (8,000 – 7,150) × £10 = £8,500 ADV

ii) Planning and Operational Variances

With hindsight a more realistic ex-post budget for the period would have been 8,000 units less 3 days standard production, ie 8,000 – 1,200 = 6,800 units.

Thus the planning variance would be the ex-ante budget less the ex-post budget at the standard margin, ie

$$(8,000 – 6,800) \times £10 = £12,000 \text{ ADV}$$

The operational variance, which is deemed to be the controllable portion, is the difference between the more realistic ex-post budget and actual output at the standard margin thus:

$$(6,800 – 7,150) \times £10 = £3,500 \text{ FAV}$$

Planning Variance + Operational Variance = Total Variance

$$£12,000 \text{ ADV} + £3,500 \text{ FAV} = £8,500 \text{ ADV}$$

It will be seen that the above variances have used the contribution foregone as a reasonable equivalent to opportunity cost. Also it can be claimed that they show a more realistic picture of the effects of planning errors and of operating efficiency or inefficiency than traditional variances which assume that all differences arise from operational factors.

15. Benefits and problems of planning and operating variances

The segregation of traditional variances into those which are due to planning deficiencies and those which are due to controllable factors is probably not widely used in the UK but it does have certain benefits.

a) It makes standard costing and variance analysis more realistic in volatile and changing conditions.

b) Operational variances provide an up to date guide to current levels of operating efficiency as the standards have been recalculated using up to date information.

c) Having up to date standards and therefore more realistic variances is likely to make the standard costing system more acceptable and to have a positive effect on motivation.

d) It emphasises the importance of the planning function in the preparation of standards and helps to identify planning deficiencies.

e) The calculation of such variances provides a systematic method of reviewing standards and the assumptions contained within them.

As is to be expected there are problems in using such variances.

a) There is an element of subjectivity in determining after the event (ie ex-post) what is a realistic price. This makes the allocation between planning and operational causes a subjective matter susceptible to political pressures.

b) There is undeniably more clerical and managerial time involved in continually establishing up to date standards and calculating additional variances.

c) Where the planning and operating functions are carried out in the same responsibility centre there is likely to be pressure to put as much as possible of the total variance down to outside, uncontrollable factors rather than internal, controllable actions. However, these pressures exist in the interpretation of any type of variance.

16. Advantages of standard costing

a) Standard costing is an example of 'management by exception'. By studying the variances, management's attention is directed towards those items which are not proceeding according to plan. Management are able to delegate cost control through the standard costing system knowing that variances will be reported.

b) The process of setting, revising and monitoring standards encourages reappraisal of methods, materials and techniques so leading to cost reductions.

c) Standard costs represent what the parts and products should cost. They are not merely averages of past performances and consequently they are a better guide to pricing than historical costs. In addition, they provide a simpler basis of inventory valuation.

d) A properly developed standard costing system with full participation and involvement creates a positive, cost effective attitude through all levels of management right down to the shop floor and thereby increases motivation and goal congruence.

17. Disadvantages of standard costing

a) It may be expensive and time consuming to install and to keep up to date.

b) In volatile conditions with rapidly changing methods, rates and prices, standards quickly become out of date and thus lose their control and motivational effects. This can cause resentment and loss of goodwill. A possible method of overcoming this problem is by the use of planning and operational variances but this involves more subjectivity and more work.

c) There is research evidence to show that overly elaborate variances are imperfectly understood by line managers and thus they are likely to be ineffective for control purposes.

d) Virtually all aspects of setting standards involves forecasting and subjective judgements with inherent possibilities of error and argument.

e) The usefulness of a number of variances relating to overheads, sales margins, mix and yield is questionable.

f) All forms of variance analysis are post mortems on past events. Obviously the past cannot be altered so that the only value variances can have is to guide management if identical or similar circumstances occur in the future. This implies stable, repeating situations which is not always a reflection of reality. Indeed if the conditions were as stable as postulated then simpler 'point of action' controls and checks are likely to have more effect than variance reporting. For example, if a purchase order was being contemplated at above standard price then it could be arranged that the order would need to be countersigned (and investigated) by the Purchasing Director. This type of control is likely to be more effective than reporting an adverse price variance weeks or months after the event.

g) The philosophy behind Standard Costing, ie setting a predetermined standard cost and assuming that actual production is satisfactory if the standard is met, is increasingly being challenged. It is claimed that such a philosophy is inappropriate in modern manufacturing environments where there is a continual drive for improvement. Furthermore, where production is rapidly changing and small batches is the norm, the conditions for standard costing ie long runs of repetitive production just do not apply. This is explored in more detail in Chapter 23 covering Advanced Manufacturing Technology and Management Accounting.

18. Cost reduction

Budgetary Control and Standard Costing are examples of cost control techniques which have the broad objective of containing costs within a pre-determined target. On the other hand cost reduction has the aim of reducing costs from some previously accepted norm or standard whilst at the same time maintaining the effectiveness or performance of the product or service. Cost reduction is an active, dynamic concept which attempts to extract more from the factors of production without loss of effectiveness.

The most effective cost reduction programmes are those which embrace all aspects of the firm's operations, systems and products and are those which have full top management support and co-operation. Significant cost reductions can often be made simply by the application of common sense but there are several formal techniques which have been found to be of value in improving products, reducing waste, streamlining systems and thereby reducing costs. Some of the more important ones are explained briefly below – variety reduction, value analysis, work study and organisation and methods.

19. Variety reduction

Examination of the product range may show that it is too extensive and that some of the products are uneconomic because they are produced in small quantities. Variety reduction when applied to components is often called standardisation and is widely used because it is often cost effective to be able to produce a range of finished products from a common, relatively small, pool of components. In general fewer varieties makes for easier production, increases the scope for automation, and is likely to reduce costs. It goes without saying that the sales and marketing aspects of variety reduction must be closely considered otherwise any production gains may be nullified.

20. Value analysis

Value analysis or value engineering is an assessment process carried out by a team during the design stages of a product. The team would consist of engineering, technical and production personnel together with an accountant and has as its objective the task of designing a product which meets the essential design objectives at minimum cost. Value analysis is a systematic, conscious attempt to eliminate inessentials and unnecessary costs and is carried out by detailed questioning of every aspect of the products functions, materials, methods of manufacture, components, finish etc.

Typical of the questions to be asked are the following:

❐ Can the function of the product be achieved in some other way?

❐ Are all of the functions of the product essential?

❐ Can the product be made lighter, smaller or from cheaper material?

❐ What standardisation of components, materials, methods of manufacture etc. can be made?

❐ Can the design be modified so that product can be made more easily and cheaply?

and so on.

The full application of value analysis would mean that periodically each product in the firm would come under searching scrutiny and thereby there would be a continual, planned search for cost reduction.

21. Work study

This is a technique used in factories to determine the most efficient methods of using labour, materials and machinery. The main subdivisions of work study are *method study* and *work measurement*. Method study is the recording and analysis of existing methods of doing work and comparing these with proposed methods in order to implement new and more effective procedures. Work measurement is the process of establishing times for a qualified worker to carry out a task at a defined level of performance. It will be apparent from this that Work Study is the basis of much of standard costing.

Work Study is a valuable technique for improving efficiency and reducing waste in factories and can be applied in many areas including: Factory layouts and work flow, materials handling, tool design, scheduling, line balancing, workplace methods and layout.

22. Organisation and methods (O & M)

O & M has been described as 'work study in the office' and the broad objectives of the two techniques are similar. Administrative and overhead costs are a significant proportion of the costs of an organisation and are a fruitful area for cost reduction programmes. O & M is the systematic analysis of administrative and office procedures in order to produce more efficient methods. O & M is carried out by a process of investigation, analysis, design and implementation of improved methods, equipment and procedures and there are many areas where it can be applied in the office. These include: form design, office layout, departmental procedures, office mechanisation, work flows, paperwork elimination, telephone and communication services and many other examples.

A development of O & M called *systems analysis* has evolved to deal with those procedures which require the use of computers. Whilst having the same broad objectives as O & M and using the same questioning approach, naturally there are many differences in the technical expertise required.

23. Cost reduction – conclusion

Any or all of the above techniques may be used in cost reduction programmes often with great success. However, of probably greater importance is the motivation of all levels of staff to achieve more effective results from every facet of their work. This is an aspect of goal congruence and it is essential that the accounting system supports, not hinders, this process.

It is important that long term as well as short term factors are kept in mind when seeking cost reductions as some cost reduction activities may be counter-productive in the long term. There are numerous examples where short term savings are easily made but which are likely to produce significant adverse results in the longer term. Examples include maintenance, advertising, staff development, research and development.

There is increasing realisation that the key area for cost reduction is Product Design, ie before the product enters manufacturing. Once it has entered manufacturing there is much less scope for cost reduction especially where there is largely automated production.

24. Summary

a) Where it can provide useful information the material usage variance can be subdivided into a mix variance and a yield variance.

b) These are variances which arise due to the actual mixture/yield varying from the standard mixture/yield where mixture means proportions.

c) Sales margin variances have the objective of helping to control the profit, ie margin, on sales.

d) The standard sales margin is the difference between the standard selling price and the standard cost of an item.

e) The total sales margin variance can be subdivided into Price and Quantity variances. Where more than one product is sold, the Quantity variance can be subdivided into mixture and volume variances.

f) The method of calculating the sales margin variances is very similar to the methods used for calculating materials variances.

g) Standard costing can employ marginal costing principles and becomes known as Standard Marginal Costing. Fixed costs are not absorbed into individual units of production.

h) A standard marginal cost is the total of all standard variable costs. A standard contribution is added to give a standard selling price.

i) Using standard marginal costing, variance analysis is simplified because all fixed overhead variances disappear, except for the fixed overhead expenditure variance.

j) Material, labour and variable overhead variances are identical and, with the exception that the standard contribution becomes the sales margin, so are the sales variances.

k) Traditional variances can be separated into planning variances and operational variances.

l) Planning variances seek to measure that part of the total variance which is due to planning deficiencies whilst the operating variances seek to measure operating results as compared to a realistic, current standard.

m) Cost reduction seeks to extract more from the factors of production without loss of effectiveness.

n) Techniques of cost reduction include: variety reduction, value analysis, work study, organisation and methods, systems analysis.

25. Points to note

a) The decision to make a detailed investigation into a particular variance is a cost/benefit appraisal depending on the cost of investigation compared with a subjective assessment of the benefits expected to result, having due regard to the probabilities involved.

b) It is important that higher management help to generate a positive attitude towards variances rather than the adverse reaction from operating management which will inevitably occur if variances are always associated with apportioning blame and criticism. The approach to be fostered is that variances and variance analysis are a way of learning how to do better in the future.

c) There is evidence that there is a tendency in practice to adopt an asymmetric approach to variances giving unfavourable variances more attention than favourable ones of similar magnitude. This may mean that opportunities are lost to improve operations by investigating the reasons for favourable variances.

d) A positive cost reduction programme having due regard to the long term effects, is essential for every organisation. It is not sufficient merely to have cost control procedures.

e) The greatest possible care is necessary when interpreting variances even ones that are apparently straightforward. For example, an adverse price variance may be due to the Purchasing Department buying in advance of a much larger price increase which is astute purchasing rather than the below par performance conventionally associated with an adverse variance.

f) Conventional variance analysis does not illustrate the interdependencies which abound in every organisation. These interdependencies makes interpretation of *any* variance a difficult task.

Additional reading

Topics in Management Accounting; *Arnold, Carsberg and Scapens* – Philip Allan

Contemporary Cost Accounting and Control; *ed. Benston* – Dickenson

Cost Accounting – a Managerial Emphasis; *Horngren & Foster* – Prentice Hall

Advanced Management Accounting; *Kaplan* – Prentice Hall

Cost Control in the 1990s; *Paxty and Lyall*– CIMA

Studies in Cost Analysis; *Solomons* – Sweet & Maxwell

Self review questions

1. When would mix and yield variances be calculated? What are their formulae? (2 & 4)
2. Why do mix and yield variances occur? (2-4)
3. What are the deficiencies of conventional mix and yield variances? (5)
4. What product cost is used in sales margin variance analysis? (5)
5. What is the standard sales margin? (6)
6. What is the standard sales contribution? (6)
7. What are the sub divisions of the total sales margin variance? (7)
8. What drawbacks are there in sales margin variance analysis? (8)
9. Distinguish between sales variances and sales margin variances. (9)
10. What are the major differences between standard marginal costing and standard costing based on total absorption costing principles? (10)
11. What is the purpose of planning and operating variance analysis? (12)
12. How is the planning variance calculated?, the operating variances? (13-14)
13. What are the benefits of planning variances? What are their limitations? (15)
14. What is cost reduction? (18)
15. What is the objective of variety reduction and standardisation? (19)
16. What is value analysis? (20)
17. Distinguish between work study and O & M. (21 & 22)

12 Stock control

1. Objectives

After studying this chapter you will:

❑ understand the principles of stock control;

❑ know why stocks are held;

❑ be able to describe stock-holding costs, ordering costs and holding costs;

❑ know the meaning of: lead time, demand, physical and free stock, buffer stock, re-order level and re-order quantity;

❑ understand the distinction between re-order level and periodic review systems;

❑ be able to calculate the Economic Order Quantity (EOQ);

❑ know the EOQ formula;

❑ be able to find the re-order quantity when discounts are available;

❑ understand how to calculate the level of safety stock.

2. Types of inventory

A convenient classification of the types of inventory is as follows:

a) Raw materials – the materials, components, fuels etc. used in the manufacture of products.

b) Work-in-progress – W-I-P – partly finished goods and materials, sub-assemblies etc. held between manufacturing stages.

c) Finished goods – completed products ready for sale or distribution.

The particular items included in each classification depend on the particular firm. What would be classified as a finished product for one company might be classified as raw materials for another. For example, steel bars would be classified as a finished product for steel mill and as raw material for a nut and bolt manufacturer.

3. Reasons for holding stocks

The main reasons for holding stocks can be summarised as follows:

a) to ensure that sufficient good are available to meet anticipated demand;

b) to absorb variations in demand and production;

c) to provide a buffer between production processes. This is applicable to work-in-progress stocks which effectively decouple operations;

d) to take advantage of bulk purchasing discounts;

e) to meet possible shortages in the future;

f) to absorb seasonal fluctuations in usage or demand;

g) to enable production processes to flow smoothly and efficiently;

h) as a necessary part of the production process, eg the maturing of whiskey;

i) as deliberate investment policy particularly in times of inflation or possible shortage.

4. Alternative reasons for stocks

The reasons given in para 3. above are the logical ones based on deliberate decisions. However, stocks accumulate for other, less praiseworthy reasons, typical of which are the following:

a) Obsolete items are retained in stock.

b) Poor or non existent inventory control resulting in over-large orders, replenishment orders being out of phase with production, etc.

c) Inadequate or non-existent stock records.

d) Poor liaison between the Production Control, Purchasing and Marketing departments.

e) Sub-optimal decision making, eg the Production Department might increase W-I-P stocks unduly so as to ensure long production runs.

5. Stock costs

Whether as a result of deliberate policy or not, stock represents an investment by the organisation. As with any other investment, the costs of holding stock must be related to the benefits to be gains. To do this effectively, the costs must be identified and this can be done in three categories: costs of holding stock, costs of obtaining stock, and stockout costs.

6. Costs of holding stock

These costs, also known as carrying costs, include the following:

a) Interest on capital invested in the stock.

b) Storage charges (rent, lighting, heating, refrigeration, air conditioning, etc).

c) Stores staffing, equipment maintenance and running costs.

d) Handling costs.

e) Audit, stocktaking or perpetual inventory costs.

f) Insurance and security.

g) Deterioration and obsolescence.

h) Pilferage, vermin damage, etc.

7. Costs of obtaining stock

These costs, sometimes known as ordering costs, include the following:

a) The clerical and administrative costs associated with the Purchasing, Accounting, and Goods Received departments.

b) Transport costs.

c) Where goods are manufactured internally, the set up and tooling costs associated with each production run.

Note: Some students consider ordering costs to include only those costs associated with ordering external to the firm. However, internal ordering (ie own manufacture) may involve high cost for production planning, set-up, and tooling.

8. Stockout costs

These are the costs associated with running out of stock. The avoidance of these costs is the basic reason why stocks are held in the first instance. These costs include the following:

a) Lost contribution through the lost sale caused by the stockout.

b) Loss of future sales because customers go elsewhere.

c) Loss of customer goodwill.

d) Cost of production stoppages caused by stockouts of W-I-P or raw materials.

e) Labour frustration over stoppages.

f) Extra costs associated with urgent, often small quantity, replenishment purchases.

Clearly, many of these costs are difficult to quantify, but they are often significant.

223

9. Objective of inventory control

The overall objective of inventory control is to maintain stock levels so that the combined costs, detailed in paras 6, 7 and 8 above, are at a minimum. This is done by establishing two factors, when to order and how many to order. These factors are the subject of the rest of the chapter but before these factors can be explained in detail some basic terminology must be dealt with.

10. Basic terminology

Brief definitions of common inventory control terms are given below and are illustrated in para 11.

a) **Lead or Procurement time.** The period of time, expressed in days, weeks, months, etc. between ordering (either externally or internally) and replenishment, ie when the goods are available for use.

b) **Demand.** The amount required by sales, production, etc. Usually expressed as a rate of demand per week, month or year. Estimates of the rate of demand during the lead time are critical factors in inventory control systems. This is dealt with in more detail in para 28.

c) **Economic Ordering Quantity (EOQ) or Economic Batch Quantity (EBQ).** This is a calculated ordering quantity which minimises the balance of cost between inventory holding costs and reorder costs. The rationale of EOQ and derivation of the EOQ formulae are dealt with in para 20.

d) **Physical stock.** The number of items physically in stock at a given time.

e) **Free stock.** Physical stock plus outstanding replenishment orders minus unfulfilled requirements.

f) **Buffer Stock or Minimum Stock or Safety Stock.** A stock allowance to cover errors in forecasting the lead time or the demand during the lead time. Buffer stock is further explained in para 28.

g) **Maximum Stock.** A stock level selected as the maximum desirable which is used as an indicator to show when stocks have risen too high.

h) **Reorder level.** The level of stock at which a further replenishment order should be placed. The reorder level is dependent upon the lead time and the demand during the lead time.

i) **Reorder Quantity.** The quantity of the replenishment order. In some types of inventory control systems this is the EOQ, but in some other systems a different value is used. This aspect is dealt with in detail in para 15.

11. A simple stock situation illustrated

Figure 12.1 shows a stock situation simplified by the following assumptions: regular rates of demand, a fixed lead time, and replenishment in one batch.

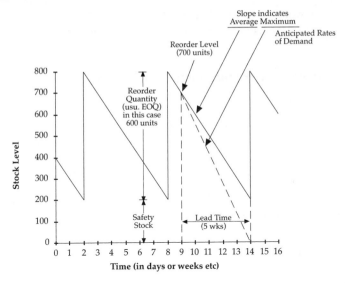

Figure 12.1 Stock Terminology Illustrated

Notes:

a) It will be seen from Figure 12.1 that the safety stock in this illustration is needed to cope with periods of maximum demand during the lead time.

b) The lead time as shown is 5 weeks, the safety stock 200 units, and the reorder quantity 600 units.

c) With constant rates of demand, as shown, the average stock is the safety stock *plus* $\frac{1}{2}$ Reorder quantity; for example, in figure 1 the average stock is:

$$200 + \tfrac{1}{2}(600) = 500 \text{ units}$$

12. Major types of inventory control systems

There are two broad divisions of inventory control systems, the *Reorder Level* and the *Periodic Review* systems. These systems are examined below but naturally many hybrid systems exist in practice and many variants of the basic types will be found.

13. Reorder level system

This system is also known as the two-bin system. Its characteristics are as follows:

a) A predetermined re-order level is set for each item.

b) When the stock level falls to the re-order level, a replenishment order is issued.

c) The replenishment order quantity is invariably the EOQ.

d) The name 'two-bin' system comes from the simplest method of operating the system whereby the stock is segregated into two bins. Stock is initially drawn from the first bin and a replenishment order issued when it becomes empty.

e) Most organisations operating the re-order level system maintain stock records with calculated re-order levels which trigger off the required replenishment order.

Note: The illustration in para 11. was of a simple re-order level system. The re-order level system is widely used in practice and is the subject of frequent examination questions.

14. A simple manual reorder system illustrated

The following data relate to a particular stock item.

Normal usage	110 per day
Minimum usage	50 per day
Maximum usage	140 per day
Lead Time	25 – 30 days
EOQ (Previously calculated)	5000

Using this data the various control levels can be calculated.

Re-order Level
= Maximum Usage × Maximum Lead Time
= 140×30
= _4,200 units_

Minimum Level
= Re-order Level – Average Usage for Average Lead Time
= $4,200 - (110 \times 27.5)$
= _1,175 units_

Maximum Level
= Re-order Level + EOQ – Minimum Anticipated Usage in Lead Time
= $4,200 + 5,000 - (50 \times 25)$
= _7,950 units_

Notes:

a) The three levels would be entered on a stock record card and comparisons made between the actual stock level and the control levels each time an entry was made on the card.

b) The re-order level is a definite action level, the minimum and maximum points are levels at which management would be warned that a potential danger may occur.

c) The re-order level is calculated so that if the worst anticipated circumstances occurs, stock would be replenished in time.

d) The minimum level is calculated so that management will be warned when demand is above average and accordingly buffer stock is being used. There may be no danger, but the situation needs watching.

e) Maximum level is calculated so that management will be warned when demand is the minimum anticipated and consequently the stock level is likely to rise above the maximum intended.

f) In a manual system if warnings about maximum or minimum level violations were received, then it is likely that the re-order level and/or EOQ would be recalculated and adjusted. In a computer based system such adjustments would take place automatically to reflect current and forecast future conditions.

15. Periodic review system

This system is sometimes called the constant cycle system. The system has the following characteristics:

a) Stock levels for all parts are reviewed at fixed intervals, eg every fortnight.

b) Where necessary a replenishment order is issued.

c) The quantity of the replenishment order is not a previously calculated EOQ , but is based upon: the likely demand until the next review, the present stock level and the lead time.

d) The replenishment order quantity variable quantities at fixed intervals as compared with the re-order level system, described above, where fixed quantities are ordered at variable intervals.

16. A periodic review system illustrated

A production control department maintains control of the 500 piece parts used in the assembly of the finished products by the periodic review system. The stock levels of all 500 parts are reviewed every 4 weeks and a replenishment order issued to bring the stock of each part up to a previously calculated level. This level is calculated at six-monthly intervals and is based on the anticipated demand for each part.

Based on the above system, Figure 12.2 shows the position for one of the piece parts, part No. 1101x, over a period of 16 weeks.

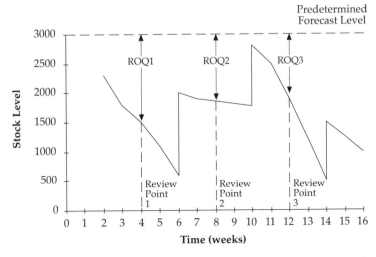

Figure 12.2 Stock levels of part no. 1101x

Notes:

a) The re-order quantities, based on the agreed system are 1500 units, 1000 units, and 1400 units.

b) It will be seen that the rates of usage are assumed to be variable and the lead time has been assumed to be 2 weeks.

c) The above illustration is merely one way of operating a periodic review system and many variants exist, particularly relating to the method of calculating the re-order quantities.

17. Periodic review system – advantages and disadvantages

Advantages:

a) All stock items are reviewed periodically so that there is more chance of obsolete items being eliminated.

b) Economies in placing orders may be gained by spreading the purchasing office load more evenly.

c) Larger quantity discounts may be obtained when a range of stock items is ordered at the same time from a supplier.

d) Because orders will always be in the same sequence, there may be production economies due to more efficient production planning being possible and lower set up cost. (This is often a major advantage and results in the frequent use of some form of periodic review system in production control systems in firms where there is a preferred sequence of manufacture, so that full advantage can be gained from the predetermined sequence implied by the periodic review systems.)

Disadvantages:

a) In general, larger stocks are required, as re-order quantities must take account of the period between reviews as well as lead times.

b) Re-order quantities are not at the optimum level of a correctly calculated EOQ.

c) Less responsive to changes in consumption. If the rate of usage changes shortly after review, a stockout may well occur before the next review.

d) Unless demands are reasonably consistent, it is difficult to set appropriate periods for review.

18. Re-order level system advantages and disadvantages

Advantages:

a) Lower stocks on average.

b) Items ordered in economic quantities via the EOQ calculation.

c) Somewhat more responsive to fluctuations in demand.

d) Automatic generation of a replenishment order at the appropriate time by comparison of stock level against re-order level.

e) Appropriate for widely differing types of inventory within the same firm.

Disadvantages:

a) Many items may reach re-order level at the same time, thus overloading the re-ordering system.

b) Items come up for re-ordering in a random fashion so that there is no set sequence.

c) In certain circumstances (eg variable demand, ordering cost etc), the EOQ calculation may not be accurate. This is dealt with in more detail later in the chapter.

19. Hybrid systems

The two basic inventory control systems have been explained above but many variations exist in practice. A firm may develop a system to suit their organisation which contains elements of both systems. In stable conditions of constant demand, lead times, and costs, both approaches are likely to be equally effective.

20. The economic order quantity (EOQ)

The EOQ has been previously defined as the ordering quantity which minimises the balance of cost between inventory holding costs and re-order costs. To be able to calculate a basic EOQ certain assumptions are necessary.

a) That there is a known, constant stockholding cost,

b) That there is a known, constant ordering cost,

c) That rates of demand are known and constant,

d) That there is a known, constant price per unit, ie there are no price discounts.

e) That replenishment is made instantaneously, ie the whole batch is delivered at once.

Notes:

a) It will be apparent that the above assumptions are somewhat sweeping and they are a good reason for treating any EOQ calculation with caution.

b) Some of the above assumptions are relaxed later in the chapter.

c) The rationale of EOQ ignores buffer stocks which are maintained to cater for variations in lead time and demand.

21. Example 1 (Graphical EOQ)

The following data will be used to develop a graphical solution to the EOQ problem.

Example 1

A company uses 50,000 widgets per annum which are £10 each to purchase. The ordering and handling costs are £150 per order and carrying costs are 15% per annum, ie it costs £1.50 p.a. to carry a widget in stock (£10 × 15%).

To graph the various costs involved the following steps are necessary:

where

Total Costs p.a. = Ordering Cost p.a. + Carrying Cost p.a.

where:

Ordering cost p.a. = No. of orders × £150

$$\text{No. of orders} = \frac{\text{Annual Demand}}{\text{Order Quantity}}$$

(For example, if the order quantity was 5,000 widgets,

$$\text{No. of orders} = \frac{50,000}{5,000} = 10$$

Ordering cost p.a. = 10 × £150 = £1,500)

and

$$\text{Carrying cost p.a.} = \text{average stock level} \times £15$$

$$\text{Average stock level} = \frac{\text{order quantity}}{2}$$

(For example if the order quantity is 5,000:

$$\text{Carrying costs p.a.} = \frac{5,000}{2} \times £1.15 = £3,750)$$

Based on the above principles, the following tables gives the cost for various order quantities.

Column I	II	III	IV	V	VI
Order Quantity	Average No of orders p.a	Annual Ordering Cost	Average Stock	Stock Holding Cost p.a.	Total Stock
	$\frac{50,000}{\text{Col I}}$	Col. II × £150	$\frac{\text{Col I}}{2}$	Col. IV × £1.5	Cols III +V
		£		£	£
1000	50	7500	500	750	8250
2000	25	3750	1000	1500	5250
3000	$16\frac{2}{3}$	2500	1500	2250	4750
4000	$12\frac{1}{2}$	1875	2000	3000	4875
5000	10	1500	2500	3750	5250
6000	$8\frac{1}{3}$	1250	3000	4500	5750

Table 1 Ordering and Stock Holding Costs for various Order Quantities

The costs in Table 1 can be plotted in a graph and the approximate EOQ ascertained.

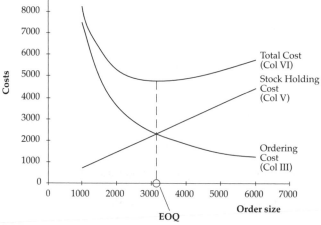

Figure 12.3 Graph of data in Table 1

From the graph it will be seen that the EOQ is approximately 3,200 widgets, which means that an average of slightly under 16 orders will have to be placed a year.

Notes:

a) From a graph closer accuracy is not possible and is unnecessary anyway.

b) It will be seen from the graph that the bottom of the total cost curve is relatively flat, indicating that the exact value of the EOQ is not too critical.

22. The EOQ formula

It is possible, and more usual, to calculate the EOQ using a formula. The formula method gives an exact answer, but do not be misled into placing undue reliance upon the precise figure. The calculations are based on estimates of costs, demands, etc. which are, of course, subject to error. The EOQ formula is given below and should be learned. The mathematical derivation is given in Appendix 1 of this chapter.

Basic EOQ formula:

$$EOQ = \sqrt{\frac{2 \times C_o \times D}{C_c}}$$

where: C_o = Ordering cost per order

D = Demand per annum

C_c = Carrying cost per item per annum

Using the data from Example 1, the EOQ can be calculated.

We have: Co = £150; D = 50,000 widgets; Cc = £10 × 15% = £1.50 per widget.

This gives: $EOQ = \sqrt{\dfrac{2 \times 150 \times 50,000}{1.5}}$

$= \sqrt{10,000}$

$= $ **3162 widgets.**

Notes:

a) The closest value obtainable from the graph was approximately 3,200 which is very close to the exact figure.

b) Always take care that demand and carrying costs are expressed for the same period. A year is the usual period used.

c) In some problems the carrying cost is expressed as a percentage of the value whereas in others it is expressed directly as a cost per item. Both ways have been used in this example to provide a comparison.

23. EOQ with gradual replenishment

In the example above the assumption was that the widgets were ordered externally and that the order quantity was received as one batch, ie instantaneous replenishment as shown in Figure 12.4.

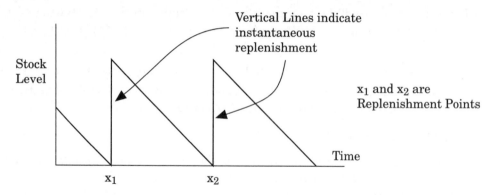

Figure 12.4 Stock levels showing instantaneous replenishment

If however, the widgets were manufactured internally, they would probably be placed into stock over a period of time resulting the pattern shown in Figure 12.5.

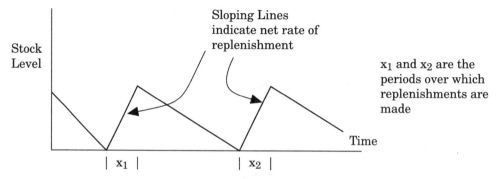

Figure 12.5 Stock levels showing non-instantaneous replenishment

The net rate of replenishment is determined by the rate of replenishment and the rate of usage during the replenishment period. To cope with such situations, the basic EOQ formula needs modification thus:

$$\text{EOQ (with gradual replenishment)} = \sqrt{\frac{2 \times C_o \times D}{C_c\left(1 - \dfrac{D}{R}\right)}}$$

where: R = Production rate per annum, ie the quantity that would be produced if production of the item was carried on the whole year.

All other elements in the formula have meanings as previously defined.

Note:

The derivation of the above formula is given in Appendix 2 of this chapter.

24. Example 2 (EOQ with gradual replenishment)

Assume that the firm described in Example 1 has decided to make the widgets in its own factory. The necessary machinery has been purchased which has a capacity of 250,000 widgets per annum. All other data are assumed to be the same.

$$\text{EOQ with gradual replenishment} = \sqrt{\frac{2 \times C_o \times D}{C_c\left(1 - \dfrac{D}{R}\right)}}$$

$$= \sqrt{\frac{2 \times 150 \times 50,000}{1.5\left(1 - \dfrac{50,000}{250,000}\right)}}$$

$$= \sqrt{12,500,000}$$

$$= \textbf{3535 widgets}$$

Notes:

a) The value obtained above is larger than the basic EOQ because the usage during the replenishment period has the effect of lowering the average stockholding cost.

b) As pointed out in para 7 the ordering costs for internal usually include set up and tooling costs as well as paper work and administration costs.

25. EOQ with discounts

A particularly unrealistic assumption with the basic EOQ calculation is that the price per item remains constant. Usually some form of discount can be obtained by ordering increased quantities. Such price discounts can be incorporated into the EOQ formula, but it becomes much more complicated. A simpler approach is to consider the costs associated with the normal EOQ and compare these costs with the costs at each succeeding discount point and so ascertain the best quantity to order.

26. Financial effects of discounts

Price discounts for quantity purchases have three financial effects, two of which are beneficial and one adverse.

Beneficial Effects: Savings come from:

a) Lower price per item

b) The larger order quantity means that fewer orders need to be placed so that ordering costs are reduced.

Adverse Effects:

a) Increased costs arise from the extra stockholding costs caused by the average stock level being higher due to the larger order quantity.

Example 3 – Example of EOQ with Discounts.

A company uses a special bracket in the manufacture of its products which it orders from outside suppliers. The appropriate data are

$$\begin{aligned}
\text{Demand} &= \text{2000 per annum} \\
\text{Ordering cost} &= \text{£20 per order} \\
\text{Carrying cost} &= \text{20\% of item price} \\
\text{Basic item price} &= \text{£10 per bracket}
\end{aligned}$$

The company is offered the following discounts on the basic price:

For order quantities | 400 – 799 | less 2%
800 – 1599 | less 4%
1600 and over | less 5%

It is required to establish the most economical quantity to order.

Solution

This problem can be answered using the following procedure:

A. Calculate the EOQ using the basic price.

B. Compare the savings from the lower price and ordering costs and the extra stock-holding costs at each discount point (ie 400, 800, and 1600) with the costs associated with the basic EOQ, thus

$$\text{Basic EOQ} = \sqrt{\frac{2 \times 2000 \times 20}{10 \times 0.2}}$$

= 200 brackets

Based on this EOQ the various costs and savings comparisons are given in the following table:

Order Quantity	200(EOQ)	400	800	1600	Line No.
Discount	-	2%	4%	5%	1
Average No. of Orders p.a.	10	5	2.5	1.25	2
Average No. of orders saved p.a.	–	5	7.5	8.75	3
Ordering cost Savings p.a.	–	(5 × 20) = £100	(7.5 × 20) = £150	(8.75 × 20) = £175	4
Price saving per item per annum	–	20p (2000 × 20p) = 400	40p (2000 × 40p) = 800	50p (2000 × 50p) = 1000	5
TOTAL GAINS		£500	£950	£1175	6
Stockholding Cost p.a.	(100×10×0.2) = £200	(200×9.8×0.2) = £392	(400×9.6×0.2) = £768	(800×9.5×0.2) = £1520	7
Additional costs incurred by increased order quantity	–	(£392 – £200) = £192	(£768 – £200) = £568	(£1520 – £200) = £1320	8
NET GAIN/(LOSS)	–	£308	£382	(£145)	9

Table 2 Cost/Savings Comparisons EOQ to Discount Points

From the above table it will be seen that the most economical order quantity is 800 brackets, thereby gaining the 4% discount.

Notes:

a) Line 2 is $\dfrac{\text{demand of 2000}}{\text{order quantity}}$

b) Line 7 is the cost of carrying the average stock,

ie $\dfrac{\text{order quantity}}{2} \times \text{cost per item} \times \text{carrying cost } \%$.

c) Line 9 is Line 6 minus Line 8.

27. Marginal costs and EOQ calculations

It cannot be emphasised too strongly that the costs to be used in EOQ calculations must be true marginal costs, ie the costs that alter as a result of a further order or carrying another item in stock. It follows therefore that fixed costs should not be used in the calculations. In the examples used in this chapter the costs have been clearly and simply stated. In examination questions this is not always the case and considerable care is necessary to ensure that the appropriate costs are used.

28. Safety stock and re-order levels

So far it has been assumed that the demand and the lead time have been known with certainty. In such circumstances the re-order level is the rate of demand times the lead time. This means that *regardless of the length of the lead time or of the rate of demand* no buffer stock is necessary when there are conditions of certainty. This results in a stock profile as follows:

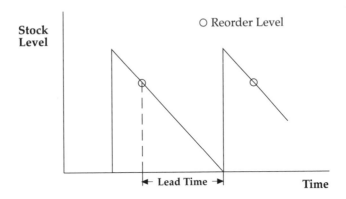

Figure 12.6 Re-order level in conditions of certainty (no safety stock)

It will be seen from Figure 12.6 that, in conditions of certainty, the re-order level can be set so that stock just reaches zero and is then replenished. When demand and/or lead time vary, the re-order level must be set so that, on average, some safety stock is available to absorb variations in demand and/or lead time. In such circumstances the re-order level calculation can be conveniently considered in two parts:

a) the normal or average rate of usage *times* the normal or average lead time (ie as the re-order level calculation in conditions of certainty) PLUS

b) the safety stock.

29. Safety stock calculation by cost tabulation

The amount of safety stock is the level where the total costs associated with safety stock are at a minimum. That is, where the safety stock holding plus the stock-out cost is lowest. (It will be noted that this is a similar cost situation to that previously described in the EOQ derivation). The appropriate calculations are given below based on the following illustration.

Example 4

An electrical company uses a particular type of thermostat which costs £5. The demand averages 800 p.a. and the EOQ has been calculated at 200. Holding costs are 20% p.a. and stock out costs have been estimated at £2 per item that is unavailable. Demand and lead times vary, but fortunately the company has kept records of usage over 50 lead times as follows:

(a) Usage in Lead time	(b) Number of times Recorded	(c) Probability $\frac{b}{50}$
25 – 29 units	1	.02
30 – 34 units	8	.16
35 – 39 units	10	.20
40 – 44 units	12	.24
45 – 49 units	9	.18
50 – 54 units	5	.10
55 – 59 units	5	.10
Total	50	1.00

Table 3

From the above the re-order level and safety stock should be calculated.

Step 1

Using the mid point of each group calculate the average usage in the lead time.

x	t	tx
27	1	27
32	8	256
37	10	370
42	12	504
47	9	423
52	5	260
57	5	285
	50	2125

Average usage $= \dfrac{2125}{50} = 42.5$

Table 4

Step 2

Find the holding and stock out costs for various re-order levels.

A Re-order Level	B Safety Stock (A-42.5)	C Holding Cost (B × £1) £	D Possible Shortages (Mid Points Table 2-A)	E Probability (From Table 1)	F No. of Orders p.a. (800÷ 200)	G Shortage Cost (D×E×F×£2) £	H Total Cost (C+G) £
45	2.5	2.50	2	.18	4	2.88	
			7	.10	4	5.60	
			12	.10	4	9.60	20.58
50	7.5	7.50	2	.10	4	1.60	
			7	.10	4	5.60	14.70
55	12.5	12.50	2	.10	4	1.60	14.10
60	17.5	17.50					17.50

Table 5

From Table 5 it will be seen that the most economic re-order level is *55 units*. This re-order level, with the average demand in the lead time of 42.5, gives a safety stock of $12\frac{1}{2}$ units, say *13 units*.

30. Safety stock calculation by statistical methods

The method of calculating safety stocks explained above was based on the relationship between holding and stock out costs but on occasions these costs are not known. In such circumstances statistical methods can be used to determine the safety stock for a given risk level. For example, management may decide that there are prepared to accept a 5% possibility of a stock out and a safety stock level would be calculated so that for 95% of all demand and lead time combinations there would be sufficient safety stock. A typical method of calculating safety stocks by statistical methods is shown below.

Example 5

Using the data from Example 4, it was found that the average demand during the lead time was $42\frac{1}{2}$ units.

The company has carried out further analysis and has found that this average lead time demand is made up of an average demand (D) of 3.162 units per day over an average lead time (L) of 13.44 days. Both demand and lead time may vary and the company has estimated that the standard deviation of daily demand (σ_D) is 1.4 units and the standard deviation of lead time (σ_L) is 2.75 days. The company are prepared to accept a 5% risk of a stock out and wish to know the safety stock required in the following three circumstances:

(i) Where demand varies and lead time is constant

(ii) Where the lead time varies and demand is constant

(iii) Where both demand and lead time vary.

In each of these circumstances the average usage is $D \times L$, ie $3.162 \times 13.44 = 42$ units.

(i) Safety stock given variable demand and constant lead time.

From Normal Area Tables it will be found that 5% of the area lies above the mean + 1.64 σ.

$$\therefore \text{ Safety Stock } = 1.64 \times \text{standard deviation of demand for 13.44 days}$$
$$= 1.64 \times \left(1.4 \times \sqrt{13.44}\right)$$
$$= \underline{8.42}$$

Note: The standard deviation of daily demand, 1.4, is multiplied by $\sqrt{13.44}$ and not 13.44 because standard deviations are not additive.

(ii) Safety stock given variable lead time and constant demand.

$$\therefore \text{ Safety stock } = 1.64 \times \text{standard deviation of lead time for a demand of 3.162}$$
$$= 1.64 \, (2.75)$$
$$= \underline{4.51}$$

(iii) This is a combination of the two previous sections and is the sum of the separate safety stocks previously calculated.

$$\therefore \text{ Safety stock } = 8.42 + 4.51$$
$$= \underline{12.93}$$

31. Pareto or ABC analysis

This has already been described and is sometimes called the 80: 20 rule. As applied to stocks it means that, say, 80% of stock value is represented by 20% of the stock items.

In many organisations there are thousands of items and materials to be stored. Detailed control applied to all items regardless of value, would be pointless and needlessly expensive. Accordingly it is normal to group items by purchase value into three groups, A,B and C. When this is done most control attention is concentrated on the relatively few items that account for most value. The following table illustrates a common position.

	Number of items		Total value	
Class	No	%	£	%
A	1500	10	3,750,000	75
B	3000	20	800,000	16
C	10,500	70	450,000	9
Total	15,000	100	5,000,000	100

Obviously most control attention would be given to Class A items.

32. Changing approaches to stock

The earlier part of this chapter has described what may be called the conventional approach to stocks and stock control. There are numerous questions in examinations covering this approach so students must become familiar with the principles.

However many changes are taking place in industry and the attitude to stock has also changed. The newer production management techniques notably Just- in- Time (described in detail in Chapter 22) endeavour to eliminate stocks entirely. Goods and materials are ordered 'just-in-time' for production and production is organised so that WIP stocks are minimal. These newer approaches together with the integration of purchasing and production in Materials Requirements Planning (MRP) Systems (covered in Chapter 22) are rendering the use of traditional re-order level methods and EOQ calculations redundant.

33. Summary

a) Stocks may conveniently be classified in Raw Materials, Work-In-Progress, and Finished Goods. The exact classification of any item depends on the nature of the firm.

b) Stocks are held to satisfy demands quickly, to allow unimpeded production, to take advantage of bulk purchasing, as a necessary part of the production process, and to absorb seasonal and other fluctuations.

c) Stocks accumulate unnecessarily through poor control methods, obsolescence, poor liaison and sub-optimal decision making.

d) The cost associated with stock are: holding costs, costs of obtaining stock, and stockout costs.

e) The overall objective of inventory control is to maintain stocks at a level which minimises total stock costs.

f) There are two basic inventory control system, the re-order level or two-bin system and the periodic review system.

g) The re-order level system usually has three control levels, re-order level, maximum level and minimum level.

h) In the re-order level system the usual replenishment order quantity is the EOQ.

i) The re-order level system results in fixed quantities being ordered at variable intervals dependent upon demand.

j) The periodic review system means that all stocks are reviewed at fixed intervals and replenishment orders issued to bring stock back to predetermined level.

k) The replenishment order quantity is based upon estimates of the likely demand until the next review period.

l) The period review system results in variable quantities being ordered at fixed intervals.

m) The EOQ is the order quantity which minimises the total costs involved which include holding costs and ordering costs.

n)   The basic EOQ calculation is based on constant ordering and holding costs, constant demand and instantaneous replenishment.

o)   The basic EOQ formula is

$$EOQ = \sqrt{\frac{2 \times C_o \times D}{C_c}}$$

p)   Where replenishment is not instantaneous, eg where the part is manufactured, the formula becomes

$$\sqrt{\frac{2 \times C_o \times D}{C_c \left(1 - \dfrac{D}{R}\right)}}$$

q)   Where replenishment is not instantaneous, the EOQ calculated is larger than the basic EOQ.

r)   Where larger quantities are ordered to take advantage of price discounts, stock-holding costs increase, but savings are made in the price reductions and reduced ordering costs.

s)   The costs to be used in EOQ calculations must be marginal costs. Fixed costs should not be included.

t)   Safety stocks are necessary because of demand and/or lead time variations.

u)   Re-order level is the average demand over the average lead time plus safety stock.

v)   The safety stock level can be established by comparing the safety stock holding cost and the stock out cost at various re-order levels.

w)   Where it is necessary to calculate the safety stock level to cater for a given risk of stock out, statistical methods, based on areas under the normal curve, can be used.

34. Points to note

a)   Forecasting is an integral part of inventory control systems. The typical forecasting system is an adaptive one using some form of exponential smoothing.

b)   Typically the bottom of the total cost curve used for determining the EOQ is relatively flat indicating that the EOQ calculated is relatively insensitive to changes in the values of the parameters (order cost, demand, carrying cost). In OR terms the EOQ calculation would be termed 'robust' as opposed to 'sensitive'.

c)   Risk and uncertainty are ever present in all business situations and this is equally applicable to inventory control. Variabilities in demand and lead times make buffer stocks necessary.

Additional reading

Operations Managemen; Bennett, *Lewis and Oakley* – Philip Allen

Management of working Capital; *Firth* – Macmillan

Cost Accounting – a management emphasis; *Horngren & Foster* – Prentice Hall

Quantitative Techniques; *Lucey* – Letts Educational (formerly DP Publications)

Operational Reasearch : Analysis and Applications; *Wilkes* – McGraw-Hill

Self review questions

1. Give 6 reasons why stocks are held. (3)
2. Why do unwanted stocks accumulate? (4)
3. What items are included in the costs of holding stocks? (6)
4. What are ordering costs? (7)
5. What is the overall objective of inventory control? (9)
6. Define: lead time, EOQ, Free Stock, Buffer Stock, Reorder Level. (10)
7. What are the characteristics of the re-order system? (13)
8. What is the periodic review system? (15)
9. Contrast the advantages and disadvantages of the re-order level and the periodic review systems. (17 and 18)
10. What are the assumptions behind the basic EOQ calculation? (20)
11. What is the basic EOQ formula? (22)
12. What is the formula for the EOQ with gradual replenishment? (23)
13. What are the financial effects of receiving discounts? (25)
14. What type of costs should be used in EOQ calculations? (27)
15. What level of safety stock is necessary when the demand and lead time is known with certainty? (28)
16. How is the safety stock calculated if management are required to accept a 10% possibility of a stockout? (30)

Appendix 1

Derivation of basic EOQ formula.

Let:
D = annual demand

Q = order quantity

C_o = cost of ordering for one order

C_c = carrying cost for one item p.a.

Then: $$\text{Average Stock} = \frac{Q}{2}$$

$$\text{Total annual stock holding cost} = \frac{Q.Cc}{2}$$

$$\text{Number of orders per annum} = \frac{D}{Q}$$

$$\text{Annual ordering costs} = \frac{D.Co}{Q}$$

Therefore: Total Cost (TC) = Total annual stock holding cost + Annual ordering costs

$$= \frac{Q.Cc}{2} + \frac{D.Co}{2}$$

The order quantity which makes the total cost (TC) a minimum is obtained by differentiating TC with respect to Q and equating this derivative to zero.

$$\frac{dTC}{dQ} = \frac{Cc}{2} - \frac{D.Co}{Q^2}$$

and when:

$$\frac{dTC}{dQ} = 0$$

$$\frac{Cc}{2} - \frac{D.Co}{Q^2} = 0$$

and to find Q:

$$\frac{Cc}{2} = \frac{D.Co}{Q^2}$$

$$Q^2.Cc = 2.D.Co$$

giving:

$$Q^2 = \frac{2.D.Co}{Cc}$$

Thus:

$$Q = EOQ = \sqrt{\frac{2 \times C_o \times D}{C_c}}$$

Appendix 2

Derivation of formula for EOQ with gradual replenishment.

It will be recalled that gradual replenishment results in a stock level profile of the following shape where replenishment is taken over time, t, at rate R.

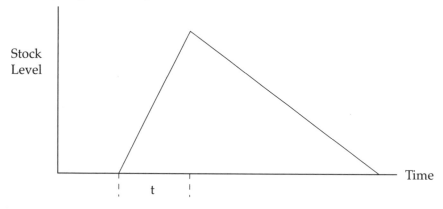

Since: no. of batches $\times R \times t = D$

we have: $\dfrac{D}{Q} \times R \times t = D$

Thus: $t = \dfrac{Q}{R}$

The average stock is half the height of the triangle and the height is determined by the rate of replenishment less the demand over the replenishment time.

Thus: $$\text{Average stock} = \frac{t(R-D)}{2}$$

and, substituting for t: $$\text{average stock} = \frac{\frac{Q}{R}(R-D)}{2}$$

$$= \frac{Q\left(1-\dfrac{D}{R}\right)}{2}$$

Therefore: Total annual stockholding cost $$= \frac{Q\left(1-\dfrac{D}{R}\right)C_c}{2}$$

This expression can be substituted for the corresponding expression in Appendix 1, and the identical steps following will result in a modified EOQ formula thus:

$$\textbf{EOQ (with gradual replenishment)} = \sqrt{\frac{2 \times C_o \times D}{C_c\left(1-\dfrac{D}{R}\right)}}$$

Assessment and revision section 3

Examination questions with answers

A1. Traditional budgeting systems are incremental in nature and tend to focus on cost centres. Activity-based budgeting links strategic planning to overall performance measurement aiming at continuous improvement.

a) Explain the weaknesses of an incremental budgeting system.

b) Describe the main features of an activity-based budgeting system and comment on the advantages claimed for its use.

ACCA, Information for Control and Decision Making.

A2. You are employed as a management accountant on the staff of the Finance Director of a diversified Group.

The Group has recently acquired a very successful high technology company from the three directors who founded the company, and who now wish to retire, and the venture capitalists who had backed them for many years. The company will be managed as a division of the Group, which has not been involved in any high technology industry in the past. New managers will be recruited to succeed the founders within the next year.

You have been asked to review the control procedures for R&D, and have discussed the problems with one of the three original directors. This was helpful as he was in a position to explain the present limited systems, having been in charge of R&D since the company had been founded.

He explained that R&D had never been analysed beyond the detail required for financial accounting. Total staff was just over 100, of whom 60% were highly qualified scientists, and the rest support staff. There was a loose matrix structure of some senior staff being responsible for specialisms and others responsible for projects, but lines were often blurred.

There were, he explained, broadly four sorts of output:

❏ work on major projects, which could last several years, and which may or may not be successful. This he commissioned on the basis of his and his fellow directors' knowledge of trends.

❏ work on specific minor product modifications requested by customers or by the marketing department. These projects were normally completed in 6 to 12 months.

❏ technical support to production and engineering departments.

❏ review of current technological development in areas broadly relevant to the product range.

Projects were not documented, and he allocated resources according to his knowledge of the industry.

At the end of the discussion he commented that he supposed more paperwork was inevitable in large groups, but that he would be surprised if it led to better decision making or performance.

Required:

Write a report to the Finance Director explaining what control procedures are required AND how they will contribute to better management of the research and development function.

In your report, explain how the control procedures you propose would apply to expenditure on each of the four types of output from R&D.

CIMA, Management Accounting Control Systems.

A3. Acca-chem Co plc manufacture a single product, product W, and have provided you with the following information which relates to the period which has just ended:

Standard cost per batch of product W

Materials:	Kilos	Price per kilo	Total
		£	£
F	15	4	60
G	12	3	36
H	8	6	48
	35		144
Less: Standard loss	3		
Standard yield	32		

Labour:	Hours	Rate per hour	
		£	
Department P	4	10	40
Department Q	2	6	12
			196

Budgeted sales for the period are 4,096 kilos at £16 per kilo. There were no budgeted opening or closing stocks of product W.

The actual materials and labour used for 120 batches were:

Materials:	Kilos	Price per kilo £	Total £
F	1,680	4.25	7,140
G	1,650	2.80	4,620
H	870	6.40	5,568
	4,200		17,328
Less: Actual loss	552		
Actual yield	3,648		

Labour:	Hours	Rate per hour £	
Department P	600	10.60	6,360
Department Q	270	5.60	1,512
			25,200

All of the production of W was sold during the period for £16.75 per kilo.

Required:

a) Calculate the following material variances:
   – price
   – usage
   – mix
   – yield.

b) Prepare an analysis of the material mix and price variances for each of the materials used.

c) Calculate the following labour variances:
   – cost
   – efficiency
   – rate

   for each of the production departments.

d) Calculate the sales variances.

e) Comment on your findings to help explain what has happened to the yield variance.

ACCA, Managerial Finance.

A4. A pharmaceuticals company has recently developed a new drug called KABO, which is made using a continuous microbiological process. The process manager is responsible for material procurement.

Four material ingredients (K, A, B and O) are used in the processing of KABO, all of which are obtainable from a variety of sources. The standard material requirements of 1 kg of KABO are as follows:

K	0.33 kg	at £104.00 per kg	£34.32
A	0.28 kg	at £49.00 per kg	£13.72
B	0.23 kg	at £186.00 per kg	£42.78
O	0.42 kg	at £72.50 per kg	£30.45
Total	1.26 kg		£121.27

Process losses occur at an even rate throughout the processing operation and tend to rise if impurities are present in the ingredients. The effectiveness of KABO depends on the quality of the ingredients being used and the maintenance of the ingredient mixture within close limits of that specified above.

At the start of April 1995 318.6 kg of 40% processed KABO were held in the division. At the end of April 426.3 kg of 52% processed KABO were held. During April 831.0 kg of fully-processed KABO were transferred from the division to stores.

During April the following materials were acquired and input to the process:

K   291.6 kg at a cost of £30,006

A   242.6 kg at a cost of £12,421

B   198.2 kg at a cost of £37,262

O   392.0 kg at a cost of £26,719

Required:

As management accountant to the pharmaceuticals company,

a) in regard to the material input in April 1995, calculate

❏ the materials total cost variance,

❏ the materials price variance,

❏ the materials usage variance,

❏ the materials mixture variance, and

❏ the materials yield variance.

Present these variances in the form of a financial control report for presentation to the company's management. You may assume that the opening and closing work-in-progress are subject to normal process losses only.

b) critically comment upon the following statement made by the company's finance director in regard to your report:

'This is an excellent report which tells us all we need to know for both financial and quality control purposes. We should pay the divisional manager a monthly performance bonus based on the cost variances that are reported.'

CIMA, *Management Accounting Applications.*

A5. You have been provided with the following operating statement which represents an attempt to compare the actual performance for the quarter which has just ended with the budget:

	Budget	Actual	Variance
Number of units sold (000s)	640	720	80
	£000	£000	£000
Sales	1,024	1,071	47
Cost of sales: (all variable)			
Materials	168	144	
Labour	240	288	
Overheads	32	36	
	440	468	(28)
Fixed labour cost	100	94	6
Selling and distribution costs:			
Fixed	72	83	(11)
Variable	144	153	(9)
Administration costs:			
Fixed	184	176	8
Variable	48	54	(6)
	548	560	(12)
Net profit	36	43	7

Required:

a) Using a flexible budgeting approach, re-draft the operating statement so as to provide a more realistic indication of the variances, and comment briefly on the possible reasons (other than inflation) why they have occurred.

b) Explain why the original operating statement was of little use to management.

c) Discuss the problems associated with the forecasting of figures which are to be used in flexible budgeting.

ACCA, Managerial Finance.

A6. A nursing home has a maximum capacity of 80 beds. Budgeted information for the year ended 31 December 1995 is as follows:

(i) Budgeted costs for the year assuming 100% capacity utilisation are as follows:

	£
Administration	92,000 (100% fixed)
Catering	164,000 (70% variable, 30% fixed)
Cleaning	32,000 (20% variable, 80% fixed)
Laundry	80,000 (100% variable)
Medical supervision	260,000 (30% variable, 70% fixed)
Sundry overheads	100,000 (25% variable, 75% fixed)

(ii) Variable costs vary in proportion to the number of beds occupied.

(iii) Fixed costs are incurred equally in each of four quarters of the year.

(iv) The budgeted charge at which residents are invoiced is £30 per day. Each quarter is treated as 90 days for invoicing purposes.

(v) The budgeted occupancy rate is 90% for the year to 31 December 1995.

Actual information for the *quarter* ended 30 June 1995 is as follows:

(i) Actual costs incurred for the quarter are:

	Variable £	Fixed £
Administration		22,000
Catering	27,500	12,400
Cleaning	1,525	6,200
Laundry	19,380	
Medical supervision	18,525	43,600
Sundry overheads	6,000	18,000

(ii) Average occupancy during the quarter was 76 beds per day.

(iii) Fee income from residents during the quarter was increased by short-term residents who agreed to pay a premium rate of £35 per day and who were invoiced in total for 700 bed days.

A number of permanent changes were acknowledged at the start of the quarter ended 30 June 1995 which would affect the budgeted costs:

1. A rearrangement of the administration staff requirement reduces salaries by £2,000 per quarter.

2. Catering variable costs will be increased by 3% because of food price increases.

3. Cleaning fixed costs will increase by £240 per quarter in order to comply with new legislation.

4. Laundry costs will be reduced by 5% as the result of a policy of contracting-out the laundry service.

5. Medical supervision variable costs will be reduced by 5% through the rationalisation of drug requirements.

6. Sundry overhead fixed costs will be reduced by £5,000 per quarter through a rationalisation of the night duty staff requirement.

A summary operating statement for the quarter ended 30 June 1995 which recognises planning and operational variances is presented as follows:

	£	£
Original budgeted contribution		125,955
Revision variances		1,003 (F)
Revised budget contribution		126,958
Less: Fixed costs (total):		
Original budget	105,950	
Revision variance	6,670 (F)	99,190
Revised budget profit		27,768

	Variable	Fixed	
Occupancy variance (contribution gain or loss)			7,053 (F)
Other variances:	Variable	Fixed	
	£	£	
Residents fees	3,500 (F)		
Cost variances (total)	1,741 (A)	3,010 (A)	
	1,759 (F)	3,010 (A)	1,251 (A)
Actual net profit			33,570

Note: (F) = favourable (A) = adverse

Required:

a) Using the information in the question, prepare detailed workings to show how each of the figures in the operating statement for the quarter ended 30 June 1995 have been calculated.

b) Estimate the occupancy rate (%) for ;the six months ending 31 December 1995 which will result in a net profit of £65,000 for the six month period if the actual cost and revenue statistics are as per those applicable in quarter 2 other than:

  (i) Operational variances for costs are reduced to 40% of the rate at which they were incurred in quarter 2.

  (ii) Fee income premium for short stay residents will boost overall fees by 5% of the budget bed day fee.

c) Explain to the nursing home owners the ways in which the planning and operational variance model enhances their ability to implement feedback and feed forward control.

  (No quantitative data required.)

  ACCA, Information for Control and Decision Making.

A7. CD Ltd sells an electric motor but finds that it runs out of stock on occasions and thus loses the contribution on missed sales.

The following information is available:

Estimated demand	12,000 per year
Purchase price	£100 each
Selling price	£155 each
Lead time	5 days guaranteed
Cost of holding a motor	£20 per year
EOQ	1,200 motors

The company works a five-day week for 48 weeks a year, i.e. 240 days. The demand figures have been analysed for the last 27 weeks:

Motors sold	Number of days level of sales occurred
30	10
40	20
50	50
60	30
70	15
80	5
90	5
	135

At present CD Ltd uses a re-order level of 250 motors and does not carry any safety stock because of the guaranteed delivery time. Ideally it wishes to satisfy customers on average at least 95% of the time whilst minimising the associated costs.

You are required:

a) to estimate the annual stock-out costs of using the present re-order level;

b) to calculate what re-order level would enable the company to meet its 95% requirement.

CIMA, Management Accounting Techniques.

A8. A firm has recently commenced using a standard costing system but the manager is having some difficulty in identifying significant variances, i.e. those that require further analysis and investigation.

You are required:

a) to describe the factors which determine whether or not a variance is significant;

b) to suggest ways in which significant variances could be more easily identified;

c) to explain what changes, if any, there would be to your previous answers if the variances were sub-divided into planning and operational variances.

CIMA, Management Accounting Techniques.

A9. Milbao plc make and sell three types of electronic game for which the following budget/standard information and actual information is available for a four-week period:

Model	Budget sales	Selling price	Variable cost	Actual sales
	(units)	£	£	(units)
Superb	30,000	100	40	36,000
Excellent	50,000	80	25	42,000
Good	20,000	70	22	18,000

Standard unit data

Budgeted fixed costs are £2,500,000 for the four-week period. Budgeted fixed costs should be charged to product units at an overall budgeted average cost per unit where it is relevant to do so.

Required:

a) Calculate the sales volume variance for each model and in total for the four-week period where (i) turnover (ii) contribution and (iii) net profit is used as the variance valuation base.

b) Discuss the relative merits of each of the valuation bases of the sales volume variance calculated in a) above.

c) Calculate the TOTAL sales quantity and sales mix variances for Milbao plc for the four-week period, using contribution as the valuation base. (Individual model variances are not required.)

d) Comment on why the individual model variances for sales mix and sales quantity may provide misleading information to management. (No calculations are required.)

e) The following additional information is available for the four-week period:

1. The actual selling prices and variable costs of Milbao plc are 10% and 5% lower respectively, than the original budget/standard.

2. General market prices have fallen by 6% from the original standard. Short-term strategy by Milbao plc accounts for the residual fall in selling price.

3. 3% of the variable cost reduction from the original budget/standard is due to an over-estimation of a wage award, the remainder (i.e. 2%) is due to short-term operational improvements.

(i) Prepare a summary for a four-week period for model Superb ONLY, which reconciles original budget contribution with actual contribution where planning and operational variances are taken into consideration.

(ii) Comment on the usefulness to management of planning and operational variance analysis in feedback and feed forward control.

ACCA, Information for Control and Decision Making.

Examination questions without answers

B1. One common approach to organisational control theory is to look at the model of a cybernetic system. This is often illustrated by a diagram of a thermostat mechanism.

You are required:

a) to explain the limitations of the simple feedback control this model illustrates, as an explanation of the working of organisational control systems;

Note: A diagram is *not* required.

b) to explain

(i) the required conditions (pre-requisites) for the existence of control in an organisation, which are often derived from this approach to control theory;

(ii) the difficulties of applying control in a not-for-profit organisation (NPO).

CIMA, Management Accounting – Control and Audit.

B2. In the operation of a standard costing system, variances may occur between the original standards for labour cost and the actual costs incurred. Such variances may be analysed into planning and operational categories.

a) Explain the calculation and relevance of the range of variances which may appear in a summary profits statement where standard marginal costing with planning variances and operational variances is in operation, which stem from labour costs differing from the original standards.

b) Suggest ways in which the variances may be useful to management for feedback and feed forward control purposes.

ACCA, Information for Control and Decision Making.

B3. You have been asked to examine the budgeting system at QED Limited - manufacturers of a range of small kitchen appliances.

QED Limited has a budgeting system which is being developed to include flexible budgeting. Some preliminary work has been carried out, and you find the following data available for the Production Department:

Expense	Estimated cost behaviour	
Indirect labour	Semi-variable	$(32{,}000 + £0.5x)$
Quality control	Semi-variable	$(£17{,}500 + £0.00001x^2)$
Maintenance	Semi-variable	$(£24{,}500 + £0.3x)$
Storekeeping	Semi-variable	$(£8{,}200 + £0.25x)$
Administrative salaries	Fixed	$(£35{,}500)$
Depreciation	Fixed	$(£29{,}000)$
Space charges	Fixed	$(£18{,}750)$

(where x = labour hours)

Product standard cost data

Can openers	1.20 labour hours per unit
Whisks	1.75 labour hours per unit
Juice extractors	2.30 labour hours per unit
Food mixers	6.90 labour hours per unit

You find that the actual results for last period were as follows:

Actual labour hours: 66,250

Actual production:

5,280	Can openers
4,164	Whisks
8,940	Juice extractors
3,950	Food mixers

Actual costs:

	£
Indirect labour	64,875
Quality control	58,110
Maintenance	43,625
Storekeeping	25,908
Administrative salaries	36,205
Depreciation	29,000
Space charges	18,250

The budget holder, who is the Production Manager, thinks that the budget should be flexed on actual labour hours, but the Managing Director has doubts about this.

You are required:

a) to produce a flexed budget for the period, based on the Production Managerís suggestion, and show the budget variances from actual;

b) to produce a flexed budget based on different principles to those used in a), and show the budget variances from actual;

c) to explain why the results of your answers to a) and b) are different, and to state, with reasons, which you recommend should be adopted.

d) If the cost behavioural characteristics had not been supplied, explain how they could be derived.

CIMA, Management Accounting Techniques.

B4. a) If an organisation applies zero-based budgeting, (ZBB), it is essential that all levels of management understand the 'decision package' concept.

Explain briefly what the decision package concept is and how it is used in ZBB.

b) The following cost information relates to product ZIM 3A, which is produced in one continuous process by Chemacca Ltd:

	£
Actual quantity of materials at standard price	103,500
Actual quantity of materials at actual price	103,250
Actual yield at standard materials cost	102,500
Standard yield from actual input of materials at standard cost	100,000

Required:

Calculate and present the following material cost variances:

– price; usage; mix and yield,

and comment briefly on your findings.

ACCA, Managerial Finance (part question).

B5. (i) A company uses 12,000 units of component X in a year. Component X is currently made in 30 batches of 400 units on a machine that makes 8 units per hour.

The company operates for 2,000 hours per year and it costs £60 to set up the machine, irrespective of batch size. For work-in-progress purposes, component X is valued at £10. The Operations Manager has supplied the following formulae:

$$\text{Economic Batch Quantity (EBQ)} = \sqrt{\frac{2dc}{v\left(1-\dfrac{d}{p}\right)}}$$

$$\text{and manufacturing cost} = \left[\left(\frac{dc}{\text{EBQ}}\right)+\left(\frac{\text{EBQ}}{2}\right)v\left(1-\frac{d}{p}\right)\right]$$

where d = annual usage

p = annual production rate

c = set-up cost

v = valuation for WIP purposes

a) **You are required** to investigate whether the existing production plan is optimum and, if not, to suggest a new plan showing what savings are possible.

(ii) It has been said that Just-in-Time (JIT) is a total manufacturing philosophy, not just a technique.

You are required:

b) to describe the main features of Just-in-Time and its value to the firm;

c) to explain how batch manufacture using Just-in-Time differs from the classic EBQ model.

CIMA, Management Accounting Techniques.

B6. It is common practice to flex a budget linearly according to the volume of production, using labour or machine hours as a proxy, yet this often results in a budget which is inaccurate and is thus less useful for control purposes.

You are required:

a) to explain why inaccuracies may result from the procedures commonly used to flex a budget;

b) to explain how these inaccuracies detract from effective control;

c) to discuss alternative ways of budgeting which might improve both accuracy and control.

CIMA, Management Accounting Techniques.

B7. The Perseus Co Ltd, a medium sized company, produces a single product in its one overseas factory. For control purposes, a standard costing system was recently introduced and is now in operation.

The standards set for the month of May were as follows:

Production and sales	16,000 units
Selling price (per unit)	£140

Materials

Material 007,	6 kilos per unit at £12.25 per kilo
Material XL90,	3 kilos per unit at £3.20 per kilo

Labour

4.5 hours per unit at £8.40 per hour

Overheads (all fixed)

£86,400 per month, they are not absorbed into the product costs.

The actual data for the month of May, is as follows:

Produced 15,400 units which were sold at £138.25 each.

Materials

Used 98,560 kilos of material 007 at a total cost of £1,256,640 and used 42,350 kilos of material XL90 at a total cost of £132,979.

Labour

Paid an actual rate of £8.65 per hour to the labour force. The total amount paid out, amounted to £612,766.

Overheads (all fixed)

£96,840

Required:

a) Prepare a standard costing profit statement, and a profit statement based on actual figures for the month of May.

b) Prepare a statement of the variances which reconciles the actual with the standard profit or loss figure.

c) Explain briefly the possible reasons for inter-relationships between material variances and labour variances.

ACCA, Managerial Finance.

Decision Making

The next six chapters cover various facets of the all important activity of decision making. A significant part of the task of the management accountant is to supply information for decision making purposes and it is essential that there is full awareness of the decision process and of the techniques that may be of help in choosing between alternatives.

Throughout this section the importance of *relevancy* is stressed again and again. The characteristics of relevant information are described and the stages in the decision process are explained.

Formal decision rules such as expected value are described and short run decision criteria based on marginal costing and cost-volume-profit analysis are analysed in typical decision making situations. The particular requirements of pricing decisions are dealt with in detail including the theoretical economic background and the important resource allocation technique of Linear Programming and the way it can provide assistance to the management accountant, is described and exemplified.

Long run decision making or investment appraisal is covered in some depth including the use of discounted cash flow and methods for dealing with risk, inflation, and capital rationing.

13 Decision making – an introduction

1. Objectives

After studying this chapter you will:

❏ understand the decision process and the importance of relevant information;

❏ know the features of relevant information

❏ be able to identify what costs are relevant to a decision;

❏ understand typical decision rules, such as expected value, maximin, maximax and minimax regret criterion;

❏ know the relationship between opportunity loss and expected value;

❏ be able to draw and evaluate decision trees;

❏ understand the backward and forward passes.

2. Background to decision making

Decision making is an all pervasive activity taking place at every level in the organisation covering both the short and long term. Plans are activated by decisions and a significant number of decisions require some form of financial or quantitative analysis in order that a rational choice can be made. It is because of this that the practising management accountant is heavily engaged in producing relevant information for decision making purposes. A knowledge of the decision process, the importance and meaning of relevancy and of the techniques which can provide assistance with the analysis of information for decision making are vital knowledge for the student of management accounting and are the subject of the next six chapters.

The emphasis in this book is on decisions which have a quantitative basis. However, it must be realised that regardless of the amount of quantitative information available, the actual decision process invariably includes consideration of qualitative, psychological, behavioural and social factors as well as the quantitative ones. Some decisions, often of great importance, are based entirely on qualitative factors, for example, staff appointments, new designs for a fashion house and other of a similar nature. In spite of this there is a vast range of business situations for which quantitative and financial analysis plays a crucial part in making rational decisions.

These range from long-term strategic decisions such as acquisitions, launching new products or buying capital equipment to shorter term tactical problems such as product planning, make or buy, product pricing and so on. A common element of all these problems is that they rely on information on costs and revenues which is correctly specified in economically relevant terms for the particular decision being considered. This is the overriding requirement of the information that should be supplied. Consistency of treatment in the traditional accounting sense is not possible in these circumstances, relevancy is all important. What are relevant costs and how they can be identified are dealt with in detail later in this chapter.

Decision making can be defined as making choices between future, uncertain alternatives. It must be emphasises that *all decision making* relates to the *future* and that a decision is a *choice* between *alternatives* in pursuit of an objective(s). Where no alternatives exist no decision can be made and nothing can be done now that will alter the past. These fundamentals of decision making are of critical importance in determining what information the management accountant should supply to the decision maker.

3. The decision process

The overall decision process can be subdivided into stages although in practice the divisions between the stages may be blurred. The stages are:

a) definition of objective(s)

b) consideration of alternatives

c) evaluation of alternatives in the light of the objective(s)

d) selection of the course of action.

The whole process may extend over a long period – for example, there were several years of analysis and exploration before the final decision to drill for oil in the North Sea – or it may take place within seconds for some routine, operational decision.

The stages in the decision process are expanded below.

4. Definition of objectives

The decision maker must be aware of the objective(s) of the organisation which should be stated in explicit terms. An organisation may have multiple objectives and where this situation exists it is essential that they are consistent with one another. For example, it may be inconsistent to pursue the objective of maximising profits whilst at the same time attempting to maximise market share.

Although the single objective of profit maximisation appears to be the norm, particularly for examination purposes, students should be aware that research by H.A. Simon and others indicates that *satisficing behaviour* (ie acceptance of a satisfactory level of achievement) appears to be more usually encountered in practice than the 'optimising' behaviour implied by profit maximisation. This is probably a realistic acceptance of the practical difficulties of information feedback, computation, and forecasting in a typical organisation.

The link between plans, objectives and decisions is that plans are the embodiment of the organisation's objectives and decisions are the implementation of plans. Wherever possible the objectives should be quantified and indeed this is essential if one or other of the powerful mathematical decision models is to be used as a basis for choosing the best alternative. Where the objective can be quantified it is known as an *objective function*. As previously stated, this book concentrates on those decision problems which lend themselves to quantitative analysis so it follows that we are only concerned with problems where the objective(s) can be quantified and an objective function established.

The definition of objectives will inevitably cause initial consideration to be given to the constraints or limitations of the problem. Constraints may be shortages of labour, materials, space, machine capacity, finance or they may be requirements on sales or stock levels or they may be the need to achieve particular results. For example, the organisation's objective may be to maximise sales turnover subject to the constraint that the return on capital employed is 15% or more. If a given constraint limits the values of the objective function it is called a *binding constraint* or a *limiting factor*. Constraints are dealt with further when the ways that alternatives can be evaluated are discussed.

5. Consideration of alternatives

Decision making always involves predictions and this is also true when selecting the set of alternatives from which the final decision will be made. There is the possibility that, although the best choice will hopefully be made from the selected set of alternatives, there exists some other alternative which would better fulfil the organisation's objectives. Attractive alternatives do not automatically submit themselves to the decision process, they have to be continuously and actively sought out. An aid to this process is the development of effective information systems which gather information from external internal sources in order to ensure that opportunities are not overlooked.

On occasions there may appear to be only one action open to the organisation and it might thus appear that the necessary conditions for decision making (ie choice between alternatives) do not exist. This is not true because one of the alternatives should be to take no action now in order to be in a position to undertake a more attractive alternative in the future which uses the same resources.

Ideally, the set of alternatives to be considered should be an exhaustive list but because of information deficiencies and uncertainty this is rarely, if ever, possible. The effect of this is that so called 'optimal' solutions produced by various techniques are only optimal in a restricted sense.

6. Evaluation of alternatives

Although the management accountant must be familiar with the whole of the decision process, undoubtedly his major contribution is in that part of the process concerned with making quantitative comparisons between the alternatives so that the decision maker is provided with a relevant and correctly specified financial basis for the ultimate decision.

To carry out this task effectively the management accountant must be totally familiar with a range of concepts and techniques including: the determination of economically relevant costs and revenues, the use of various formal decision rules or models, the use of probabilities in decision analysis, the construction of decision trees, the use of Cost-Volume-Profit analysis, resource allocation using linear programming, and the use of investment appraisal techniques such as Discounted Cash Flow (DCF). DCF, linear programming and Cost-Volume-Profit analysis are dealt with in subsequent chapters whilst the other material is dealt with later in this chapter.

An important part of the evaluation of alternatives is concerned with the assessment of risk and uncertainty. Because all decision making is concerned with the future, uncertainty is ever present and in general it would be misleading to present information for decision making purposes which ignored the possible consequences of such matters as: competitor's actions, inflation, imperfect forecasting, interest and finance changes, new government legislation, possible material/labour shortages, possible industrial disputes and all the factors which contribute to uncertainty. This chapter and subsequent ones cover a range of methods of incorporating uncertainty into the appraisal process.

7. Selection of the course of action

This is the stage where the actual choice between the alternatives is made. Decisions have been classified by Simon into *programmed* and *non-programmed* categories.

Programmed. These are relatively structured decisions within a clearly defined operational area. The decision rules are known and generally there is a clear cut, single objective. Because of the nature of these decisions they are the first to be incorporated into computer based information systems because they can be made automatically, given normal circumstances.

A typical example of a programmed decision is a replenishment decision based on usage and re-order levels in an inventory control system.

Non-programmed. These are decisions for which decision rules and procedures cannot or have not yet been devised. Generally they involve non-repetitive circumstances and may include a number of external and internal factors many of which have a substantial degree of uncertainty. As a consequence there is the necessity to supply a variety of information tailored to the particular situation rather than the narrower, restricted range of information suitable for programmed decisions.

Ad-hoc decision problems are severe tests for information systems and as a consequence there is the tendency to try to make the decision problem under consideration fit existing decision rules or models so that a decision can be made more easily. This approach is only correct when the current problem is *truly suitable* for the decision model envisaged. An example of this is the assumption, frequently made, that all the costs and factors in a problem behave in a linear fashion. If this assumption is made then various solution techniques exist, ranging from simple contribution and cost-volume-profit analysis to linear programming models. If the linearity assumption is valid then the techniques will be of value but if the assumption is invalid then an incorrect decision could easily be made.

The *real* situation must be studied and only information and techniques *relevant* to the *actual problem* should be used.

An important factor in decision making is the individual's attitude to risk. Individual attitudes range from *risk seeking* to *risk aversion* so in consequence, given the same information, different individuals are quite likely to make different decisions. Research has shown that people making business decisions tend towards risk aversion and as a result do not necessarily choose alternatives which have the highest calculated returns if those returns are associated with significant chances of failure. The importance of this for the management accountant is that it is essential to provide information for decision making which shows the effects of risk and uncertainty and the range of likely outcomes. In this way the decision maker is better able to appreciate the background to the alternatives and hopefully will be able to make more informed decisions.

8. Relevant costs and revenues

The importance of relevancy for decision making has already been stressed and it is now time to consider in detail what are relevant costs and revenues for decision making purposes. In summary, relevant information concerns:

a) Future costs and revenues.

Decision making is concerned with the future so that it is expected future costs and revenues which are of importance to the decision maker. This means that past costs and revenues are only useful insofar as they provide a guide to future values. Costs which have already been spent in the past, known as *sunk costs,* are irrelevant for decision making..

b) Differential costs and revenues.

Only those costs and revenues which alter as a result of a decision are relevant. Where factors are common to all of the alternatives they can be ignored; only the differences are relevant. In many short run situations the fixed costs remain constant for each of the alternatives being considered so that the marginal costing approach showing sales, marginal cost and contribution is useful. However great care is necessary when dealing with traditional accounting classifications of cost in order not to mislead or be misled. So called 'fixed' costs can and do change and thus become relevant factors for the decision being considered. This is the key factor and not the recorded cost classification – with its implied behaviour patterns – contained within the cost accounting system.

Differential costs and revenues are *costs* that can be *avoided* or *revenues foregone* if the particular alternative is not adopted. The differential approach is an essential one for decision making and can be used for both short and long run decision making. The major operational difference between the two is that for long run decisions, usually called investment decisions, the time value of money has to be considered and discounting techniques need to be used. Investment decisions are dealt with later in the book.

9. Opportunity cost

So far the economically relevant costs for decision making have been defined as future, avoidable costs but in economic theory the correct cost for evaluating a decision is termed the *opportunity cost*. Opportunity cost can be defined as the value of the next best alternative, ie it is the net receipts foregone by not accepting the best available alternative. It will be noted that the definition of opportunity cost emphasises *alternatives* which, of course, are the basis of decision making.

Thus there would seem to be two types of relevant costs for decision making – opportunity costs and avoidable costs. However, this is not so as the two are identical and are merely different ways of looking at the same thing.

Economically relevant cost ≡ opportunity cost ≡ avoidable cost.

In a given problem where there are exchange transactions (buying or selling) then opportunity costs are measured by the money outlays. In other circumstances where the resources used are not represented by outlay costs it may be necessary to impute a value for opportunity cost.

Whether it is best to use solely avoidable (differential) costs or avoidable costs plus imputed opportunity costs depends entirely on what is more convenient in a given problem. Properly used, either method will give the correct decision.

A number of examples follow which illustrate typical problems encountered in determining relevant costs.

10. Relevant cost examples

Example 1

A 1 year contract has been offered which will utilise an existing machine that is only suitable for such contract work. The machine cost £25,000 five years ago and has been depreciated £4,000 per year on a straight line basis and thus has a book value of £5000. The machine could be sold now for £8000 or in 1 year's time for £1000. Four types of material would be needed for the contract as follows:

| | Units | | | Price per Unit | |
Material	In Stock	Required for Contract	Purchase Price of Stock	Current Buying-in Price	Current Resale price
			£	£	£
W	1200	300	1.80	1.50	1.20
X	200	1100	0.75	2.80	2.10
Y	3000	600	0.50	0.80	0.60
Z	1800	1200	1.80	2.00	1.90

W and Z are in regular use within the firm. X could be sold if not used for the contract and there are no other uses for Y, which has been deemed to be obsolete.

What are the relevant costs in connection with the contract (ignoring the time value of money)?

Solution

Machine costs. The historic cost is a sunk cost and is not relevant. The depreciation details given relate to accounting conventions and are not relevant.

The relevant cost is the opportunity cost caused by the reduction in resale value over the one year duration of the contract, ie £8000 – 1000 = £7000.

Material costs

W

Although there is sufficient in stock the use of 300 units for the contract would necessitate the need for replenishment at the current market price.

∴ Relevant cost　＝　300 × £1.50　＝　£450

X

If the contract were not accepted 200 units of X could be sold at £2.10 per unit. The balance of 900 units required would be bought at the current buying-in price of £2.80.

$$
\begin{array}{rcl}
 & & £ \\
\text{∴ Relevant cost} \;=\; 200 \times £2.10 \;=\; & & 420 \\
900 \times £2.80 \;=\; & & 2520 \\
& & £2940 \\
\end{array}
$$

Y

If the 600 units were used on the contract they could not be sold so the opportunity cost is the current resale price of £0.60 per unit.

∴ Relevant cost　＝　600 × £0.60　＝　£360

Z

Similar reasoning to W, ie replenishment at current buying-in price

∴ Relevant cost　＝　1200 × £2　＝　£2400

Note: It will be seen from the above examples that the recorded historical cost, which is the 'cost' using normal accounting conventions, is not the relevant value in any of the circumstances considered.

Example 2

A decision has to be taken by a firm whether or not to initiate manufacture of a new product called Wizzo. The following data have been established.

a) A market research study carried out three months ago into the sales potential of Wizzo cost £25,000.

b) A new machine would require to be purchased at a cost of £100,000 solely to make Wizzo. A nil scrap value is anticipated and it is the firm's policy to write of depreciation on a straight line basis over 5 years.

c) Wizzo would be manufactured in a factory owned by the firm, the annual depreciation charge of which is £8,000. At present the factory is sub-let at £17,500 p.a.

d) The labour requirements for Wizzo are:

	Hours/Unit of Wizzo	Normal Wage Rates/Hour	
		First Year	Subsequent Years
		£	£
Skilled	4	3.00	3.50
Semi-Skilled	3	2.20	2.60
Unskilled	2	1.80	1.85

It is expected that there will be shortage of skilled labour in the first year only so the manufacture of Wizzo will make it necessary for the skilled labour to be diverted from other work on which a contribution of £4.50 per hour is earned, net of wage costs. The firm currently has a surplus of semi-skilled labour paid at full rate but doing unskilled work. The labour concerned could be transferred to provide sufficient labour for the manufacture of Wizzo and would be replaced by unskilled labour.

e) Overhead costs are allocated to manufacture at the rate of £18 per skilled labour hour as follows:

	£
Fixed overheads	13.00
Variable overheads	5.00
	18.00

f) The manufacture and sale of Wizzo is expected to cause sales of an existing product, Bango, to fall by 3000 units per annum. The contribution on Bango is £9 per unit.

g) The manufacture of Wizzo would require the services of an existing manager who would be paid £12,000 p.a. If not required for Wizzo the manager would be made redundant and would receive £3,000 p.a. under a service agreement.

What are the relevant costs from the above data in deciding whether or not to manufacture Wizzo (ignoring the time value of money)?

Solution

a) The market research cost of £25,000 is a sunk cost and is irrelevant to the current decision.

b) The purchase of the machine is a relevant cash flow. The depreciation charges are non-cash flows and are irrelevant to the current decision.

   Machinery:- Relevant Cost £100,000

c) Manufacture of Wizzo would mean that the present rental received would be foregone so it is a relevant cost. The depreciation charge is not relevant.

   Factory:- Relevant Cost £17,500 p.a.

d) The out of pocket wages costs per unit of Wizzo are as follows:

		£	1st Year £	Subsequent Years £
Note (i)	Skilled	4 × 3.50		14.00
Note (ii)	Semi-skilled	3 × 1.80	5.40	
		3 × 1.85		5.55
Note (iii)	Unskilled	2 × 1.80	3.60	
		2 × 1.85		3.70

Notes:

i) There is a shortage of skilled labour in year 1 so there will be no additional cash flow for wages but there will be an opportunity cost of alternative work foregone (see Note iv)

ii) The relevant cost of the semi-skilled labour is the replacement cost of the new unskilled labour.

iii) The relevant costs are the normal wage rates.

iv) The diversion of skilled labour to Wizzo causes a loss of net contribution of £4.50 per hour plus a loss of the recoupment of skilled wages of £3.00 per hour, ie a total opportunity cost of £7.50 per hour making a total cost per unit of Wizzo of 4 × £7.50 = £30.

∴ Relevant wages and opportunity costs of labour are:

Year 1 = £5.40 + 3.60 + 30.00 = £39 per unit

Year 1 = £14 + 5.55 + 3.70 = £23.25 per unit

e) It is assumed that the fixed overhead proportion of the overhead rate relates to existing fixed overheads which do not change. Accordingly the relevant costs are the variable overheads, thus

Overheads:- Relevant cost = 4 × £5 = £20 per unit

f) If the manufacture of Wizzo causes a sales loss elsewhere then this is a relevant cost applicable to the Wizzo decision

Sales loss:- Relevant cost = 3000 × £9 = £27,000 p.a.

g) If Wizzo is manufactured then the manager will have to be paid £12,000 p.a. However, employing him full time will avoid the £3,000 p.a. redundancy payment which is an opportunity benefit arising from the manufacture of Wizzo. Thus the net avoidable cost of the manager is £12,000 – 3000 = £9,000 p.a.

Manager:- Relevant cost = £9,000 p.a.

11. Formal decision rules

It is often considered useful to process the alternatives being considered according to particular decision rules or decision models. In this way the ultimate decision maker is presented with a ranking of the alternatives according to some previously agreed criteria so making the actual decision a more routine matter, provided of course that the decision maker considers the particular rule appropriate for the decision being considered.

The decision rules covered in this book are Expected Value, the Maximin rule, the Maximax rule and the Minimax regret criterion.

12. Expected value (EV)

Expected value is an averaging process which can be used where the alternatives being considered have two or more possible outcomes and where, objectively or subjectively, a probability can be assigned to each outcome. Thus, expected value is a simple way of bringing some of the effects of uncertainty into the appraisal process.

Rarely are objective probabilities (ie those verifiable by repeated tests, eg tossing coins) available in business so that the probabilities with which we are invariably concerned are *subjective probabilities,* which are the quantification of judgements and assessments by the people involved. Once assigned, subjective probabilities obey the normal rules of probability.

The expected value of an event is the total of the *probability* of each possible outcome times the value of each possible outcome.

Example 3

Three alternatives are being considered each of which has several outcomes with associated probabilities and it is required to calculate the Expected Values.

Alternative A Outcomes		Alternative B Outcomes		Alternative C Outcomes	
Probability	Contribution £	Probability	Contribution £	Probability	Contribution £
		0.1	2,500		
0.2	6,000	0.2	5,000	0.4	8,000
0.6	10,000	0.4	9,000	0.6	11,500
0.2	12,500	0.2	11,500		
		0.1	16,000		

Solution

Expected Values

A $(0.2 \times 6,000) + (0.6 \times 10,000) + (0.2 \times 12,500)$ = £9,700

B $(0.1 \times 2,500) + (0.2 \times 5,000) + (0.4 \times 9,000) + (0.2 \times 11,500) + (0.1 \times 16,000)$ = £8,750

C $(0.4 \times 8,000) + (0.6 \times 11,500)$ = £10,100

∴ on basis of expected value C would be preferred and the ranking would be CAB.

Notes:

a) In each case it will be seen that the probabilities total 1 which indicates that all outcomes have been included.

b) The number of outcomes can vary as shown in this example but a commonly encountered situation is that depicted for Alternative A where there are three outcomes: often termed Optimistic, Most Likely and Pessimistic.

c) Expected value calculations use the two basic rules of probability. It will be recalled from foundation statistics that these are the multiplication rule (AND) and the addition rule (OR).

d) The reporting of the expected value alone may mislead the decision maker because it has the effect of masking the characteristics of the underlying distribution of outcomes and probabilities. Where more information is required on the uncertainties additional information can be supplied utilising various statistical techniques. Examples of such techniques are dealt with later in the book.

13. Expected value – advantages and disadvantages

Expected Value is a useful summarising technique, but suffers from similar advantages and disadvantages to all averaging methods.

Advantages:

a) Simple to understand and calculate.

b) Represents whole distribution by a single figure.

c) Arithmetically takes account of the expected variabilities of all outcomes.

Disadvantages:

a) By representing the whole distribution by a single figure it ignores the other characteristics of the distribution, eg the range and skewness.

b) Makes the assumption that the decision maker is risk neutral, ie he would rank equally the following two distributions:

	£	p	
Distribution 1			
Pessimistic Outcome	18000	0.25	
Most likely Outcome	20000	0.50	
Optimistic Outcome	22000	0.25	EV = £20,000
Distribution 2			
Pessimistic Outcome	6000	0.20	
Most likely Outcome	18000	0.60	
Optimistic Outcome	40000	0.20	EV = £20,000

It is of course unlikely that any decision maker would rank them equally due to his personal attitude to risk and, assuming a typical 'risk aversion' attitude, the first of the above distributions would normally be preferred.

Although it appears to be widely used for the purpose, the concept of expected value is not particularly well suited to one off-decisions. Expected value can strictly only be interpreted as the value that would be obtained if a large number of similar decisions were taken with the same ranges of outcomes and associated probabilities. Hardly a typical business situation!

14. Optimisation of levels of activity under conditions of uncertainty

Expected Value concepts can be used to calculate the maximum stock or profit level when demand is subject to random variations over a period.

Example 4

A distributor buys perishable articles for £2 per item and sells them at £5. Demand per day is uncertain and items unsold at the end of the day represent a write off because of perishability. If he understocks he loses profit he could have made.

A 300 day record of past activity is as follows:

Daily Demand (units)	No. of Days	p
10	30	0.1
11	60	0.2
12	120	0.4
13	90	0.3
	300	1.0

What level of stock should he hold from day to day to maximise profit?

Solution

It is necessary to calculate the *Conditional Profit* (CP) and *Expected Profit* (EP). CP = profit that could be made at any particular conjunction of stock and demand, eg if 13 articles were bought and demand was 10 then:

$$CP = (10 \times 5) - (13 \times 2) = £24$$

$$EP = CP \times \text{probability of the demand}$$

and since the CP above is £24 and p (demand = 10) = 0.1, we have:

$$EP = £24 \times 0.1 = £2.4$$

Stock Options

Demand	p	10 CP £	10 EP £	11 CP £	11 EP £	12 CP £	12 EP £	13 CP £	13 EP £
10	0.1	30	3	28	2.80	26	2.60	24	2.40
11	0.2	30	6	33	6.60	31	6.20	29	5.80
12	0.4	30	12	33	13.20	36	14.40	34	13.60
13	0.3	30	9	33	9.90	36	10.80	39	11.70
	1.0		30		32.50		*34.00		33.50

* = Optimum

Table 1 Conditional and expected profit table

The optimum stock position, given the pattern of demand, is to stock 12 units per day.

15. Value of perfect information

Assume that the distributor in Example 4 could buy market research information which was perfect, ie it would enable him to forecast the exact demand on any day so that he could stock up accordingly. How much would the distributor be prepared to pay for such information? To solve this type of problem, the profit with perfect information is compared with the optimum EP from Table 1.

Profit with perfect Information

				£
When demand is 10, stock 10	Profit	=	$(10 \times £3) \times .1$	=	3.0
When demand is 11, stock 11	Profit	=	$(11 \times £3) \times .2$	=	6.6
When demand is 12, stock 12	Profit	=	$(12 \times £3) \times .4$	=	14.4
When demand is 13, stock 13	Profit	=	$(13 \times £3) \times .3$	=	11.7

$$35.7$$

As the EP from Table 1 was £34, the distributor could pay up to £1.70 (£35.7 – 34) for the information. The principles behind this type of problem seem to be the subject of frequent examination questions so clear understanding is vital. The shortfall between the *expected value* of outcome and the *maximum possible* outcome with perfect information is the upper limit of the amount that would be paid for such information.

Obviously there is no such thing as perfect information and the calculation of the amount to pay for such information would seem to be a totally theoretical exercise with no practical value. This is not so, because the calculation provides the upper limit which any information could be worth. Having this ceiling value relates the costs of information production to the maximum value which could possibly be obtained. It makes explicit the fact that producing more information, with the resulting increase in costs, is not automatically worthwhile. The extra costs must be compared with the extra benefits expected.

16. Alternative decision rules

The rule so far covered in this chapter is to choose the alternative which maximises the expected value. This is the most commonly encountered decision rule and is the one which should be used unless there are clear instructions to the contrary. However alternative rules do exist and these include:

❑ the *maximin* rule

❑ the *maximax* rule

❑ the *minimax regret* rule

These rules are illustrated using the following payoff table showing potential profits and losses which are expected to arise from launching various products in three market conditions thus.

	£'000s		
	Boom Conditions	Steady State	Recession
Product A	+ 8	1	– 10
Product B	– 2	+ 6	+ 12
Product C	+ 16	0	– 26

Table 2 Pay Off Table

The probabilities are, Boom 0.6, Steady State 0.3 and Recession 0.1 so that the expected values are

Product A	$= (0.6 \times 8) + (0.3 \times 1) + (0.1 \times -10)$	$= 4.1$
Product B	$= (0.6 \times -2) + (0.3 \times 6) + (0.1 \times 12)$	$= 1.8$
Product C	$= (0.6 \times 16) + (0.3 \times 0) + (0.1 \times -26)$	$= 7.0$

So using the expected value rule the ranking would be C, A, B.

What are the rankings using the alternatives?

MAXIMIN the 'best of the worst'

This is a cautious decision rule based on maximising the minimum loss that can occur. The worst losses are:

A	-10
B	-2
C	-26

∴ Ranking using the MAXIMIN rule is B, A, C.

MAXIMAX the 'best of the best'

This is an optimistic rule and maximises the maximum that can be gained.

The maximum gains are:-

A	$+8$
B	$+12$
C	$+16$

∴ ranking using the *maximax* rule is C, B, A.

17. Minimax regret

This decision seeks to 'minimise the maximum regret' that there would be from choosing a particular strategy. To see this clearly it is necessary to construct a *regret table* based on the payoff table, Table 2. The regret is the *opportunity loss* from taking one decision given that a certain contingency occurs; in our example whether there is boom, steady state, or recession.

	Boom	Steady State	Recession
Product A	8	5	22
Product B	18	0	0
Product C	0	6	38

Table 3 Regret Table in £'000s

Note: The above opportunity losses are calculated by setting the best position under any state to zero and then calculating the amount of shortfall there is by not being at that position. For example, if there is a recession product B gains +12 but if Product A had been chosen there is a loss of –10 making a total shortfall, as compared with B, of 22, which is the opportunity loss.

The maximum 'regrets' are:-

$$
\begin{array}{ll}
\text{A} & 22 \\
\text{B} & 18 \\
\text{C} & 38
\end{array}
$$

∴ ranking using the *minimax* regret rule is B, A, C.

18. Opportunity loss and expected value

As a loss is the negative aspect of gain it is to be expected that opportunity loss and expected value are related. This is indeed so and the opportunity losses multiplied by the probabilities, ie the expected opportunity loss (EOL) can be used to arrive at the same ranking as the expected value (EV) rule except that where the maximum EV is chosen, the minimum EOL is required.

∴ *minimising* EOL gives the same decision as *maximising* EV.

For example, the EOL'S of Table 3 are:

$$
\begin{array}{lll}
\text{A} & (0.6 \times 8) + (0.3 \times 5) + (0.1 \times 22) & = & 8.5 \\
\text{B} & (0.6 \times 18) + (0.3 \times 0) + (0.1 \times 0) & = & 10.8 \\
\text{C} & (0.6 \times 0) + (0.3 \times 6) + (0.1 \times 38) & = & 5.6
\end{array}
$$

∴ ranking in order of minimum EOL gives C, A, B, which is identical to the ranking given by the expected value method.

19. Use of decision rules

The calculation of expected value or a ranking based on the alternative decision rules is but one input of information to the ultimate decision maker. The calculations may give some broad guidance but in practice it is unlikely that the recommended decisions would be automatically adopted in all cases. There are too many political, behavioural and other factors involved in a typical business situation to allow the act of decision making to become an automatic process dictated by a simple decision criterion. However, if no guidance is given in an examination, then the use of some form of expected value would be recommended, although it would be prudent to mention some of the inherent limitations of the technique.

20. Decision trees

These are a pictorial method of showing a sequence of inter-related decisions and outcomes and can provide assistance in the clarification of complex decisions. They invariably involve multiple outcomes and associated probabilities and are usually based on expected values although, in principle, there is no reason why any other decision rule could not be used.

21. Structure of decision trees

The structure and typical components of a decision tree are shown in the following illustration:

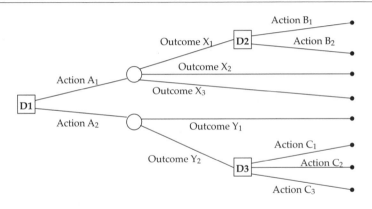

Figure 13.1

Notes:

a) It will be seen that there are two types of nodes. Decision nodes depicted by squares and Outcome nodes depicted by circles.

b) The Decision nodes are points where a choice exists between alternatives and a managerial decision is made based on estimates and calculations of the returns expected.

c) The Outcome nodes are points where the events depend on probabilities, eg assume that Action A_1 in Figure 1 was – Build branch factory – then outcomes, X_1, X_2, and X_3 could represent various possible sales: high, medium, and low, each with an estimated probability.

22. Drawing decision trees

The procedure for drawing decision trees and evaluating the returns expected will be illustrated by using the following example.

Example 5

A firm making widgets have been considering the likely demand for widgets over the next 6 years and think that the demand pattern will be as follows:

Situation	Probability
High demand for 6 years	0.5
Low demand for 6 years	0.3
High demand for 3 years followed by Low demand for 3 years	0.2

(No possibility is envisaged of Low demand followed by High demand).

Enlargement of capacity is required and the following options are available:

Option A Install fully automatic facilities immediately at a cost of £5.4m.

B Install semi-automatic facilities immediately at a cost of £4m.

C Install the semi-automatic facilities immediately as in B and upgrade to fully automatic at an additional cost of £2m in 3 years time providing demand has been high for 3 years.

The returns expected for the various demand and capacity options are estimated to be

		if high demand	*if low demand*
Option	A	£1.6m p.a.	£0.6m p.a.
	B	£0.9m p.a. for 3 years then £0.5m p.a. for 3 years	£0.8m p.a.
	C	£0.9m p.a. for 3 years then £1.1m for 3 years	£0.8m p.a. for 3 years then £0.3m p.a. for 3 years

What decision(s) should the firm take assuming that the objective is to maximise expected value (ignoring the time value of money)?

Solution

The decision tree is developed in two stages, the forward pass and the backward pass which are described in the following two sections.

23. Forward pass

Draw the decision tree starting from the left showing the two Decision points and the various demand options thus:

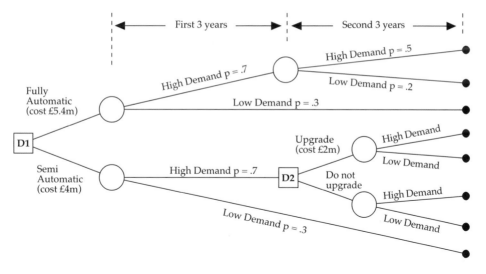

Figure 13.2

24. The backward pass

It will be seen that there are two decision points D_1 at the start and D_2 at the end of the first three years. To evaluate D_1 it is necessary to evaluate D_2 first, because the values of the D_1 actions depend upon the D_2 values. This is why this stage is known as the *backward pass*, ie evaluate the decision points from right to left.

D_2 can be depicted as follows:

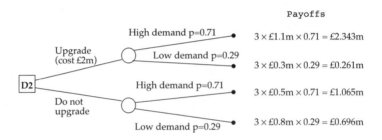

Figure 13.3

∴ The expected value of upgrading is £2.343 + £0.261 = **£0.604m**

The expected value of NOT upgrading is £1.065 + £0.696 = **£1.761m**

∴ the D_2 decision is 'do not upgrade' with an EV of £1.761m.

Note:

The probability of high demand being 0.71 as shown in Figure 13.3 is obtained by the following reasoning. D_2 will only be reached if there is high demand for the first three years. The probability that high demand will be following by high demand is 0.5 and by low demand 0.2.

$$\therefore \text{ P(High demand in second 3 years)} = \frac{0.5}{0.5 + 0.2} = 0.71$$

Figure 13.2 can now be redrawn with D_2 having an expected value of £1.761m.

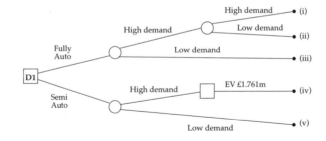

Figure 13.4

	Payoffs		*EV*
i)	$6 \times £1.6m \times 0.5$	=	£4.8000m
ii)	$(3 \times £1.6m + 3 \times £0.6m) \times 0.2$	=	£1.3200m
iii)	$6 \times £0.6m \times 0.3$	=	£1.0800m
			£7.2000m
iv)	$(3 \times £0.9m + £1.76m) \times 0.7$	=	£3.122m
v)	$6 \times £0.8m \times 0.3$	=	£1.440m
			£4.562m

The expected value of being fully automatic = £7.2m – £5.4m = £1.8m

and the expected value of being semi-automatic = £4.562m – £4m = £0.562m

The D_1 decision would be go for A, ie put in the fully auto machinery at the outset.

25. Summary

a) Plans are activated by decisions and the decision process includes consideration of political, psychological and social factors as well as quantitative and financial ones.

b) Relevancy is the all important characteristic of information supplied for decision making.

c) Decision making is making choices between future, uncertain alternatives. Where no alternatives exist no decision making is possible.

d) The decision process consists of: the definition of objectives, the consideration of alternatives, the evaluation of alternatives and the selection of the course of action.

e) Risk and uncertainty are ever present in business and so the information presented must clearly show the effects of uncertainty. Single value profit or contribution figures can be positively misleading if some or all of the factors involved are uncertain.

f) The relevant costs and revenues for decision making are differential future costs and revenues. Sunk costs are irrelevant.

g) Opportunity cost is the value of the next best alternative and, properly specified, is equivalent to future avoidable costs.

h) In appropriate circumstances formal decision rules can be useful. The rules include: expected value, maximin, maximax, and the minimax regret criterion.

i) Expected value is value × probability and is a useful averaging technique but suffers from several disadvantages.

j) Maximin is a cautious decision rule, maximax is an optimistic rule and minimax regret seeks to minimise the maximum regret that could occur.

k) Decision trees are a pictorial method of showing an interrelated series of decisions and outcomes. Generally they are evaluated using expected value.

l) Decision trees are developed in two stages the forward pass (when the tree is drawn) and the backward pass (when the tree is evaluated).

26. Points to note

a) Programmed decisions, as defined by Simon, are the ones in which the use of formal decision rules (expected value, minimax regret and so on) is likely to be the most appropriate.

b) It is a common misconception to assume that all decision making in conditions of certainty (ie where all outcomes and values are known) is trivially easy. This is not so because there are some problems where there are thousands or indeed millions of possible combinations and where the optimum choice is by no means obvious. Some of these types of problems can be solved by mathematical programming techniques, one of which, Linear Programming, is dealt with later in the book.

c) The importance of relevancy for costs and revenues in decision making has been emphasised in this chapter. Where there is difficulty in establishing relevant costs or revenues ask the basic question: 'Will it change?' If the cost or revenue item does alter as a result of the decision, then it is relevant.

Additional reading

Management Accounting: a conceptual approach; *Amey and Egginton* – Longman

Topics in Management Accounting; Arnold, *Scapens and Carsberg* – Philip Allan

Economics of Business Decisions; *Carsberg* – Penguin

Managing for Results: Economic tasks and risk taking decisions; *Drucker* – Heinemann

Information for decision making; *Rappaport* – Prentice Hall

Studies in Cost Analysis; *Solomons* – Sweet &Maxwell

Self review questions

1. What is the relationship between objectives, plans and decisions? (2)
2. What are the stages in the decision process? (3)
3. What is 'satisficing' behaviour? (4)
4. What are constraints or limitations? (4)
5. Why should the analysis of decisions include the effects of uncertainty? (6)
6. Distinguish between programmed and non-programmed decisions. (7)
7. Define relevant cost and revenues. (8)
8. What are opportunity costs? (9)
9. Explain expected value and its use in decision making. (12)
10. What is conditional profit? (14)
11. How is the value of perfect information calculated? (15)
12. Define the maximin, maximax, and the minimax regret rules. (16 & 17)
13. What is opportunity loss? (18)
14. What is a decision tree and what are the types of nodes it contains? (21)
15. How is a decision tree drawn? (22)

14 Marginal costing & C-V-P analysis

1. Objectives

After studying this chapter you will:

❏ understand the importance of marginal costing in short-run decision making;

❏ know what is a key factor and how this changes the decision process;

❏ be able to use marginal costing in typical short-run decisions, such as make or buy, limiting factor, dropping a product;

❏ understand Cost-Volume-Profit (CVP) analysis;

❏ know basic CVP formulae;

❏ be able to draw traditional and contribution break-even charts;

❏ understand profit graphs;

❏ be able to contrast the accountant's and economist's view of CVP analysis;

❏ know the assumptions and limitations of CVP analysis.

2. Uses of the marginal costing approach

The principles of marginal costing – the separation of costs into fixed and variable, the calculation of contribution, and the treatment of fixed costs as period costs – was introduced in Chapter 2 where the effects of using marginal costing in the routine cost accounting system was explored. The key aspect of the approach, that of the separation of fixed and variable elements of cost, is widely used in cost and management accounting. Examples include: forecasting cost behaviour (dealt with in Chapter 3), flexible budgeting (dealt with in Chapter 7), transfer pricing (dealt with later) and short run decision making which is dealt with in this chapter.

3. Short run tactical decisions

These are decisions which seek to make the best use of existing facilities. Typically, in the short run, fixed costs remain unchanged so that the marginal cost, revenue and contribution of each alternative is relevant.

In these circumstances *the selection of the alternative which maximises contribution* is the correct decision rule. In the long term (and sometimes in the short term) fixed costs do change and accordingly the differential costs must include any changes in the amount of fixed costs. Where there is a decision involving no changes in fixed costs normal marginal costing principles apply. Where the situation involves changes in fixed costs a more fundamental aid to decision making called differential costing is used. Marginal costing is covered first in this chapter and then differential costing.

4. Alternative concepts of marginal cost

To the economist, marginal cost is the additional cost incurred by the production of one extra unit. To the accountant, marginal cost is average variable cost which is presumed to act in a linear fashion, ie marginal cost per unit is assumed to be constant in the short run, over the activity range being considered.

These views can be contrasted in the following graphs:

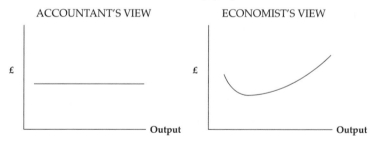

Figure 14.1 Marginal Cost per Unit

This difference of viewpoint regarding marginal cost per unit results in the following alternative views of a firm's total cost structure.

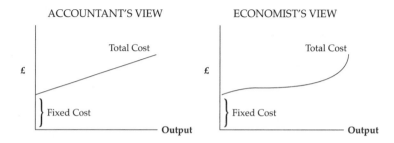

Figure 14.2 Total Cost Structures

The economic model is an explanation of the cost behaviour of firms in general, whereas the accounting model is an attempt to provide a pragmatic basis for decision making in a particular firm. However, it is likely that differences between the two view-points are more apparent than real. A number of investigations have shown that marginal costs are virtually constant per unit over the range of activity changes studied. Accordingly for short run decision making purposes the marginal cost per unit is normally assumed to be constant. Thus if the marginal cost per unit was £5 per unit, the total marginal cost for

100 units would be	£500
150 units would be	£750
200 units would be	£1000
...	

and so on.

Great care must be taken not to make this assumption unless it is realistic. Where economies or diseconomies of scale are expected or if there is any other factor which will make the costs behave in a non-linear fashion then the traditional assumption of linearity should not be made and a deeper analysis should be undertaken to determine the true underlying cost function.

5. Key factor

Sometimes known as a *limiting factor* or *principal budget factor*. This is a factor which is a binding constraint upon the organisation, ie the factor which prevents indefinite expansion or unlimited profits. It may be sales, availability of finance, skilled labour, supplies of material or lack of space. Where a single binding constraint can be identified, then the general objective of maximising contribution can be achieved by selecting the alternative which *maximises the contribution per unit of the key factor.* It will be apparent that from time to time the key factor in an organisation will change. For example, a firm may have a shortage of orders. It overcomes this by appointing salesmen and then finds that there is a shortage of machinery capacity. The expansion of the productive capacity may introduce a problem of lack of space and so on.

Note: The 'maximising contribution per unit of the limiting factor' rule can be of value, but can only be used where there is a single binding constraint and where the constraint is continuously divisible, ie it can be altered one unit at a time. Where several constraints apply simultaneously, the simple maximising rule given above cannot be applied because of the interactions between constraints.

In such circumstances mathematical techniques can be used to establish the optimal position. One of the more important mathematical techniques that can be used for such problems, known as Linear Programming (LP), is described later in the book. LP represents a readily available means of extending C-V-P analysis to cope with practical problems.

6. Example of decisions involving marginal costing

Several typical problems in which marginal costing can provide useful information for decision making are given below. Once the general principles are understood, they can be applied in any other similar circumstances.

The steps involved in analysing such problems are as follows:

a) Check that fixed costs are expected to remain unchanged.

b) If necessary separate out fixed and variable costs.

c) Calculate the revenue, marginal costs and contribution of each of the alternatives.

d) Check to see if there is a single limiting factor which will be a binding constraint and if so, calculate the contribution per unit of the limiting factor.

e) Finally, choose the alternative which maximises contribution.

The situations shown below are decisions involving acceptance of a special order, dropping a product, choice of product where a limiting factor exists and make or buy.

7. Acceptance of a special order

By this is meant the acceptance or rejection of an order which utilises spare capacity, but which is only available if a lower than normal price is quoted. The procedure is illustrated by the following example.

Example 1

Zerocal Ltd manufacture and market a slimming drink which they sell for 20p per can. Current output is 400,000 cans per month which represents 80% of capacity. They have the opportunity to utilise their surplus capacity by selling their product at 13p per can to a supermarket chain who will sell it as an 'own label' product.

Total costs for the last month were £56,000 of which £16,000 were fixed costs. This represented a total cost of 14p per can.

Based on the above data should Zerocal accept the supermarket offer?

What other factors should be considered?

Solution

The present position is as follows:

		£	
	Sales (400,000 × 20p) =	80,000	
less	Marginal cost	40,000	(= 0.10p/can)
=	Contribution	40,000	
less	Fixed Costs	16,000	
=	NET PROFIT	£24,000	

On the assumption that fixed costs are unchanged, the special order will produce the following contribution

			£
	Sales (100,000 × 13p)	=	13,000
less	Marginal cost (100,000 × 10p)	=	10,000
=	CONTRIBUTION		£3,000

∴ the new order brings in more contribution which, because fixed costs are already covered, results in increased net profit. Thus, purely on the cost figures, the order would be acceptable.

However, there are several other factors which would need to be considered before a final decision is taken.

a) Will the acceptance of one order at a lower price lead other customers to demand lower prices as well?

b) Is this special order the most profitable way of using the spare capacity?

c) Will the special order lock up capacity which could be used for future full price business?

d) Is it absolutely certain that fixed costs will not alter.

Notes:

a) Although the price of 13p is less than the total cost of 14p per can, it does provide some contribution, so may be worthwhile.

b) The process of marginal cost pricing to utilise spare capacity is widely used, eg hotels provide cheap weekend rates, railways and airlines have cheap fares for off peak periods, many manufacturers of proprietary goods produce own label products and so on.

c) The contribution from the special order can also be calculated by multiplying the quantity by the contribution per can, ie 100,000 × 3p = £3,000.

8. Dropping a product

If a company has a range of products one of which is deemed to be unprofitable, it may consider dropping the item from its range.

Example 2

A company produces three products for which the following operating statement has been produced:

	Product X	Product Y	Product Z	Total
	£	£	£	£
Sales	32,000	50,000	45,000	127,000
Total Costs	36,000	38,000	34,000	108,000
Profit/(Loss)	(4,000)	12,000	11,000	19,000

The total cost comprise $\frac{2}{3}$ variable $\frac{1}{3}$ fixed.

The directors consider that as Product X shows a loss it should be discontinued.

Based on the above cost data should Product X be dropped?

What other factors should be considered?

Solution

First calculate the fixed costs, as: $\frac{1}{3}(36,000) + \frac{1}{3}(38,000) + \frac{1}{3}(34,000) = £36,000$

Rearranging the operating statement in marginal costing form products:

	Product X	Product Y	Product Z	Total
	£	£	£	£
Sales	32,000	50,000	45,000	127,000
less Marginal Cost	24,000	25,333	22,667	72,000
= CONTRIBUTION	8,000	24,667	22,333	55,000
less Fixed Costs				36,000
= NET PROFIT				19,000

From this it will be seen that Product X produces a contribution of £8,000. Should it be dropped the position would be:

	£
Contribution Product Y	24,667
Contribution Product Z	22,333
Total Contribution	47,000
less Fixed Costs	36,000
= NET PROFIT	11,000

Thus dropping Product X with an apparent loss of £4,000 reduces total profits by £8,000 which is, of course, the amount of contribution lost from Product X.

Other factors which need to be considered:

a) Although Product X does provide some contribution, it is at a low rate and alternative, more profitable products or markets should be considered.

b) The assumption above was that the fixed costs were general fixed costs which would remain even if X was dropped. If dropping X results in the elimination of the fixed costs originally apportioned to X, then the elimination would be worthwhile. However, this is unlikely.

9. Choice of product where a limiting factor exists

This is the situation where a firm has a choice between various types of products which it could manufacture and where there is a single, binding constraint.

Example 3

A company is able to produce four products and is planning its production mix for the next period. Estimated cost, sales, and production data are given below.

Product		W		X		Y		Z
		£		£		£		£
Selling Price/unit		20		30		40		36
	£		£		£		£	
Labour (@ £2/hr)	6		4		14		10	
Materials (@ £1 kg)	6	12	18	22	10	24	12	22
Contribution		8		8		16		14
Resources/Unit								
Labour (hours)		3		2		7		5
Materials (Kgs)		6		18		10		12
Maximum Demand (Units)		5000		5000		5000		5000

Based on the above data, what is the most appropriate mix under the two following assumptions?

a) If labour hours are limited to 50,000 in a period or

b) If material is limited to 110,000 Kgs in a period.

Whatever products have a positive contribution and there are no constraints, there is a prima facie case for their production.

However, when, as in this example, constraints exist, the products must be ranked in order of contribution per unit of the constraint and the most profitable product mix established.

Accordingly, the contribution per unit of the inputs is calculated.

Product	W	X	Y	Z
	£	£	£	£
Contribution/Unit	8.00	8.00	16.00	14.00
Contribution/Labour Hour	2.67	4.00	2.29	2.80
Contribution/Kg of Material	1.33	0.44	1.60	1.17

Solution

a) *Labour hours restriction.* To make all the products up to the demand limit would require:

$$(5000 \times 3) + (5000 \times 2) + (5000 \times 5) = 85,000$$

labour hours but as there is a limit of 50,000 hrs in a period, the products should be manufactured in order of attractiveness related to labour hours which is X, Z, W and finally Y.

Produce			
	5000 units X using	10,000	labour hours
	5000 units Z using	25,000	labour hours
	5000 units W using	15,000	labour hours
and no units of Y which uses the total of		50,000	hours available.

b) *Material restriction.* If the constraint is 110,000 kgs of material, then a similar process produces a ranking of Y, W, Z and finally X which will be noted is the opposite of the ranking produced if labour is the constraint.

When material is the constraint, the optimum production mix is:

	5000 units of Y using	50,000	Kgs material
	5000 units of W using	30,000	Kgs material
	2500 units of Z using	30,000	Kgs material
and no units of X which uses the total of		110,000	Kgs material

Notes:

a) The above process of maximising contribution per unit of the limiting factor can only be used where there is a single binding constraint.

b) Most practical problems involve various constraints and many more factors than the example illustrated. In such circumstances, if linearity can be assumed, linear programming will indicate the optimum solution.

c) In general where no constraint is identified, a reasonable decision rule is to choose the alternative which maximises contribution per £ of sales value.

10. Make or buy decisions

Frequently management are faced with the decision whether to make a particular product or component or whether to buy it in. Apart from overriding technical reasons, the decision is usually based on an analysis of the cost implications.

In general, the relevant cost comparison is between the marginal cost of manufacture and the buying in price. However, when manufacturing the component displaces existing production, the lost contribution must be added to the marginal cost of production of the component before comparison with the buying in price. The two situations are illustrated below.

Example 4

A firm manufactures component BK 200 and the costs for the current production level of 50,000 units are:

Costs/unit

	£
Materials	2.50
Labour	1.25
Variable overheads	1.75
Fixed overheads	3.50
Total cost	9.00

Component BK 200 could be bought in for £7.75 and, if so, the production capacity utilised at present would be unused.

Assuming that there are no overriding technical considerations, should BK 200 be bought in or manufactured?

Solution

Comparison of the buying in price of £7.75 and the full cost of £9.00 might suggest that the component should be bought in.

However, the correct comparison is between the MARGINAL COST of manufacture (ie £5.50) and the buying in price of £7.75. This indicates that the component should be manufactured, not bought in.

The reason for this is that the fixed costs of £175,000 (ie 50,000 units at £3.50) would presumably continue and, because the capacity would be unused, the fixed overheads would not be absorbed into production.

If BK 200 was bought in, overall profits would fall by £112,500, which is the difference between the buying in price and the marginal cost of manufacture, ie (£7.75 – 5.50) × 50,000.

Example 5

A firm is considering whether to manufacture or purchase a particular component 2543. This would be in batches of 10,000 and the buying in price would be £6.50. The marginal cost of manufacturing Component 2543 is £4.75 per unit and the component would have to be made on a machine which was currently working at full capacity. If the component was manufactured, it is estimated that the sales of finished product FP97 would be reduced by 1000 units. FP97 has a marginal cost of £60/unit and sells for £80/unit.

Should the firm manufacture or purchase component 2543?

Solution

A superficial view, based on the preceding example, is that because the marginal cost of manufacture is substantially below the buying in price, the component should not be bought in and thus further analysis is unnecessary. However, such an approach is insufficient in this more realistic situation and consideration must be given to the loss of contribution from the displaced product.

Cost analysis – Component 2543 in batches of 10,000

		£
Marginal Cost of manufacture = £4.75/unit × 10,000		47,500
+ Lost contribution for FP97 = £20/unit × 1000		20,000
		67,500
Buying in price = £6.50/unit × 10,000		65,000

There is a saving of £2,500 per 10,000 batch by buying in rather than manufacture.

Note: The lost contribution of £20,000 is an example of an opportunity cost discussed in the previous chapter. This is the value of a benefit sacrificed in favour of some alternative course of action. Where there is no alternative use for the resource, as in Example 4, then the opportunity cost is zero and can thus be ignored.

11. Differential costing

This is a term used in the preparation of ad-hoc information when all the cost and income differences between the various options being considered are high-lighted so that clear comparisons can be made of all the financial consequences. In one sense differential costing is a wider concept than marginal costing because all cost changes are considered, both fixed and variable, whereas the presumption when marginal costing is used is that only variable costs change.

A simple example of the application of differential costing is as follows.

A company is considering whether to expand activities by 20% (Option B) or remain at their present level (Option A). The expansion will increased fixed costs and, because of overtime, also marginal costs. To sell the extra output some selling price reductions will be necessary. Summaries of the positions and of the differential between them are shown below:

	Option A Current Activity	Option B Current Activity + 20%	Differential B – A
	£	£	£
Sales	300,000	350,000	50,000
less Marginal Cost	180,000	220,000	40,000
= Contribution	120,000	130,000	10,000
less Fixed Costs	90,000	96,000	6,000
= Net Profit	30,000	34,000	4,000

Thus, on the basis of the figures and with the usual caveats regarding the quality of estimates the expansions would seem to be worthwhile.

This simple procedure should be recognised as merely a restatement of the relevant cost principles discussed in Chapter 13, that is the relevant costs and revenues are those which will *change as a result of the decision.*

12. Cost-volume profit (C-V-P) analysis

C-V-P analysis, sometimes termed Break-Even analysis, is an application of marginal costing and seeks to study the relationship between costs, volume and profit at differing activity levels and can be a useful guide for short-term planning and decision making. It is more relevant where the proposed changes in activity are relatively small so that established cost patterns and relationships are likely to hold good. With greater changes in activity and over the longer term, existing cost structures, eg the amount of fixed costs and the marginal cost per unit, are likely to change so C-V-P analysis is unlikely to produce useful guidance.

Typical short run decisions where C-V-P analysis may be useful include: choice of sales mix, pricing policies, multi-shift working and special order acceptance.

13. C-V-P analysis assumptions

Before any formulae are given or graphs drawn, the major assumptions behind C-V-P analysis must be stated. These are:

a)   All costs can be resolved into fixed and variable elements.

b)   Fixed costs will remain constant and variable costs vary proportionately with activity.

c)   Over the activity range being considered costs and revenues behave in a linear fashion.

d)   That the only factor affecting costs and revenues is volume.

e)   That technology, production methods and efficiency remain unchanged.

f)   Particularly for graphical methods, that the analysis relates to one product only.

g)   There are no stock level changes or that stocks are valued at marginal cost only.

h)   There is assumed to be no uncertainty.

It will be apparent that these are over simplifying assumptions for most practical situations so that C-V-P analysis should be used with caution and only as an approximate guide for decision making.

14. C-V-P analysis by formula

C-V-P analysis can be undertaken by graphical means which are dealt with later in this chapter, or by simple formulae which are listed below and illustrated by examples

(a)   Break-even point (in units) $= \dfrac{\text{Fixed Costs}}{\text{Contribution/unit}}$

(b)   C/S Ratio $= \dfrac{\text{Contribution/ unit}}{\text{Sales Price/unit}} \times 100$

(c)   Break-even point (£ sales) $= \dfrac{\text{Fixed Costs}}{\text{Contribution/unit}} \times \text{Sales Price/unit}$

$= \text{Fixed Costs} \times \dfrac{1}{\text{C/S Ratio}}$

(d)   Level of sales to result in target profit (in units) $= \dfrac{\text{Fixed Costs} + \text{Target Point}}{\text{Contribution/unit}}$

(e) Level of sales to result in target profit after tax (in units)

$$= \frac{\textbf{Fixed Cost} + \left(\dfrac{\textbf{Target Profit}}{\textbf{1 - Tax Rate}} \right)}{\textbf{Contribution / unit}}$$

(f) Level of sales to result in target profit (£ sales)

$$= \frac{\textbf{(Fixed Cost + Target Profit)} \times \textbf{Sales Price / unit}}{\textbf{Contribution / unit}}$$

Note: The above formulae relate to a single product firm or one with an unvarying mix of sales. With a multi product firm it is possible to calculate the break even point as follows:

$$\text{Break-even point (£ sales)} = \frac{\textbf{Fixed Costs} \times \textbf{Sales Value}}{\textbf{Contribution}}$$

Example 6

A company makes a single product with a sales price of £10 and a marginal cost of £6. Fixed costs are £60,000 p.a.

Calculate

a) Number of units to break even

b) Sales at break-even point

c) C/S ratio

d) What number of units will need to be sold to achieve a profit of £20,000 p.a.?

e) What level of sales will achieve a profit of £20,000 p.a.?

f) As (d) with a 40% tax rate.

g) Because of increasing costs the marginal cost is expected to rise to £6.50 per unit and fixed costs to £70,000 p.a. If the selling price cannot be increased what will be the number of units required to maintain a profit of £20,000 p.a. (ignore tax)?

Solution:

Contribution	= Selling Price – Marginal Cost
	= £10 – £6
	= £4
a) Break-even point (units)	$= \dfrac{£60,000}{£4}$
	= 15,000
b) Break-even point (£ sales)	= 15,000 × £10
	= £150,000
c) C/S ratio	$= \dfrac{£4}{£10}$
	= 40%

d) Number of units for target profit $= \dfrac{£60,000 + £20,000}{£4}$

$= \underline{20,000}$

e) Sales for target profit $= 20,000 \times £10$

$= \underline{£200,000}$

(Alternatively, this figure can be deduced by the following reasoning. After break-even point the contribution per unit becomes net profit per unit, so that as 15,000 units were required at break-even point, 5000 extra units would be required to make £20,000 profit.

∴ total units = 15,000 + 5,000 = 20,000 × £10 = £200,000)

f) Number of units for target profit with 40% tax $= \dfrac{£60,000 + \left(\dfrac{£20,000}{1 - 0.4} \right)}{£4}$

$= \underline{23,333}$

g) Note that the fixed costs, marginal cost and contribution have changed

No. of units for target profit $= \dfrac{£70,000 + £20,000}{£3.50}$

$= \underline{25,714 \text{ units}}$

Note: The C/S ratio is sometimes known as the P/V ratio.

15. Graphical approach

This may be preferred

a) Where a simple overview is sufficient.

b) Where there is a need to avoid a detailed, numerical approach when, for example, the recipients of the information have no accounting background.

The basic chart is known as a Break Even chart which can be drawn in two ways. The first is known as the *traditional approach* and the second as the *contribution approach*. Whatever approach is adopted, all costs must be capable of separation into fixed and variable elements, ie semi-fixed or semi-variable costs must be analysed into their components.

16. The traditional break-even chart

Assuming that fixed and variable costs have been resolved, the chart is drawn in the following way:

a) Draw the axes

❏ Horizontal: showing levels of activity expresses as units of output or as percentages of total capacity.

❏ Vertical: showing values in £'s or £000s as appropriate for cost and revenues.

b) Draw the cost lines

❏ Fixed cost. This will be a straight line parallel to the horizontal axis at the level of the fixed costs.

❏ Total cost. This will start where the fixed cost line intersects the vertical axis and will be a straight line sloping upward at an angle depending on the proportion of variable cost in total costs.

c) Draw the revenue line

This will be a straight line from the point of origin sloping upwards at an angle determined by the selling price.

Example 7

A company makes a single product with a total capacity of 400,000 litres p.a. Cost and sales data are as follows:

Selling price	£1 per litre
Marginal cost	£0.50 per litre
Fixed costs	£100,000

Draw a traditional break-even chart showing the likely profit at the expected production level of 300,000 litres.

Solution

From Figure 14.3 it will be seen that break-even point is at an output level of 200,000 litres and that the width of the profit wedge indicates the profit at a production level of 300,000. The profit is £50,000.

Notes: The 'margin of safety' indicated on the chart is the term given to the difference between the activity level selected and break-even point. In this case the margin of safety is 100,000 litres.

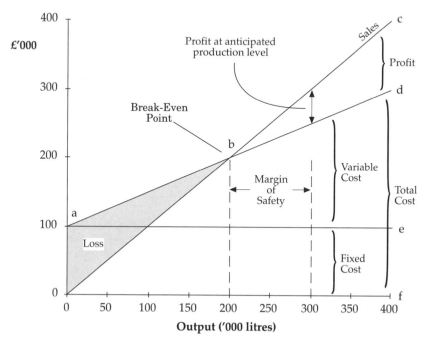

Figure 14.3 Traditional Break-Even Chart

17. The contribution break-even chart

This uses the same axes and data as the traditional chart. The only difference being that variable costs are drawn on the chart before fixed costs resulting in the contribution being shown as a wedge.

Example 8

Repeat Example 7 except that a contribution break-even chart should be drawn.

Solution (see Figure 14.4)

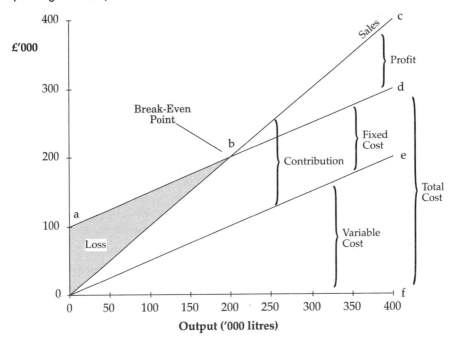

Figure 14.4 Contribution Break-Even Chart

Notes:

a) The area c.o.e. represents the contribution earned. There is no direct equivalent on the traditional chart.

b) The area of d.a.o.f. represents total cost and is the same as the traditional chart.

c) It will be seen from the chart that the reversal of fixed costs and variable costs enables the contribution wedge to be drawn thus providing additional information.

An alternative form of the contribution break-even chart is where the net difference between sales and variable cost, ie total contribution, is plotted against fixed costs. This is shown in Figure 14.5 once again using the same data from Example 7.

Notes:

a) Sales and variable costs are not shown directly.

b) Both forms of contribution chart. Figures 14.4 and 14.5, show clearly that contribution is first used to meet fixed costs and when these costs are met, the contribution becomes profit.

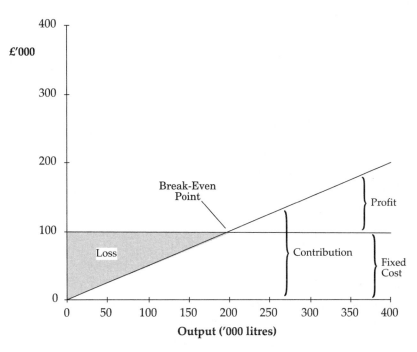

Figure 14.5 Alternative Form of Contribution Break-Even Chart

18. Profit chart

This is another form of presentation with the emphasis on the effect on profit of varying levels of activity. It is a simpler form of chart to those illustrated so far because only a contribution line is drawn.

The horizontal axis is identical to the previous charts, but the vertical axis is continued below the point of origin to show losses. A contribution line is drawn from the loss at zero activity, which is equivalent to the fixed costs, through the break-even point.

The contribution line is drawn by plotting the amount of contribution at various sales levels which is readily calculated using the CS ratio; 50% in Example 7. By commencing the line at the amount of the fixed costs, 'loss' and 'profit' wedges are shown which are identical to those in the earlier charts.

This type of chart is illustrated in Fig 14.6 using, once again, the data from Example 7.

Note: Lines for variable and fixed costs and sales do not appear, merely the one summary profit line.

19. Changes in costs and revenues

Several of the main types of chart have been described and it should be apparent that they are all able to show cost/revenue/volume/profit relationships in a simple, effective form. It is also possible to show the effect of changes in costs and revenues by drawing additional lines on the charts.

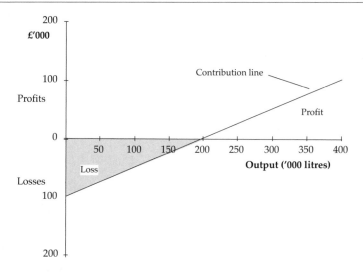

Figure 14.6 Profit Chart

The changes are of two types:

a) Fixed cost changes. Increases or decreases in fixed costs do not change the slope of the line, but alter the point of intersection and thus the break-even point.

b) Variable cost and sales price changes. These changes alter the slope of the line thus affecting the break-even point and the shape of the profit and loss 'wedges'.

These changes are illustrated below using a Profit Chart.

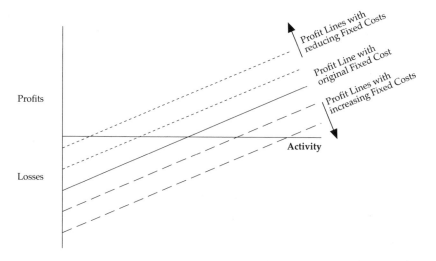

Figure 14.7 Profit Chart Showing Changes in Fixed Costs

Note: The above chart shows the effect of variable cost and/or sales price changes which have a net effect on contribution. If, say, an increase in variable costs was exactly counterbalanced by an increase in sales price, the contribution would be the same and the original profit line would still be correct.

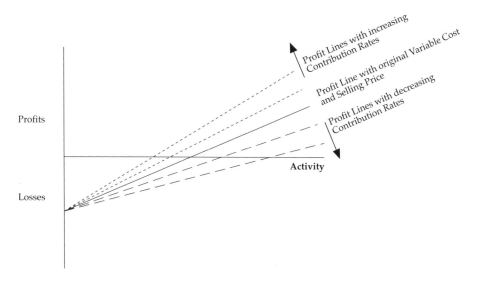

Figure 14.8 Profit Chart Showing Changes in Contribution Ratio

20. A multi-product chart

All of the charts illustrated so far have assumed a single product. Equally they could have illustrated a given sales mix resulting in an average contribution rate equivalent to a single product. An alternative method is to plot the individual products each with their individual C/S characteristics and then show the resulting overall profit line. This is shown below:

Example 9

A firm has fixed costs of £50,000 p.a. and has three products, the sales and contribution of which are shown below.

Product	Sales	Contribution	C/S ratio
	£	£	
X	150,000	30,000	20%
Y	40,000	20,000	50%
Z	60,000	25,000	42%

Plot the products on a profit chart and show the break-even sales.

Solution

The axes on the profit chart are drawn in the usual way and the contribution from the products, in the sequence of their C/S ratio, ie Y, Z, X, drawn on the chart.

Notes:

a) The solid lines represent the contributions of the various products.

b) The dotted line represents the resulting profit of this particular sales mix and C/S ratios.

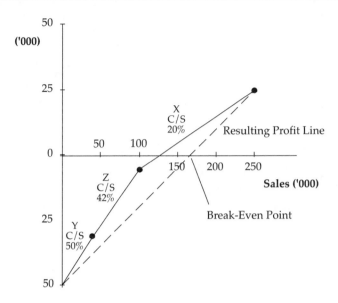

Figure 14.9 Multi-Product Profit Chart

c)   Reading from the graph the break-even point is approximately £170,000. The exact figure can be calculated as follows:

Product	Sales	Contribution
	£	£
X	150,000	30,000
Y	40,000	20,000
Z	60,000	25,000
Totals	250,000	75,000

Overall C/S ratio $= \dfrac{£75,000}{£250,000} = 30\%$

Break-even point $= \dfrac{\text{Fixed Costs}}{\text{C/S Ratio}} = \dfrac{£50,000}{0.3} = \underline{£166,667}$

The above result could also be found using the formula for a multi product firm given earlier in the Chapter thus:

Breakeven point for multi-product firm $= \dfrac{\text{Fixed Costs} \times \text{Sales Value}}{\text{Contribution}}$

$$= \dfrac{£50,000 \times £250,000}{£75,000}$$

$$= £166,667$$

21. Limitations of break-even and profit charts

The various charts depicted show cost, volume and profit relationships in a simplified and approximate manner. They can be useful aids, but whenever they are used the following limitations should not be forgotten.

a) The charts may be reasonable pointers to performance within normal activity ranges, say 70% – 120% of average production. Outside this relevant range the relationship depicted almost certainly will not be correct. Although it is conventional to draw the lines starting from zero activity, as they have been drawn in this chapter, relationships at the extremes of activity cannot be relied upon. A typical relevant range of activity could be shown as follows.

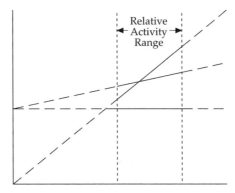

Figure 14.10 Break-Even Chart Showing Relevant Activity Range

b) Fixed costs are likely to change at different activity levels. A stepped fixed cost line is probably the most accurate representation.

c) Variable costs and sales are unlikely to be linear. Extra discounts, overtime payments, the effect of the learning curve, special price contracts and other similar matters make it likely that the variable cost and revenue lines are some form of curve rather than a straight line.

d) The charts depict relationships which are essentially short term. This makes them inappropriate where the time scale spans several years.

e) C-V-P analysis, like marginal costing, makes the assumption that changes in the level of output are the sole determinant of cost and revenue changes. This is likely to be a gross over-simplification in practice although volume changes, of course, do have a significant effect on costs and revenues.

f) It is assumed that either, there is a single product or a constant mix of products or a constant rate of mark-up on marginal cost.

g) Risk and uncertainty are ignored and perfect knowledge of cost and revenue functions is assumed.

h) It is assumed that the firm is a price taker, ie a perfect market is deemed to exist.

i) It is assumed that revenues and all forms of variable cost (materials, labour and all the components of variable overheads) vary in accordance with the same activity indicator. This is an over-simplification in most realistic situations.

22. Alternative forms of break-even charts

So far the charts depicted have had conventional linear cost and revenue functions but as pointed out in the previous paragraph, these are not always realistic. There is no reason why the charts should not be drawn using other, perhaps more appropriate representations of costs and revenues, eg stepped costs and revenues, curvi-linear functions, linear functions with variable slopes and so on. The permutations and possibilities are endless and a few of the possibilities are shown below.

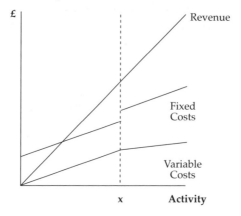

Figure 14.11 Chart with Stepped Linear Cost Function

Figure 14.11 shows a stepped increase in fixed costs at activity x and a reduction in the variable cost slope from that point. A possible cause might be the introduction of equipment which increases fixed charges but reduces labour costs.

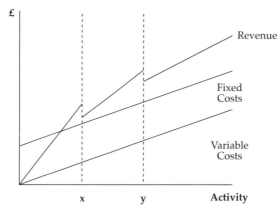

Figure 14.12 Chart with Stepped Linear Revenue Function

Figure 14.12 shows a stepped revenue function with break points at x and y and reductions in the slope at these two points. A possible explanation is that the points x and y represent discount break points and that to increase sales it is necessary to reduce unit selling prices as well as have discounts.

Figure 14.13 shows a curvi-linear revenue function caused by having to reduce prices to increase sales and a stepped cost function at activity q. The effect of these two functions is to produce three break-even points at p, r and s.

The various characteristics shown could be combined in different ways and many other representations could be drawn.

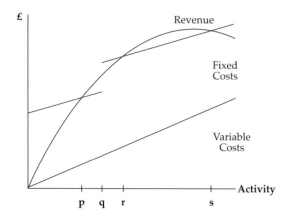

Figure 14.13 Chart with Curvilinear Revenue Function and Multiple Breakeven Points

23. Economist's view of C-V-P analysis

Economists have given considerable attention to the problems of determining the optimal level of activity of the firm. Given the objective of profit maximisation the optimal level of activity is when marginal cost (MC) equals marginal revenue (MR).

A typical representation of short run economic relationships under conditions of imperfect competition is shown in Figures 14.14 and 14.15.

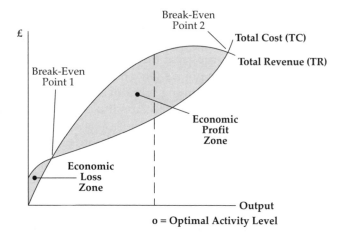

Figure 14.14

The following characteristics should be noted regarding the economist's approach compared with that of the accountant.

a) The economic model, like the accountant's model assumes that volume is the sole determinant of cost and revenue changes.

b) Economic theory treats the total cost function as curvi-linear as opposed to the simpler accounting assumption of linearity. The economic model reflects decreasing marginal cost at lower output levels and increasing marginal cost at higher levels. Although there are conflicts between the assumptions contained in both models regarding input prices and production efficiencies, probably the major reason for the differences between the cost functions is the range of activity levels encompassed by the models. The economic model covers a range of outputs sufficient to cause significant changes in efficiency whereas the simpler cost-volume relationships assumed in the accounting model would only be valid over a smaller activity range.

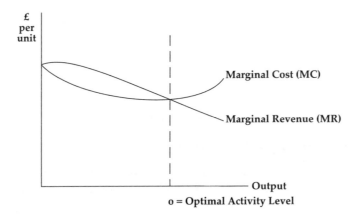

Figure 14.15

c) The economic model is based on opportunity costs which include a normal rate of profit. A normal rate of profit is considered by economists to be a cost that has to be met if the firm is to stay in business. Profit is a reward to one of the factors of production (eg the entrepreneurial input supplied by shareholders) for risk-taking and for enterprise. This means that Break-Even point No 1 in Figure 14.14 is *not* equivalent to the break-even point shown in a typical accounting break-even chart such as Figure 14.3. The accounting break-even point would be to the left of the economist's break-even point No 1 because it does not include any profit element being merely the balancing of accounting costs and revenues. The accounting break-even chart should be based, like all information for decision making purposes, on expected future costs and revenues not on historical costs.

d) The point o in Figures 14.14 and 14.15 indicates the optimal level of activity where profit is at a maximum. The 'envelope' between the two break-even points, in Figure 14.14 represents the 'super-profit' potential which, according to conventional economic theory, could only be achieved over a short period in a competitive market. In the long run it would be expected that firms would earn the normal level of profits included at the first break-even point assuming free entry to the market. The typical accounting break-even chart has a single break-even point and, because of the linearity assumptions, predicts – unrealistically – that profits can continually be increased by expanding output. Without further analysis, the traditional accounting break-even approach cannot be used to establish the optimum output level.

e) The conventional accounting break-even model has a linear revenue function with a constant price per unit at all production levels and therefore profit increases proportionately with output. The assumption is that the firm operates under perfect competition and is a price taker. The particular economic model depicted assumes a curvi-linear function which shows increasing profits at low activity levels and decreasing profits at higher levels.

The model shown in Figure 14.14 assumes imperfect market conditions where pricing and output decisions are inter-dependent. The validity of either model depends upon the type of market in which the firm operates although in practice the position is more complicated than the simplistic assumptions contained in both of the models. Product differentiation, promotion policies, tactical pricing, changes in the marketing mix, foreign competition at subsidised prices and other such operating disturbances all tend to cloud the clear cut relationships embodied in both models.

f) The economist's approach produces a general analytical model which is designed to produce predictions about the behaviour of market variables (price, output, etc.) whereas the accountant's model has the more limited objective of attempting to provide practical assistance for decision making within a given firm. Both models suffer from the disadvantage that they are based on single cost and revenue values for every output level and thus ignore the uncertainties which exist in every planning and decision making situation. Provided that the relevant activity range is being considered and the cost and revenue functions are valid then both models are likely to give similar solutions to a given problem although care will be needed in the interpretation because of the inclusion of normal profits in the cost function of the economic model.

24. Optimising the level of activity

Where the cost and/or revenue functions are curvi-linear, for example as shown in Figure 14.14, then it is possible to determine the optimal level of activity in accordance with the objectives of the firm. This can be done in two ways, either by drawing graphs of the functions as in Figure 14.14 and 14.15 or more directly by the use of differential calculus. It will be recalled that the process of differentiation provides a ready means of finding the rates of change of curvi-linear functions and of their turning points. If the curvi-linear functions represent cost and revenue then the rates of change are marginal cost and marginal revenue respectively and the turning points of the functions are the point of minimum cost and maximum revenue respectively.

The following example uses differentiation to find the optimal activity level.

Example 10

A firm has the following cost and revenue functions:

Variable cost function, $c = £\left(\frac{1}{2}q^2 + 10q\right)$

Demand function, $p = £\left(150 - \frac{3}{4}q\right)$

where p = price in £'s

c = variable cost in £'s

q = number of units sold per period

The fixed costs are £1,000 per period

It is required to determine:

a) The price, quantity and resulting profit if the firm's objective is to maximise sales revenue.

b) The price, quantity and resulting profit if the firm's objective is to maximise profit.

Solution

a) Let R = revenue.

Then

$$R = pq$$
$$= (150 - \tfrac{3}{4}q)q$$
$$= 150q - \tfrac{3}{4}q^2$$

For maximum revenue, $\dfrac{dR}{dq} = 0$ (with a negative second derivative).

Thus: $\qquad 150 - 1\tfrac{1}{2}q = 0$

(Note that $\dfrac{d^2R}{dq^2} = -1\tfrac{1}{2}$, i.e negative, as required for a maximum point)

$$\therefore \quad q = 100 \text{ at maximum revenue point.}$$
$$\therefore \quad p = £(150 - \tfrac{3}{4}q)$$
$$= £(150 - \tfrac{3}{4}(100))$$
$$= £75$$
$$\therefore \quad R = pq$$
$$= £(75 \times 100)$$
$$= £7500$$

Profit at maximum revenue point is:

		£
	Revenue	7,500
less	Costs = $£[\tfrac{1}{2}(100)^2 + 10(100) + 1,000]$	7,000
	Profit per period	500

b) For maximum profit, marginal revenue should equal marginal cost.

i.e. $\qquad \dfrac{dR}{dQ} = \dfrac{dC}{dQ}$

[But $\dfrac{dR}{dQ} = 150 - 1\tfrac{1}{2}q$ and $\dfrac{dC}{dQ} = q + 10$]

$$\therefore 150 - 1\tfrac{1}{2}q = q + 10$$

giving, after some rearrangement: $q = 56$ at maximum profit point.

The resulting price per unit is: $\qquad p = £(150 - \tfrac{3}{4}q)$
$$= £108$$

Profit at maximum profit point is:

		£
	Revenue = £(56 × 108)	6,048
less	Costs = £[$\frac{1}{2}$ (56)^2 + 10(56) + 1,000]	3,128
	Profit per period	2,920

Note: If the processes of differentiation are unfamiliar to you or you wish to revise the principles you are advised to refer to a suitable text book covering this topic, eg *Quantitative Techniques, T. Lucey,* DP Publications.

25. Summary

a) The principles of marginal costing (the separation of fixed and variable costs and the calculation of contribution) have many uses in management accounting including short run decision making.

b) To the accountant marginal cost is average variable cost which is generally assumed to behave linearly whilst to the economist it is the cost incurred by the production of one extra unit.

c) The key factor is a binding constraint upon the organisation. Where a single binding constraint can be identified then maximising contribution per unit of the limiting factor will produce the maximum contribution. LP is necessary to deal with more than one constraint.

d) Marginal costing principles can be used for numerous types of short run decisions, eg special order acceptance, make or buy, expansions or contraction of activity and other similar problems.

e) Care must be taken in identifying the relevant costs and revenues that an applicable opportunity cost is not overlooked.

f) Cost-volume-profit (CVP) analysis is an application of marginal costing principles and seeks to estimate the profit or loss at differing activity levels. Basic CVP analysis has many simplifying assumptions and any results must be viewed with caution.

g) CVP analysis can be dealt with by the use of formulae or by using charts which are generally termed break-even charts.

h) Break-even charts can be drawn in a variety of ways and probably the most informative way is known as the contribution break-even chart where variable costs are drawn first and the contribution 'wedge' is produced.

i) Profit charts are simpler representations whereby a single line representing profit is drawn commencing at the loss value equivalent to fixed costs. Multi-product charts can also be drawn based on their C/S ratios.

j) Traditionally drawn break-even charts have many limitations including: linearity assumptions, based on single products or constant product mixes, risk and uncertainty are ignored.

k) The economist's view of C-V-P analysis is based on curvi-linear functions. One of the other major differences in approach is the inclusion of a normal rate of profit in economic costs.

l) The inclusion of curvi-linear functions enables the optimal level of activity to be determined either graphically or by means of differential calculus.

m) Given the assumptions contained in the economic model the price, quantity and profit can be established whether the firm's objective is sales or profit maximisation.

26. Points to note

a) Marginal costing and C-V-P analysis can be useful guides in short-term decision making but they are based on a number of restrictive assumptions. These must be thoroughly understood so that the techniques are not used in circumstances where they could give misleading information.

b) Finding the optimal price, quantity and profit values as illustrated for the economist's approach to C-V-P analysis has a satisfying air of completeness but it must be remembered that the information upon which the analysis is based is rarely, if ever, fully available. This applies particularly to the revenue functions.

c) Providing that linearity of all factors can be assumed then Linear Programming (LP) provides a powerful extension to basic C-V-P analysis. LP is able to deal with many more factors, numerous binding constraints and, because most computers have LP packages, the effects of uncertainty can readily be incorporated into the analysis.

Additional reading

Management Accounting: A decision emphasis; *De Coster and Schafer* – Wiley

Statistical Cost Accounting; *Johnston* – McGraw Hill

Quantitative Techniques; *Lucey* – DP Publications

Information for Decision Making; *Solomons* – Prentice Hall

Contempory issues in Cost Accounting; *Anton and Firmin* – Houghton Mifflin

Self review questions

1. Why is the marginal costing approach suitable for analysing short run decisions? (3)
2. What are the differences between the accountant's and economist's views of marginal cost? (4)
3. What is the limiting factor and what is the basic decision rule where a limiting factor exists? (5)
4. What are the general steps involved in analysing a decision when marginal costing is to be used? (6)
5. When should costs and opportunity costs be considered? (10)
6. What is differential costing? (11)
7. What are the assumptions behind C-V-P analysis? (13)
8. What are the formulae for: break-even point (units); break-even point (sales); level of sales to achieve a target profit? (14)

9. Draw a traditional break-even chart. (16)
10. How does the contribution break-even chart differ from the traditional one? (17)
11. What is a profit chart? (18)
12. What would be the effect on a chart of altering fixed costs? Variable costs? (19)
13. How is a multi-product profit chart drawn? (20)
14. What are the limitations of break-even and profit charts? (21)
15. What alternative representations could be included in such charts? (22)
16. What are the major differences between the accountant's and economist's views of C-V-P analysis? (23)
17. Using differential calculus what are the main steps in establishing the price, quantity and profit if the firm's objective is to maximise profit? (24)

15 Pricing decisions

1. Objectives

After studying this chapter you will:

❒ understand the factors which may be considered in pricing decisions;

❒ know the theoretical economic background to pricing;

❒ be able to use differential calculus to find the optimal price;

❒ understand the limitations of classical theory;

❒ be able to use cost-plus pricing;

❒ know the differences between full cost pricing, rate of return pricing and marginal pricing.

2. Internal and external pricing

A firm may be concerned with two types of pricing decisions. Those for sales external to the firm, ie to its customers and those relating to prices used for internal transfers between parts of the same organisation. This latter process is known as *transfer pricing* and is dealt with in this book in the section on Performance Appraisal.

Pricing decision for external sales are dealt with in the rest of this chapter.

3. The pricing problem

The pricing problem is a complex one with numerous, interacting factors and no simplistic solution. Typical of the factors which may need to be considered – explicitly or implicitly – in a pricing decision are the following:

The firm's objective(s).

Is the firm a profit or revenue maximiser or is it pursuing satisficing objectives?

The market in which the firm operates.

Perfect or imperfect competition or oligopolistic or monopolistic conditions?

The demand for the firm's product.

Are the quantities known which are expected to be sold at various prices?

The elasticity of demand for the product.

Is the demand elastic or inelastic?

The cost structure of the firm and the product.

What are the expected future marginal costs, fixed costs?

The competition.

What is the extent and nature of the competition?

The product.

What is the stage in the product life cycle?

The relative position of the firm.

Is the firm dominant enough to be a price maker or is it a price taker?

Level of activity.

Will the firm be working at full or below capacity? What is the position of competitors?

Government restrictions or legislation.

Are there regulations or laws governing prices?

Inflation

Is inflation rising, falling, high, low?

The availability of substitutes.

Is the product clearly differentiated or are there close substitutes?

Naturally not all these points are explicitly considered in every pricing decision and it is quite possible for some factor not included above to be significant for a particular situation.

4. Theoretical background to pricing

Micro-economics has provided much of the theoretical background to pricing and, whilst there are difficulties in applying the basic theory in practice, it serves as a useful starting point.

The theory states that firms should seek the price which maximises profit and will thereby obtain the most efficient use of the economic resources held by the firm. This price is at that level of sales where the addition to total revenue from the sale of the last unit (the marginal revenue, MR) is equal to the addition to total costs resulting from the production of that last unit (the marginal cost, MC).

This is illustrated below in relation to one particular type of market; that where there is monopolistic or imperfect competition and differentiated products thus enabling the firm to pursue an independent pricing policy.

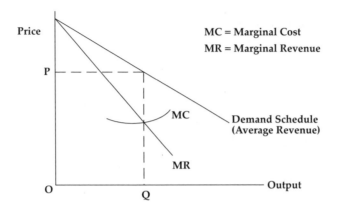

Figure 15.1 Optimum Pricing in Imperfect Competition

At price P, output is the level of Q and profit is at a maximum. The optimal price P represents the price ceiling in any situation. The price floor could theoretically be zero if the goods are already produced, or if it is still to be produced and there is spare capacity, the price floor could be marginal cost. If there are scarce resources then the price floor will include the opportunity cost of the scarce resources.

It follows from Figure 15.1 that the firm operating in imperfect competition can determine either price or output but not both. This also applies to the monopolist. A firm operating under conditions of perfect competition, where the price is determined by the market, can only determine its output. In an oligopolistic market (where there are few sellers) firms recognise their interdependence and are influenced by each other's decisions, particularly regarding prices. All the oligopolists will tend to charge similar prices even if there is no overt collusion and in such market structures there is likely to be a price leader who will provide the bench mark for the prices of the whole industry.

In such market conditions there is likely to be considerable non-price competition, eg advertising, hidden discounts, extended credit and similar activities.

5. Establishing the theoretical optimal price

Assuming that the required information on demand and cost functions is available the optimal price can be determined easily by the use of differential calculus.

For example, assume that a firm has the following demand and cost functions:

Demand function:

$P = 80 - 3Q$, where P is the unit selling price and Q is quantity in thousands.

Cost function:

$TC = Q^2 + 2OQ + 100$, where TC is total cost in £'000s.

What is the optimal price to maximise profits? What is the maximum profit and what is the sales revenue at that point?

Solution

If: demand function $= P$ $= 80 - 3Q$

then: Total Revenue $= TR$ $= Q(80 - 3Q)$

$= 80Q - 3Q^2$

and Marginal Revenue is obtained by using differential calculus thus:

Marginal Revenue $= MR = \dfrac{dTR}{dQ} = 80 - 6Q$

Also: Total Cost function $= TC$ $= Q^2 + 20Q + 100$

Therefore: Marginal Cost $= MC = \dfrac{dTC}{dQ} = 2Q + 20$

To find the output level (and hence price) to maximise profits:

MR $= MC$

That is: $80 - 6Q$ $= 2Q + 20$

and: 60 $= 8Q$

$\therefore Q$ $= 7.5$ ie **7,500 units**

To find the optimal price the value obtained for Q is substituted in the demand functions,

P $= 80 - 3Q$

$= 80 - 3(7.5)$

$\therefore P$ $=$ **£57.50**

The total sales revenue at this point will be $7500 \times £57.5 = $ **£431,250**

The total profit is TR – TC and it is maximised when $Q = 7.5$, (units of 1,000).

That is, total profit $= (80Q - 3Q^2) - (Q^2 + 20Q + 100)$

and thus: maximum profit $= (600 - 168.75) - (56.25 + 150 + 100)$

$= 125$, which converted into '000s $=$ **£125,000.**

6. Price elasticity of demand

An important consideration for a supplier is the reaction of consumers to alterations in price. The concept of price elasticity of demand has been developed to provide a measure of the degree to which demand responds to a change in price.

The basic formula is:

Price Elasticity of Demand $= \dfrac{\text{% change in quantity demanded}}{\text{% change in price}}$

Note: It is important to remember that it is the *percentage changes* in quantity and price that are used and *not absolute changes*. Price elasticity is normally negative but by convention the minus sign is omitted.

The measurement of elasticity can range from zero to infinity; from perfect inelasticity to perfect elasticity but naturally the extremes of values have only theoretical interest. Three important ranges of values are discussed below.

Elasticity of demand greater than 0 but less than 1

A commodity with this value is said to have an INELASTIC demand. This means that a fall in price results in a less than proportionate extension of demand and thus total revenue falls.

Elasticity of demand = 1

Such a value is known as UNIT elasticity which means that a percentage fall in price is exactly matched by a percentage extension of demand so total revenue remains constant.

Elasticity of demand greater than 1 but less than infinity

In these circumstances the demand is said to be ELASTIC. The demand changes by a greater proportion than the change in price and accordingly the total revenue rises when price falls. The greater the elasticity the greater the effect on revenue from a reduction in price.

Although the concept of elasticity of demand is of considerable importance there are obvious practical problems in obtaining realistic values. Two particular difficulties which arise are the differing reactions to large and to small price movements and to the fact that it is unlikely for a demand curve to have constant elasticity along its entire length.

Whilst the price elasticity of demand is the most important measure of the sensitivity of demand, two other types of elasticity are associated with changes in the condition of demand, the formulae of which are given below:

$$\textbf{Cross elasticity of Demand} = \frac{\textbf{\% change in quantity of X demanded}}{\textbf{\% change in price of Y}}$$

This shows the effect of a change in the price of one good on the demand for another good.

$$\textbf{Income elasticity of Demand} = \frac{\textbf{\% change in quantity demanded}}{\textbf{\% change in income}}$$

This shows the effect on demand of a change in income.

7. Limitations to the classical theory

The classical theoretical approach, often called marginal analysis, has numerous limitations which makes practical application of the pure theory difficult. The following are some of the main limitations.

a) Marginal analysis assumes perfect knowledge of all the factors involved. The practical difficulties of finding such information are great particularly relating to knowledge of the demand schedule, ie how much will be sold at any price. Finding the true marginal cost also poses considerable difficulties.

b) Marginal analysis assumes a single maximising objective with the firm acting with complete economic rationality. Studies of practical situations show that firms do not pursue single objectives and satisficing rather than maximising behaviour appears to be commonly encountered.

c) Marginal analysis assumes that changes in the volume of sales are solely a function of price changes where as many non-price factors, eg advertising and sales promotion and changes in the conditions of demand such as income changes, produce significant changes in sales volume.

d) Marginal analysis assumes rational decision guided by purely economic factors. Decision makers in practice are influenced by moral, social, political as well as economic considerations. The behavioural factors which impinge upon decision makers are reflected in such common phrases as 'a fair price' or 'a reasonable rate of return'.

Despite the limitations outlined above, economic analysis makes an important contribution to pricing theory by emphasising the interaction of demand and cost information and directs attention to the importance of marginal changes in costs and revenues. This emphasis has encouraged more flexible pricing policies and has caused traditional accounting 'cost-based' pricing methods to be reassessed and to be used in a more circumspect manner.

8. Pricing in practice

Like many other types of problem the pricing decision suffers from the lack of accurate and relevant information. This is particularly so in relation to demand information and many firms incur considerable costs in an attempt to discover likely demand and how demand will vary with changes in price – its elasticity. Ways in which this is done include: surveys, market research, econometric analysis, test marketing, simulation models, representative's feedback and other such methods.

However difficult the task may be, it is important to try to establish some form of information on demand because it is a crucial element. Pricing is not simply a cost based decision which has been a traditional view and accounts for the frequent use of some form of cost plus system.

Pricing is always an important decision although the frequency of such decisions and the level at which they are taken varies from firm to firm. For example, the price for a car would be a decision taken at Board level in a car manufacturers and, even in inflationary conditions, would only be infrequently altered. On the other hand, in a jobbing engineering company making a variety of items to order, pricing decisions are frequent and likely to be delegated to a relatively low level in the organisation. It is in such organisations that pricing formulae and prescribed mark ups are found. In this way senior management attempt to control pricing policy whilst at the same time avoiding the detailed, day to day work of setting individual prices.

9. Cost plus pricing system

Empirical studies have shown that firms frequently employ some form of formula based on costs to arrive at a selling price. In general these systems are concerned with two elements – what is the relevant cost to include in the price?, and – what is the 'profit' margin which must be added to the costs to arrive at the selling price?

Two cost plus systems are described below: full-cost pricing and rate of return pricing.

10. Full cost pricing

This system, sometimes known as absorption cost pricing, uses conventional cost accounting principles to establish the total cost for a product to which is added a mark up, say 20%, to arrive at a selling price. The total cost includes all the variable costs, the measurement of which should present few problems, plus apportioned fixed costs based on normal volumes and normal production mixes. It is this latter point which causes the major problems. The costs so established will only be appropriate when the actual volume/mix is the same as the estimated volume/mix even assuming there was some non-arbitrary way of assigning fixed costs to products which there is not. Alterations in selling prices affect the volume of sales which in turn affect the unit fixed costs which raises the possibility of further price changes thus causing a circular problem to be ever present when full-cost pricing is employed. A further problem with this method of pricing, which is common to all cost-plus systems, is the amount of the mark-up.

There are numerous factors which govern the mark-up percentage. For example, the mark-up may be related to risk and rates of stock turnover (eg higher for jewellers than greengrocers), it may be influenced by general market conditions and the expected elasticity of demand for the product and it may be governed by what is normal for a given trade.

The most inflexible system would be where a fixed percentage is applied to the total cost of each product regardless of changes in conditions. This approach could cause a firm that is operating below capacity to turn away business which is available at less than normal price even though such business may be priced above marginal cost and would thus make a contribution to fixed cost.

However, it must be realised that in the long run prices must be sufficiently high to recover all costs, both fixed and variable, together with a reasonable rate of profit otherwise the survival of the firm will be in jeopardy.

11. Rate of return pricing

Where an organisation uses the concept of return on capital employed,

$$\text{i.e.} \quad \frac{\text{Profit}}{\text{Capital Employed}} \, \%$$

as a measure of performance, management may wish to know what selling price would be necessary to achieve a given rate of return on capital employed. This procedure involves deciding upon a target rate of return on capital employed, estimating the total costs for a 'normal' production year, and the amount of capital employed. These figures can be used in the following formula:

% mark-up on cost =

$$\frac{\text{Capital Employed}}{\text{Total Annual Costs}} \times \text{Planned Rate of Return on Capital Employed}$$

For example, assume that the target rate of return on capital employed is 18%, the amount of capital employed is £1.5m and the estimated annual total costs are £2.25m, what is the required mark up on cost?

$$\text{Mark up } \% = \frac{1.5}{2.25} \times 18\%$$

$$= 12\%$$

Notes:

a) The ratio Capital employed: Total Annual Costs is known as the capital turnover ratio.

b) Return on capital employed (ROCE) is fully described later in the book.

This method of calculating a mark-up does have the advantage of relating pricing to longer term financial objectives but it will be apparent that it is only a variant of full-cost pricing with the same potential inflexibility. The claim is sometimes made that the method removes the arbitrary element from establishing what is a 'fair' mark up, but the arbitrariness is simply transferred to the target rate of return. A further element of arbitrariness is that in order to make the calculation in a multi-product firm it would be necessary to apportion capital employed by product group which could only be done in an arbitrary manner.

Both full-cost and rate of return pricing are essentially long-term pricing strategies which, rigidly applied, lack the flexibility to deal with short-term pricing decisions.

12. Using cost plus systems

A number of criticisms can be levelled at cost plus systems particularly when they are used in a mechanical fashion.

The main ones are as follows:

a) The systems do not take demand explicitly into account and assume that prices are solely cost related.

b) Where the systems are incorporated in routine decision making there is the tendency to base the costs on past cost levels rather than consider what the costs will be in the future.

c) Cost plus systems tend to ignore the inherent arbitrariness of fixed cost allocation and absorption procedures and the apportionment of capital employed in a multi-product organisation.

d) Cost plus is a long run pricing concept which lacks flexibility in dealing with short run pricing where the interaction of volume, price and profit are all important.

Frequently, of course, cost plus systems are used in a more flexible fashion and the notional cost plus price is but the starting point in a pricing decision. Management may vary the mark up percentage by some intuitive consideration of demand, competition, capacity and other relevant matters, thus adjusting the price to suit current circumstances.

13. Cost plus system and ABC

In the discussion so far it has been assumed that the 'cost' to be used in cost-plus pricing has been calculated using conventional absorption costing. Of course this need not be the case and the cost could be derived using Activity-Based Costing (ABC) principles. It is claimed that conventional absorption costing tends to overcost high volume products and undercost low volume items. The effect of this is that, using cost-plus pricing, the low-volume items will have lower selling prices than they should have.

This is claimed to be one of the factors which have lead to the development of ABC by CAMI (Computer Assisted Manufacturing International). Many of the companies in CAMI work in the US Defence industry where cost-plus pricing is used extensively and consequently there is a need for product costs which more accurately reflect the underlying influences on costs.

14. Marginal pricing

This method of pricing, sometimes referred to as the variable cost or contribution method of pricing, is simply the application of cost-volume-profit analysis to pricing decisions. Using marginal pricing, the firm sets prices so as to maximise contribution towards fixed cost and profit.

As in any decision the costs and revenues to be used for pricing are FUTURE costs and revenues. All past outlays are inescapable, they are sunk costs. For short-term decisions marginal pricing can increase pricing flexibility and profits but needs to be used judiciously.

A typical example of its application in practice is where hotel chains cater for full price business during the week and offer the spare capacity at weekends at some price above marginal cost, but less than normal price, thus increasing profits. This process is known as *price discrimination* and enables the firm to sell at different prices in different markets. A further example of marginal pricing is the familiar one where a firm is experiencing reduced demand and obtains the best possible price above marginal cost in order to provide some contribution to fixed costs.

Marginal pricing policies may also be relevant when dealing with the variables involved in managing marketing strategies. For example, a typical product moves through what is known as the product life-cycle, ie introduction, growth, maturity, saturation and decline. At each stage management will require marginal cost and separable period cost data relevant to that stage in the cycle in order to make appropriate pricing decisions. Because volumes will vary at each stage the marginal approach will assist in choosing the most appropriate combination of price, advertising and, where necessary, price discrimination without the issue being clouded by the inclusion of unit fixed costs.

Marginal pricing makes explicit the consideration of demand and volume and thus more nearly approaches the theoretical framework of classical economics dealt with in the early part of the chapter. However, few if any firms are able to optimise prices by the MC = MR equation.

Used with care, marginal pricing can assist in short run price setting but care must be taken that marginal pricing does not become the long run norm. It is worth restating that in the long run prices must cover all costs plus a reasonable margin of profit.

Marginal pricing differs from the cost plus systems in that there is no automatic percentage mark up on cost to arrive at a selling price. When the marginal cost is known, the selling price is established in order to maximise contribution having regard to the expected demand, volume and other factors.

15. Alternative ways of influencing demand

So far, this chapter has concentrated on pricing as the sole means by which a firm can influence demand for its products but pricing is only one way of influencing demand; others include advertising, improving quality, better service, more representatives and numerous other devices. Where markets are oligopolistic or near oligopolistic, common in industrial societies, price is not generally considered a competitive device and advertising and other forms of sales promotion become all important.

Advertising is invariably associated with product branding and seeks to shift the demand curve of the firm to the right and/or to make it more inelastic thus giving the firm more flexibility in its pricing. The possible effect of a successful advertising campaign is shown below.

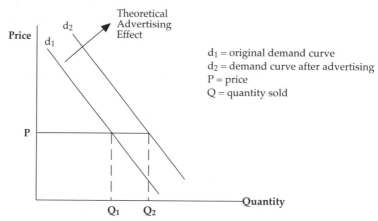

Figure 15.2 Demand Curves and Advertising

Figure 15.2 shows the position where the demand curve is moved to the right thus moving the quantity sold from Q_1 to Q_2. It will be noted that the price is unchanged and also that in this illustration the elasticity of demand (the slope) is unchanged.

If advertising has any success then there are two possible results. One is a *market widening effect* where the total market is expanded and increased sales by a single firm are not at the expense of others. The other is a *substitution or market sharing* effect where the result is a revision of market share. As is to be expected, the two effects may well interact in practice.

16. Summary

a) Pricing is a complex problem with numerous interacting factors including: objectives, markets, demand and demand elasticity, costs, competition, level of activity and so on.

b) Economic theory states that firms should seek the price which maximises profit. Given the demand schedule the intersection of the marginal cost and marginal revenue is the optimum point and either price or output (but not both) can be determined.

c) If the appropriate functions are known, the optimal price can be determined using differential calculus.

d) Price elasticity of demand is a measure of the degree to which demand responds to price changes. Price elasticity can vary from zero (perfectly inelastic demand) to infinity (perfectly elastic demand).

e) Marginal analysis is difficult to apply in practice. Difficulties include: lack of information, multiple objectives, non-price factors influencing demand.

f) A typical pricing system used in practice is full cost pricing where a mark-up, say 30%, is added to total cost. There are difficulties associated with the fixed element of the cost and with the amount of mark up.

g) Rate of return pricing is but a variant of full cost plus pricing. Both these pricing policies are essentially long-term strategies which may lack flexibility in the short term.

h) Marginal or variable cost or contribution pricing is the application of cost-volume-profit analysis to pricing decisions where management aims to maximise contribution. It increases pricing flexibility but should be considered only as a short run policy if applied to all products and services.

i) Advertising is another means of influencing demand and has the general objective of pushing the demand schedule to the right. Advertising may have a market widening or a market sharing effect.

17. Points to note

a) One particular use of full cost plus pricing is in some Government contracts where the price is determined by a formula whereby the firm recovers all its agreed costs plus a percentage mark-up.

b) Like all decision making, pricing decisions must be concerned with future costs and revenues.

c) 'Standby' air tickets are a well publicised example of marginal pricing in practice.

d) Two possible pricing policies are price skinning and pricing penetration. Price skimming is where a firm exploits the market by charging a high initial price perhaps to capitalise on the novelty appeal of a product. Price skimming is not feasible when there are already numbers of close substitutes and the high profits, if successful, may induce competitors to enter the market. Pricing penetration is in effect the opposite policy where low prices are charged initially in order to gain a large part of the market.

e) Target costing is a new approach that integrates marketing and product costing. It is described in detail in Chapter 22 but in outline, market analysis is used to determine the selling price which should enable the firm to gain the desired market share. Target product costs are derived from the selling price which Production Management are then expected to meet over time. Thus the target cost involves working backwards from the target competitive price. Cost-plus pricing is not used at all.

Additional reading

Pricing and output decisions; *Arnold* –Haymarket

The Pricing decision – economic theory and business practice; *Dorward* – Harper& Row

Pricing –principles and practice; *Gabor* – Heinemann

Pricing in business; *Hague* – Allen & Unwin

Advanced Management Accounting; *Kaplan* – Prentice-Hall

Insight into management accounting; *Sizer* – Pitman

Studies in cost analysis; *Ed Solomons* –Sweet & Maxwell

Self review questions

1. Give twelve factors which may need to be considered in a pricing decision. (3)
2. Given a profit maximising objective what is the theoretically optimum level of sales? (4)
3. Define price ceiling and price floor. (4)
4. How can calculus be used to determine the optimal price? (5)
5. What is the price elasticity of demand and why is it important? (6)
6. What is the characteristic of sales revenue when the price elasticity of demand is unity? (6)
7. What are the major limitations associated with theoretical marginal analysis? (7)
8. What are the characteristics of cost plus systems? (9)
9. What is full cost pricing and what are the problems associated with the system? (10)
10. What is 'rate of return' pricing and what are its advantages and disadvantages? (11)
11. What criticisms can be made of cost plus pricing systems? (12)
12. What is marginal pricing and when is it best applied? (13)
13. What is the main objective of advertising? (14)

16 Linear programming

1. Objectives

After studying this chapter you will:

❒ be able to define linear programming (LP) and know where it can be used;

❒ know the features of problems that can be solved by LP;

❒ be able to define LP problems in a standard manner;

❒ understand how to solve LP problems with graphs;

❒ know the elements of the Simplex method of solving LP problems

❒ be able to interpret Simplex solutions;

❒ understand how to deal with minimising LP problems;

❒ know what is meant by a shadow price;

❒ understand how sensitivity analysis can be applied to LP problems.

2. LP definition

LP is a mathematical technique to optimise the allocation of scarce resources. Many management decisions are essentially resource allocation decisions and LP enables optimal solutions to be found to a range of problems where the number of factors involved and their relationships would make simpler solution methods difficult, if not impossible. LP can be used for a range of problems and typical applications include: product mix problems, production planning, capital rationing and aspects of financial modelling. LP is an important technique for the management accountant because it provides an extension of cost-volume-analysis capable of dealing with practical problems which, because of the large number of interactions and the presence of more than one binding constraint, cannot be solved by the more basic approaches.

3. Requirements for LP

LP is a technique to optimise the value of some objective (eg to maximise contribution) when the factors involved (eg labour hours) are subject to some constraint or limitation.

Thus LP can be used to solve problems which have the following characteristics:

a) Can be stated in numeric terms.

b) All factors have linear relationships, ie if one unit requires 5 man hours, 2 units require 10 hours and so on. It must be stressed that every relationship in the problem must be linear or able to be linearly approximated.

c) The problem must permit a choice or choices between alternative courses of action.

d) There must be one or more restrictions on the factors involved. These may be restrictions on the availability of resources, for example, only 3,000 machine hours are available per week or they may relate to particular characteristics, for example, a fertiliser mix must contain a minimum of 15% phosphates and 25% nitrogen.

e) Fractional solutions must be feasible.

4. Expressing LP problems in a standard manner

Before considering methods of solving LP problems it is necessary to be able to express any given problem in a standardised manner. This is a common examination requirement which facilitates the solution and ensures that no important element of the problem is overlooked. The two main aspects of this process are determining the objective (and hence the objective function) and the *limitations* or *constraints*.

5. The objective function

This is the objective of the problem expressed in a simple mathematical form. The objective may be to maximise contribution or net present value or profit or it may be to minimise cost or time or some other appropriate measure. Examples follow of both maximising and minimising problems.

Example 1

A company produces three products A, B and C with contributions of £10, £15 and £20 per unit respectively and it is required to maximise total contribution.

The objective function is:

$$10x_1 + 15x_2 + 20x_3$$

which should be *maximised*

where: x_1 = number of units of A produced

x_2 = number of units of B produced

x_3 = number of units of C produced

Note: This problem has three unknowns or decision variables: x_1, x_2 and x_3.

Example 2

A company mixes four raw materials to produce a plastic. Material W costs 40p per kilogram, material X costs £1.20 per kilogram, material Y cost 90p per kilogram and material Z cost £2.60 per kilogram. Each of the materials contribute some essential quality to the plastic and it is required to use the least cost mix.

The objective function is:

$$40x_1 + 120x_2 + 90x_3 + 260x_4 \text{ (in pence)}$$

or

$$0.4x_1 + 1.20x_2 + 0.90x_3 + 2.60x_4 \text{ (in £s)}$$

either of which should be *minimised.*

where: x_1 = kgs of W

x_2 = kgs of X

x_3 = kgs of Y

x_4 = kgs of Z

Note: This problem has four decision variables.

It is necessary to be clear about the number of decision variables because this influences the choice of solution method. It must be emphasised that an LP problem can only pursue one objective at a time. If the objective is changed it becomes a new problem.

6. Limitations or constraints

The limitations in any given problem must be clearly identified, quantified, and expressed mathematically. To be able to use LP they must, of course, be linear.

The following example follows the typical pattern for maximising problems.

Example 3

A company produces three products and wishes to plan production to maximise contribution.

The objective function is

$$16x_1 + 8x_2 + 5.5x_3$$

which should be *maximised.*

where: x_1 = number of units of A

x_2 = number of units of B

x_3 = number of units of C

and the coefficients of the objective function (16, 8 and 5.5) represent the contributions per unit of the products.

The company employs 150 skilled and 80 unskilled workers and works a 40 hour week. The times to produce 1 unit of each product by the types of labour are shown as follows

Products

	A	B	C
Skilled Labour Hours	3	2.5	1
Unskilled Labour Hours	3.5	6	4

The three products are made from two raw materials, Argon and Zenon. There are limitations on the availability of the materials and only 25,000 kgs of Argon and 18,000 kgs of Zenon are available in a period. The usage of the materials in the products is as follows:

Products

	A	B	C	
Argon	3	2.5	1	kgs/unit
Zenon	3.5	6	4	kgs/unit

Labour and material limitations expressed in the standard manner

$$3x_1 + 2.5x_2 + x_3 \leq 6000 \text{ (skilled labour)}$$
$$3.5x_1 + 6x_2 + 4x_3 \leq 3200 \text{ (unskilled labour)}$$
$$7.5x_1 + 3x_2 + 4.5x_3 \leq 25000 \text{ (Argon)}$$
$$6x_1 + 5x_2 + 3x_3 \leq 18000 \text{ (Zenon)}$$

In addition there is a general limitation applicable to all maximising problems which is a formal means of ensuring that negative quantities of a product do not result, ie

$$x_1, x_2, x_3 \geq 0$$

Notes:

a) The above constraints are all of the 'less than or equal to' type ($\leq$) which are the most commonly encountered in maximising problems.

b) 'Greater than or equal to' ($\geq$) constraints can also occur. For example if in Example 3 it was necessary to produce at least 500 units of product C to fulfil a contract a new restriction would have to be included thus:

$$x_3 \geq 500 \text{ (contract restriction)}$$

7. Fixed costs

LP is concerned with changes in cost and revenues so it follows that a factor such as fixed costs which would be unchanged over the range of output being considered should not be included in the LP formulation. To eliminate the effect of fixed costs and to maintain linear relationships it is normal to use contribution (ie sales less marginal cost) rather than profit in the objective functions.

8. Solving LP problems

When the problem has been expressed in the standardised manner it can be solved by either of two methods. If there are only TWO unknowns or decision variables then the problem can be solved by graphical methods. If there are THREE or more unknowns then the usual solution method is the Simplex technique. Graphical methods are dealt with first followed by a description of the Simplex method.

9. Graphical LP solutions

Graphical methods are the simplest to use and should be employed wherever possible. The following are the major features of the approach.

a) Can only be used where there are 2 unknowns.

b) Graphical methods can deal with any number of limitations but as each limitation is a line on the graph a large number of lines may make the graph difficult to read. This is rarely a problem in examination questions.

c) Both maximising and minimising problems can be dealt with graphically and the method can deal with constraints of the 'greater than or equal to' ($\geq$) type and the 'less than or equal to ($\leq$) type.

d) The axes of the graph represents the unknowns and each constraint is drawn as a straight line on the graph. The area on the graph which does not contravene any of the constraints is known as the feasible region.

e) The solution point is always at a vertex of the constraints on the edge of the feasible region. If a line is drawn representing the objective function the solution point for maximising problems is the corner of the feasible region furthest to the right which can be touched by the objective function line; for minimising problems it is the corresponding point furthest to the left of the feasible region. When the solution point is found the values of the decision variables can be read directly from the axes of the graph.

10. Graphical LP example

Example 4

A manufacturer produces two products, Klunk and Klick. Klunk has a contribution of £3 per unit and Klick £4 per unit. The manufacturer wishes to establish the weekly production plan which maximises contribution.

Production data are as follows:

	per unit		
	Machining (Hours)	Labour (Hours)	Material (kgs)
Klunk	4	4	1
Klick	2	6	1
Total Available per week	100	180	40

Because of a trade agreement sales of Klunk are limited to a weekly maximum of 20 units and to honour an agreement with an old established customer at least 10 units of Klick must be sold per week.

Solution

It will be seen that this is a problem with two unknowns (the quantities of the two products) and five constraints (machining hours, labour hours, materials and the two sales constraints). Four of the constraints are of the ≤ type whilst the sales constraint for Klick is of the ≥ type.

The problem in the standardised format is as follows:

maximise $\qquad\qquad\qquad 3x_1 + 4x_2$ (objective function)

subject to constraints:

A	$4x_1$	$+$	$2x_2$	$\leq$	100	(Machining hours constraint)
B	$4x_1$	$+$	$6x_2$	$\leq$	180	(Labour hours constraint)
C	x_1	$+$	x_2	$\leq$	40	(Materials constraint)
D	x_1			$\leq$	20	(Klunk sales constraint)
E			x_2	$\geq$	10	(Klick sales constraint)
	x_1			$\geq$	0	

where: $\quad x_1$ = number of units of Klunk

$\qquad\quad x_2$ = number of units of Klick

Note: As it is impossible to make negative quantities of the products it is necessary formally to state the non-negative constraint (ie $x_1 \geq 0$). Constraint E, being of the ≥ type already ensures that negative quantities of x_2 will not appear in the solution.

The optimal solution is 15 units of x_1 and 20 units of x_2 giving a contribution of £(15(3) + 20(4)) = £125.

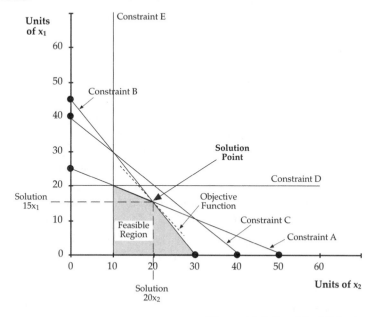

Figure 16.1 Graphical Solution to Example 4

Notes:

a) Each constraint is plotted on the graph as an equality. Using Constraint A as an example, the plotting points are found as follows.

Constraint: $4x_1 + 2x_2 = 100$

Plotting point on x_1 axis = $\dfrac{100}{4} = 25$

Plotting point on x_2 axis = $\dfrac{100}{2} = 50$

The area to the left of each $\leq$ constraint, ie A to D, and the area to the right of the $\geq$ constraint E, is the area which does not violate that particular constraint. As each constraint is drawn the area that does not violate any constraint – the feasible region – generally becomes smaller.

b) The values of x_1 and x_2 at the optimal activity can be inserted into the constraints to find out the utilisation of each constraint thus,

Resource Constraint A $4(15) + 2(20) = $ 100 (Machining hours fully utilised)

Resource Constraint B $4(15) + 6(20) = $ 180 (Labour hours fully utilised)

Resource Constraint C $1(25) + 1(20) = $ 35 (5 lbs material spare)

Sales Constraint D $1(15)$ $= $ 15 (Sales agreement honoured)

Sales Constraint E $1(20) = $ 20 (Sales agreement honoured)

It will be seen that the two resource constraints which are fully utilised, A and B, formed the vertex at the optimum point. Constraint C which is not fully utilised did not touch the feasible region and is an example of a redundant or non-binding constraint.

c) The line representing the objective function is sloped to reflect the relative contributions of the two unknowns. Such a line is known as an Iso-profit or Iso-cost line and the line shown is only one of an infinite number of such lines that can be drawn. The lines could be drawn, parallel to each other, increasingly further to the right from the point of origin of the graph. For maximising problems the optimum point is that vertex of the feasible region furthest to the right that can be touched by an iso-profit line.

In many examples, including Figure 16.1, the optimal point is obvious without drawing the iso-profit line but students are advised *always* to draw the iso-profit line which can help to determine the optimum point where there are a number of vertices close together. Also, in examinations, more marks will be gained for a complete graph. Similar principles apply to minimising problems except that the converse applies, ie the optimum point is the point furthest to the *left* that can be touched by an iso-profit line.

d) Although Example 1 produced whole number solutions (15 and 20) fractional solutions are possible and frequently occur when solving LP questions.

11. Simplex method

The Simplex method is an iterative arithmetic method of solving LP problems and can be used for problems with any number of unknowns and any number of constraints. A typical examination question using the Simplex method would typically have three or four unknowns but practical problems may contain dozens, hundreds and even thousands of unknowns and constraints. Such problems are invariably solved by computers which use techniques based on the Simplex method. The main practical involvement of management accountants with LP, and a typical examination requirement, is calculating contributions, establishing constraints, expressing the problem in the standardised manner and interpreting the computer produced results. Accordingly, this book concentrates on these aspects and does not deal with the detailed processes of the Simplex method. The method is straightforward but somewhat lengthy and tedious and students wishing to have a full explanation of the technique are advised to study an appropriate text book (For example, Quantitative Techniques, *T. Lucey*, Letts Educational (formerly DP Publications))

The Simplex method can be used for both minimising and maximising problems, constraints of the ≤ and ≥ type and situations where the both types of constraint are included in the same problem.

12. Simplex maximising example

The following example will be used as a basis for explaining the use of the Simplex method. The explanations include: expressing the problem in the standardised manner, setting up the first Simplex tableau and finally how the final solution tableau can be interpreted.

Example 5

A company can produce three products, A, B and C. The products yield a contribution of £8, £5 and £10 respectively.

The products use a machine which has 400 hours capacity in the next period. Each unit of the products uses 2, 3 and 1 hour respectively of the machine's capacity.

There are only 150 units available in the period of a special component which is used singly in products A and C.

200 kgs only of a special alloy is available in the period. Product A uses 2 kgs per unit and Product C uses 4 kgs per unit.

There is an agreement with a trade association to produce no more than 50 units of Product B in the period.

The company wishes to find out the production plan which maximises contribution.

Solution

As always, the first step is to express the problem in the standardised manner as described in the first part of the chapter.

The standardised format is shown on the following page.

Objective function (to be *maximised*):

$$8x_1 + 5x_2 + 10x_3$$

subject to:-

$$
\begin{array}{llll}
2x_1 & + \ 3x_2 & + \quad x_3 & \leq 400 \ \text{(Machine hours constraint)} \\
x_1 & & + \quad x_3 & \leq 150 \ \text{(Component constraint)} \\
2x_1 & & + \ 4x_3 & \leq 200 \ \text{(Alloy constraint)} \\
& x_2 & & \leq 50 \ \text{(Sales constraint)} \\
x_1 & & & \geq 0 \\
& x_2 & & \geq 0 \\
& & x_3 & \geq 0
\end{array}
$$

where: x_1 = no. of units of Product A
          x_2 = no. of units of Product B
          x_3 = no. of units of Product C

It will be seen that this is a problem with 3 unknowns and four constraints which are all of the $\leq$ type.

The next stage is to change the inequalities in the constraints into equalities by adding a slack variable in each constraint. This is done so that arithmetic can take place on the constraints during the Simplex iterations. The slack variables represent the spare capacity in the constraints and the Simplex method automatically assigns a value to the slack variables. The values can range from the full amount of the constraint when there is no production to a value of zero when the constraint is fully utilised. For example when a slack variable, s_1, is added to the machining constraint the constraint appears as follows

$$2x_1 + 3x_2 + x_3 + s_1 = 400$$

The slack variable, s_1, can take any value between:

400 hours ie the position of zero production and therefore maximum unused
          capacity

and   0 hours ie the position of full production and zero unused capacity.

The full formulation with slack variables is as follows:

maximise: $8x_1 + 5x_2 + 10x_3$

subject to:

$$
\begin{array}{lllll}
2x_1 + & 3x_2 + & x_3 + & s_1 & = 400 \\
x_1 & & + \ x_3 + & s_2 & = 150 \\
x_1 & & + \ x_3 + & s_3 & = 200 \\
& x_2 & + & s_4 & = 50
\end{array}
$$

Note: s_1, s_2, s_3, s_4 are the slack variables and represent the spare capacity in the limitations.

The initial Simplex tableau can now be set up ready for the step-by-step solution method to take place.

Initial simplex tableau

Solution Variable	Products			Slack Variables				Solution Quantity
	x_1	x_2	x_3	s_1	s_2	s_3	s_4	
s_1	2	3	1	1	0	0	0	400
s_2	1	0	1	0	1	0	0	150
s_3	2	0	4	0	0	1	0	200
s_4	0	1	0	0	0	0	1	50
Z	8	5	10	0	0	0	0	0

Table 1

Notes:

a) It will be seen that the values in the body of the table are the values from the objective function and constraints in the formulation where the slack variables were added.

b) The variable 'Z' has been used for the objective function and represents total contribution.

c) The tableau shows that $s_1 = 400$, $s_2 = 150$, $s_3 = 200$, $s_4 = 50$ and $Z = 0$.

d) The tableau shows a feasible solution, that of nil production, nil contribution, and maximum unused capacity as represented by the values of the slack variables.

e) It will be seen that the columns under the slack variables contain a single figure 1 with the rest of the column being zeros. In a Simplex tableau the solution value for a variable is ALWAYS found opposite the figure 1 where the rest of the column is zeros.

f) Although this initial Simplex tableau does show a feasible solution – as does every succeeding tableau – it can obviously be improved upon and this is the task of the Simplex solution technique. After a number of iterations the optimum solution is reached giving a final tableau as follows.

Solution Variable	Products			Slack Variables				Solution Quantity
	x_1	x_2	x_3	s_1	s_2	s_3	s_4	
s_1	0	0	-3	1	0	-1	-3	50
s_2	0	0	-1	0	1	$-\frac{1}{2}$	0	50
x_1	1	0	2	0	0	$\frac{1}{2}$	1	100
x_2	0	1	0	0	0	0	1	50
Z	0	0	-6	0	0	-4	-5	-1050

Table 2

Note: This is recognised as the optimum position because there are no positive values in the bottom row, ie no further gains in contribution can be made by altering production levels.

Interpreting the final tableau

The solution can be read directly from Table 2 in each row where there is a figure 1 in a column of zero's, ie

$$s_1 = 50; \quad s_2 = 50; \quad x_1 = 100; \quad x_2 = 50$$

This means that the optimum production plan is:

100 units of Product A (ie x_1)

50 units of Product B (ie x_2)

This production plan results in a contribution of £1050 found in the Table at the end of the Z row. Because s_1 and s_2, the slack variables, have values at optimum this means that there is some unused capacity, ie

$s_1 = 50$ – means that there are 50 hours of unused machine capacity

$s_2 = 50$ – means that there are 50 unused components.

It will be realised that x_3, s_3 and s_4 do not have values in the final volume of Table 2. This means that, at optimum,

❏ there is no production of x_3

❏ that the 200 kgs of special alloy are fully utilised

❏ that the sales constraint is binding

Note: This minus sign against the £1050 contribution in the Z row is merely a result of the Simplex arithmetic and can be ignored.

The values shown for the production plan, contribution and unused capacities can be verified as follows

At optimum when $x_1 = 100$ and $x_2 = 50$

Contribution	=	£(100(8) + 50(5))	=	£1050
Machining hours	=	100(2) + 50(3)	=	350 leaving 50 spare
Components usage	=	100(1)	=	100 leaving 50 spare
Alloy usage	=	100(2)	=	200 fully utilised

Further information can be obtained from Table 2 which is of considerable importance from an accounting viewpoint. It will be seen the bottom row of Table 2 contains three minus figures

x_3 column –6; s_3 column –4; s_4 column –5

The values, which are an automatic and useful by-product of the Simplex method, are known as shadow prices or shadow costs or dual prices and are discussed below.

13. Shadow prices

The shadow price of a scarce resource is the increase in the value of the objective function which would be achieved if one more unit of the resource was available. In the terms of Example 2 above, if one more kilogramme of the special alloy was made available, contribution would increase by £4 (ie the s_3 value).

The shadow price of a resource is the opportunity cost of that resource and the valuation produced by the Simplex method results from the effects of one more unit of the resource on the output of the products: A and B in our example.

At the margin, shadow prices can provide guidance to decision makers on, for example, the value to the business of relieving existing constraints, but they will normally only apply to relatively small changes in the resource levels. If the change in the amount of the resource is of a significant magnitude then the problem should be re-solved using the revised resource levels when new shadow prices will result.

A constraint only has a shadow price when it is binding. Where resources are not fully utilised the shadow price is zero. This accords with common sense for there can be no benefit in increasing the amount of a resource of which there is already a surplus.

Reverting to the interpretation of Table 2 the shadow prices and interpretations are as follows.

x_3 shadow price £6

> This means that if any units of Product C were manufactured (it will be recalled that it was not in the optimal production plan) overall contribution would FALL by £6.

s_3 shadow price £4

> This means every extra kilogramme of the alloy would INCREASE contribution by £4.

s_4 shadow price £5

> This means that if the sales constraint could be lifted every extra unit of product B that could be sold would increase overall contribution by £5.

Machine hours and components, slack variables s_1 and s_2, have zero shadow prices as shown in Table 2. This is to be expected as there are surplus machine hours and components available.

The shadow prices of the binding constraints can be used to prove the contribution, thus:

Alloy constraint	$200 \times £4$	=	£800
Sales constraint	$50 \times £5$	=	£250
Total contribution		=	£1050

14. Primal and dual problems

Every LP problem has an equal but opposite formulation. For every maximising problem there is an equal but opposite minimising problem and for every minimising problem, an equal but opposite maximising problem. Correctly interpreted the same answers can be obtained from either formulation. The original problem is known as the *primal problem* and the equal but opposite formulation as the *dual* or *inverse*. For example, in a given set of circumstances, the same optimal plan for the organisation might be obtained from either a primal problem to maximise contribution or the dual problem to minimise cost.

A particular use of the dual formulation is concerned with minimisation problems which it is required to solve by the Simplex method. The method can be used to solve both minimising and maximising problems but because solving maximising problems by the Simplex method is a more straight forward process, it is normal to convert a minimising problem into a maximising one and solve the resulting dual formulation by the usual Simplex technique. This is illustrated below.

15. Minimisation example

Example

A plastics manufacturer can utilise three raw materials, Poly, Gimp and Mox in varying proportions to produce three products A, B and C. The firm wishes to produce at least 200 units of A, 300 units of B and 80 units of C.

Each kilo of Poly yields 4 of A, 3 of B and 2 of C

Each kilo of Gimp yields 5 of A, 6 of B and 1 of C

Each kilo of Mox yields 1 of A, 3 of B and 1 of C.

If Poly costs 20p a kilo, Gimp costs 30p per kilo and Mox costs 50p what is the minimum purchase plan to produce the required output?

Solution

Step 1

Express the problem in the standardised manner, ie

minimise: $\qquad 20x_1 + 30x_2 + 50x_3$

subject to:-

$4x_1$	+	$5x_2$	+	x_3	≥ 200	Product A
$3x_1$	+	$6x_2$	+	$3x_3$	≥ 300	Product B
$2x_1$	+	x_2	+	x_3	≥ 80	Product C

$$x_1, x_2, x_3 \geq 0$$

where: x_1 = kgs of Poly

x_2 = kgs of Gimp

x_3 = kgs of Mox

Step 2

Form the *dual* and *inverse* of the formulation above. make the problem into a *maximising* one by making a column for each *limitation* and a *constraint* row for each *element* in the objective function, thus:

maximise: $\qquad 200A + 300B + 80C$

subject to:-

4A	+	3B	+	2C	≤ 20
5A	+	6B	+	1C	≤ 30
1A	+	3B	+	1C	≤ 50

It will be seen that the original quantity column has become the objective function row and that the original costs (20, 30 and 50) have become the amounts of the constraints.

It will also be noted that the constraints are of the $\le$ type, ie as a normal maximising problem.

Step 3

Set up the first Simplex tableau complete with slack variables.

Initial Simplex tableau

Solution Variable	A	B	C	s_1	s_2	s_3	Cost
s_1	4	3	2	1	0	0	20
s_2	5	6	1	0	1	0	30
s_3	1	3	1	0	0	1	50
Quantity	200	300	80	0	0	0	0

Step 4

The normal Simplex procedure for maximising is worked through resulting in the following optimum position.

Final Simplex tableau

Solution Variable	A	B	C	s_1	s_2	s_3	Cost
C	1	0	1	$\frac{2}{3}$	$-\frac{1}{3}$	0	$3\frac{1}{3}$
B	$\frac{2}{3}$	1	0	$-\frac{1}{9}$	$\frac{1}{9}$	0	$4\frac{4}{9}$
s_3	-2	0	0	$-\frac{1}{3}$	$-\frac{2}{3}$	1	$33\frac{1}{6}$
Quantity	-80	0	0	-20	-40	0	-1600

The above is the normal result of a maximising problem. However, to obtain the solutions to the original minimising problem some differences in the usual interpretation are required.

Quantities to be purchased

These are the figures under the slack variable columns, ie

$$s_1 = -20 \text{ Purchase 20 kgs of Poly}$$
$$s_2 = -40 \text{ Purchase 40 kgs of Gimp}$$
$$s_3 = 0 \quad \text{Nil purchases of Mox}$$

Total Cost

This is the value at the bottom right hand corner, ie £1600, which can be verified as follows:

$$£(20 \times 20 + 30 \times 40) = \underline{£1600}$$

Shadow Prices

These are read from the cost column, ie

$$C = 3\tfrac{1}{3}; \quad B = 4\tfrac{4}{9}; \quad s_3 = 33\tfrac{1}{6}$$

Explanations. If either of the two quantity constraints C or B is changed by one unit then the total cost will change by £$3\tfrac{1}{3}$ or £$4\tfrac{4}{9}$ respectively.

The s_3 valuation means that if any of the material, Mox, is purchased, total cost will increase by £$33\tfrac{1}{6}$ per kg purchased .

Overproduction

The −80 under column A indicates an overproduction of Product A by 80 units.

> Proof: 20 kgs Poly + 40 kgs Gimp yields
> Product A: 80 units + 200 units = 280 units, ie 80 surplus
> Product B: 60 units + 240 units = 300 units, ie minimum required
> Product C: 40 units + 40 units = 80 units, ie minimum required

16. Calculating the shadow prices

As explained above, the Simplex method produces the shadow prices as an automatic by-product. However, on occasions it is required to calculate the shadow prices for problems that have been solved graphically, ie those with two unknowns. The shadow prices cannot be read from the graph and some simple calculations are required. It will be recalled from para 14 that every primal problem has a dual. The dual formulation of a problem gives the shadow prices so all that is necessary for a two decision variable problem is to form the dual and to solve by simultaneous equations.

The problem given in Example 4, Figure 1 will be used to exemplify the method.

The objective function and the two binding constraints (the only ones that can have shadow prices) were as follows:

maximise $3x_1 + 4x_2$ (objective function)

subject to:

$$4x_1 + 2x_2 \leq 100 \quad \text{(machining)}$$
$$4x_1 + 6x_2 \leq 180 \quad \text{(labour)}$$

and the optimal solution was 15 units of x_1 and 20 units of x_2 giving a contribution of £125.

The shadow prices are found thus (see next page):

If   M = shadow price per machining hour

and   L = shadow price per labour hour

the dual formulation is:

$$4M + 4L = 3 \quad \ldots\ldots\ldots\ldots \text{Equation 1}$$
$$2M + 6L = 4 \quad \ldots\ldots\ldots\ldots \text{Equation 2}$$

Equation 2:	2M + 6L	= 4
Divide Equation 1 by 2:	2M + 2L	= 1.5

Subtracting gives:	4L	= 2.5
i.e.:	L	= 0.625
and substituting gives:	M	= 0.125

Thus the shadow prices are £0.125 per machining hour and £0.625 per labour hour. These values can be verified by evaluating the total availability of the two resources by their respective shadow prices thus:

Contribution   = £(100 × 0.125 + 180 × 0.625)

                = **£125**

17. Sensitivity analysis

In practice, management are interested in more than just the solution to the LP problem as indicated either graphically or by the Simplex method. They need to know about the sensitivity of the solution. An optimal solution may hold for only a narrow range of constraint or contribution values and would thus be termed as sensitive solution. Alternatively, the indicated solution may hold good over a wide range of values and would be termed robust. The examination over which range of values the original solution still applies is termed sensitivity analysis. The output of LP packages on computers usually provides sensitivity analysis information which gives guidance on the amount of variation that can be tolerated before there is a change in the solution.

For smaller problems sensitivity analysis can be carried out by making some simple calculations. As an illustration assume that having found the solution to Example 4, shown on Figure 16.1, you are asked the following question.

What is the maximum contribution to which Klick can be raised without the original solution of 15 units of Klunk and 20 units of Klick being changed? (The contribution of Klunk is to remain at £3 per unit).

Examination of Figure 16.1 will show that the angle of the objective function (determined by the relative contributions) can be increased to that of constraint B before a change in solution occurs.

∴ Ratio of constraint B = 45 : 30 = $1\frac{1}{2}$: 1

∴ As Klunk is to remain at the same contribution, Klick can increase in the ratio of $1\frac{1}{2}$:1 in relation to the £3 contribution of Klunk.

Putting the contribution of Klick as x, we have:

$$x : £3 = 1\frac{1}{2} : 1$$

$$\therefore x = £4.50$$

Klick can increase up to £4.50 without the solution changing. When the contributions are £4.50 and £3 exactly the objective function is at the same angle as constraint B and there is an infinite number of solutions ranging from the original solution $(15x_1, 20x_2)$ to $30x_2$. When the price of Klick goes above £4.50 there will be a single solution of $30x_2$, ie 30 units of Klick and no production of x_1.

18. Limitations of LP

LP is a useful, practical technique but naturally there are some drawbacks to its use. The main ones are summarised below.

a) Assumption of certainty. The LP model is a deterministic one where certain knowledge is assumed of the input values and the uncertainties surrounding most business situations are not included. (Sensitivity analysis is a means of attempting to include some of the problem's uncertainties).

b) Assumption of linearity. The objective function and the constraints must all be linear or capable of being approximated by a linear function. This may not be appropriate for many practical problems which may be better represented by curvilinear functions.

c) Assumption of continuity. In ordinary LP it is assumed that the functions are continuous variable. In some situations only whole number solutions are realistic and rounding of Simplex or Graphical solution values may cause serious errors.

d) Single objectives. An LP formulation can only pursue one objective at a time whereas a practical problem may have multiple objectives.

It will be apparent that a number of the limitations of LP apply with equal or greater force to management accounting techniques such as marginal costing or C-V-P analysis. Consequently it is important to be aware of the limitations of ANY technique used for decision making.

19. Summary

a) LP is a resource allocation technique which provides a valuable extension to cost-volume-profit analysis.

b) The major requirements of problems which can be solved by LP are: numeric, linearity, alternatives must exist, restrictions or constraints must exist.

c) Before solving, LP problems must be expressed in a standardised manner whereby the objective function and the constraints are clearly set out in mathematical form.

d) LP is concerned with changes in costs and revenues so fixed costs are not included. It is because of this that maximising contribution rather than profit is generally the objective.

e) If there are only 2 unknowns or decision variables LP problems can be solved by graphical means regardless of the number of constraints.

f) The axes represent the unknowns and each constraint is drawn as a straight line. The area which does not contravene any constraint is known as the feasible region.

g) The optimum point is always a vertex of the constraints at the edge of the feasible region, the furthest to the right for maximising problems and the furthest to the left for minimising problems.

h) The Simplex method is an iterative, arithmetic method of solving LP problems which can be used for problems of any size and for maximising and minimising problems.

i) A typical examination requirement is to interpret the final Simplex tableau which shows: the solution quantities, the value of the objective function, the unused capacities or resources, and the shadow prices.

j) The shadow price of a scarce resource (ie fully utilised at optimum) is the opportunity cost of the constraint and is a valuable by-product of the Simplex method.

k) For every LP problem there is an equal but opposite formulation known as the primal and dual formulations, respectively. Although there are different layouts in the final tableau, the required results can be obtained from either formulation.

l) Shadow prices cannot be read directly from a graphical solution but can be obtained by simple calculation.

m) Sensitivity analysis is the process of varying factors in the problem to see the effect on the solution and to see the range of variation permitted before the solution changes.

n) The major limitations of LP are: the assumptions of linearity, certainty and continuity.

20. Points to note

a) The importance of opportunity costs (ie shadow prices) has already been mentioned. These are automatically produced by the Simplex method of solving LP problems and can be easily determined from graphical solutions. This makes LP an extremely useful technique for the management accountant when advising on resource allocation problems.

b) LP is a valuable extension of C-V-P analysis using similar principles and assumptions.

Additional reading

Introduction to mathematical programming for accountants; *Carlsberg* – Allen & Unwin

Economics of business decision; *Carlsberg* – Penguin

Advanced management accounting; *Kaplan & Atkinson* – Prentice Hall

Quantitative Techniques; *Lucey* – Letts Educational (formerly DP Publications)

Linear programming in financial planning; *Salkin & Kornbluth* – Prentice Hall

Self review questions

1. What is LP and why is it of value to the management accountant? (2)
2. What are the characteristics of problems that can be solved by LP? (3)
3. How are problems expressed in the standardised manner? (4-6)
4. When can graphical solution methods be used and how is the graph drawn? (9)

5. How is the graph interpreted? (10)
6. When is the Simplex method used? (11)
7. What are slack variables and why are they necessary? (12)
8. How is the final tableau recognised and how is it interpreted? (12)
9. What are shadow prices and what constraints have shadow prices? (13)
10. Distinguish between the primal and dual. (14)
11. What differences in interpretation are necessary when considering the final tableau of a maximising dual formulation of a primal minimising problem? (15)
12. How can shadow prices be obtained when the Simplex method has not been used to find a solution? (16)
13. What is a sensitive solution and what is sensitivity analysis? (17)

17 Investment appraisal I

1. Objectives

After studying this chapter you will:

❒ have been introduced to long-run decision making or investment appraisal;

❒ understand the two main traditional methods of appraisal: accounting rate of return and payback;

❒ know the principles of Discounted Cash Flow (DCF);

❒ be able to calculate the Net Present Value (NPV) of an investment;

❒ understand the meaning of NPV;

❒ know how to calculate the Internal Rate of Return (IRR) of an investment;

❒ understand how to use NPV and IRR in varying circumstances;

❒ be able to calculate the profitability index;

❒ know what is meant by the cost of capital;

❒ be able to calculate the weighted average cost of capital;

❒ understand the capital asset pricing model.

2. Long-run decision making

Investment decisions are long-run decisions where consumption and investment alternatives are balanced over time in the hope that investment now will generate extra returns in the future. There are many similarities between short-run and long-run decision making, for example, the choice between alternatives, the need to consider future costs and revenues and the importance of incremental changes in costs and revenues but there is the additional requirement for investment decisions that, because of the time scale involved, the time value of the money invested must be considered. The time scale also makes the consideration of uncertainty and inflation of even greater importance than when considering short term decisions.

Assuming that finance is available the decision to invest will be based on three major factors:

a) The investor's belief in the future. In business the beliefs would be based on forecasts of internal and external factors including: costs, revenues, inflation and interest rates, taxation and numerous other factors.

b) The alternatives available in which to invest. This is the stage at which the various techniques used to appraise the competing investments would be used. The various techniques are covered in detail in this chapter.

c) The investor's attitude to risk. Because investment decisions are often on a large scale, analysis of the investor's attitude to risk and the project uncertainty are critical factors in an investment decision and are dealt with in the following chapter.

Investment decision making is invariably a top management exercise. This is because of the scale and long term nature of the consequences of such decisions. The accountant's task is to gather the essential data from various sources, consider the financing and taxation implications, analyse the data using one or more of the appraisal techniques and present the decision maker with the results of the exercise so that the decision maker may make more informed and hopefully better decisions.

There is strong research evidence that overly elaborate appraisal methods, notwithstanding their theoretical correctness, are seen by practical decision makers as largely irrelevant. What is crucial is that the accountant should provide information which improves real investment decision making.

3. Traditional investment appraisal techniques

Two particular methods of comparing the attractiveness of competing projects have become known as the 'traditional techniques'. These are the *Accounting Rate of Return* and *Payback* which are described below.

4. Accounting rate of return

This is the ratio of average annual profits, after depreciation, to the capital invested. This is a basic definition only and variations exist, for example

❐ profits may be before or after tax

❐ capital may or may not include working capital

❐ capital invested may mean the initial capital investment or the average of the capital invested over the life of the project.

Note: An alternative term is return on Capital Employed (ROCE). The use of ROCE in divisional performance appraisal is dealt with later in the book.

Example 1. Accounting Rate of Return

A firm is considering three projects each with an initial investment of £1000 and a life of 5 years. The profits generated by the projects are estimated to be as follows:

	After tax and depreciation profits		
Year	Project I	Project II	Project III
	£	£	£
1	200	350	150
2	200	200	150
3	200	150	150
4	200	150	200
5	200	150	350
Total	1000	1000	1000

Calculate the accounting rate of return (ARR) on

a) Initial Capital

b) Average Capital

Solution

Accounting rate of return on Initial Capital:

| | Project I | Project II | Project III |

Average Profits £ $\dfrac{1000}{5}$ £200 p.a.   £ $\dfrac{1000}{5}$ £200 p.a.   £ $\dfrac{1000}{5}$ £200 p.a.

ARR $\dfrac{200}{1000} = 20\%$ $\dfrac{200}{1000} = 20\%$ $\dfrac{200}{1000} = 20\%$

Accounting rate of return on Average Capital:

| | Project I | Project II | Project III |

Average Capital £ $\dfrac{1000}{2}$ £500 p.a.   £ $\dfrac{1000}{2}$ £500 p.a.   £ $\dfrac{1000}{2}$ £500 p.a.

ARR $\dfrac{200}{500} = 40\%$ $\dfrac{200}{500} = 40\%$ $\dfrac{200}{500} = 40\%$

Note: Average capital is calculated according to the usual accounting convention that the initial investment is eroded steadily to zero over the life of the project so that:

$$\text{average capital invested} = \frac{\text{Initial Investment}}{2}$$

5. Advantages and disadvantages of ARR

The only advantage that can be claimed for the ARR is simplicity of calculation, but the disadvantages are more numerous.

Disadvantages:

a) Does not allow for the timing of outflows and inflows. The three projects in Example 1 are ranked equally even though there are clear differences in timings.

b) Uses as a measure of return the concept of accounting profit. Profit has subjective elements, is subject to accounting conventions and is not as appropriate for investment appraisal purposes as the cash flows generated by the project.

c) There is no universally accepted method of calculating ARR.

6. Payback

Numerous surveys have shown that payback is a popular technique for appraising projects either on its own or in conjunction with other methods. Payback can be defined as the period, usually expressed in years which it takes for the project's net cash inflows to recoup the original investment. The usual decision rule is to accept the project with the shortest payback period. The following example demonstrates the technique.

Example 2

Calculate the payment periods for the following three projects:

Net Cash Flows

Year	Project I		Project II		Project III	
	Cash Flow	Cumulative Cash Flow	Cash Flow	Cumulative Cash Flow	Cash Flow Flow	Cumulative Cash Flow
0	−1500	−1500	−1500	−1500	−1500	−1500
1	+ 600	− 900	+ 400	−1100	+ 300	−1200
2	+ 500	− 400	+ 500	− 600	+ 500	− 700
3	+ 400	NIL	+ 600	NIL	+ 400	− 300
4	–		–		+ 300	NIL
5	–		–		+ 300	+300
6	–		–		+ 300	+600

Note: The usual investment appraisal assumptions are adopted for the above table and all subsequent examples, that Year 0 means now, Year 1 means at the end of 1 year, year 2 the end of 2 years and so on, and that a negative cash flow represents a cash outflow and a positive sign represents a cash inflow).

Payback Periods   Project I   = 3 years
Project II = 3 years
Project III = 4 years

7. Advantages and disadvantages of payback

Advantages:

a) Simple to calculate and understand.

b) Uses project cash flows rather than accounting profits and hence is more objectively based.

c) Favours quick return projects which may produce faster growth for the company and enhance liquidity.

d) Choosing projects which payback quickest will tend to minimise those risks facing the company which are related to time. However, not all risks are related to time.

Disadvantages:

a) Payback does not measure overall project worth because it does not consider cash flows after the payback period. In Example 2, Project III is ranked after Projects I and II, even though it produces cash flows over a 6 year period.

b) Payback provides only a crude measure of the timing of project cash flows. In example 2, Projects I and II are ranked equally, even though there are clear differences in the timings of the cash flows.

In spite of any theoretical disadvantages, payback is undoubtedly the most popular appraisal criterion in practice.

8. Discounted cash flow (DCF)

There is growing use of DCF techniques for appraising projects and for assisting invest-ment decision making. The use of DCF overcomes some of the disadvantages of the traditional techniques but it must be stressed that DCF itself has problems and contains many assumptions so that it should be used with care and with an awareness of its limitations. The main DCF techniques of Net Present Value (NPV) and Internal Rate of Return (IRR) are described in this chapter but it is necessary first to consider two features common to all DCF methods: the use of cash flows and the time value of money.

9. Use of cash flows

All DCF methods use cash flows and not accounting profits. Accounting profits are invariably calculated for stewardship purposes and are period orientated (usually monthly, quarterly or annually) thus necessitating accrual accounting with its atten-dant conventions and assumptions. For investment appraisal purposes a project orien-tated approach using cash flows is to be preferred for the following reasons.

a) Cash flows are more objective and in the end are what actually count. Profits cannot be spent.

b) Accounting conventions regarding revenue/capital expenditure classifications, depreciation calculations, stock valuations become largely redundant.

c) The whole life of the project is to be considered, therefore it becomes unnecessary and misleading to consider accounting profits which are related to periods.

d) The timing or expected timing of cash flows is more easily ascertained.

10. What cash flows should be included?

The all embracing answer to this question is the net after tax incremental cash flow effect on the firm by accepting the project, ie the comparison of cash flows with and without the project. Many of the cash flow items are readily identifiable, eg the initial outlay on a new machine, but others are less easily identified yet are nevertheless just as relevant, eg the increase or reduction in sales income of an existing product when a new product is introduced. Typical cash flow items include:

a) Cash Inflows
   i)   The project revenues
   ii) Government grants
   iii) Resale or scrap value of assets
   iv) Tax receipts
   v)   Any other cash inflows caused by accepting the project.

b) Cash Outflows
   i)   Initial investment in acquiring the assets
   ii) Project costs (labour, materials etc)

    iii) Working capital investment

    iv) Tax payments

    v) Any other cash outflow caused by accepting the project.

Notes:

a) The relevant costs in investment decisions, as with all other decisions, are opportunity costs and not historical accounting costs. For example, if a project occupies storage space rented by the firm at £5/square metre which could be sublet by the firm at £7/square metre, then the relevant cash flow is the benefit foregone of £7/square metre.

b) It will be noted that depreciation is not included. Depreciation is NOT a cash flow but an accounting convention. The capital outlay is already represented by the cash outflow of the initial investment, so to include depreciation would involve double counting. The only role of depreciation in investment appraisal is in determining the tax payments of the project, which are, of course, real cash flows.

c) Similarly, interest payments are not included because the discounting process itself takes account of the time value of money and to include interest payments and to discount would be to double count.

11. Time value of money

Investment appraisal is concerned with long-run decisions where costs and income arise at intervals over a period. Monies spent or received at different times cannot be compared directly, they must be reduced to equivalent values at some common date. This could be at any time during the the project life but appraisal methods which take account of the time factor use either now, the present time, or the end of the project as the common date.

Both discounting and compounding methods allow for the time value of money and could thus be used for investment appraisal but on the whole discounting methods are more frequently used. In general it is preferable to receive a given sum earlier rather than later because the sum received earlier can be put to use by earning interest or some productive investment within the business, ie money has a time productivity.

It should be noted that the time value of money concept applies even if there is zero inflation. Inflation obviously increases the discrepancy in value between monies received at different times but it is not the basis of the concept.

12. Assumptions in basic DCF appraisal

In describing the two main DCF methods certain assumptions are made initially so that the underlying principles can be more easily understood. These are as follows:

a) Uncertainty does not exist

b) Inflation does not exist

c) The appropriate discount rate to use is known

d) A perfect capital market exists, ie unlimited funds can be raised at the market rate of interest.

Subsequently these assumptions will be removed and the problems of dealing with uncertainty, inflation, choosing a discount rate and capital rationing dealt with.

13. Net present value (NPV)

The NPV method utilises discounting principles which should be familiar to management accounting students from earlier studies but for those whose knowledge is incomplete in this area the principles of discounting and the use of discount tables are reviewed in Appendix I of this chapter.

The NPV method calculates the present values of expected cash inflows and outflows (ie the process of discounting) and establishes whether in total the present value of cash inflows is greater than the present value of cash outflows. The formula is

$$NPV = \sum_{i=0}^{i=n} \frac{C_i}{(1+r)^i}$$

where C = the net cash flow in the period,

          i = the period number

          r = discount rate.

Where the discount rate is the cost of capital of the firm (described in para 22) the usual decision rule, given the assumptions in para 12, is that a *project is acceptable if it has a positive NPV*.

Example 3

An investment is being considered for which the net cash flows have been estimated as follows:

Year 0	Year 1	Year 2	Year 3	Year 4
–9,500	+3,000	+4,700	+4,800	+3,200

What is the NPV if the discount rate is 20%? Is the project acceptable?

Note: Conventional year end cash flows have been assumed, ie Year 0 means now, Year 1 means that the cash flow is received after 1 year and so on.

Solution

From Table A the discount factors are 0.833, 0.694, 0.579 and 0.482.

∴   NPV = − 9,500 + (0.833 × 3,000) + (0.694 × 4,700) + (0.579 × 4,800) + (0.482 × 3,200)

i.e.   NPV = + **£582**

and, given the assumptions contains in the basic DCF model the investment would be acceptable.

14. Meaning of NPV

If the NPV of a project is positive this can be interpreted as the potential increase in consumption made possible by the project valued in present day terms. This is illustrated by Table 1 based on Example 3 which shows the position if £9,500 is borrowed at 20% p.a. to finance the project on overdraft terms where interest is paid on the balance outstanding at the end of each year.

	Amount Owing b/fwd	+	Year's Interest	−	Year's Cash Flow	=	Balance o/s c/fwd
End year 1	9500	+	1900	−	3000	=	8400
End Year 2	8400	+	1680	−	4700	=	5380
End Year 3	5380	+	1076	−	4800	=	1656
End Year 4	1656	+	331	−	3200	=	1213

giving a final surplus of £1213

Table 1

This shows that if £9500 is borrowed at 20% the principal and interest could be repaid from the project cash flows leaving a cash balance at the end of Year 4 of £1213. This balance is known as the Net Terminal Value and has a present value of £584 (£1213 × 0.482) which, allowing for the approximations contained in three figure tables, is the NPV of Example 3.

15. Internal rate of return (IRR)

Alternative names for the IRR include: DCF yield, marginal efficiency of capital, trial and error method, discounted yield and the actuarial rate of return.

The IRR can be defined as the *discount rate which gives zero NPV*. Except by chance the IRR cannot be found directly; it can be found either by drawing a graph known as a present value profile or, more normally, by calculations involving linear interpolation. Both methods are illustrated below using the data from Example 3.

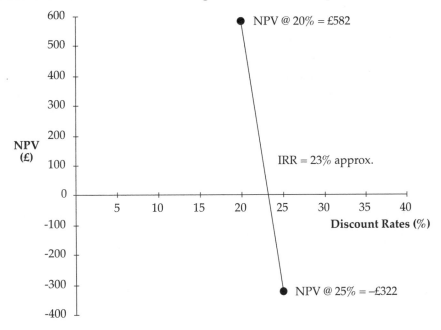

Figure 17.1 Present Value Profile

Notes on Figure 17.1

a) At least one discount rate must be chosen which gives a negative NPV so that the present value line crosses the horizontal axis.

b) The present value line crosses the axis at approximately 23% which is a close enough estimate for most practical purposes.

16. Finding the IRR by linear interpolation

Based on the data from Example 3 the IRR can be calculated as follows:

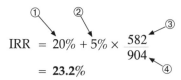

$$\text{IRR} = 20\% + 5\% \times \frac{582}{904}$$

$$= \mathbf{23.2\%}$$

where:

① = discount rate which gives a positive NPV. In this example 20% gives £582.

② = difference between ① and the rate which gives a negative NPV. In this example 25% − 20% = 5%.

③ = positive NPV at the discount rate chosen in ①. In this example it is £582.

④ = total range of NPV at the rates chosen. In this example +582 to −322 is a range of £904.

Notes:

a) A simple way of obtaining a rough estimate of the IRR is to take the reciprocal of the payback periods. With short payback periods as in Example 3 the method is a poor estimator.

b) As there is a non-linear relationship between discount rates and NPV, linear interpolation does not give a strictly accurate results. However, where the two discount rates that give positive and negative results are fairly close then the result is accurate enough for all practical and examination purposes.

17. Decision rule using IRR

Where the calculated IRR is greater than the company's cost of capital then the project is acceptable, given the assumptions already mentioned. In the majority of cases where there are conventional cash flows, ie an initial outflow followed by a series of inflows, then the IRR gives the same accept or reject decision as the NPV which is the case in Example 3 above. This does not follow for all cash flow patterns and the two techniques do not necessarily rank projects in the same order of attractiveness.

18. NPV and IRR compared

In many circumstances either of these decision criteria can be used successfully but there are differences in particular situations which are dealt with below.

a) *Accept/reject decisions*

Where projects can be considered independently of each other and where the cash flows are conventional then NPV and IRR give the same accept/reject decision.

	Accept project	*Reject project*
NPV	Positive NPV	Negative NPV
IRR	IRR above cost of capital	IRR below cost of capital

b) *Absolute and relative measures*

NPV is an absolute measure of the return on a project whereas IRR is a relative measure relating the size and timing of the cash flows to the initial investment. Thus the NPV reflects the scale of a project whereas the IRR does not.

Example 4

Assume a project has the following cash flows:

	Year 0	Year 5
Project X	–£20,000	+£40,241

$$\text{NPV @ 10\%} = \textbf{£4,990}$$
$$\text{IRR} = \textbf{15\%}$$

∴ Project acceptable by both methods – assuming 10% is the cost of capital.

Now assume that the project is scaled up by a factor of 10

	Year 0	Year 5
Project 10X	–£200,000	+£402,410

$$\text{NPV @ 10\%} = \textbf{£49,900}$$
$$\text{IRR} = \textbf{15\%}$$

The NPV method clearly discriminates between Project X and Project 10X whereas the IRR remains unchanged at 15%.

c) *Mutually exclusive projects*

An important class of projects is that concerned with mutually exclusive decisions, eg where only one of several alternative projects can be chosen. For example, where several alternative uses of the same piece of land are being considered, when one is chosen the other are automatically excluded.

Mutually exclusive decisions are commonly encountered and make it necessary to rank projects in order of attractiveness and to choose the most profitable. In such circumstances NPV and IRR may give conflicting rankings.

Example 5 (Mutually exclusive projects of differing scale)

A property company wishes to develop a site it owns. Three sizes of property are being considered and the costs and revenues are as follows:

	Year 0 Expenditure £m	Year 1 to perpetuity Rentals p.a. £m
Small development	2	0.6
Medium development	4	1
Large development	6	1.35

The cost of capital is 10% and it is required to rank the projects by NPV and IRR and to select the most profitable. The projects are mutually exclusive because the building of one size of development excludes the others.

Solution

	Expenditure £m	P.V. of rentals £m	NPV £m	IRR %
Small	2	6	4	30
Medium	4	10	6	25
Large	6	13.5	7.5	22.5

The ranking obtained by NPV and IRR differ and in such circumstances the NPV ranking is preferred (ie large development in this example) because it leads to the greatest increase in wealth for the company.

Although safer and simpler to rank by NPV, IRR can be used by adopting an incremental approach and comparing the incremental IRR at each increment with the cost of capital. Example 5 is reworked using this approach.

	Incremental Expenditure £m	Incremental Rental £m	Incremental IRR %
Stage 1 (small)	2	0.6	30
Stage 2 (medium-small)	2	0.4	20
Stage 3 (large-medium)	2	0.35	17.5

It will be seen that the IRR of each successive stage, although declining, is greater than the 10% cost of capital so that each successive increment is worthwhile. Although this method leads to the correct conclusion it is cumbersome and the simpler, more direct NPV method is preferable.

Example 6 (Mutually exclusive projects, same scale)

Two mutually exclusive investments have cash flows as follows:

	Year 0	Year 1	Year 2	Year 3
Project A	−24000	+8000	+12000	+16000
Project B	−24000	+16000	+10000	+8000

The cost of capital is 10%.

The NPV and IRR of these projects is as follows:

	NPV @ 10%	IRR
		%
Project A	+5200	20.65
Project B	+4812	22.8

Thus it will be seen that the rankings differ and, assuming that 10% is the appropriate discount rate, the ranking given by the NPV, ie Project A being preferred, gives the maximum wealth to the company at the cost of capital.

Note: The conflict in ranking shown is but a reflection of the differing time profile of the project cash flows. Such time profiles produce different NPV rankings using different discount rates; for example, the NPV's of the above projects at 20% discount rate are £256 and £900 respectively, giving a B – A ranking instead of the A – B ranking at 10%.

19. Non-conventional cash flows (the multiple rate problem)

The projects considered so far have had conventional cash flows, ie an initial outflow followed by a series of inflows. Where the cash flows vary from this they are termed non-conventional. The following are examples.

Example 7 *(Non-Conventional Cash-flow Patterns)*

	Year 0	Year 1	Year 2
Project X	–2000	+4700	–2750
Project Y	+2000	–4000	+4000

Project X has 2 outflows and is thus non-conventional

Project Y has an outflow in a year's time instead of now and is thus non-conventional.

When a project has non-conventional cash flows it may have

i)   one IRR   ii)   multiple IRR's   iii)   no IRR

Multiple Rates

If the present value profile for Project X in Example 7 is drawn it can be seen that it is a multiple IRR project having two IRR's, at 10% and 25%.

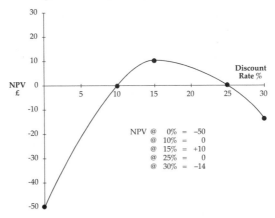

Figure 17.2 Present Value Profile of Project X

No IRR

Project Y in Example 7 above is an example of a project where it is not possible to calculate a real rate of return.

To be able to calculate a real IRR it is necessary to solve for i in the following expression:

$$+2000 - \frac{4000}{(1+i)^1} + \frac{4000}{(1+i)^2} = 0$$

Solving for i produces $i = \sqrt{(-1)}$ which is not a real number.

Where there are non-conventional cash flow patterns which produce multiple IRR's or no real IRR the use of IRR is not recommended.

The NPV method gives clear, unambiguous results whatever the cash flow pattern.

Project X above has positive NPV's at discount rates between 10% and 25% and negative NPV's at lower and higher rates. Project Y has a positive NPV at any discount rate.

20. Summary of NPV and IRR comparison

a) NPV is technically superior to IRR and is simpler to calculate.

b) Where cash-flow patterns are non-conventional there may be nil or several internal rates of return making the IRR impossible to apply.

c) NPV is superior for ranking investments in order of attractiveness.

d) With conventional cash flow patterns both methods give the same accept or reject decision.

e) Where discount rates are expected to differ over the life of the project such variations can be readily incorporated into NPV calculations, but not in those for the IRR.

f) Notwithstanding the technical advantages of NPV over IRR, IRR is widely used in practice so that it is essential that students are aware of its inherent limitations.

21. Excess present value index (EVPI) or profitability index

The EVPI is merely a variant of the basic NPV method and is the ratio of the NPV of a project to the initial investment

$$\text{i.e. } \textbf{EVPI} = \frac{\textbf{NPV}}{\textbf{Initial Investment}}$$

Thus the index is a measure of relative and not absolute profitability. Because of this it suffers from the same general criticisms when used for ranking purposes as the IRR. The EVPI is not suitable for ranking mutually exclusive projects, but because it is a measure of relative profitability it can be used where there are a number of divisible projects (ie fractional parts of projects may be undertaken) which cannot all be implemented because of a shortage of capital in the current period.

In such circumstances the projects can be ranked in order of their EVPI's and implemented in order of attractiveness until the capital available is exhausted. If, however, the projects being considered covered two or more periods where funds were limited then the EVPI could not be used. In general the EVPI is of limited usefulness and the use of NPV is considered safer.

22. Cost of capital

So far in this chapter the discount rate or the target rate of return has been assumed. Obviously in practice the rate is not automatically provided and it is necessary to estimate or calculate some appropriate discount rate. This rate is known as the *cost of capital*. The calculation of the cost of capital is a complex subject involving many aspects of financing and company financial structures. Inevitably there are many subjective judgements to be made even in the most sophisticated calculations and there is empirical evidence that many businessmen estimate the cost of capital in an intuitive manner without too much regard for theoretical niceties.

In spite of this it is necessary for accountancy students to be aware of some of the more generally accepted theoretical background to cost of capital calculations. Two possible approaches to this problem are discussed in this book, one based on the estimated costs of the elements which make up the overall supply of capital known as the *Weighted Average Cost of Capital* and a more theoretical view based on the relationship in the capital market between risk and return known as the *Capital Asset Pricing Model*.

23. The weighted average cost of capital approach

Companies, particularly large ones, are complex entities and are funded from a large number of sources. These range from long term sources such as equity capital to short term sources such as bank overdrafts. They also range from those with a fixed contractual rate of interest such as debentures and preference shares to those with no specified cost such as ordinary shares. It is this diversity which complicates the situation, but fortunately there are two generally accepted principles which help to clarify the situation somewhat. These are that long term funds only should be included in the cost of capital calculation and that the cost of capital should be representative of the overall pool of long term capital.

a) Long term funds only. The reasoning behind this is that investment appraisals are essentially concerned with long-term investments and short-term finance, for example, bank overdrafts, is not generally available for these investments. Short-term finance such as bank overdrafts and hire purchase provide valuable ancillary forms of finance and can be taken into account in the cash flows of the project, ie as changes in the working capital requirements or as the cash payments under the hire purchase agreements.

b) Representative Cost of Pool of long-term Capital. It is generally considered incorrect to identify the particular source of capital with particular projects. It is incorrect to discount one project, financed by an issue of debentures, at the cost of those debentures and some other project at an imputed cost of equity capital. The reasons for this are that the coupon cost of the debentures almost certainly does not reflect the overall impact on the company's cost of capital, and also because the matching of projects with particular sources of funds is very much a random matter. What is more important is that projects earn at least the average cost of capital of the pool of long-term capital resources available to the firm. This cost of capital is known as the weighted average cost of capital (WACC).

Note: The above principles are not absolute rules and differences exist in practice and in examination questions. A typical variation is for a regularly occurring bank overdraft (normally considered a short term method of finance) to be included in the pool of capital resources available for investment purposes and thus the cost of the bank over-draft would need to be included in the weighted average cost of capital calculation.

The WACC is found by calculating the average of the cost of each component of the firm's finance (equity, preference, debentures) weighted according to its proportionate share of the total pool of capital available. The weighting normally used is the current market valuation of the shares and loan stock, not the nominal book values.

Example 8

Acropolis Ltd has the following long term sources of capital:

10 million £1 Ordinary shares with a current market price of £1.40

2 million £1 Preference shares with a current market price of 92.5p

£7.5 million Debenture Stock with a current market price of £90 per £100 nominal value.

The individual component costs have been estimated at 16%, 12% and 8% respectively.

Calculate the WACC using market value weighting.

Solution

Component	Market Value		Proportion	Individual Cost	Weighted Cost %	
Ord. Shares	10m × £1.4 =	£14m	62%	16%	0.62 × 16% =	9.92
Pref. Shares	2m × 0.925 =	£1.85m	8%	12%	0.08 × 12% =	0.96
Debentures	7.5m × 0.9 =	£6.75m	30%	8%	0.3 × 8% =	2.4
		£22.6m total			Total =	13.28%

∴ Weighted average cost of capital = **13.28%**.

In the example above, the individual component costs were provided but normally these have to be estimated or calculated. The major factors to be considered in this process are discussed below.

24. The cost of components of WACC

Preference shares and debentures have known costs associated with them, either the dividend rate of the shares or the fixed rate of interest attached to the debentures. Accordingly, having due regard to the different taxation treatment of debentures and preferences shares, an estimate of their costs can be made relatively easily. The position is more complicated with ordinary shares or equity and many more assumptions are required.

Debentures and preference shares are dealt with first followed by discussion of the problems associated with estimating the cost of equity.

25. Fixed interest capital (debentures and preference shares)

Fixed interest sources of funds, debentures and preference shares, may be irredeemable or redeemable at a given date. Interest paid on debentures, unlike preference divi-dends, is an allowable charge against corporation tax. These factors give rise to four possible situations shown below.

	Irredeemable	Redeemable
Preference Shares	Case 1	Case 2
Debentures	Case 3	Case 4

Except for the taxation deduction Case 1 and Case 3 are identical and so are Case 2 and Case 4.

26. Irredeemable sources (Cases 1 and 3)

The cost of a perpetuity is:

$$r = \frac{a}{v} = 100\%$$

where r = rate of interest or dividend

a = annual income

v = current market value.

This simple formula is used in the examples below.

Example 9 (Case 1)

A company finds that its £1 nominal value 9% Preference shares are currently quoted at 82p. What is the effective cost?

Solution

$$= \frac{a}{v} \times 100\%$$

$$= \frac{0.09}{0.82} \times 100\%$$

$$= 10.97\% \text{ say } 11\%$$

Example 10 (Case 3)

Assume the same data as in Example 9 except that debentures are involved and the corporation tax rate is 55%.

Solution

The after tax cost of interest = $r(1 - c)$

where c = corporation tax rate

∴ Based on Example 9 data and 55% corporation tax:

After tax cost of interest $= 11(1 - 0.55)$

$$= 4.95$$

$$= \text{say } 5\%$$

27. Redeemable sources of capital

The cost of redeemable debentures and preference shares consists of two elements.

a) The costs of servicing, by interest or dividends, the loan stock for a finite number of years and,

345

b) The redemption costs at the end of the stated number of years.

The annual servicing costs can be considered as an annuity and, if debenture interest is involved, are an allowable charge against corporation tax. The redemption costs at the end of the period are not tax deductible so must be included gross in the cost of capital calculation.

Example 11 (Case 2)

Assume the same data as in Example 9 except that the stock is redeemed at par (£1) after 20 years. No taxation is involved because the stock is in the form of preference shares.

The cost to the company is the discount rate (x) which equates the future income and amount of the redemption to the current purchase price, ie

$$0.09 \times A_{\overline{n}|r} + 1.0 \times \frac{1}{(1+x)^{20}} - 0.82 = 0$$

(with labels ① over $A_{\overline{n}|r}$, ② over $\frac{1}{(1+x)^{20}}$, ③ over 0.82)

Notes:

① = the present value of a 20 year annuity of the 9p income at $x\%$ (Table B)

② = the present value of the amount redeemed (£1) after 20 years at $x\%$ (Table A)

③ = the current price.

To find the value of x we try a given percentage in the equation above. Try 12%.

$$0.09 \times 7.47 + 0.104 - 0.82 = -0.0437$$

∴ 12% is too high. Try 10%.

$$0.09 \times 8.514 + 0.149 - 0.82 = +0.0953$$

∴ 10% is too low.

As usual the value is found by linear interpolation:

$$x = 10 + 2\left(\frac{0.0935}{0.1390}\right)$$

$$= 11.37\%$$

Example 12 (Case 4)

Once again the position is as Example 11 except that debentures are involved and thus the taxation aspects must be considered. Because of the differing tax treatments of the two elements which make up the total cost to the firm (ie interest – allowable against tax, redeemable element – not allowable) it is necessary to consider the elements separately.

Effective interest rate for 10 years of interest payments at 9% nominal when purchased at 82p is found as follows:

$$0.82 = 0.09 \times 20 \text{ year annuity factor at } x\%$$

But: $\dfrac{0.82}{0.09} = 9.11$

and looking along the 20 year annuity line the rate will be seen to be between 8% and 10% (ie between 9.818 and 8.514). This rate can be approximated as follows:

$$8\% + 2\%\left(\frac{0.60}{1.304}\right) = 8.92\%, \text{ say } 9\%$$

∴ After tax interest rate $= 9(1 - 0.55)\% = 4\%$

The redemption yield for a 20 year debenture paying a 9% coupon rate redeemable at par is made up of the interest payments over the 20 years plus the amount received at redemption, ie 11.37% as calculated in Example 11.

As the interest payments account for 9% of this, the extra non tax allowable element is 2.37% (11.37 − 9).

∴ the overall, net, after tax cost to the firm is $4\% + 2.37\% = 6.37\%$ say $6\frac{1}{2}\%$

28. Equity capital

Although of great importance in the financial structures of most organisations equity capital does not have a known, fixed rate of dividend associated with it but obviously it does have a cost. There is general acceptance that the returns to equity should be higher than the returns to fixed interest investments such as debentures, and also that there is a relationship between the returns to equity shareholders and the risk class of the company – the higher the risk, the higher the expected return.

One approach to the estimation of the cost of equity is the use of the *Gordon growth model*, sometimes termed the *dividend valuation model*.

29. Gordon growth model

This is a theory of share price movements based on the assumption that the sole determinant of the price of shares (and thus the return received by the investor) is the present value of the anticipated future stream of dividends. The model is based on numerous assumptions the major ones of which are:

a) Investors act rationally with regard to future returns.

b) Investors all have the same time preference which can be evaluated by discounting at the investor's personal discount rate.

c) There is no inflation or taxation and that the future is known with certainty by all investors.

Clearly these assumptions may make the model totally invalid in practice, but the application of the theory may be a useful starting point in the estimation of the cost of equity. Two further assumptions frequently made for examination purposes which considerably simplify the calculations, involved are that either constant dividends are paid each year to perpetuity, or that there is a constant compound growth rate of dividends to perpetuity, ie the dividend each year increases by the same percentage. The formulae for the dividend valuation model are as follows:

i) Constant dividends to perpetuity

$$i = \frac{d}{v}$$

ii) Constant compound growth rate of dividends to perpetuity

$$i = \frac{d(1 + g)}{v} + g$$

where: v = current market value for share

          d = dividend per share

          i = personal discount rate

          g = growth rate of dividends.

Example 13

Pitprop Ltd has just paid a dividend of 35p on its ordinary shares which are currently priced at £3.20. What is the investor's personal discount rate if:

a)   dividends are expected to remain constant?

b)   dividends are expected to grow at 15% compound p.a.?

Solution

a) $i = \dfrac{d}{v}$

$$= \frac{0.35}{3.20}$$

$$= 10.93\% \text{ say } \mathbf{11\%}$$

b) $i = \dfrac{d(1 + g)}{v} + g$

$$= \frac{0.35\,(1 + 0.15)}{3.20} + 0.15$$

$$= 27.58\%, \text{ say } \mathbf{27\tfrac{1}{2}\%}$$

Notes:

a)   The investor's personal discount rate is known as the *Cost of Equity Capital.*

b)   With constant dividends it will be recognised that the cost of equity capital is the dividend yield.

c)   If a company was entirely equity financed, as postulated in the basic Gordon model, then the cost of capital to be used for discounting should be the cost of equity as outlined above and thus the NPV of projects is directly related to their impact on share prices as shown in Example 14.

d)   Estimates of g, the growth factor, may be based on past growth rates of dividends or on the expected results of current and future investment opportunities and changes in the financing strategies of the firm.

Example 14

Wye Ltd is financed entirely by equity and has 5000 £1 shares in issue which have a market price of £4 each. From existing projects a constant dividend of 50p per share has been and can continue to be paid. A new project is being considered which has an outlay now of £2000 and which is expected to generate £650 p.a. cash flows to perpetuity. Assuming that the finance for the new project is raised by a right issue and that all project proceeds will continue to be paid out as dividends, calculate:

a) the new dividends per share

b) the new market value per share assuming a 2 : 5 rights issue

c) the overall gain to the shareholders.

Solution

Shareholders personal discount rate (cost of equity) $= \dfrac{50p}{£4}$

$$= 0.125$$
$$= 12\tfrac{1}{2}\%$$

a) New dividend per share $= \dfrac{\text{old dividend payment + project proceeds}}{\text{new number of shares}}$

$$= \dfrac{£(5000 \times 0.50) + 650}{7000}$$

$$= \textbf{45p/share}$$

b) New market value per share $= \dfrac{\text{new dividend}}{\text{cost of equity}}$

$$= \dfrac{45}{0.125}$$

$$= \textbf{£3.60}$$

c) Overall gain to shareholders

Project NPV $= \dfrac{650}{0.125} - 2000$

$$= \textbf{£3,200}$$

which is reflected in the changed market valuation of the company thus:

		£	£
Net Market Valuation = 7000 × £3.60 =			25,200
less Old Market Valuation	20,000		
Cost of Rights Issue	2,000		22,000
Gain to Shareholders			3,200

Note: The actual terms of the rights issue whether 2:5. 1:2 or whatever, are irrelevant because the overall valuation and the amount to be contributed by shareholders is unaffected. The project NPV is obtained by calculating the present value of a £650 p.a. perpetuity and deducting the original investment of £2,000.

30. New issues, rights issues and retained earnings

There are various forms in which equity finance may appear. These may be public issues to the market, rights issues to existing shareholders and the use of retained earnings which are an alternative to the payment of dividends. In general, some estimate of the cost of each source could be based on the 'growth model' but there are detail differences. For example, both rights issues and public issues incur issue costs which may be considerable.

On the other hand, retained earnings have no issue expenses and reduce the tax liability on income for shareholders. However, if the retained earnings can only be obtained by reduction in anticipated dividends then there may be a fall in the share price and a loss of confidence in the firm.

In general all types of equity are relatively expensive forms of finance compared with, for example, the tax allowable interest on debentures.

31. Gearing and the WACC

The relationship between fixed interest capital sources (debentures and preferences shares) and equity sources is known as the *gearing* of the firm (leverage in American terminology) and is usually expressed as percentage. Various gearing ratio formulae exist. Typical examples are:

$$\text{Capital Gearing} = \frac{\text{Fixed interest capital}}{\text{Fixed interest capital} + \text{Equity capital}}$$

The fixed interest capital and the equity capital may be expressed either in terms of Book Values or Market Values.

$$\text{Income Gearing} = \frac{\text{Fixed interest charges}}{\text{Operating profit before fixed interest charges and taxation}}$$

Because many variants of the gearing ratio exist students must take particular care when comparing gearing ratios of different companies that they are calculated on the same basis.

32. Effects of changes in gearing

The general effect of increases in the gearing ratio is to increase the risks of both equity and fixed interest investors but particularly those of the equity shareholder, because of the fixed interest entitlement whether or not profits are made or whether profits are high or low. Thus, as the gearing ratio increases, holders of both equity and fixed interest capital are likely to require higher returns to compensate for the increased vulnerability of their dividends or interest. What gearing ratio to aim for, that is, the optimum financial structure of the company, is a matter of some debate with two contrasting positions, what has become known as the 'traditional view' and the Modigliani-Miller hypothesis.

33. The traditional view of gearing and WACC

Because fixed interest investors historically have not required such a high return as equity investors, making a company more highly geared by introducing fixed interest capital, such as debentures and preferences shares, lowers the WACC at least in the early stages. As the gearing increases equity holders start to demand a higher return to compensate for the increased risks involved and at even higher gearing ratios the fixed interest investors start to demand higher returns so that eventually the WACC starts to rise. This movement results in a U shaped WACC curve indicating that for a given company there is some optimum mix of debt and equity. This is summarised in Figure 17.3.

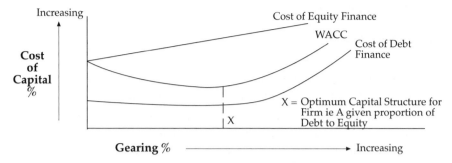

Figure 17.3 Traditional View of Gearing and WACC

34. The modigliani-miller hypothesis (MM)

The essential core of the MM view is that firms of the same size with the same operating risks will have the same total value and hence WACC regardless of their individual gearing ratios. Their view that the proportion of debt to equity does not affect the WACC results in a straight line WACC rather than a U shaped curve as in the traditional view. The MM view is shown in Figure 17.4.

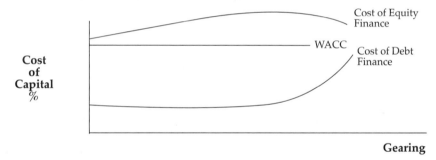

Figure 17.4 Modigliani Miller View of Gearing and WACC

To obtain a straight line WACC, MM advance two basic arguments.

a) The issue of more debt causes the return required by equity shareholders to rise so that the advantages of using the cheaper debt finance is exactly offset. This process they suggest works by investors altering their own personal gearing through personal borrowing, and switching investments. This process is known as *arbitrage*.

b) At high levels of gearing, risk seeking investors will buy shares for the first time.

The MM view is based on a number of assumptions the major ones of which are that there is no taxation and capital markets are perfect. In practice the market is not perfect and taxation does exist which has the effect of reducing the cost of debt finance substantially. Since the early 1960's when MM first published their thesis much academic discussion and empirical research has taken place to verify or disprove their arguments. So far this has been inconclusive.

From a student's point of view the importance of the MM view is that it prevents too ready acceptance of the apparently common-sense 'traditional view'. It should be clear that a broad view of the cost of fixed interest capital should include not only the effective rate of interest calculations as shown above but also the effect on the returns required by equity investors.

35. WACC – a summary

The WACC appears to be a commonly used method of obtaining the discounting rate for use in investment appraisal but it must be recognised simply as an operational tool with a number of subjective elements and theoretical limitations.

If the WACC is based simply on historical capital structures then its use can be severely criticised because it is the anticipated future structures that are relevant particularly if the capital for the proposed project makes a significant change in the financial structure of the company, for example by changing the gearing ratio. In general, WACC would seem to be more appropriate when the proposed investment is of a similar nature to existing operations so that the general business risk is unchanged. WACC makes the implicit assumption that the two types of risk with which the company is concerned, (ie business risks caused by trading and operations and financial risks which are a function of gearing) remain unchanged.

Although there is an accounting logic to WACC, whereby the average value of the various elements is used, it will be apparent that the estimated cost of an important element, the equity based sources, is dependent on the validity of the dividend valuation model with its inherent assumptions and estimates, eg the estimate for g and the assumption that dividends are the sole determinant of share price.

These and other problems lead a number of writers, eg Williams and Gordon and others, to doubt if the cost of capital can be measured in the real world. Whilst such authorities are no doubt correct, that is little comfort to the practising management accountant faced with the task of deciding upon a realistic discounting rate. It is because of such realities that the WACC is often used as a base valuation with appropriate adjustments made for such matters as the risk elements caused by the project, future interest and taxation changes and other practical considerations.

36. Capital asset pricing model (CAPM)

The CAPM is an alternative approach to the problem of measuring the cost of capital. The model attempts to measure the relationship between risk and return in the capital market. Underlying the model is the assumption that the return to an investor is made up of two parts: a risk free rate of interest to which is added a premium to cater for the particular level of risk in a given security. Where the risk is greater so is the additional premium. The premium is calculated by using what is known as the β (Beta) coefficient.

The beta-coefficient is a measure of the volatility of the individual security's returns relative to market returns and thus, when a risk-return profile for the market is calculated, the cost of capital for a given company can be established. Assuming that such a value is available, it can be used as the discount rate being a fair approximation of opportunity cost representing as it does the market's expected rate of return for shares in its risk class.

The CAPM was developed as an aid to optimal portfolio selection whereby, according to the attitude to risk of the investor, a capital market line would be established such that all efficient portfolios (ie preferred trade-offs between risk and return) lie on the capital market line.

From the capital market line the security market line is developed which relates to individual securities and firms. From this line, using the Beta coefficients, an estimate is made of the cost of capital.

Although this process is involved and somewhat theoretical it is an attempt to obtain an objective estimate of the required return of shareholders and seeks to measure the very real trade-off that exists between risk and return in the capital market. Like all theoretical models the CAPM incorporates numerous assumptions which may limit its application in practical situations. Some of the major assumptions are:-

a) Investors are wealth maximisers who base their choice of portfolios on the mean and variance (ie the measure of risk) of the returns expected from the security.

b) All investors can borrow or lend unlimited amounts at a given risk free rate of interest.

c) All investors have identical subjective estimates of the return and variance of return (riskiness) of a particular security.

d) There are no transaction costs and no taxes.

e) All investors are price takers. This means that no investor operates on a scale large enough to have any significant influence on the price of a security.

Note: These are restrictive assumptions and the CAPM can be criticised on these grounds but it should be remembered that some criticisms can be made against ALL investment appraisal techniques.

37. Using CAPM to estimate the cost of equity

The steps involved in using CAPM to estimate the cost of equity capital are as follows:

1. Estimate the market parameters.

   That is the risk-free rate of return, the expected return on the market and the variance of the market return.

2. Estimate the firm's beta coefficient.

   This is based on an historical analysis of the shares performance, ie the prices, price changes, dividend yields, variances of return and covariances with market returns over as long a period as possible. Risk-less securities have beta coefficients equal to nil; an average security has a beta value of 1.0; lower risk securities have values less than 1 and relatively higher risk securities have beta values greater than 1.

3. Estimate the cost of equity using the market parameters and the firm's beta coefficient.

   Figure 17.5 provides a representation of the process.

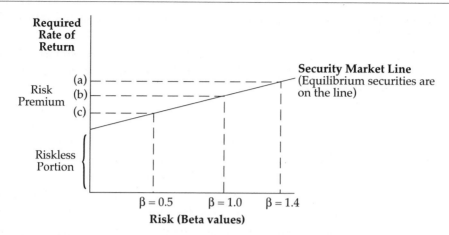

Figure 17.5 Security market line showing trade-off between risk and return

Notes on Figure 17.5: Three possible beta values have been shown which result in three estimates of the required rate of return.

a) Beta value 1.4 – higher than average return and risk

b) Beta value 1.0 – security with an average return and risk

c) Beta value 0.5 – lower than average return and risk.

The intercept with y axis is the riskless rate of return and is generally taken as the return on government stocks.

The appropriate equation for establishing the expected return is as follows:

$$R_a = R_f + (R_m - R_f)\beta$$

where: R_a = the expected return on the security

R_f = the risk free interest rate

R_m = the expected return on a market portfolio

β = the beta coefficient which measures the volatility of the security's return relative to market return.

For example, if the risk free interest rate is 9%, the market return 13% and the beta coefficient is 1.4 then:

$$R_a = 9 + (13 - 9)1.4$$
$$= \mathbf{18.2\%}$$

which would be the cost of capital estimate according to the Capital Asset Pricing Model.

Note: The β coefficient is found by dividing the covariance of the return on the new investment and the return on the market portfolio by the variance of the market return,

$$\text{ie } \beta = \frac{\text{Cov } (R_a.R_m)}{\text{Variance } (R_m)}$$

38. Life cycle costing – a definition

Life cycle costing or terotechnology can be defined as:

' The practice of obtaining over their life-times, the best use of physical assets at the lowest total cost to the entity (terotechnology). This is achieved through a combination of management, financial, engineering and other disciplines'   *Terminology*

The concept of terotechnology was originally publicised by the Department of Industry with the aim of getting industry to take account of the total cost of acquiring, operating and eventually disposing of an asset over its whole life rather than merely concentrate on one aspect of cost, that of acquisition. Of course enlightened management have always taken the long view and have avoided the trap of making undue economies at the purchasing stage to the detriment of operating and maintenance costs later on. This is false economy but is all too prevalent. The original concept addressed only physical assets (see definition above) but the more modern view is that the principles of life cycle costing should apply equally to products and services as well as conventional fixed assets.

39. Typical life cycle costs

In general all costs incurred over the full life cycle of an asset from the original idea for purchase or design through to disposal or withdrawal from the market are life cycle costs.

Examples include:

a) *Acquisition costs*

  ❐ if made by the firm these might include research and development costs, design costs, consultancy fees, testing, production and so on.

  ❐ if purchased; purchase price, any purchasing costs, testing, installation, etc.

b) *Operating costs*

  including; servicing and maintenance, training costs, cost of standby facilities, energy costs, overhead costs attributable to asset, spare parts, warehousing and inventory costs for spares, etc.

c) *Retirement or disposal costs*

  including; dismantling and salvage costs, site reclamation (if applicable), any other form of termination costs.

At any of the stages there may be fees for technical services or costs to bring the equipment up to current legal standards. Examples include the costs of eliminating excess noise, fumes or noxious discharges and waste products and of meeting more stringent safety regulations.

40. Optimising life cycle costs

It will be apparent that the aim is to minimise the overall costs over the asset's life cycle. This will be achieved best by considering the impact of, and interactions between, all costs prior to acquisition rather than considering the elements in a piecemeal fashion. All too often the initial capital costs are considered in isolation in a conventional project appraisal and the budgeting of maintenance and operating costs are considered separately after the asset has been acquired. If the interactions between the two are studied it may well be cost effective to incur higher initial capital costs to reduce later servicing and maintenance charges and to ensure more trouble free production.

To keep life cycle costs to a minimum, apart from initial acquisition costs, three areas need close examination.

Utilisation: What is the proportion of time that the asset is capable of functioning or producing to the required standard?

Maintainability: How easy is the asset to service and maintain and what is the availability and cost of parts?

Disposal: What will be the costs and problems of disposal or destruction?

Each of these areas requires technical, engineering, scientific and production expertise; they cannot be assessed by accountants alone. If any of these vital areas are overlooked it is unlikely that life cycle costs will be minimised. As an example of the problems encountered, consider the difficulties and costs faced by the Nuclear Industry in decommissioning obsolete reactors and disposing of nuclear waste.

An important point for accountants to remember is that reports and cost analyses should be related to the variable length of an asset's life cycle and not to the conventional reporting periods of months and years commonly encountered. Terotechnology does not involve any new accounting techniques or principles; rather it is a way of integrating types of information in order to examine a problem in its entirety.

41. Example – life cycle costs

A firm with a 10% cost of capital is considering the purchase of two machine tools, X and Y. Both can produce the same component at identical rates per working hour and the relevant data on the machines is as follows:

	Machine X	Machine Y
Capital Cost	£100,000	£160,000
Operating costs per working hour		
Energy	£3	£5
Consumables	£6	£8
Variable overheads	£6	£7
Maintenance Costs		
Service intervals	12 p.a.	10 p.a.
Cost of Services	£1000	£800
Random breakdowns	3 p.a.	1 p.a.
Cost of breakdowns	£2000	£3000
Expected Availability		
(working hours per annum)	1500	2000
Contribution from production per hour		
(excluding mc. costs)	£50	£50
Expected life	5 years	5 years
Net salvage value at the end of year 5	£10,000	£25,000

Solution

		Machine X		Machine Y	
	Gross contribution/hour		£50		£50
less	Operating costs		£15		£20
	Contribution/hour		£35		£30
	Hours available		1500		2000
		£	£	£	£
	Total contribution p.a.		52,500		60,000
less	Maintenance				
	Service	12000		8000	
	Breakdowns	6000	18,000	3000	11,000
	Net contribution p.a.		£34,500		£49,000

$\therefore$ PV of X $= -100,000 + 3.791 \times 34,500 + 0.621 \times 10,000 =$ **£37,000**

PV of Y $= -160,000 + 3.791 \times 49,000 + 0.621 \times 25,000 =$ **£41,284**

Thus machine Y would be preferred because, although having a greater capital cost, it is available for more hours per year for production, it has lower servicing costs and a greater resale value. Over the whole life cycle it is more cost effective.

42. Summary

a) Investment decisions are long-run decisions where consumption and investment opportunities are balanced over time.

b) The decision to invest is based on many factors including: the investor's beliefs in the future, the alternatives available and his attitude to risk.

c) The 'traditional' investment appraisal techniques are the accounting rate of return and payback. Payback is shown by recent surveys to be the most widely used technique.

d) Payback is the number of period's cash flows to recoup the original investment. The project chosen is the one with the shortest payback period.

e) Discounted Cash Flow (DCF) techniques use cash flows rather than profits and take account of the time value of money.

f) The formula for Net Present Value is:

$$\text{NPV} = \sum_{i=0}^{i=n} \frac{C_i}{(1+r)^i}$$

and given the assumption of the basic model, a project is acceptable if it has a positive NPV.

g) NPV can be interpreted as the potential increase in consumption made possible by the project valued in present day terms.

h) Internal Rate of Return (IRR) is the discount rate which gives zero NPV and can be found graphically or by linear interpolation.

i) With conventional projects IRR and NPV give the same accept or reject decision. NPV is an absolute measure whereas IRR is a relative one.

j) NPV is a more appropriate measure for choosing between mutually exclusive projects and in general is technically superior to IRR.

k) The discount rate used in DCF calculations is known as the cost of capital.

l) The Weighted Average Cost of Capital (WACC) approach is based on the theory that long term funds only should be included in the cost of capital which should be representative of the overall pool of capital available.

m) The WACC is found by weighting (according to market values) each of the component costs of the sources of capital.

n) Fixed interest funds such as debentures and preferences shares have known costs associated with them but equity does not.

o) One approach to estimating the cost of capital is by the use of the Gordon growth or dividend valuation model.

p) The dividend valuation model postulates that the sole determinant of the price of shares is the present value of the anticipated future stream of dividends.

q) Changes in gearing (the relationship between fixed interest and equity capital) is deemed to affect the WACC according to the 'traditional' view whereas the Modigliani-Miller (MM) hypothesis states that the proportion of debt to equity does not affect the WACC.

r) The Capital Asset Pricing Model (CAPM) attempts to measure the relationship between risk and return in the capital market and is an alternative approach to the measurement of the cost of equity capital. The CAPM, like all investment appraisal techniques, has numerous assumptions.

s) Using the CAPM involves: estimating the market parameters and the firm's beta coefficient and using these values to calculate the expected return on the security using the formula

$$R_a = R_f + (R_m - R_f)\beta$$

t) Life cycle costing or terotechnology aims to obtain the best use of an asset over the whole life taking into account acquisition, maintenance, operating and disposal costs.

43. Points to note

a) It is arguable that the existence of a stream of potentially worthwhile investment opportunities is of far greater importance to the firm than the particular appraisal method used.

b) A number of surveys of capital budgeting practices have shown that a majority use Payback as an appraisal method, often in conjunction with other techniques. This would seem to suggest that much of the academic preoccupation with refining measurement techniques may be misplaced.

c) Successful investment appraisal is entirely dependent on the accuracy of cost and revenue estimates. No appraisal technique can overcome significant inaccuracies in this area.

d) The CAPM was developed to assist in portfolio management which has the general objective of maintaining an efficiently diversified portfolio of investments. This means studying the relationship between risk and return in the market place. The research has indicated that risk consists of two elements; systematic or undiversifiable risk, ie the volatility or movements of the market as a whole, and unsystematic or diversifiable risk, ie the volatility of operations and investments specific to the firm. This is the type of risk measured by the beta coefficient.

Additional reading

Principle of Corporate Finance; *Brealy and Myers* – McGraw Hill

Economics of capital budgeting; *Bromwich* – Pitman

Capital Investment and Financial Decisions; *Levy & Sarnat* – Prentice Hall

Investment Appraisal and Financing Decisions; *Lumby* – Van Nostrand Reinhold

Capital budgeting in the 1990's; *Pike & Wolfe* – CIMA.

Self review questions

1. Why are investment decisions important? (2)
2. Define the accounting rate of return and give its advantages and disadvantages. (4)
3. What is payback and what is the normal decision rule using payback? (6)
4. Why are cash flows used in DCF calculations and not accounting profits? (9)
5. What cash flows should be included in the appraisal? (10)
6. Why has money a time value? (11)
7. Define NPV and state the basic formula. (13)
8. What is Net Terminal Value? (14)
9. What is the Internal Rate of Return and how is it calculated? (15 and 16)
10. What are the major differences between NPV and IRR? (18)
11. What is the multiple rate problem? (19)
12. What is the EVPI or Profitability Index and when can it be used effectively? (21)
13. What are the two general principles underlying the WACC approach? (23)
14. Given the individual element costs how is the WACC calculated? (23)
15. What is the difference in the calculation of the cost of debentures and preference shares? (25)
16. How is the cost calculated of redeemable sources of capital? (27)
17. What is the Gordon growth model and what are its major assumptions? (29)
18. What is gearing and what is the 'traditional' view of gearing and the WACC? (31-33)
19. What is the MM hypothesis? (34)
20. What is the CAPM? (36)
21. Describe the steps in using the CAPM in estimating the cost of equity capital. (37)
22. What is terotechnology? (38)

Appendix to Chapter 17

Review of discounting formulae and the use of discount tables

1. Compound interest

The principles of compound interest form the basis of discounting and annuity calculation so must be understood.

The basic compounding formula is

$$S = P(1 + r)^n$$

where S = a sum arising in the future

     r = rate of interest usually expressed as an interest rate per annum, eg 10%. It appears in the formula as a decimal, ie 10% = 0.10

     n = number of interest bearing periods, usually expressed in years

Example 1

How much will £5000 amount to at 10% compound over 6 years?

$$S = £5000 (1 + 0.10)^6$$
$$= £5000 \times 1.772$$
$$= £8860$$

Note: The compound interest factor $(1 + 0.10)^6$, can be found using a calculator or logarithms but tables are more normally used. Look up in Table D under 10% for 6 years and the factor is 1.772.

Example 2

How long will it take for a given sum to treble itself at 17% p.a. compound?

i.e. to find n such that: $3 = 1(1 + 0.17)^n$

Table D can be used as a shortcut solution method. Look under 17% to find the factor closest to 3. This will be found to be 3.001 opposite 7 years.

∴ a given sum will treble itself in almost exactly 7 years at 17% p.a. compound.

2. Discounting

Compounding looks forward from a known present sum which, with the addition of re-invested interest, equals some future value. On occasions the future sum is known (or estimated) and it is required to calculate the present value. This process is known as discounting and is effectively the obverse of compounding.

The compounding formula given in para 1 can be restated in terms of *discounting* to a present value thus:

$$P = \frac{S}{(1 + r)^n}$$

Example 3

What is the present value of £15000 received in 10 years time with a discount rate of 14%?

$$P = \frac{S}{(1+r)^n}$$

$$= \frac{£15,000}{(1+0.14)^{10}}$$

$$= £4050$$

Note: Once again the expression could be evaluated by calculator or logarithms but tables are normally used. Table A shows the discount factors,

$$\text{i.e.} \quad \frac{1}{(1+r)^n}$$

and at 14% for 10 years the factor is 0.270. Thus the answer to this problem is £15000 × 0.270 = £4050.

3. Discounting a series

The most important application of discounting is in connection with investment appraisal and the normal requirement is to discount a series of cash flows and not just a single figure. In such circumstances the formula given in para 2 becomes

$$\text{NPV} = \sum_{i=0}^{i=n} \frac{C_i}{(1+r)^i}$$

where C = the net cash flow in the period,

   i = the period number

   r = discount rate.

Example 4

What is the present value of the following cash flows, which are deemed to arise at the end of each year, when the discount rate is 15%.

Period:	Now	after 1 year	after 2 years	after 3 years
Cash Flow	− 2000	+ 800	+ 1000	+ 1300

$$\therefore \text{NPV} = \frac{-2,000}{(1+0.15)^0} + \frac{800}{(1+0.15)^1} + \frac{1,000}{(1+0.15)^2} + \frac{1,300}{(1+0.15)^3}$$

The expression has been given in full for illustrative purposes only and is not normally necessary as the discount factors from Table A can be used thus:

$$\text{NPV} = -2000 + 800 \times 0.870 + 1000 \times 0.756 + 1300 \times 0.658 = + £307.4$$

Where the cash flows vary from year to year, as in Example 4, a separate calculation has to be made for each year but where the cash flows are constant for all years, ie an annuity, the discounting process is simplified considerably.

4. Annuities

Where a constant cash flow is received each year the series is known as an annuity. The present value could be found by separately discounting each year but the series can be brought together into one expression, as follows:

$$P = \frac{A\left(1-(1+r)^{-n}\right)}{r}$$

where: A is the regular cash receipt, ie, the annuity.

Example 5

What is the present value of an annuity of £1000 p.a. received for 10 years when the discount rate is 12%?

$$P = \frac{1000\left(1-\dfrac{1}{(1+0.12)^{10}}\right)}{0.12}$$

$$= \textbf{£5,650}$$

Because annuities are commonly encountered tables are available for the annuity factor, ie

$$\frac{1-(1+r)^{-n}}{r} \quad \text{(See Table B)}$$

From Table B the factor under 12% for 10 years is 5.650 (It will be noted that the Annuity factors are simply the summation of the discount factors from Table A).

∴ present value is £1000 × 5.650 = **£5,650.**

A shorthand way of expressing the annuity factor is $A_{\overline{n}|}\,r$ which means the annuity factor for n years at r rate of interest. Thus Example 5 could be shown as:

$$£1000 \; A_{\overline{10}|}\,0.12 \; = £5,650.$$

Example 6

Evaluate

a)   £500 $A_{\overline{5}|}\,0.10$

b)   £2000 $A_{\overline{8}|}\,0.20$

c)   £4500 $A_{\overline{6}|}\,0.12$

Solution

a)   £500 $A_{\overline{5}|}\,0.10$ = £500 × 3.791 = £1895.5

b)   £2000 $A_{\overline{8}|}\,0.20$ = £2000 × 3.837 = £7674

c)   £4500 $A_{\overline{6}|}\,0.12$ = £4500 × 4.111 = £18499.5

Example 7

A firm agrees to pay an employee the following amounts at the end of each year

Year	1	2	3	4
Amount	£6,000	£7,500	£9,000	£10,000

However, the employee prefers to receive the same amount in each of the years. What is the amount given that the discount rate is 10%?

Solution

It is necessary first to find the NPV of the payments.

NPV $= 6000 \times 0.909 + 7500 \times 0.826 + 9000 \times 0.751 + 10000 \times 0.683 = $ **£25,238**

From Table B the annuity factor for 4 years at 10% is 3.170.

$\therefore$ Equal payment in each of the 4 years $= \dfrac{25238}{3.170}$

$$= \textbf{£7961.51}$$

Note: This process is known as *annualising* and is a useful procedure for dealing with replacement problems where there are various possible life cycles. If the annualised equivalent to each of the cycles is found a direct comparison is possible.

5. Cash flows growing (or declining) at a compound rate

It is sometimes necessary to find the present value of a stream of cash flows which are expected to increase (or reduce) at a compound rate. This is as follows:

Let $g = \%$ growth p.a. and $A' = \dfrac{A}{1+g}$

then: $\qquad P = A'_{\overline{n}|r_0}$

where: $\qquad r_0 = \dfrac{r-g}{1+g}$

Example 8

What is the present value of rentals which are expected to commence in a year's time with a rental of £1155 p.a. and thereafter increase at 5% p.a. compound? The rentals will last 10 years and the discount rate is 26%.

Solution

$$r_0 = \frac{r-g}{1+g}$$

$$= \frac{0.26 - 0.05}{1.05}$$

$$= \textbf{0.20}$$

and: $\quad \dfrac{A}{1+g} = \dfrac{1155}{1.05}$

$$= \text{£}1100$$

$\therefore \qquad P = \text{£}1100.\ A'_{\overline{10}|\,20\%}$

$$= \text{£}1100 \times 4.192$$

$$= \textbf{£4611.20}$$

Example 9

Assume the same problem as Example 8 except that the rental will reduce by 5% p.a.

$$g = -0.05$$

$$r_0 = \frac{0.26 + 0.05}{1 - 1.05}$$

$$= 32.63\%, \text{ say } \mathbf{33\%}$$

and

$$\frac{A}{1+g} = \frac{1155}{0.95}$$

$$= 1215.7$$

∴

$$P = £1215.7 \; \mathbf{A'}_{\overline{10}|\,33\%}$$

$$= £1215.7 \times 2.937$$

$$= \mathbf{£3570.51}$$

6. Perpetuities

Where a stream of cash flows goes on for ever the expression in the outer brackets in the annuity formula given in para 4 reduces to 1 and the formula simplifies considerably to

$$P = \frac{A}{r}$$

Example 10

What is the present value of a perpetual annuity of £1000 at 20% which could alternatively be shown as £1000. $\mathbf{A}_{\overline{\infty}|\,20\%}$

$$P = \frac{A}{r}$$

$$= \frac{1000}{0.2}$$

$$= \mathbf{£5000}$$

7. Compounding/discounting at intervals other than annual

Conventionally, particularly in examinations, it is assumed that all compounding and discounting is at yearly intervals. This need not be so and discounting or compounding can take place at any interval, eg monthly, quarterly, half yearly or continuously.

Continuous discounting or compounding requires special tables but the normal tables (Tables A, B and D) can be used for discrete periods other than yearly as shown in the following example.

Example 11

What is the present value of £30,000 received in 3 years time discounted at half yearly intervals at 20% p.a.?

Solution

Calculate the discount rate per period $= \dfrac{\text{Discount rate p.a.}}{\text{No. of periods p.a.}}$

$= \dfrac{20\%}{2}$

$= \mathbf{10\%}$

Look up in Table A for 6 periods at 10% (ie treat the year's column as periods). The discount factor will be found to be 0.564.

$\therefore$ Present value $= £30,000 \times 0.564$

$= \mathbf{£16920}$

Similar principles apply to compounding problems. The more frequently a value is discounted/compounded the more smaller/larger will be the result.

Note: The rule given above only provides an approximate answer. If an exact answer is required the following formula can be used.

$$\textbf{True annual rate of interest} = \left[\left(1+\frac{r}{n}\right)^{n}-1\right] \times 100\%$$

where: $n =$ number of times compounded in a year

          $r =$ nominal yearly rate

Example 12

What is the true annual rate of interest if the nominal rate is 10% p.a. but interest is paid half yearly at 5%?

$$\text{true rate} = \left[\left(1+\frac{0.1}{2}\right)^{2}-1\right] \times 100\%$$

$$= \mathbf{10.25\%}$$

18 Investment appraisal II

1. Objectives

After studying this chapter you will:

❐ understand how inflation affects investment appraisal;

❐ know what is meant by synchronised and differential inflation;

❐ be able to describe the ways taxation affects project appraisal;

❐ know how to deal with uncertainty;

❐ understand payback, risk premium, and finite horizon;

❐ be able to use probability in project appraisal;

❐ know how sensitivity analysis can be used in project appraisal;

❐ understand portfolio risk;

❐ be able to distinguish between risk seeking and risk averting behaviour;

❐ know the effects of capital rationing and possible project selection methods.

2. Inflation

Inflation can be simply defined as an increase in the average price of goods and services. The accepted measure of general inflation in the UK is the Retail Price Index (RPI) which is based on the assumed expenditure patterns of an average family. General inflation is a factor in investment appraisal but of more direct concern is what may be termed *specific inflation*, ie the changes in prices of the various factors which may up the project being investigated, eg wage rates, sales prices, material costs, energy costs, transportation charges and so on.

Every attempt should be made to estimate specific inflation for each element of the project in as detailed a manner as feasible. General, overall estimates based on the RPI are likely to be inaccurate and misleading.

3. Synchronised and differential inflation

Differential inflation is where costs and revenues change at differing rates of inflation or where the various items of cost and revenue move at different rates. This is the normal situation but the concept of *synchronised inflation* – where costs and revenues rise at the same rate – although unlikely to be encountered in practice, is useful for illustrating various facets of project appraisal involving inflation.

4. Money cash flows and real cash flows

Money cash flows are the actual amounts of money changing hands whereas 'real' cash flows are the purchasing power equivalents of the actual cash flows. In a world of zero inflation there would be no need to distinguish between money and real cash flows as they would be identical. Where inflation does exist then a difference arises between money cash flows and their real value and this difference is the basis of the treatment of inflation in project appraisal.

5. Inflation in investment appraisal

The following example will be used to illustrate the way that inflation is dealt with in investment appraisal.

Example 1

A labour saving machine costs £60,000 and will save £24,000 p.a. at current wage rates. The machine is expected to have a 3 year life and nil scrap value. The firm's cost of capital is 10%.

Calculate the project's NPV

a) With no inflation

b) With general inflation of 15% which wage rates are expected to follow (ie synchronised inflation)

c) With general inflation of 15% and wages rising at 20% p.a. (ie differential inflation)

Solution

a) No inflation.

$$\text{NPV} = -60{,}000 + 24000.\ A_{\overline{3}|10\%}$$
$$= -60{,}000 + 24000 \times 2.487$$
$$= -£312$$

∴ Project unacceptable as it has a negative NPV at company's cost of capital.

b) General inflation 15%, wages increasing at 15%.

Wage savings p.a. with no inflation	Wage savings p.a. with 15% inflation
24000	27600
24000	31740
24000	36501

With no inflation the appropriate discounting rate was 10%. With inflation at 15%, the 10% discounting rate is insufficient to bring cash sums arising at different periods into equivalent purchasing power terms. Without inflation £1 now was deemed equivalent to £1.10 a year hence. With a 15% inflation rate the sum required would be £1.10(1.15) = £1.265, thus the discount rate to be used is $26\frac{1}{2}$ %.

Project NPV with 15% synchronised inflation

Year	Cash Flow £	$26\frac{1}{2}$% Discount Factors	Present Value £
0	−60,000	1.000	−60,000
1	+27,600	0.792	21,859
2	+31,740	0.624	19,806
3	+36,501	0.494	18,031
		NPV =	−304

∴ Project unacceptable

It will be seen that the answers with no inflation and with 15% synchronised inflation are virtually the same, (the difference being due to roundings in three figure tables). This equivalence is to be expected, as with synchronised inflation the firm, in real terms, is no better or no worse off.

c) Project with 15% general inflation and wages rising at 20% p.a. (differential inflation).

Wages per annum

Year 1 $24000 \times (1.20)$ $= £28,800$

2 $24000 \times (1.20)^2$ $= £34,560$

3 $24000 \times (1.20)^3$ $= £41,472$

Project NPV with differential inflation

Year	Cash Flow	$26\frac{1}{2}\%$ DiscountFactors	Present Value
	£		£
0	−60,000	1.000	−60,000
1	+28,800	0.792	22,810
2	+34,560	0.624	21,565
3	+41,472	0.494	20,487
		NPV =	**+4,862**

∴ Project acceptable.

Thus it will be seen that with differential inflation the project is acceptable. In this case this is to be expected because it was a labour saving project so that, in real terms, the firm is better off if the rate of wage inflation is greater than the general rate of inflation.

Frequently differential inflation works to the disadvantage of the firm, for example, when costs are rising faster than prices. Each case is different and detailed, individual analysis is required – not generalised assumptions.

6. Money and real discount rates

The $26\frac{1}{2}$ % discount rate used in Example 1 was a money discount factor and was used to discount the money cash flows of the project. The relationship between real and money discount factors is as follows:

$$\textbf{Real discount factor} = \frac{1 + \textbf{Money discount factor}}{1 + \textbf{Inflation rate}} - 1$$

Using the data from Example 1 the real discount factor can be calculated.

Real discount factor

$$= \frac{1 + 0.265}{1 + 0.15} - 1$$

$$= 0.1 \text{ i.e. } \textbf{10\%}$$

In this case, of course, the real discount factor was already known and the above calculation is for illustrative purposes only.

The real discount factor can be used providing that the money cash flows are first converted into real cash flows by discounting at the general inflation rate as follows.

Example 2

Rework part (c) of Example 1 using real cash flows and the real discount factor.

Solution

Real Cash Flow Evaluation

Year	Money Cash Flow	General Inflation 15% discount factors	Real Cash Flows	Real Discount Factors 10%	Present Values
0	−60,000	1.000	−60,000	1.000	−60,000
1	+28,800	0.870	25,056	0.909	22,776
2	+34,560	0.756	26,127	0.826	21,581
3	+41,472	0.658	27,289	0.751	20,494
				NPV =	4,851

From which it will be seen that (table rounding differences apart) the two methods give identical results.

Thus there are two approaches to investment appraisal where inflation is present.

Single discounting – money cash flows discounted by money discount factor

Two stage discounting – money cash flows discounted by general inflation rate and the real cash flows produced discounted by real discount factor

The two approaches produce the same answer because the money discount factor includes the inflation allowance. Because of this and because money cash flows are the most natural medium in which estimates will be made, it is recommended that money cash flows should be discounted at an appropriate money discount factor. Take great care never to discount money cash flows by a real discount factor or real cash flows by a money discount factor. If real cash flows are directly provided in a question take care to discount once only using a real discount factor.

7. Taxation and investment appraisal

Because taxation causes a change in cash flows it is a factor to be considered in project appraisal. Indeed in some practical situations the taxation implication are dominant influences on the final investment decision. The following paragraphs cover the general impact of taxation on the appraisal process but make no claim to cover the intricacies of company taxation.

8. Treatment of taxation in principle

It will be recalled that project appraisal should be based on the net, after tax, incremental cash flows arising from the project. It follows therefore that the general treatment of taxation in project appraisal involves estimating the cash outflows or inflows arising in respect of taxation, incorporating them in the project cash flow estimates, and discounting in the usual manner.

Because of the complexities of the taxation system the tax cash flows resulting from a project may have adverse (ie cause a cash outflow) or beneficial (ie product a cash inflow or reduce an outflow) effects on a project. In addition, as project appraisal is concerned with both the amount and timing of cash flows, the inclusion of the effects of taxation may significantly alter project returns because of the timing of taxation payments.

9. The major taxation effects upon project appraisal

Taxation effects a project in numerous ways, but probably the most significant three effects are:

a) Corporate taxes on project profits and losses

b) Investment incentives (cash grants and/or capital allowances), where applicable.

c) The reduction of the WACC because interest payments are allowable against tax.

It is somewhat ironic that, notwithstanding what has been said earlier about the inappropriateness of conventionally prepared accounting profits for investment appraisal purposes, it is usually necessary in practical problems to calculate accounting profits to assess the taxation effects on cash flows. This is, of course, because taxation is assessed upon conventionally prepared accounts, not on cash flows. In most examination questions this distinction is usually ignored and project cash flows are deemed to be the appropriate figures on which to base taxation.

10. Corporation taxes on profits and losses

Where a project produces profits these are taxed at the appropriate ruling rate of Corporation Tax and payable 9 months after the end of the period in which the profits were earned. Because project appraisal deals with both the timing and amount of cash flows it is necessary to allow for this time lag and to bring the taxation cash outflow into the appropriate period. Typically in examination questions a one year lag is assumed, ie tax payments are deemed to be paid in the year following that in which profits are earned. Where a specific time lag is not given assume a one year period.

Where a project produces losses, the overall taxation of the firm will be affected as follows:

a) Where the firm has sufficient profits from other operations the loss on the project will reduce the overall taxation liability of the firm. This reduction of tax is equivalent to a cash inflow to the project (ie loss × corporation tax rate) suitably time lagged.

b) Where the project loss causes an overall loss, the resulting cash inflow from the loss can be either

  i)   Carried back to the three previous profit making years. In this case the equivalent cash inflow should be shown against the project in the year in which the reduction of tax liability was possible.

  ii) Carried forward to a future profit making year. Similarly the equivalent cash inflow will be shown against the project in the future year when sufficient profits become available.

11. Investment incentives

Although details of investment incentives are altered frequently, the overall objective says the same, ie to encourage investment in fixed assets though the tax system. There are two basic types of investment incentives; cash grants (currently only payable in development areas), and accelerated depreciation allowances (known as capital allowances).

i) Cash grants. When these are receivable they should be brought into the project appraisal in the period in which they are receivable.

ii) Capital allowances. These allowances have an equivalent cash inflow value of capital allowance × corporation tax rate assuming sufficient profits are being earned to cover all the allowances. The cash inflow effect will be lagged an appropriate period. One year should be assumed unless stated to the contrary.

12. Tax and the WACC

This has already been dealt with in the previous chapter where it was explained that because debenture interest is tax deductible, the WACC is thereby reduced. This concession does not apply to dividends or to the capital redemption portion of the yield on redeemable debentures.

13. Imputation system and advance corporation tax (ACT)

The current U.K. system means that the timing of tax payments is affected by the company's dividend policy. The payment of dividends to shareholders is regarded as the net equivalent of a grossed up amount currently at the lower tax rate of 20%. The difference must be paid by the company as ACT under the quarterly account system and the amount of ACT paid has the effect of reducing the corporation tax to be paid subsequently (subject to the limitations imposed by the Taxes Acts). Thus, the imputation tax system favours the use of retained earnings since the payment of ACT can be delayed. From the examination point of view it is considered that the combination of investment appraisal, dividend policy, and ACT is unlikely to be encountered.

14. Project appraisal involving taxation

Example 3

Electronic Ltd is considering the purchase of a die casting machine at a cost of £20,000. The project cash flows are estimated as follows

Year 0	Year 1	Year 2	Year 3	Year 4
−20,000	+7,000	+5,000	+11,000	+5,000

The following may be assumed

a) the existence of other taxable profits.

b) 25% writing down allowances (on the reducing balance method).

c) 35% rate of Corporation Tax.

d) The machine was sold for £4,500 at the end of 4 years.

e) 1 year lag on all tax effects.

The company requires a 10% return after tax.

Calculate the NPV of the project.

Solution

Year	Project Cash Flows	Tax effect of WDA	Tax on profits	Net after Tax Cash Flows	Discount Factors	Present Values
	£	£	£	£		£
0	−20,000			−20,000	1.000	−20,000
1	+ 7,000	+1,750		+ 8,750	0.909	+ 7,954
2	+ 5,000	+1,312	−2,450	+ 3,862	0.826	+ 3,190
3	+11,000	+ 984	−1,750	+10,234	0.751	+ 7,686
4	+ 5,000	+ 738	−3,850	+ 6,388	0.683	+ 4,363
	+ 4,500					
5		+ 640	−2,450	− 1,810	0.621	− 1,124
						+ 2,069

Note: The tax effect of the WDA is calculated thus:

	£			£
Capital Cost	20,000			
25% WDA	5,000	@ 35%	=	1,750
WDV	15,000			
25% WDA	3,750	@ 35%	=	1,312
WDV	11,250			
25% WDA	2,812	@ 35%	=	984
WDV	8,438			
25% WDA	2,109	@ 35%	=	738
WDV	6,329			
Sold for	4,500			
∴ Balancing allowance	1,829	@ 35%	=	640

It will be seen that the project has a positive NPV of £2,069 and, subject to the usual qualifications, the project is acceptable.

15. Uncertainty in investment appraisal

Uncertainty is a major factor to be considered in all types of decision making. It is of particular importance in investment appraisal because of the long time scale and amount of resources involved in a typical investment decision.

In general, risky or uncertain projects are those whose future cash flows, and hence the returns on the project, are likely to be variable – the greater the variability, the greater the risk. Unfortunately, elements of uncertainty can exist even if future cash flows are known with certainty. For example, if a lease is being appraised the future cash flows are known and fixed but their value may vary because of changes in the rate of inflation.

There are three stages of the overall appraisal and decision process in which risk and uncertainty merit special attention:

a) The risk and uncertainty associated with the individual project.

b) The effect on the overall risk and uncertainty of the firm when the project being considered is combined with the rest of the firm's operations – the portfolio effect.

c) The decision maker's attitude to risk and its effect on the final decision. These three elements are dealt with below.

16. Uncertainty and the individual project

Various methods of considering the uncertainty associated with projects are described below. They have the general objective of attempting to assess or quantify the uncertainty surrounding a project by some form of analysis which goes beyond merely calculating the overall return expected from the project. In this way further information is provided for the ultimate decision maker so that, hopefully, a better decision will be made. It must be emphasised however, that the methods do not of themselves reduce the uncertainties surrounding a proposed investment. If this is feasible, it can only be done by management action.

The methods to be described can be separated into three groups.

a) Time based

b) Probability based

c) Sensitivity analysis and simulation.

17. Time based

The three methods of incorporating uncertainty which are based on time are Payback, Risk Premium and Finite Horizon. These methods rest on the assumption that project risks and uncertainty are related to time, ie the longer the project the more uncertain it is. Whilst it is reasonable to assume that uncertainty does often increase with time it is by no means universally true and there are many projects which are shortlived and risky whilst others are long term and relatively safe. The three methods are described below.

18. Payback

This is the number of periods cash flows required to recoup the original investment. Apart from its use as an accept/reject criterion, payback can be used as a measure of risk, often in conjunction with a DCF measure such as NPV or IRR. If two projects A and B had approximately the same NPV and A had the shorter payback period then A would be preferred.

Advantages

a) Simplicity of calculation.

b) General acceptability and ease of understanding.

Disadvantages

a) Assumes that uncertainty relates only to the time elapsed.

b) Assumes that cash flows within the calculated payback period are certain.

c) Makes a single blanket assumption – that uncertainty is a function of time – and does not attempt to consider the variabilities of the cash flows estimated for the particular project being appraised.

19. Risk premium

On occasions the discount rate is raised above the cost of capital in an attempt to allow for the riskiness of projects. The extra percentage being known as the risk premium. Such an inflated discounted rate raises the acceptance hurdle for projects and can be shown to treat risk as a function of time by more heavily discounting later cash flows as demonstrated in the following example.

Example 4

The cash flows for a project are shown below. The cost of capital is 10% and as the project is considered to be risky, a risk premium of 5% is to be added to the basic rate. The effects of the two discount rates are shown.

Year	0	1	2	3	4	5	NPV
Estimated Cash Flows	−10,000	+2,000	+3,000	+2,500	+3,000	+3,500	
10% Discount Factors	1.000	0.909	0.826	0.751	0.683	0.621	
P.V. @ 10%	−10,000	1818	2478	1877	2049	2173	+395
15% Discount Factors	1.000	0.870	0.756	0.658	0.572	0.495	
P.V. @ 15%	−10,000	1740	2268	1645	1716	1732	−899
Percentage reduction of P.V.s caused by risk premium		4%	8%	12%	16%	20%	

Table 1

The bottom line shows the progressively increased discounting which takes place on later cash flows demonstrating that the risk premium concept treats uncertainty as being related to time elapsed.

Advantages of a risk premium.

a) Simple to use.

Disadvantages of a risk premium.

a) Makes the implicit assumption that uncertainty is a function of time.

b) By making the same overall, blanket assumption for all projects it does not consider the individual project characteristics nor does it explicitly consider the variability of the project cash flows.

c) It creates the problem of deciding upon a suitable risk premium. Should it be the same for all projects or should it be adjusted for different projects?

Note: One of the theories relating to business profit is that it is the reward for taking uninsurable risks. If this is correct, and it has some intuitive appeal, then a more subtle and long term effect of using a risk premium is that the firm will tend to move towards a portfolio of projects which, although potentially high yielding, have high risks – which is the opposite effect to that intended.

20. Finite horizon

In this method which is the simplest of all to apply, project results beyond a certain period (eg 10 years) are ignored. All projects are thus appraised over the same time period.

Advantage:

a) Simplicity.

Disadvantages:

a) The establishment of any fixed time horizon is arbitrary. Projects do vary in length and this should be reflected in the appraisal.

b) Project cash flows within the time horizon are considered certain.

c) Does not explicitly consider the variabilities of cash flows.

21. Summary of time-based methods of considering uncertainty

These methods are simple to apply and require little, if any, extra calculation. They are for the most part arbitrary and unreliable. Although obviously uncertainty tends to increase with time there is not a straightforward relationship and the time based methods fail to examine the characteristics of individual projects and merely make one blanket assumption covering all projects. The whole purpose of investment appraisal is to distinguish between projects and accepting one overall assumption is likely to mask rather than highlight the differences between the investment opportunities being considered.

22. Probability-based methods of assessing uncertainty

The methods to be described rest on the assumption that realistic estimates of the subjective probabilities associated with the various cash flows can be established. For example, the project analyst might ask a manager to make three estimates of the cash flow of a period (optimistic, most likely, pessimistic) instead of just a single estimate, and in addition ask the manager to assess the likelihood of each of three estimates. Following such a request the manager might make the following estimate:

Cash Flow in Period x

Optimistic	£8,000	with a probability of 10% (0.1)
Most likely	£4,500	with a probability of 65% (0.65)
Pessimistic	£3,000	with a probability of 25% (0.25)

The estimates thus obtained form a probability distribution of the cash flows. It follows that if the individual cash flows are expected to vary then the overall return for the project will also vary. The main objectives of probability-based methods is to demonstrate the likely variation in the result, whether NPV or IRR, due to the estimated variations in the cash flows. In this way the effects of uncertainty are more clearly shown and it is hoped that a more informed decision may be taken. The three methods to be described which use subjective probabilities are *Expected Value, Discrete Probabilistic Analysis* and *Continuous Probabilistic Analysis*.

23. Expected value (EV)

This has been covered in detail in Chapter 13. It will be recalled that EV is Probability × Value and EV can be used for individual cash flows or project NPV's. The following simple example illustrates the technique.

Example 5

The cash flow and probability estimates for a project are shown below.

Calculate

a) Expected value of the cash flows in each period and

b) Expected value of the NPV when the initial project outlay is £11,000 and the cost of capital is 15%.

Cash Flow and probability estimates

| | Probability | Cash Flows | | | |
| | | Period 1 | Period 2 | Period 3 | Period 4 |
		£	£	£	£
Optimistic	0.3	5000	6000	4500	5000
Most likely	0.5	3500	4000	3800	4500
Pessimistic	0.2	3200	3600	3100	4000
Expected value of cash flows		*3890	4520	3870	4550

* Each of the periods' expected values are found in the usual way. For example, the expected value for period $1 = (5000 \times 0.3) + (3500 \times 0.5) + (3200 \times 0.2) = 3890$.

The NPV is found by discounting the expected value of cash flows in the normal manner.

$NPV = -11,000 + (3890 \times 0.870) + (4520 \times 0.756) + (3870 \times 0.658) + (4550 \times 0.572) = £950$

The advantages and disadvantages of expected value as a decision criterion have already been covered in Chapter 13 and these apply equally to the use of Expected Value in investment appraisal.

It is worth repeating that expected value, in spite of its limitations, is the decision rule which should normally be employed unless the problem clearly indicates something to the contrary.

24. Discrete probabilistic analysis (DPA)

DPA can be considered as an extension of the expected value procedure described above. As its basis it requires similar estimates of cash flows and associated probabilities, but instead of merely averaging these estimates it uses the component parts of the estimates to show the various outcomes and probabilities possible. The following example illustrates the technique.

Example 6

The NPV of Example 5 was £950 and management consider this somewhat marginal and wish to explore the range of outcomes possible. Further investigation reveals that two capital costs are possible; the £11,000 as stated with a probability of 0.8 and £15,000 with a probability of 0.2. This results in a new expected NPV of +£150 using the new expected capital cost of £11,800. The full range of outcomes and probabilities is shown in Table 2.

	Most Likely Capital Cost P = 0.8 £11,000		Pessimistic Capital Cost P = 0.2 £15,000	
Optimistic Cash Flows P = 0.3	3707	(0.24)	−293	(0.06)
Most Likely Cash Flows P = 0.5	*143	(0.4)	−3857	(0.1)
Pessimistic Cash Flows P = 0.2	−1167	(0.16)	−5167	(0.04)

Table 2

The table shows the NPV resulting from each possible combination of the original estimates of cash flows and the capital costs and gives the probability of the combination occurring. For example, the cell marked* is calculated thus

£

Present value of most likely cash flows	=	11,143	
less most likely capital cost		11,000	
NPV	=	**143**	

The combination has a probability of $0.5 \times 0.8 = \mathbf{0.4}$

From Table 2 it will be seen that the outcomes range from +£3707 to −£5167 and that the probability of making a loss is $0.16 + 0.06 + 0.1 + 0.04 = 0.36$ or alternatively, the probability of at least breaking even is 0.64.

Management now has more information on which to base a decision.

Advantages of DPA.

a) Simple to apply and understand.

b) Gives some indication of the range of possible outcomes and their probabilities.

c) Considers the detailed variations in the cash flows and investment required for a project rather than merely making one overall assumption such as that uncertainty is directly related to time elapsed.

Disadvantages of DPA.

a) Uses discrete estimates whereas a continuous distribution may be a better representation of a particular project.

b) Increases the amount of subjective estimation necessary.

25. Continuous probabilistic analysis (CPA)

CPA has the same overall objective as DPA which has been described above. That is, to show the variability of the project outcome which results from the variability of the individual cash flows thus enabling the analyst to make probability assessments of the likelihood of various outcomes. It differs from DPA in that continuous distributions and aspects of statistical theory are used instead of the discrete estimates which are a feature of DPA.

CPA can be shown diagrammatically as follows

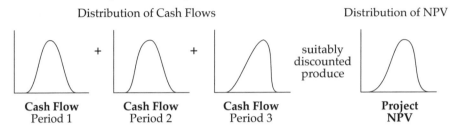

Figure 18.1

To be able to combine the distributions as shown and to be able to make probability statements about the project outcome, it is first necessary to establish the mean (or most likely value) and a measure of the dispersion of each of the individual period's cash flows.

26. Establishing the means and dispersion of cash flows

In general, there is little problem in estimating the mean of the period's cash flows, this being equivalent to the most likely value. A more significant problem is to establish a suitable measure of the variability or dispersion of the period's cash flows. The most useful measure for statistical purposes is the *standard deviation* in the conventional statistical manner so that some form of subjective estimation becomes necessary.

This could be done as follows:

Assume that the most likely value of the cash flow in a given period was estimated to be £30,000 and it was considered that there was likely to be some variability.

The manager responsible for the estimate could be asked a question similar to the following.

'Given that the most likely value of the cash flow is £30,000, within what limits would you expect the cash flow to be 50% of the time?'

Assume that the answer to the above question was £25,000 to £35,000.

It is known from Normal Area Tables that 50% of a distribution lies between the mean $\pm \frac{2}{3}\sigma$ (approximately)

$\therefore$ £10,000 (ie 35,000 – 25,000) $= \frac{4}{3}\sigma$

i.e. $\sigma = £7500$

An alternative to the question asked above would be ask the manager, 'what is the total range of cash flow that might be expected?'

If the manager was consistent he would answer, '£7,500 to £52,500'.

It is known that the whole of a normal distribution is within the range of the mean $\pm 3\sigma$ (approximately). Accordingly, the estimate of the standard deviation would be:

$$\sigma = \frac{\pounds(52,500 - 7,500)}{6} = \pounds7,500$$

It is clear that the estimation process outlined above is crude and lacks statistical rigour. However, subjective estimation is an unavoidable aspect of all investment appraisals and the procedure does enable some sort of assessment to be made of the probability of achieving various outcomes.

Having obtained the estimates of the means and standard deviations these must be combined to give the mean and standard deviation of the overall project NPV.

27. Combining the means and standard deviations of the cash flows

There is little problem in obtaining the mean of the project NPV. This is simply the means, or most likely values, of the cash flows discounted in the usual manner. The project standard deviation is obtained by combining the discounted standard deviations of the individual cash flows using what is known as the statistical sum.

Standard deviations cannot be combined directly but it is possible to add variances. When this is done the square root of the result can be taken thus establishing the standard deviation of the project's NPV, ie σ_{NPV}.

By definition:
$$\sigma^2_{NPV} = \sum \left[\frac{\sigma_i}{(1+r)^i} \right]^2$$

$$= \sum \frac{\sigma_i^2}{(1+r)^{2i}}$$

Taking the square root of both sides gives:
$$\sigma_{NPV} = \sqrt{\sum \frac{\sigma_i^2}{(1+r)^{2i}}}$$

This formula is used in the following example.

Example 6

The means and standard deviations of the cash flows of a project are shown below and it is required to calculate.

a) The project NPV (ie the mean)

b) The variability of the project NPV (ie σ_{NPV})

c) The probability of obtaining
- ❐ a negative NPV
- ❐ a NPV of at least £20,000

It can be assumed that the cash flows in each period are independent, ie variations in one period are independent of variations in others and that the cost of capital is 10%

Period	0	1	2	3	4	5
Net cash flow (most likely value)	−200,000	+55,000	+48,000	+65,000	+70,000	+40,000
Variability expected (ie Standard deviation of cash flow)	0	4,000	4,500	3,500	4,500	3,000
Discount Factors @ Cost of Capital of 10%	1.00	0.909	0.826	0.751	0.683	0.621

Solution

a) The project NPV is found in the usual way.

Project NPV (ie the mean)

$$= -200,000 + (55,000 \times 0.909) + (48,000 \times 0.826) + (65,000 \times 0.751)$$
$$+ (70,000 \times 0.683) + (40,000 \times 0.621)$$
$$= \text{£11,108}$$

b) The standard deviation of the NPV is found by inserting the various estimated cash flow standard deviations into the formula.

$$\sigma_{NPV} = \sqrt{\sum \frac{\sigma_i^2}{(1+r)^{2i}}}$$

$$= \sqrt{\frac{4000^2}{(1+0.1)^2} + \frac{4500^2}{(1+0.1)^4} + \frac{3500^2}{(1+0.1)^6} + \frac{4500^2}{(1+0.1)^8} + \frac{3000^2}{(1+0.1)^{10}} +}$$

$$= \text{£6,847}$$

It will be seen that the squaring of the denominator has the effect of requiring discount factors at 2, 4, 6, 8 and 10 years instead of the usual 1, 2, 3, 4 and 5 years.

c) The probability of obtaining a negative NPV (or the probability of any value of NPV) is found by using standard statistical tests of normal area, ie find the 'z' score or standardised variate and obtain the resulting probability from Normal Area Tables as follows.

$$z = \left| \frac{\text{£}(11,108 - 0)}{6,847} \right|$$

$$= 1.622$$

and from the Tables we find that the probability of the NPV being above zero is 0.9474 (ie 0.5 + 0.4474) thus there is approximately a **5.3% chance** (1 − 0.9474) of there being a negative NPV.

The probability of there being at least £20,000 NPV is found by a similar process.

$$z = \frac{£(20,000 - 11,108)}{6,847}$$

$$= 1.299$$

and using the Tables we find that the probability of obtaining at least £20,000 NPV is approximately **9.7%**.

The distribution of the project NPV can also be shown diagrammatically as in Figure 18.2.

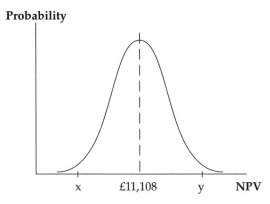

Figure 18.2 Probability Distribution of Project

Point x on the diagram is approximately £11,108 – (3 × 6847) = **–£ 9433** and point y is approximately £11,108 + (3 × 6847) = **£31,649**

28. Comparison of projects using CPA

Having calculated the means and standard deviations of various projects the project distributions can be compared quite simply. The distributions could be drawn on the same graph and visually examined or the relative variability of the distributions could be calculated using their *coefficients of variation.*

The coefficient of variation is found as follows:

$$\textbf{Coefficient of variation} = \frac{\sigma}{\bar{x}} \times 100\%$$

For example, two projects have estimated results as under

Project A: mean = £80,000   s.d. = £12,500
Project B: mean = £130,000   s.d. = £17,500

What are the coefficients of variation and which is the relatively less risky project?

$$\text{Coefficient of variation A} = \frac{12,500}{80,000}$$

$$= \textbf{15.6\%}$$

$$\text{Coefficient of Variation B} = \frac{17,500}{130,000}$$

$$= \textbf{13.5\%}$$

381

∴ Project B is relatively less risky assuming that the standard deviation is a reasonable measure of risk for the projects.

29. Summary of CPA

The analysis outlined above can be extended to cover situations where projects are not independent and/or where the individual distributions are not normal or near normal. All the methods have the same overall objects, which is to find the mean and variability (riskiness) of the project NPV.

Advantages of CPA

a) Produces a distribution of the NPV rather than a single figure.

b) Enables probability statements to be made about the project's outcome which reflect the variabilities expected in each period's cash flows.

c) Enables the NPV distributions of competing projects to be compared.

d) Uses the more realistic assumption of continuous rather than discrete values.

Disadvantages of CPA

a) Introduces a further element of subjective estimation.

b) More complex than DPA, so therefore may not be properly understood or used by decision makers.

30. Sensitivity analysis

This is a practical way of showing the effects of uncertainty by varying the values of the key factors (eg sales volume, price, rates of inflation, cost per unit) and showing the resulting effect on the project. The objective is to establish which of the factors affect the project most. When this is done it is management's task to decide whether the project is worthwhile, given the sensitivity of one or more of the key factors. It will be seen that this method does not ask for subjective probability estimates of likely outcomes, but attempts to provide the data upon which judgements may be made. The method is illustrated by the following example.

Example 7

Assume that a project (using single valued estimates) has a positive NPV of £25,000 at a 10% discounting rate. This value would be calculated by the normal methods using particular values for sales volume, sales price, cost per unit, inflation rate, length of life etc, etc.

Once the basic value (ie the NPV of £25,000) has been obtained the sensitivity analysis is carried out by flexing, both upwards and downwards, each of the factors in turn.

An abstract of the results of a sensitivity analysis for the project above might be as follows:

Sensitivity Analysis Abstract

Original NPV = £25,000

A	B	C	D	E	F
Element to be varied	Alteration from Basic	Revised NPV	Increase + Decrease −	Percentage Change	Sensitivity Factor
		£	£		E÷B
Sales	+15%	46,000	+21,000	84	5.6
Volume	+10%	33,000	+ 8,000	32	3.2
(Basic Value	−10%	17,000	− 8,000	32	3.2
8000 units in Period 1,	−15%	14,000	−11,000	44	2.9
8500 in Period 2 etc)	−20%	9,000	−16,000	64	3.2
Sales	+20%	42,000	+ 17,000	68	3.4
Price	+10%	31,000	+ 6,000	24	2.4
(Basic Value	−10%	17,000	− 8,000	32	3.2
£6 unit in Period 1,	−15%	11,000	−14,000	56	3.73
£6.25 in Period 2 etc)	−20%	2,000	−23,000	92	4.6
Cost/Unit	+25%	−12,000	−37,000	148	5.9
(Basic Value	+10%	6,000	−19,000	76	7.6
£2.50 in Period 1	−5%	34,000	+ 9,000	36	7.2
£2.60 in Period 2 etc)	−10%	47,000	+22,000	88	8.8

Table 3

From such an analysis the more sensitive elements can be identified. Once identified further analysis and study can take place on these factors to try to establish the likelihood of variability and the range of values that might be expected so as to be able to make a more reasoned decision whether or not to proceed with the project.

Advantages of Sensitivity Analysis

a) Shows the effect on project outcome of varying the value of the elements which make up the project (eg Sales, Costs, etc).

b) Simple in principle.

c) Enables the identification of the most sensitive variables.

Disadvantages of Sensitivity Analysis

a) Gives no indication of the likelihood of a variation occurring.

b) Considerable amount of computation involved.

c) Only considers the effect of a single change at a time which may be unrealistic.

31. Risk and the portfolio effect

So far in this Chapter we have studied the risks associated with each project considered in isolation. This is an important matter but it will be apparent that of greater significance to the firm is the aggregate risk from all projects accepted which could be termed its *portfolio of projects*.

The effect on the firm of the risks of individual projects may be neutralised or enhanced when all the individual projects are considered together. A simple example would be where a firm is operating in a cyclical industry with variable (ie risky) returns on its existing projects. A new project is being considered which, although variable or risky, is expected to follow a different cyclical pattern to existing operations. When existing operations are experiencing low activity the new project is expected to have substantial activity so that the overall risk to the firm from its portfolio, including the new project, will be minimised. This is, of course, a major reason why firms diversify their operations.

The analysis of this aspect of risk and uncertainty was developed for stock market investment portfolio analysis by Markowitz and others and has already been briefly alluded to when the Capital Asset Pricing Model was discussed earlier. There are many restrictive assumptions behind the analysis and there are some difficulties in applying it to project investment within the firm but the general reasoning is valid and is of considerable importance.

32. Assessing the portfolio risk

The general procedure for assessing the extent to which the proposed project(s) add to or subtract from the risk of existing operations is to calculate the covariance between the returns of the project(s) and returns of existing operations and to use the covarance(s) to obtain the coefficient of correlation between the project(s) returns and the returns of existing operations.

The interpretation of the correlation coefficients is as follows:-

Coefficient of correlation

$$\text{Coefficient of correlation} = \begin{cases} -1, & \text{risk fully neutralised} \\ 0, & \text{risk unaltered} \\ +1, & \text{risk fully enhanced} \end{cases}$$

The following example illustrates the general procedure.

Example 8

A firm with £100,000 to invest is considering two projects, X and Y each requiring an investment of £100,000. The returns from the proposed projects and from existing operations under three possible views of expected market conditions are shown in Table 4 together with the calculated standard deviations of returns, ie the measure of riskiness used by the company.

Market state	I	II	III
Probability of market state	0.3	0.4	0.3
Rate of return Project X	20%	20%	$-1\frac{2}{3}\%$
Standard deviation of returns, Project X = 22%			
Rate of Return Project Y	-2%	15%	27%
Standard deviation of returns, Project Y = 15%			
Rate of Return of existing operations	-9%	$18\frac{1}{4}\%$	28%
Standard deviation of returns on existing operations = 18%			

Table 4

The firm considers that the risk and return of their existing operations are similar to the market as a whole and that a reasonable estimate of a risk free interest rate is 8%.

Which, if either, of the two proposed investments should be initiated and why?

Solution

The first stage is to calculate the expected returns for X and Y and existing operations.

Expected Returns (R)

Project X: $\overline{R}_x$ $= (0.20 \times 0.3) + (0.20 \times 0.4) + (-0.01667 \times 0.3)$

$= 0.135$

$= \textbf{13.5\%}$

Project Y: $\overline{R}_y$ $= (-0.02 \times 0.3) + (0.15 \times 0.4) + (0.27 \times 0.3)$

$= 0.135$

$= \textbf{13.5\%}$

Existing Operations: $\overline{R}_o$ $= (-0.09 \times 0.3) + (0.1825 \times 0.4) + 0.28 \times 0.3)$

$= 0.13$

$= \textbf{13\%}$

It will be seen that the expected returns of Projects X and Y are the same and as the standard deviation of Project Y is lower than Project X then Project Y is the preferred project if the projects are considered in isolation from existing operations.

However, this is too superficial a view and further analysis is required on the effect of adding either project to the existing portfolio.

It will be recalled that a project's risk can be separated into two elements – systematic and unsystematic risk. The unsystematic risk is the diversifiable risk which can be reduced or eliminated when the project is part of an appropriate portfolio. The systematic risk is the proportion which cannot be eliminated (it applies to the economy or market as a whole) and thus the project's returns must be considered against this residual element.

Portfolio analysis can be used to find the minimum required return for Projects X and Y given their risk levels by calculating the covariances between project returns and existing operations and using these values to calculate the correlation coefficients thus:

Covariance between Project X return (R_x) and Company Return (R_o)

		$*(R_x - \overline{R}_x)$	$*(R_o - \overline{R}_o)$	Market state probability	Covariance
		(1)	(2)	(3)	$= (1) \times (2) \times (3)$
State	I	0.065	−0.22	0.3	−0.00429
	II	0.065	0.0525	0.4	0.001365
	III	−0.15167	0.15	0.3	−0.00682
				Covariance =	**−0.009745**

*These values are found by deducting the calculated expected return $\overline{R}$ from the actual return given in Table 4. For example the value −0.15167 is found as follows:

$$(-0.01667 - 0.135) = -0.15167.$$

The value of the co-variance is then used to find the correlation coefficient between Project X returns and returns from existing operations (O).

Correlation coefficient between X and O $\quad =$ correlation (x,o)

$$= \frac{\text{covariance } (x,o)}{\sigma_x . \sigma_o}$$

$$= \frac{-0.009745}{0.22 \times 0.18}$$

$$= \mathbf{-0.246}$$

Covariance between Project Y return (R_y) and Company Return (R_o)

		$*(R_y - \overline{R}_y)$	$*(R_o - \overline{R}_o)$	Market state probability	Covariance
		(1)	(2)	(3)	$= (1) \times (2) \times (3)$
State	I	−0.155	−0.22	0.3	0.01023
	II	0.015	0.0525	0.4	0.000315
	III	0.135	0.15	0.3	0.006075
				Covariance =	**+0.01662**

Correlation coefficient between Y and O $\quad =$ correlation (y,o)

$$= \frac{\text{coveriance } (y,o)}{\sigma_y . \sigma_o}$$

$$= \frac{+0.01662}{0.15 \times 0.18}$$

$$= \mathbf{+0.615}$$

These values can be used to calculate the required return from projects X and Y given that the risk free interest rate is 8%. (RF)

Required return of Project X $\quad = R_F + \dfrac{R_o - R_F}{\sigma_o} \times \sigma_x \times$ correlation (x,o)

$$= 0.08 + \frac{0.13 - 0.08}{0.18} \times 0.22 \times -0.246$$

$$= 0.08 - 0.015$$

$$= \mathbf{6.5\%}$$

Required return of Project Y $\quad = R_F + \dfrac{R_o - R_F}{\sigma_o} \times \sigma_y \times$ correlation (y,o)

$$= 0.08 + \frac{0.13 - 0.08}{0.18} \times 0.15 \times 0.615$$

$$= 0.08 + 0.0256$$

$$= \mathbf{10.56\%}$$

Based on the Portfolio analysis, Project X is the preferred project for the following reasons.

a) Project X provides the greatest excess of actual return over minimum return, ie 13.5% c.f. 6.5% whereas Project Y is 13.5% c.f. 10.56. Thus Project X maximises the company's wealth.

b) The negative correlation coefficient of Project X, –0.246 means that its pattern of returns to some extent neutralise the overall portfolio risk when Project X is combined with current operations. Although Project Y has a lower individual risk its correlation coefficient of +0.615 means that it enhances risk when combined with current operations.

Note: It will be seen that the decision following analysis of the Portfolio effects is the opposite to that when the project's riskiness is considered in isolation.

It is feasible to work manually through a problem with as few projects as Example 8 but the number of relationships rises dramatically as the number of projects increases so it is likely that the application of the above principles to any practical sized problem would require computer assistance.

33. Decision maker's attitude to risk

Having dealt with the riskiness of individual projects and of combinations of projects, the third aspect of risk in investment appraisal can now be considered; that of the decision maker's attitude to risk and its influence on the final investment decision.

Surveys and studies have shown that individual differ in their attitudes to risk and that for serious decision making such as investment appraisals in business, decision makers are *risk averters*. This means that in general, decision makers would prefer a less risky (less variable) investment even though it may have a lower expected value than a higher return yet riskier investment.

This may be demonstrated by the following example.

Two investments are being considered.

Investment A   Return of £100,000 with a probability of 1, ie certainty

Investment B   Return of £300,000 with a probability of 0.5

Return of zero with a probability of 0.5

The expected returns are:

Investment A   £100,000

Investment B   (£300,000 × 0.5) + (0 × 0.5) = £150,000

It will be apparent that virtually every investor would prefer the certainty of Investment A to the uncertainty or risk involved in Investment B even though it has the higher expected value. Such behaviour is risk aversion.

Implicit in such behaviour is an assumption about the utility or satisfaction derived from money. The utility function of a risk averter declines as the level of income or wealth rises, ie a declining marginal utility. A 'risk neutral' investor regards each increment of income or wealth as having the same value whereas a 'risk seeker' is a person whose utility function increases as his level of income or wealth increases. These three possibilities are shown in Figure 18.3.

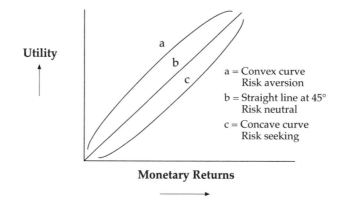

Figure 18.3 Utility Function of Money

34. Utility and certainty equivalent

Utility theory applied to decision making in risky conditions postulates that individuals attempt to optimise something termed *utility* and assumes that for any individual a formal, quantifiable relationship can be established between utility and money.

The theoretical way that an individual's utility function is established is by the use of certainty equivalents. These are derived in the following fashion.

Assume that an individual owns a sweepstake ticket which offers a 50% chance of winning £200,000 and a 50% chance of winning nothing. He would be asked what amount of cash he would accept for the lottery ticket. If he would sell the ticket for

£75,000 this is the certainty equivalent, ie the value at which he is indifferent between the certain £75,000 and the chance of winning £200,000. This certainty equivalent would be assigned a utile value of 0.5 (a utile is the unit of utility). From such questions the person's utility function can be derived and then asked to make choices in investment decisions.

However, whilst these processes have theoretical appeal they are virtually impossible to apply in practice because of the extreme difficulty of establishing any form of meaningful utility function. However, risk aversion and varying individual attitudes to risks are very real phenomena although difficult to quantify. Accordingly, it is essential that the project analyst produces some form of risk analysis, both for projects in isolation and in combination, so that the decision maker has more information upon which to make a decision. There are variable or risky elements of every project and to ignore this aspect in the project appraisal can be positively misleading to the decision maker.

35. Capital rationing – definition

This is where the firm is unable to initiate all projects which are apparently profitable because insufficient funds are available. Under the assumption given for the basic DCF model, a perfect capital market was presumed, ie as much finance as required could be raised at the market rate of interest. In imperfect capital market conditions capital may be raised, but at increasing rates of interest; but there will be some point where there is an absolute limit to the amount that could be raised. Such a situation is known as external capital rationing.

Alternatively, the effects of *capital rationing* may develop for internal purposes, for example, it may be decided that investment should be limited to the amount that can be financed solely from retained earnings or kept within a given capital expenditure budget. The external and internal factors which impose quantitative limits have led to two opposing viewpoints developing, known as the 'hard' and 'soft' views of capital rationing. The 'hard' view is that there is an absolute limit on the amount of money a firm may borrow or raise externally whereas the 'soft' view is that rationing by a quantitative limit such as an arbitrary capital expenditure budget should only be seen as a temporary, administrative expedient because such a limit is not determined by the market (the assumption being that any amount of funds is available at a price) and such a limit would not be imposed by a profit maximising firm.

Whatever the causes of the limited capital supply available for investment purposes it means that, not only must each project cover the cost of capital, but that the project or batch of projects selected must maximise the return from the limited funds available, ie some form of ranking becomes necessary.

Before considering solution methods some definitions need to be made.

a) Single period capital rationing – where there is a limit on the funds available now but where it is anticipated that funds will be freely available in subsequent periods.

b) Multi-Period Capital rationing – where the limitation of funds extends over a number of periods or possibly indefinitely.

c) Divisible projects – projects where the whole project or any fraction may be undertaken. If a fractional part is undertaken, then it is assumed that the initial outlay and subsequent cash inflows and outflows are reduced pro rata. Although for most industrial projects this situation seems somewhat hypothetical, the assumption of divisibility is frequently made in solving capital rationing problems, particularly in examination questions.

d) Indivisible projects – where the whole project must be undertaken or not at all.

36. Project selection under capital rationing

Where capital rationing exists the normal DCF decision rule, ie accept all projects which have a positive NPV at the cost of capital, is insufficient to make the appropriate project selection.

The objective where capital rationing exists is to maximise the return from the batch of projects selected having regard to the capital limitation. This means that the investment decision changes from simply being 'accept or reject' to what is in effect a ranking problem. Ways of achieving this objective are shown below for the following rationing possibilities.

❑ single period capital rationing with divisible projects

❑ single period capital rationing with divisible projects where some are mutually exclusive

❑ single period capital rationing with indivisible projects

❑ multi period capital rationing with divisible projects.

37. Single period capital rationing – divisible projects

This is the simplest case and the solution method is to rank the projects in order of their EVPI (ie NPV per £ of outlay as described earlier) and to choose projects, or fraction of a project, until the supply of capital for investment is exhausted.

Example 9

CR Ltd has a cost of capital of 15% and has a limit of £100,000 available for investment in the current period. It is expected that capital will be freely available in the future. The investment required, the NPV at 15% and the EVPI for each of the 6 projects currently being considered are shown below.

What projects should be initiated?

Project	Outlay	NPV @ 15%	$EVPI = \dfrac{NPV}{Outlay}$
	£	£	
A	20,000	8,000	0.4
B	40,000	28,000	0.7
C	35,000	37,500	1.07
D	50,000	31,500	0.63
E	15,000	3,500	0.23
F	45,000	–5,000	–0.11

Solution

Ranking by EVPI is C, B, D, A and E. Project F cannot be considered because it fails the initial hurdle of achieving a positive NPV.

∴ Optimal Investment Plan:

Project	Fraction undertaken	Investment	NPV
		£	£
C	1.00	35,000	37,500
B	1.00	40,000	28,000
D	0.50	25,000	15,750
		£100,000	£81,250

It will be seen that this solution method uses the well known management accounting principle of maximising return per unit of the limiting factor – in this case NPV per £ of capital available for investment. It will be recalled that this principle is appropriate where there is a single constraint only – in this example, investment finance for one period.

38. Single period capital rationing with mutually exclusive divisible projects

Where two or more of the projects are mutually exclusive the solution method of ranking by EVPI can still be used but the projects have to be divided into groups each containing one of the mutually exclusive projects. This is shown below.

Example 10

Assume the same data as Example 9 except that projects B and D are mutually exclusive.

What projects should be initiated?

Solution

It is necessary to divide the projects into two groups, rank by EVPI, select projects up to the capital limit and to compare the total NPV obtainable from each group.

	Group I			Group II	
Project	Investment	EVPI	Project	Investment	EVPI
	£			£	
A	20,000	0.4	A	20,000	0.4
B	40,000	0.7	C	35,000	1.07
C	35,000	1.07	D	50,000	0.63
E	15,000	0.23	E	15,000	0.23

Ranking the groups and choosing the projects up to the investment limit produces the following:

| | | Group I | | | | Group II | |
Project	Fraction	Investment	NPV	Project	Fraction	Investment	NPV
		£	£			£	£
C	1	35,000	37,000	C	1	35,000	37,500
B	1	40,000	28,000	D	1	50,000	31,500
A	1	20,000	8,000	A	$\frac{3}{4}$	15,000	6,000
E	$\frac{1}{3}$	5,000	1,167				
		£100,000	£74,667			£100,000	£75,000

It will be seen that, by a narrow margin, Group II with the proportion indicated, has the greater NPV and would be chosen.

39. Single period capital rationing – indivisible projects

Where projects have to be accepted in their entirety or not at all, then the EVPI ranking procedure does not necessarily produce the optimal solution. Providing that relatively few projects are involved a trial and error approach can be used to find a solution. Where projects are indivisible then it is likely that some of the capital available for investment may be unused and in such circumstances a full analysis should include the returns from external investment of under-utilised funds.

Example 11

Lloyds Ltd has a cost of capital of 10% and has a limit of £100,000 available for investment in the current period. Capital is expected to be freely available in future periods. The following indivisible projects are being considered.

Project	Initial Investment	NPV @ 10%
	£	£
A	35,000	17,500
B	40,000	22,500
C	65,000	38,000
D	48,000	31,500
E	23,000	9,000

It is required to calculate the optimal investment plan when:

a) where there are no alternative investments available for any surplus funds

b) where surplus funds can be invested to produce 12% in perpetuity.

Solution

a) Various combinations are tried to see which combination produces the maximum NPV. Table 5 shows a few examples.

Project Combinations	Total Outlay for Combinations	Surplus Funds	Total NPV of Combination
	£	£	£
AC	100,000	–	55,500
ABE	98,000	2,000	49,000
AD	83,000	17,000	49,000
BD	88,000	12,000	54,000
BE	63,000	37,000	31,500
CE	88,000	12,000	47,000
DE	71,000	29,000	40,500

Table 5

It will be seen from Table 5 that the best investment plan is A and C which utilises all the funds available and produces a combined NPV of £55,500.

b) When surplus funds can be invested externally each of the combinations in Table 5 which have surplus funds must be examined to see if the project NPV plus the return on external investment is greater than £55,500.

Each £1,000 invested at 12% in perpetuity yields:

$$\text{NPV} = \frac{1,000 \times 0.12}{0.1} - 1,000 = £200$$

The project combinations and total NPV (Projects + External Investment) are shown in Table 6.

Combination	Total Project Outlay	Funds Externally Invested	External Investment NPV	Project NPV	Total NPV
	£	£	£	£	£
ABE	98,000	2,000	400	49,000	49,400
AD	83,000	17,000	3,400	49,000	52,400
BD	88,000	12,000	2,400	54,000	*56,400
BE	63,000	37,000	7,400	31,500	38,900
CE	88,000	12,000	2,400	47,000	49,400
DE	71,000	29,000	5,800	40,500	46,300

Table 6

*When external investment is considered then projects B D should be initiated and £12,000 invested externally to produce a total NPV of £54,500. It will be seen that this is slightly better than the A C combination shown in Table 5.

Note: Although ranking by EVPI in conditions of single-period capital rationing with indivisible projects does not necessarily produce the correct ranking it usually provides an excellent guide to the best group of projects.

40. Multi-period capital rationing

This has been previously defined as the position where investment funds are expected to be limited over several periods. In such circumstances it becomes difficult to choose the batch of projects (some starting immediately, some one period hence, two periods hence, etc.) which yield the maximum return and yet which remain within the capital limits. The problem becomes one of optimising a factor (eg NPV) where resources are limited, ie the funds available over the periods being considered. This will be recognised as a problem where Linear Programming (LP) can be used and LP has been used successfully in solving Multi-Period Capital Rationing problems.

41. Multi-period rationing – LP solution

To use LP as a solution method means making the assumption that projects are divisible, ie fractional parts can be undertaken. This is not necessarily a realistic assumption, but it is one frequently made for examination purposes. The following example will be used to illustrate the LP formulation, solution and interpretation of multi-period capital rationing problems.

Example 12

Trent Ltd has a cost of capital of 10% and is considering which project or projects it should initiate. The following projects are being considered:

Project	Estimated Cash Flows				
	Year 0	Year 1	Year 2	Year 3	Year 4
A	−15,000	−25,000	30,000	30,000	20,000
B	−25,000	−15,000	30,000	29,000	30,000
C	−35,000	−15,000	40,000	44,000	30,000

Capital is limited to £40,000 now and £35,000 in Year 1. The projects are divisible.

Solution

Step 1. Calculate the project NPV's in the usual manner.

These are as follows:

$$A = £23,245$$
$$B = £28,414$$
$$C = £37,939$$

Step 2. Formulate the problem in LP terms which means defining the objective function and the constraints. The objective for Trent Ltd is to maximise NPV and this may be expressed as:

$$\text{maximise: } 23,245X_A + 28,414X_B + 37,939X_C$$

where: X_A is the proportion of Project A to be initiated

           X_B is the proportion of Project B to be initiated

           X_C is the proportion of Project C to be initiated

The constraints in this problem are the budgetary limitations in Periods 0 and 1.

Capital at time 0: $15,000X_A + 25,000X_B + 35,000X_C \leq 40,000$

Capital at time 1: $25,000X_A + 15,000X_B + 15,000X_C \leq 35,000$

In addition it is necessary to specify the formal constraints regarding the proportions of projects accepted to ensure that a project cannot be accepted more than once or that 'negative' projects are accepted.

ie $\qquad\qquad\qquad\qquad\qquad X_A, X_B, X_C \leq 1$

and $\qquad\qquad\qquad\qquad\qquad X_A, X_B, X_C \leq 1$

The whole formula appears thus:

maximise:	$23,245X_A$	$+$	$28,414X_B$	$+$	$37,939X_C$		
subject to	$15,000X_A$	$+$	$25,000X_B$	$+$	$35,000X_C$		$\leq 40,000$
			$25,000X_B$	$+$	$15,000X_B$	$+$ $15,000X_C$	$\geq 35,500$
	X_A						≤ 1
				X_B			≤ 1
						X_C	≤ 1
	X_A						≥ 0
				X_B			≥ 0
						X_C	≥ 0

Step 3. Solve the LP Problem.

The above formulation can then be solved by the Simplex method as described previously. It will be apparent that even with a highly simplified problem such as this manual solution methods are exceedingly tedious and accordingly it is unlikely that a student would have to work through the method in examinations.

However, formulation of the problem and interpretation of results are possible topics.

The solution of the above problem is as follows:

Project	Fraction accepted
A	0.988
B	0
C	0.719

Value of objective function **£50,244.**

Shadow prices: 1st constraint (ie £40,000 Year 0 budget) $=$ **0.922**

2nd constraint (ie £35,000 Year 1 budget) $=$ **0.3755**

Step 4. Interpretation of Solution

The solution indicates that 0.988 of Project A and 0.719 of Project C should be initiated. This investment plan uses all the funds available in Years 0 and 1.

The shadow prices indicate the amount by which the NPV of the optimal plan (ie £50,244) could be increased if the budgetary constraints could be increased. For every £1 relaxation of the constraint in Period 0, £0.922 extra NPV would be obtained. The shadow prices indicate that extra funds in Period 0 are worth approximately three times those in Period 1. This fact may give management some guidance in their consideration of various alternative sources of capital.

Note: It will be remembered the assumption made in this example is that these projects are divisible. This is not necessarily a very practical assumption, but it appears to be one frequently made in examinations. Being divisible the NPV is scaled down by the proportion of the project accepted. This is a way of checking the result obtained. In this example the value of NPV obtained is £50,244, ie $(0.988 \times £23,245) + (0.719 \times 37,939)$.

Where projects are not divisible the only feasible solution method is Integer Programming which is outside the scope of the syllabuses at which this book is aimed.

42. Reservations over the LP method of solving capital rationing problems

There is no doubt that in the right circumstances LP can be a useful method of dealing with multi-period capital rationing problems. There are, however, numerous assumptions and limitations which must be kept in mind if the use of the technique is being considered. The major ones are as follows:

a) Is the assumption of linearity for all functions realistic?

b) Are projects truly divisible and capable of being scaled in a linear fashion?

c) Are all investment opportunities included for each of the periods contained in the model?

d) Are all projects and constraints independent of one another as assumed in the LP model?

e) Are all cash flows, resources, constraints known with the certainty assumed in the model? (The way that uncertainty is ignored is possibly the most significant reservation).

f) Is the choice of discount rate a realistic one? Under 'hard' capital rationing (ie externally imposed) the opportunity cost of funds cannot be known until the investments plan is formulated which, of course, requires the cost of funds to be known – a classic circular argument!

43. Summary

a) Specific inflation is of more direct concern in investment appraisal and differential inflation is commonly encountered.

b) The general treatment of inflation in investment appraisal is concerned with distinguishing between the real and nominal value of money and can be dealt with by either single or double discounting.

c) Because taxation affects the cash flows of a project it is a factor to be considered. It affects a project in three ways: taxes on profits, investment incentives, and its effect on the cost of capital.

d) Some taxation implications have beneficial effects on projects, eg investment incentives and the fact that interest payments are an allowable charge.

e) Uncertainty and risk are important factors to be considered in investment appraisal. Three aspects are of special concern: individual project uncertainty, the 'portfolio' effect, and the decision makers' attitude to risk.

f) Individual project uncertainty can be analysed by three groups of techniques: time-based, probability-based, and sensitivity analysis and simulation.

g) The main problem with the time based methods is that they do not explicitly consider the variability of cashflows.

h) The probability-based methods use subjective probabilities and range from expected value through to methods employing statistical analysis based on the properties of distributions.

i) Arguably of more importance than individual project risk is the aggregate risk of the firm's portfolio of projects. New projects may, to some extent, neutralise or enhance existing risks.

j) Using the covariance of project returns and returns on existing operations the correlation coefficients of new and existing projects can be calculated.

k) The decision maker's attitude to risk is of critical importance but is extremely difficult to quantify. In general, decision makers are risk averters.

l) Capital rationing is where all apparently profitable projects cannot be initiated because of shortage of capital.

m) The decision rule where capital rationing exists is to maximise the return from the project(s) selected rather than simply accept/reject decisions of projects in isolation.

n) Single period rationing with divisible projects is dealt with by ranking in order of EVPI, having due regard to mutually exclusive projects. Where the projects are indivisible then a trial and error combination approach can be used.

o) Multi-period capital rationing with divisible projects is usually solved by LP which produces the optimal solution quantities (ie the projects to be initiated) the value of the objective function (ie the total NPV) and the shadow costs (ie opportunity costs of the binding constraints).

p) Although useful there are a number of reservations of using LP for solving capital rationing problems.

44. Points to note

a) The treatment of such matters as inflation and uncertainty have been dealt with in this chapter in the context of investment appraisal. However the concepts and techniques described have a much wider application than just investment decisions. For example, the uses of expected values, sensitivity analysis and the concept of the real as opposed to the nominal value of money are applicable in virtually every area of planning and decision making.

b) Because of the amount of data involved and the complexity of the techniques used, computers are widely employed for investment appraisals, particularly in the area of risk evaluation and sensitivity analysis. to obtain the maximum benefit from the computer packages it is essential that the management accountant is totally familiar with the appraisal principles and concepts upon which the programs are based.

c) Valuable information can sometimes be gleaned from carrying out a post audit of a capital project. This should include a review of the forecasts and out-turns for all the factors involved, eg cash flows, length of life, inflation rates and so on as well as the appraisal methods used.

d) A common application of investment appraisal is the analysis of purchase c.f. leasing. Frequently the decision to purchase or lease depends on the taxation rules in operation at the time. In general, when an organisation leases an item the leasing payments are fully tax deductible but the firm (the lessee) loses the capital allowances which accrue to the leasing company (the lessor). Each case is different and individual analysis is required which should follow the following pattern.

i) Calculate the present value of the lease arrangement with the necessary adjustments for taxation including the time lags.

ii) Calculate the present value of outright purchase including the taxation effects of capital allowances and any loan repayments made if it is necessary to raise a loan to purchase the asset.

iii) Choose the cheapest acquisition method between (i) and (ii), both of which will show negative present values.

iv) Calculate the present value of the trading operations of the asset and project with the usual taxation adjustment for profits and/or losses. This present value will be positive and care must be taken NOT to include any form of acquisition costs (purchase or lease) in this part of the analysis. This has been dealt with in steps (i) and (ii).

v) Compare the best present value of lease or purchase, ie (i) or (ii) with the trading present value form (iv) to decide whether the project is worth while initiating.

Additional reading

Economics of Capital Budgeting; *Bromwich* – Pitman

Business decisions under inflation; *Carlsberg & Hope* – ICA.

Capital investment and financial decisions; *Levy & Sarnat* – Prentice Hall

Investment appraisal and Financing decisions; *Lumby* – Chapman & Hall

Capital budgeting in the 1990s; *Pike & Wolfe* – CIMA

Financial Management & Policy; *Van Horne* – Prentice Hall

Investment Appraisal and Inflation; *Westwick and Shohet* – ICA.

Self review questions

1. What is specific inflation and why is it important in investment appraisal? (2)
2. Distinguish between money and 'real' cash flows. (4)
3. What is the relationship between real and money discount factors? (6)
4. Why is it necessary to consider taxation in investment appraisal and in what ways does taxation affect a project? (7-9)
5. What are the steps in considering taxation in project appraisals? (14)
6. In which stages of the appraisal and decision process should uncertainty and risk be considered? (15)

7.   What are the time based methods of considering uncertainty? What is their underlying assumption and their major limitation? (17-21)

8.   Describe the method of using Expected Value in project appraisals. (23)

9.   How does discrete probabilistic analysis extend the expected value technique? (24)

10. What is continuous probabilistic analysis and, if used, how are the means and dispersions of the cash flows established? (25 & 26)

11. How is the standard deviation of the NPV established and how is this used? (27)

12. What is the objective of sensitivity analysis and how is it carried out? (30)

13. Why is it important to consider not only the risks of individual projects but the aggregate risk of combinations of projects? (31)

14. What is the general procedure for assessing the portfolio risk? (33)

15. What are risk averters? (33)

16. What is a certainty equivalent? (34)

17. What is the difference between 'hard' and 'soft' capital rationing? (35)

18. How would the investment decision be made if single period rationing existed with divisible projects? (37)

19. How would the answer to 18 change if some of the projects were mutually exclusive? (38)

20. What is multi-period capital rationing and what is a possible solution method? (40)

21. What reservations existing regarding the use of LP to solve capital rationing problems? (42)

Assessment and revision section 4

Examination questions with answers

A1   You are a Management Accountant in a large broadcasting organisation. At present the various service departments provide services on demand to users within the organisation at no charge. The managers are considering introducing an internal charging system within the organisation and have asked for your advice.

You are required:

a)   to describe the advantages and disadvantages of the current system;

b)   to explain what would be the likely motivational, control, and administrative effects of internal charging for services;

c)   to suggest three possible bases of charging that could be used, together with their advantages and disadvantages.

CIMA, Management Accounting Techniques.

A2. The over-riding feature of information for decision making is that it should be relevant for the decision being taken. However, decision making varies considerably, at different levels within an organisation, thus posing particular difficulties for the management accountant.

You are required:

a) to describe the characteristics of decision making at different levels within an organisation;

b) to explain how the management accountant must tailor the information provided for the various levels;

c) to give an example of a typical management decision, state at what level this would normally be taken and what specific information should be supplied to the decision maker.

CIMA, Management Accounting Techniques.

A3. Explain how each of the undernoted quantitative ideas and techniques may improve the budgetary planning process, suggesting a specific aspect of budgetary planning in which each may be used:

a) Learning curve

b) Linear regression analysis

c) Linear programming

d) Economic order quantity

e) Probability estimates.

(Note that detailed technical descriptions of each of a) to e) is NOT required.

ACCA, Information for Control and Decision Making.

A4. CD Ltd has for some years manufactured a product called the C which is used as a component in a variety of electrical items. Although the C remains in demand, the technology on which its design is based has become obsolete. CD Ltd's engineers have developed a new product called the D which incorporates new technology. The D is smaller and more reliable than the C but performs exactly the same function.

The management of CD Ltd is considering whether to continue production of the C or discontinue the C and start production of the D. CD Ltd does not have the means to produce both products simultaneously.

If the C is produced then unit sales in year 1 are forecast to be 24,000, but declining by 4,000 units in each subsequent year. Additional equipment costing £70,000 must be purchased now if C production is to continue.

If the D is produced then unit sales in year 1 are forecast to be 6,000, but a rapid increase in unit sales is expected thereafter. Additional equipment costing £620,000 must be purchased now if D production is to start.

Relevant details of the two products are as follows:

	C	D
	£	£
Variable cost per unit	25	50
Selling price per unit	55	105

CD Ltd normally appraises investments using a 12% per annum compound cost of money and ignores cashflows beyond five years from the start of investments.

Required:

a) Advise CD Ltd's management on the minimum annual growth in unit sales of the D needed to justify starting D production now – using CD Ltd's normal investment appraisal rules. Support your advice with a full financial evaluation.

b) Advise CD Ltd's management on the number of years to which its investment appraisal time horizon (currently five years) would have to be extended in order to justify starting D production now if the forecast annual increase in D sales is 2,800 units.

c) State and explain any factors not included in your financial evaluation that CD Ltd should consider in making its decision.

Note: You should ignore inflation, and the residual values of equipment.

CIMA, Management Accounting Applications.

A5. Bushworks Ltd convert synthetic slabs into components AX and BX for use in the car industry. Bushworks Ltd is planning a quality management programme at a cost of £250,000. The following information relates to the costs incurred by Bushworks Ltd both before and after the implementation of the quality management programme:

1. *Synthetic slabs*

Synthetic slabs cost £40 per hundred. On average 2.5% of synthetic slabs received are returned to the supplier as scrap because of deterioration in stores. The supplier allows a credit of £1 per hundred slabs for such returns. In addition, on receipt in stores, checks to ensure that the slabs received conform to specification costs £14,000 per annum.

A move to a just-in-time purchasing system will eliminate the holding of stocks of synthetic slabs. This has been negotiated with the supplier who will deliver slabs of guaranteed design specification for £44 per hundred units, eliminating all stock-holding costs.

2. *Curing/moulding process*

The synthetic slabs are issued to a curing/moulding process which has variable conversion costs of £20 per hundred slabs input. This process produces sub-components A and B which have the same cost structure. Losses of 10% of input to the process because of incorrect temperature control during the process are sold as scrap at £5 per hundred units. The quality programme will rectify the temperature control problem thus reducing losses to 1% of input to the process.

3. *Finishing process*

The finishing process has a bank of machines which perform additional operations on type A and B sub-components as required and converts them into final components AX and BX respectively. The variable conversion costs in the finishing process for AX and BX are £15 and £25 per hundred units respectively. At the end of the finishing process 15% of units are found to be defective. Defective units are sold for scrap at £10 per hundred units. The quality programme will convert the finishing process into two dedicated cells, one for each of component types AX and BX. The dedicated cell variable costs per hundred sub-components A and B processed will be £12 and £20 respectively. Defective units of components AX and BX are expected to fall to 2.5% of the input to each cell. Defective components will be sold as scrap as at present.

4. *Finished goods*

A finished goods stock of components AX and BX of 15,000 and 30,000 units respectively is held throughout the year in order to allow for customer demand fluctuations and free replacement of units returned by customers due to specification faults. Customer returns are currently 2.5% of components delivered to customers. Variable stock holding costs are £15 per thousand component units.

The proposed dedicated cell layout of the finishing process will eliminate the need to hold stocks of finished components, other than sufficient to allow for the free replacement of ;those found to be defective in customer hands. This stock level will be set at one month's free replacement to customers which is estimated at 500 and 1,000 units for types AX and BX respectively. Variable stockholding costs will remain at £15 per thousand component units.

5. *Quantitative data*

Some preliminary work has already been carried out in calculating the number of units of synthetic slabs, sub-components A and B and components AX and BX which will be required both before and after the implementation of the quality management programme, making use of the information in the question. Table 1 summarises the relevant figures.

	Existing situation		Amended situation	
	Type A/AX (units)	Type B/BX (units)	Type A/AX (units)	Type B/BX (units)
Sales	800,000	1,200,000	800,000	1,200,000
Customer returns	20,000	30,000	6,000	12,000
Finished goods delivered	820,000	1,230,000	806,000	1,212,000
Finishing process losses	144,706	217,059	20,667	31,077
Input to finishing process	964,706	1,447,059	826,667	1,243,077

	2,411,765	2,069,744
Curing/moulding losses	267,974	20,907
Input to curing/moulding	2,679,739	2,090,651
Stores losses	68,711	–
Purchase of synthetic slabs	2,748,450	2,090,651

Table 1

Required:

a) Evaluate and present a statement showing the net financial benefit or loss per annum of implementing the quality management programme, using the information in the question and the data in Table 1.

(*All relevant workings must be shown.*)

b) Explain the meaning of the terms internal failure costs, external failure costs, appraisal costs and prevention costs giving examples of each.

ACCA, Information for Control and Decision Making.

A6. EZ Limited, well established in the express parcel delivery business, is evaluating a new venture – the establishment of a motorcycle courier service offering same-day delivery.

The venture would require the purchase of a building for £250,000, payable immediately. The building would need extensive alterations costing £150,000 to enable it to become the control and distribution centre for the venture. The alterations would take a year, and operations could not commence until the building was ready. Immediately after completion of the building EZ Limited would take delivery of 100 motorcycles at £4,000 each and engage riders.

Running costs of the operation in current prices are expected to be fixed costs of £750,000 per annum and a variable cost of £1 per packet. Fixed costs are expected to increase by 8% per year and variable costs by 5% per year. £50,000 of working capital would need to be injected immediately prior to the completion of the building.

A market research survey, undertaken at a cost of £40,000, suggests that the price per packet should be £5 or £8. At these prices the following numbers of packets are forecast:

Expected packets per year (000)

Probability of demand	Price £5	Price £8
0.10	175	160
0.20	275	190
0.40	350	210
0.20	375	230
0.10	400	260

The above prices are at current price levels and are expected to increase by 5% at the end of each year.

Over the next five years, EZ Limited's cost of capital is expected to be 15% per annum, constant. The board wishes to evaluate the venture over the first five years of operations, at the end of which the realisable value of the venture as a going concern is expected to be £1m.

Unless otherwise stated, assume all cash flows take place at the end of the year. Ignore tax.

You are required:

a) to decide, with reasons, which price for the packets would maximise profit;

b) to calculate the expected net present value of the venture for the first five years of operations;

c) to discuss any limitations of the methods and data used and to state what recommendation you would make about the venture.

CIMA, Management Accounting Techniques.

A7. Armcliff Ltd is a division of Shevin plc which requires each of its divisions to achieve a rate of return on capital employed of at least 10% p.a. For this purpose, capital employed is defined as fixed capital and investment in stocks. This rate or return is also applied as a hurdle rate for new investment projects. Divisions have limited borrowing powers and all capital projects are centrally funded.

The following is an extract from Armcliff's divisional accounts:

Profit and loss account for the year ended 31 December 1994

	£m
Turnover	120
Cost of sales	(100)
Operating profit	20

Assets employed as at 31 December 1994

	£m	£m
Fixed (net):		75
Current assets (inc. stocks £25m)	45	
Current liabilities:	(32)	13
Net capital employed		88

Armcliff's production engineers wish to invest in a new computer-controlled press. The equipment cost is £14m. The residual value is expected to be £2m after four years operation, when the equipment will be shipped to a customer in South America.

The new machine is capable of improving the quality of the existing product and also of producing a higher volume. The firm's marketing team is confident of selling the increased volume by extending the credit period. The expected additional sales are:

Year 1	2,000,000 units
Year 2	1,800,000 units
Year 3	1,600,000 units
Year 4	1,600,000 units

Sales volume is expected to fall over time due to emerging competitive pressures. Competition will also necessitate a reduction in price by £0.5 each year from the £5 per unit proposed in the first year. Operating costs are expected to be steady at £1 per unit, and allocation of overheads (none of which are affected by the new project) by the central finance department is set at £0.75 per unit.

Higher production levels will require additional investment in stocks of £0.5m, which would be held at this level until the final stages of operation of the project. Customers at present settle accounts after 90 days on average.

Required:

a) Determine whether the proposed capital investment is attractive to Armcliff, using the average rate of return on capital method, as defined as average profit-to-average capital employed, ignoring debtors and creditors.

   (Note: Ignore taxes)

b) (i) Suggest *three* problems which arise with the use of the average return method for appraising new investment.

   (ii) In view of the problems associated with the ARR method, why do companies continue to use it in project appraisal?

c) Briefly discuss the dangers of offering more generous credit, and suggest ways of assessing customers' credit worthiness.

ACCA, Managerial Finance.

A8. Trenset plc has a semi-automated machine process in which a number of tasks are performed. A system of standard costing and budgetary control is in operation. The process is controlled by machine minders who are paid a fixed rate per hour of process time. The process has recently been reorganised as part of an ongoing total quality management programme in the company. The nature of the process is such that the machines incur variable costs even during non-productive (idle time) hours. Non-productive hours include time spent on the rework of products. *Note that gross machine hours = productive hours + non-productive (idle time) hours.*

The standard data for the machine process are as follows:

(i) Standard non-productive (idle time) hours as a percentage of gross machine hours is 10%.

(ii) Standard variable machine cost per gross hour is £270.

(iii) Standard output productivity is 100% i.e. one standard hour of work is expected in each productive machine hour.

(iv) Machine costs are charged to production output at a rate per standard hour sufficient to absorb the cost of the standard level of non-productive time.

Actual data for the period August to November has been summarised as follows:

	Aug.	*Sept.*	*Oct.*	*Nov.*
Standard hours of output achieved	3,437	3,437	4,061	3,980
Machine hours (gross)	4,000	3,800	4,200	4,100
Non-productive machine hours	420	430	440	450
Variable machine costs (£000)	1,100	1,070	1,247	1,218
Variance analysis:	£	£	£	£
Productivity	42,900(A)	?	?	99,000(F)
Excess idle time	6,000(A)	?	?	12,000(A)
Expenditure	20,000(A)	?	?	111,000(A)
Variance analysis (in % terms)	%	%	%	%
Productivity	4.2(A)	?	7.4(F)	?
Excess idle time	5.0(A)	?	4.8(A)	?
Expenditure	1.9(A)	?	10.0(A)	?

Required:

a) Calculate the machine variances for productivity, excess idle time and expenditure for each of the months September and October.

b) In order to highlight the trend of the variances in the August to November period, express each variance in percentage terms as follows:

Productivity variance: as a percentage of the standard cost of production achieved.

Excess idle time variance: as a percentage of the cost of expected idle time.

Expenditure variance: as a percentage of hours paid for at standard machine cost per hour.

(Note that the August and October calculations are given in the question.)

c) Comment on the trend of the variances in the August to November period and possible inter-relationships, particularly in the context of the total quality management programme which is being implemented.

d) Management are considering an investigation of the excess idle time variance during December. The decision whether to investigate will be made on the basis of the following estimated figures:

(i) The average excess idle time variance will be eliminated at the end of March as the existing total quality management programme takes effect. Until that time it is estimated that the excess idle time variance will continue to occur each month at a level equal to 75% of the November variance. The December idle time variance will remain unaffected irrespective of the action taken, and should not be included in your calculations.

(ii) The additional investigation will have an initial cost of £1,500 to determine whether the variance is controllable in the January to March period.

(iii) The cost of taking control action will be £7,000 per month which would eliminate the variance from January onwards if the variance responds to the planned control action. The variance may not respond to the control action and remain unchanged.

(iv) The probability that the variance is controllable in the January to March period is 0.4.

(v) The probability that the variance will respond to the proposed control action is 0.8.

Advise management of the expected net cost or benefit of the investigation proposal and comment on the reliability of the results obtained. Your answer should include a decision tree illustration of the situation.

ACCA, Information for Control and Decision Making.

A9. MNO Ltd produces two products – W and B. Both are components that have a wide range of industrial applications. MNO Ltd's share of the market for W is insignificant but is one of a limited number of suppliers of B. W is a long-established product and B is a new product.

The market price of W is £128 and that of B £95. MNO Ltd is unable to influence these prices.

The resource requirements for producing one unit of each of the two products are:

	process hours	kgs of material	labour hours
W	4	8	21.8
B	3	14.25	7.5

Materials cost £3 per kg and labour costs £3.20 per hour. Other costs are fixed.

During the coming period the company will have the following resources available to it:

> 1,200 process hours
> 4,000 kgs of material
> 6,000 labour hours

You are required, as MNO Ltd's management accountant,

a) to advise the company of the output combination of W and B that will maximise its profit in the coming period (support your advise with full financial analysis);

b) to write a memorandum suitable for circulation to MNO Ltd's board of directors explaining the commercial limitations of the model you have used in your answer to part (a).

CIMA Management Accounting – Decision making

Examination questions without answers

B1. For some time the BB company has sold its entire output of canned goods to super-market chains which sell them as 'own label' products. One advantage of this arrangement is that BB incurs no marketing costs, but there is continuing pressure from the chains on prices and margins are tight.

As a consequence, BB is considering selling some of its output under the BB brand when margins will be better but there will be substantial marketing costs.

The following information is available:

	Current years results - 1992 (adjusted to 1993 cost levels)	Forecast for 1993 (assuming all 'own labels' sales)
Sales (millions of cans)	18	19
	£million	£million
Sales	5.94	6.27
Manufacturing costs	4.30	4.45
Administration costs	1.20	1.20
Profit	0.44	0.62

For 1993 the unit contribution on BB brand sales is expected to be $33\frac{1}{3}$% greater than own label sales, but variable marketing costs of 2p per can and fixed marketing costs of £400,000 will be incurred.

You are required:

a) to prepare a contribution break-even chart for 1993 assuming that all sales will be own label;

b) to prepare a contribution break-even chart for 1993 assuming that 50% of sales are own label and 50% are of the BB brand;

Note: The break-even points and margins of safety must be shown clearly on the charts.

c) to comment on the positions shown by the charts and your calculations and to discuss what other factors management should consider before making a decision.

(Ignore inflation)

CIMA, Management Accounting Techniques.

B2. a) In an attempt to win over key customers in the motor industry and to increase its market share, BIL Motor Components plc have decided to charge a price lower than their normal price for component TD463 when selling to the key customers who are being targeted. Details of component TD463's standard costs are as follows:

Standard cost data	Component TD463 Batch size 200 units			
	Machine Group 1	Machine Group 7	Machine Group 29	Assembly
	£	£	£	£
Materials (per unit)	26.00	17.00		3.00
Labour (per unit)	2.00	1.60	.75	1.20
Variable overheads (per unit)	.65	.72	.80	.36
Fixed overheads (per unit)	3.00	2.50	1.50	.84
	31.65	21.82	3.05	5.40
Setting-up costs per batch of 200 units	£10	£6	£4	–

Required:

Compute the lowest selling price at which one batch of 200 units could be offered, and critically evaluate the adoption of such a pricing policy.

b) The company is also considering the launch of a new product, component TDX489, and have provided you with the following information:

Product TDX489	Standard cost per box
	£
Variable cost	6.20
Fixed cost	1.60
	7.80

Market research - forecast of demand

Selling price (£)	13	12	11	10	9
Demand (boxes)	5,000	6,000	7,200	11,200	13,400

The company only has enough production capacity to make 7,000 boxes. However, it would be possible to purchase product TDX489 from a sub-contractor at £7.75 per box for orders up to 5,000 boxes, and £7 per box if the orders exceed 5,000 boxes.

Required:

Prepare and present a computation which illustrates which price should be selected in order to maximise profits.

c) Where production capacity is the 'limiting factor', explain briefly the ways in which management can increase it without having to acquire more plant and machinery.

ACCA, Managerial Finance.

B3. EX Limited is an established supplier of precision parts to a major aircraft manufacturer. It has been offered the choice of making either Part A or Part B for the next period, but not both.

Both parts use the same metal, a titanium alloy, of which 13,000 kilos only are available, at £12.50 per kilo. The parts are made by passing each one through two fully-automatic computer-controlled machine lines - S and T - whose capacities are limited. Target prices have been set and the following data are available for the period:

Part details:		
	Part A	Part B
Maximum call-off (units)	7,000	9,000
Target price	£145 per unit	£115 per unit
Alloy usage	1.6 kilos	1.6 kilos
Machine times		
Line S	0.6 hours	0.25 hours
Line T	0.5 hours	0.55 hours

Machine details:		
	Line S	Line T
Hours available	4,000	4,500
Variable overhead per machine hour	£80	£100

You are required:

a) to calculate which part should be made during the next period to maximise contribution;

b) to calculate the contribution which EX Limited will earn and whether the company will be able to meet the maximum call-off.

As an alternative to the target prices shown above, the aircraft manufacturer has offered the following alternative arrangement:

Target prices less 10% plus £60 per hour for each unused machine hour.

c) **You are required** to decide whether your recommendation in a) above will be altered and, if so, to calculate the new contribution.

CIMA, Management Accounting Techniques.

B4. Recyc plc is a company which reprocesses factory waste in order to extract good quality aluminium. Information concerning its operations is as follows:

(i) Recyc plc places an advance order each year for chemical X for use in the aluminium extraction process. It will enter into an advance contract for the coming year for chemical X at one of three levels - high, medium or low, which correspond to the requirements of a high, medium or low level of waste available for reprocessing.

(ii) The level of waste available will not be known when the advance order for chemical X is entered into. A set of probabilities have been estimated by management as to the likelihood of the quantity of waste being at a high, medium or low level.

(iii) Where the advance order entered into for chemical X is lower than that required for the level of waste for processing actually received, a discount from the original demand price is allowed by the supplier for the total quantity of chemical X actually required.

iv) Where the advance order entered into for chemical X is in excess of that required to satisfy the actual level of waste for reprocessing, a penalty payment in excess of the original demand price is payable for the total quantity of chemical X actually required.

A summary of the information relating to the above points is as follows:

Level of reprocessing	Waste available	Probability	Chemical X costs per kg		
			Advance order	Conversion discount	Conversion premium
	000 kg		£	£	£
High	50,000	0.30	1.00		
Medium	38,000	0.50	1.20		
Low	30,000	0.20	1.40		
Chemical X: order conversion:					
Low to medium				0.10	
Medium to high				0.10	
Low to high				0.15	
Medium to low					0.25
High to medium					0.25
High to low					0.60

Aluminium is sold at £0.65 per kg. Variable costs (excluding chemical X costs) are 70% of sales revenue.

Aluminium extracted from the waste is 15% of the waste input. Chemical X is added to the reprocessing at the rate of 1kg per 100kg of waste.

Required:

a) Prepare a summary which shows the budgeted contribution earned by Recyc plc for the coming year for each of nine possible outcomes.

b) On the basis of maximising expected value, advise Recyc plc whether the advance order for chemical X should be at low, medium or high level.

c) State the contribution for the coming year which corresponds to the use of (i) maximax and (ii) maximin decision criteria, and comment on the risk preference of management which is indicated by each.

d) Recyc plc are considering employing a consultant who will be able to say with certainty in advance of the placing of the order for chemical X, which level of waste will be available for reprocessing.

On the basis of expected value, determine the maximum sum which Recyc plc should be willing to pay the consultant for this information.

e) Explain and comment on the steps involved in evaluating the purchase of imperfect information from the consultant in respect of the quantity of waste which will be available for reprocessing.

ACCA, Information for Control and Decision Making.

B5. Assume that you are the financial controller of a large manufacturing company, which produces clothing for large retail stores.

The production director has a problem in interpreting the summarised management accounts for 1993 compared with 1992. He fully understands that in the clothing business margins are small and efficiency is vital. He does not consider himself responsible for the losses on labour efficiency, overheads and production volume.

	1992	1993
	£000	£000
Sales	61,858	57,008
Direct material	32,208	30,620
Direct labour	11,438	10,633
Factory overhead	14,569	14,697
Selling overhead	3,492	3,312
Total cost	61,707	59,262
Profit/(loss)	151	(2,254)

He considers that the losses in 1993 against 1992 arise from

1. making more styles, in smaller quantities per style,
2. making a large number of sample (or experimental) garments in very small quantities to show to the store buyers.

Each style is made up in a single batch and thus has only a single set up.

He has some statistics on quantities produced and costs associated with the production, as follows:

	Styles (and set ups)		Production (dozens)	
	1992	1993	1992	1993
Samples	470	740	1,410	2,960
Short production runs	280	504	117,600	206,800
Long production runs	90	52	182,000	68,600

	Annual Costs			
	1992		1993	
Set up related costs	£000	£000	£000	£000
Mechanics: normal pay	322		384	
overtime	67	389	108	492
Direct labour: extra payment for learning new style: double pay for first 5 dozen garments of a style		124		219

Analysis of factory overheads: Variable with volume 15%; Fixed 85%.

You should assume that samples are sold at normal selling prices. Selling overhead should be assumed to be fixed costs.

a) You are required to analyse the data given above and comment on the causes of the losses and the production director's explanations.

b) The production director considers that it may be beneficial to change the batch sizes for non-sample runs. He has provided further data for the three categories of production:

(i)   Short production run garments: 75% of short production run garments for immediate sale to customers, holding cost 10% of cost

(ii) Short production run garments: 25% of short production run garments held in finished goods stock until needed, holding cost 20% of cost

(iii) Long production run garments: All held in finished good stock until needed, holding cost 20% of cost

You are required to analyse the data for 1993 for *each* of the *three* categories of production given above and advise whether the current policy of making garments of the same style in one production run is appropriate for 1994.

Use the simple version of the EOQ/EBQ formula $\sqrt{\dfrac{2CoD}{Ch}}$

c) Considering that there may be problems in this approach, you also look at data being collected as part of an internal study on Activity Based Costing

Cost	*Cost Driver*
Direct material	Volume
Direct labour (excluding learning)	Volume
Learning	Number of production runs
Set up	Number of production runs
Design	Number of styles (= number of production runs)
Planning and control	Number of production runs
Finished stock	Number of garments put in stock
Factory overhead	Volume

Annual factory overhead 1993

	£000
Garment design	974
Production planning and control	2,512
Mechanics	492
Finished stock handling	870
Production related costs	9,849
	14,697

You are required:

(i)   to calculate the costs of small and large production runs and samples using the ABC study data,

(ii) to compare these costs with the average conventional costs,

(iii) to comment on the differences between these results and those in a) and the extent to which they explain the production director's problems.

d) Explain how, in the implementation of an ABC system, cost drivers should be selected, and what factors determine how many cost drivers are required.

CIMA, Management Accounting - Control and Audit.

B6. a) Distinguish between hard and soft capital rationing, explaining why a company may deliberately choose to restrict its capital expenditure.

b) Filtrex plc is a medium-sized, all equity-financed, unquoted company which specialises in the development and production of water- and air-filtering devices to reduce the emission of effluents. Its small but ingenious R and D team has recently made a technological breakthrough which has revealed a number of attractive investment opportunities. It has applied for patents to protect its rights in all these areas. However, it lacks the financial resources required to exploit all of these projects, whose required outlays and post-tax NPVs are listed in the table below. Filtrex's managers consider that delaying any of these projects would seriously undermine their profitability, as competitors bring forward their own new developments. All projects are thought to have a similar degree of risk.

Project	(£) Required outlay	(£) NPV
A	150,000	65,000
B	120,000	50,000
C	200,000	80,000
D	80,000	30,000
E	400,000	120,000

The NPVs have been calculated using as a discount rate the 18% post-tax rate of return which Filtrex required for risky R & D ventures. The maximum amount available for this type of investment is £400,000, corresponding to Filtrex's present cash balances, built up over several year' profitable trading. Projects A and C are mutually exclusive and no project can be sub-divided. Any unused capital will either remain invested in short-term deposits or used to purchase marketable securities, both of which offer a return well below 18% post-tax.

Required:

(i) Advise Filtrex plc, using suitable supporting calculations, which combination of projects should be undertaken in the best interests of shareholders, and

(ii) Suggest what further information might be obtained to assist a fuller analysis.

c) Explain how, apart from delaying projects, Filtrex plc could manage to exploit more of these opportunities.

ACCA, Managerial Finance.

B7. Zerochance Ltd manufactures gaming machines and is exploring the possibility of making and selling a new machine.

Estimates have been made of the net cash flows (in £ million) of the project, and of their variability expressed as the standard deviation of the cash flows, as follows:

Year	0	1	2	3	4	5
Most likely value of net cash flow	-5	1.3	1.8	2.1	1.4	1.7
Standard deviation of cash flows	0	0.13	0.19	0.34	0.34	0.46

As an alternative to the risky investment in the new machine, Zerochance Ltd is able to invest the £5 million initial cost on the money markets, for which it would receive a five-year annuity of £1.31926 million per year, commencing after one year.

The money market investment is virtually risk-free.

You are required:

a) to calculate the NPV of the new machine project, using the risk-free return as the discount rate;

b) to calculate the standard deviation of the new machine project's NPV.

c) Zerochance Ltd has rules of thumb when analysing risky investments. Its rules are that the risky investment must have a most likely NPV of at least £1 million, and that there must be at least an 85% chance of obtaining a positive NPV.

   You are required to assess the risky investment according to Zerochance Ltd's decision rules and to recommend whether it should be initiated.

   Note: You are reminded that the formula for the standard deviation of NPV is

$$\sigma_{NPV} = \sqrt{\Sigma\left(\frac{\sigma_i}{(1+r)^i}\right)^2}$$

CIMA, Management Accounting Techniques.

Performance Appraisal

The work of the management accountant can range from the analysis of detailed aspects of operations such as calculating variances or job costs, to consideration of performance at a broader, macro level. This may involve assessing the performance of autonomous or semi-autonomous divisions of the same firm or considering the performance and stability of whole companies perhaps for the purpose of investment or acquisition. Alternatively it may involve assessing and measuring the performance of a non-profit organisation such as a Local Authority.

This section of the book deals with aims, techniques and limitations of performance appraisal systems in both the public and private sectors. There is detailed coverage of transfer pricing which becomes necessary when divisions of the same company trade with each other and it is desired to assess the profitability of each division. Ratio analysis relating to internal efficiency, solvency and investment is explained and the section concludes with an outline of value -added statements as an aid to performance appraisal.

19 Divisional performance appraisal

1. Objectives

After studying this chapter you will:

❑ understand the decision process and the importance of relevant information;

❑ know why performance appraisal is necessary in divisionalised concerns;

❑ understand the benefits and problems of decentralisation;

❑ be able to describe cost centres, profit centres and investment centres;

❑ know the various types of profitability measures used for performance appraisal;

❑ be able to calculate residual profit;

❑ understand the advantages and disadvantages of Return on Capital Employed (ROCE);

❑ know the problems of performance measurement in not-for-profit organisations and the Public Sector;

❑ be able to calculate efficience measures;

❑ understand value for money audits.

2. Divisionalisation and performance appraisal

Particularly in large companies, there has been substantial decentralisation of managerial decision making from central management to the operating divisions of the company. This has occurred in existing single companies and also as a consequence of merger activity. Typically, mergers result in a large, diversified group consisting of a number of operating divisions, with various degrees of autonomy, answerable to the holding company or the main board of directors. As a result of such structural changes the financial control of divisions by central management has become a complex and vital task. It is one in which the practising management accountant, particularly at senior levels, has a key role in the design and operation of performance appraisal systems which assist central management to ensure that the company as a whole – including the divisions – fulfils overall company objectives.

Before examining the techniques and methods of performance appraisal it is necessary to consider the reasons why decentralisation occurs and to discuss the potential problems which may arise if the process works imperfectly and there is inadequate monitoring.

3. What is decentralisation?

As organisations grow in size and complexity top management find themselves unable to make all the decisions. In such circumstances authority for certain types of decision-making is delegated to subordinate managers and thus some decision making moves away from the centre and decentralisation takes place.

The amount of decentralisation can vary widely. In theory, total decentralisation could occur whereby a division operated completely autonomously with authority to make all types of decisions and would thus in effect be a separate entity. Of course, such a situation is unlikely to be encountered and whilst the amount of delegated authority varies considerably, certain types of decisions invariably seem to be retained by central management. Typically these include: major investment decisions, senior staff appointments and salaries and pricing decisions although in certain types of industries, for example, retailing and jobbing engineering, pricing may be considered an operational responsibility. If central management delegated these and other such major decisions it would lack strategic control of the enterprise.

The main areas of divisional responsibility are connected with the day to day actions of manufacturing, selling and promotion, labour appointments and utilisation, maintenance, and customer and supplier relationships.

There are no absolute standards to judge the extent to which an organisation is decentralised. An organisation may have numerous operating divisions but with all decisions of any significance taken at the centre whilst another may have few or no identifiable divisions yet has genuine, decentralised decision making. The natural consequence of a policy of decentralisation is the creation of semi-autonomous operating divisions where the local management has considerable, but not absolute, discretion and has responsibility for divisional profitability. It is in such circumstances that formal performance appraisal and monitoring systems become necessary.

4. Objectives of decentralisation

The general purpose of decentralisation and the creation of divisional structures is to enhance the efficiency of the enterprise as a whole and to make it more capable of meeting overall objectives.

Properly organised and controlled, decentralisation should:

a) Improve local decision making.

   Divisional management are in close touch with day to day operations and are in a position to make more informed and speedier decisions.

b) Improve strategic decision making.

Central management are relieved of much lower level and routine decision making and thus able to concentrate on strategic considerations.

c) Increase flexibility and reduce communication problems.

The ability to take decisions near the point of action reduces response time and means that adjustments can be made more swiftly to cope with changes in market or supply conditions. The shorter communication lines mean quicker decisions and fewer chances of errors caused by communication channels.

d) Increase motivation of divisional management.

This is a key feature of decentralisation and arguably is the most important factor contributing to increased efficiency. Research shows that people value greater independence and respond in a positive manner to increased responsibility particularly when this is linked to the reward system of the organisation. An important factor in the design of performance appraisal systems is to ensure that motivation is not stifled and that goal congruence is encouraged.

e) The spread of genuine decision making and the increased responsibility this entails provides better training for junior management. In many organisations there are movements within divisional management and between divisional and central management thus enhancing career opportunities for able and ambitious managers. The existence of these opportunities helps to attract people of the right calibre and increases morale and motivation.

The process of decentralisation i.e. moving decision making away from the centre is not confined to the private sector. A feature of government policy in the 1980's and 1990's has been to create more local autonomy in the Public sector. Examples include the establishment of Trust Hospitals in the National Health Service and Local Management of Schools. Accordingly much of the general material on decentralisation and performance appraisal applies equally to the public and private sectors. The special features of public sector performance appraisal are dealt with later in the chapter.

5. Possible problems with decentralisation

The major potential problem with decentralisation, particularly where the divisions are highly interdependent, is that of sub-optimal decision making. This is caused by decisions where benefits to one division are more than offset by costs or loss of benefits to other divisions. Where there is a lack of congruence between the overall objectives of the organisation and the goals and aims of the local decision maker then sub-optimal decision making is likely unless there is a relevant and well design appraisal system.

Other problems and extra costs which may occur with decentralisation are the duplication of certain services in the divisions and at headquarters, eg market research, computing services, personnel functions. In addition, it is likely that decentralisation will require more sophisticated information systems. Friction may also occur between divisional managements, particularly where the performance of one division is dependent on that of another division. This problem is aggravated when financial considerations which affect divisional performance are concerned. A particular example of this is the problem of setting transfer prices for goods and services supplied by one division to another. The price at which goods or services are transferred affects the financial performance of both divisions involved and is a possible area in which sub-optimal decisions may be taken. The setting of transfer prices and the problems associated with them are discussed in detail in the following chapter.

6. Objectives of performance appraisal

When central management have decided that decentralisation should take place and operating divisions are established, some system of control or performance appraisal becomes necessary. As with any form of information system the performance appraisal system should assist management to plan and control activities, and to make decisions which enable the objectives of the organisation as a whole to be met. In particular, performance appraisal systems for monitoring divisions with substantial delegated powers, ideally should:

a) Promote goal congruence.

   The performance appraisal system and criteria employed should help local management to direct operations and to make decisions in ways that fulfil overall company objectives. Ideally the goals of local managements should coincide with overall company goals – perfect goal congruence – but of course this is a difficult state to achieve in its entirety.

b) Provide relevant and regular feedback to central management.

   Central management need regular feedback of appropriate information in order to judge the capability of local management and also to assess the economic worth of the division as an operating unit. These two aspects may be related but involved distinctively different considerations and information requirements.

c) Encourage initiative and motivation.

   The performance appraisal system should not be narrowly conceived or so rigidly applied that it stifles initiative. For example, if local management see an opportunity which would increase overall company profits but which would reduce the profits of their own division, then the system should be flexible enough for this to take place without local management feeling that they will be penalised. Local management must be encouraged to feel that, within the prescribed limits, they have genuine autonomy.

d) Encourage long run views rather than short-term expedients.

   The long-term success of the organisation is the primary objective and the performance appraisal systems and measures should encourage decision making which contributes to this objective. An over emphasis on short run considerations may cause adverse long-term effects. Short-term improvements in results are relatively easily made by, for example, forgoing proper maintenance, hiring poorer quality but cheaper staff, reducing product quality and other similar expedients. Maintaining improved results over a period is quite a different matter.

7. Responsibility centres

In Chapter 2 one type of responsibility centre was discussed. This was the cost centre which, it will be recalled, is a department or section or function over which a designated individual has responsibility for expenditure. Cost centres generally form the basis of budgetary control systems which are one form of performance appraisal usually with the emphasis on cost items.

When setting up systems to monitor the performance of semi-autonomous operating divisions the basic principles of responsibility accounting are developed beyond cost centres to what are called *profit centres* and *investment centres*.

Profit centre – this is a unit of the organisation, often called a division, which is responsible for expenditures, revenues and profits.

Investment centre – this is a profit centre for which the designated manager is responsible for profit in relation to the capital invested in the division. It should be noted that the term does not necessarily mean that the manager is responsible for the investment decisions within the division. As previously pointed out, above a fairly low limit, investment decisions are frequently the prerogative of central management.

The following table summarises the types of responsibility centres:

Centre type:	Cost Centre	Profit Centre	Investment Centre
Responsible for:			
Costs	✓	✓	✓
Revenues		✓	✓
Profits		✓	✓
Profits in relation to investment			✓

In practice it appears the the term profit centre is frequently used whether the division is responsible for just profit or profit in relation to the capital invested in the division.

8. Choice of financial appraisal measures

Having decided that a division's performance must be monitored the measures to be used need to be chosen. Should the division's performance be judged by its profit and if so on what basis should this be calculated? Or should the basis be some quite different measure such as sales growth? The considerations affecting these and other measures are dealt with below but it must be realised that no single measure can fulfil all the requirements of an ideal appraisal criterion nor can any one measure satisfactorily monitor all aspects of the multi-faceted nature of divisional operations.

Two categories of financial performance measures appear to be commonly used – those based on absolute values which are usually profitability criteria of one kind or another, and those based on relative values which are generally some form of return on investment or capital employed. These measures are dealt with below.

9. Profitability measures of performance

Profit is a widely used absolute measure of performance and is one familiar to management and acceptable to them; which is an important behavioural consideration. When profit is used as a performance measure it provides a means by which division can be compared with division and one division's performance can be compared period by period. However used, there are substantial control advantages when actual profit is compared with planned or budgeted profit.

When profit is used as measure of performance appraisal it may be defined in a variety of ways and a number of the more important variants are described below, including: controllable profit, divisional profit, net profit, controllable residual profit, and net residual profit.

After the descriptions of each type of profit a table is given showing their relationships. In addition, a worked example is provided showing the calculations necessary for each measure.

10. Controllable profit

This can be defined as revenues less costs controllable at the divisional level. The rationale for this concept is sound in that the measure includes only those costs and revenues for which local management has primary responsibility. What costs and revenues to include depends on the degree of tactical responsibility that has been delegated. Particular items that are included or excluded are dealt with below:

Variable items (costs and revenues)

In general those items of cost and revenues which are dependent on local decisions are included, for example, sales income, costs of labour, materials, operating expenses including short run interest charges relating to controllable working capital items such as debtors and inventories.

Divisional overheads

Where the items are controllable locally they would be included. This would include items which are fixed in relation to activity but can be varied by management action. Examples include administrative and supervisory costs and, where delegated to the division, advertising costs.

Depreciation and fixed asset costs

Normally these items should be excluded because the investment and disinvestment of fixed assets and hence depreciation charges are a strategic responsibility and outside the control of local management. Also, depreciation charges are based on past investment decisions and often on historical costs so do not reflect current conditions. Note that if fixed asset investment is controllable by local management then depreciation on controllable items would be included.

Apportioned items

Frequently a portion of central administration costs or part of the costs of facilities used jointly by divisions (eg computer costs) are charged to the division. By definition these are non-controllable and all such apportioned costs are excluded.

11. Divisional profit

Sometimes known as traceable profit or direct profit. This is the profit that arises from divisional operations which can be calculated without arbitrarily apportioned central costs. It is equivalent to controllable profit less depreciation on divisional assets and other non-controllable divisional overheads. It follows that a number of the costs which are identifiable with the division are not controllable by the division.

12. Net profit

This can be defined as revenues less controllable divisional costs and apportioned central administration costs.

The use of this method does allow local management to be aware of all the costs of the division and of its net effect on the group results. However, all methods of apportioning costs are arbitrary and local management have no control over the amount of costs apportioned which may be at a significant level. In such circumstances appraisal by divisional net profit may have adverse behavioural effects, reduce motivation and may lead to sub-optimal decision making.

Conceptually this method does not seem as sound as controllable profit although it appears to be commonly used.

13. Controllable residual profit or income

This is sales revenue less controllable divisional costs and interest imputed on the divisional investment. Using residual profit as a performance measure assumes that the level of divisional investment is a responsibility of divisional management. This should be contrasted with the view taken when controllable profit is used as a performance measure that the investment level is a central, strategic responsibility. It follows that depreciation should be charged on fixed assets controlled by the division when residual income is calculated. The imputed interest charge on the amount invested represented the opportunity cost of funds and is normally based n the firm's cost of capital.

It will be apparent that residual profit is a broader concept than any of the simpler profit variants and rests upon a firmer theoretical base.

The advantages and disadvantages and some of the problems associated with the application of controllable residual profit are given below.

Advantages of controllable residual profit

a) Goal congruence is encouraged because the process of charging the divisions with the firm's cost of capital ensures that managers are aware of the opportunity cost of funds and that divisional decisions, particularly relating to investment, are compatible with the aims of the organisation as a whole.

b) The use of a clear cut objective such as 'maximise residual profit' could have a strong motivating influence and would ensure that growth opportunities will not be missed providing they earn a rate of return above the cost of capital.

c) Residual profit concepts take a long run view of divisional performance. Also, an objective expressed in terms of maximising an absolute figure avoids the situation which may occur when investment opportunities would be rejected if they lowered the average divisional rate of return, expressed in relative terms, even though such opportunities earn a rate of return above the company's cost of capital. This is directly analogous to the arguments for NPV as compared with IRR discussed earlier particularly in relation to mutually exclusive investment.

Note: Return on capital employed, which is a relative measure of performance has strong affinities with Residual Profit and is discussed in para 18 in this chapter.

d) Controllable residual profit is a reasonable measure, albeit with many imperfections, of the performance of local management. The inclusion of controllable items plus the imputed interest charge on controllable divisional investment is a genuine attempt to separate managerial performance from the overall performance of the division as an economic unit.

Disadvantages of controllable residual profit.

a) Although central management may like the idea of imputing a cost to the division for use the use of local assets, they may not favour the assumption on investment powers contained within the residual profit approach. It will be recalled that it is assumed that local management are able to take their own investment decisions which is a power that central management may not wish to relinquish.

b) Residual profit includes, without distinction, the effects of both past investment decisions and of current operation performance. This is because the depreciation charges included in the residual profit calculations should represent the true loss in economic value of the asset(s), whereas the calculation is usually based on historic values or less frequently on inflation adjusted values, neither of which necessarily reflect any economic changes specific to the assets(s).

Ideally, the effects of past decisions, which are by definition unalterable, should be separated from the effects of current operations, but there are obvious practical difficulties in this process.

c) The difficulties of estimating the firm's cost of capital have been discussed earlier but, notwithstanding the problems, the use of the weighted average cost of capital for calculating residual profit is frequently advocated. The WACC, an estimate of the current opportunity cost of funds, is applied to the book value (gross or net) of divisional assets which are the results of past investment decisions. Thus there is an incompatibility in that the interest charge, as conventionally calculated, is a form of review of the past usage of assets rather than a correctly specified opportunity cost relevant for taking decisions about the asset's future.

This may lead to sub-optimal decision making on the part of local management. For example, local management may dispose of an asset which in the short run does not meet the required return even though it may be in the long run interest of the firm as a whole to retain the asset within the division.

14. Net residual profit

This is controllable residual profit less interest on non-controllable divisional assets and apportioned head office charges. This performance measure attempts to appraise the economic worth of the division as a whole from the viewpoint of the group. It combines both the performance of local management (appraised by controllable residual profit) and an evaluation of the investment in the division and its total costs, including an appropriate share of central charges.

15. Relationship of the appraisal measures based on profit

The various definitions of profit have been discussed in the preceding paragraphs. What measure to use is a matter of judgement which depends on a variety of factors including: company objectives, degree of decentralisation and divisionalisation, quality of local management, the efficiency of available information systems including the accounting systems, the type of industry and other such considerations.

Table 1 summaries the various measures and shows their relationships. It will be seen that after controllable profit there is a divergence of philosophy whereby divisions are considered either as profit centres or, when imputed interest is involved, as investment centres.

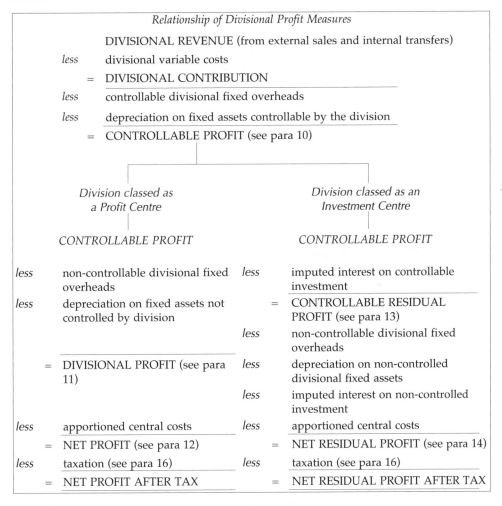

Table 1

16. Should profit be before or after tax?

Whatever the particular variant of profitability used there is the problem of deciding whether performance should be appraised on a before or after tax basis.

It can be argued that a before tax basis should be used for the divisions because the final tax assessment is based on the results of the company or group as a whole and therefore tax could only be charged to the divisions on some arbitrary basis. An alternative view is that it may be the investment decisions of a particular division which earn the capital allowances or generate the taxable income so that the division concerned should have the appropriate credit or charge. This is particularly relevant for investment centres which have substantial control over investment policies.

Although the decision to appraise on a before or after tax basis is complex and will in practice be based on the circumstances of the particular situation, on balance it would seem that a before tax basis is preferred. The main reasons for this are:

a) The whole purpose of appraisal systems is to appraise the performance of local management and the performance of the division as an economic unit. The effects of the tax system through timing differences, capital allowances and changing rates may obscure the actual underlying managerial and economic performance.

b) Tax planning is frequently a central function which, quite properly, may impose constraints or cause local decisions to be adjusted for the good of the firm as a whole. Accordingly local performance levels may be misrepresented if based on after-tax considerations.

c) In many circumstances the apportionment to divisions of a share of the taxation charge or credit may be on an arbitrary basis.

17. Profitability calculations

Example 1

The following data have been collected relating to the WYMEX division of the MULTI-CELL group.

Data for WYMEX *division*

		£
Sales Revenue	– external customers	600,000
	– internal transfers	350,000
Variable operating costs	– labour	95,000
	– materials	160,000
	– overheads	42,500
Fixed operating costs	– controllable by division	78,000
	– controllable centrally	41,000
Divisional management cost		26,500
Fixed Assets (at cost)	– divisional purchases	450,000
	– central purchases	250,000
Total central administration and management costs		684,210

(These are apportioned on the basis of sales revenue which was £5.2m for the group as a whole)

The group's weighted average cost of capital is estimated at 15% and it is group policy to calculate depreciation on a straight line basis at 25% and to impute interest on a gross investment basis.

Solution

		£	£
	Divisional Revenue		950,000
less	Variable costs		
	labour	95,000	
	materials	160,000	
	overheads	42,500	297,500
=	Divisional contribution		652,500
less	controllable fixed overheads		78,000
less	controllable depreciation		112,500
=	CONTROLLABLE PROFIT		462,000

Profit Centre Approach

		£	
	CONTROLLABLE PROFIT b/f	462,000	
less	non-controllable fixed overhead	41,000	
less	non-controllable depreciation	62,500	
=	DIVISIONAL PROFIT	358,500	
less	Apportioned central charges		
	$\dfrac{684,210}{5,200,000} \times 950,000$	125,000	
=	NET PROFIT before tax	£233,500	

Investment Centre Approach

		£
	CONTROLLABLE PROFIT b/f	462,000
less	imputed interest on controllable investment (15% of £450,000)	67,500
=	CONTROLLABLE RESIDUAL PROFIT	394,500
less	non-controllable overheads	41,000
less	non-controllable depreciation	62,500
less	non-controllable imputed interest	37,500
less	apportioned central charges	125,000
=	NET RESIDUAL PROFIT before tax	£128,500

18. Return on capital employed (ROCE)

Return on capital employed, alternatively termed return on investment (ROI), is a commonly used relative measure of divisional performance appraisal. It has the appeal of simplicity in that a single percentage figure, prepared from readily available and understood financial information, is used both as a measure of divisional performance and as a basis of comparison with other divisions and other opportunities available to the firm. However, ROCE has numerous limitations and needs to be used with caution.

ROCE can be defined in various ways but the basis of all the variants is the simple formula:

$$\text{ROCE} = \frac{\text{Profit}}{\text{Investment}} \times 100\%$$

This formula can be disaggregated as follows:

$$\text{ROCE} = \frac{\text{Sales}}{\text{Investment}} \times \frac{\text{Profit}}{\text{Sales}} \times 100\%$$

or **ROCE = Capital turnover × Profit percentage on sales**

Profit and investment can be defined in a variety of ways, which are discussed below, but such variations are relatively unimportant compared with the potential problems which may arise from the fact that any form of ROCE is a ratio measure. It will be recalled in the discussion of NPV and IRR, that any ratio measure, improperly used, is unsuitable for ranking investments so that improper use of ROCE may cause local management to make sub-optimal decisions. ROCE measures the average return on divisional investment and local management can only improve their ROCE by investing in projects which earn above the existing ROCE or by ceasing existing projects which earn below their average ROCE. This is a safety first policy which means that local management may act in a manner detrimental to the interests of the firm as a whole. For example, they may reject an investment which, although lowering their divisional ROCE, has a return in excess of the firm's WACC and therefore should be accepted.

The use of ROCE as a divisional appraisal measure makes the same assumption over investment powers as that discussed in para 13 on residual profit, that is divisional management have control over their own investments. When divisional management do not have such control, the denominator (investment) of the ratio is a constant as far as divisional management is concerned so that maximising ROCE is equivalent to maximising profit and the use of the ratio becomes unnecessary.

Any value that ROCE may have as an appraisal measure of divisional performance can only arise when local management have control over both the denominator (investment) and the numerator (profit) of the ratio.

As conventionally calculated (using normal profits and book values of assets) ROCE overstates the rate of return, which may have serious repercussions if decisions are based on the calculated figure. This arises because, in inflationary conditions, profits are overstated owing to depreciation charges being based on historical costs, whilst at the same time the bottom half of the ratio, the capital employed, is understated being the same original costs. The overall effect of this two way bias can be seriously to over-state the ROCE. It follows from this that some form of inflation adjustment should be made, both to profits and to asset values, if a more realistic ROCE figure is required.

19. Profit in ROCE calculations

Depending on circumstances and the objectives of the appraisal process any of the profit measures described in relation to profit centres, as shown on Table 1, could be used in ROCE calculations. This includes Controllable Profit, Divisional Profit and Net Profit. It will be apparent that residual profit already takes account of the investment in the division, via the imputed interest charge, and to use such a profit figure in the ROCE calculation would double count the impact of the investment.

ROCE is an investment centre approach and uses one of the profit measures mentioned applied to the divisional investment. The factors governing the choice of profit measures and whether they should be before or after tax have already been discussed. These factors apply equally to their use in ROCE calculations.

20. Defining the investment base in ROCE calculations

Several different bases are used to value the capital employed in a division, for example, gross book value, net book value or current replacement cost. Whatever method is used, great care is needed that bias from accounting procedures does not mask the underlying level of operational efficiency. For example, if original cost is used as the base, a division with old assets may be shown to have a higher rate of return than a division with more modern assets, simply as a result of lower original costs. The valuation of assets on an historical basis invariably means that the asset base is an amalgam of assets acquired at different times with correspondingly different monetary values which inevitably creates anomalies.

Consideration of the three valuation bases mentioned above follow:

Gross book value:

If this basis is used comparisons between divisions may be difficult and local management may be induced to make sub-optimal decisions. For example, when a new asset is replaced the gross book value of divisional assets will increase by the difference between the cost of the new asset and the original cost of the old asset. The relevant capital cost for investment appraisal purposes is the new asset cost less the scrap value of the old asset. As the scrap value is likely to be far less than the original cost of the old asset, the capital cost of the new asset is understated when gross book values are used in the ROCE calculation.

This means that replacement decisions which did not meet normal investment targets (eg a DCF return above the weighted average cost of capital of the firm) may improve a division's ROCE. The use of gross book values may also cause a manager to dispose of assets which earn less than the divisional average ROCE even though their retention can be justified when the overall return of the company is considered.

Net book values:

The use of net book values has the effect of showing an increasing rate of return over time simply by the diminution of the capital employed base as each period's depreciation is deducted. There is little logic in this and such a result may cause local management to discourage new investment which would reduce an overstated return on capital employed. Such a policy might show increasing rates of return on capital employed whilst at the same time profits could actually be falling.

Current replacement cost:

The theoretically correct valuation for the assets employed is their opportunity cost or economic value to the business. This involves a range of subjective judgements which may be unacceptable to the managements concerned.

Accordingly, a number of firms use the current replacement cost of the assets as an approximation of their economic value. Replacement costs are usually estimated by the use of specially prepared indices which measure the changing costs of various groups of assets. The indices are applied to the historical costs to produce a current valuation. There is no doubt that this method is more defensible than gross or net book values although there are still a number of subjective elements and appropriate indices or estimates of current values will not always be readily available. It follows that if current values are used for the assets employed, profits will have to be adjusted to current values.

Note: Whatever basis is used, it appears to be common practice to use the average value for the year, and not year end values. It will be realised that this is a minor refinement which does not solve the fundamental problems mentioned above.

21. ROCE c.f. residual profit

These are the two most frequent advocated financial performance measures, both of which include the impact of the amount invested in the division, one in a relative way – ROCE – and one using absolute values – RESIDUAL PROFIT. Both have numerous limitations but both are defensible as practical performance measures when used with an awareness of their deficiencies and particularly when they are supported by other appraisal information.

Which is to be preferred? The balance of the theoretical argument would favour residual profit. It is a better ranking device and it encourages management to invest in assets which will produce a return greater than the imputed interest charge and thus increase residual income. Also it avoids the problems which may occur when a division is earning a high rate of return on existing assets and is reluctant to invest in lower return yet still worthwhile projects.

In spite of these arguments ROCE is the more widely used measure in practice so it is important that the measure is used in its most appropriate form and close attention is given to signs of any sub-optimal decision making based on ROCE computations.

22. Target level of performance

Notwithstanding their limitations, ROCE and residual profit are used as performance measures so that it is necessary to set some level or standard of performance to be used as the divisional target.

Setting any form of performance target is a controversial exercise with many subjective elements but typical factors which would be considered include:

a) The company's cost of capital. This, of course, is the absolute minimum acceptable rate of return and the target level would normally be set higher than this.

b) The returns being achieved by efficient competitors in the same industry. Interfirm comparisons and other published data can provide guidance in this area.

c) The risk level of the industry, company and division. In general the higher the risk levels the higher the target.

d) The nature of the industry, the degree of competition and the position of the firm within the industry.

e) The general economic climate and the extent of under/over capacity within the industry and the firm.

It does not follow that a standard rate or target should be set for all the divisions of a firm. Although this appears to be a 'fair' and consistent approach it must be remembered that the objective of performance appraisal measures and the targets set is to motivate local management into making decisions in accordance with the overall interests of the firm. If divisions operate in different markets with differing risk levels it is extremely likely that different target levels, appropriate to individual divisional conditions, will be more efficient than an overall blanket rate.

23. Appraising multiple objectives

ROCE and residual profit are useful summary appraisal measures and, in spite of deficiencies, make a significant contribution to the assessment of financial performance and financial objectives. However, no single measure can hope to assess all of the various objectives that might be set for a company or division. This is in accordance with the Law of Requisite Variety, discussed previously, and means that for full control of a division, ROCE or residual profit should be supported by other appraisal measures appropriate to the particular objective being considered.

Examples of areas in which objectives might be set and possible appraisal measures are as follows:

Objectives set in connection with:	*Possible appraisal measures:*
Sales	Sales turnover and trends by product, product range, area, type of distribution etc.
Market share	Proportion of market for individual product and product ranges. Trends and comparison with overall market.
Growth	Appropriately adjusted for inflation, comparisons and trends for sales, assets employed, profits, number of employees, etc.
Labour relations	Labour turnover, absenteeism statistics, number of promotions, transfers, grievances. Number of apprentices and trainees, courses and support.
Productivity	Labour and machine hours per unit, output per shift and hour. Material utilisation. Overheads per £ of sales, value added statistics.
Quality and Reliability	Quantifiable measures include number of goods returns, guarantee claims, item and product acceptability. Percentage of re-worked parts.
Social responsibilities	Difficult to quantify but possible measures include: number of local employees, support given to local institutions, number of school visits, sponsorships, amount spent on anti-pollution measures.

It is likely that objectives will be set in some or all of the above areas, particularly where the firm practices 'management by objectives' (MBO). This phrase was first publicised by Drucker who emphasises the multiple aspects of managerial performance and the need to harmonise individual aspects of managerial performance and the need to harmonise individual managerial goals with organisational goals. Where MBO is practiced, informally or formally, appraisal of performance will be required in many areas outside the strictly financial measures discussed in this chapter.

24. Conventional appraisal measures and DCF

The appraisal methods discussed so far use historical values based on the conventions and assumptions of accrual accounting. The methods include the various categories of profit, ROCE and residual profit. A particular problem which arises is the conflict between the recommended use of DCF criteria for making investment decisions, and the use of conventional accounting information for appraising the performance of past investment decisions. In effect, managers are recommended to use one method to choose between investments, yet the progress of the investments is judged by quite different criteria.

In certain circumstances the choice of the correct investment using DCF criteria can lead to a short-run fall in profits and ROCE as conventionally calculated. This may lead a manager to reject a project which would lower his ROCE, even though it had a positive NPV at the cost of capital and is thus in the group's interest. Alternatively, a manager whose existing ROCE is below the cost of capital may be tempted to accept a project which increases his own ROCE, even though the project may have a negative NPV at the group's cost of capital. In consequence the use of ROCE as an appraisal method is less satisfactory in those circumstances where the manager has a direct influence on investment decisions.

In general, the use of residual profit as the appraisal method mainly avoids the potential problems of ROCE. In the long run the use of residual profit will influence managers to make investment decisions consistent with those that would be made using NPV. However, if conventional methods of depreciation are used (straight line or reducing balance) then short-run residual profit calculations do not necessarily lead to decisions consistent with those that would be made using NPV. Where there are constant, or near constant, cast flows then the use of *annuity depreciation* in the residual profit calculations will produce decisions consistent with those using NPV. Annuity depreciation is described below.

25. Annuity method of depreciation

The annuity (or compound interest) method of calculating depreciation produces a value for the yearly depreciation charge which results in a constant residual profit. In addition the present value of the residual profits will equal the NPV of the project as calculated using normal DCF rules. The annual depreciation charge using the annuity method is the capital element of an annuity sufficient to repay the projects initial investment at the appropriate cost of capital. The procedures will be illustrated using the following example.

Example 2

A firm is considering a project with an initial investment of £50,000. The project will produce cash inflows of £17,300 per year for 4 years. The cost of capital is 10% and there is nil scrap value.

Required:

a) Calculate the NPV of the project.

b) Calculate the residual profit of the project in year 1 using straight-line depreciation.

c) Calculate the residual profit per year using the annuity method of depreciation.

Solution

a) Using Table B the NPV $= -50,000 + (3.170 \times 17350)$

$$= +\textbf{5000}$$

∴ project acceptable according to normal DCF criteria.

b) *Residual profit in Year 1 using straight-line depreciation*

Depreciation p.a. $= \dfrac{£50,000}{4} = £12,500$

	£
Income	17,350
– Depreciation	12,500
	4850
– Int. in investment	5000 (ie 10% × £50,000)
= Residual profit	**(150)**

Thus, using conventional measures the project would show a loss in Year 1 and the manager may not wish to initiate the project even though it has a positive NPV at the cost of capital.

c) *Residual profits using annuity depreciation*

In order to calculate this we first have to find the value of the 4-year annuity which has a present value of £50,000, ie the initial investment. From Table B the 4-year annuity factor at 10% is 3.170,

∴ annuity $= \dfrac{£50,000}{3.170} = £15,773$

This value is used in the following table and the capital element of the annuity calculated. This is the depreciation charge required.

	Calculated Annuity (A)	10% interest on capital o/s (B) (B=10% × D)	Capital Repayment (C) (C=A–B)	Capital outstanding (D) (D=D–C)
Year 0				£50,000
1	£15,773	£5000	£10,773	39,227
2	15,773	3923	11,850	27,377
3	15,773	2738	13,035	14,342
4	15,773	1434	14,339	3

Notes:

(i) Column C is the capital repayment and is the depreciation using the annuity method. It will be noted that it increases each year.

(ii) The £3 capital outstanding in Year 4 is due to rounding errors.

Calculation of residual profits using the annuity depreciation charges

	Capital outstanding (A) (from above)	Project In flows (B)	10% interest on capital o/s (C) (C=10% × A)	Depreciation (D) (from above)	Residual Profit (E) (E=B–C–D)
Year 1	£50,000	£17,350	£5000	10,773	1577
2	39,227	17,350	3923	11,850	1577
3	27,377	17,350	2738	13,035	1577
4	14,342	17,350	1434	14,339	1577

Notes:

(i) It will be seen that the use of annuity depreciation results in a constant residual profit of £1577 per year.

(ii) The present value of the residual profit is £1577 × 3.170 = £5000, which is the project NPV.

(iii) By using Annuity Depreciation in Residual Profit calculations the manager will take investment decisions which correspond to those using NPV.

It should be noted the method outlined above does not ensure consistent decision making if the cash inflows of the project vary from year to year.

In general the annuity method of depreciation appears not to be widely used in practice. This may be because it produces an increasing charge for depreciation over the years, and, especially in the early years, the market values of assets are not likely to coincide with book values. Also, whilst any method of depreciation may be used for internal management, the use of annuity depreciation is not acceptable for financial reporting as laid down in SSAP12.

26. Multi-national performance appraisal

An extreme form of divisionalisation occurs in multi-national organisations and companies who typically operate on a world wide scale with operating divisions dispersed in numerous countries and even continents. Whilst in general the principles covered in this chapter apply to such organisations it is obvious that the scale of operations, the diversity of conditions and personnel, and the distances involved make control of such organisations a complex and exacting task.

Typical of the additional problems that these organisations face are the following (not in order of importance).

a) Distance and remoteness from headquarters which increase delays and information problems.

b) Variability in the quality of management and workers in the various countries.

c) Differing local taxation and company rules.

d) Local trade and government policies and restrictions.

e) Local pricing and tariff regulations.

f) Currency exchange difficulties and rate fluctuations.

g) Transportation delivery problems and transfer pricing difficulties concerned with trade between divisions.

h) Differences in accounting standards and policies.

i) Motivation problems with local management remote from headquarters.

27. Non-profit organisations and performance measurements

Non-profit (or not-for-profit) organisations (NPO's) are organisations for social, educational and philanthropic purposes. They include: schools and colleges, charities, churches, hospitals, local and central government and many others.

Measuring the performance of NPO's is important, especially for those in the Public Sector of the economy where accountability to national and local taxpayers is of concern. A major problem with many NPO's is that precise objectives are difficult to define in a quantifiable way and actual accomplishments cannot be readily measured in monetary terms. The availability, quality and level of service are of paramount importance for most NPO's and these are factors which are not easily assessed or measured without a degree of subjectivity and making value judgements.

In spite of these problems assessment of progress is important and considerable attention is being paid by the Government and the Treasury to performance appraisal and measurement in the Public Sector.

28. Problems of performance measurement in the public sector

The first problem is that measures of output quantity are often crude and of little meaning by themselves (for example, number of patients treated at a hospital) and measures relating to quality are often subjective.

Public Sector services differ from the private sector in that:

a) The key decisions about funds and allocations are made by central government and the Treasury.

b) spending decisions are implemented by local and central government departments and by officials in other public services

c) the main beneficiaries of the spending are the general public

These mean that information about the aims and results of public spending derives from a variety of disparate sources and it is often difficult to obtain information which is not disputed by one or other of the groups. An example is the long running argument about the funding of the National Health Service (NHS). The government claims that it is better funded than ever whilst health professionals and many of the public claim it is grossly underfunded.

In an attempt to improve flexibility and quality there have been numerous changes in public sector organisations over recent years. Examples include; the establishment of self governing hospitals, the internal market in the NHS, doctors becoming fund holders, the local management of schools and so on.

In general performance can be measured by:

❏ the progress towards meeting objectives

❏ the progress in improving efficiency

❏ assessing the control over spending

Objectives must be accepted as appropriate by all groups and the activities undertaken must be defined at the outset. There is little point in meeting inappropriate objectives or becoming more efficient at carrying out unnecessary activities.

In summary, whilst performance measurement is desirable in the Public sector there are major problems thus:

a) Output measurement is difficult and attaching costs to the outputs is even more difficult.

b) It is difficult to establish cause and effect relationships especially where there are interactions between various activities or one activity may contribute to more than one objective e.g. the provision of a youth training centre may reduce local unemployment and also reduce street crime.

c) Simple, quantitative, performance measures may be misleading.

In spite of the problems Performance Measurement is widely practised in the Public Sector.

29. Measuring efficiency

Efficiency is a ratio measure relating inputs to output. The inputs are the resources (e.g. manpower, capital investment) which are transformed through activities into the outputs. Inputs are usually expressed as £s and the outputs as some appropriate physical units e.g., miles travelled, arrests made, students graduating, meals served and so on. The influences of any efficiency measurement is enhanced when it is compared with a target or standard or with a value from some other similar organisation.

For example, assume that data have been collected on library costs and issues in Loamshire District Council. This information could be compared with the National Standard and the neighbouring Gravelton D.C thus:

$$\frac{\text{Actual Input}}{\text{Actual Output}} \quad \text{compared with} \quad \frac{\text{Standard Input}}{\text{Standard Output}}$$

	Loamshire D.C	Gravelton D.C	National Standard
	$\dfrac{£126,000}{85000 \text{ issues}}$	$\dfrac{£115,000}{82500 \text{ issues}}$	
	£1.48 per issue	£1.39 per issue	£1.25 per issue
Efficiency	84%	90%	100%

This simple example illustrates the important point that comparison with agreed standards and other suitable organisations greatly enhances the value of any performance measure. Also the plotting of the measures over time enables trends to be monitored.

30. Comparative statistics

As examples of the areas in which comparisons might be made the following statistics are suggested by the Local Authorities Code of Practice.

Comparative statistics suggested in the Code of Practice

For the authority's total expenditure and for each function	Net cost per 1000 population Manpower per 1000 population
Primary education Secondary education	Pupil/teacher ratio Cost per pupil
School meals	Revenue/cost ratio Pupils receiving free meals as a proportion of school roll
Children in care	As a proportion of total under 18 population Cost per child in care
Care of elderly	Residents of council homes as a proportion of total over-75 population Cost per resident each week
Home helps	Contact hours per 1000 population over 65
Police	Population per police officer Serious offences per 1000 population
Fire	Proportion of area at high risk
Public transport	Passenger journeys per week per 1000 population
Highways	Maintenance cost per kilometre
Housing	Rents as a proportion of total cost Management cost per dwelling per week Rent arrears as a percentage of year's rent income Construction cost per dwelling completed
Trading services	Revenue/gross cost ratio

Although performance measurement has always been done within individual Public Sector organisations it is becoming of greater national significance with the concentration on Value For Money (VFM) in the public sector. The idea behind VFM is to examine how NPO's use their funds to produce *inputs* (e.g. staff time and other resources), how the inputs are used to produce *outputs* (goods and services) and how the outputs produce *outcomes* (effects on users).

Part of the drive towards obtaining better value for money is the VFM audit.

31. Value for money audits

VFM audits can be defined thus;

> 'An investigation into whether proper arrangements have been made for securing economy, efficiency and effectiveness in the use of resources'   Terminology.

(Note Economy, Efficiency and Effectiveness are known as the 3 E's)

Effectiveness is concerned with whether the organisation is achieving its objectives

Efficiency is concerned with the relationships between inputs and outputs. Is the organisation using its resources to fulfil its objectives in an efficient manner?

Economy is concerned with seeing that the minimum quantity and quality of resources are used to achieve the desired outputs. The emphasis is on reducing costs or inputs.

VFM audits are usually associated with local authorities and central government departments. However VFM audits are also used for profit seeking organisations and are sometimes known as *efficiency audits*.

VFM audits are wide ranging and pay particular attention to good management practice. These include examining and analysing such things as:

❏ Manpower management including recruitment, training, motivation

❏ Systems for planning, budgeting and controlling expenditure

❏ Managerial decision making including the tactical allocation of existing resources and strategic matters

❏ Proper management of all assets including, land, building, finance

❏ Organisation structures including responsibilities, authority and accountability

❏ Specific initiatives to improve economy, effectiveness and efficiency

❏ The ways performance is monitored and compared with objectives and standards.

32. Steps in a VFM audit

In outline, a VFM audit would have the following six steps:

Step 1. Find out the objectives of the NPO, department or system being examined. What is it trying to achieve?

Step 2. Examine the systems and controls used to achieve the objectives. How are the objectives achieved? How are the achievements monitored and measured?

Step 3. Document in detail the system/department being audited. This includes the identification and evaluation of the key controls.

Step 4. Verify and test the system in operation. Are the controls too strong or too weak. Is there scope for cost savings (economy)?

Step 5. Examine the *efficiency* of the system. Are too many resources being used? Are the performance indicators used the best for monitoring efficiency? (Links with Step 2)

Step 6. Appraise the effectiveness of the organisation, Does the system meet its objectives. (Links with Step 1)

33. Summary

a) The growth of divisionalisation has produced a need for performance appraisal and financial control systems.

b) Decentralisation takes place when authority is delegated.

c) Decentralisation should: improve local and strategic decision making, increase flexibility, increase motivation, improve training.

d) Decentralisation may bring problems. These include: sub-optimal decision making, duplication, more expensive information systems.

e) Ideally, performance appraisal systems should promote goal congruence, provide meaningful feedback, encourage initiative and the longer term view.

f) Profit centres are responsible for expenditures, revenues and profits. Investment centres are profit centres where profit is assessed in relation to capital invested.

g) Financial performance appraisal measures are either absolute measures (some form of profit) or relative measures (return on capital employed).

h) Controllable profit is revenues less costs controllable at divisional level.

i) Divisional profit is the divisional profit without apportioned central costs.

j) Controllable residual profit is revenue less controllable costs and interest imputed on the divisional investment. This measure assumes that divisional investment is the responsibility of divisional management. This measure is a reasonable measure of managerial performance albeit with some limitations.

k) In general, a before tax basis for profits is preferred because the general objective of performance appraisal is to assess managerial operating efficiency which may be masked by after-tax profit figures.

l) Return on Capital Employed (ROCE) is a commonly used relative measure of performance appraisal but has numerous limitations which must be understood before its use is advocated.

m) Any of the profit measures could be used as the numerator of the ROCE ratio with their previously stated meanings.

n) The investment base may be based on historical asset values on a gross or net basis or may be based on replacement values.

o) On balance residual profit is technically to be preferred but ROCE is widely used and can be a useful, practical tool provided there is an awareness of its inherent limitations.

p) Whatever appraisal measure is used a target level of performance must be set. Factors to be considered include: cost of capital, risks, interfirm comparisons, economic conditions and so on.

q) To control all the facets of divisional operations other appraisal measures should be set in such areas as: sales, growth, productivity, labour relations, quality.

r) Performance appraisal is a vital process in the Public Sector although there are many problems.

s) The usefulness of any performance measure is enhanced when it is compared with a standard and measures from similar organisations.

t) Value for money seeks to assess how *inputs* produce *outputs* and how outputs produce *outcomes*.

u) VFM audits assess the 3 E's (Economy, Efficiency and Effectiveness).

34. Points to note

a) To design effective performance appraisal systems the objectives and problems associated with decentralisation and divisionalisation should be thoroughly understood.

b) Divisional performance appraisal can assess the performance of the division as an operating unit jointly with the performance of divisional management. However this need not be so and the performance of the division could be assessed using the measures outlined in this chapter, separately from the performance of the management who could be judged against agreed targets in all the areas for which they have responsibility.

c) A problem which may occur in performance appraisal is the conflict between the (recommended) use of DCF for investment decision making and the use of conventional accrual accounting conventions for overall performance appraisal. In certain circumstances the choice of the correct project using DCF criteria can lead to a short run fall in profits and ROCE, as conventionally calculated. This may lead a manager into not making an investment which is in the overall group interest because it will have no apparently adverse effect on divisional performance. The potential for this problem always exists but can be mitigated to some extent by the use of residual profit as an appraisal measure and by head office management taking a long run view.

Additional reading

Accounting for management control;*Emmanuel, Merchant and Otley* – Chapman & Hall

Management Control in non-profit organisations;*Anthony & Herzlinger* – Irwin

Performance measurement in the manufacturing sector – CIMA

Performance measurement in service industries; *Fitzgerald et al* – CIMA

Measuring corporate performance; *Lothian* – CIMA

Management control decisions; *Patz & Rowe* – Wiley

Divisional performance : Measurement & control; *Solomons* – Irwin

Self review questions

1. What is decentralisation? (3)
2. What type of decision making is usually retained by central management? (3)
3. What are the objectives of decentralisation? (4)
4. What are the possible problems which may arise with decentralisation? (5)
5. Where operating divisions exist what are the objectives of performance appraisal? (6)
6. Distinguish between profit and investment centres. (7)
7. What are the two major categories of financial performance appraisal measures? (8)
8. Define: controllable profit, divisional profit, net profit, controllable residual profit and net residual profit. (9-14)
9. What are the arguments as to whether appraisal should be based on profits before or after tax? (16)
10. How can ROCE be defined? (18)
11. Why do conventionally calculated ROCE ratios overstate the return? (18)
12. What are the various investment bases which can be used in ROCE calculations and what are their characteristics? (20)
13. Contrast ROCE and residual profits as financial performance measures. (21)
14. What factors are involved in setting target performance levels? (22)

15. What non-financial appraisal measures could be used for divisional performance appraisal? (23)
16. What is annuity depreciation and why is it used? (25)
17. What are the main problems of Performances Measurement for non-profit organisations? (27 & 28)
18. What enhances the value of any performance measure calculated? (30)
19. What is Value For Money (VFM)? (30)
20. What is a VFM audit? (31)

20 Transfer pricing

1. Objectives

After studying this chapter you will:

❑ know why transfer pricing (TP) is necessary;

❑ understand the objectives TP should attempt to meet;

❑ know the theoretical economic background to TP;

❑ understand the problems of TP in practice;

❑ know the advantages and disadvantages of market based TP;

❑ be able to use cost-based TP;

❑ understand the problems associated with negotiated TP.

2. Why is transfer pricing necessary

Transfer pricing is the process of determining the price at which goods are transferred from one profit centre to another profit centre within the same company. Such internal trading is more prevalent within horizontally and vertically integrated companies than conglomerate operations with their heterogenous groupings.

If profit centres are to be used, transfer prices become necessary in order to determine the separate performances of both the 'buying' and 'selling' profit centres. If transfer prices are set too high, the selling centre will be favoured whereas if set too low the buying centre will receive an unwarranted proportion of the profits.

In general terms, transfer pricing is purely an internal, bookkeeping exercise which does not affect the overall profitability of the firm. However, in certain circumstances, transfer pricing may have an indirect effect on overall company profitability by influencing the decisions made at divisional level. For example, based on the proposed transfer price, a divisional manager may decide to purchase an item externally rather than accept the internal transfer even though such a decision may reduce overall company profitability.

3. Objectives which transfer prices should meet

Ideally, transfer prices should be set in a manner and at a level which fulfil three objectives:

a) *Goal congruence*. The prices should be set so that the divisional management's desire to maximise divisional earnings is consistent with the objectives of the company as a whole. The transfer prices should not encourage sub-optimal decision making.

b) *Performance appraisal*. The prices should enable reliable assessments to be made of divisional performance. The prices form part of information which should

❏ guide decision making

❏ appraise managerial performance

❏ evaluate the contribution made by the division to overall company profits

❏ assess the worth of the division as an economic unit.

c) *Divisional autonomy*. The prices should seek to maintain the maximum divisional autonomy so that the benefits of decentralisation (motivation, better decision making, initiative, etc) are maintained. The profits of one division should not be dependent on the actions of other divisions.

In practice there are extreme difficulties in establishing prices which meet all these objectives. If prices are set centrally at levels where overall company objectives are met, then the autonomy of divisions is jeopardised, motivation may diminish and some of the benefits of decentralisation will be lost. Alternatively, where divisions act autonomously and freely set transfer prices, sub optimal decision making is hard to avoid. There is no completely satisfactory solution to this problem but research studies suggest that companies are prepared to accept a certain level of sub-optimal decision making on the part of divisions in order to gain the more than compensating advantages which they perceive arise from decentralisation.

4. Theoretical background to transfer pricing

Before considering the various methods used in practice for setting transfer prices it is useful to consider the relevant aspects of economic analysis which indicate the theoretically optimum price.

Given a profit maximising objective, economic theory states that the marginal net revenue product of each resource throughout the company should be the same. This means that the equilibrium transfer price would be the marginal cost of the selling division for that output level at which this marginal cost equals the buying division's marginal revenue product from the use of the resource or item transferred.

This can be shown graphically as follows.

Example 1

A company has two divisions, S and B. S makes an intermediate product which can be sold to division B or on the open market which is perfectly competitive. Division B has complete freedom to buy from S or on the open market. It can be assumed:

a) that there is perfect knowledge of all cost and revenue functions;

b) that the buying and selling costs on the open market are the same as for internal buying and selling;

c) that the firm has a profit maximising objective.

Let   S = supplying division

   B = buying division

   p_i = open market price of intermediate product

   mc_S = marginal cost function of S

   nmr_B = net marginal revenue function of B

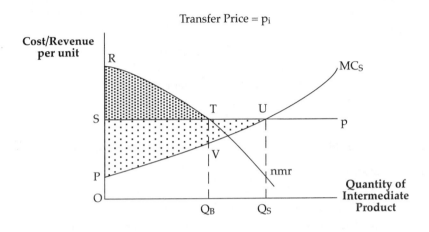

Figure 20.1

Notes on Figure 20.1

a) The net marginal revenue function (nmr_B) is the difference between the selling price of the final product and division B's own marginal cost, ie excluding the cost of the intermediate product transferred from Division S.

b) OQS represents the total output of intermediate products from Division S. OQB represents the amount of output transferred to Division B whilst the difference between QS and QB represents the amount sold on the open market.

c) The shaded area, PSRTU, represents total profits for the company as a whole which could be distributed as follows:

Area RST to division B

Area SUP to division S

The reasoning for this is that RTU is the net marginal revenue function for the firm as a whole resulting from sales of the final product, so that the area above pi (transfer price of intermediate product) represents the marginal revenue resulting from the inclusion of the intermediate product into the final product. The area SUP shows the difference between the marginal cost of the intermediate product and the price obtained for the intermediate product either as part of the final product (area STVP) or as direct sales of the intermediate product (area TUV).

d) The optimal quantities, QB and QS, are found by the usual method of equating marginal revenue to marginal cost. QB corresponds to the intersection of the net marginal revenue division B with pi. QS corresponds to the intersection of pi and the marginal cost of division S.

It will be recalled that in conditions of perfect competition, as assumed in this case, the selling price per unit = average revenue = marginal revenue.

In this particular case, division S will be indifferent as to whether to transfer internally or sell on the open market. Similarly division B can buy internally or externally as desired and in each case the price would be pi. It should be noted that in other circumstances it may be necessary for the firm to specify that internal transfers should take place up to certain levels in order to avoid sub-optimal decision making. This is dealt with in paras 5 to 8.

e) Transfer pricing policies are based on the marginal costs of the supplying division plus any opportunity costs to the whole organisation. In this case no opportunity costs were identified so that the optimal transfer price is the stated intermediate product market price, pi, which also enables the two quantities, QB and QS, to be determined.

5. Unequal intermediate product buying and selling prices

The theoretical background to transfer pricing can be developed to deal with the problems which occur when there are transaction costs involved in the buying and/or selling of the intermediate product on the external market.

For example, whilst there may be, in all other respects, a perfect intermediate product market with a given selling price per unit, buyers may have to pay packing and delivery charges which effectively creates separate buying and selling prices as far as a firm such as described in Example 1 is concerned.

The analysis to deal with this situation follows the same broad principles covered in paragraph 4 and is shown in connection with Example 2.

Example 2

A company has two divisions, S and B. S makes an intermediate product which can be transferred to division B or sold on the open market. The open market for the intermediate product is perfectly competitive except that if division B buys on the open market it will have to pay packaging and delivery costs. The effect of this as far as the whole firm is concerned is that there are two prices for the intermediate product; POS which is the price for outside sales from division S and POP which is the price for outside purchases by division B. It follows that POP > POS.

For each of the three cases specified below it is required to:

a) derive the optimal transfer price;

b) show the total profits accruing to each of the divisions and to the firm as a whole;

c) show the optimum output level of the intermediate product;

d) state any restrictions central management may place upon divisional management's autonomy in order to avoid sub-optimal decision making.

Case 1. Where the intersection of the marginal cost function of division S(mcS) and the net marginal revenue function of division B (nmrB) is below POS.

Case 2. Where the intersection of mcS and nmrB is between POS and POP.

Case 3. Where the intersection of mcS and nmrB is above POP.

In each case a diagram is used which follows the same pattern as Figure 20.1.

6. Solution case 1

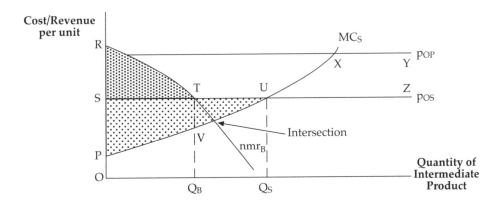

Figure 20.2 Intersection below POS

a) Optimal transfer price is POS.

b) The profits accruing to the firm as a whole and the distribution is identical to that shown in Figure 20.1, ie

    area PSRTU = total profits

    area RST   = profit to division B

    area SUP   = profit to division S

c) The total output of the intermediate product is QS and QB will be transferred to division B. The difference between QB and QS will be sold on the open market at price POS.

d) Some central management intervention is required because although division B will always prefer to buy internally at price POS rather than buy on the open market at price POP, the intermediate products may not always be available. Accordingly, management must monitor the situation so that division S always has sufficient (quantity QB) to supply all division B's requirements. Division S will be indifferent between selling externally and internal transfers at price, POS, but to maximise overall company profits it is important that sufficient quantities of the intermediate product are available for internal transfer thus avoiding division B having to buy externally at price POP.

Note: The net marginal revenue function of the firm as a whole is RTUZ and the firm's intermediate marginal cost function is PXY.

7. Solution case 2

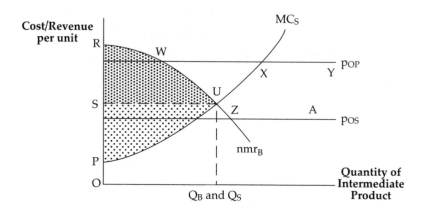

Figure 20.3 Intersection between POS and POP

a) The transfer price will be set at OS, ie at the intersection of the marginal cost of the supplying division and the net marginal revenue of the buying division.

b) The profits accruing to the company as a whole are represented by area PRU. The proportion accruing to division B is area RSU and the proportion to division S is area PSU.

c) The optimum output level and the number to be transferred internally are the same, at point QS/QB. No intermediate product will be sold externally.

d) No central management intervention will be required as the price OS is always preferred by both divisions. For division S it is higher than the price it can sell externally, POS, and for division B the price OS is lower than it can purchase externally, POP.

Note: The net marginal revenue function of the firm as a whole is RZA and the firm's intermediate marginal cost function is PXY.

8. Solution case 3

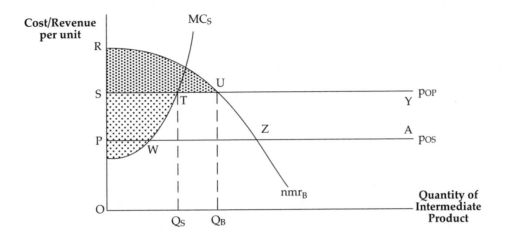

Figure 20.4 Intersection above POP

a) As mc_S and nmr_B intersect above the buying in price, POP, the transfer price must set at POP.

b) The profits are as follows:

area PSRUT	=	total company profits
area RUS	=	profit to division B
area PST	=	profit to division S

c) The total output of division S, quantity QS, must all be transferred to division B. Division B's total requirements is QB so the division will have to purchase the difference between QS and QB on the open market at price POP. This situation should be contrasted with Case 1, Figure 2, particularly in respect of the positions of QS and QB.

d) Some central management intervention is required to ensure that quantity QS is made and transferred internally because the marginal cost of the intermediate product is below the buying in price up to point T. It will be apparent that division B will be indifferent between internal transfers and external purchases because these are at the same price, POP. Accordingly, some central management intervention will be required to avoid sub-optimal decision making. Division S would produce only up to Point W if selling on the open market at POS.

Note: The net marginal revenue function of the firm as a whole is RZA and firm's intermediate marginal cost function is PTY.

9. Transfer pricing in practice

Generally there is insufficient information to set prices using the economic analysis previously described. Firms need to use methods for setting transfer prices which are feasible, which use information that is available without undue costs, and which meet as many of the objectives described in para 3 as possible.

The methods utilised can be divided into three categories:

a) market based pricing

b) cost-based pricing

c) negotiated pricing.

10. Market-based transfer pricing

Where a market exists outside the firm for the intermediate product and where the market is competitive (ie the firm is a price taker) then the use of market price as the transfer price between divisions would generally lead to optimal decision making. Such a price would meet all the objectives described in para 3, ie

☐ Goal congruence would be achieved as the divisions could act in their own best interest without reducing overall company profits.

☐ Performance evaluation would be possible in a realistic manner.

☐ The autonomy of the divisions would be maintained as the selling division could sell on the open market or internally and the buying division would have the option of purchasing in the market place or internally.

Where significant external buying and selling costs exist then a transfer price may be set somewhat lower than market price to reflect the cost savings from internal transfers. These circumstances may lead to negotiated market prices where the total cost savings are apportioned between the buying and selling divisions. In such circumstances an arbitration procedure may be required but too much central intervention of this nature could undermine the autonomy of divisions.

Where appropriate market prices exist then their use represents a feasible ideal. However there are difficulties in applying the concept universally. These include the following:

a) Frequently there is no market for the intermediate product or service being considered. This is typically the case for specialised components, materials, parts or services.

b) Even where some form of intermediate market does exist it may be difficult to obtain an appropriate price. A price is only strictly comparable when all features are identical – quality, delivery, finish, and so on.

c) Where a market does exist it may not be perfectly competitive, which means that the market is affected by the pricing decisions of divisional managers. Where there is an interdependence between output and pricing decisions there is no such thing as a single market price.

d) The market prices that are available may be considered unrepresentative. For example, there may be considerable excess capacity in the intermediate market so that current quotations are well below long run average prices. In such circumstances the use of either the current, abnormally low, price or the long run 'normal' price may lead to sub-optimal decision making on the part of the supplying divisional management or to loss of motivation and autonomy of the purchasing division.

11. Cost-based pricing

Cost-based transfer pricing systems are commonly used because the conditions for setting ideal market prices frequently do not exist; for example, there may be no intermediate market or the market which does exist may be imperfect.

Without the necessary conditions for establishing market prices there is no simple decision rule which leads to optimal decision making and which meets all the objectives for the ideal transfer price described in para 3. Providing that the required information is available, a rule which would lead to optimal decisions for the firm as a whole, would be to transfer at marginal cost up to the point of transfer, plus any opportunity cost to the firm as a whole.

Even assuming that variable outlay costs as conventionally recorded in accounting systems, are a reasonable approximation of economic marginal costs the imposition of such a rule would undermine the concept of profit centres in that the profitability of divisions required to transfer at marginal cost could not be appraised, and the autonomy of divisions would be affected.

Given all the difficulties in establishing ideal prices, firms have to find some answer to the transfer pricing problem so that methods based on costs which are readily available from the normal accounting systems are frequently used. A general problem which arises in such circumstances is that the costs may include inefficiencies of the selling division which would thus be passed on to the buying division. Accordingly standard, rather than actual, costs should be used as the basis of the transfer price in order not to burden the buying department with the inefficiencies of the supplying department.

The two main cost derived methods are those based on *full cost* and *variable cost*.

12. Full cost transfer pricing

This method, and the variant, which is full costs plus a profit markup, has the disadvantage that sub-optimal decision making may occur particularly when there is idle capacity within the firm.

The full cost (or cost plus) is likely to be treated by the buying division as an input variable cost so that external selling price decisions, if based on costs, may not be set at levels which are optimal as far as the firm as a whole is concerned.

A simple example of this follows.

Division S sells to division B at full cost + $33\frac{1}{3}\%$ and division B sells externally at a similar mark up. The following data are available.

Division S	£	Division B	£
Variable costs per unit	26	Transfer Price	48
Fixed costs per unit	10	Own variable costs per unit	15
Total Cost per unit	36	Fixed costs per unit	9
Mark up	12		72
		Mark up	24
Transfer Price	£48	Selling Price	£96

Thus, based on the stated pricing rules, division B would be attempting to sell at £96. If spare capacity exists then B may try to obtain any price above marginal cost but is likely to treat marginal cost as the variable costs of the division, ie £63 (£48 + 15). As far as the firm as a whole is concerned the marginal cost is the variable cost in each division, £41 (£26 + £15) so that the firm may lost a contribution margin if £63 is deemed to be the minimum acceptable figure for marginal pricing.

Full cost transfer pricing suffers from a number of other limitations.

a) The calculated cost is only accurate at one level of output.

b) The validity of any pricing decision based on past costs is questionable.

c) When transfers are made at full cost plus a profit markup the selling division is automatically given a certain level of profit rendering genuine performance appraisal difficult.

d) When the selling division is inefficient or working at low volume the costs may be unacceptably high as far as the buying division is concerned.

13. Variable cost transfer pricing

Using this system transfers would be made at the (standard) variable costs up to the point of transfer. Assuming that the variable cost is a good approximation of economic marginal cost then this system would enable decisions to be made which would be in the interests of the firm as a whole as pointed out in para 4. However, variable cost-based prices will result in a loss for the selling division so performance appraisal becomes meaningless and motivation will be reduced.

A possible way of resolving this dilemma is to use a variable cost-based transfer price so that sub-optimal decision making is minimised and, as a separate exercise, credit the supplying division with a share of the overall profit which eventually results from the transferred item. This dual transfer price approach has an apparent fairness in that credit for profits earned are shared between divisions but performance appraisal based on arbitrarily apportioned profit shares has obvious shortcomings and administrative difficulties.

14. Negotiated transfer pricing

As an alternative to setting prices based on rules or formulae, transfer prices could be set by negotiation between the buying and selling divisions. This would be appropriate if it could be assumed that such negotiations would result in decisions which were in the interests of the firm as a whole and which were acceptable to the parties concerned.

However, there are difficulties in this approach because it is unlikely that the parties concerned have equal bargaining power and protracted negotiations may be time consuming and divert management energies away from their primary tasks. Disagreements, which are all too likely, will require some form of arbitration by central management which itself undermines the autonomy of divisions and may cause resentment. It must be remembered that the objective of divisionalisation is to enhance the overall efficiency of the organisation so that care must be taken not to nullify any benefits through inter-divisional wrangling over transfer prices.

15. Example of transfer pricing

To illustrate some of the factors that need to be considered in a typical transfer pricing examination question an example follows, drawn from CIMA, Management Accounting – Decision Making paper.

Example 3

A group has two companies:

K Ltd, which is operating at just above 50% capacity, and

L Ltd, which is operating at full capacity (7,000 production hours).

L Ltd produces two products, X and Y, using the same labour force for each product. For the next year its budget capacity involves a commitment to the sale of 3,000 kgs of Y, the remainder of its capacity being used on X.

Direct costs of these two products are:

	X	Y
Direct materials	18	14
Direct wages	15 (1 production hour)	10 ($\frac{2}{3}$ production hour)

The company's overhead is £126,000 per annum relating to X and Y in proportion to their direct wages at full capacity, £70,000 of this overhead is variable. L Ltd prices its products with a 60% mark-up on its total costs.

For the coming year, K Ltd wishes to buy from L Ltd 2,000 kgs of product X which it proposes to adapt and sell, as product Z, for £100 per kg. The direct costs of adaptation are £15 per kg. K Ltd's total fixed costs will not change but variable overhead of £2 per kg will be incurred.

You are required to recommend, as group management accountant,

a) at what range of transfer prices, if at all, 2,000 kgs of X should be sold to K Ltd;

b) what other points should be borne in mind when making any recommendations about transfer prices in the above circumstances.

Solution

a) Some preliminary calculations are required to establish costs, profits and 'normal' selling prices, thus:

Profit statement for product X

Variable costs		
Direct materials	18	
Direct wages	15	(one manhour)
Variable overhead	10	$\frac{£70,000}{7,000}$
	43	
Fixed overhead	8	$\frac{£56,000}{7,000}$
Total cost	51	
Profit	30.6	60% of total cost
Selling price	81.6	

If L Ltd sells to K Ltd at the existing price of £81.6 per kg then K Ltd makes a profit of £100 – (81.6 + 15 + 2) = £1.4 per kg and on the total order of 2,000 kgs the profit would be £2,800.

Providing that there are no adverse affects, 2,000 kgs of X should be sold to K Ltd.

Range of transfer prices

The market price of £81.6per kg leaves L in an identical position to selling outside. Thus, £81.6 is the top of the price range. Without more information it is difficult to set a floor price. Theoretically this should be set at an amount representing the saving in the company overheads of £10 per kg, gained by selling within the group. If this was, say £3, then the transfer price would reduce by £3 + 60% = £4.80. Thus the range would be £81.6 to 76.8.

b) The main points that should be considered relate to the viability, or otherwise, of the new product Z. Is it a one-off order or has it a good future? Will transferring 2,000 kgs of X internally (and thus not selling externally) cause customers to take their business for other products elsewhere?

16. Summary

a) Transfer pricing is the pricing of internal transfers between profit centres.

b) Ideally the transfer prices should: promote goal congruence, enable effective performance appraisal, and maintain divisional autonomy.

c) Economic theory suggests that the optimum transfer price would be the marginal cost of the selling division for that output level at which the marginal cost equals the buying divisions marginal revenue product. Transfer prices should always be based on the marginal costs of the supplying division plus the opportunity costs to the organisation as a whole.

d) Because of information deficiencies, transfer pricing in practice does not always follow theoretical guidelines. Typically prices are market based, cost based or negotiated.

e) Where an appropriate market price exists then this is an ideal transfer price. However there may be no market for the intermediate product, the market may be imperfect, or the prices considered unrepresentative.

f) Where cost-based systems are used then it is preferable to use standard costs to avoid transferring inefficiencies.

g) Full cost transfer pricing (or full cost plus a mark up) suffers from a number of limitations; it may cause sub-optimal decision making, the price is only valid at one output level, it makes genuine performance appraisal difficult.

h) Providing that variable cost equates with economic marginal cost then transfers at variable cost will avoid gross sub-optimality but performance appraisal becomes meaningless.

i) Negotiated transfer prices will only be appropriate if there is equal bargaining power and if negotiations are not protracted.

17. Points to note

a) There is a tendency to think of transfer pricing solely in terms of goods or parts being transferred between manufacturing divisions. This is not so, because the principles apply equally to the transfer of services between divisions and to the provision of services from the centre to divisions. A particular example of the latter is the provision of computer services from headquarters to divisions and the problem that arises of determining the level of charges that should be made to the profit centres. This is a form of transfer pricing to which the general principles outlined in this chapter apply.

b) The use of transfer prices is fundamental to the profit centre concept where there is significant interdependence between divisions. The rationale for decentralisation and profit centres depends on the local management's freedom and interdependence. Imposed transfer prices and/or lack of buying and selling options severely limits the significance of any form of divisional performance appraisal.

Additional reading

Management Control System; *Anthony and Dearden* – Irwin

Accounting for Management Control;
Emmanuel, Otley and Merchant – Chapman & Hall

Cost Accounting : A Managerial Emphasis; *Horngren and Foster* – Prentice Hall

Divisional Performance : Measurement and Control; *Solomons* – Irwin

Financial Planning in Divisionalised Companies; *Tomkins* – Haymarket

Self review questions

1. Why do transfer prices become necessary? (2)
2. What objectives should transfer prices attempt to meet? (3)
3. What is the theoretically optimum transfer price? (4)
4. In what circumstances should central management intervene in setting transfer prices or transfer quantities? (6-8)
5. What is market based transfer pricing and why might there be difficulties in using this approach? (10)
6. Describe full cost transfer pricing and its characteristics. (12)
7. What is variable cost transfer pricing and how might any possible disadvantages be overcome? (13)
8. What is negotiated transfer pricing? (14)

21 Ratio analysis

1. Objectives

- ❏ After studying this chapter you will:
- ❏ know what ratio analysis (RA) is and why it is used;
- ❏ understand the ratio pyramid;
- ❏ be able to calculate various profit ratios and asset turnover ratios;
- ❏ know the importance of solvency ratios;
- ❏ be able to distinguish between short-term and long-term solvency ratios;
- ❏ understand various ratios covering earnings, dividends and share prices;
- ❏ know the key value-added ratios.

2. What is ratio analysis and why is it used

Ratio analysis is the systematic production of ratios from both internal and external financial reports so as to summarise key relationships and results in order to appraise financial performance. Ratio analysis as a practical means of monitoring and improving performance is greatly enhanced when

a) Ratios are prepared regularly and on a consistent basis so that trends can be highlighted and the changes investigated.

b) Ratios prepared for an individual firm can be compared with other firms in the same industry. This process is greatly facilitated when the firm has ready access to comparative ratios prepared in a standardised manner. Some Trade Associations prepare ratios for their member companies and the Centre for Inter firm Comparison, established by the British Institute of Management and the British Productivity Council, provides such a service on a national basis.

c) Ratios are prepared showing the inter-locking and inter-dependent nature of the factors which contribute to financial success. Typically this is done using the so-called 'pyramid of ratios' which is described in detail in para 4.

The information value of any given ratio, considered in isolation, is small. For example, if it is known that the return on capital employed for a company is 12% in a given year, this is not very informative. However if we find that the figure was 18% five years ago and has been declining, or that the average percentage for similar firms in the same industry is 15% then this information becomes of much greater significance and further analysis would be urgently required.

Ratio analysis may direct attention to areas where there are inefficiencies and this it provides a valuable service but it cannot say how the deficiencies will be made good. That can only be done by managerial action.

3. What ratios should be prepared?

The simple answer to this question is, any ratio which will assist management to plan, control or make decisions. This means that some ratios will be prepared that are unique to the individual firm whilst others will have universal applicability. It will be recalled that this is a similar position to that discussed in the chapters on standard costing variances.

Ratio analysis can be directed towards various aspects of company performance including:

☐ the financial performance of the company in terms of income generation, ie profitability. Ratios in this area include return on capital employed and the analysis of this ratio into component ratios relating to sales and assets (covered in para 4 to 10).

☐ the analysis of company solvency. Ratios in this area include those relating to current assets and current liabilities and the breakdown of these measures to show the effects of cash flows, inventory changes and movements in debtors and creditors (covered in paras 11 to 14).

☐ the assessment of the company's performance in terms of its value to investors. Ratios dealing with this area include PE (price/earnings) ratio, dividend yields and other such investment criteria (covered in paras. 15 and 16).

4. The profitability ratios

For comparative purposes the key ratio in this area is the return on capital employed (ROCE) already discussed. The ROCE is the primary ratio and the factors involved (Profit and Capital Employed or Total Assets) can be progressively subdivided into more and more detailed ratios which highlight the influence of sales, the types of assets, and the various types to costs, on overall company performance as expressed by the ROCE.

Typically the ROCE and supporting ratios are shown as a pyramid of ratios as depicted in Figure 21.1 which should be studied in conjunction with the paragraphs indicated on the diagram.

Note on Figure 21.1: The chart shows some typical ratios which can be calculated to show the relationships which exist between the factors which affect the overall return the company obtains on operating assets, ie the operating capital employed. The major division of the ROCE is into the rate of asset turnover and the percentage operating profit on sales, ie

$$\frac{\text{Operating Profit}}{\text{Operating Assets}} = \frac{\text{Operating Profit}}{\text{Sales}} \times \frac{\text{Sales}}{\text{Operating Assets}}$$

$$= \text{Percentage Profit} \times \text{Rate of Asset Turnover}$$

This division illustrates that a low return on operating assets is due to either low profit margins or a low rate of asset turnover or both these factors combined. The subsidiary ratios attempt to pinpoint the reasons why there are low profit margins and/or why the asset turnover is low.

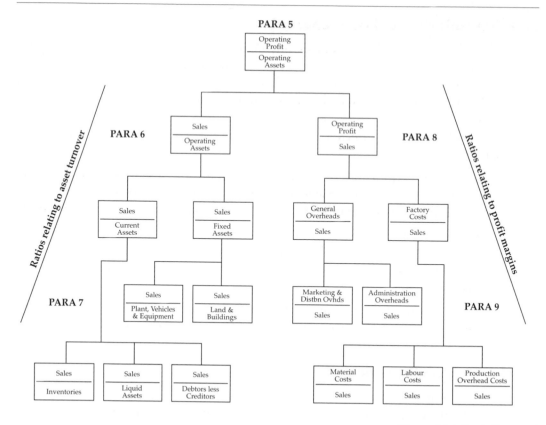

Figure 21.1 Ratio Pyramid

5. ROCE – the primary ratio (see Figure 21.1)

This ratio is the ROCE and as previously discussed this can be defined in various ways. The definition to be used depends on the purpose of the ratio analysis and what external figures are available for comparative purposes. The most realistic return will be shown when all assets are included at current valuations not historic costs. Naturally, for any form of inter-firm comparison the bases used must be same for all participants, and this requirement usually determines the basis to be adopted in a particular firm.

Various definitions of the 'capital employed' part of the ratio can be used and these include:

a) *Total capital* represented by total share capital, reserves, long-term liabilities, current liabilities.

b) *long-term capital* represented by total capital less current liabilities.

c) *Shareholders' total capital* represented by total share capital plus reserves.

d) *Shareholders' equity capital* represented by ordinary share capital plus reserves.

Where a firm has investments unconnected with their normal trading it is usual practice to exclude these from capital employed when assessing internal efficiency. It follows that the income from such investments would be excluded from operating profits in order that the ratio analysis can concentrate upon the assessment of operating efficiency.

Of the above four types of capital employed (a) and (b) are more appropriate for assessing the firm's efficiency in generating profitability with a preference for (a) representing as it does the total operating assets of the company. Definitions (c) and (d) are more useful for relating net income to the value of shareholder's capital. The basis most appropriate for the pyramid of ratios shown in Figure 21.1, which seek to assess the internal efficiency of the company, is basis (a), ie total operating assets.

The numerator of the ROCE ratio, profit or income, can also be defined in various ways and it is vital to have the correctly specified profit for the particular capital employed base being used. Again, if a firm is a participant in an interfirm comparison scheme then the factors involved in the profit calculation would be specified in detail to ensure comparability and consistency. Failing such guidelines then the following definitions might typically be used.

	Capital Employed base	*Appropriate profit*
a)	Total capital	Operating profit before tax, long-term loan interest and bank interest.
b)	long-term capital	Operating profit before tax and long-term loan interest.
c)	Shareholders' total capital	Operating profits plus other income, less tax.
d)	Shareholders' equity capital	Operating profits plus other income less tax and preference dividends.

The factors governing the choice of before or after tax profits have already been discussed previously.

6. Rate of asset turnover (see Figure 21.1)

This ratio measures the use being made of assets and draws attention to the intensity with which assets are employed. The ratio gives an assessment of past managerial efficiency in the deployment of company assets and is considered to be a good guide to the likely level of future profits.

7. Subsidiary asset ratios (see Figure 21.1)

The various subsidiary ratios shown (and others which could be calculated) attempt to answer the question, 'What are the detailed reasons why the rate of asset turnover has declined/increased?' For example, a firm may have too much working capital in relation to sales or it may not have made effective use of the various types of fixed assets. As with all ratios, trends in this area are of great importance and adverse movements should receive close attention so that remedial action can be taken.

8. Profitability margin (see Figure 21.1)

This ratio assesses the overall margin on sales which, together with the rate of asset turnover, is a major factor in the return that the company receives on capital employed. Because the margin on sales varies greatly from industry to industry (compare, for example, a clothing manufacturer and a heavy machine tool manufacturer) it is important that comparisons are made only with firms within the same industry or with the previous performance of the same firm.

9. Subsidiary margin ratios (see Figure 21.1)

These ratios relate the various costs, which determine the overall margin, to sales. The ratios are useful measures of internal operating efficiency and may provide guidance as to where further analysis would be worthwhile. The ratios shown are but typical examples and many other more specialised ratios might be calculated to suit particular firms or industries. For example, in a particular industry one raw material may be considered to be of great importance so that a special ratio may be calculated relating that material to the sales value of production.

10. Profitability ratios example

Example 1

Using the Final Accounts given below calculate the profitability ratios shown in Figure 1 for Relationships plc.

Relationships plc
Profit and loss account for year ended 31st December 19..

		£('000s)	£('000s)
	Sales		6,500
less	Factory Cost of Sales		
	Materials	2,610	
	Labour	1,140	
	Production Overheads	725	4,475
=	GROSS PROFIT		2,025
less	Administration Overheads	666	
	Marketing & Distribution Overheads	426	
	Bank Interest	65	
	Loan Interest	240	1,397
=	NET PROFIT BEFORE TAX		628
less	Tax		116
	PROFIT AFTER TAX		512
less	Dividends		
	10% Preference	50	
	Ordinary – Interim (paid)	180	
	Ordinary – Final (proposed)	180	410
	TRANSFERRED TO RESERVES		102

Relationships plc

Balance Sheet as at 31st December 19..

		£('000s)	£('000s)	£('000s)
FIXED ASSETS				
	Goodwill	50		
	Patents	175		
	Land and Buildings	2,500		
	Machinery and Equipment	3,750		
	Vehicles	595		7,070
CURRENT ASSETS				
	Stocks: Finished Goods	265		
	W-I-P	195		
	Raw Materials	320		
	Debtors	1,025		
	Cash and Bank	95	1,900	
less CURRENT LIABILITIES				
	Bank overdraft	850		
	Creditors	824		
	Taxation payable	116		
	Proposed dividend	180	1,970	(70)
				£7,000

		£
Represented by		
SHARE CAPITAL		
	Ordinary Shares £1 each	2,750
	10% Preference Shares £1 each	500
RETAINED PROFIT		1,750
DEBENTURES		
	12% loan stock	2,000
		£7,000

Solution

As explained in para 5 various definitions of 'Capital Employed' are possible with Total Capital being the most appropriate for the calculation of the efficiency ratios as depicted in Figure 21.1.

Relationships plc total capital = £7,070,000 + 1,900,000

= **£8,970,000**

The appropriate profit to use is also given in para 5 and is operating profit before tax, long-term loan interest and bank interest, ie

appropriate profit = £628,000 + 305,000

= <u>£933,000</u>

$$\therefore \quad ROCE = \frac{£933,000}{£8,970,000}$$

$$= 10.4\%$$

The various supporting ratios can now be calculated.

Asset turnover ratios

$$\frac{Sales}{Operating\ Assets} = \frac{6,500,000}{8,970,000} = 0.72{:}1$$

$$\frac{Sales}{Current\ Assets} = \frac{6,500,000}{1,900,000} = 3.42{:}1$$

$$\frac{Sales}{Fixed\ Assets} = \frac{6,500,000}{7,070,000} = 0.92{:}1$$

$$\frac{Sales}{Inventories} = \frac{6,500,000}{780,000} = 8.33{:}1$$

$$\frac{Sales}{Liquid\ Assets} = \frac{6,500,000}{1,120,000} = 5.80{:}1$$

$$\frac{Sales}{Debtors\ less\ Creditors} = \frac{6,500,000}{201,000} = 32.34{:}1$$

Profit margin ratios

$$\frac{Operating\ Profit}{Sales} = \frac{933,000}{6,500,000} = 14.35\%$$

$$\frac{General\ Overhead}{Sales} = \frac{1,092,000}{6,500,000} = 16.8\%$$

$$\frac{Factory\ Costs}{Sales} = \frac{4,475,000}{6,500,000} = 68.8\%$$

$$\frac{Marketing\ Overheads}{Sales} = \frac{426,000}{6,500,000} = 6.5\%$$

$$\frac{Administration\ Overheads}{Sales} = \frac{666,000}{6,500,000} = 10.25\%$$

$$\frac{Material\ Cost}{Sales} = \frac{2,610,000}{6,500,000} = 40.15\%$$

$$\frac{Labour\ Cost}{Sales} = \frac{1,140,000}{6,500,000} = 17.54\%$$

$$\frac{Production\ Overheads}{Sales} = \frac{725,000}{6,500,000} = 11.5\%$$

Note:

The calculation of the above ratios is only the first step in the full process of Ratio Analysis. Comparisons would be made with the ratios of previous years of Relationships plc, trends would be identified, reasons established for adverse movements and so on. In addition, comparisons would be made with ratios from other similar companies with the overall objective of identifying and rectifying weaknesses.

11. Solvency ratios

The analysis of solvency (or potential insolvency) can be assisted by the judicious use of ratio analysis but such analysis has certain limitations. Ratio analysis is of necessity based on normal financial reports (balance sheets, operating statements, profit and loss accounts) so that any ratios prepared relate to past conditions whereas solvency relates to the present. Conditions may have changed dramatically since the last balance sheet date and a firm which was solvent then may be currently having difficulties, perhaps because of credit facilities being withdrawn. Accordingly, any solvency ratios need to be interpreted with care and adjustments made in the light of more up-to-date information.

Solvency ratios can be grouped into two categories, those relating to short-term factors and those concerned with the long-term ability of the firm to meet all financial liabilities including those not currently payable.

12. Short-term solvency ratios

Certain of the short-term solvency ratios, particularly the 'current' and 'quick' ratios, are considered to be of great importance in judging the financial stability of companies particularly by financial analysts, investors, bankers and creditors.

Two groups of ratios have been found to be of value: those which relate current assets to current liabilities and those which indicate the rate at which short-term assets such as stock and debtors are turned into cash.

Group 1. Ratios concerned with current assets and liabilities.

$$\text{Current ratio} = \frac{\text{Current Assets}}{\text{Current Liabilities}}$$

Quick (or Acid test) ratio =

$$\frac{\text{Current Assets} - \text{Stocks (sometimes known as } Quick\ Assets)}{\text{Current Liabilities}}$$

The current ratio effectively assesses the working capital of the firm and is generally expected to be within a band of values appropriate for a given industry. It is wrong to be dogmatic about the 'ideal' value for the current ratio but it appears that analysts consider values in the range of 1.8:1 to 2:1 to be acceptable.

The current ratio considers those assets and liabilities which have life cycles measured in months rather than weeks and whilst this aspect of solvency is of great importance the immediate liquidity position, say the next 6/10 weeks, also needs to be considered. This is assessed by the quick ratio which excludes stocks and thus concentrates attention on more liquid assets such as cash and debtors. Again, whilst there can be no precise norm, it appears that an acceptable range of values for the acid test ratio is between 1:1 and say 0.8:1 (Quick assets: Current liabilities).

If the current liabilities include a bank overdraft which it is known will not be recalled within the short time scale being considered then a more useful ratio would be to calculate the following adjusted acid test ratio.

$$\text{Adjusted acid test ratio} = \frac{\text{Quick Assets}}{\text{Current Liabilities} - \text{Bank Overdraft}}$$

This would compare assets and liabilities with approximately the same life cycles.

Note: This principle could also apply to a tax liability with a known payment date.

Group 2. Cash conversion ratios

The firm's day to day liquidity position is largely dependent upon the rate at which cash flows into the business from normal operations. These operations include the conversion of stocks into sales and therefore debtors and the subsequent rate of conversion of debtors into cash.

The two following ratios provide some guidance to the firm's ability to generate cash from normal trading.

$$\text{Average stock turnover ratio} = \frac{\text{Costs of goods sold in period}}{\text{Average stock held during the period}}$$

$$\text{Average collection period} = \frac{\text{Debtors as at balance sheet date}}{\text{Average daily credit sales during period}}$$

Whilst the average stock turnover ratio varies greatly between different industries, comparison with broadly similar companies and with previous periods of the same firm can provide useful guidance. Increasing competition, dated marketing policies and products, unnecessarily high prices and other such factors are likely to be reflected in a deterioration in the average stock turnover ratio.

An important element in cash flow management is to monitor continually the average time that debtors take to settle. The calculation of the average collection period should be only part of a firm's total credit and cash management system. The system would normally include such matters as: regular reminder letters, use of debt collection agencies if necessary, cash discounts, trade discounts related to creditworthiness, prompt invoicing and banking procedures, age analysis of debtors and the application of Pareto analysis (ie the 80:20 rule) to the individual debtors so that the important items can be monitored closely.

13. Long-term solvency ratios

These ratios concentrate on the longer term financial stability and structure of the firm and are generally of most interest to financial analysts and investors.

A number of ratios can be calculated in this area and these include:

a) $$\text{Gearing ratio} = \frac{\text{Fixed Interest Capital}}{\text{Fixed Interest Capital} + \text{Equity Capital}}$$

b) Shareholders equity to assets ratio ratio

$$= \frac{\text{Shareholders Equity (capital plus reserves)}}{\text{Total Assets}}$$

c)   **Non-equity claims to assets ratio** $= \dfrac{\textbf{Long-Term Debt plus Current Liabilities}}{\textbf{Total Assets}}$

d)   **Interest coverage ratio** $= \dfrac{\textbf{Profit before tax and interest}}{\textbf{Interest Charges for period}}$

Ratios (a), (b) and (c) are closely related and are merely facets of the same relationship. Analysts consider that too high a gearing ratio is potentially unstable indicating as it does undue dependence on external sources for long-term financing. It is important to calculate these longer term solvency factors because favourable short-term ratios may disguise a worsening financial position. For example, if a firm incurs a long-term liability in the form of debentures this has the effect of improving the current ratio (current assets : current liabilities) but it worsens the firm's gearing and interest coverage ratios. With fluctuating profits this could cause substantial variations in the dividends paid to shareholders which is considered by the market to be one of the signs of financial instability.

The interest coverage ratio assesses the ability of the company to meet the recurring interest charges which arise when long-term and short-term loans are contracted.

14. Solvency ratios example

Example 2

Using the data from Example 1 calculate the short-term and long-term solvency ratios for Relationships plc. It can be assumed that the stock values given in the balance sheet approximate to average stocks held during the year.

Solution

$$\text{Current ratio} = \frac{\text{Current assets}}{\text{Current Liabilities}} = \frac{1,900,000}{1,970,000} = \textbf{0.96:1}$$

Note: With a 'normal' range of 1.8:1 to 2:1 this would be considered an alarming value.

$$\text{Acid test} = \frac{\text{Quick assets}}{\text{Current Liabilities}} = \frac{1,120,000}{1,970,000} = \textbf{0.57:1}$$

If it could be assumed (or ascertained by enquiry) that the bank overdraft will not be recalled then the adjusted acid test ratio could be calculated.

$$\text{Adjusted acid test ratio} = \frac{\text{Quick assets}}{\text{Current Liabilities} - \text{Overdraft}} = \frac{1,120,000}{1,120,000} = \textbf{1:1}$$

Cash conversion ratios

$$\text{Average stock turnover} = \frac{\text{Cost of Goods Sold}}{\text{Average Stock}} = \frac{4,475,000}{780,000} = \textbf{5.74 times}$$

$$\text{Average collection period} = \frac{\text{Debtors}}{\text{Average Daily Sales}} = \frac{1,025,000}{17,808} = \textbf{57.56 days}$$

Note: In the stock turnover ratio average stock is invariably used. Where beginning and end stock values are unrepresentative it may be necessary to calculate an average based on monthly stock values.

Long-term solvency ratios

$$\text{Gearing ratio} = \frac{\text{Fixed Interest Capital}}{\text{Fixed Interest} + \text{Equity Capital}} = \frac{2,000,000}{7,000,000} = \mathbf{28.6\%}$$

Note: The above ratio is based on book values. Alternatively the ratio could be based on market values as shown in para 16.

$$\text{Equity to assets ratio} = \frac{\text{Shareholders Equity}}{\text{Total Assets}} = \frac{5,000,000}{8,970,000} = \mathbf{55.74\%}$$

$$\text{Non-equity claims to assets ratio} = \frac{\text{Long-Term Debt} + \text{Current Liabilities}}{\text{Total Assets}}$$

$$= \frac{3,970,000}{8,970,000} = \mathbf{44.26\%}$$

$$\text{Interest coverage ratio} = \frac{\text{Profit before tax and interest}}{\text{Interest Charges}} = \frac{933,000}{305,000} = \mathbf{3.06 \ times}$$

Note: Once again trends and comparisons are all important. Based on the conventionally accepted norms Relationships plc would appear to be having severe solvency problems, particularly in the short term.

15. Investment ratios

The overall objective of calculating the various investment ratios is to assess the company in terms of its potential and stability as an equity investment.

The ratios typically calculated cover earnings, dividends and share prices as follows:

$$\textbf{a) Earnings per share} = \frac{\textbf{Profits after tax less Preference Dividend (Gross)}}{\textbf{Number of ordinary shares issued}}$$

SSAP 3 recommends that this ratio should be shown in the accounts of all listed companies and students are advised to refer to the Standard for guidance on how to deal with the complications which occur in practice.

$$\textbf{b) Dividend yield} = \frac{\textbf{Nominal Share Value} \times \textbf{Dividend \%}}{\textbf{Market price per share}}$$

This ratio measures the rate of return on the amount invested.

$$\textbf{c) Dividend cover (or Payout ratio)} = \frac{\textbf{Profit after tax} - \textbf{Preference Dividend (gross)}}{\textbf{Gross Equity Dividend}}$$

This ratio gives a measure of the margin of available earnings that is available to meet the current dividend declared on ordinary shares. The higher the dividend cover the more certain it is that the dividends on ordinary shares will be maintained.

$$\textbf{d) Price earnings (PE) ratio} = \frac{\textbf{Market price per share}}{\textbf{Earnings per share}}$$

The PE ratio relates earnings to market price and is generally taken as measure of the growth potential of an investment. Company earnings after tax and preference dividends, are available to pay ordinary dividends and to plough back into the company. The PE ratio is equivalent to the number of years' purchase of latest earnings, represented by the share price at any given time. The reciprocal of the PE ratio shows the earnings yield, ie

e)   **Earnings yield** $= \dfrac{\textbf{Earnings per share}}{\textbf{Market price per share}} \times 100\%$

$= \textbf{Dividend cover} \times \textbf{dividend}$

In addition to the above ratios an investor or analyst will also be interested in the gearing of the company (already mentioned in connection with the long-term solvency para 13) and to the investor, gearing ratios based on market values are likely to be the most relevant, ie

f)   **Capital gearing ratio (market values)**

$= \dfrac{\textbf{Total market value preference shares} + \textbf{Market value of debentures}}{\textbf{Total equity market value}}$

Unduly low gearing ratios indicate that the company is failing to take full advantage of the tax relief available on debenture interest whilst excessively high gearing will force up the cost of debentures (the market will require higher interest rates to compensate for the extra risk) and cause equity earnings to become volatile.

16. Investment ratios example

Example 3

Using the data from Example 1 calculate the investment ratios for Relationships plc. The market price for Ordinary Shares is £1.80; for Preference Shares 80p; and debentures are quoted at 92.

Solution

Earnings per share $= \dfrac{\text{Profit after tax less Preferences Dividend}}{\text{No. of Ordinary Shares}} = \dfrac{462{,}000}{2{,}750{,}000} = \textbf{16.8p}$

Dividend Yield $= \dfrac{\text{Nominal Value} \times \text{Dividend \%}}{\text{Market Price}} = \dfrac{£1 \times 13.1\%}{£1.80} = \textbf{7.28\%}$

Payout ratio $= \dfrac{\text{Profit after tax less Preference Dividend}}{\text{Equity Dividend}} = \dfrac{462{,}000}{360{,}000} = \textbf{1.28 times}$

Price earnings ratio $= \dfrac{\text{Market price per share}}{\text{Earnings per share}} = \dfrac{£1.80}{16.8p} = \textbf{10.7}$

Earnings yield $= \dfrac{1}{\text{P/E Ratio}} = \dfrac{1}{10.7} = \textbf{9.3\%}$

alternatively: $= \text{Payout ratio} \times \text{Dividend yield} \% = 1.28 \times 7.28\% = \textbf{9.3\%}$

Capital gearing $= \dfrac{\text{Market value preference} + \text{debentures}}{\text{Market value equity}}$

$= £\dfrac{400{,}000 + 1{,}840{,}000}{4{,}950{,}000}$

$= \textbf{45.25\%}$

Note: Comparisons with alternative yields, cover, earnings and gearing are available from financial analysts, journals and stockbrokers.

17. Developments in ratio analysis

Historical ratio analysis as described so far in this chapter appears to be a useful management technique, particularly when used on a comparative, interfirm basis but it is not without limitations. Consequently a number of attempts have been made to refine ratio analysis in order to make it more effective and forward looking. The general aim being to provide predictors of future performance instead of analysing the past. A number of researchers have worked in this area including; Altman, Tafler, Robertson and Koh and Killough.

For example, Altman and other workers have developed a technique based on identifying a small, selected group of 5 ratios which are combined using calculated weightings to produce a single value, known as Z or Zeta score. The procedure, which is a form of multiple discriminant analysis, is designed to replace the conventional norms which are used in traditional ratio analysis, by empirically tested weights and groups that provide a clear datum level above which the firm is likely to be healthy and profitable and below which there are likely to be financial crises.

The original equation developed by Altman was,

$$Z = 0.012X_1 + 0.014X_2 + 0.033X_3 + 0.006X_4 + 0.010X_5$$

where X_1 to X_5 are the particular ratios chosen by Altman as the most significant predictors of performance and financial health and the coefficients (0.012 et al) are the constant weightings derived from empirical studies.

18. The five key ratio

The ratios selected by Altman were those which his researches indicated as the best collective predictor of financial stability and hence survival. The detailed make up of each ratio and the definitions used are based on American practice but require little or no adjustment for UK conventions. The selected ratios are:

$$X_1 = \frac{\text{Gross Current Assets}}{\text{Gross Total Assets}}$$

This means that current liabilities are not deducted to establish the working capital which is a normal UK convention.

$$X_2 = \frac{\text{Retained Earnings}}{\text{Gross Total Assets}}$$

$$X_3 = \frac{\text{Profits (before interest and tax)}}{\text{Gross Total Assets}}$$

This is the ROCE ratio which, to be expected, has the highest weighting (0.033) in arriving at the Z score.

$$X_4 = \frac{\text{Market Value of Equity}}{\text{Book Value of Total Debt}}$$

$$X_5 = \frac{\text{Sales}}{\text{Gross Total Assets}}$$

Using the above ratios and weights Altman established two indicator values for the Z score; above 3% (0.03) there is a high probability that the company would not fail, below 1.8% (0.018) failure was very likely and would probably happen within two years. Obviously there is a grey area between these two values but any value below 3% should be cause for serious concern for the firm in question.

Developments in the procedure have enabled claims to be made that it is possible to make successful predictions as much as five years ahead and the process has been further refined by calculating differing values for the Z score indicators for different industries.

The ability of ratio models to make accurate predictions has been studied extensively. A recent study by Houghton and Woodliffe found that there was some evidence that they could but not, of course, with 100% accuracy. The researchers used a group of 13 ratios shown in Figure 21.2

Working capital / Total assets

Retained earnings / Total assets

Profit before tax / Total assets

Market value / Total debt

Sales / Total assets

Profit before tax / Current liabilities

Working capital / Total debt

Current liabilities / Total assets

No credit interval / Operating costs

Cash flow / Total debt

Total debt / Total assets

Current ratio

Acid test ratio

Figure 21.2 Summary of choice of ratios

The researchers found that there was a high degree of accurate discrimination of the companies studied into various categories e.g. Successful, At risk, Failures and so on. They found that the ratio's which were the best discriminators were those based on the ability to generate profits.

19. Value added (or added value)

Value added is the difference between sales income and bought in goods and services. Value added statements can help to assess the relative efficiency of the firm without the analysis being obscured by external input costs which may be largely uncontrollable. Value added is the wealth that a firm creates by its own efforts. The value added performance of a company is a good measure of the overall productivity of the firm and it is out of the total amount of the value added that the firm rewards all interested parties, including shareholders, staff, Inland Revenue and others.

Value added is defined by CIMA thus

> ' *Sales value less the cost of purchased materials and services. This represents the worth of an alteration in form, location or availability of a product or service.'*   Terminology

The Corporate Report advocated that a statement of Added Value should be prepared as this was considered to be the simplest and most effective way of putting profit into proper perspective in relation to the amount of value added paid out to employees, shareholders, the Government, and suppliers of loan capital.

A typical format of a Value Added Statement is shown in Table 1.

Statement of Added Value
for year to . . . . .

			£
	SALES		6,500,000
less	Bought in goods and services		4,250,000
=	ADDED VALUE		2,250,000
	APPLIED AS FOLLOWS		£
	To employees (Wages, pensions, and other benefits)		1,750,000
	To suppliers of capital	£	
	Dividends to shareholders	140,000	
	Interest on loans	75,000	215,000
	To pay Government Taxation		50,000
	To provide for maintenance and expansion of assets		
	Depreciation		100,000
	Retained profits		135,000
=	ADDED VALUE		2,250,000

Table 1

20. Value added ratios

In addition to the production of a summary value added statement such as that shown in Figure 2 the concept of value added can be included in ratio analysis.

Value added is a prime measure of productivity and ratios using value added could easily be included in the pyramid of ratios shown in Figure 21.1. Typical ratios involving value added include:

Value added / Fixed Assets

Value added / Current Assets

Value added / Per Employee

Value added / per £ of direct wages

and others of a similar nature.

21. Value added and motivation

It can be argued that value added is a better measure of performance than profit and if this viewpoint is accepted then there is likely to be more favourable motivational effects if performance is judged on value added rather than profit. To change the whole range of management accounting reports and statements from conventional profits and contributions to statements of value added would be a formidable task but on a selective basis it might be worthwhile.

22. Ratio analysis – a summary

Ratio analysis, particularly when used in a comparative manner, is a useful broad indicator to weaknesses in company operations and policies. All companies can derive some benefits from properly conducted ratio analysis and comparison but clearly the less efficient firms are likely to gain the most pertinent information. Participation in properly organised inter-firm comparison schemes, where consistent bases are employed and information is used that is unavailable from normal published accounts, eliminates many of the difficulties that may occur when comparisons are made based on ratios prepared on an ad hoc basis using information only from published accounts. In such circumstances ratio analysis may be of limited value for a number of reasons, including:

a) The accounting rules and conventions used for matters such as stock valuations, depreciations, revenue/capital distinctions etc are likely to differ from company to company.

b) Where accounts are prepared on an historical cost basis without current value and inflation adjustments, comparisons become more difficult and the ratios themselves have less meaning.

c) Where a company is part of a group, transfer pricing policies and financing arrangements make it difficult to establish genuine operating results for the individual company.

Regular ratio analysis to determine trends within a given company is always likely to be of some value and it would be normal to include inter-related ratio analysis as part of the overall performance appraisal systems of the firm.

A development of the principle of formal inter-firm comparison schemes mentioned above, is that of *benchmarking*. This is a technique where a firm's performance is compared with other companies, preferably industry leaders across a range of financial and non-financial performance indicators. Traditional inter-firm comparison schemes tend to concentrate only on financial aspects of performance and less on key operational matters such as lead times, productivity and quality measures. Sometimes because of the difficulty in obtaining sensitive information from competitors, *process benchmarking* is carried out. This means identifying critical processes within the firm and looking for non-competitive firms which use, and excel in, that particular process. Benchmarking and inter-firm comparison schemes can contribute to efficiency and cost reduction by making management more aware of areas/techniques/processes which need attention and can be improved to bring them up to the standard of the industry leaders.

23. Summary

a) Ratio analysis uses financial reports and data and summarises key relationships, eg profit to sales, in order to appraise financial performance.

b) The effectiveness of ratio analysis is greatly improved when trends are identified, comparative ratios are available, and inter-related ratios are prepared.

c) Ratios can be subdivided into many groups and three typical ones are: profitability ratios, solvency ratios, and investment ratios.

d) The key ratio dealing with profitability is the ROCE. Typically this is supported by other ratios which progressively analyse asset turnover and profitability.

e) Key supporting ratios are sales: Operating Assets and Operating profit:Sales.

f) Solvency ratios can be concerned with the short-term and the long-term.

g) The main ratios concerned with short-term solvency are the current ratio and the 'quick' ratio or acid test. Also, cash conversion ratios such as the average stock turnover and average collection period are useful aids.

h) The long-term solvency ratios concern the financial stability and structure of the firm. Several of the ratios relate to the firm's gearing and others concern interest coverage.

i) The investment ratios include: earnings per share, dividend yield and cover and the price-earnings ratio.

j) Conventional ratio analysis has been refined by Altman by developing a value known as the Z score, based on five key ratios. Indicator values have been developed which it is claimed provide good predictors of financial stability or instability.

k) Value Added is the wealth that a company creates by its own efforts and value added statements and ratios can provide guidance on the productivity and performance of an organisation with the issue being clouded by input costs.

24. Points to note

a) Ratio analysis, using inter-related ratios, avoids giving undue emphasis to one isolated aspect of company operations and emphasises that financial success is the result of the interaction of numerous contributory factors.

b) Comparison between ratios for widely differing types of organisation are usually pointless and misleading. For example the ROCE for a capital intensive food processing company might be 12% whilst the ROCE for a knowledge based organisation (eg designers, architects, solicitors) with virtually no capital assets, might be 2000%.

c) There are firms who specialise in publishing ratios for particular trades supported by forecasts and analyses of trends which are likely to affect that sector of the economy.

Additional reading

Application of classification techniques in business, banking and finance;
Altman – JAI Press

Performance measurement in the manufacturing sector – CIMA

Performance measurement in services businesses – CIMA

Financial ratios: prediction of corporate success or failure;
Houghton & Woodliffe – Journal of Business Finance and Accounting

Financial Statement & Analysis; *Lev* – Englewood Cliff

Positive accounting theory; *Watts & Zimmerman* – Englewood Cliff

Self review questions

1.   How can ratio analysis be most effective? (2)
2.   What broad groups of ratios can be prepared? (3)
3.   What is the 'pyramid' of ratios and what ratios are typically included? (4)
4. . In what ways can the 'capital employed' and 'profit' parts of the ROCE ratio be defined? (5)
5.   What are the asset ratios? (6 & 7)
6.   What are the profitability ratios? (8 & 9)
7.   What are the main short-term solvency ratios and what are considered 'good' ranges of values? (12)
8.   What are the key long-term solvency ratios? (13)
9.   Define the main investment ratios and show their relationships. (15)
10. What is the objective of calculating the Z score developed by Altman? What are the five key ratios? (17)
11. What is the value added and what is the typical layout for a value added statement? (19)
12. What are the reasons why ad hoc ratio analysis may be of limited value? (22)

22 AMT and management accounting

1. Objectives

After studying this chapter you will:

☐   understand key developments in Advanced Manufacturing Technology (AMT) and how they affect management accounting;

☐   be able to describe, in outline computer-aided design and manufacturing, material requirements planning and just-in-time systems;

☐   know the importance of total quality control;

☐   understand the relationship of activity-based costing and AMT;

☐   know the key principles of throughput accounting;

☐   understand backflush accounting;

☐   know the principles of target costing;

☐   be able to use physical measures for performance appraisal.

2. Why study AMT?

Advanced manufacturing technology (AMT) is revolutionising the way products are manufactured especially in what are termed World-Class Manufacturers (WCM).

AMT is a general expression encompassing; Automated production technology, computer assisted design and manufacturing (CAD/CAM), Flexible manufacturing systems (FMS), robotics, Total Quality Control (TQC), advances in Production Management including Materials requirement and Manufacturing Resources Planning Systems (MRP), Just-in-Time (JIT) systems and so on.

The various items in the above definition are covered in more details below but it is first necessary to examine why a knowledge of AMT is essential for the management accountant.

It has been argued by a number of academics, consultants and industrialists that traditional management accounting systems and performance measures are inappropriate and misleading for firms using AMT. Indeed Professor Kaplan has claimed that traditional management accounting produces '...simply the wrong measures. They move the company in the wrong direction, reward managers for damaging the business and provide no incentive for improvement. The best we can do is to switch them off, just stop doing them!'

Before looking at the claimed deficiencies of management accounting in detail we must first study the main elements of AMT.

3. Objectives of AMT

Companies need to compete in fast moving, sophisticated world markets. The use of AMT helps them to do this. It increases their capability to produce high-quality goods at low cost and thus provide high levels of customer satisfaction. Firms need to be innovative and flexible and to be able to deal with short product life cycles. They need to be able to offer greater product variety whilst maintaining or reducing their costs. They wish to reduce set-up times and inventories and have the greatest possible manufacturing flexibility. AMT helps them to do this.

The various facets making up AMT are now examined.

4. Computer-aided design (CAD)

This is product/component design and testing using a computer terminal. The interaction between the designer, the computer and the database enables many more options and designs to be considered in order to achieve the greatest efficiency and simplicity at the lowest cost. An important facility is the interrogation of the CAD database to identify standard parts and methods thus simplifying product design, reducing the number of product parts, and thus helping to minimise inventories.

5. Computer-aided manufacture (CAM)

This is a wide ranging expression to cover the use of computers for the programming and control of production machines. It includes the use of robots, numerically controlled (NT) machines and computer numerically controlled (CNC) machines.

Because of the ability to re-programme as required, CAM offers many advantages including;

❑ flexibility i.e. ability to perform a variety of operations and produce a range of parts

❑ greater control over manufacturing

❑ reduced set-up times

❑ better, more consistent quality

❑ fewer reworked items and less scrap

❑ less reliance on direct labour

In many companies CAD and CAM are integrated thus helping to reduce the lead time from the initial produce idea through to the market place.

6. Flexible manufacturing systems (FMS)

This is a highly-automated manufacturing system which is computer controlled and capable of producing a 'family ' of parts in a flexible manner. The main essence is a mixture of CNC machines, robots and automated materials handling equipment to move the components from tool to tool.

The final stage in automation would be the complete automation of the whole factory, known as computer-integrated manufacturing (CIM). This stage has not yet been reached as even the most advanced of today's factories contain islands of automation (IAs) linked by human bridges.

7. Production management systems

In addition to improvements in machines and technology there have been major advances in the planning and control of production. Some of these management changes have been so sweeping that they have changed the whole manufacturing culture, especially in WCM companies. Some of the systems, especially Just-in-Time (JIT) have challenged traditional views of manufacture and, it is claimed, have been largely instrumental to the success of Japanese manufacturers.

Two of the main production management systems are described below.

❑ Materials Requirement Planning (MRP)

❑ Just-in-Time (JIT)

8. Materials requirement planning (MRP)

MRP is a computerised information, planning and control system which has the objective of maintaining a smooth production flow.

It is concerned with:

❑ maximising the efficiency in the timing of orders for raw materials or parts that are placed with external suppliers

❑ efficient scheduling of the manufacture and assembly of the final product.

The operation of an MRP System requires the following:

a) A master production schedule showing the quantities and timings required for the finished product(s).

b) A Bill of Materials (BOM) which shows the breakdown of each finished product into sub-assemblies components and raw materials.

c) An Inventory file containing the balance on hand, scheduled receipts and numbers already allocated for each sub-assembly, component and type of raw material.

d) A parts manufacturing and purchasing file containing lead times of all purchased items and lead times and production sequences of all sub-assemblies and components produced internally.

MRP has evolved into MRPII which attempts to integrate material resource planning, factory capacity planning and labour scheduling into a single manufacturing control system.

9. Just-in-time systems

JIT systems developed in Japan, notably at Toyota, and are considered as one of the main contributions to Japanese manufacturing success.

The aim of JIT systems is to produce the required items, of high quality, exactly at the time they are required: JIT systems are characterised by the pursuit of excellence at all stages with a climate of continuous improvement.

A JIT environment is composed of the following:

❐ a move towards zero inventory

❐ elimination of non-value added activities

❐ an emphasis on perfect quality i.e. zero defects

❐ short set-ups

❐ a move towards a batch size of one

❐ 100% on time deliveries

❐ Demand-pull manufacture

It is this latter characteristic which gives rise to the name of Just-in-Time. Production only takes place when there is actual customer demand for the product so JIT works on a *pull-through* basis which means that products are not made to go into stock.

Contrast this with the traditional manufacturing approach of *production-push* where products are made in large batches and move into stock.

There are two aspects to JIT systems, JIT Purchasing and JIT Production.

10. Just-in-time Purchasing

This seeks to match the *usage* of materials with the *delivery* of materials from external suppliers. This means that material stocks can be kept at near-zero levels. For JIT purchasing to work requires the following:

a) Confidence that suppliers will deliver exactly on time.

b) That suppliers will deliver materials of 100% quality so that there will be no rejects, returns and consequent production delays.

The reliability of suppliers is all-important and JIT purchasing means that the company must build up close working relationships with their suppliers. This is usually achieved by doing more business with fewer suppliers and placing long-term purchasing orders in order that the supplier has assured sales and can plan to meet the demand.

11. JIT production

JIT production works on a demand-pull basis and seeks to eliminate all waste and everything which does not add value to the product. As an example consider the lead times associated with making and selling a product. These include:

Inspection time – Transport time – Queueing time – Storage time – Processing time

Of these, only processing time adds value to the product whereas all the others add cost, but not value.

The ideal for JIT systems is to convert materials to finished products with a lead time equal to processing time so eliminating all activities which do not add value. A way of emphasising the importance of reducing throughput time is to express the above lead times as follows:

Throughput time = Value-added time + Non-value added time

The JIT pull system means that components are not made until requested by the next process. The usual way this is done is by monitoring parts consumption at each stage and using a system of markers (known as kanbans) which authorise production and movement to the process which requires the parts. A consequence of this is that there may be idle time at certain work stations but this is considered preferable to adding to work-in-progress inventory.

Poor and uncertain quality is a prime source of delays hence the drive in JIT systems for zero defects and Total Quality Control (TQC). When quality is poor, higher WIP is needed to protect production from delays caused by defective parts. Higher inventory is also required when there are long set-up and changeover times. Accordingly there is continual pressure in JIT systems to reduce set-up times and eventually eliminate them so that the optimal batch size can become one. With a batch size of one, the work can flow smoothly to the next stage without the need to store it and schedule the next machine to accept the item.

12. JIT production implications

To operate JIT manufacturing successfully and achieve the targets of low inventories and on-time deliveries means that:

a) The production processes must be shortened and simplified. Each product family is made in a work-cell based on flowline principles. The JIT system increases the variety and complexity within work cells. These contain groups of dissimilar machines which thus require workers to be more flexible and adaptable.

b) Using JIT the emphasis is on 'doing the job right the first time' thus avoiding defects and reworking. JIT systems require quality awareness programmes, statistical checks on output quality and continual worker training.

473

c) Factory layouts must be changed to reduce movement. Traditionally machines were grouped by function; all the drilling machines together, the grinding machines and so on. This meant a part had to travel long distances moving from one part of the factory to another often stopping along the way in a storage area. All these are non-value added activities which have to be reduced or eliminated.

d) There must be full employee involvement. As an example it has been reported that the 60,000 employees of Toyota produced a total of 2.6 million improvement suggestions per annum. In most cases, after line management approval, the working groups simply get on with implementing their ideas. Arguably one of the most important behavioural implications of JIT is that the status quo is continually challenged and there is a never ending search for improvements.

13. Benefits from JIT

Successful users of JIT systems are making substantial savings. These arise from numerous areas:

a) Lower investment required in all forms of inventory.

b) Space savings from the reduction in inventory and improved layouts.

c) Greater customer satisfaction resulting from higher quality better deliveries and greater product variety.

d) The buffers provided by traditional inventories masked other areas of waste and inefficiency. Examples include; co-ordination and work flow problems, bottlenecks, supplier unreliability and so on. Elimination of these problems improves performance dramatically.

e) The flexibility of JIT and the ability to supply small batches enables companies to respond more quickly to market changes and to be able to satisfy market niches.

14. Total quality control (TQC)

AMT and JIT systems have a total quality control philosophy in which the only acceptable quality level is zero defects. Prominence is given in JIT systems to all defects found so that the reason(s) for the defect can be discovered and put right. A defect found is a learning opportunity.

On the other hand, in many Western manufacturers using conventional management accounting, activities and costs associated with poor quality are obscured by the common practice of including in standard costs and process costs 'normal' allowances for scrap, waste and reworks. Thus, as long as the production process turned out high volumes and kept within the 'normal' scrap levels all was thought to be well. The conventional wisdom was that there was an optimal percentage of defects with a quality-cost trade-off. This is shown in Figure 22.1.

Contrast this approach with the TQC view of cost trade off and quality as shown in Fig. 22.2.

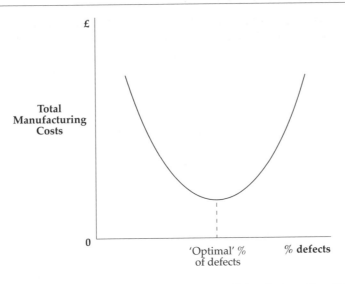

Figure 22.1 *Traditional view of quality-cost trade off*

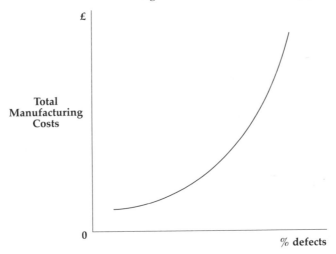

Figure 22.2 *Total quality control view of quality-cost trade off*

The traditional views and systems associated with quality can be illustrated by using a pop-up toaster as an analogy for a production system. If, from time to time, the toaster pops up slices of burnt toast the traditional approach was to set up an elaborate recording system to count the number of burnt slices (called the Quality Control Dept.) and an expensive system to scrape them (called re-working). The Japanese approach is to fix the toaster as soon as the first burnt slice is discovered.

15. Moving towards TQC

Companies operating TQC measure defects not as a percentage of outgoing items but as a parts-per-million (PPM) ratio of defects to items produced. They realise that many things have to be done correctly to achieve continual reductions in PPM defect rates.

The most important thing is to realise that quality has to be designed in, not inspected in. TQC has to be considered at every stage starting with the initial product idea. It is not something which is solely the concern of Inspectors at the end of the production line.

The following are the key points at which TQC must operate:

Product design

Probably the key stage. Product design should have price, performance, ease of manufacturing and quality in mind throughout the design stage. An important factor is simplicity; fewer parts preferably of standard design. Product designers should also liaise closely with manufacturing and process engineers. A well designed product not only works well, it is easy to manufacture. During the design stage the technique of value analysis is used extensively. This is the systematic examination of cost factors in order to devise ways of achieving the specified purpose, most economically, at the required standard of quality and reliability.

Production engineering

This is the process of designing the methods for making a product to the design specification. This also includes the tools and processes to be used, the tolerances and finishes required, assembly sequences and so on.

Manufacturing

Manufacturing considerations must be part of product design because it is estimated that only 20% of quality defects can be traced to the production line. The other 80% being attributable to design factors or poor purchasing. In JIT systems the responsibility for defects has moved away from quality control inspectors to the operatives. Operators are expected to maintain their equipment and produce zero defect output. They are, of course, aided in this by CNC machines and automatic equipment which often incorporates computerised gauging and measuring devices. In addition, there is extensive use of Statistical Process Control and Control Charts.

JIT systems emphasise in-process checks rather than waiting until the product is fully completed before it gets a final inspection. This was the traditional method and is still widely used even though it is a less efficient system.

(Note: Statistical Process Control and Control Charts are covered in detail in Quantitative Techniques by T. Lucey, DP Publications.)

Goods inwards

The quality of output depends on the quality of input materials. This means that Quality requirements are also imposed on suppliers to ensure quality and no inspection is performed on incoming supplies.

Output inspection

Final inspection is being replaced by in-process checking. Final inspection, based on sampling, does still take place mainly to satisfy management that quality control in production is being maintained.

When TQC is properly applied and the incidence of defects decrease, total manufacturing costs, including warranty and service costs, decrease.

This is not surprising because if items are made correctly first time money is saved from the avoidance of detection, reworking, scrapping, repairing in the field and so on.

Higher quality means lower costs.

16. Total quality management and BS.EN.ISO 9000 (formerly BS5750)

Total quality management is where there is a defined culture of quality improvement in every process and department of the organisation.

In the UK, organisations can be accredited under British Standard 5750 if they meet stringent quality requirements throughout the organisation. BS5750 applies to service organisations as well as manufacturing firms and there are numerous businesses who have obtained accreditation. These include; solicitors, travel agencies, architects, transport firms, tyre and exhaust fitters as well as a wide range of manufacturers.

17. Management accounting and AMT

Now that the basics of AMT have been outlined we can examine the deficiencies that traditional management accounting approaches have been claimed to possess when they are applied to companies using AMT.

These deficiencies are said to be so severe that a number of leading commentators have stated that much of traditional management accounting is based on incorrect principles and provides misleading information to managers, especially when applied to AMT.

The main problem areas identified are:

Absorption costing – the traditional methods of calculating product costs use absorption costing based on production-volume related absorption rates (direct labour hours or machine hours). These methods are considered inappropriate in an AMT environment.

Cost behaviour – traditional management accounting classifies costs as fixed or variable in relation to production volume. In AMT many overheads costs are for support which are related to activities and factors other than production volume. Traditionally, the longer-term variability of many costs has been largely ignored. Labour costs are a declining proportion of total costs so the treatment and understanding of overheads becomes increasingly important.

Standard costing – standard costing and variance analysis are widely used traditional control techniques whose usefulness for AMT and JIT environments have been questioned. The doubts arise from both the general philosophy and detailed operation of standard costing. The idea that performance is deemed satisfactory if it meets predetermined standards is at odds with the philosophy of continual improvement in AMT. Also, standard costing variances focusing on financial numbers produced with a time lag are likely to be of little or no value in a fast changing AMT environment. Many individual variances lose their relevance entirely when AMT is used. For example purchase price variances have little meaning when prices are determined by long-term contracts where quality and supplier reliability are dominant factors. Bulk purchasing to achieve lower material prices contradicts the AMT philosophy of maintaining near zero inventory levels.

Short-term financial measures – much of the output of traditional management accounting consists of short-term financial performance measures, e.g. costs, production efficiency measured by cost per unit, variances and so on. Many of these are produced long after the event and are too narrowly focused. A much wider view is necessary for AMT together with the realisation that more speedily available, non-financial performance measures are required. For example, those relating to quality, equipment failures, reject-rates, maintenance and so on.

Cost accounting methods – traditional cost accounting traces raw materials to various production stages, via WIP, to the next stage through to finished goods. This is supported by literally thousands of transaction entries. With JIT this becomes needlessly expensive and uninformative when production flows through the factory on a continual basis with near-zero inventories and very low batch sizes. In addition all piecework payments at the individual worker level and local efficiency measures become pointless. With JIT the only worthwhile efficiency measure relates to the entire JIT line and not to individual stations in the line. Thus cost accounting and recording systems can be greatly simplified. For example, Hewlett-Packard reported a drop in accounting transactions for materials from 100,000 per month to 5000 when an accounting system suited to JIT operations was introduced.

Whether all the above criticisms are well founded is, of course, debatable. What is undeniable is that changes and developments in Management Accounting are taking place in order to meet the challenge of AMT.

A number of the more important developments are dealt with below including; Activity-Based Costing, Throughput Accounting, Backflush Accounting, Target Costing Non-Financial Performance Measures.

18. Activity-based costing (ABC) and AMT

The principles of ABC have been covered earlier. Here we discuss ABC's suitability for AMT environments and some possible problems which may be encountered.

Companies using AMT have a high level of overhead costs, especially relating to support services such as industrial engineering, maintenance, production planning, data processing etc. By the use of carefully chosen cost drivers ABC traces these overheads to product lines in a more logical and less arbitrary manner than absorption on production volume.

Also, many costs previously included in general overheads, and absorbed by a percentage uplift of factory cost can be traced to specific JIT lines. This improves product costing and cost management as the costs are made the responsibility of the line manager. Further, the determination and use of cost drivers helps to measure and improve the efficiency and effectiveness of the support departments.

It forces the company to ask searching questions. For example, what does the department achieve? Does it add value? Why is the department needed? What causes the demand for the activity? Are there better ways of meeting this demand? and so on.

ABC systems may also encourage reductions in throughput time, inventory reductions and quality improvements thus helping to achieve the objectives of AMT.

It would appear that ABC has much to offer firms using AMT although, as is to be expected, there are problems with ABC. For example, a key element in JIT philosophy is the drive towards simplicity yet ABC systems by using multiple cost pools and a variety of cost drivers can lead to more complexity. Another example is to do with set-ups. JIT seeks to reduce set-up times so that very small batches (ideally one part only) can be made economically. The aim of set-up time reduction is to allow more set-ups not merely to reduce set-up costs. The use of a cost-driver based on the number of set-ups will therefore work against JIT principles as it will tend to encourage larger batches.

All in all however, the use of ABC seems to be more logical and does remove the patent illogicalities and major inaccuracies of traditional product costing applied to AMT.

19. Throughput accounting

Throughput accounting is a system of performance measurement and costing which traces costs to throughput time. It is claimed that it complements JIT principles and forces attention to the true determinants of profitability; the rate at which goods can be produced to satisfy customers' orders.

Throughput accounting is defined as follows:

> *'A method of performance measurement which relates production and other costs to throughput. Throughput accounting product costs relate to the usage of key resources by various products.'* *Terminology*

Throughput Accounting (TA) is based on three concepts:

Concept 1

With the exception of material costs, in the short-run, most factory costs (including direct labour) are fixed. These fixed costs can be grouped together and called Total Factory Costs (TFC).

Concept 2

With JIT products should not be made unless there is a customer waiting for them because the ideal inventory level is zero. The effect of this is that there will be unavoidable idle capacity in some operations, except for the operation that is the bottleneck of the moment. Working on output just to increase WIP or finished goods stocks creates no profit and so would not be encouraged.

As Galloway and Waldron have stated 'If the resource cannot be exploited fully because of the bottleneck's limited capacity then letting it stand idle when it has completed the work required, costs nothing'.

This means that profit is inversely proportional to the level of inventory in the system. This can be expressed thus:

$$\text{Profit} = f\left(\frac{1}{MRT}\right)$$

where *MRT* is the manufacturing response time.

Concept 3

Profitability is determined by how quickly goods can be produced to satisfy customer's orders. Producing for stock does not create profits. Improving the throughput of bottleneck operations will increase the rate at which customer demand can be met and will thus improve profitability.

Contribution in its traditional form (sales – variable costs) is not a good guide to profitability because capacity factors and the rate of production are ignored.

Using TA, product returns should be measured thus:

$$\text{Return per factory hour} = \frac{\text{Sales Price – Material Cost}}{\text{Time on key resource (ie the bottleneck)}}$$

Product costs are measured thus:

$$\text{Cost per factory hour} = \frac{\text{Total factory costs (TFC)}}{\text{Total time available on the key resource}}$$

The Returns and Cost per Factory hour are combined into the Throughput Accounting (TA) ratio thus:

$$\text{TA ratio} = \frac{\text{Return per factory hour (or Minute)}}{\text{Cost per Factory Hour (or Minute)}}$$

The TA ratio should be greater than 1. If it is less than 1 the product will lose money for the company and the company should consider withdrawing it from the market.

Using TA, value is not created until products are sold. Thus items made for stock produce no return and depress the TA ratio. This should encourage managers to use their limited bottleneck resource to produce products for which customer demand exists.

The TA ratio can also be considered in total terms and compares the total return from the throughput to the TFC i.e.

$$\text{Primary TA ratio} = \frac{\text{Return from total throughput (ie Sales – Material Costs)}}{\text{TFC (ie all costs other than materials)}}$$

20. Bottlenecks and overhead attribution

A bottleneck is an activity that places a restriction on a production line or factory. A typical bottleneck being the capacity of a key machine. On occasions there may be a 'wandering ' bottleneck. This means that the identified key bottleneck is not fully utilised because of a temporary limitation elsewhere, caused by poor production planning and control. If there is a wandering bottleneck the actual time on the key resource is used, not the actual time on the wandering bottleneck.

TA suggests that overheads be attributed to product costs according to their usage of bottleneck resources:

$$\text{Throughput Cost} = \frac{\text{Standard minutes of throughput}}{\text{(usage of bottleneck resource)}} \times \frac{\text{Budgeted TFC cost per minute}}{\text{of bottleneck resource}}$$

Based on this, an efficiency percentage can be calculated thus:

$$\text{Efficiency \%} = \frac{\text{Throughput cost}}{\text{Actual TFC}} \text{\%}$$

This will fall below 100% if:

a) actual output is less than budgeted e.g. if there was a wandering bottleneck in production or poor quality *or*

b) actual factory costs exceed budget.

Labour efficiency can be measured as:

$$\text{Labour Efficiency \%} = \frac{\text{Throughput cost}}{\text{Actual total labour cost}} \%$$

21. Examples using throughput accounting

The following examples illustrate various aspects of throughput accounting.

Example 1

A factory has a key resource (bottleneck) of Facility A which is available for 6260 minutes per period.

Budgeted Factory costs and data on two products, X and Y, are shown below.

Product	Selling price/unit	Material cost/unit	Time in Facility A
	£	£	Mins
X	7	4	1
Y	7	3.50	2

Budgeted Factory costs per week

	£
Direct Labour	5,000
Indirect Labour	2,500
Power	350
Depreciation	4,500
Space costs	1,600
Engineering	700
Administration	1,000

Calculate:

❑ Total Factory Costs (TFC)

❑ Cost per Factory Minute

❑ Return per Factory Minute for both products

❑ TA ratios for both products

Solution

Total Factory Costs = Total of all costs except materials

= 5,000 + 2,500 +350 +4,500 +1,600 + 700 + 1,000

= **£15,650**

$$\text{Cost per Factory Minute} = \frac{\text{TFC}}{\text{Minutes available in bottleneck}}$$

$$= \frac{15,650}{6,260}$$

= **£2.5**

$$\text{Return per bottleneck minute for Product X} = \frac{\text{Selling Price} - \text{Material cost}}{\text{Minutes in bottleneck}}$$

$$= \frac{£7-4}{1}$$

$$= £3$$

$$\text{Return per bottleneck minute for Product Y} = \frac{£7-3.5}{2}$$

$$= £1.75$$

$$\text{Throughput Accounting (TA) Ratio for Product X} = \frac{\text{Return per minute}}{\text{Cost per minute}}$$

$$= \frac{£3}{£2.5}$$

$$= 1.2$$

$$\text{TA ratio for Product Y} = \frac{£1.75}{£2.5}$$

$$= 0.7$$

The TA ratios show that if we only made Product Y we would make a loss as its TA ratio is less than 1; when we make Product X we make money.

Example 2

Based on the data in Example 1 above during a week actual production was 4,750 units of Product X and 650 units of Product Y. Actual factory costs were £15,650.

Calculate:

❏ Throughput cost for the week

❏ Efficiency percentage

and comment on the possible reasons(s) for the efficiency percentage calculated.

Solution

Workings

Standard minutes of throughput for the week = $(4,750 \times 1) + (650 \times 2)$

$$= 6,050$$

Throughput cost for week = $6,050 \times £2.5$ per min (from Example 1)

$$= £15,125$$

$$\text{Efficiency \%} = \frac{\text{Throughput cost}}{\text{Actual TFC}} \%$$

$$= \frac{£15,125}{£15,650}$$

$$= 96.6\%$$

The bottleneck resource of Facility A is available for 6,260 minutes per week but produced only 6,050 standard minutes. This could be due to:

a) the presence of a 'wandering' bottleneck causing Facility A to be under-utilised or

b) inefficiency in Facility A.

22. Throughput accounting – conclusion

It will be seen that the TA approach has certain similarities with the well established management accounting approach of maximising contribution per unit of scarce resource.

However there are important differences. In TA, return is defined as sales less material costs in contrast to contribution which is sales less all variable costs (material, labour and variable overheads). The assumption in TA is that all costs, except materials, are fixed in relation to throughput in the short run.

Professors Kaplan and Shank have criticised TA for its short-term emphasis but TA does appear to be useful in JIT environments. TA helps to direct attention to bottlenecks and forces management to concentrate on the key elements in making profits namely; inventory reduction and reducing the response time to customer demand.

Note: The outline of throughput accounting given above has been based mainly on the series of articles by Waldron and Galloway in Management Accounting (November 1988 to February 1989). For further details students are recommended to read all the articles themselves.

23. Backflush accounting

This is defined as

> 'A cost accounting system which focuses on the output of the organisation and then works backwards to allocate costs between cost of goods sold and inventory'.
> Terminology

In essence, backflush accounting is a simpler book-keeping system designed to reflect key aspects of JIT systems i.e. little or no Work-in-Progress and demand pull. There are several variants of backflush accounting (BFA); a popular one being the replacement of separate Raw Materials and WIP accounts with a single account; Raw and In Process (RIP) account. When items are sold the standard cost for the materials in the finished goods would be credited (or back-flushed) to the RIP account. All conversion costs (labour and materials) would be applied to the cost of finished goods production, none would be applied to WIP.

Example 3

In a period a company has the following transactions:

	£
Purchase of raw materials	85,000
Conversion costs	68,600
	units
Production	4,900
Sales	4,850

There were no opening stocks of raw materials, WIP or finished goods. The standard cost per unit is £31 (£17 materials + £14 conversion cost). There was no closing WIP at the end of the period.

Show the Journal entries for a back-flush accounting system using a Raw Materials and In Progress (RIP) account.

Solution

	£	£
RIP account	85,000	
Creditors		85,000
Purchase of raw materials on credit		
Finished Goods Stock	151,900	
RIP a/c		83,300
Conversion cost control a/c		68,600
Cost of goods produced (4,900 units)		
Cost of sales	150,350	
Finished Goods Stock		150,350
Cost of goods sold (4,850 units)		

At the end of the period there will be two separate stock balances:

	£
RIP account (85,000 – 83,300)	1,700
Finished Goods (50 @ £31)	1,550

Notes:

a) All the entries shown above are at standard cost.

b) For simplicity the figures have been chosen so that no variances arise.

24. Advantages of backflush accounting

a) It is simpler. Materials are not tracked through the production process as is done traditionally. There is no separate accounting for WIP.

b) There are far fewer accounting entries, supporting vouchers, work flow documents and so on.

c) The system may discourage managers in producing for stock. Working on material does not add value if it moves into stock.

25. Target costing

Target costing is widely used in Japan. It is a market driven approach where market research establishes the performance requirements and target selling price required to gain the desired market share for a proposed product. The required profit margin is subtracted from the target selling price to arrive at the *target cost* for the product. This is cost which, in the long run, must be met. Thus accounting practice is driven by the requirements of the market place.

Using the target cost approach, product designers, purchasing and manufacturing specialists work together to determine the product and process features which will enable the long-run target cost to be achieved.

Figure 22.3 outlines the whole process.

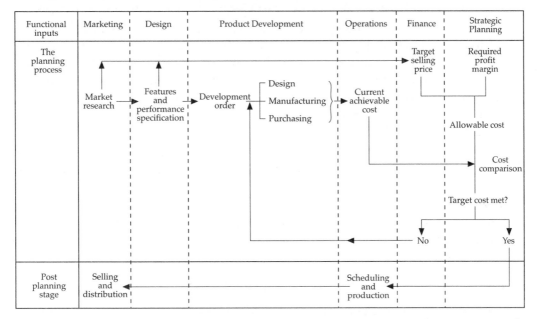

Figure 22.3 Target costing outline

The importance of the target costing approach is that it focuses attention on the product design stage i.e. prior to release to manufacturing.

Most costs are committed or locked in early in the life cycle of the product. Once the product is released to manufacturing it becomes much harder to achieve significant cost savings although some savings are possible, for example by the learning curve effect.

Target costing, which is a form of life cycle costing, is an example of *feed-forward* control.

26. AMT and performance measurement

Traditional accounting performance measures e.g. cost per unit, material and labour variances and so on, are being severely criticised as sending the wrong messages to management, focusing on only one aspect i.e. the financial, and encouraging short-termism.

More specifically the criticisms include:

a) Failure to monitor key aspects of performance. By focusing solely on cost and financial results there is a tendency to ignore vital aspects such as; lead times, quality, customer satisfaction, reliability and so on.

b) Incorrect signals from the misleading use of efficiency measures and absorption costing. Traditional efficiency measures encourage large batches. Absorption costing encourages high volumes in order to reduce under-absorption of overheads. Thus reported profits actually increase when stocks rise even though the stocks may never be sold.

c) Inappropriate use of standard costing. Variances relating to individual labour efficiencies, material price and overhead volume serve little or no purpose in JIT environments and may actually encourage managers to take inappropriate decisions.

d) Delayed reporting. Much traditional feedback information is produced far too late to be effective. A typical traditional control cycle is monthly whereas what managers really need is more frequent feedbacks, perhaps daily, much of it in non-financial form with an emphasis on yields, quality, throughput times and so on.

To overcome these deficiencies a much broader range of performance measures are used in AMT environments. Many are in non-financial forms such as hours, ratios, percentage.

This has a number of advantages including:- speed of production, greater understandability, comparability without the distorting effects of price level changes, and greater impact.

The key feature of the newer performance measures is that they are designed to foster improvement rather than just to monitor. Operational and manufacturing control is achieved largely by non-financial measures relating to *quality, delivery, flexibility* and *process times.*

27. Physical measures and non-financial indices in AMT

There is increasing recognition that a variety of measures are required to monitor and control complex environments. In Systems Theory this is known as the *Law of Requisite Variety*. This is not just an abstract, theoretical idea but is being applied throughout the world. As an example, J. G. Miller carried out an international survey on the measures being used to monitor and control production in Europe, USA and Japan. The key results are summarised in Figure 22.4.

	Europe	*United States*	*Japan*
1	Outgoing quality	Incoming quality	Manufacturing lead times
2	Unit manufacturing costs	Inventory accuracy	Direct labour productivity
3	Unit material cost	Direct labour productivity	WIP turnover
4	Overhead costs	Manufacturing leadtimes	Incoming quality
5	On-time deliveries	Vendor leadtime	Vendor leadtime
6	Incoming quality	Set-up times	Indirect productivity
7	Direct labour productivity	WIP turnover	Material yield

Figure 22.4 Performance measures listed in order of importance

Examples of non-financial measures

Manufacturing cycle efficiency

$$= \frac{\textbf{Processing time}}{\textbf{Processing time + waiting time + transport time + inspection time}}$$

Ideally the above ratio should be 1. Progress in moving towards this should be monitored. This is a useful summary ratio for a JIT factory or line as it relates value added time to non-value added time.

$$\text{Machine availability} = \frac{\text{Machine down time}}{\text{Total machine hours}}$$

Useful to monitor machine availability, usage and efficiency.

$$\text{In-coming quality} = \frac{\text{Rejected parts (numbers, weights as appropriate)}}{\text{Purchased parts}}$$

This could be used to monitor the quality of existing and new suppliers.

Customer satisfaction is the ultimate measure of product/service quality. This can be measured in a variety of ways including:-

$$\frac{\text{Customer rejects/returns}}{\text{Total sales}}$$

and/or **Percentage of sales which are repeat sales to existing customers**

$$\text{Delivery performance} = \frac{\text{Deliveries late}}{\text{Deliveries on Schedule}}$$

Applied to *sales* this provides a measure of the efficiency of production and production scheduling. Applied to *purchasing* it monitors supplier reliability.

In addition to ratios, many AMT performance measures are expressed in real terms; such as hours, minutes, quantities, weights and so on. The trends in these can be followed easily and have real and immediate meaning for everybody associated with production.

Examples include:

❏ Process times

❏ Set-up times

❏ Distance parts/materials travel

❏ No. of on time deliveries

❏ No. of lost machine time

❏ PPM defects

and so on.

28. Summary

a) AMT is altering the way manufacturing takes place and the way it is organised and it is claimed that traditional management accounting has become misleading when AMT is used.

b) AMT consists of Computer Aided Design and Manufacture (CAD/CAM), Flexible Manufacturing Systems (FMS) and employs advanced production management including; Materials Requirements Planning (MRP) and Just-in-Time (JIT) Systems.

c) JIT aims for zero inventory and perfect quality and operates by demand-pull. JIT consists of JIT purchasing and JIT production.

d) JIT results in; lower investment requirements, space savings, greater customer satisfaction and increased flexibility.

e) The Total Quality Control (TQC) seeks to incorporate perfect quality at every stage starting at Product Design and moving through Production Engineering, Manufacturing and Goods Inward. Higher quality means lower costs.

f) The main criticisms of traditional management accounting applied to AMT are in the areas of absorption costing methods, cost behaviour analysis, standard costing and the preoccupation with short-term financial measures.

g) It is claimed that Activity-Based Costing is more relevant for AMT environments because of the increase in support overheads.

h) Throughput accounting is a system which relates production and other costs to throughput and relates to the usage of key resources (bottlenecks) by products.

i) Throughput accounting has similarities with the well established management accounting approach of maximising contribution per unit of scarce resource but there are key differences.

j) Backflush accounting works backwards from the output to allocate costs between the cost of goods sold and inventory.

k) A popular variant of back-flush accounting replaces separate Raw Materials and WIP accounts with a single account; Raw and In Process account.

l) Target costing is a method of deriving product costs from a market price. The product cost becomes a target which must be met.

m) A much broader range of performance measures are required to control adequately AMT systems. These include many non-financial indicators covering such things as quality, lead times, customer satisfaction and so on.

Additional reading

Management Accounting – evolution not revolution; *Bromwich & Bhimani* – CIMA

Management Accounting : The challenge of technological innovation – CIMA

Management accounting in advanced manufacturing environments – CAM – I

Activity-based costing ; *Innes & Mitchell* – CIMA

Managerial accounting changes for the 1990's; *Lee* – Addison Wesley

Issues in Management Accounting; *Ed Ashton et al* –Prentice Hall

Self review questions

1. What is AMT? (1)
2. What criticisms have been made of traditional management accounting in AMT? (1)
3. What is CAD/CAM? (3 & 4)
4. What are Flexible Manufacturing Systems? (5)
5. What is Materials Requirement Planning? (6)
6. What are the key features of Just-in-Time Systems? (8)
7. What is demand-pull? (10)

8. What are the benefits of JIT? (12)
9. What is Total Quality Control? (13)
10. What is BS5750? (15)
11. What are the main problem areas of traditional management accounting applied to AMT environments? (16)
12. Is Activity-Based Costing appropriate for AMT? (17)
13. Explain Throughput Accounting. (18)
14. What are the three concepts underlying Throughput Accounting? (18)
15. What are the advantages claimed for Throughput Accounting? (21)
16. Define Backflush accounting. (22)
17. What is an RIP account? (22)
18. What is Target costing? (24)
19. What is the importance of Target costing? (24)
20. What criticisms have been made of traditional performance measures and AMT? (25)
21. Give examples of non-financial measures used in AMT. (26)

23 Management accounting and computers

1. Objectives

After studying this chapter you will:

❑ understand some of the ways computers can assist management accounting;

❑ know the distinction between data processing and decision support systems;

❑ be able to describe transaction processing;

❑ know the criteria necessary for the successful use of decision support systems;

❑ understand what databases are and how they are used;

❑ be able to describe spreadsheet packages;

❑ know what is meant by Executive Information Systems;

❑ understand the principles of prototyping.

2. Background computer knowledge

All students taking management accounting examinations will either be concurrently studying computers and data processing or will be exempt from the subject because of their previous studies.

Accordingly no attempt will be made in this book to explain what computers are or how they operate. The emphasis will be on highlighting some of the ways they can be used for management accounting purposes and the resulting advantages and disadvantages. It is assumed that students are familiar with the more common terms used in data processing; for example, hardware, software, files, VDU, disk storage, terminal, on-line, application packages, printers, program, and so on.

Students unfamiliar with these terms or who wish to study computers and data processing in more detail are advised to consult a comprehensive book on the subject, for example *Data Processing* by Oliver and Chapman, D P Publications Ltd. Any question in a management accounting examination which involve computers are thought unlikely to require much detailed technical computer knowledge, rather it is expected that they will test understanding of the application of computers to various facets of management accounting.

3. Why are computers useful for management accounting?

Computers can be valuable tools for management accounting purposes for the same reasons as they are for all other applications, namely, speed, accuracy, filing and retrieval abilities, calculating and decision making capabilities, input and output facilities.

These points are expanded below:

❒ *Speed*

Relative to manual methods, all aspects of computer operations (except the initial manual input of data via the keyboard) take place at very high speeds. Whether the computer is calculating an overhead variance, making an entry on a job cost file, printing an actual/budget statement or carrying out some other task the computer does this in a minute fraction of the time it would take manually.

❒ *Accuracy*

All computers incorporate inbuilt checking features which ensure for all practical purposes 100% accuracy in following a program. If a program has been thoroughly tested and produces the required output or performs the correct calculations, then this will be followed faithfully time after time after time.

On occasions computer systems do produce errors but investigations invariably show that these errors arise from such factors as errors contained in the data input or programming errors or an unforeseen combination of circumstances not allowed for in the program and not from computer malfunction.

❒ *Filing and retrieval abilities*

Computer files, nowadays invariably maintained on some type of disk storage, and the associated software file handling systems, permit the rapid updating, amendment, cross-referencing and retrieval of huge volumes of data that would be virtually impossible using any manual system. Computer backing storage systems are becoming physically smaller, cheaper and permit faster access. These developments mean that accountants and managers can have more and more information readily available for instantaneous display on their terminal.

❒ *Calculating and decision making capability*

Computer calculating speeds are measured in millionths of a second and are the heart of their power. In computer terms, the calculations required for management accounting purposes are very modest yet these same calculations done manually are tedious and time-consuming. Take for example the calculations required for apportioning various items of overhead expenditure over cost centres, which is a routine but necessary task. Each calculation is simple but the overall task, including cross and down totalling, can be lengthy when done manually, yet is ideally suited to the computer where it would be done virtually instantaneously.

Allied to the calculating power of the computer is its ability to test different values or conditions and depending on the results, take different actions. It is this ability which enables the computer to make decisions and makes it qualitatively different from other machines. The speed, calculating power and decision-making ability of the computer enables the accountant to extend the scope of his analysis beyond that which would be feasible manually, except for a special once-off exercise. As an example, manually-prepared variance statements typically highlight variances above a certain value (say, £1000) or those more than a given percentage (say ± 5%) away from standard. The computer could be programmed to do this and also to analyse the variance and its significance by statistical methods – including the calculation of the standard deviation – and, where a significant variance is detected, to retrieve the history of this variance for comparison and to ascertain trends.

In short, a more detailed analysis could routinely be undertaken, where required, without extra effort on the part of the accountant who would know that all truly significant variances would be highlighted so leaving more time for any personal investigations felt necessary. This, incidentally, is the key to effective use of computers for management accounting (or any other) purposes. They should be used, where feasible for all forms of routine ledger keeping, calculating, searching, periodic statement/report production and so on in order that there is more time for activities requiring the human touch; for example interpretation of results, special investigations, planning, interviewing and so on.

❏ *Input and output facilities*

Computers can read and search files, print results or display information on VDU's at very high speeds. With modern software, report layouts can be altered at will, results can be displayed using a range of diagrammatic and graphical displays, often in full colour, and displays can be interrogated and manipulated by the user without leaving his desk. Taken together the various facilities provide a far more flexible and speedy service than would be possible using manual means.

4. Management accounting and management information systems (MIS)

Management accounting is only one part of the overall MIS of the organisation. Because of the integration of tasks and the need to use files of data in common for various purposes rarely is a management accounting application dealt with separately by the computer system.

Management Accounting information is usually produced in conjunction with, or as a by-product of, some other computer application. As an example, information on material usage and wastage is likely to be produced in conjunction with the main inventory control and re-ordering system. The material usage and wastage information would then be used as the basis of computer produced variance analysis and product costing information. The inter-relationship of management accounting and the rest of the organisation's information is receiving increasing recognition in examinations. Accordingly it is not sufficient merely to examine the role of computers for management accounting purposes only but to widen the study to include the role of computers in management information system (MIS) generally.

5. Are computers essential for MIS?

The short answer to this question is, not essential but they can be very useful. The study of MIS is not about the use of computers, it is about the provision and use of information relevant to the user. Computers are one – albeit important – means of producing information and concentration on the means of producing information and concentration on the means of production rather than the needs of the user can lead to expensive mistakes. There is undoubtedly an important and growing role for computers in MIS but the technology must be used with discretion.

Computers are good at rapid and accurate calculations, manipulation, storage and retrieval but less good at unexpected or qualitative work or where genuine judgement is required. It has been suggested that computers can be used to best advantage for processing information which has the following characteristics:

a)   a number of interacting variables

b)   speed is an important factor

c)   there are reasonably accurate values

d)   accuracy of output is important

e)   operations are repetitive

f)   large amount of data exist

These characteristics can be related to the needs of the various management levels as shown in Figure 23.1.

The unshaded are of Figure 23.1 represents unstructured problems and decisions where human involvement is essential. The division between computer and human tasks is constantly changing. As software and hardware develops and organisations gain more skill in using computers, tasks previously requiring managerial expertise and judgement become worthwhile computer jobs.

An example is the now widespread use of 'credit scoring' in banks. An applicant for a loan fills in a detailed questionnaire and the answers are input into a computer. The program carries out a series of checks and tests and decides whether or not the loan should be granted. Previously all loan applications required a managerial decision which is now needed only for unusual requests, large loans or industrial applications.

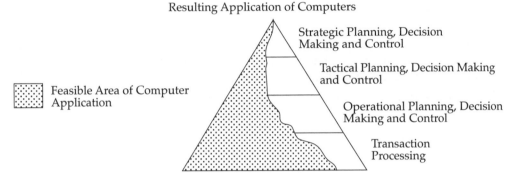

Information Characteristics	Presence in Management Information		
	Operational Level	Tactical Level	Strategic Level
Interacting Variables	Frequent ⟶		Always
Speed Important	Usually ⟶		Rarely
Data Accuracy	High ⟶		Low
Output Accuracy	Always ⟶		Rarely
Repetition	Usually ⟶		Rarely
Data Volume	High ⟶		Low

Resulting Application of Computers

Strategic Planning, Decision Making and Control

Tactical Planning, Decision Making and Control

Feasible Area of Computer Application

Operational Planning, Decision Making and Control

Transaction Processing

Figure 23.1 Feasibility of computer application by management level

6. Computers and information systems

Although the boundaries between them are blurred and there is substantial overlap it is possible to distinguish two major areas of application of computers in information systems. These are

❒ Data Processing (or Transaction Processing)

❒ Decision Support Systems (or End User Computing)

These categories are shown in Figure 23.2 and developed in following paragraphs.

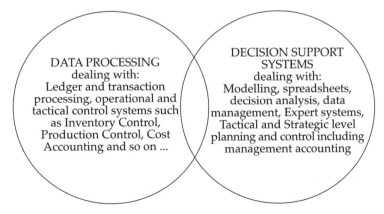

DATA PROCESSING
dealing with:
Ledger and transaction processing, operational and tactical control systems such as Inventory Control, Production Control, Cost Accounting and so on ...

DECISION SUPPORT SYSTEMS
dealing with:
Modelling, spreadsheets, decision analysis, data management, Expert systems, Tactical and Strategic level planning and control including management accounting

Figure 23.2 Computers and information systems

7. Data processing systems

These systems perform the essential role of collecting and processing the daily transactions of the organisation, hence the alternative term, transaction processing. Typically these include: all forms of ledger keeping, accounting receivable and payable, invoicing, credit control, rate demands, stock movements and so on.

These types of systems were the first to harness the power of the computer and originally were based on centralised mainframe computers. In many cases this still applies, especially for large volume repetitive jobs, but the availability of micro and mini computers has made distributed data processing feasible and popular. Distributed data processing has many variations but in essence means that data handling and processing are carried out at or near the point of use rather than in one centralised location.

Transaction processing is substantially more significant in terms of processing time, volume of input and output than say, information production for tactical and strategic planning. Transaction processing is essential to keep the operations of the organisation running smoothly and provides the base for all other internal information support. This is shown in Figure 23.3.

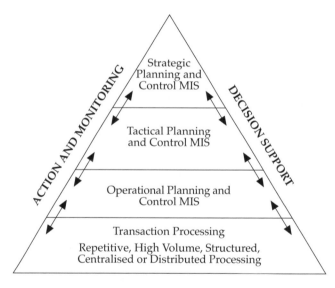

Figure 23.3 Transaction processing as a base for MIS

8. Characteristics of data processing systems

These systems are 'pre-specified'; that is their functions, decision rules and output formats cannot usually be changed by the end user. These systems are related directly to the structure of the organisation's data. Any change in the data they process or the functions they perform usually requires the intervention of information system specialists such as system analysts and programmers.

Some data processing systems have to cope with huge volumes and a wide range of data types and output formats. As an example consider the Electricity and Gas Board

Billing and Payment Handling systems, the Clearing Bank's Current Accounting Systems, the Motor Policy handling systems of a large insurer and so on. The systems and programming work required for these systems represents a major investment. For example, the development of a large scale billing system for a public utility represents something like 100 man years of effort.

Of course, data processing also takes place on a more modest scale and the ready availability of application packages – ie software to deal with a particular administrative or commercial task – means that small scale users have professionally written and tested programs to deal with their routine data processing. The better packages provide for some flexibility and the user can specify – within limits – variations in output formats, data types and decision rules.

9. Scope of transaction processing

Transaction processing is necessary to ensure that the day to day activities of the organisation are processed, recorded and acted upon. Files are maintained which provide both the current data for transactions; for example the amount invoiced and cash received during the month for statement preparation, and which also serve as a basis for operational and tactical control and for answering enquiries.

Transaction processing can be sub-divided into:

a) Current activity processing

b) Report processing

c) Inquiry processing

Figure 23.4 shows in outline these sub-divisions with examples of the various processing types drawn from inventory and materials processing.

A routine data processing system is not in itself an MIS because it does not support all the management functions of the organisation nor does it have the decision focus which is the primary objective of MIS. Nevertheless it should be apparent that routine transaction processing is essential for day-to-day activities and provides the indispensable foundation upon which the organisation's MIS is built. For example, there would be little point in developing a sophisticated flexible budgeting system complete with detailed variance analysis if the routine, but essential, cost analysis and recording system was not working perfectly.

10. Decision support systems (DSS)

DSS are alternatively termed end-user computing systems. Their objective is to support managers in their work, especially decision making.

DSS tend to be used in planning, modelling, analysing alternatives and decision making. They generally operate through terminals operated by the user who interacts with the computer system. Using a variety of tools and procedures the manager (ie the user) can develop his own systems to help perform his functions more effectively. It is this active involvement and the focus on decision making which distinguishes a DSS from a data processing system. The emphasis is on support for decision making not on automated decision making which is a feature of transaction processing.

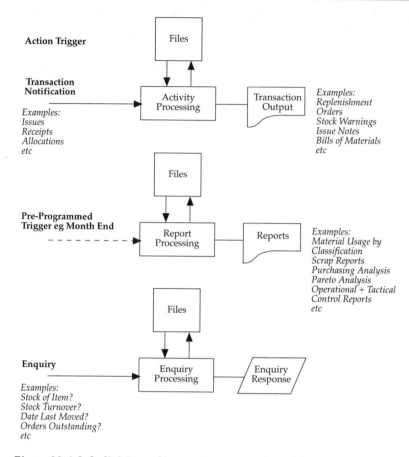

Figure 23.4 Sub-divisions of transaction processing with inventory control examples)

DSS are especially useful for semi-structured problems where problem solving is improved by interaction between the manager and the computer system. The emphasis is on small, simple models which can easily be understood and used by the manager rather than complex integrated systems which need information specialists to operate them.

The main characteristics of DSS are:

a) The computer provides support but does not replace the manager's judgement nor does it provide pre-determined solutions.

b) DSS are best suited to semi-structured problems where parts of the analysis can be computerised but the decision maker's judgement and insight is needed to control the process.

c) Where effective problem solving is enhanced by interaction between the computer and the manager.

11. Where to apply DSS

DSS are man/machine systems and are suitable for semi-structured problems. The problem must be important to the manager and the decision required must be a key one. In addition if an interactive computer-based system is to be used then some of the following criteria should be met.

a) *There should be a large data base*

A data base is an organised collection of structured data with a minimum duplication of data items. The data base is common to all users of the system but is independent of the programs which use the data. If the data base is too large for manual searching then a computer-supported approach may be worthwhile.

b) *Large amount of computation or data manipulation*

Where analysis of the problem requires considerable computation or data manipulation, computing power is likely to be beneficial.

c) *Complex inter-relationships*

Where there is a large data base or where there are numerous factors involved it is frequently difficult to assess all the possible inter-relationships without computer assistance.

d) *Analysis by stages*

Where the problem is an iterative one with stages for re-examination and re-assessment it becomes more difficult to deal with manually. The computer-based model can answer the question, 'What if?' quickly and effectively.

e) *Judgement required*

In complex situations judgement is required both to determine the problem and the solution. Unaided, no computer system can provide this.

f) *Communication*

Where several people are involved in the problem solving process, each contributing some special expertise, then the co-ordinating power of the computer can be of assistance.

It follows from the above criteria that DSS are inappropriate for unstructured problems and unnecessary for completely structured problems because these can be dealt with wholly by the computer and man/machine interaction is unnecessary.

In outline DSS require a database, the software to handle the database and decision support programs including, for example, modelling, spread sheet and analysis packages, expert systems and so on. The above elements of DSS are dealt with in the paragraphs which follow.

In a study of DSS used in organisations, Alter found they fell into 7 main groups. These are shown in Figure 23.5.

DSS Classification	Type of Operation	Examples and Comments
File Drawer Systems	Access of data items	Data oriented systems. Basically on-line computerised versions of manual filing systems e.g. account balance, stock position queries, monitoring loads and capacities.
Data Analysis Systems	Ad hoc analysis of data files	Data oriented systems. Used to analyse files containing current or historical data e.g. analysing files for overdue account, bad payers.
Analysis Information Systems	Ad hoc analysis using databases and small models	Data oriented systems. Extension of data analysis systems to include internal and external databases with limited modelling e.g. a marketing support DSS could include internal sales data, customer data and market research data.
Accounting Models	Estimating future results using accounting rules	Model oriented systems. Typically these generate estimates of cash, income, costs etc based on accounting relationships and rules e.g. cash and expenditure budgeting, balance sheet projections.
Representational Models	Estimating results, consequences where risk exists	Model oriented systems. These generate results using probability based simulation models e.g. risk analysis for new project, traffic simulation with variable flows
Optimisation Models	Calculating optimal results where constraints exist	Model oriented systems. These are used for structured decisions where constraints exist and there is a clear objective e.g. machine loading, material usage, production planning.
Suggestion Models	Producing suggested results where decision rules are known	Model oriented systems. These compute suggested decisions for semi-structured problems. Expert systems are one of the tools e.g. credit authorisations, insurance rate calculations.

Figure 23.5 Alter's DSS classifications

12. The database concept

A database was defined earlier as a collection of structured data, with minimum duplication, which is common to all users of the system but is independent of programs which use the data. The database can grow and change and is built up stage by stage within the organisation. It will actually comprise several databases, each providing the anticipated information for several logically related management information systems where the data can be accessed, retrieved and modified with reasonable flexibility.

The data structures and relationships require highly technical software – known as the Data Base Management System (DBMS) – to deal with them. Fortunately the user is shielded, to a large extent, from the complexity and is able to access the data base with the minimum of technical knowledge.

Figure 23.6 shows the relationship between the database, transaction processing, decision support systems and the DBMS.

The database concept allows data to be captured once at source and to be available for numerous applications. Redundancy and duplication are reduced and potentially there is more flexibility and an increase in data reliability, accuracy and consistency. It also means that the same data will support both transaction processing and serve as a reservoir for management use in decision support systems.

Where the only form of data storage possible was unrelated, unique files for each application, this engendered a narrow, parochial view of information. The reality is that management need information which crosses functions, applications and levels and the flexibility of databases and the linkages possible make the concept a powerful one and essential for decision support systems.

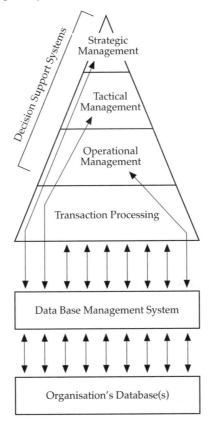

Figure 23.6 Databases and decision support systems

13. Data base management systems (DBMS)

The DBMS is a complex software system which constructs, expands and maintains the database. It also provides the link or interface, between the user and the data in the base. Figure 23.7 provides a summary of the three main elements of DBMS – definition, processing and enquiry.

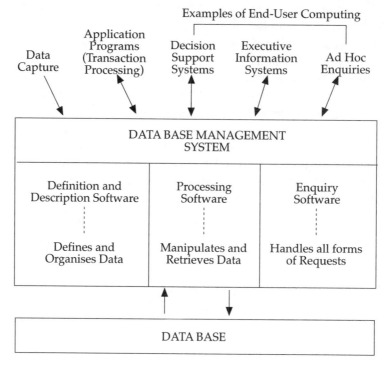

Figure 23.7 Database Management Systems

The three primary categories of DBMS are:

❐ *Relational*

Where each type of record is represented as existing in a table of file of like records. For example, there could be customer records, product records, order records and so on. These systems are relatively simple and are suitable for manipulation by non-data processing personnel (as in a DSS) but their technical efficiency may be poor.

❐ *Hierarchial*

This is a system having in-built linkages whereby there are 'owner' records which 'own' numerous 'member' records.

❐ *Network*

These are further developments of linkage systems with many more record types and linkages.

Both the linkage systems require the user to know what linkages have been established in order to know on what basis data can be retrieved. The linkage systems are technically more efficient but do require greater data processing knowledge so their use tends to be restricted to information specialists.

14. Decision support packages

The existence of the database and a DBMS to handle it means that the manager can interrogate and access a mass of data at will. He then needs to be able to use this data in exploring alternatives and making decisions. To do this there is an enormous range of packages available. These include packages for:

a) Modelling and simulation

b) Spreadsheets

c) Statistical analyses of all types

d) Forecasting

e) Non-Linear and Linear Programming

f) Regression analysis

g) Financial modelling

h) Sensitivity and risk analysis

i) Expert systems

and so on.

It is clearly beyond the scope of this book to describe all these types of packages in detail but three of the more relevant ones are briefly described below, namely, spreadsheets, expert systems and sensitivity analysis.

15. Spreadsheet packages

A general outline of modelling and simulation has already been given together with an explanation of how modelling can help the manager and accountant in planning and decision making. One useful practical way of modelling is to use a spreadsheet package to show the results of different actions.

The basis of a spreadsheet package is an electronic worksheet whereby data can be stored and manipulated at will. The spreadsheet is a matrix of locations which can contain values, formulae and relationships. The key feature is that all elements in the matrix are changed automatically when one or more of the key assumptions are changed.

For example a series of interlocking departmental operating statements culminating in an overall projected profit and loss account may have been prepared on the spreadsheet. If one or more of the variables (rates of pay, output levels, sales, absorption rates and so on) needs to be altered then the new value needs only to be entered once and a the whole of the matrix is recalculated virtually instantaneously with all relationships, sub-totals and totals automatically catered for. This facility allows a series of outcomes to be explored, providing answers to the 'what if' questions which are so essential to the manager. For example, what would be the effect on profit of a change in inflation rate/cost per unit/contribution margin/scrap rates or whatever factor need to be explored. Used in this way spreadsheet packages perform a modelling function and this facility is greatly expanded in the latest spreadsheet packages.

16. Spreadsheets and budgeting

One of the important tasks of tactical level management is concerned with budgeting. Spreadsheets can be of great assistance in exploring the effect on a budget of different values and assumptions so that the manager can make more effective decisions. As one example, consider the Accountant dealing with cash budgeting.

Cash budgets are examples of routine but highly essential reports which need frequent updating to reflect current and forecast conditions, changes in credit behaviour, anticipated gains or expenditures and so on. Each period (weekly, monthly, quarterly, as required) changes and up-to-date information are input and, in combination with the brought forward file data, the cash budget will be automatically projected forward by the spreadsheet program with highlighted surpluses and/or deficiencies, balances carried forward from one period to another and all the usual contents of a cash budget. The budget could be shown in both an abbreviated and detailed format and could also be displayed in a graphical form.

Figure 23.8 shows the possible output of a Summary Cash Budget and a corresponding graphical display, the facility for which is increasingly being included in modern spreadsheet packages.

17. Expert systems

At the present time, Expert Systems represent the most advanced stage of decision support systems. An Expert System is a computer system which embodies some of the experience and specialised knowledge of an expert or experts. An Expert System enables a non-expert to achieve comparable performance to an expert in the field. It uses a reasoning process which bears some resemblance to human thought.

The unique feature of an Expert System is the knowledge base, which is a network of rules which represents the human expertise. These rules and linkages are derived from discussions with experts and analysis of their decision making behaviour. Attempts are made to include the effects of uncertainty and judgement and clearly such an approach is likely to be costly and time consuming. Expert Systems are much more sophisticated and powerful than simply automating a typical structured decision but conversely, they are very much more difficult to implement.

Expert Systems have been developed in a number of fields of which the following are examples:

Medical diagnosis; Personal tax planning; Product pricing; Selection of selling methods; Statutory Sick Pay Entitlement and Claims; Credit approval in banking; Air crew scheduling and so on.

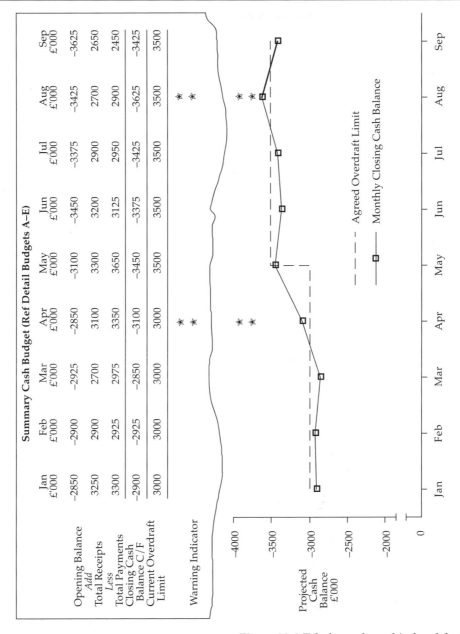

Summary Cash Budget (Ref Detail Budgets A–E)

	Jan £'000	Feb £'000	Mar £'000	Apr £'000	May £'000	Jun £'000	Jul £'000	Aug £'000	Sep £'000
Opening Balance	-2850	-2900	-2925	-2850	-3100	-3450	-3375	-3425	-3625
Add Total Receipts	3250	2900	2700	3100	3300	3200	2900	2700	2650
Less Total Payments	3300	2925	2975	3350	3650	3125	2950	2900	2450
Closing Cash Balance C/F	-2900	-2925	-2850	-3100	-3450	-3375	-3425	-3625	-3425
Current Overdraft Limit	3000	3000	3000	3000	3500	3500	3500	3500	3500
Warning Indicator				**				**	

Projected Cash Balance £'000

- - - Agreed Overdraft Limit
——— Monthly Closing Cash Balance

Figure 23.8 Tabular and graphical cash budget

18. Sensitivity analysis

Dealing with uncertainty is an inescapable part of planning and decision-making. Accordingly the accountant must show the effects of uncertainty in the information provided to decision makers insofar as this is possible. It can be positively misleading to produce information for a decision which shows only a single value of profit or contribution or NPV when the factors which are involved in the decision – costs, sales expected, purchase prices and so on – cannot be forecast with certainty. Ideally the decision maker would like to know the expected result and how sensitive or robust is the solution. A robust solution is one which will still remain acceptable in spite of substantial variations in the factors involved whilst a sensitive solution is one that is vulnerable to minor variations in the factors which, in practice, is all too likely.

Sensitivity analysis is a practical way of assessing the degree of sensitivity of the solution for many types of decision for which the accountant provides information. The general procedure is simple; all the factors except one are held constant and the value of the one being studied is altered, increment by increment, in both an upwards and downwards direction. At each alteration the effect on the result (ie the profit, contribution, NPV or whatever) is noted. This process is then repeated for each of the factors in the problem and the sensitivity of the solution to changes in the values of each of the factors is thus identified. Although in principle a simple idea it can mean an enormous number of calculations hence the importance of computer assistance.

Many computer packages incorporate sensitivity analysis facilities and where these are not automatically provided a similar effect can be obtained by the multiple insertion of the input data suitably adjusted on each occasion. Typical of the areas where computer based sensitivity analysis will be found to be of value for management accounting purposes are:

> LP models for
>
> Capital rationing
>
> Product planning
>
> Ingredient mix problems
>
> Investment appraisals
>
> Financial modelling
>
> Budget planning
>
> Pricing models
>
> Decision analysis

and so on.

19. Executive Information Systems (EIS)

These are forms of data retrieval systems that provide selected and summarised information for senior executives. They assist top management by providing information on critical areas of the organisation's activities drawn from both internal and external databases. EIS are becoming, more widely available and organisations such as British Airways, ICI, BP, Glaxo and others are enthusiastic users.

The key features of an EIS are:

❏ *Easy to use.* The system must be fast and extremely simple to use as it will be used by busy executives. The use of touch screens, mice and icons, pop-up menus etc. is normal.

❏ *Access to data.* There must be unhindered rapid access to data permitting vertical and horizontal exploration. This is known as drilling down the data.

❏ *Data analysis*. Having obtained the data the EIS should provide facilities for such things as; ratio and trend calculations, data integration, forecasts and so on.

❏ *Quality presentation*. The system should provide interest-ing and understandable formats using colour, graphs, dia-grams and so on.

A typical way that an EIS works is by exception reporting and *drilling down* to investi-gate the causes. For example a director may be alerted that a particular department is well over budget. (An exception to budget or target is known as a *'hot-spot'* and would be highlighted by the EIS). The manager would then drill down the data by pursuing lower and lower levels of detail. He might first seek a breakdown of the departmental budget and actual expenditure into broad categories such as; Material, Labour and Overheads. If he discovered that the major overspend was in over-heads he would access the detailed expenditure on the various items of overhead cost such as; Salaries, Depreciation, Telephones, Insurance and so on. In this way the executive can explore at will and is thus provided with better assistance in planning and con-trolling.

EIS are used personally by managers and it is thus essential that the system reflects their requirements. The managers must be involved in the development and imple-mentation of the system. By their nature top level information and data requirements are difficult to specify precisely in advance and are subject to change. As a consequence a technique known as *prototyping* is widely used in development of EIS and similar systems.

20. Prototyping

Prototyping is based on the simple idea that people can express more easily what they like or do not like about an actual working system rather than specify what they would like to see in an imagined, future system.

Prototyping consists of four steps;

1. Identify the user's basic requirements.
2. Develop an initial prototype. This is a live, working system to meet the users basic requirements. It is usually programmed using a very high level development language. The emphasis is on speed of development rather than completeness and efficiency.
3. The user works with the prototype. Using real data and problems the user works with the prototype. He thus gains hands-on experience, finds problems, sharpens his requirements, tests assumptions and so gains deeper insight. Normally the user finds problems and omissions in the initial prototype and feeds back his re-actions to the systems designer for revisions. It is thus the user who controls the process and defines the system.
4. Revise the prototype. Based on the feedback from step 3 the prototype is revised and enhanced. Steps 3 and 4 are repeated until an acceptable working system is developed.

Prototype is useful for most interactive applications especially where the user is more concerned with the format and layout of VDU screens for data entry, output and error messages than the underlying processes of the system.

21. Summary

a) Computers are useful for management accounting because of their speed, accuracy, filing and retrieval abilities, calculating and decision making capabilities.

b) Management accounting is but one facet of the general information system of the organisation.

c) Data processing, or transaction processing, deals with the routine ledger and transaction processing of the organisation and provides the base for the whole information system.

d) Decision support systems support managers in their work especially decision making.

e) DSS include; planning, modelling, simulation decision making.

f) DSS are best for semi-structured problems where the solution is improved by interaction between the user and the computer system.

g) DSS are best suited where there is a large data base, complex inter-relationships, step-by-step analysis and where judgement is necessary.

h) Spreadsheets are valuable packages for accountants and can be used for numerous tasks including; cash budgeting, variance analysis, modelling.

i) Expert systems incorporate a knowledge base which enables a non-expert to achieve comparable performance to an expert.

j) Sensitivity analysis is a practical way of assessing the effects of uncertainty and, because of the repeated calculations, requires the assistance of a computer.

k) Executive Information Systems permit rapid information retrieval and work by exception reporting and 'drilling down' the data.

22. Points to note

a) The declining real cost of computer systems makes their use cost-effective even for small, one-off jobs.

b) Increasingly the decision regarding which computer system to purchase depends on the software support for the machine, especially, the availability of application packages.

c) Problems can occur when using computers and the greatest care must be taken to obtain feedback from the users of the system, in order to overcome any difficulties which arise. Problems may include; use of generalised and inappropriate packages which do not deal adequately with specialised problems, over-abundant printouts which swamp managers with paper, delays in producing required results, antagonism from managers and staff used to manual systems, fear of the unknown, inadequate training, unexplained jargon and so on.

Additional reading

Business Data Systems; *Clifton* – Prentice Hall

Management Information Systems; *David & Olsen* – McGraw Hill

Decision Support Systems; *Finlay* – NCC Blackwell

Data Processing & Information Technology; *Oliver & Chapman* – DP Publications

Information Systems : Management in practice; *Sprague & McNurlin* – Butterworth

Self review questions

1. Why are computers useful for management accounting? (3)
2. What is the relationship of management accounting to the information system of the firm? (4)
3. What characteristics of processing make it advisable to use computers? (5)
4. How do these characteristics of processing make it advisable to use computers? (5)
5. What is a data processing system? (7)
6. What is the scope of data processing? (9)
7. What is a decision support system? (10)
8. Where can a DSS be best applied? (11)
9. What is a Data Base? a Data Base Management System? (12)
10. Give examples of packages used in DSS. (14)
11. What is a spreadsheet package? (16)
12. Describe an Expert System. (17)
13. What is a sensitivity analysis and why is the use of a computer necessary? (18)
14. What are Executive Information Systems? (19)

Assessment and revision section 5

Examination questions with answers

A1. Energy costs may include the following items in a company which manufactures and sells products:

- ❏ maintaining a statutory temperature range in the workplace
- ❏ the operation of a specially humidified materials store
- ❏ power costs per unit of output
- ❏ power costs in the movement of raw materials and work in progress
- ❏ losses from steam pipelines and steam valves
- ❏ heat losses through windows.

Explain how management may be assisted in the implementation of an energy cost reduction strategy through the application of a) zero-base budgeting and b) total quality management. Your answers to a) and b) should each refer to any *three* of the energy cost examples given in the question.

ACCA, Information for Control and Decision Making.

A2. A large local government authority in the United Kingdom has decided to seek competitive tenders for all its internal computing requirements. The present managers of the authority's Computer Services Department have decided that they wish to tender for the work, and if successful, form a company to acquire the existing assets and carry out work for the local government authority and other customers.

They think that the work that they currently do for their own local government authority is technically far in advance of that done by neighbouring local government authorities. They consider that additional volume would allow them to reward more highly the good staff who are currently employed at low public sector rates of pay.

A group of local businessmen and potential investors has discussed this proposal with the Director of Computing, who would lead the proposed management buy-out (MBO). They are quite impressed with the technical competence of the staff, and the prospects for gaining additional work.

However, they have a number of reservations, as the staff have no experience outside information technology, and no commercial experience. Their experience of budgeting is also limited. The local government authority does not subdivide its budget for the Computer Services Department. It manages this department as a cost centre, and receives reports of expenditure against budget at quarterly intervals.

The investors have asked consultants to advise on certain aspects of the proposals.

Required:

Write a report to the investors. This report should

a) recommend the form and level of detail of budgetary control required in the new company,

b) recommend the structure and formal controls required at Board level in the new company.

CIMA, Management Accounting Control Systems.

A3. You have just been appointed financial controller of an old-established family-controlled business which operates a large number of shops. These shops are located in most towns in the country. It also owns a number of factories which manufacture a variety of products, most of which are sold through the shops.

The new managing director, appointed at the same time as you, is very critical of the limited management information available for the various operations, which consists of

❏ quarterly internal financial accounts

❏ daily and weekly sales

❏ statements comparing ratios of gross profit and costs to sales.

He wishes to introduce better ways of measuring performance, as a preliminary step towards assessing the quality of the management of the various operations, and towards starting some rationalisation. His initial view is that both management and the operations are very variable in quality.

His first thoughts on defining this requirement were that it could be useful to produce statements of the return on investment (ROI) for each operation.

Required:

Write a report to the managing director which

a) explains the problems in measuring the 'investment' in the ROI and the practical problems this causes in developing and interpreting the ROI measure for the purposes envisaged.

b) explains the process of determining which performance measurements are appropriate in a particular business.

CIMA, Management Accounting Control Systems.

A4. A large organisation, with a well-developed cost centre system, is considering the introduction of profit centres and/or investment centres throughout the organisation, where appropriate. As management accountant, you will be providing technical advice and assistance for the proposed scheme.

You are required:
a) to describe the main characteristics and objectives of profit and investment centres;
b) to explain conditions necessary for the successful introduction of such centres;
c) to describe the main behavioural and control consequences which may arise if such centres are introduced;
d) to compare two performance appraisal measures that might be used if investment centres are introduced.

CIMA, Management Accounting Techniques.

A5. A non-executive director has queried progress on a new product investment. The product was estimated to have a four-year product life before being overtaken by competitive products. The results for the first two year have shown considerable losses. The original project proposal as approved by the board showed an internal rate of return (IRR) of 22% and a net present value (NPV) of £509,000 at a cost of capital of 15% These calculations were based on the following cash flows, revenues and costs:

Year	0	1	2	3	4	5
	£000	£000	£000	£000	£000	£000
Tooling and plant	(1,480)					
Design	(144)					
Research and Development	(595)					
Market research	(161)					
Working capital		(286)	(201)	(413)	107	793
Sales		1,145	1,949	3,600	3,173	
Variable manufacturing costs		(572)	(876)	(1,760)	(1,493)	
Variable selling costs		(115)	(156)	(220)	(30)	

The operating statements, and figures from the budget and strategic plan, show the following project results and forecast results:

Year	1	2	3	3
Status	Actual	Actual	Budget	Plan
	£000	£000	£000	£000
Sales	1,025	2,070	3,400	3,000
Manufacturing variable cost	570	930	1,360	1,380
Manufacturing fixed cost	150	248	340	390
Depreciation	370	370	370	370
Variable selling cost	130	180	170	60
Fixed selling cost	195	270	285	90
Administration	109	229	340	300
Profit/(loss)	(499)	(157)	535	410
Return on investment (ROI)	–	–	43.2%	41.6%

The following additional information is available:

☐ Capital expenditure incurred was as the original proposal.

☐ The Group ignores taxation for project proposals and operating statements.

☐ Working capital consists entirely of debtors; creditors offsetting stock. For the first two years debtors have been at the projected 90 days.

☐ Fixed cost *apportionments* (manufacturing, sales, and administration) are on the same conventional bases in the budget and plan as in the actual results.

☐ ROI is calculated on the basis of an average of opening and closing capital employed each year.

You are required:

a) to analyse the data available and to prepare a report to the board comparing the original project with the figures now available, and commenting on the extent to which performance on the project is in line with original expectations;

b) to explain how the high projected ROI figures for the next two years arise, and whether they reflect over-optimistic projections for the next two years;

c) to explain as clearly as possible why the original IRR figures cannot be compared with the ROI figures;

d) to write a report for the board explaining the case for post auditing all major projects and proposing a procedure for so doing.

CIMA, Management Accounting – Control and Audit.

A6. Excel Ltd make and sell two products, VG4U and VG2. Both products are manufactured through two consecutive processes – making and packing. Raw material is input at the commencement of the making process. The following estimated information is available for the period ending 31 March 1995:

(i)

	Making	Packing
	£000	£000
Conversion costs:		
Variable	350	280
Fixed	210	140

40% of fixed costs are product specific, the remainder are company fixed costs. Fixed costs will remain unchanged throughout a wide activity range.

(ii) *Product information:*

	VG4U	VG2
Production time per unit:		
Making (minutes)	5.25	5.25
Packing (minutes)	6	4
Production/sales (units)	5,000	3,000
Selling price per unit (£)	150	180
Direct material cost per unit (3)	30	30

(iii) Conversion costs are absorbed by products using estimated time based rates.

Required:

a) Using the above information,

    (i) calculate unit costs for each product, analysed as relevant.

    (ii) comment on a management suggestion that the production and sale of one of the products should not proceed in the period ending 31 March 1995.

b) Additional information is gathered for the period ending 31 March 1995 as follows:

    (i) The making process consists of two consecutive activities, moulding and trimming. The moulding variable conversion costs are incurred in proportion to the temperature required in the moulds. The variable trimming conversion costs are incurred in proportion to the consistency of the material when it emerges from the moulds. The variable packing process conversion costs are incurred in proportion to the time required for each product. Packing materials (which are part of the variable packing cost) requirement depends on the complexity of packing specified for each product.

    (ii) The proportions of product specific conversion costs (variable and fixed) are analysed as follows:

        Making process: moulding (60%); trimming (40%)

        Packing process: conversion (70%); packing material (30%)

    (iii) An investigation into the effect of the cost drivers on costs has indicated that the proportions in which the total product specific conversion costs are attributable to VG4U and VG2 are as follows:

	VG4U	VG2
Temperature (moulding)	2	1
Material consistency (trimming)	2	5
Time (packing)	3	2
Packing complexity	1	3

    (iv) Company fixed costs are apportioned to products at an overall average rate per product unit based on the estimated figures.

Required:

Calculate amended unit costs for each product where activity-based costing is used and company fixed costs are apportioned as detailed above.

c) Comment on the relevance of the amended unit costs in evaluating the management suggestion that one of the products be discontinued in the period ending 31 March 1995.

d) Management wish to achieve an overall net profit margin of 15% on sales in the period ending 31 March 1995 in order to meet return on capital targets.

    Required:

    Explain how target costing may be used in achieving the required return and suggest specific areas of investigation.

ACCA, Information for Control and Decision Making.

A7. KDS Ltd is an engineering company which is organised for management purposes in the form of several autonomous divisions. The performance of each division is currently measured by calculation of its return on capital employed (ROCE). KDS Ltd's existing accounting policy is to calculate ROCE by dividing the net assets of each division at the end of the year into the operating profit generated by the division during the year. Cash is excluded from net assets since all divisions share a bank account controlled by KDS Ltd's head office. Depreciation is on a straight-line basis.

The divisional management teams are paid a performance-related bonus conditional upon achievement of a 15% ROCE target. On 20 December 1995 the divisional managers were provided with performance forecasts for 1995 which included the following:

Forecast	Net assets at 31 December 1995	1995 operating profit	ROCE
	£	£	
Division K	4,400,000	649,000	14.75%
Division D	480,000	120,000	25.00%

Subsequently, the Manager of Division K invited members of her management team to offer advice. The responses she received included the following:

from the Divisional Administrator:

'We can achieve our 1995 target by deferring payment of a £90,000 trade debt payable on 20 December until 1 January. I should add that we will thereby immediately incur a £2,000 late payment penalty.'

from the Works Manager:

'We should replace a number of our oldest machine tools (which have nil book value) at a cost of £320,000. The new equipment will have a life of eight years and generate cost savings of £76,000 per year. The new equipment can be on site and operational by 31 December 1995.'

from the Financial Controller:

'The existing method of performance appraisal is unfair. We should ask head office to adopt residual income (RI) as the key performance indicator, using the company's average 12% cost of money for a finance charge.'

Required:

a) Compare and appraise the proposals of the Divisional Administrator and the Works Manager, having regard to the achievement of the ROCE performance target in 1995 and to any longer term factors you think relevant.

b) Explain the extent to which you agree or disagree with the Financial Controller's proposal.

c) Explain how depreciation policy might be modified in order to improve performance measurement. Explain the value and use of non-financial performance measures.

CIMA, Management Accounting Applications.

A8. a) The transfer pricing method used for the transfer of an intermediate product between two divisions in a group has been agreed at standard cost plus 30% profit markup. The transfer price may be altered after taking into consideration the planning and operational variance analysis at the transferor division.

Discuss the acceptability of this transfer pricing method to the transferor and transferee divisions.

b) Division A has an external market for product X which fully utilises its production capacity.

Explain the circumstances in which division A should be willing to transfer product X to division B of the same group at a price which is less than the existing market price.

c) An intermediate product which is converted in divisions L, M and N of a group is available in limited quantities from other divisions within the group and from an external source. The total available quantity of the intermediate product is insufficient to satisfy demand.

Explain the procedure which should lead to a transfer pricing and deployment policy resulting in group profit maximisation.

ACCA, Information for Control and Decision Making.

A9. *Statement 1:* The availability of computers and sophisticated financial software has made budgeting a routine, almost automatic, process.

Statement 2: Effective budgeting is much more than just number-crunching.

You are required:

a) to describe the different kinds of computer software which are available to assist budgeting as indicated in *Statement 1;*

b) to explain what is meant by 'effective budgeting' in *Statement 2* and what features contribute to effective budgeting;

c) to reconcile the apparent contradiction between Statements 1 and 2.

CIMA, Management Accounting Techniques.

Examination questions without answers

B1. Research on Performance Measurement in Service Businesses, report in Management Accounting, found that

'......performance measurement often focuses on easily quantifiable aspects such as cost and productivity whilst neglecting other dimensions which are important to competitive success.'

You are required:

a) to explain what 'other dimensions' you think are important measures of performance;

b) to describe what changes would be required to traditional information systems to deal with these 'other dimensions'.

CIMA, Management Accounting Techniques.

B2. The acceptability of an investment proposal at a division within a vertically integrated group may be affected by the financial performance measure used and the accounting procedures in operation within the group.

Expand on this statement incorporating the following terms into your discussion.

(i) Return on investment

(ii) Residual income

(iii) Transfer pricing

(iv) Annuity depreciation

(v) Net present value.

ACCA, Information for Control and Decision Making.

B3. a) Explain the features of a Decision Support System, and give *two* examples of such systems.

    b) Explain the methods by which the working of a Decision Support System could be checked, and set out how these would affect the two examples you have given in a).

CIMA, Management Accounting, Control & Audit.

B4. A company extracts exhaust gases from process ovens as part of the manufacturing process. The exhaust gas extraction is implemented by machinery which cost £100,000 when bought five years ago. The machinery is being depreciated at 10% per annum. The extraction of the exhaust gases enhances production output by 10,000 units per annum. This production can be sold at £8 per unit and has variable costs of £3 per unit. The exhaust gas extraction machinery has directly attributable fixed operating costs of £16,000 per annum.

The company is considering the use of the exhaust gases for space heating. The existing space heating is provided by ducted hot air which is heated by equipment with running costs of £10,000 per annum. This equipment could be sold now for £20,000 but would incur dismantling costs of £3,000. If retained for one year the equipment could be sold for £18,000 with dismantling costs of £3,500.

The conversion to the use of the exhaust gases for space heating would involve the following:

(i) The removal of the existing gas extraction machinery. This could be implemented now at a dismantling cost of £5,000 with sale of the machinery for £40,000. Alternatively it could be sold in one year's time for £30,000 with dismantling costs of £5,500.

(ii) The leasing of alternative gas extraction equipment at a cost of £4,000 per annum with annual fixed running costs of £12,000.

(iii) The conversion would mean the loss of 30% of the production enhancement which the exhaust gas extraction provides for a period of one year only, until the new system is 'run-in'.

(iv) The company has a spare electric motor in store which could be sold to company X for £3,500 in one year's time. It could be fitted to the proposed leased gas extraction equipment in order to reduce the impact of the production losses during the running-in period. This course of action would reduce its sales value to company X in one year's time to £2,000 and would incur £2,500 of fitting and dismantling costs. It would, however, reduce the production enhancement loss from 30% to 10% during the coming year (year 1). This would not be relevant in year 2 because of an anticipated fall in the demand for the product.

The electric motor originally cost £5,000. If replaced today it would cost £8,000. It was purchased for another process which has now been discontinued. It could also be used in a cooling process for one year if modified at a cost of £1,000, instead of the company hiring cooling equipment at a cost of £3,000 per annum. Because of its modification, the electric motor would have to be disposed of in one year's time at a cost of £250.

Ignore the time value of money.

Required:

a) Prepare an analysis indicating all the options available for the use of the spare electric motor and the financial implications of each. State which option would be chosen on financial grounds.

b) Prepare an analysis on an incremental opportunity cost basis in order the decide on financial grounds whether to convert immediately to the use of exhaust gases for space heating or to delay the conversion for one year.

c) Explain the steps in the construction and use of a spreadsheet model which will allow management to evaluate the financial impact of a change in one or more of the input variables on the decisions in a) and b) above.

ACCA, Information for Control and Decision Making.

B5. The chairman of your group, which is large and diversified, has expressed concern at the inadequacies of the present voluminous monthly reporting package. He acknowledges that it compares actual and forecast results for all operations with the budget, and that it contains extensive reporting of non-financial indicators of customer satisfaction and quality, and of factory performance towards attaining JIT (just-in-time manufacturing) and TQM (total quality management). However, he regards much of this as operational detail, and considers that the Board should place more emphasis on the shareholders' interests. This would be in accord with the declared group aim of maximising shareholder value in the long run.

As part of a response to the chairman's concerns, the finance director has asked you to prepare a report on certain aspects of the problem.

Required:

Write a report to the finance director

a) explaining what is meant by shareholder value, and how it can be assessed.

b) explaining what measure of measures of divisional performance would enable the management of a diversified group to assess divisional performance against the group objective of maximising shareholder value. Include in your report appropriate commentary on the role of non-financial indicators, and a possible approach to changing the reporting to the Board.

CIMA, Management Accounting Control Systems.

B6. Ewden plc is a medium-sized company producing a range of engineering products which it sells to wholesale distributors. Recently, its sales have begun to rise rapidly following a general recovery in the economy as a whole. However, it is concerned about its liquidity position and is contemplating ways of improving its cash flow.

Ewden's accounts for the past two years are summarised below.

Profit and loss account for the year ended 31 December

	1992	1993
	(£000)	(£000)
Sales	12,000	16,000
Cost of sales	7,000	9,150
Operating profit	5,000	6,850
Interest	200	250
Profit before tax	4,800	6,600

	1992	1993
	(£000)	(£000)
Taxation*	1,000	1,600
Profit after tax	3,800	5,000
Dividends	1,500	2,000
Retained profit	2,300	3,000

*After capital allowances

Balance sheet as at 31 December

	1992		1993	
	(£000)		(£000)	
Fixed assets (net)		9,000		12,000
Current assets:				
Stock	1,400		2,200	
Debtors	1,600		2,600	
Cash	1,500		100	
		4,500		4,900
Current liabilities:				
Overdraft	–		200	
Trade creditors	1,500		2,000	
Other creditors	500		200	
		(2,000)		(2,400)
10% Loan stock		(2,000)		(2,000)
Net assets		9,500		12,500
Ordinary shares (50p)		3,000		3,000
Profit and loss account		6,500		9,500
Shareholders' funds		9,500		12,500

In order to speed up collection from debtors, Ewden is considering two alternative policies. One option is to offer a 2% discount to customers who settle within 10 days of despatch of invoices rather than the normal 30 days offered. It is estimated that 50% of customers would take advantage of this offer. Alternatively, Ewden can utilise the services of a factor. The factor will operate on a service-only basis, administering and collecting payment from Ewden's customers. This is expected to generate administrative savings of £100,000 p.a. and, it is hoped, will also shorten the debtor days to an average of 45. The factor will make a service charge of 1.5% of Ewden's turnover. Ewden can borrow from its bankers at an interest rate of 18% p.a.

Required:
a) Identify the reasons for the sharp decline in Ewden's liquidity and assess the extent to which the company can be said to be exhibiting the problem of 'overtrading'.

Illustrate your answer by reference to key performance and liquidity ratios computed from Ewden's accounts.

(*Note:* it is not necessary to compile a FRS1 statement.)

b) Determine the relative costs and benefits of the two methods of reducing debtors, and recommend an appropriate policy.

ACCA, Managerial Finance.

B7. Just-in-Time (JIT) systems are coming into increasing use in manufacturing, with varying degrees of success. One result of this can be purchasing and production each period of a large number of different products in small quantities, rather than large quantities of relatively few products.

Required:

a) Explain how the benefits claimed for JIT should affect profits and product costs, AND how these benefits should appear in routine control information.

b) Explain the possible changes in routine factory accounting and control systems that may become necessary with a transition to JIT.

CIMA, Management Accounting Control Systems.

B8. a) Explain how inflation affects the rate of return required on an investment project, and the distinction between a real and a nominal (or 'money terms') approach to the evaluation of an investment project under inflation.

b) Howden plc is contemplating investment in an additional production line to produce its range of compact discs. A market research study, undertaken by a well-known firm of consultants, has revealed scope to sell an additional output of 400,000 units p.a. The study cost £0.1m but the account has not yet been settled.

The price and cost structure of a typical disc (net of royalties), is as follows:

		£
Price per unit		12.00
Costs per unit of output		
Material cost per unit	1.50	
Direct labour cost per unit	0.50	
Variable overhead cost per unit	0.50	
Fixed overhead cost per unit	1.50	
		(4.00)
Profit		8.00

The fixed overhead represents an apportionment of central administrative and marketing costs. These are expected to rise in total by £500,000 p.a. as a result of undertaking this project. The production line is expected to operate for five years and require a total cash outlay of £11m, including £0.5m of materials stocks. The equipment willl have a residual value of £2m. Because the company is moving towards a JIT stock management policy, it is expected that this project willl involve steadily reducing working capital needs, expected to decline at about 3% p.a. by volume. The production line will be accommodated in a presently empty building for which an offer of £2m has recently been received from another company. If the building is retained, it is expected that property price inflation will increase its value to £3m after five years.

While the precise rates of price and cost inflation are uncertain, economists in Howden's corporate planning department make the following forecasts for the average annnual rates of inflation relevant to the project:

Retail Price Index	6% p.a.
Disc prices	5% p.a.
Material prices	3% p.a.
Direct labour wage rates	7% p.a.
Variable overhead costs	7% p.a.
Other overhead costs	5% p.a.

Note: You may ignore taxes and capital allowances in this question.

Required:

Given that Howden's shareholders require a real return of 8.5% for projects of this degree of risk, assess the financial viability of this proposal.

c) Briefly discuss how inflation may complicate the analysis of business financial decisions.

ACCA, Managerial Finance.

Solutions to assessment and revision sections

Assessment and revision section 1

A1. (i) This can be taken more or less directly from the text. Key point is that the type of classification (e.g. by behaviour, controllability, expense, type etc.) must be consistent and fulfil a genuine management need.

(ii) The MA system seeks to provide *relevant* information for all management needs, especially for planning, control and decision making. Each of the major classifications may be relevant for planning, control or decision making, e.g.:

When planning: classification by behaviour (i.e. fixed, variable), by controllability (for setting budgets), by function (for departmental planning etc.) may all be necessary.

For control: classification by function (for identification), by behaviour (to assess allowed expenditure levels), by expense type (for standards and budgets) etc.

For decision making: classification by relevance (e.g. opportunity and incremental costs), by behaviour (to assess costs levels etc.).

A2. Relevance is the primary characteristic of useful MA information. Information should be: specific to the problem or decision being studied; appropriate for the period or level of activity being studied; classified in the necessary fashion; presented to the right person in time for it to be useful; and so on. If information has these and other appropriate characteristics it is likely to be relevant and therefore useful.

Neutrality means the information does not contain bias. Bias may take the form of omitting adverse items, excluding some of the likely outcomes, or slanting a report so as to make a particular decision or action inevitable. In general, information should seek to present an objective , rounded viewpoint, with the aim of pursuing overall organisational goals rather than sectional interests.

A3. a) *Main process account*

	Kg	£		Kg	£
Materials	10,000	15,000	P Finished goods	4,800	16,390
Direct labour	-	10,000	Q Process 2	3,600	17,210
Variable overhead	-	4,000	By-product R	1,000	1,750
Fixed overhead	-	6,000	Normal toxic waste	500	-
Toxic waste disposal (normal)	-	750	Abnormal toxic waste	100	400
	10,000	35,750		10,000	35,750

$$\text{Cost per Kg of output} = \frac{(£35,750 - £1,750)}{(4,800 + 3,600 + 100)} = £4.00$$

Joint cost apportionment:

	P	Q	Total
Sales values	£24,000	£25,200	£49,200
Apportioned costs:			
$\dfrac{24}{49.2} \times £33,600$	£16,390	£17,210	£33,600

b)

Normal toxic waste account

	£		£
Bank – disposal cost	900	Main process	750
		Abnormal toxic waste	150
	900		900

Abnormal toxic waste

	£		£
Main process	400	Profit and loss account	550
Normal toxic waste	150		
	550		550

Process 2 account

	Kg	£		Kg	£
Main process Q	3,600	17,210	Finished goods Q	3,300	26,465
Fixed cost		6,000	Closing work-in-progress	300	1,920
Variable cost*		5,175			
	3,600	28,385		3,600	28,385

*(3,300 + (300 × 0.5) × £1.50)

Equivalent units

	Main process	Conversion
Finished goods	3,300	3,300
Closing work-in-progress	300	150
	3,600	3,450
Cost	£17,210	£11,175
Cost per equivalent unit	£4.78	£3.24

Valuation:			Total
	£	£	£
Finished goods	15,776	10,689	26,465
Closing work-in-progress	1,434	486	1,920
			28,385

c) All forms of cost separation for joint costs are merely conventions. The sales value convention generally results in similar profit margins.

d)

	Per Kg £	
Sales value at separation point	4.30	
Final sales value	7.00	
Incremental revenue	2.70	Total
Incremental cost	1.50	£
Incremental benefit	1.20	4,320 (× 3,600)
Specific fixed costs avoidable		3,600
Net benefit		720

Therefore, product Q should continue to be processed into Q2 so long as the cost and revenue assumptions used above continue to hold.

A4. a) (i)

Absorption costing profit statement

Products

(£000)	XYI 000		YZT 000		ABW 000	
Sales/production (units)	50		40		30	
(£000)	£	£	£	£	£	£
Sales		2,250		3,800		2,190
Less: Prime cost	1,600		3,360		1,950	
Overheads:						
Machine dept.	120		240		144	
Assembly dept.	288.75	2,008.75	99	3,699	49.5	2143.5
Profit (loss)		£241.25		£101		£46.5

Workings for ABC statement

Cost Pools

(£000)	Machining services	Assembly services	Set-ups	Order processing	Purchasing
(£000)	357	318	26	156	84
Cost drivers	420,000 machine hours	30,000 direct labour hours	520 set-ups	32,000 customer orders	11,200 suppliers' orders
	£.85 per machine hour	£.60 direct labour hour	£50 per set-up	£4,875 per customer order	£7.50 per suppliers' order

(ii)   Activity-Based Costing Profit Statement

	XYI		YZT		ABW	
	000		000		000	
Sales/production (units)	50		40		30	
(£000)	£	£ £		£ £		£
Sales		2,250		3,800		2,190
Less Prime cost	1,600		3,360		1,950	
Cost pools:						
Machine department						
at .85	85		170		102	
Assembly department at .60	210		72		36	
Set-up costs at £50	6		10		10	
Order processing at £4.875	39		39		78	
Purchasing at £7.50	22.5	1,962,5	30	3,681 31.5		2,207.5
Profit (loss)		£287.5		£119		(£17.5)

b)   Comments can be taken from the text.

A5. a)

Cassiop plc

Calculation of fixed overhead absorption rates

	Period 1	Period 2	Period 3
	£	£	£
Budgeted FOH	10,400	19,170	17,360
Budgeted production (units)	8,000	14,200	12,400
FOH absorption rate (per unit)	1.30	1.35	1.40
Actual production	8,400	13,600	9,200
	£	£	£
FOH absorbed (actual units × rate)	10,920	18,360	12,880
Less: Actual FOH	11,200	18,320	16,740
	U/A 280	O/A 40	U/A 3,860
Effect on the profit or loss	Deducted in P & L	Added back in P & L	Deducted in P & L

U/A and O/A = under and over absorption

b)

Units in closing stock

(Units)	Period 1	Period 2	Period 3
Opening stock	2,600	1,400	2,600
Add: Production	8,400	13,600	9,200
	11,000	15,000	11,800
Less: Sales	9,600	12,400	10,200
Closing stock	1,400	2,600	1,600

Whether marginal costing (i.e. stock valued at variable cost), or absorption costing (stock valued at fixed and variable cost) produces a higher profit in a given period depends entirely on the amount of fixed overheads in opening and closing stocks. In this case the difference can be calculated as follows, by showing the fixed overhead content in opening and closing stocks in each period.

Fixed overhead content of stocks

	Period 1	Period 2	Period 3
	£	£	£
F.O. content of closing stock	1,820	3,510	2,240
	$(1,400 \times £1.30)$	$(260 \times £1.35)$	$(1,600 \times £1.40)$
less F.O. content of opening stock (given)	3,315	(period 1) 1,820	(period 2) 3,510
= Difference	(1,495)	1,690	(1,270)

∴. Therefore absorption profit lower than marginal profit in periods 1 and 3, higher in period 2.

c) Absorption costing is a product costing convention with many arbitrary assumptions and subjective assessments, e.g. analysis, apportionment and absorption of overheads, treatment of under/over absorption, the way cost centres are determined, the treatment of service cost centres. In consequence, information based on absorption costing principles is not suitable for use in decision making.

A6. a) Product cost per unit – conventional methods

	Product X	*Product Y*	*Product Z*
	£	£	£
Direct labour	3	9	6
Materials	20	12	25
Production overhead	42	28	84
	65	49	115

b) ABC principles – Total production overhead

$$(750 \times 1.5 + 1,250 \times 1 + 7,000 \times 3) \times 28 = £654,500$$

		£
Set-up cost	35%	229,075
Machining	20%	130,900
Materials handling	15%	98,175
Inspection	30%	196,350
	100%	654,500

Calculation of Cost Driver Rates:

	Total	Product X	Product Y	Product Z
	£	£	£	£
Set-up cost	229,075	25,643	39,319	164,113
Machining	130,900	6,300	7,000	117,600
Materials handling	98,175	9,817	17,181	71,177
Inspection	196,500	29,453	35,343	131,554
	654,000	71,213	98,843	484,444
Number of units		750	1,250	7,000
Production overhead per unit (rounded)		95	79	69

Note: Machining have been split in proportion to the total machine hours per product:

Product X	1,125
Product Y	1,250
Product Z	21,000
	23,375

Product cost per unit– ABC principles

	Product X	Product Y	Product Z
	£	£	£
Direct labour	3	9	6
Materials	20	12	25
Production overhead	95	79	69
	118	100	100

c) *Reasons for differences:*

❐ Product Z has fewer set-ups than X or Y;

❐ Product Z has fewer material movements than X or Y; and

❐ Product Z has fewer inspections than Y, which has fewer inspections than X. Hence, products X and Y have received proportionally more production overhead under ABC principles than under conventional product costing methods.

A7. Parts a) and c) can be taken from the text.

Diagrams for Part b)

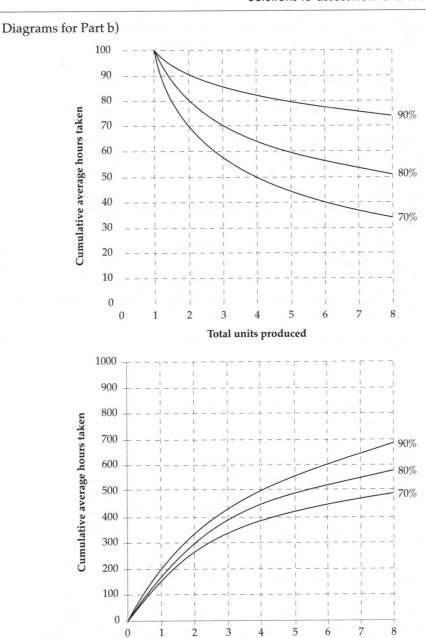

Assessment and revision section 2

A1. a) In attempting to extrapolate past performance into the future, a number of assumptions are made:

- ❑ that conditions in the past have been constant and therefore that the relationships between variables are valid;

- [ ] that the conditions in the future are the same as the past and therefore that the relationships derived from past data can be used;

- [ ] that extrapolation in terms of volumes are valid, e.g. no sudden jumps in fixed costs due to the production volume being outside the current capacity; and

- [ ] that the relationship between the variables is linear, which may not be valid outside the current planned volumes.

In so far as these assumptions are not valid, the extrapolation will not be accurate and will in some ways be misleading, especially where the business environment is changing rapidly and therefore it is difficult to predict the likely demand for the products. The greatest difficulty is when there has been a sudden change in the business environment due to, for example, foreign competition, innovative product development or a sudden change in consumer tastes.

All of the above must be taken into account when seeking to use a forecast as the basis for planning future action. The assumptions upon which such forecasts have been made must be known and taken into account by all users of the information.

b) When seeking to forecast in circumstances where the future is likely to be different to the past, a number of techniques can be employed:

- [ ] use of probabilities to assess how likely certain events are, and their effect on the forecast;

- [ ] use of simulation to evaluate alternatives;

- [ ] use of surveys – trade/industry/economic information to help assessment of future trends; and

- [ ] use of statistical techniques to form the basis for the forecast and then apply more subjective assessments to modify the forecast.

There is a tendency to give up when the future looks uncertain, but the effort of trying to forecast enables management to become more aware of the factors involved and thus to be able to adjust their actions to take account of them. The forecast also provides a control against which actual performance can be measured and the key factors affecting the company assessed.

Forecasting the future when the environment is changing rapidly requires that a company becomes more outward focused, looking at competition, new products, new markets and has a well developed information gathering system rather than being focused inwardly – relying upon internal statistics of past performance.

A2. a) Key features of strategic and operational planning can be taken from the text. These include: external orientation and analysis; management involvement; commitment; communication; creation of action plans/budgets/standards at the operational level.

b) *Unrealistic plans* may assume quicker deliveries or production than is economically justified.

Inconsistent goals, where departmental goals conflict with organisational goals.

Poor communication between functions or management hamper operations.

Inadequate performance measurement – concentration on, say, purely financial performance measures may cause poorer quality, higher stocks etc.

A3. a) Budgetary slack occurs when budgets are over-generous and thus easy to achieve. Three ways managers may attempt to achieve slack are:

❏ Cost over-estimation;

❏ Sales under-estimation;

❏ Over-estimation of difficulties expected.

b) In some circumstances managers may set budgets which are too high. This may be due to:

❏ the organisation concentrating and rewarding budget levels rather than actual achievements;

❏ managers setting individual goals;

❏ genuine mistakes;

❏ as compensation for poor past performance.

c) Contingency theory suggests that systems, including MA systems, are dependent (or contingent) upon various underlying factors present in the given unique situation. This helps to explain the various different forms systems take.

Environmental uncertainty can occur in almost infinite variety and makes the design of control systems much more difficult, e.g.: there are more disturbances and changes to consider; information is constantly changing; outcomes vary; organisations/structures/personnel constantly alter; and so on.

A4. a) *Raw materials budget (units)*

	March	April	May	June
Opening stock	100	110	115	110
Add: Purchases	80	80	85	85
	180	190	200	195
Less: Used in production	70	75	90	90
Closing stock	110	115	110	105
Finished production budget (units)				
Opening stock	110	100	91	85
Add: Production	70	75	90	90
	180	175	181	175
Less: Sales	80	84	96	94
Closing stock	100	91	85	81

b) Sales budget

					Total
(at £219 per unit)	£17,520	£18,396	£21,024	£20,586	£77,526

Production cost budget

Raw materials	*3,024	**3,321	4,050	4,050	14,445
Wages and variable costs	4,550	4,875	5,850	5,850	21,125
	£7,574	£8,196	£9,900	£9,900	£35,570

Debtors

Closing debtors = May + June sales = **£41,610**

Creditors

June, raw materials 85 units × £45 = **£3,825**

$$*\left(£4,320 \times \frac{70}{100}\right) = \textbf{£3,024}$$

$$*\left(£4,320 \times \frac{30}{100}\right) = £1,296 + 45 \text{ units at } £45 = \textbf{£3,321}$$

Closing stocks

Raw materials 105 units × £45	=	**£4,725**
Finished goods 81 units × £110	=	**£8,910**

(material £45 per unit + Lab + O.H. £65 per unit)

Cash budget

	March £	April £	May £	June £
Balance b/f	6,790	4,820	5,545	132,415
Add: Receipts				
Debtors (two month's credit)	7,680	10,400	17,520	18,396
Loan	–	–	120,000	–
Cash available	14,470	15,220	143,065	150,811
Payments				
Creditors (one month's credit)	3,900	3,600	3,600	3,825
Wages and variable overheads	4,550	4,875	5,850	5,850
Fixed overheads	1,200	1,200	1,200	1,200
Machinery	–	–	–	112,000
Interim dividend	–	–	–	12,500
Cash payments	9,650	9,675	10,650	135,375
Balance c/f	4,820	5,545	132,415	15,436

d)

Master budget

Budgeted trading and profit and loss account for the four months to 30 June 19X5

	£	£
Sales		77,526
Less: Cost of sales: Opening stock finished goods	10,450	
Add: Production cost	35,570	
	46,020	
Less: Closing stock finished goods	8,910	37,110
		40,416
Less: Expenses Fixed overheads (4 × £1,200)	4,800	
Depreciation		
Machinery and equipment	15,733	
Motor vehicles	3,500	
Loan interest (two months)	1,500	25,533
		14,833
Less: Interim dividends		12,500
		2,383
Add: Profit and loss account balance b/f		40,840
		£43,223

Budgeted balance sheet as at 30 June 19X5

Employment of Capital

Fixed assets	Cost	Depreciation to date	Net
	£	£	£
Land and buildings	500,000	–	500,000
Machinery and equipment	236,000	100,233	135,767
Motor vehicles	42,000	19,900	22,100
	778,000	120,133	657,867

Working capital

Current assets

Stock of raw materials	4,725
Stock of finished goods	8,910
Debtors	41,610
Cash and bank balances	15,436
	70,681

Less: Current liabilities			
Creditors	3,825		
Loan interest owing	1,500	5,325	65,356
			£723,223

	£
Capital employed	
Ordinary share capital £1 shares (fully paid)	500,000
Share premium	60,000
Profits and loss account	43,223
	603,223
Secured loan (7.5%)	120,000
	£723,223

e) The company's cash management could be improved in numerous ways, e.g.:

- ❐ closer credit control, especially debtors' collection;

- ❐ reducing stocks and increasing stock turnover;

- ❐ utilising surplus cash efficiently;

- ❐ consider more debt financing;

- ❐ consider disposal of surplus assets;

- ❐ reduce production lead times and possibly use sub-contractors.

A5. a) (i)   *Average net current operating assets.*

	Product A	Product B	Product C	Total
Annual volume, units	50,000	60,000	75,000	
Selling price £ per unit	4.50	6.50	3.50	
Cost of sales £ per unit	2.25	3.90	1.05	
Stock in months	1.50	2.00	1.00	
Debtors in months	2.00	3.00	1.50	
Creditors in months	2.50	2.50	1.50	
Currently:				
	£000	£000	£000	£000
Stock	14,063	39,000	6,562	
Debtors	37,500	97,500	32,813	
(Creditors)	(23,438)	(48,750)	(9,843)	
Total on current figures	**28,125**	**87,750**	**29,532**	**145,407**
Effect of volume increase				
25%/20%/30%	7,031	17,550	8,860	
Total on scenario 1	**35,156**	**105,300**	**38,392**	**178,848**
Increase debtors by a further 25%	11,719	29,250	10,664	

Total on scenario 2	46,875	134,550	49,056	230,481
Scenario 1 recap	35,156	105,300	38,392	
(reduce) debtors by 25%	(11,719)	(29,250)	(10,664)	
reduce creditors	1,172	2,340	2,559	
Total on scenario 3	24,609	78,390	30,287	133,286

(ii) Other factors include:

❒ cash payments/receipts of a non-current nature, e.g. purchase/sales of fixed assets, loan repayments or receipts etc.;

❒ distribution of tax, interest, dividends;

❒ reliability of estimates for operating assets;

❒ firm's attitude to overdraft;

❒ changes in sales/prices/costs etc. which may occur.

c) Three possible uses of cash:

❒ reduce overdraft;

❒ put on deposit;

❒ bring forward payments where discounts can be gained.

A6. a) Price elasticity of demand $= \dfrac{\% \text{ change in quantity demanded}}{\% \text{ change in price}}$

$= 1.5$

When the company's price fell by 4% in real terms, demand increased by $4\% \times 1.5$. i.e. 6%. When the company's price falls by 6% in real terms, demand will increase by $6\% \times 1.5$ i.e. 9%.

Determination of fixed and variable costs:

Adjust current period's costs to previous period's prices

$$\frac{1.077.44}{1 + 4\%} = 1,036$$

Use High/Low method to determine fixed/variable cost split

Period	units 1.000	costs £000
Current	106	1,036
Previous	100	1,000
	6	36

variable cost per unit	$= £6$
fixed cost per unit	$= £1,000 - 100 \times £6 = £400$
variable cost per unit next period	$= £6 \times (1 + 4\%) \times (1 + 6\%) = £6.6144$
fixed cost per unit next period	$= £400,000 \times (1 + 4\%) \times (1 + 6\%) = £440,960$

Budgeted position, price £13

		£
Sales:	106,000 × (1 + 9%) × £13	1,502,020
Variable costs:	106,000 × (1 + 9%) × £6.6144	(764,228)
Contribution		737,792
Fixed costs:		440,960
Profit		296,832

b) **Budgeted position, price £13 + 6%**

		£
Sales:	106,000 × £13 × (1 + 6%)	1,460,680
Variable costs:	106,000 × £6.6144	(701,126)
Contribution		759,554
Fixed costs:		440,960
Profit		318,594

c) Report would recommend increasing price by 6%, which produces higher profit.

d) Typical assumptions:

❏ that changes in volume are solely a function of price changes, i.e. are not influenced by advertising, consumer preferences, general economic conditions etc.;

❏ the decision makers, i.e. customers, are rational and are making decisions on purely economic factors;

❏ the fixed/variable cost split is constant over time;

❏ that fixed and variable costs are both affected by inflation to the same degree;

❏ that estimates of the elasticity of demand are correct.

Assessment and revision section 3

A1. This can be taken largely from the text. Key points: incremental budgeting tends to be backward looking and accepts too readily existing tasks, functions and structures; alternatives tend not to be examined.

Activity-based budgeting focuses on efficiency, effectiveness and continuous improvement. Emphasis is on activities which cause costs and non-value added activities are more easily identified. There is likely to be a more positive attitude to the identification of critical success factors and total quality management.

A2. R & D expenditure is notoriously difficult to control except in an arbitrary, cash-limited fashion. The problem is that R & D is, by nature, risky and speculative, and short-term outcomes difficult to assess.

Nevertheless, certain basic control procedures can be of value. These include:

❏ clear authorisation procedures for major items with agreed plans of work linked to strategic planes;

❏ good planning and review systems with time scales and anticipated achievement dates for stages of projects;

❏ effective costing and reporting systems showing R & D expenditure for each project department compared with budgets;

❏ regular review and re-assessment reports, especially on major projects;

❏ targets should be set (and revised) and progress compared with targets.

The general aim should be to be flexible and give as much autonomy as possible to the R & D management, yet preserve strategic oversight and control.

A3. a) Material variances

(i) Actual quantity at actual price (given) — £17,328

(ii) Actual quantity at standard price:	£	
F 1,680 × £4	6,720	
G 1,650 × £3	4,950	
H 870 × £6	5,220	
		£16,890

(iii) Standard yield × standard cost
(32 × 120) × £4.50 (W1) — £17,280

(iv) Actual yield × standard cost
3,648 × £4.50 — £16,416

Variances	£	
Price (i) – (ii)	438	A
Usage (ii) – (iv)	474	A
Cost (i) – (iv)	912	A
Mix (ii) – (iii)	390	F
Yield (iii) – (iv)	864	A
Usage (as above)	474	A

Workings

W1 Standard cost per kilo = $\dfrac{£144}{32 \text{ kilos}}$ = £4.50

Variances

A = Adverse

F = Favourable

b) *Analysis of material variances for F, G and H*

Mix	Total	F	G	H
Standard (kilos)		1,800	1,440	960
Actual (kilos)		1,680	1,650	870
		120 F	210 A	90 F
× Standard price (£)		4	3	6
	£390 F	£480 F	£630 A	£540 F

Price	Total	F	G	H
		£	£	£
Standard		4.00	3.00	6.00
Actual		4.25	2.80	6.40
		.25 A	.20 F	.40 A
× Actual kilos used		1,680	1,650	870
	£438 A	£420 A	£330 F	£348 A

c) Labour variances:

Cost variances		Total	Dept. P	Dept. Q
		£	£	£
Standard cost		6,240	4,800	1,440
Actual cost		7,872	6,360	1,512
	(i)	£1,632 A	£1,560 A	£72 A

Efficiency variances				
Standard hours			480	240
Actual hours			600	270
			120 A	30A
× Standard rate per hour (£)			10	6
	(ii)	£1,380 A	£1,200 A	£180 A

Rate variances				
			£	£
Standard rate			10.00	6.00
Actual rate			10.60	5.60
			.60 A	.40 F
× Actual hours worked			600	270
	(iii)	£252 A	£360 A	£108 F

Proof
(i) = (ii) + (iii)

d) Sales variances

		£
Budgeted sales for actual level of activity 120 × 32 × £16		61,440
Actual sales 3,648 × £16.75		61,104
		£336 A

Made up of: Volume variance		
(3,860 − 3,648 kilos) × £16	3,072	A
Price variance (£.75 × 3,648)	2,736	F
	£336	A

e) The yield variance is adverse, perhaps caused by using more of G and less of F and H as planned. Alternatively, the price variance for G (£330 F) could have been caused by a lower quality material, also affecting yield.

A4. a) It is first necessary to calculate the WIP and production:

The equivalent weight of product in the work-in-progress (WIP) is:

Opening WIP $318.6 \div \{1 + (0.26 \times (1 - 0.4)]\}$

i.e. $318,6 \div 1.156 = 275.6$ kg

Closing WIP $426.3 \div \{1 + (0.26 \times (1 - 0.52)]\}$

i.e. $426.3 \div 1.1248 = 379.0$ kg

Production of KABO from material input in April was

	kg
Production transferred to stores	831.0
Less: Opening WIP of KABO	− 275.6
Plus: Closing WIP of KABO	+ 379.0
	934.4

Materials total cost variance

	£
Standard cost of output 934.4 × 121.27	113,315
Less: Actual cost of output	106,408
	6,907 FAV

Materials price variance

	Standard price	Actual price	Actual quantity	Variance	
	£/kg	kg	£/kg	£	
K	104.00	102.90	291.6	320.8	FAV
A	49.00	51.20	242.6	533.7	ADV
B	186.00	188.00	198.2	396.4	ADV
O	72.50	68.16	392.0	1,703.3	FAV
				1,092.0	FAV

Materials usage variance

	Standard usage	Actual usage	Standard price	Variance	
	kg	kg	£/kg	£	
K	308.4	291.6	104.00	1,747	FAV
A	261.6	242.6	49.00	933	FAV
B	214.9	198.2	186.00	3,108	FAV
O	392.4	392.0	72.50	32	FAV
	1,177.3	1,124.4		5,820	FAV

Materials mixture variance

	Standard mix	Actual mix	Standard price	Variance	
	kg	kg	£/kg	£	
K	294.5	291.6	104.00	302	FAV
A	249.9	242.6	49.00	358	FAV
B	205.2	198.2	186.00	1,302	FAV
O	374.8	392.0	72.50	1,247	ADV
	1,124.4	1,124.4		715	FAV

Materials yield variance

Actual output	934.4 kg
Less: Standard output from actual input	
i.e. 1,124.4 ÷ 1.26	892.4 kg
	42.0 kg
Evaluated at standard price	£5,093 FAV

Financial control report for material input in April 1995

	£
Actual material cost	106,408
Materials price variance	+ 1,092
Materials yield variance	+ 5,093
Materials mixture variances	
K	+ 302
A	+ 358
B	+ 1,302
O	− 1,247
Rounding errors	+ 7
Standard material cost	113,315

b) The above variances relate to materials only, and a fully rounded picture should contain performance data of actual compared with budget or standard for labour, overheads and sales, together with quality control data. Thus the information supplied presents only a narrow view of operations and, because of the deficiencies of mix and yield variances (outlined in the text), it may not be particularly useful even relating to materials.

A5. a) *Flexed budget to suit actual sales of 720,000 units*

	Budget £000	Actual £000	Variance £000
Sales	1,152	1,071	(81)
Cost of sales			
Materials	189	144	45
Labour (variable)	270	288	(18)
Labour (fixed)	100	94	6
Overheads	36	36	Nil
	595	562	33
Gross profit	557	509	(48)
Other overheads			
Selling and distribution:			
Fixed	72	83	(11)
Variable	162	153	9
Administration			
Fixed	184	176	8
Variable	54	54	Nil
	472	466	6
Net profit	85	43	(42)

The main reasons for the £42,000 reduction in Net Profit are: sales lower than planned, higher labour costs, offset to an extent by savings on materials and overheads.

b) Like must be compared with like, i.e. budget must be flexed to suit the actual level of activity of 720,000 units.

c) Can be taken from the text.

A6. a) *Workings for figures in operating statement.*

	Annual budget (at 100% capacity)		Quarterly budget (at 90% capacity)		Agreed changes to budget	
	Fixed £	Variable £	Fixed £	Variable £	Fixed £	Variable £
Administration	92,000				2,000	
Catering	49,200	114,800		25,830		−775
Cleaning	25,600	6,400		1,440	−240	
Laundry		80,000		18,000		900
Medical	182,000	78,000		17,550		878
Sundry	75,000	25,000		5,625	5,000	
	423,800	304,200	105,950	68,445	6,760	1,003

Notes: Quarterly fixed cost = £423,800/4= £105,950

In revision changes a minus sign signals an increase in cost

The above workings show the values for the revision variances, fixed and variable, together with the budgeted fixed and variable costs.

Original budget for the quarter:

Resident fee income = 90 days × 80 beds × 90% × £30 =	£194,400
Less: Variable cost (as above)	68,445
Original budgeted contribution	£125,955

Occupancy variance calculations:

Revised budget variable cost at 90% capacity = £68,445 – 1,003 = £67,442

Revised budgeted contribution = £194,400 – £67,442 = £126,958

Occupancy in bed days per quarter:

Budget = 90 × 80 × 0.9 = 6,480 bed days

Actual = 90 × 80 × 0.95 = 6,840 bed days

Revised standard contribution per bed day = £126,958/6,480 = £19.5923

Occupancy variance = (6,840 – 6,480) × £19.5923 = £7,053 (F)

Operational variances:

Variable cost = flexed revised budget – actual cost

$$= £71,189^* – 72,930 = £1,741 \text{ (A)}$$

Fixed cost = £99,190 – 102,200 = £3,010 (A)

Fee income premium = 700 bed days × £5 = £3,500 (F)

*Variable cost budget adjusted to actual activity = £67,442 × 0.95/0.90 = £71,189

b)

	£
Actual fixed costs for quarter 2 =	102,200
Operational variance saving: 60% × £3,010	1,806
Revised fixed cost per quarter	100,394
Revised fixed cost for six months (×2)	200,788
Net profit required for six months	65,000
Contribution required for six months	265,788

Expected contribution per bed day for the six months to 31 December may be calculated as:

Revised standard contribution (per above)	£19.5923
Add: Fee income increase 5% × £30	1.50
Less: Residual operational variances (£1,741 × 0.4)/6,480) (adverse)	–0.1018
Estimated actual contribution per bed day	£20.9905

Hence bed days of occupancy for the six months to 31 December

$$= £265,788/£20.9905 = 12,662$$

Now 100% capacity for six months = 80 × 180= 14,400 bed days

Hence occupancy rate required to give a net profit of £65,000

$$= (12,662/14,400) \times 100 = 87.93\%$$

c) Uses of operational and planning variances, and feedback and feedforward control, can be taken from the text.

A7. *Workings:*

Units sold	No. of days	Probability	Units × Prob.
30	10	0.07	2.1
40	20	0.15	6.0
50	50	0.37	18.5
60	30	0.22	13.2
70	15	0.11	7.7
80	5	0.04	3.2
90	5	0.04 .	3.6
	135	1.00	54.3

Average demand = 54.3 (say 54) units per day

Average usage in lead time = 54 × 5 = 270 units

Orders per annum $= \dfrac{12,000}{1,200} = 10$

Stock out cost per unit = £155 – £100 = £55

a) Cost of stock outs:

Re-order Level	Safety	Holding Stock	Possible Cost £	Prob. Shortage	No. of Orders	Shortage Cost £
250	0	0	50	0.22	10	6,050
			100	0.11	10	6,050
			150	0.04	10	3,300
			200	0.04	10	4,400
				Total Cost = £19,800		
300	30	600	50	0.11	10	3,025
			100	0.04	10	2,200
			150	0.04	10	3,300
				Total Cost = £9,125		
350	70	1,400	50	0.04	10	1,100
			100	0.04	10	2,200
				Total Cost = 4,900		
400	130	2,600	50	0.04	10	1,100
				Total Cost = £3,700		
450	180	3,600	0	0.0	10	0
				Total Cost = £3,600		

Annual stock out cost of using present re-order level of 250 = £19,800 (from table)

b) 450 re-order level has the minimum cost and enable the company to meet its 95% requirement.

A8. This can be largely taken from the text. The use of operational and planning variances tends to make it more obvious which are the significant variances, because those that are outside operational control (i.e. the planning variances) are dealt with first, leaving the ones due to inefficiency and poor control (i.e. the operational variances).

A9. a)

	Superb	Excellent	Good	Total
Line1. Budget sales (units)	30,000	50,000	20,000	100,000
Line 2. Actual sales (units) in std. proportions	28,800	48,000	19,200	96,000
Line 3. Actual sales (units)	36.000	42,000	18,000	96,000
Standard unit valuations:				
Line 4. Selling price (£)	100	80	70	
Line 5. Contribution (£)	60	55	48	
Line 6. Profit (£)*	35	30	23	

*Line 6. = Line 5. – Fixed cost per unit e.g. for Superb $= 60 - \dfrac{2.5m}{100,000} = 35$

Sales volume variance:

On turnover basis

$(1-3) \times 4$ (£)	600,000 (F)	640,000 (A)	140,000 (A)	180,000 (A)

On contribution basis

$(1-3) \times 5$ (£)	360,000 (F)	440,000 (A)	96,000 (A)	176,000 (A)

On profit basis

$(1-3) \times 6$ (£)	210,000 (F)	240,000 (A)	46,000 (A)	76,000 (A)

b) The basis of valuation should be the one which management think gives them most information.

If management wish to monitor market share in sales, then the turnover basis might be used.

The contribution basis is the closest to the cash flow effect of a change in sales units. The profit basis understates the cash flow position because the fixed element will be unaffected by volume changes.

d) Different individual model variances can be calculated using individual model contributions (as above), or a weighted average contribution per unit (in this example £55.10 per unit). These two approaches produce the same total quantity and mix variances, but different model variances. Neither approach is more correct – they are simply different conventions.

e) (i)   Workings

	Original standard	Revised standard	Actual
	£	£	£
Selling price	100	94	90
Variable cost	40	38.80	38
Contribution/unit	60	55.20	52

Summary statement – Model 'Superb' for four-week period

	£	£
Original budget contribution (30,000 × £60)		1,800,000
Revision variances (planning):		
selling price 30,000 × £6	180,000 (A)	
variable cost 30,000 × £1.20	36,000 (F)	
		144,000 (A)
Revised budget contribution (30,000 × £55.2)		1,656,000
Sales volume variance (6,000 × £55.2)		331,200 (F)
Revised standard contribution		1,987,200
Residual variances (operational):		
selling price 36,000 × £4	144,000 (A)	
variable cost 36,000 × £0.8	28,800 (F)	
		115,200 (A)
Actual contribution (36,000 × £52)		1,872,000

e) (ii)   Can be taken from the text.

Assessment and revision section 4

A1. a) The advantages of the current system are:

- ❏ it is inexpensive to operate;
- ❏ it encourages the use of the service departments thus leading to more demand and possible economies of scale; and
- ❏ it avoids conflict between departments.

The disadvantages are:

- ❏ it encourages waste;
- ❏ it discourages more economic use of the resources;
- ❏ it does not promote efficiency in the service departments;
- ❏ it is difficult to monitor usage; and
- ❏ product costs may be inaccurate if particular products use proportionally more of the facilities than other.

b) *Motivational effects:*

- ❏ encourages a reduction in usage;
- ❏ causes conflict if charges are considered too high;
- ❏ may result in poor servicing of equipment and subsequent damage; and
- ❏ mistakes in recording cause conflicts.

Control effects:

❐ better recording of actual usage;

❐ better control of costs; and

❐ more accurate product costs.

Administration effects:

❐ increased administration burden: recording, analysing, reporting – increased costs;

❐ increased need for accuracy of recording; and

❐ data processing requirements may necessitate a computer system – increased costs.

c) **Three possible bases of charging:**

1 *actual hours worked @ standard cost:*

record actual time spent and charge to the department at a standard rate.

advantages:

accurate charging of actual usage

there is no need to calculate actual cost rates.

disadvantages:

cost of recording and analysis.

2 *estimated usage @ standard cost:*

based upon some surrogate measure, e.g. maintenance materials used.

advantages:

reduces the amount of recording required.

disadvantages:

not an accurate reflection of usage.

3 *actual hours worked @ actual cost:*

record actual time spent and charge to the department at actual rate.

advantages:

accurate charging of actual usage.

disadvantages:

cost of recording and analysis, particularly the calculation of actual cost rates, passes on service department inefficiencies to other departments.

A2. a) One possible classification of the different decision levels within an organisation is: Strategic, Tactical and Operational.

❐ Strategic decisions are made by the top levels of management and relate to the longer term, say three – five years or longer. They tend to be non-programmed in nature i.e. ends can be defined, but not the means of achieving them.

❐ Tactical decisions are made by middle managers and relate to the shorter term, say within one year. They are programmed and non-programmed.

    ❑ Operational decisions are made by the lowest level of management and relate to day-to-day operations. They tend to be programmed in nature i.e. there is a clear means-end relationship.

b)   The information requirement varies at the different levels.

    ❑ Strategic decisions require information which is external, qualitative, highly summarised. Plans tend to be long-term. Feedback is quarterly and annually.

    ❑ Tactical decisions require information which is both external and internal, quantitative and qualitative, summarised. Plans tend to be for the year. Feedback is monthly.

    ❑ Operational decisions require information which is internal, quantitative and detailed. Plans are daily or weekly. Feedback is daily or weekly.

    ❑ The management accountant must tailor the information provided for the various levels to meet the above requirement for type of information, level of detail and frequency of reporting.

c)   A strategic decision to manufacture a new product would require a large amount of external information i.e. market surveys, competitor analysis, general economic conditions, exchange rate etc. This information would be supported by financial information on projected cash flows and expected returns. The NPV of projected cash flows could be used to evaluate alternative strategies. This would be used as one of the decision criteria, but other more qualitative information would also be required.

    The information for this project would be very different from that required for the replacement of an existing machine where the focus would be on cost savings and operational efficiency.

A3.   Note: each of the techniques is fully described in the text.

Ways that they could improve budgetary planning:

a)   Learning curves: more accurate assessment of labour times for future production.

b)   Linear regression as an aid to forecasting such things as overheads, costs etc.

c)   Linear programming: producing an optimum solution to a variety of resource allocation problems, e.g. product planning, ingredient mix etc.

d)   EOQ: deciding the least cost order quantity for parts or materials.

e)   Probability estimates: enable uncertainty to be incorporated into planning procedures.

A4.   The simplest way to determine the minimum annual growth in D is by trial and error and interpolation, thus:

Try D increasing by 6,000 units p.a.

Time	Net investment	Contribution forgone from C (@£30/unit)	Contribution from D (@£55/unit)	Net cashflow	Discount factor	Present value
Years	£	£	£	£		£
0	-550,000			-550,000	1.0000	-550,000
1		-720,000	330,000	-390,000	0.8929	-348,200
2		-600,000	660,000	60,000	0.7972	47,800
3		-480,000	990,000	510,000	0.7118	363,000
4		-360,000	1,320,000	960,000	0.6355	610,000
5		-240,000	1,650,000	1,410,000	0.5674	800,100
						922,800

Try, say D, increasing by 3,000 units p.a.

Time	Net investment	Contribution forgone from C (@£30/unit)	Contribution from D (@£55/unit)	Net cashflow	Discount factor	Present value
Years	£	£	£	£		£
0	-550,000			-550,000	1.0000	-550,000
1		-720,000	330,000	-390,000	0.8929	-348,200
2		-600,000	495,000	-105,000	0.7972	-83,700
3		-480,000	660,000	180,000	0.7118	128,100
4		-360,000	825,000	465,000	0.6355	295,500
5		-240,000	990,000	750,000	0.5674	425,600
						-132,700

As the NPV is negative the rate of increase is between 3,000 and 6,000:

$$3,000 + 3,000 \; \frac{132,700}{1,055,500} \approx 3,377 \text{ units.}$$

Thus D will be worthwhile, with any annual increase > 3,377 units (assuming usual caveats re estimates etc.).

b) With a 5 year horizon D's sales will have to increase at 3,377 p.a.

Accordingly, if the increase is only 2,800 units then the project will have to last longer than 5 years to be worthwhile. This is calculated in the table at the top of the following page.

Time	Net investment	Contribution forgone from C (@£30/unit)	Contribution from D (@£55/unit)	Net cashflow	Discount factor	Present value
Years	£	£	£	£		£
0	-550,000			-550,000	1.0000	-550,000
1		-720,000	330,000	-390,000	0.8929	-348,200
2		-600,000	484,000	-116,000	0.7972	-92,500
3		-480,000	638,000	158,000	0.7118	112,500
4		-360,000	792,000	432,000	0.6355	274,500
5		-240,000	946,000	706,000	0.5674	400,600
					NPV =	-203,100
		-120,000	1,100,000	980,000	0.5066	496,500

Thus, the investment appraisal time horizon is extended by approximately $\frac{203,100}{496,500} = 0.41$ of a year, say 5 months, to 5 years and 5 months.

c) Other factors include: extent of competition; reliability of all estimates; the market; inflation; is technology proven? etc.

A5. a) *Workings:*

Variable cost reduction

Existing cost	£
Type AX 964,706 × £15/100 =	144,706
Type BX 1,447,059 × £25/100 =	361,765
	506,471

Amended cost	
Type AX 826,667 × £12/100	(99,200)
Type BX 1,243,077 × £20/100	(248,615)
Net reduction in cost	158,656

Financial (cost)/benefit of proposed changes:

Elimination of synthetic slabs stock:	£
stores losses 68,711 units × £1/100	(687)
specification check	14,000
Savings on purchase quantity of synthetic slabs:	
(2,748,450 – 2,090,651) × £40/100	263,120
Less: increased price: 2,090,651 × £4/100	(83,626)
Curing/moulding processes costs:	
variable cost reduction	
(2,679,739 – 2,090,651) × £20/100	117,818
Scrap sub-component sales foregone	
(267,974 – 20,907) × £5/100	(12,353)

	£
Finishing process cost reduction:	
variable cost reduction (see workings)	158,656
scrap sales foregone $(361,765 - 51,744) \times £10/100$	(31,002)
Finished goods stock:	
holding costs $(45,000 - 1,500) \times £15/1,000$	653
	426,579
Less: cost of quality management programme	250,000
Net (cost)/benefit of proposed changes	176,579

b) Internal failure costs are problems/losses discovered *before* despatch, e.g. material losses, yield losses etc.

External failure costs are those incurred *after* despatch, e.g. warranty claims.

Appraisal costs are those internal costs required to check that required standards/specifications are achieved, e.g. inspection costs.

Prevention costs are those associated with the implementation of a total quality management programme, the general aim of which is to 'get it right first time'.

A6. a) *Price*

Since the variable cost is the same for each option and increases at the same rate as the price, the price which maximises revenue will also maximise contribution.

Expected revenue:

£5.00 $(0.10 \times 175 + 0.20 \times 275 + 0.40 \times 350 + 0.20 \times 375 + 0.10 \times 400) \times £5.00 \times 1,000$
$= 327,500 \times £5 = £1,637,500$

£8.00 $(0.10 \times 160 + 0.20 \times 190 + 0.40 \times 210 + 0.20 \times 230 + 0.10 \times 260) \times £8.00 \times 1,000$
$= 210,000 \times £8 = 1,680,000$

Therefore the price which maximises the expected revenue contribution is £8.00 per packet.

b) *Expected NPV over first five years of operation*

@ *£8.00 per packet – expected demand of 210,000 packets*

Operations can only start in twelve months time, therefore fixed and variable costs are first brought into the appraisal two years from now and so will have two years inflation applicable.

Cashflow in £000

	0	1	2	3	4	5	6
				Year			
Building	(250)						
Alterations		(150)					
Motor Cycles			(400)				
Fixed Costs			(875)	(945)	(1,020)	(1,102)	(1,190)
Expected Variable Costs			(232)	(243)	(255)	(268)	(281)
Working Capital		(50)					
Revenue			1,852	1,945	2,042	2,144	2,251
Realisable Value							1,000
Net Cash Flow	(250)	(200)	345	757	767	774	1,780

				Year			
	0	1	2	3	4	5	6
Discount Factor @ 15%	1	0.87	0.76	0.66	0.57	0.50	0.43
PV	(250)	(174)	262	500	437	387	765

∴ Therefore expected NPV = £1,927,000

c) Limitations include: reliability of all estimates; ignores competition effect on parcel service; prices and inflation rates may not be realistic etc.

A7. a) Current return on capital employed:

= Operating profit/capital employed = £20m/(£75m + £25m)

= £20m/£100m = 20%

Analysis of the project

Project capital requirements are £14m fixed capital plus £0.5m stocks. The annual depreciation charge (straight line) is:

(£14m – expected residual value of £2m)/4 = £3m p.a.

Profit calculations:

Year	1	2	3	4
Sales	$(5.00 \times 2m)$	$(4.50 \times 1.8m)$	$(4.00 \times 1.6m)$	$(3.50 \times 1.6m)$
	= 10.00	= 8.10	= 6.40	= 5.60
Op. costs	(2.00)	(1.80)	(1.60)	(1.60)
Fixed costs	(1.50)	(1.35)	(1.20)	(1.20)
Depreciation	(3.00)	(3.00)	(3.00)	(3.00)
Profit	3.50	1.95	0.60	(0.20)
Capital employed (start-of-year):				
Fixed	14.00	11.00	8.00	5.00
Stocks	0.50	0.50	0.50	0.50
Total	14.50	11.50	8.50	5.50

$$\text{Average rate of return} \quad \frac{\text{Average profit}}{\text{Average capital employed}} = \frac{£5.85/4}{£40.0/4} = \frac{£1.46}{£10.0} = 14.6\%$$

Although the ARR of 14.6% is above the 10% threshold, it is below the current ROCE of 20%, which would thus be lowered. Accordingly it is possible that the new press should not be purchased.

b) (i) & (ii) can be largely taken from the text. Possibly the main reasons why ARR is used are simplicity, and the use of well-known accounting values, but ARR has numerous technical limitations.

c) Extending credit terms to increase sales may cause: more bad debts; higher costs through discounts and interest; more financially unstable companies to become customers.

Creditworthiness can be assessed in various ways: references from bankers and other suppliers; analysis of financial statements; credit reports from credit assessment agencies; information from others in the industry, and trade associations.

A8. a) *Workings*

Standard rate per machine allowing for idle time at standard rates

$$= \frac{£270}{0.9} = £300 \text{ per hour}$$

Machine variances

Productivity variance

= (standard hours produced – useful machine hours) × standard rate per hour

Sept. = (3,437 – (3,800 – 430)) × £300

= £20,100 (F)

Oct. = (4,061 – (4,200 – 440)) × £300

= 90,300 (F)

Excess idle time variance

= (expected idle time – actual idle time) × standard rate per hour

Sept. = ((3,800 × 10%) – 430) × £300

= £15,000 (A)

Oct. = ((4,200 × 10%) – 440) × £300

= £6,000 (A)

Expenditure variance

= (gross machine hours × standard rate per hour) – actual cost

Sept. = (3,800 × £270) – £1,070,000

= £44,000 (A)

Oct. = (4,200 × £270) – £1,247,000

= £113,000 (A)

b) *Percentage calculations*

	Aug	Sept	Oct	Nov
1. Standard hours of production	3,437	3,437	4,061	3,980
2. Gross machine hours	4,000	3,800	4,200	4,100
3. Expected idle time hours (row 2 × 10%)	400	380	420	410
4. Standard cost of production (row 1 × £300)	1,031,100	1,031,100	1,218,300	1,194,000
5. Expected cost of idle time (row 3 × £300)	120,000	114,000	126,000	123,000
6. Standard cost of machine time (row 2 × £270)	1,080,000	1,026,000	1,134,000	1,107,000
Variances: (from question and answer a))				
7. Productivity (£)	(42,900)	20,100	90,300	99,000
8. Excess idle time (£)	(6,000)	(15,000)	(6,000)	(12,000)
9. Expenditure (£)	(20,000)	(44,000)	(113,000)	(111,000)

Variances: (as percentages)

Productivity (row 7/row 4)	−4.2%	1.9%	7.4%	8.3%
Excess idle time (row 8/row 5)	−5.0%	−13.2%	−4.8%	−9.8%
Expenditure (row 9/row 6)	−1.9%	−4.3%	−10.0%	−10.0%

c) Typical comments on variances:
  - ❒ expenditure has increased;
  - ❒ excess idle time has been adverse in every month;
  - ❒ productivity has improved.

  Possible inter-relationships:
  - ❒ the productivity improvements may be due to the increased expenditure on machine minders; alternatively the improvement may be due to impact of the TQM programme;
  - ❒ the idle time in excess may be due to production planning problems and/or difficulties with materials.

d)

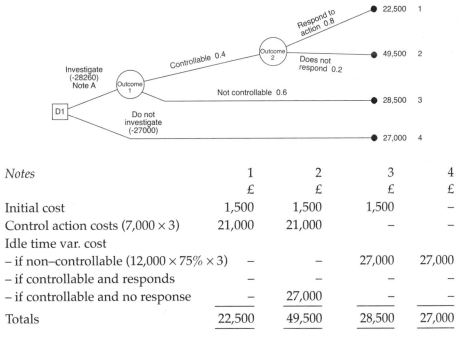

Notes	1	2	3	4
	£	£	£	£
Initial cost	1,500	1,500	1,500	–
Control action costs (7,000 × 3)	21,000	21,000	–	–
Idle time var. cost				
– if non–controllable (12,000 × 75% × 3)	–	–	27,000	27,000
– if controllable and responds	–	–	–	–
– if controllable and no response	–	27,000	–	–
Totals	22,500	49,500	28,500	27,000

Note A

Cost of investigation

Outcome 2 EV $= (0.8 \times 22,500 + 0.2 \times 49,500)$
       $= \mathbf{27,900}$

Outcome 1 EV $= (0.4 \times 27,900 + 0.6 \times 28,500)$
       $= \mathbf{28,260}$

∴. Therefore better not to investigate.

A9.

Contribution of products

	W	B
	£	£
Material £3/kilo	24	42.75
Labour £3.2/hour	69.76	24.00
	93.76	66.75
Selling price	128	95
Contribution	34.24	28.25

Expressing the problem in the standard manner

Maximise: 34.24W + 28.25B

subject to: (process hours)   4W + 3B ≤ 1,200
             (material)   8W + 14.25B ≤ 4,000
             (labour hours)   21.8W + 7.5B ≤ 6,000

Where   W = output Product W
         B = output Product B

The constraints are graphed and the contribution line drawn at a slope of 1.212W:1B (i.e. 34.24:28.25)

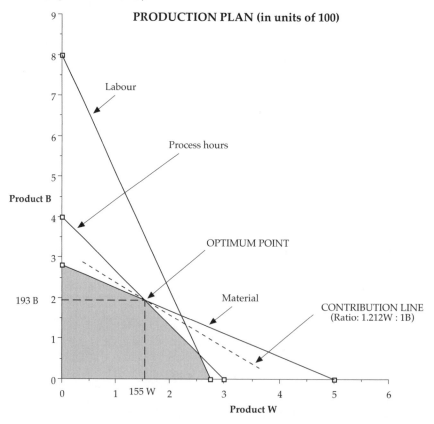

PRODUCTION PLAN (in units of 100)

Figure A9/4

Maximum contribution is

$$155(34.24) + 193(28.25) = 10,759.45$$

b) Limitations of LP model

It is unlikely that the production resources are in fixed supply particularly as sales do not appear to be a restriction.

The data given ignore marketing factors. It is unlikely that all factors will have the linear relationships given.

Assessment and revision section 5

A1. a) Whereas traditional incremental budgeting uses last year's budget as a starting point, zero-base budgeting (ZBB) theoretically starts from zero and makes it more likely that expenditure is justified. Thus, in the energy area the starting point is zero energy costs and increments justified stage by stage. For example, the first stage may be legally determined, i.e. to maintain the statutory workplace temperature. ZBB provides a systematic way of focusing attention on various facets of energy expenditure.

b) Total Quality Management (TQM) is an approach which emphasises such things as:

- ❏ waste elimination;
- ❏ minimising cost;
- ❏ zero defects at lowest cost;
- ❏ elimination of non-value added activities, and so on.

TQM is thus another systematic way of focusing attention on waste elimination, improving productivity. Energy related examples include: alternative ways of producing heat or insulating premises; reduction of movements to save energy; elimination of heat losses etc.

A2. Typical points to be made in the report regarding the management buy-out (MB0) and controls include:

MBO

The budgeting system must be tailored to suit the organisation's structures, operating procedures and so on. Probably a conventional budgeting system for key indicators reporting monthly would be a basis with more detailed analyses carried out every quarter. Ideally there should be separation of costs and budgets for development and special jobs, especially long-term ones. Cost over-runs and cost authorisations must be closely monitored.

Controls at Board level

There should be a clear-cut system of delegation, with a reporting system to match to ensure that Board members have an over-view of operations.

There should be quality, time, volume and other quantitative information as well as for costs and revenues.

Consideration should be given to the establishment of profit and investment centres in the organisation, as well as cost centres. There should be a comprehensive cash budgeting and reporting system on a rolling basis to monitor liquidity.

A3. The main problems of using ROI (or ROCE) can be taken from the text.

The process of determining what performance indicators suit a particular firm includes:

- ❏ gaining a thorough understanding of the way the firm operates, its markets, its suppliers and purchases;
- ❏ analysing operations to discover the critical success factors, e.g. quality, lead times, costs, advertising etc.;
- ❏ considering other firms in the industry, trade associations and so on;
- ❏ producing numerous test indicators and, in conjunction with the managers concerned, assessing their usefulness over several periods.

In summary, whilst there are common indicators that are generally useful, e.g. residual income, ROCE, profit : sales etc. there are specific indicators which are critical for a given firm.

A4. a) Profit centres have control of costs and revenue and can therefore be measured on profit in both absolute terms and as return on sales. Objectives can be set in terms of profit maximisation and growth rather than just costs against budget. Investment centres have, in addition to control of costs and revenue, control of investment. Objectives can therefore be set in terms of return on investment and capital utilisation.

Investment centres are best suited to decentralised organisations where local management are given a high degree of autonomy. They form a structure for providing performance measures relating to revenues, profits and asset utilisation.

b) In order to introduce profit centres, managers must have control of costs and revenue. This may mean the introduction of a system of transfer prices if the cost centres are inter-dependent with the output of one being the input of another.

In addition, investment centre managers must have autonomy in terms of capital investment, and some measure of autonomy in the area of cash and funds management. The apportionment of central charges may also limit the actual degree of control which can be exercised by local management.

- ❏ The main conditions for the successful introduction of profit centres and investment centres are:
- ❏ acceptance by local management of the extra responsibility;
- ❏ acceptance by central management that a reasonable degree of local autonomy is essential otherwise performance evaluation is meaningless;
- ❏ ability to calculate/estimate profit and asset values (investment centres) in a realistic manner for each of the sub units; and
- ❏ some control over their asset decisions by managers of investment centres.

c) With the move away from cost centres to profit centres and investment centres, managers are given more autonomy. They feel that they have more control over their company and thus are motivated to achieve better results. The objectives set by head office are in terms of profit or profit growth in the case of a profit centre and profitability (e.g. Return on Capital Employed (ROCE)) for an investment centre. The actual means of achieving these objectives are largely at the discretion of the manager. In order to maintain control, head office will need to introduce a report system which monitors actual performance against the set objectives, otherwise certain dysfunctional behaviour may become evident e.g. sub-optimal decisions made by local management to increase their performance at the expense of the company as a whole. Also friction may result due to transfer prices, head office charges, asset valuations and central policies.

d) Two performance appraisal measures which can be used for investment centres are ROCE and Residual Income (RI). ROCE is the profit before interest and tax divided by the capital employed to generate the profit. It is a relative measure of performance. RI is the profit before interest and tax minus an imputed capital charge, which is calculated as the capital employed multiplied by the required return on capital. It is an absolute measure of performance and is judged by many to be superior to ROCE. This is due to the possible sub-optimal decisions which may result when the return of a project is above the company's required return, but below the subsidiaries actual return. Both suffer from the same problem of calculating the profit and asset values in a realistic manner.

A5. a) Revised project calculations based on actual results for Year 1 and 2 and budget and plan for Years 3 and 4.

Cash Flows ('000s)

	Actual	Actual	Actual	Budget	Plan	
years	0	1	2	3	4	5
Tooling and Plant	−1,480					
Design	−144					
Research and Development	−595					
Market Research	−161					
Sales		1,025	2,070	3,400	3,000	
Manufacturing Variable Cost		−570	−930	−1,360	−1,380	
Variable Selling Cost		−130	−180	−170	−60	
Increase in Working Capital		−256	−262	−332	100	750
Total Cash Flow	−2.380	69	698	1,538	1,660	750
Present Value Factors @ 15%	1	0.870	0.756	0.658	0.572	0.497
Present Value	−2,380	60	528	1,012	950	373
Net Present Value	543					
Working Capital		256	518	850	750	
Change		256	262	332	−100	−750

Notes:

1. The cash flows are the out-of-pocket costs, and exclude all fixed cost apportionments.

2. Each year the working capital = 90 days debtors, i.e. 3 months, e.g. Year 1, £1,025,000 × $\frac{3}{12}$ ≈ 256,000.

The individual figures are then cumulatively summed.

Comments

Although the project apparently shows losses (presumably based on normal accounting conventions), if the actual figures are combined with the budget and plan then there is a reasonable NPV of £543,000. All in all, provided that expectations for the next 2 year are met, the project seems worthwhile.

b)

		Years			
	0	1	2	3	4
Calculation of ROI					
Sales		1,025	2,070	3,400	3,000
Variable Costs		700	1,110	1,530	1,440
Contribution		325	960	1,870	1,560
Fixed Costs		824	1,117	1,335	1,150
Net Profit		−499	−157	535	410
Contribution to Sales		31.7%	46.4%	55%	52%
Fixed Assets Year End	1,480	1,110	740	370	0
Working Capital Year End		256	518	850	750
Total Assets Year End	1,480	1,366	1,258	1,220	750
Total Assets Beginning Year		1,480	1,366	1,258	1,220
Average Assets		1,423	1,312	1,239	985
ROI		−35.1%	−12.0%	43.2%	41.6%

Note that fixed cost apportionments are included in the ROI calculations.

The higher ROI figures in year 3 and 4 are due to the higher profits and falling asset base. A query which should be raised is the substantial variation in fixed costs over the years.

c) ROI and IRR cannot be compared because they are prepared on quite different principles. See text.

d) Can be taken from the text.

A.6 a) (i) *Workings:*

Total estimated minutes:

Making: $8,000 \times 5.25$ $= 42,000$

Packing: $5,000 \times 6 + 3,000 \times 4 = 42,000$

Absorption rate per product unit (both products):

Making: variable $(£350,000/42,000) \times 5.25$ $= £43.75$

fixed $(£210,000/42,000) \times 5.25$ $= 26.25$

Packing cost per minute:

variable £280,000/42,000 $= £6.666$

fixed £140,000/42,000 $= £3.333$

Unit costs are determined as cost per minute × minutes per unit.

e.g. VG4U variable cost $= £6.666 \times 6$ minutes $= £40$

VG2 fixed cost $= £3.333 \times 4$ minutes $= £13.33$ (split 40% specific 60% company).

Cost statement

		VG4U	VG2
		£	£
Direct material		30	30
variable conversion cost	– Making	43.75	43.75
	– Packing	40.00	26.67
		113.75	100.42
Product specific fixed costs:			
Making		10.50	10.50
Packing		8.00	5.33
Total product specific cost		132.25	116.25
Company fixed cost:			
Making		15.75	15.75
Packing		12.00	8.00
Total cost		160.00	140.00
Selling price		150.00	180.00
Profit (loss)		(10.00)	40.00

(ii) VG4U makes a loss of £10 per unit, but makes a contribution over specific costs of £150 – 132.25= £17.75 towards meeting general company fixed costs. This represents a total contribution of 5,000 × £17.75= £88,750 for the period so that the product should be continued unless there is an alternative use for the capacity which produces more contribution.

b) Workings using ABC

		Total	VG4U	VG2
Product units			5,000	3,000
	(%)	£	£	£
Variable conversion cost:				
Moulding (temperature)	(60)	210,000	140,000	70,000
Trimming (consistency)	(40)	140,000	40,000	100,000
Packing (time)	(70)	196,000	117,600	78,400
Packing material (complexity)	(30)	84,000	21,000	63,000
			318,600	311,400
Variable cost per product unit			63.72	103.80
Product specific fixed costs:				
Moulding (60% × £84,000)		50,400	33,600	16,800
Trimming (40% × £84,000)		33,600	9,600	24,000
Packing (70% × £56,000)		39,200	23,520	15,680
Packing material (30% × £56,000)		16,800	4,200	12,600
Specific fixed cost per product unit			14.18	23.03

Company fixed costs $= £210,000 + 140,000 - 70,920 - 69,080$

$= £210,000$

Overall average cost per unit $= £210,000/8,000$

$= £26.25$

Cost summary

	VG4U	VG2
	£	£
Direct material cost	30.00	30.00
Variable conversion costs	63.72	103.80
	93.72	133.80
Product specific fixed costs	14.18	23.03
	107.90	156.83
Company fixed cost	26.25	26.25
	134.15	183.08
Selling price	150.00	180.00
Profit (loss)	15.85	(3.08)

c) *Comments*

ABC is a different convention and therefore give different costs. It is claimed to be more realistic. All that can be said in this case is that both products have a margin over specific costs (£42.10 and 23.17) and thus contribute to meeting general fixed costs. They should be continued until higher earning products can be found.

d) Comments on target costing can be taken from the text.

A7. a) The proposal to defer payment would have the following effects;

1995 Net assets at year end will be reduced to £4,310,000 and operating profit will be reduced by the late payment penalty of £2,000.

$$\therefore \text{ROCE} = \frac{647,000}{4,310,000} \times 100 = 15.01\%$$

This meets the target so management will adopt this proposal and receive their bonuses.

1996 No effect

The proposal to replace the oldest machine tools would have the following effects:

1995 Net assets at year end increased by £320,000 and no effect upon operating profit.

$$\therefore \text{ROCE} = \frac{649,000}{4,720,000} \times 100 = 13.75\%$$

1996 Extra depreciation charges £40,000 and operation saving £76,000

$$\therefore \text{ROCE for the proposal is } \frac{36,000}{280,000} \times 100 = 12.9\%$$

This will not help to achieve an overall Divisional ROCE of 15%.

The proposal to delay payment incurs expensive finance costs:

$\dfrac{2{,}000}{900{,}000} \times 100 = 2.2\%$ for 12 days (or $\frac{1}{30.4}$) of a year) (approximately 94% p.a.)

In the short term the replacement of all assets will decrease the Divisional ROCE, but by 1998 (because of the declining capital base) it will rise to over 16%. The new equipment has an IRR of approximately 17%, well above the 12% cost of capital, so is worthwhile to the organisation as a whole, yet the project is likely to be rejected because of the short-term reduction of ROCE.

b) The arguments for and against residual income can be taken from the text.

The residual income of the divisions is as follows:

Division		K		D
Profit		649,000		120,000
Interest on assets 12% × £4.4m		528,000	12% × £0.48m	57,600
= Residual income		121,000		62,400

Thus, K has twice the RI of D, although using up many more assets.

c) This part relates to the use of Annuity Depreciation, which can be taken from the text.

A8. a) Most of this answer can be taken from the text. Using planning and operational variances where there has been a genuine change in conditions (i.e. the planning variances), it would be normal for these to be incorporated into the price charged to the transferee division.

b) Market price (which is the theoretical ideal) would be reduced by any savings from internal transfers, e.g. transport, packing costs etc.

c) Where there are shortages LP can be used to indicate the optimum transfers.

A9. a) There are a number of computer software packages which can assist the preparation of budgets. These fall into a number of categories: general accounting packages, forecasting software, spreadsheets, financial modelling software and database software.

❒ *General accounting packages* provide facilities for the collection and analysis of actual accounting transactions. These data can be summarised to provide the basis of forecasts. Some packages provide rudimentary forecasting and budgeting as an integral part.

❒ *Forecasting software* uses past data to predict trends and seasonalities, often by automatically selecting the best formulae to fit the data. Such forecasts have as their basic assumption that the future will be similar to the past. In today's business environment this is not a very valid assumption, so facilities to adjust the forecast must be provided.

❒ *Spreadsheets* can be used to perform many tasks including basic accounting, forecasting and budget preparation. They are flexible and relatively easy to use and have become very popular in recent years particularly with the advent of the personal computer. They lack the power of the more specific packages, but provide sufficient facilities for many businesses.

❏ *Financial modelling software* provides facilities for building complex models of the business. They are more difficult to operate than spreadsheets, but provide as standard many of the more complex operations. Reporting can also be more sophisticated than from simple spreadsheets.

❏ *Database software* enables rapid retrieval and cross-referencing of the records of the organisation.

b) Effective budgeting is concerned with the setting of realistic standards for each area within the business. Such realistic standards cannot just be based upon previous years' data, nor can setting such standards be seen as a mathematical exercise. In order for the budget to be effective, it must be based upon the present and future business environment and the company's response to the opportunities and threats which this presents. Computers can provide tools which assist managers in this process, but cannot do the decision making for them. Alternative responses must be considered and the decisions made incorporated into the budget. Computer modelling can assist in this by quickly evaluating alternative courses of action, but the choice is left to managers.

c) The availability of computers and sophisticated software has made the collection and analysis of data and the modelling of alternative courses of action a more routine, almost automatic, process, but effective budgeting involves management in making choices between these alternatives, not just in the mindless acceptance of computer forecasts. The computer is a very powerful management tool, but like all tools it must be used appropriately and with skill.

Tables

Table A

Present value factors. Present value of £1 $(1 + r)^{-n}$

Periods (n)	Interest rates (r)%								
	1%	2%	4%	6%	8%	10%	12%	14%	15%
1	0.990	0.980	0.962	0.943	0.926	0.909	0.893	0.877	0.870
2	0.980	0.961	0.925	0.890	0.857	0.826	0.797	0.769	0.756
3	0.971	0.942	0.889	0.840	0.794	0.751	0.712	0.675	0.658
4	0.961	0.924	0.855	0.792	0.735	0.683	0.636	0.592	0.572
5	0.951	0.906	0.822	0.747	0.681	0.621	0.567	0.519	0.497
6	0.942	0.888	0.790	0.705	0.630	0.564	0.507	0.456	0.432
7	0.933	0.871	0.760	0.665	0.583	0.513	0.452	0.400	0.376
8	0.923	0.853	0.731	0.627	0.540	0.467	0.404	0.351	0.327
9	0.914	0.837	0.703	0.592	0.500	0.424	0.361	0.308	0.284
10	0.905	0.820	0.676	0.558	0.463	0.386	0.322	0.270	0.247
11	0.896	0.804	0.650	0.527	0.429	0.350	0.287	0.237	0.215
12	0.887	0.788	0.625	0.497	0.397	0.319	0.257	0.208	0.187
13	0.879	0.773	0.601	0.469	0.368	0.290	0.229	0.182	0.163
14	0.870	0.758	0.577	0.442	0.340	0.263	0.205	0.160	0.141
15	0.861	0.743	0.555	0.417	0.315	0.239	0.183	0.140	0.123
16	0.853	0.728	0.534	0.394	0.292	0.218	0.163	0.123	0.107
17	0.855	0.714	0.513	0.371	0.270	0.198	0.146	0.108	0.093
18	0.836	0.700	0.494	0.350	0.250	0.180	0.130	0.095	0.081
19	0.828	0.686	0.475	0.331	0.232	0.164	0.116	0.083	0.070
20	0.820	0.675	0.456	0.312	0.215	0.149	0.104	0.073	0.061
21	0.811	0.660	0.439	0.294	0.199	0.135	0.093	0.064	0.053
22	0.803	0.647	0.422	0.278	0.184	0.123	0.083	0.056	0.046
23	0.795	0.634	0.406	0.262	0.170	0.112	0.074	0.049	0.040
24	0.788	0.622	0.390	0.247	0.158	0.102	0.066	0.043	0.035
25	0.780	0.610	0.375	0.233	0.146	0.092	0.059	0.038	0.030

Periods (n)	Interest rates (r)%								
	16%	18%	20%	22%	24%	25%	26%	28%	30%
1	0.862	0.847	0.833	0.820	0.806	0.800	0.794	0.781	0.769
2	0.743	0.718	0.694	0.672	0.650	0.640	0.630	0.610	0.592
3	0.641	0.609	0.579	0.551	0.524	0.512	0.500	0.477	0.455
4	0.552	0.516	0.482	0.451	0.423	0.410	0.397	0.373	0.350
5	0.476	0.437	0.402	0.370	0.341	0.328	0.315	0.291	0.269
6	0.410	0.370	0.335	0.303	0.275	0.262	0.250	0.227	0.207
7	0.354	0.314	0.279	0.249	0.222	0.210	0.198	0.178	0.159
8	0.305	0.266	0.233	0.204	0.179	0.168	0.157	0.139	0.123
9	0.263	0.225	0.194	0.167	0.144	0.134	0.125	0.108	0.094
10	0.227	0.191	0.162	0.137	0.116	0.107	0.099	0.085	0.075
11	0.195	0.162	0.135	0.112	0.094	0.086	0.079	0.066	0.056
12	0.168	0.137	0.112	0.192	0.076	0.069	0.062	0.052	0.043
13	0.145	0.116	0.093	0.075	0.061	0.055	0.050	0.040	0.033
14	0.125	0.099	0.178	0.062	0.049	0.044	0.039	0.032	0.025
15	0.108	0.084	0.065	0.051	0.040	0.035	0.031	0.025	0.020
16	0.093	0.071	0.054	0.042	0.032	0.028	0.025	0.019	0.015
17	0.080	0.060	0.045	0.034	0.026	0.023	0.020	0.015	0.012
18	0.069	0.051	0.038	0.028	0.021	0.018	0.016	0.012	0.009
19	0.060	0.043	0.031	0.023	0.017	0.014	0.012	0.009	0.007
20	0.051	0.037	0.026	0.019	0.014	0.012	0.010	0.007	0.005
21	0.044	0.031	0.022	0.015	0.011	0.009	0.008	0.006	0.004
22	0.038	0.026	0.018	0.013	0.009	0.007	0.006	0.004	0.003
23	0.033	0.022	0.015	0.010	0.007	0.006	0.005	0.003	0.002
24	0.028	0.019	0.011	0.008	0.006	0.005	0.004	0.003	0.002
25	0.024	0.016	0.010	0.007	0.005	0.004	0.003	0.002	0.001

Table B

Present value annuity factors. Present value of £1 received annually for n years $\dfrac{1-(1+r)^{-n}}{r}$

Periods	Interest rates (r) %								
(n)	1%	2%	4%	6%	8%	10%	12%	14%	15%
1	0.990	0.980	0.962	0.943	0.926	0.909	0.893	0.877	0.870
2	1.970	1.942	1.886	1.833	1.783	1.736	1.690	1.647	1.626
3	2.941	2.884	2.775	2.675	2.577	2.487	2.402	2.322	2.283
4	3.902	3.808	3.610	3.465	3.312	3.170	3.037	2.914	2.855
5	4.853	4.713	4.452	4.212	3.996	3.791	3.605	3.433	3.352
6	5.795	5.601	5.242	4.917	4.623	4.355	4.111	3.889	3.784
7	6.728	6.472	6.002	5.582	5.206	4.868	4.564	4.288	4.160
8	7.652	7.325	6.733	6.210	5.747	5.335	4.968	4.639	4.487
9	8.566	8.162	7.435	6.802	6.247	5.759	5.328	4.946	4.772
10	9.471	8.983	8.111	7.360	6.710	6.145	5.650	5.216	5.019
11	10.368	9.787	8.760	7.887	7.139	6.495	5.988	5.453	5.234
12	11.255	10.575	9.385	8.384	7.536	6.814	6.194	5.660	5.421
13	12.114	11.343	9.986	8.853	7.904	7.103	6.424	5.842	5.583
14	13.004	12.106	10.563	9.295	8.244	7.367	6.628	6.002	5.724
15	13 865	12.849	11.118	9.712	8.559	7.606	6.811	6.142	5.847
16	14.718	13.578	11.652	10.106	8.851	7.824	6.974	6.265	5.954
17	15.562	14.292	12.166	10.477	9.122	8.022	7.120	6.373	6.047
18	16.328	14.992	12.659	10.828	9.372	8.201	7.250	6.467	6.128
19	17.226	15.678	13.134	11.158	9.604	8.365	7.366	6.550	6.198
20	18.046	16.351	13.590	11.470	9.818	8.514	7.469	6.623	6.259
21	18.857	17.011	14.029	11.764	10.017	8.649	7.562	6.687	6.312
22	19.660	17.658	14.451	12.042	10.201	8.772	7.645	6.743	6.369
23	20.456	18.292	14.857	12.303	10.371	8.883	7.718	6.792	6.399
24	21.243	18.914	15.247	12.550	10.529	8.985	7.784	6.815	6.434
25	22.023	19.523	15.622	12.783	10.675	9.077	7.843	6.873	6.464

Periods	Interest rates (r) %								
(n)	16%	18%	20%	22%	24%	25%	26%	28%	30%
1	0.862	0.847	0.833	0.820	0.806	0.800	0.794	0.781	0.769
2	1.605	1.566	1.528	1.492	1.457	1.440	1.424	1.392	1.361
3	2.246	2.174	2.106	2.042	1.981	1.952	1.923	1.868	1.816
4	2.798	2.690	2.589	2.494	2.404	2.362	2.320	2.241	2.166
5	3.274	3.127	2.991	2.864	2.745	2.689	2.635	2.532	2.436
6	3.685	3.498	3.326	3.167	3.020	2.951	2.885	2.759	2.643
7	4.039	3.812	3.605	3.416	3.242	3.161	3.083	2.937	2.802
8	4.344	4.078	3.837	3.619	3.421	3.329	3.421	3.076	2.925
9	4.607	4.303	4.031	3.786	3.566	3.463	3.366	3.184	3.019
10	4.833	4.949	4.192	3.923	3.682	3.571	3.465	3.269	3.092
11	5.029	4.636	4.327	4.035	3.766	3.656	3.544	3.335	3.147
12	5.197	4.793	4.439	4.127	3.851	3.725	3.606	3.387	3.190
13	5.342	4.910	4.533	4.203	3.912	3.780	3.656	3.427	3.223
14	5.468	5.008	4.611	4.265	3.961	3.824	3.965	3.459	3.249
15	5.575	5.092	4.675	4.315	4.001	3.859	3.726	3.483	3.268
16	5.669	5.162	4.730	4.357	4.033	3.887	3.751	3.503	3.283
17	5.749	5.222	4.775	4.391	4.059	3.910	3.771	3.518	3.295
18	5.818	5.273	4.812	4.419	4.080	3.928	3.786	3.529	3.304
19	5.877	5.316	4.844	4.442	4.097	3.942	3.799	3.539	3.311
20	5.929	5.353	4.870	4.460	4.110	3.954	3.808	3.546	3.316
21	5.973	5.384	4.891	4.476	4.121	3.963	3.816	3.551	3.320
22	6.011	5.410	4.909	4.488	4.130	3.970	3.822	3.556	3.323
23	6.044	5.432	4.925	4.499	4.137	3.976	3.827	3.559	3.325
24	6.073	5.451	4.937	4.507	4.143	3.981	3.831	3.562	3.327
25	6.097	5.467	4.948	4.514	4.147	3.985	3.834	3.564	3.329

Table C *

Areas under the Standard Normal curve from 0 to Z

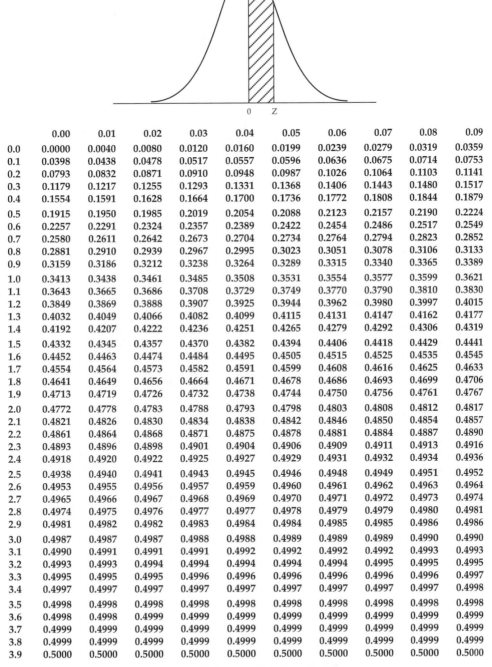

	0.00	0.01	0.02	0.03	0.04	0.05	0.06	0.07	0.08	0.09
0.0	0.0000	0.0040	0.0080	0.0120	0.0160	0.0199	0.0239	0.0279	0.0319	0.0359
0.1	0.0398	0.0438	0.0478	0.0517	0.0557	0.0596	0.0636	0.0675	0.0714	0.0753
0.2	0.0793	0.0832	0.0871	0.0910	0.0948	0.0987	0.1026	0.1064	0.1103	0.1141
0.3	0.1179	0.1217	0.1255	0.1293	0.1331	0.1368	0.1406	0.1443	0.1480	0.1517
0.4	0.1554	0.1591	0.1628	0.1664	0.1700	0.1736	0.1772	0.1808	0.1844	0.1879
0.5	0.1915	0.1950	0.1985	0.2019	0.2054	0.2088	0.2123	0.2157	0.2190	0.2224
0.6	0.2257	0.2291	0.2324	0.2357	0.2389	0.2422	0.2454	0.2486	0.2517	0.2549
0.7	0.2580	0.2611	0.2642	0.2673	0.2704	0.2734	0.2764	0.2794	0.2823	0.2852
0.8	0.2881	0.2910	0.2939	0.2967	0.2995	0.3023	0.3051	0.3078	0.3106	0.3133
0.9	0.3159	0.3186	0.3212	0.3238	0.3264	0.3289	0.3315	0.3340	0.3365	0.3389
1.0	0.3413	0.3438	0.3461	0.3485	0.3508	0.3531	0.3554	0.3577	0.3599	0.3621
1.1	0.3643	0.3665	0.3686	0.3708	0.3729	0.3749	0.3770	0.3790	0.3810	0.3830
1.2	0.3849	0.3869	0.3888	0.3907	0.3925	0.3944	0.3962	0.3980	0.3997	0.4015
1.3	0.4032	0.4049	0.4066	0.4082	0.4099	0.4115	0.4131	0.4147	0.4162	0.4177
1.4	0.4192	0.4207	0.4222	0.4236	0.4251	0.4265	0.4279	0.4292	0.4306	0.4319
1.5	0.4332	0.4345	0.4357	0.4370	0.4382	0.4394	0.4406	0.4418	0.4429	0.4441
1.6	0.4452	0.4463	0.4474	0.4484	0.4495	0.4505	0.4515	0.4525	0.4535	0.4545
1.7	0.4554	0.4564	0.4573	0.4582	0.4591	0.4599	0.4608	0.4616	0.4625	0.4633
1.8	0.4641	0.4649	0.4656	0.4664	0.4671	0.4678	0.4686	0.4693	0.4699	0.4706
1.9	0.4713	0.4719	0.4726	0.4732	0.4738	0.4744	0.4750	0.4756	0.4761	0.4767
2.0	0.4772	0.4778	0.4783	0.4788	0.4793	0.4798	0.4803	0.4808	0.4812	0.4817
2.1	0.4821	0.4826	0.4830	0.4834	0.4838	0.4842	0.4846	0.4850	0.4854	0.4857
2.2	0.4861	0.4864	0.4868	0.4871	0.4875	0.4878	0.4881	0.4884	0.4887	0.4890
2.3	0.4893	0.4896	0.4898	0.4901	0.4904	0.4906	0.4909	0.4911	0.4913	0.4916
2.4	0.4918	0.4920	0.4922	0.4925	0.4927	0.4929	0.4931	0.4932	0.4934	0.4936
2.5	0.4938	0.4940	0.4941	0.4943	0.4945	0.4946	0.4948	0.4949	0.4951	0.4952
2.6	0.4953	0.4955	0.4956	0.4957	0.4959	0.4960	0.4961	0.4962	0.4963	0.4964
2.7	0.4965	0.4966	0.4967	0.4968	0.4969	0.4970	0.4971	0.4972	0.4973	0.4974
2.8	0.4974	0.4975	0.4976	0.4977	0.4977	0.4978	0.4979	0.4979	0.4980	0.4981
2.9	0.4981	0.4982	0.4982	0.4983	0.4984	0.4984	0.4985	0.4985	0.4986	0.4986
3.0	0.4987	0.4987	0.4987	0.4988	0.4988	0.4989	0.4989	0.4989	0.4990	0.4990
3.1	0.4990	0.4991	0.4991	0.4991	0.4992	0.4992	0.4992	0.4992	0.4993	0.4993
3.2	0.4993	0.4993	0.4994	0.4994	0.4994	0.4994	0.4994	0.4995	0.4995	0.4995
3.3	0.4995	0.4995	0.4995	0.4996	0.4996	0.4996	0.4996	0.4996	0.4996	0.4997
3.4	0.4997	0.4997	0.4997	0.4997	0.4997	0.4997	0.4997	0.4997	0.4997	0.4998
3.5	0.4998	0.4998	0.4998	0.4998	0.4998	0.4998	0.4998	0.4998	0.4998	0.4998
3.6	0.4998	0.4998	0.4999	0.4999	0.4999	0.4999	0.4999	0.4999	0.4999	0.4999
3.7	0.4999	0.4999	0.4999	0.4999	0.4999	0.4999	0.4999	0.4999	0.4999	0.4999
3.8	0.4999	0.4999	0.4999	0.4999	0.4999	0.4999	0.4999	0.4999	0.4999	0.4999
3.9	0.5000	0.5000	0.5000	0.5000	0.5000	0.5000	0.5000	0.5000	0.5000	0.5000

* From Statistics by SPIEGEL, Copyright 1972 McGraw-Hill Publishing Co. Ltd
Used with kind permission of McGraw-Hill Book Company

Table D

Compound interest. Table shows value of £1 at compound interest $(1+r)^n$

Years (n)	Interest rates (r) %									
	1	2	3	4	5	6	7	8	9	10
1	1.010	1.020	1.030	1.040	1.050	1.060	1.070	1.080	1.090	1.100
2	1.020	1.040	1.061	1.082	1.103	1.124	1.145	1.166	1.188	1.210
3	1.030	1.061	1.093	1.125	1.158	1.191	1.225	1.260	1.295	1.331
4	1.041	1.082	1.126	1.170	1.216	1.262	1.311	1.360	1.412	1.464
5	1.051	1.104	1.159	1.217	1.276	1.338	1.403	1.469	1.539	1.611
6	1.062	1.126	1.194	1.265	1.340	1.419	1.501	1.587	1.677	1.772
7	1.072	1.149	1.230	1.316	1.407	1.504	1.606	1.714	1.828	1.949
8	1.083	1.172	1.267	1.369	1.477	1.594	1.718	1.851	1.993	2.144
9	1.094	1.195	1.305	1.423	1.551	1.689	1.838	1.999	2.172	2.358
10	1.105	1.219	1.344	1.480	1.629	1.791	1.967	2.159	2.367	2.594
11	1.116	1.243	1.384	1.539	1.710	1.898	2.105	2.332	2.580	2.853
12	1.127	1.268	1.426	1.601	1.796	2.012	2.252	2.518	2.813	3.138
13	1.138	1.294	1.469	1.665	1.886	2.133	2.410	2.720	3.066	3.452
14	1.149	1.319	1.513	1.732	1.980	2.261	2.579	2.937	3.342	3.797
15	1.161	1.346	1.558	1.801	2.079	2.397	2.759	3.172	3.642	4.177
20	1.220	1.486	1.806	2.191	2.653	3.207	3.870	4.661	5.604	6.727
25	1.282	1.641	2.094	2.666	3.386	4.292	5.427	6.848	8.623	10.835

Years (n)	Interest rates (r) %										
	11	12	13	14	15	16	17	18	19	20	25	30
1	1.110	1.120	1.130	1.140	1.150	1.160	1.170	1.180	1.190	1.200	1.250	1.300
2	1.232	1.254	1.277	1.300	1.323	1.346	1.369	1.392	1.416	1.440	1.563	1.690
3	1.368	1.405	1.443	1.482	1.521	1.561	1.602	1.643	1.685	1.728	1.953	2.197
4	1.518	1.574	1.630	1.689	1.749	1.811	1.874	1.939	2.005	2.074	2.441	2.856
5	1.685	1.762	1.842	1.925	2.011	2.100	2.192	2.288	2.386	2.488	3.052	3.713
6	1.870	1.974	2.082	2.195	2.313	2.436	2.565	2.700	2.840	2.986	3.815	4.827
7	2.076	2.211	2.353	2.502	2.660	2.826	3.001	3.185	3.379	3.583	4.768	6.275
8	2.305	2.476	2.658	2.853	3.059	3.278	3.511	3.759	4.021	4.300	5.960	8.157
9	2.558	2.773	3.004	3.252	3.518	3.803	4.108	4.435	4.785	5.160	7.451	10.604
10	2.839	3.106	3.395	3.707	4.046	4.411	4.807	5.234	5.695	6.192	9.313	13.786
11	3.152	3.479	3.836	4.226	4.652	5.117	5.624	6.176	6.777	7.430	11.642	17.922
12	3.498	3.896	4.335	4.818	5.350	5.936	6.580	7.288	8.064	8.916	14.552	23.298
13	3.883	4.363	4.898	5.492	6.153	6.886	7.699	8.599	9.596	10.699	18.190	30.288
14	4.310	4.887	5.535	6.261	7.076	7.988	9.007	10.147	11.420	12.839	22.737	39.374
15	4.785	5.474	6.254	7.138	8.137	9.266	10.539	11.974	13.590	15.407	28.422	51.186
20	8.062	9.646	11.523	13.743	16.367	19.461	23.106	27.393	32.429	38.338	86.736	190.050
25	13.585	17.000	21.231	26.462	32.919	40.874	50.658	62.669	77.388	95.396	264.698	705.641

Appendix 1

Management Accounting Case Studies

by

G.S. Clinton, M.Soc.Sc., F.C.M.A., A.C.I.S., M.B.I.M.
University of Aberystwyth

Case Study 1

Country Brews Ltd

A comprehensive variance accounting case covering sales and cost variances including mixture and yield, together with an introduction to standard marginal costing. The questions should allow for practise in variance calculations in the less familiar setting of a family brewery.

Country Brews Ltd is based in Shropshire at Diddlebury-in-Corvedale. There has been a tradition of beermaking on a small scale in this part of Shropshire for generations and, until recently, as much difference between one beer and another in the dale as between grape wines in France. One explanation for quality of the beer may well lie in the unpolluted waters of the rivers Corve and Onny – the two left bank tributaries of the Teme which, in analysis, shows a high proportion of gypsum, or calcium sulphate. Corvedale itself is so near the industrial region of Coalbrookdale and yet it has left the dale itself undisturbed. Indeed it is so different from the rest of the country as to be almost a 'country' conserving traditions which are more typical of old Shropshire. Long before the advent of mass production brewing with the branded name and the tied house, Corvedale boasted ales and beers as glorious as any in the land.

The difficult part of making beer is in the malting of the barley. This can be very tricky and requires space, time and a lot of experience as well as carefully regulated heat on kilns and floors. Bill Bowen had a talent amounting to genius for brewing and its attendant processes and it was he who formed Country Brews Ltd late in the 1930s. He knew that the secret lay with having the best barley, fully ripe and flowery, indicating its low nitrogen content. Local farmers were encouraged to grow the right barley for the malting which old Bill still personally supervises, although responsibility for the company's affairs is now in the hands of Bill's two sons, Grant and Mark.

The father had held strong views on the size of his company, maintaining its employee strength and turnover at roughly the same levels for 20 years. It was his view that increased organisation size was the basis of many of the ills in present manufacturing society. He had felt that the inevitable impersonality, the fragmentation of jobs and most important of all, the alienation of lower level members of the organisation must lead to a deterioration in morale and employee behaviour.

Grant Bowen is chiefly concerned with administration and overall financial control and under his guidance the company has grown steadily, its sales per week now reaching some 2,000 crates of Country Brew and distributed as far away as the Welsh coast towns. Growth has not been restricted to that of the orthodox ale. Much has been done to rekindle demand for the specialist season drinks which were so renowned a century ago in Dickens's day. There was now an established call for Mulled Ale (at Christmas), Midsummer Ale and harvest brew. One most fearsome drink, 'Cock Brew' based upon a centuries-old recipe, has been reintroduced with quite remarkable interest. The normal procedure with these specialists drinks is to take half a mashing of Country Brew and reprocess by adding various ingredients. The company has been able to utilise the byproducts of the brewing process: brewers' grain is distributed locally to farmers (at £10 per wet tonne) and various yeast products, manufactured in conjunction with a firm at Ludlow, are distributed nationally through health shops.

Growth has brought many financial problems. There has been a reluctance to modernise the production process, as much of the increased demand has been due to the individual nature of the beer as compared to the conventional watery ales which can be obtained from any town brewery. In some ways growth has been regretted and there are dangers that, even though the company has increasingly provided much needed local employment, its present size may dictate its joining a group of companies, with consequential loss of identity and the inevitable souring of employee relations. In an effort to obtain closer financial control Grant has installed a standard costing system over the mashing and bottling operations to complement the budgetary system already operating.

In the mashing process, the enzyme cytase dissolves the protective cellulose coating of the barley and thus the starch is liquefied and converted. This enzyme activity can be extremely sensitive to temperature changes, and so any variation in the conditions will affect the wort and so the resultant beer. The ingredients for the mashing process are malt, sugar and hops and anticipated prices over the next six months are:

Malt £300 per tonne

Sugar £250 per tonne

Hops £50 per 50 kilos

The relatively lower price to be paid for hops compared with previous periods arises out of the purchase of a hop farm at Tenbury Wells and the growing of Hallertauer hops (of Bavarian origin) which should improve the head retention of the beer.

The standard proportions for 450 litres of Country Brew are:

Malt 70 kilos

Sugar 36 kilos

Hops 2 kilos

The standard quantity for one mashing is 4,500 litres (1,000 gallons). Assume for the purpose of this case study that there is no loss in this process.

It can be seen that the proportion of sugar is higher than many conventional beers and this increased content results in a stronger drink perhaps more similar to Barley Wine. Country Brew is indeed an acquired taste but once acquired other beer seems pale and insipid.

The labour time is largely dictated by the mashing process and some shift work is necessary to maintain the coverage. From experience an attainable high performance standard would be a total of 200 labour hours per mashing for all the workers concerned. The current wage rate for all production employees is £2 per hour.

Country brews Ltd recovers production and bottling overhead on the basis of mashings. The budget for the next six-month period (April to September) totals £19,200 and has been analysed as shown below. The normal production capacity suggests that 120 mashings will be achieved in this six-month period (ie six standard months of four weeks, each week producing two mashings of brew).

Production and bottling overhead

	Variable	Fixed	Total
Labour overhead (holiday pay, NHI employer contributions etc.)	£400	£3,400	£3,800
Power, lighting and heating	1,800	800	2,600
Depreciation of equipment	1,400	1,400	
Consumable supplies including additives	6,100	1,100	7,200
Clerical and other wages	1,700	1,700	
Repairs and maintenance	700	1,800	2,500
	£9,000	£10,200	£19,200

After the beer has fermented out it is bottled. Every mashing of production is expected to fill 8,000 bottles with the wort. The anticipated labour cost is £0.01 per bottle and each of the bottles is £0.03 to buy.

Administration, selling and distribution costs budgeted for the six months are absorbed on a crate basis, each crate containing 20 bottles.

Administration, selling and distribution costs budgets April to September

	Variable	Fixed	Total
Administration		£18,000	£18,000
Selling and distribution	12,000	18,000	30,000
	£12,000	£36,000	£48,000

Shown in Figure 1 is a blank standard cost card for Country Brew. The agreed selling price that would hold throughout the six-month period was £4.50 per crate.

The usual method of analysing overhead items between fixed and variable is by scattergraph. For example a study of a particular distribution expense (after adjustments for price changes) over recent years disclosed:

Year	No. of crates delivered	Distribution expense
1 (last year)	48,000	£8,000
2	42,000	7,300
3	38,000	7,000
4	30,000	6,200
5	28,000	6,100
6	24,000	5,700
7	20,000	5,150

Per mashing

Ingredients

	Quantity	Price (£)		Total(£)
Malt	....	kilos at...........................	=	
Sugar	....	kilos at...........................	=	
Hops	....	kilos at...........................	=	

Labour

	Quantity	*Rate*	
	....	hours at £	=

Production overhead

      Variable

      Fixed

                 Standard cost per mashing

Per crate   £

      Mashing cost

      Bottle cost

      Bottling cost

      Administration, selling and distribution overhead

            Variable

            Fixed

                 Standard cost per crate

                 Standard cost per bottle

Figure 1 Standard cost card for Country Brew

22 mashings produced and all crates sold		£39,600
Ingredients		
15,500	kilos of malt	4,960
8,000	kilos of sugar	1,840
450	kilos of hops	450
Mashing labour		
4,400 hours		8,888
Production overhead		
Variable		1,600
Fixed		1,850
Bottle costs		5,000
Bottling labour costs		2,000
Administration, selling, distribution overhead		
Variable		2,200
Fixed		6,200

Figure 2 Actual results for the month of May

33	kilos of honey at £1 per kilo
5	kilos of horehound at £0.20 per kilo
6	kilos of gentian root at £2.30 per kilo
6	kilos of other herbs at £1.50 per kilo

The resultant 150 litres of wort are added to half a mashing of Country Brew at standard cost.

Figure 3 Standard data for Harvest Brew

35	kilos of honey at £1.20 per kilo
5	kilos of horehound at £1.10 per kilo
6	kilos of gentian at £2.50 per kilo
4	kilos of other herbs at £1.50 per kilo

This resulted in 150 litres of wort being added to 2,250 litres of Country Brew. The quantity of Harvest Brew which remained after fining was 2,050 litres.

Figure 4 Actual data for Harvest Brew (July)

The production and sale of Country Brew proceeded very much as planned. Actual results were compared monthly with the budgets and standards and and the resultant variances investigated. Shown in Figure 2 are the actual results for the month of May which were subject to close examination.

In this particular month, as an experiment, variances were calculated not only in the conventional way but also on a marginal basis. One of the reasons for the experiment was the inadequate information which appears to be provided by the fixed overhead variances themselves. It was resolved that in some later month an attempt might be made to analyse the conventional volume variance between capacity and productivity.

In anticipation of the seasonal demand for Harvest Brew, half a mashing of Country Brew was reprocessed during the month of July. This reprocessing is achieved through two stages: first, the additional ingredients are fused to produce 150 litres of wort: second the wort is added to half a mashing of Country Brew. Due to the nature of the ingredients, Harvest Brew requires considerable gelatine fining and consequently an allowance is made for a 10 per cent loss from the total quantity. The standard proportions of ingredients together with the standard prices are shown in Figure 3 and the actual figures incurred in Figure 4.

What do you think?

You are asked to give some thought to the following questions and perhaps prepare some of the figures and statements concerned:

1. Prepare a scattergraph and identify the approximate fixed element which lies in the distribution expense as described.

2. Complete the blank standard cost card (Figure 1).

3. a) Prepare a detailed budget for the month of May.
    b) Calculate the actual profit for the month utilising the data given in Figure 2.
    c) Calculate the following variances:
        Sales margin price variance;
        Sales margin quantity variance;
        Mashing ingredients price variance;
        Mashing usage variance;
        Mashing labour rate variance;
        Mashing labour efficiency variance;
        Mashing variable overhead expenditure variance;
        Mashing fixed overhead expenditure variance;
        Mashing fixed overhead volume variance;
        Bottle cost variance; Bottling labour cost variance;
        Admin/selling overhead variable expenditure variance;
        Admin/selling overhead fixed expenditure variance;
        Admin/selling overhead fixed volume variance.
    d) Prepare a statement that reconciles, through the variances calculated in (c), the budgeted with the actual profit.

4. Name and calculate any *new* or *different* variances that will have arisen in May when the experimental standard marginal cost system was tried.

5. What do you understand by volume capacity and volume productivity variances and what data would be necessary for their calculation?

6. In relation to the production of Harvest Brew in July, calculate:
   a) Total variance
   b) Price variance
   c) Mixture variance
   d) Yield variance.

Case Study 2

Haltwhistle Manufacturers Ltd

All businesses require, from time to time, to make decisions about long-term capital expenditure. This case offers the opportunity to study investment appraisal and make judgements about relevant costs. It will be seen how deceptive quite simple figures can prove when presented in different ways and how important interest rates are for investment decision. The aspects of taxation introduced are comparatively simple.

Haltwhistle Manufacturers Ltd is a member of the Dalting group of companies whose members are largely based in the northern counties of England. The group is organised on entirely autonomous lines with complete freedom of management decision-making permitted even as to capital-investment schemes, although company overall performance is evaluated carefully. Profitability is considered the key to non-interference in the long term.

It is understandable in this environment that the general manager, John Pelenski, should look carefully at all new investment schemes. This was very much the situation in 1989 when the latest proposal involved an entirely new product called Aluflex which provided an alternative to the conventional ceiling work of prestige buildings. Produced in aluminium strip sections in a variety of metal dye finishes, the whole ceiling could be assembled in hours rather than the weeks required for traditional ceiling methods. The ability to introduce flexures and curvatures was very much to the modern architectural style and taste.

Aluflex had proved extremely successful in American and Canada and it was, in fact, a Canadian machine capable of forming and processing 500,000 metres of Aluflex each year which was now offered to Haltwhistle for £360,000. Technology was likely to be subject to some change and therefore a four-year life was envisaged for the machine with little salvage value. Contribution per metre from Aluflex was budgeted at £0.39 and this figure subsequently proved accurate.

One attraction and real benefit of the scheme was that Aluflex would replace lost contributions of declining products. Applying the apportionment method established as equitable for the other company products, it could fairly receive £125,000 of the existing fixed administrative overhead. Figures were prepared for Pelenski which demonstrated clearly that it was a profitable project and the order was duly placed with the Canadian supplier.

Inevitably some delay occurred before the installation of the machine. Haltwhistle was grateful for these months to solve machining manning problems and settle arrangements with Alston Ltd (another member of the Dalting group) for installation work on the forthcoming contracts.

At the time, many of the problems appeared insurmountable. Union representatives were reluctant to accept the new machine unless wage rates were made comparable with non-automatic machine process. Eventually a compromise was reached but this had repercussions on costs and a renegotiation of prices was necessary. Alston suffered from these cost changes and its margin for fixing on some contracts was reduced. The

Alston management was openly critical of the way in which the whole scheme had been handled.

In January 1990 just three hours after production of Aluflex had commenced, the managing director of Alston telephoned Pelenski with the news that a new German machine was immediately available which was superior in every respect ... he was driving over that day to help in the reappraisal of the scheme. Pelenski commented to his accountant that he was certain that Alstons had been aware of this machine for some months and this latest development was aimed at embarrassing the Haltwhistle management, perhaps leading to censure and criticism from the group board.

As the day progressed the following information was established regarding the German machine. Its purchase price would be £440,000 and it would have the effect of reducing operating costs by £150,000 per annum. Demand for Aluflex in the foreseeable future was hardly likely to exceed the 500,000 metre output and no case could be made for having two machines.

Other crucial facts emerged. The Canadian machine, although virtually unused, could only be resold for £50,000 ... any new machine sales would be of the German variety! Another disquieting observation was that if the old machine were sold at a low figure to a competitor, this might lead to unfavourable competition. Also the new machine, being more efficient, would consume fewer hours in operation, leading to a smaller absorption of company overhead.

Haltwhistle's accountant prepared the two statements shown below for the meeting held late that day.

1 Profit/loss budget for 1990

	Canadian Machine £000)	German Machine (£000)
Sales	1,000	1,000
Additional operating costs	805	655
Depreciation	90	110
Loss on sale of machinery		* 310
	895	1,075
Profit(Loss)	105	(75)

* Purchase of the Canadian machine for £360,000 less possible sale for £50,000

2 Profit/loss budget over four years (if the change were made)

	£
Cost of German machine	440,000
Loss on sale of Canadian machine	310,000
Total cost	750,000
Savings (four years at £150,000 per annum)	600,000
Loss on replacement	150,000

It was with immense relief to Haltwhistle's management that the figures demonstrated that there should be no change. Alston's managing director, too, was pacified – he had made his point and 'they' well understood his views on the handling of the project and the blunder in purchasing the Canadian machine. He could well see that the £105,000 p.a. profit in the first statement was very satisfactory ... Not many days passed before be broached the subject of profit margins on installation with Pelenski!

In January 1990 the question of replacement arose again. The original Canadian machine now required an overhaul/modification costing £50,000 to continue working efficiently. The modification would assure a further working life of four years until 1997. The machine by this date had been written down in the Haltwhistle books to £90,000.

Surely this was the opportunity to replace with the more efficient German machine, whose present purchase price was £475,000? Changes had taken place over the years and the extra contribution which might confidently be expected was £145,000 per annum. The supplier was prepared to take the old machine off their hands for £25,000. Pelenski reasoned that the extra contribution in the first year alone would cover any loss on sale.

Whichever scheme were pursued it would be necessary for Haltwhistle to borrow money for finance purposes. Interest rates had varied somewhat in recent times and it seemed prudent to assess the situation allowing for overdraft rates to range between 15 and 20% per annum.

The Dalting group had for some time been concerned with control over capital investment schemes. Changes were now planned so that projects could only be sanctioned by the group board. A further proposal was that a post audit team should be created to monitor the performance of capital schemes made by group members.

What do you think?

You are asked to give some thought to the following questions and perhaps prepare some of the figures and statements concerned:

1. a) Calculate the return (before tax) that the original Canadian machine would give to Haltwhistle based on the figures budgeted in 1990.
   b) To provide further information, calculate the net present value of the project after tax, assuming an interest rate of 20 per cent (corporation tax is 50 per cent payable on year later and Haltwhistle has sufficient profit to absorb the 100 per cent depreciation allowance).

2. a) Prepare cumulative budgeted profit and loss accounts for four years as viewed from 1990 for both the Canadian and German machines, showing clearly the difference in profit over the project lifetime (do not include 1993 replacement data at this stage).
   b) Prepare a cumulative cash flow statement over the same period showing the budgeted difference in cash between the two machines.
       Ignore interest rates for question 2.)

3. Comment on the irrelevant items that appear in the case study and your financial statements.

4. Advise Pelenski whether to retain or replace the Canadian machine in 1993 (ignore taxation considerations).

5. Discuss the benefits of the post audit scheme proposal and comment on some of the difficulties that might be encountered.

Case Study 3

The Whangamata Assignment

A wide ranging case in financial planning including network analysis and normal curve theory, cost-volume-profit analysis, opportunity and relevant costs. The questions on beta probability distributions and the use of curve tables should prove a fair challenge to final level students. The break-even calculations, although commonsense, provide an opportunity to demonstrate logical thought and presentation.

Normal Stannard qualified as an engineer with the Central Electricity Generating Board in the early 1970s. Ambitious and enterprising, he soon realised that often the successful engineer was a person who had ceased to be one! He set about progressively widening his knowledge by means of management courses and made a special study of the mystical world of accounting and management accounting. The financial expertise was in the future to provide a platform for many interesting jobs and assignments.

Normal was rather on the small side with a round cherubic face and snub nose supporting professional steel-framed spectacles. His swathe of dark curling unkept hair reminded one at times of the legs of large black insects. Outside his working hours he was never happier than when 'roughing it' on some mountainous terrain with his scout troup in tow. There was in Norman a restless desire for new jobs and different surroundings and the day was always begun by scouring the paper for new opportunities. It was no surprise that he chose to emigrate to New Zealand in 1984 and his friends were privately of the view that it would not be long before he went properly 'native'.

New Zealand at this time was planning a considerable diversification in its export trade. This was a natural consequence of Britain's joining the Common Market and the reality that New Zealand would be unwise to rely so substantially on agricultural exports in the long term. The skills developed in carpet, crockery and wallpaper manufacture were finding attractive markets throughout the world. One very considerable potential in this diversification programme was the encouragement of tourism. The increasing affluence of industrialised countries and the tendency towards cheaper package tours and cut-price air flights opened up the possibilities of attracting tourists on a much greater scale than in previous times. By the mid 1970s the New Zealand Tourist Board, with government finance, had embarked on an ambitious programme to improve tourist facilities throughout North Island.

1990 saw Norman Stannard as a special projects manager to the New Zealand Board with a wide job description and closely concerned with the Whangamata Leisure Complex assignment. Traditionally a camping and boating centre, Whangamata seemed a natural starting point to provide facilities which might attract tourists and provide a base to tour North Island. The size and ambitiousness of the scheme were relatively large but the most worrying feature at this stage was whether the Stage II accommodation buildings would be ready for the summer season. Already there had been a curtailment of the advertising programme in case they would not be ready to open on 1 November.

On Monday morning Norman was pouring over plans and costs at his office in St Paul's Road, Hamilton. Now if an old CEGB engineer is good at anything he is good at networks! It was not long before the remaining crucial stages were identified, the facts and figures tabulated and the resultant network drawn (Table 1).

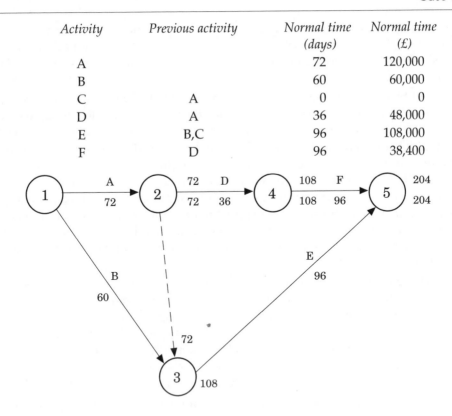

Activity	Previous activity	Normal time (days)	Normal time (£)
A		72	120,000
B		60	60,000
C	A	0	0
D	A	36	48,000
E	B,C	96	108,000
F	D	96	38,400

Table 1

Note: Earliest and latest event times are shown respectively above and below each event.

Clearly the critical path for Stage II of the Leisure Project was A, D and F, with a duration of 204 days and at a cost of £374,400.

This project time was just not good enough: the work had to be completed in 180 days ... time was of the essence. Normal called a meeting with the various parties at which he insisted on a completion date of six months. However, to his dismay the Tourist Board budget officer opposed the use of 'excessive funds' to meet this target date. 'There must be a judicious balance between time and money for me to authorise expenditure'. After lengthy discussions Norman was able to prepare a second table of figures to reflect the minimum times and costs that could be expected (Table 2).

Activity	Minimum time (days)	Minimum time cost (£)
A	48	168,000
B	60	60,000
C	0	0
D	24	60,000
E	84	144,000
F	48	96,000

Table 2

Fortunately the nature of the project allowed for reduction from normal to minimum time in small graduations with the associated costs being in proportion to the time saved. Thus a satisfactory compromise was agreed ... a completion date in 180 days at a minimum cost.

Norman Stannard still remained very troubled. He had not until this meeting been aware of the uncertainty that surrounded the time estimates for activity E. According to the contractors this time could fall anywhere between 72 and 120 days. Agreed ... by committing another £28,000, twelve days might be saved. On other occasions Norman had tended to treat estimates as if they were absolute and then add a safety factor of between 10 and 20 per cent. This situation clearly did not lend itself to this treatment. Perhaps a three-estimate approach using the Burman system* might be employed; assuming that the distribution was approximately normal a beta-distribution could be used. Irrespective of what the budget officer had said, if the accommodation centre was not completed in 180 days then they would suffer lost bookings and compensation that could well total £30,000.

The Whangamata Leisure Centre would have many facilities available for the visitor. It was always the intention of the New Zealand Tourist Board, however, that it should be operated on commercial lines and very serious thought had been given to the financial planning, the setting of prices and the creation of systems to control costs. There was little doubt that the whole scheme would be financially successful ... already an offer of £100,000 by Kiwi International (New Zealand's leading travel firm) to operate the complex for five years had been firmly turned down by the Tourist Board.

As the first season approached a final review of financial budgets was authorised. The data are offered below under separate headings.

*The reader is recommended to consult Precedence networks for project planning and control by P. J. Burman p.103-109; McGraw-Hill (or other suitable text).

Guest accommodation centre

20 double rooms at £15 per day.

50 single rooms at £8 per day.

Variable costs approximately £5 per person per day.

Fixed costs (for the summer season) £30,850.

Self service cafeteria

revenue approximately £4 per person per day.

Variable food and other consumables £3 per person per day.

Fixed costs (for the summer season £10,860).

Recreation centre (swimming, boating, badminton, squash, etc)

All guests to pay a standard £14 per week to give access to the recreation facilities. An extra contribution would come from the centre's sports shop and also from special letting fees estimated at £5.60 per person per week.

Fixed salary costs etc. for the season were budgeted at £23,438, of which some £10,032 could be attributed to the running of the sports shop.

The summer season was from November to March and the Leisure Complex would be open seven days a week for 22 weeks. Recently it had been decided to make a surcharge of £3 for accommodation (per person per week) for the five-week peak period. Another recent decision was to allow casual visitors access to the recreation centre. It was intended to charge them £3 per day and it was estimated that on average 25 casuals per day would take advantage of this offer.

Because of the uncertainty about completion of the single rooms in time for the first season Norman had restricted the booking programme. Consequently the single room bookings for 1980 were down on full capacity, although doubles were fully booked and singles also for the peak period. It was anticipated that future seasons would be entirely sold out in advance of each season.

The Tourist Board had been subject to mounting pressure to open the centre in the winter months for schools, youth clubs, scouts, etc. to use for adventure holidays. This suggestion had been thoroughly supported by most youth organisations and there had been growing support even at Government level. If the scheme went ahead the centre would be operated on a non-profit making basis for the winter. Norman Stannard has compiled the following relevant data.

Winter season

Adventure holidays scheme

Open for 140 days or 20 weeks.

All costs are as the summer season with the exception of:

a) extra heating costs £2,100 for the season;

b) additional instructor fees, £3,126;

c) approximately half of the summer season's fixed costs are annual charges and can be considered to be borne by the summer season's prices.

The New Zealand government indicated that it was likely to support the scheme by offering a subsidy of £16 per person per week resident. As regards occupancy, in view of the number of younger residents it was intended, by the use of portable beds, to increase the total capacity by approximately one half. In view of these numbers it would not be possible to allow casual visitors access in the winter season. It was intended to charge one composite fee per week to reach resident and therefore there would be no income from special lettings or from meals etc .... although the sports shop would still operate independently giving an estimated contribution of £4 per week for each person resident. There was every sign that such an adventure holiday scheme would be a complete success.

Working life through those winter months of 1990 was hectic indeed but happily the important issues seemed to have been resolved. August involved a series of meetings to consider the next stage of the complex. The Tourist Board had earlier in 1989 purchased a further adjacent site for £160,000 to build chalets. With all the development work on the complex it could easily now be sold for £300,000 although a sale was not seriously contemplated. Two schemes were being considered for the site .... either to build a block of flats or erect a number of chalets and at this earlier stage the possibility of their own development and erection, employing their own labour, was also under consideration. At the first meeting in August Norman presented the following estimate.

Estimate 1

	Chalets (£000)	Flats (£000)
Cost of Land	160	160
Material cost	300	300
Labour cost	300	200
Subcontractor	100	
Supervisory costs	40	45
Overhead (apportioned on a time basis)	20	25
	820	830

Already materials costing £40,000 had been delivered to the site which could be used for the chalet project. However, if the scheme were now changed to flats, they would not be used, but in this circumstance they could be sold for £50,000 (less haulage and transport costs of 5 per cent). If the chalet project were approved the materials could be used and effectively reduce the material cost to £255,000. The labour costs are likely to be variable although the supervision cost by contrast could be considered as fixed. Most of the overhead represents an apportionment of part of the fixed costs of the whole complex and it is fair to assume that these costs would remain unaltered whether the development took place or not. Included also in the overhead figure is a specific depreciation charge calculated in relation to the plant to be used. The plant register disclosed the following regarding this equipment:

Cost (£)	Cumulative depreciation after 3 years)	Written down value (£)	Replacement Cost (£)
20,000	10,000	10,000	40,000

The nature of the contracts suggest that at completion, the plant is not likely to be worth more than £8,000 or £4,000 for the chalet and flat scheme respectively.

It soon became apparent that there were too many problems in the own-erection notion which were quite beyond the skill and knowhow of the Tourist Board staff and so any idea of own-development was abandoned and the contract offered out for tender. It was also decided that chalets would blend more naturally into the wooded background of the site and therefore the chalet scheme was environmentally more acceptable.

So it was that Stage IV of the Leisure Complex would be a development consisting of 100 chalets expected to have a life of 25 years. By November planning and architects fees committed amounted to £15,000. Norman received the following communication from Auckland regarding the scheme:

'Serious consideration is being given as to whether to commence the chalet project in January 1991. We estimate construction costs to be £600,000 payable:

	£
1/1/1991	200,000
1/1/1992	200,000
1/1/1993	200,000
	600,000

The chalets would be ready and available for tenancy on 1 January 1994. We are very concerned to have your estimate of the *minimum* rental charge to be paid annually in arrear to the booking agents. These agents will be adding 10 per cent to this figure to cover their charges. Rental charges will be held constant over the years (as far as possible) but you must allow a 10 per cent rate of inflation to be reflected in your calculation. We are at present negotiating possible finance for construction but every indication is that we shall be charged approximately 16.6 per cent. All other figures we believe are known to you.'

What nonsense .... assume inflation at a rate of 10 per cent! What was the point? Interest rates and inflation were so uncertain that projections three months ahead were fraught with grave danger of error. In the present age the manner and presentation of calculations, as long as approached in an apparent scientific way, will satisfy most employers.

What do you think?

You are asked to give some thought to the following questions and perhaps attempt some of the calculations involved.

1. Utilising the data from Tables 1 and 2, what programme should be followed to achieve project completion in 180 days at a minimum cost?

2. a) Apply a three-estimate approach to the uncertainty surrounding activity E and by use of a beta probability distribution advise between the extra expense of achieving the completion date as opposed to the risk involved with non-action.

   b) Advise similarly but utilising curve tables.

3. a) Approximately how many single rooms need to be let in the off peak period to ensure that break-even position exists in 1989 at the guest accommodation centre?

   b) Would the cafeteria be profitable in these weeks and with these numbers?

4. From a financial standpoint is the tourist Board wise in rejecting the offer of £100,000 for the rights to operate the complex for the next five years? Assume the Tourist Board is borrowing money at 15 per cent rate of interest and that in 1990 ten single rooms were not let outside of the peak period.

5. What profit per week is made by the sports shop when the complex is fully occupied?

6. Assuming full bookings what charge per head needs to be made in the winter season to achieve a break-even situation?

7. Prepare a table of items (as Estimate 1) comparing the development costs of chalets and flats from the standpoint of 'relevant opportunity cost' and make brief notes on your reasoning for your choice of figures.

8. Prepare *your* estimate of the minimum rental charge to be paid annually for each chalet on Stage IV of the complex.

Case Study 4

The Kirkland-Carrigill Group

This case is much concerned with 'modern' topics in management accounting – Gap Analysis, Probability Theory, Graphical and Simplex Linear Programming and incorporates the teaching of certain techniques. Although the Simplex method is not covered in the manual it should be familiar from previous studies and this case study will provide useful revision and demonstrates an alternative method of solution of LP problems.

Cedric Lea is management accountant to the Kirkland-Carrigill group. An experienced and popular man, he has an infectious enthusiasm for new ideas and a perceptive understanding of the problems with which many of the accountants throughout the group are faced.

As a new working week began he reflected nostalgically over the many changes he had seen in the 20 years spent with the company. Fifteen years ago he was almost entirely concerned with historical cost accounting and much of that little more than the collection, coding and recording of basic data.

Today's responsibilities were so much different; the emphasis was very much on problem-solving accountancy incorporating as much mathematical programming and statistics as traditional budgeting and profit forecasts. As applied mathematics and computing facilities become more widespread it had been necessary continually to improve his knowledge to keep abreast of developments so as to exercise his judgement as to the value and limitations of such techniques not only for accounting systems but also for their impact on organisational structures.

At the present time long range planning and corporate modelling were very much his preoccupation with projections five years ahead analysed by profit, product and cash .... had he been able to achieve this analysis 'historically' in 1980 it would have been highly acclaimed. Certainly he could see that the modern accountant was committed to a life-long process of learning and education. However there had been compensations compared with the 'straight jacket' within which the financial accountants (with their pledge to external reporting) had been constrained. The focus of his task had always been in helping managers to make better decisions.

Something which he had learnt early in his career was how accounting systems inevitably had enormous influence on the behaviour of employees. Thus when Lea had introduced young accountants into the organisation, he had always made it very clear that they were under the sole jurisdiction of the dencentralised company manager with whom they were placed. Consequently they become 'one of the company' and carried out their duties in helping that organisation to make better decisions without any conflicting loyalty to the group.

Cedric Lea's appointment book for the coming week revealed the following daily assignments.

Tuesday: Dufton Manufacturing Ltd (at Teesdale Works) hopefully to finalise the investment decision on the 'electronic ignition and engine conditions recorder' project (called EIECR project). [It is interesting to note that this investment scheme arose from the systematic corporate planning gap-analysis programme that he had initiated.]

Thursday: An informal discussion with the financial director at headquarters on continuing the present growth policy of the group on a conglomerate strategy.

Friday: To give a lecture/seminar and set practical assignments on mathematical programming at the group's in-service training course being held at Coanwood Hall.

Dufton Manufacturing Ltd (EIECR project)

This was an interesting scheme with many political overtones. The figure side of the story looked straightforward enough as far as making decisions based upon forecasts was concerned. It was so important today to be able to present the arguments clearly and in accordance with investment appraisal procedure (he secretly wondered whether tossing a coin in decision making situations would be just as likely to give a successful decision and save a lot of expense).

The market survey data for EIECR over the next ten years could be summarised as follows:

	chance
10 years continuing higher demand	50%
2 years higher demand and then 8 years lower demand	10%
10 years lower demand	40%

The investment decision was complicated by the possibility of expanding the Teesdale Works in two years' time. The expected cash flows from the different courses of action were as follows:

	Annual Cash Flow	
	First two years	Remaining eight years
New plant for ten years:		
10 years high demand	£225,000	£150,000
2 years higher demand and then 8 years lower demand	225,000	180,000
10 years lower demand	180,000	180,000
New plant expanded after two years:		
10 years higher demand	225,000	360,000
2 years higher demand and then 8 years lower demand	225,000	42,000

Investment costs are predicted to run:

New plant	£650,000
The later expansion	£1,100,000

When Lea arrived at the Teesdale Works that Tuesday he found a changed situation – there was no talk of a new factory and plant at Swindale to help ease the unemployment situation.

Wednesday was spent in his own office. He gave some thought to the discussion the following day but Friday's assignment at Coanwood Hall gave him some disquiet. He intended to illustrate some graphical and simplex linear programming to fairly experienced production staff drawn from various member companies. On these occasions he felt that a mathematician would be a more appropriate person but when this had been done it had left the participating members in a bewilderment of Greek symbols and complex algebra. He prepared his talk carefully keeping in his mind that the audience was more likely to be experienced in pressure and gravity diecasting procedures rather than mathematics. After giving a background to the subject the main talk (and hand-out) would be as follows:

Graphical and simplex linear programming

Linear programming is mathematically complex and the procedures are usually time-consuming and thus require computer aid. However a number of simple situations have arisen within Kirkland-Carrigill of recent years and by illustrating these it may enable us to have a better insight into the computer-based world.

The simplest technique is that of graphical linear programming where only, say, two products are involved. The following problem arose regarding profit maximisation with two products which passed through three manufacturing departments. The correct solution was 'guessed' but we might usefully use the figures for an illustration. (As a matter of fact the *solution* was overridden for very good sales strategy reasons.)

Products		x	y	Capacity hours
Dept A		10h	5h	8000
Dept B		6h	10h	9000
Dept C		12h	12h	12000
Contribution		£10	£8	
Fixed costs	£2000			

The correct mix can easily be seen by drawing a graph illustrating the production barriers which arise. The steps that should be followed are:

1. Designate a product to each axis, calculating the maximum points of scale required, ie

$$x = \frac{9000}{6} = 1500$$

$$y = \frac{8000}{5} = 1600$$

Take Department A and calculate the numbers of each product that could be manu-factured, ie

Dept A $\frac{8000}{10} = 800$ of x or $\frac{8000}{5} = 1600$ of y

Similarly:

Dept B $\frac{9000}{6} = 1500$ of x or $\frac{9000}{10} = 900$ of y

Dept C $\frac{12000}{12} = 1000$ of x or $\frac{12000}{12} = 1000$ of y

3. Now plot these points on our graph and join with straight lines (See Figure 1).

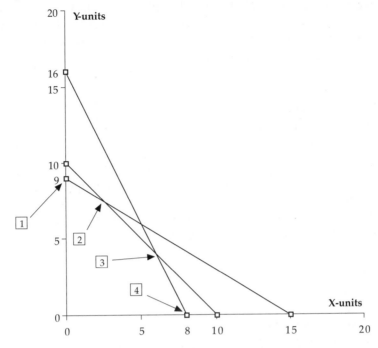

Figure 1

4. The area of feasible solution must lie within all production barriers. The best mix will be found at one of the points of the feasible area. Although there is a short cut method it is just as easy to test each point:

From the graph

Corner	x	y		Contribution
1	0	900	900 × £8	£7,200
2	250	750	(250 × £10) + (750 × £8)	8500
3	600	400	(600 × £10) + (400 × £8)	9200
4	800	0	800 × £10	8000

Maximum profit will therefore be obtained by producing 600 of x and 400 of y, ie a £9200 contribution less a fixed cost of £2000 = £7200 net profit.

To ensure that the technique had been properly mastered the delegates would then be broken into working groups and asked to tackle two problems (these had arisen with the Kirkland Carrigill group). These are shown in examples 1 and 2. If some groups found example A too easy they should turn their attention to B, where it should be added that a 'four-dimensional graph' is not required.

Example A:

The Teesdale works has an assured market for any quantities of two products which are processed on one machine and then finished by hand. Machine capacity is 1200 units per week of either product or a combination of the two and no time is lost in changing over from one product to the other. However under the present

583

employment legislation machine operators cannot be discharged and are thus treated as fixed overhead. The finishing labour supply is limited to 2400 direct labour hours per week. Finishing labour is a fixed cost in the short run as no other work is available if machine output is delayed for any reason. Standard product costs and selling prices are as follows:

	Product A	Product B
Direct material	£2	£2
Finishing labour at £3 per hour	£9	£3
Fixed overhead 1/3 labour cost	£3	£1
Selling price	£16	£8

Example B

Keilder Ltd has drawn up a production budget as follows:

Product	A	B	C	D
Selling price per unit	£55	£53	£97	£86
Direct material per unit	£17	£25	£19	£11
Labour hours				
Grade 1	10	6		
Grade 2			10	20
Grade 3			12	6
Variable overheads	£6	£7	£5	£6

Fixed overheads of the firm amount to £35,500 per annum. Each grade of labourer is paid £1.50 per hour but skills are specific to a grade so that an employee in one grade cannot be used to undertake the work of another grade. The annual supply of each grade is limited to the following maximum: Grade 1:9000 hours, Grade 2: 14500 hours, Grade 3: 12000 hours. There is no effective limitations on the volume of sales of any product.

It was planned that the course should reassemble at 2 pm and Lea would then continue with his paper (giving first some background to mathematical programming).

The basic simplex technique

This will normally only be used where there are more than two products and two or more constraints, so that it becomes difficult to see what product mix will maximise profit. We will continue using figures from our previous graphical illustration ... a slightly more difficult problem will be offered later for the working sessions.

The following algebraic expressions cover our problem:

$$10x + 5y \leq 8{,}000$$
$$6x + 10y \leq 9{,}000$$
$$12x + 12y \leq 12{,}000$$

We now require the introduction of slack variables to enable us to change figures within a matrix (to convert the inequalities into equations). Therefore introducing slack variables P, Q, R we have:

$$10x + 5y + P \leq 8{,}000$$
$$6x + 10y + Q \leq 9{,}000$$
$$12x + 12y + R \leq 12{,}000$$

Clearly the profit to be achieved will be:

$$10x + 8y - 2000$$

and this is called the objective function and designated B.

If we now rewrite our equations, ie

$$P = 8 - 10x - 5y$$

We can produce our first matrix or tableau:

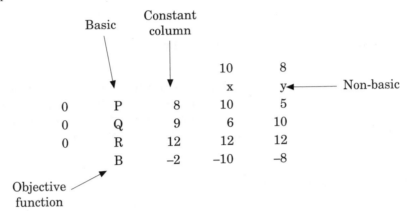

Here the non-zero 'basic' variables table each row and the zero 'non-basic' variables each column.

The simplex technique is a set of rules for interchanging the rows and columns (basic and non-basic variables) until the *best* solution has been achieved. This optimum position is reached when the B row co-efficients are all positive.

The first step is to find the pivot:

Note preferred to the row transformation approach). Identify the column with the largest negative figure in the B row, ie –10. Moving up the –10 column identify the *smallest* positive ratio by dividing the constant figure by the coefficient in that row, ie

$$\frac{12}{12} \quad \text{or} \quad \frac{9}{6} \quad \text{or} \quad \frac{8}{10} \ldots \text{clearly} \quad \frac{8}{10}$$

Therefore 10 is the pivot.

Now interchange the variables:

i) Exchange x and P (the variables in the pivot row and column).

ii) Replace the pivot by its reciprocal $\frac{1}{10}$.

iii) Divide the other pivot row figures by the pivot.

iv) Divide the other pivot column figure by the pivot and change their sign.

Tableau example at this stage:

$$
\begin{array}{ccccc}
 & & & 0 & \\
 & & & P & \\
10x & \dfrac{8}{10} & & \dfrac{1}{10} & \dfrac{5}{10} \\[2mm]
 & & & \dfrac{6}{10} & \\[2mm]
 & & & \dfrac{12}{10} & \\[2mm]
 & & & 1 &
\end{array}
$$

v) All other values must now be replaced by:

$$
\text{Figure} \quad \dfrac{\begin{array}{c}\text{Figure in the same column corresponding to}\\ \text{the pivot row minus figure in the same row}\\ \text{correspondent to the pivot column}\end{array}}{\text{Pivot (note not reciprocal)}}
$$

Examples: to replace 9 (below $\dfrac{8}{10}$)

$$
9 \;-\; \frac{8\times 6}{10} \;=\; \frac{42}{10}
$$

and to replace –2 (the fixed cost appearing in the SW corner)

$$
-2 \;-\; \frac{8\times -10}{10} \;=\; -2 \;-\; \left(-\frac{80}{10}\right) \;=\; -2 \;+\; \frac{80}{10} \;=\; 6
$$

The completed tableau appears as follows:

$$
\begin{array}{cccc}
 & 0 & 8 & \\
 & P & y & \\
x & \dfrac{8}{10} & \dfrac{1}{10} & \dfrac{5}{10} \\[2mm]
Q & \dfrac{42}{10} & \dfrac{6}{10} & 7 \\[2mm]
R & \dfrac{24}{10} & \dfrac{12}{10} & 6 \\[2mm]
B & 6 & 1 & -3
\end{array}
$$

It can be seen that the B row is not yet positive so therefore we must prepare a second tableau (pivot will be 6).

$$
\begin{array}{ccccc}
 & & 0 & 0 & \\
 & & P & R & \\
10 & x & \dfrac{6}{10} & \dfrac{2}{10} & -\dfrac{5}{60} \\[2mm]
 & Q & \dfrac{14}{10} & \dfrac{8}{10} & -\dfrac{7}{6} \\[2mm]
8 & y & \dfrac{4}{10} & -\dfrac{2}{10} & \dfrac{1}{6} \\[2mm]
 & B & \dfrac{72}{10} & \dfrac{4}{10} & \dfrac{3}{10}
\end{array}
$$

The B row is now positive and so we can read (scaling up by 1,000):

Produce 600 of x $\left(\dfrac{6}{10} \times 1,000\right)$ and 400 of y $\left(\dfrac{4}{10} \times 1,000\right)$

to achieve a profit of £7,200 $\left(\dfrac{72}{10} \times 1,000\right)$

Lee pondered over the typescript of his paper and wondered just fleetingly, whether to continue with a 'revised' simplex approach and explain concepts of duality and prices. After reflection he decided to leave this for another time. Finally, he constructed a linear programming problem (shown in Example C) in which he intended to involve the course members on Friday.

Example C:

Standard per unit

Product	x	y	z
Direct material	£4.50	£5.75	£6.25
Direct labour hours			
Dept A	2	3	1
Dept B	2	1	3
Selling price	£30	£28	£35

Other Budget figures

Department	A	B
Direct labour wage rates	£2	£2.25
Direct labour hours per annum	90,000	150,000
Overhead costs		
Variable	£2 per labour hr	£3 per labour hr

Fixed £150,000 in total

What do you think?

You are asked to give some thought to the following questions and perhaps prepare some of the figures and graphical statements concerned.

1. What do you understand by 'systematic gap analysis' in a corporate planning context?
2. What matters do you think may arise in a discussion concerning diversification on a conglomerate strategy?
3. Advise the Dufton Manufacturing Ltd whether or not to expand their Teedsdale Plant after two years.
    i)   without discounting;
    ii) discounting at a 15 per cent rate of interest.
4. Prepare graphical solutions to the problems that are given in Examples A and B.
5. Provide a 'simplex' solution to the problem shown in Example C, showing the number of units of each product to be produced together with the associated profit.

Case Study 5

The Ditton Corvedale Company Ltd

A study of transfer pricing and performance evaluation within a group of companies. The case draws attention to difficulties in comparing and accurately evaluating the performance of member companies. Not only are methods of evaluation seen to conflict, but alternative transfer pricing techniques shown to compound the problems.

The Ditton Corvedale Co Ltd is a diverse group of companies whose activities are largely concerned with gas and electric domestic appliances but include a number of companies in such fields as metal finishing and small-tool manufacture. The group head office is maintained in London but most manufacturing plants are located in the Midlands and the South West. The group in title has been in operation for a number of years but, even so, the group image is not strong. It is to this end of strengthening group cohesiveness that in recent years a number of executive appoints have been made, including that of Robin Hollingsclough as group management accountant. It should be stressed that overall there is reasonable profitability and a health growth potential which is partly traceable to the assured market of inter-company trading.

Until Hollingsclough's appointment, accounting had been of variable standards. The first phase he embarked on what the creation of monthly and quarterly statements and, by careful appointment and development of staff throughout the group, be continued this to 'departmental' reporting. When satisfied with the accuracy of cost data he was able to achieve 'profit' reporting by means of sales analysis. The next step was the analysis of capital employed to the profit centres. This proved difficult and at times very arbitrary and working capital was a particularly difficult problem. It had been a long hard task but 1992 at last saw monthly statements to the group board and centres disclosing both absolute profit and profit related to capital employed. Inevitably there were some controversies and disputes.

Performance evaluation and transfer pricing

A controversy arose within the gas appliance companies where, it must be explained, accounting had previously been strong and performance measurements quite regularly made. There are two separate companies manufacturing cookers and gas fires. Previously assessments were based on total profit only. However, they did charge an imputed rate of interest of 10 per cent on net capital employed before arriving at these final figures. Hollingsclough's new method was simply to measure profit to net capital employed as a percentage. The general manager of the cooker company was upset and complained, commenting that even if a higher and more realistic imputed rate of interest were charged this would be better than the new measurement which was manifestly unfair. Also neither method truly reflected the utilisation of fixed assets because of differing depreciation policies. The summary figures for 1992 were as follows:

Balance Sheet as at 31 December 1992 (£000)

	High Speed Fires Ltd		Jackson Cookers Ltd	
Fixed assets at cost		570		1,900
Less Depreciation		400		1,000
Written-down value		170		900
Current assets	50		130	
Less Current liabilities	20	30	30	100
		200		1,000
Income Statement (Extract)				
Net Profit	40		150	
Less Corporation Tax	19	21	70	80
Balance at 1 January 1982		15		30
		36		110
Transfers to reserve		26		55
Balance at 31 December 1982		10		55

The most controversial area of the group affairs has always been transfer pricing. The effect of the creation of new profit centres, greater disclosure of accounting data and the evaluation of managers by performance has heightened the controversy. Two of the problems which arose are now shown, the first of which was a simple dispute but serves to illustrate the confused thinking of the time.

The general manager of the small-tools company had insisted that, where transfers were made between centres within the company, this should be at marginal cost. This was understandable as most centres had a saleable output and transfers did not occur on any large scale.

In this instance an electric drill (B7) whose product cost in the 'small drill' centres is shown below, had previously been sold to an outside wholesaler for approximately £14. The volume of sales reached 4,000 drills in the previous period.

Small drill centre

Product cost statement – B7 Electric drill

	£	
Direct materials	2	
Direct labour	6	(£3 per hour)
	8	
Prime cost	8	
Variable overhead	1	
Fixed overhead (apportioned)	2	
Total cost	11	

It appears that the product could now be further processed by the 'special attachments' centre incurring a further variable cost of £16.25 per drill. The process itself would take five hours to complete. They only extra material necessary, however, is a small handle costing £1.25 per drill. The selling price would then be raised to £29 and the sales volume would probably reach 6,000 per period. If the further processing operation does not take place then there is a possibility of a substitute produce, a B27 multi-purpose sharpener being manufactured. This would take the same hours to complete and have marginal cost and selling prices of £18 and £23 respectively. A sales volume of 5,000 could be anticipated.

The second problem arose in the plating and anodising company. Here a special decorative finishing strip had been developed which was used to advantage by both the gas and electric appliance companies. An outside customer had also been obtained who took approximately one-third of the output. The income statement for 1992 was shown below.

Plating and anodising company

	Inter-group company transactions		Outside company transactions	Total
	Gas	Electric	Vector Ltd	
Sales				
Metres sold	500,000	500,000	500,000	
Price per metre	£0.70	£0.70	£1	
Sales value	£350,000	£350,000	£500,000	£1,200,000
Cost of sales				
Variable cost £0.50 per metre	£250,000	£250,000	£250,000	£750,000
Fixed cost	£75,000	£75,000	£75,000	£225,000
	£325,000	£325,000	£325,000	£975,000
Profit	£25,000	£25,000	£175,000	£225,000

The outside market price was £1 but internally a special concessionary price of £0.70 per metre was used, calculated on the basis of savings in selling and administration overheads. The general managers of the gas and electric companies put forward strong arguments for a reduction in price in view of increasing competition. They suggested a reduction to £0.65 per metre. The plating company's management was naturally resistant to the change and went as far as stating that, although there was little possibility of increasing sales outside, it would rather curtail its own production than supply 'at a price at which there is simply no profit for us'. The gas and electric companies were equally adamant, claiming that they had to achieve cost reductions to maintain market share.

The decentralised accounting system has not been without its critics and some of the profits per department were not as they were thought to be. Overall, Hollingsclough is well satisfied with the first year and remains confident that this must be the best approach for such a diverse group of companies. The most pertinent problem for 1983 is transfer pricing and it is his intention to review all possible ways of establishing equitable prices which relate profitability to efficiency. A procedure must be devised whereby inter-centre disputes can be handled without the recriminations which have arisen during the last year.

What do you think?

You might give some thought to the following questions and perhaps jot down points and figures which you consider appropriate.

1. Which do you consider to be the most successful company – Jackson Cooker or Highspeed Fire? Indicate the various methods of performance evaluation and comment on the characteristics of each.

2. a) Illustrate with appropriate figures the benefit to the respective managers and to the group as a whole of
      i)   processing further or
      ii) not processing further
           the B7 electric drill.

   b) Is it better to process further the B7 drill or manufacture the multi-purpose sharpener?

3. Prepare figures for the plating and anodising company to show the effect of a £0.65 per metre internal selling price on
   a) profit achieved within the group and
   b) overall profit of the company.
      How critical is the reduction in price to the gas and electric companies for maintaining competitive product prices?
      Is the plating and anodising company justified in curtailing production at this price?

4. Outline the alternative methods of transfer pricing which Hollingsclough might adopt together with a recommendation as to a procedure for solving price disputes.

Appendix 2 Examination technique

1. Introduction

If you are a genius and/or can calculate and reproduce facts and figures with the speed of computer and/or know the examiner then there is no need for you to read this section. On the other hand if you do not fall into any of the above categories then you will stand more chance of passing your examinations first time if you study this section carefully and follow the simple rules.

2. Well before the examination

No amount of examination room technique will enable you to pass unless you have prepared yourself thoroughly beforehand. The period of preparation may be years or months long. It is no use expecting to pass with a feverish last minute bout of revision. Plan your study and preparation systematically. Allocate specific times for study and stick to them. At a minimum your pre-examination preparation should include the following:

a) Obtain the official syllabus of the examination.

b) Systematically follow a course of study directed towards the examination.

c) Obtain past examination papers for say the last five years.

d) Make sure you can answer every question previously set.

e) Analyse the questions. Are some topics more popular than others?

f) Make sure you enter for the examination in good time and receive official confirmation.

3. Immediately before the examination

a) Make sure you know exact time, date and location of examination.

b) Carefully check your travel arrangements. Leave yourself adequate time.

c) Check over your examination equipment:

Calculator? Spare battery? Pens? Pencils? Tables? Watch? Sweets? etc, etc.

d) Check your examination number.

4. In the examination room

If you have followed the rules so far you are well prepared; you have all the equipment you need; you did not have to rush – YOU ARE CALM AND CONFIDENT.

❐ Before you start writing:

a) Carefully read the whole examination paper including the rubic.

b) Decide what questions you are going to answer.

c) Decide the sequence you will tackle the questions. Generally, answer the easiest question first.

d) Decide the time allocation for each question. In general the time allocation should be in direct proportion to the marks for each questions.

e) Read the questions you have decided to answer again. Do you know exactly what the examiner is asking? Underline the key words in the question and keep these in your mind when answering.

❐ When you start writing:

a) Make sure you plan each question first. Make a note of the main points or principles involved. If you are unable to finish the question you will gain some marks from these points.

b) Attempt all questions required and each part of each question.

c) Do not let your answer ramble on. Be as brief as possible consistent with covering all the points you know.

d) Follow a logical sequence in your answers.

e) Write neatly, underline headings and if the question asks for a particular sequence of answer then follow that sequence.

f) If diagrams graphs or tables are required give them plenty of space, label them neatly and comprehensively, and give a key to symbols, lines etc used. A simple clear diagram showing the main points can often gain a good proportion of the marks for a question.

❐ When you have finished writing:

a) Check that you have followed the examination regulations regarding examination title, examination number, candidates number and sequence of answer sheets.

b) Make sure you include all the sheets you require to be marked.

c) If you have time carefully read each and every part of each answer and check each calculation.

❐ General points

a) Concentrate on answering the questions set not some related topic which you happen to know something about.

b) Do not leave the examination room early. use every minute for checking and rechecking or adding points to questions answered.

c) Always attempt every question set and every part of each question.

Index